PRINCIPLES OF ECONOMICS:
AN IRISH TEXTBOOK

SECOND EDITION

PRINCIPLES OF ECONOMICS:
AN IRISH TEXTBOOK
SECOND EDITION

GERARD TURLEY

and

MAUREEN MALONEY

with contributions from
Matthew Coffey, Eithne Murphy and Francis O'Toole

GILL & MACMILLAN

Gill & Macmillan Ltd
Hume Avenue
Park West
Dublin 12
with associated companies throughout the world
www.gillmacmillan.ie
© Gerard Turley, Maureen Maloney 2001
Chapters 8 and 17.3 © Eithne Murphy 2001
Chapter 9 © Francis O'Toole 2001
Chapter 18 © Matthew Coffey 2001
0 7171 3171 8

Print origination in Ireland by
Carrigboy Typesetting Services, County Cork

The paper used in this book is made from the wood pulp of managed forests. For every tree felled, at least one tree is planted, thereby renewing natural resources.

A catalogue record is available for this book from the British Library.

To my mother and the memory of my father
G.T.

To my parents
M.M.

CONTENTS

PREFACE

> 'Normality is a fiction of economic textbooks.'
>
> *Joan Robinson (1903–83)*

In 1948 the first mass-produced 'modern' textbook in economics was published. Since then, Paul Samuelson's *Economics* has sold millions of copies, being translated into over forty languages with fifteen editions. Many others, on both sides of the Atlantic, have tried to follow Samuelson's success. By the 1990s over fifty major introductory textbooks were available. American textbooks were soon adapted in order to meet the particular demands of the European market (Parkin and King's *Economics*, for example). European texts have also become popular (Burda and Wyplosz's *Macroeconomics: A European Text*, for example).

An economics textbook for the Irish third-level market is not a new idea. In the 1920s the Educational Company of Ireland published *A Groundwork of Economics*, written by Joseph Johnston. Macmillan & Co. Ltd published an Irish edition of a well-established British textbook in 1963. It was called *Textbook of Economic Analysis* and was written by Edward Nevin. At a more advanced level, Desmond Norton wrote *Economic Analysis for an Open Economy: Ireland* which was published by the Irish Management Institute in 1980. A second textbook by Norton, entitled *Economics for an Open Economy: Ireland* was published in 1994. An intermediate macroeconomic textbook, *The Macroeconomy of Ireland* by Brendan Walsh and Anthony Leddin has been updated regularly. Other introductory textbooks in economics by Irish authors include *Economics* by Noel Palmer, *Economics for Irish Students* by Murphy & Ryan and *Economics* by Seán Nagle.

Notwithstanding these welcome developments on the publishing front, we believe that there is a need for an introductory third-level economics textbook. We hope that this book fills that gap. It covers the basic theory of both microeconomics and macroeconomics in a user-friendly way. Students are introduced to economic terminology and concepts. We attempt to reinforce these ideas by applying them in 'case studies' drawn from a number of sources including journals, newspapers, policy documents and CSO publications. An Irish section is included in each of the macroeconomic chapters. Wherever possible, we have used current national data.

Additional case studies and a wide range of questions conclude each chapter. It was our intention to provide a 'complete' text, not requiring supplements. We hope that readers will find this useful, challenging and a welcome addition to the existing stock of economic textbooks already on the market.

ACKNOWLEDGMENTS

There is a large number of people whom we wish to thank. In particular, we want to say a special word of thanks to the contributors to the second edition of the textbook. They are Eithne Murphy, Matthew Coffey and Francis O'Toole. We are very grateful for your time and expertise. It was a pleasure to work with you.

We want to acknowledge the support that we received from the faculty and staff at the NUI, Galway. From the Economics Department, we thank Michael Cuddy, Aidan Kane, Brendan Kennelly and Terry McDonough. Once again, we wish to thank Imelda Howley and Claire Noone for all their assistance. The 'wheels of progress' would have ground to a halt except for the guidance of the staff of Computer Services who managed to solve our software problems. Thanks to Mary Guckian and many other staff members of the James Hardiman Library for their diligent efforts in finding the data information that we needed to update this edition. We are grateful that we received such strong support from our own university.

We were also helped by a number of people from other institutions in Ireland. In particular, our thanks go to Mary Hanley, Tony Kelleher, Peter Meany, Majella MacLennan, Martina O'Callaghan and Margot O'Reilly of the Central Statistics Office, Margaret Daly of the Central Bank of Ireland and Sue Blood, Maura Conneely, Una Dixon and John Newham of the Department of Finance.

We wish to thank everyone who adopted the first edition of the textbook. In particular, we want to acknowledge those who reviewed the book and those who completed the questionnaires. We adopted as many of your suggestions as possible in this edition.

Gerard Turley wishes to thank everybody closely associated with the Economics Department, Heriot-Watt University, Edinburgh and in particular Mark Schaffer who was kind enough to give me time off work to complete the textbook.

Maureen Maloney thanks Pauline O'Neil and Gaye Doyle, the librarians at Shannon College of Hotel Management. The faculty and staff are lucky to have you. I benefited enormously from your help and support.

We acknowledge the inspiration that our students have given us over the years. We are very grateful to the students of NUI, Galway, Shannon College of Hotel Management and St. Angela's College, Sligo. This textbook is a testament to your questions, ideas and criticisms.

As with the first edition, we want to thank our publishers, Gill & Macmillan. In particular, we wish to thank our editor, Ailbhe O'Reilly and Gabrielle Noble in the Editorial Department. When deadlines were missed, you continued to show both understanding and patience. For this, we are very grateful. We also wish to thank our copy-editor Julia Fairlie.

Finally, we wish to thank our families for the support that they have given to us over the years. The massive debt of gratitude that we referred to in the first edition has increased with time.

We bear full responsibility for all errors and omissions.

G.T. and M.M.

PROLOGUE

We are living in remarkable times. When we wrote the first edition of this book, we were emerging from a period of 'jobless growth' characterised by high rates of growth accompanied by persistently high rates of unemployment. Long-term unemployment seemed to be an unsolvable problem in the late 1980s and early 1990s.

Since then, the transformation in the labour market has been breathtaking. The 'dole' queues are much shorter. Job fairs in Australia, Canada, New Zealand and America are designed to convince emigrants to return home. In the year 2001, no young person is forced to leave Ireland to look for work.

However, rapid growth raises a new set of problems. Although Ireland has one of the highest rates of growth and one of the lowest rates of unemployment in the EU, it also has the highest rate of inflation among member states. In the year 2000, the annual inflation rate was almost 5% higher than the EU average. The high rate of inflation has placed considerable strain on the most recent national wage agreement. Many workers are not convinced that they are receiving their fair share of the income generated by the 'Celtic Tiger' economy. Inflation is eroding their negotiated wage increases. High inflation endangers Ireland's competitiveness and continued economic prosperity.

If unemployment was the problem of the 1980s and 1990s, inflation, infrastructural bottlenecks, distribution of income and labour market shortages appear to be the problems that confront us in the first few years of the new millennium. We look at these issues in detail in the second edition.

NEW SECTIONS AND CHAPTERS IN THE SECOND EDITION

Chapter 1 is an expanded version of the Introduction that appeared in the first edition. It briefly explains the schools of thought used in economics, the methods of researching economic issues and the production possibility frontier. Chapter 7 contains two new sections on the minimum wage and the national wage agreements. Chapter 9 is a new chapter written by Dr Francis O'Toole of Trinity College, Dublin. The topics covered include taxation policy and competition policy.

In the macroeconomics part of the book, the latest developments in monetary and exchange rate policy are included in Chapters 13 and 15 respectively. The unemployment section of Chapter 17 incorporates the recent dramatic events in the labour market in Ireland. Chapter 18 is a new chapter written by Matthew Coffey, formerly of NUI, Galway. In this chapter, the author examines growth theory, both in a worldwide context and in an Irish context.

All of the case studies in the second edition are new. Data are updated using the most recent information available. In response to the comments of lecturers who used the first edition, all of the answers to the case studies and questions at the end of the chapters are found on the Gill & Macmillan website for this book. This allows you to use case studies and chapter questions for assignments and tutorials. The address is http://www.gillmacmillan.ie. The website has links to sources of data found in this edition. Also, many of the diagrams contained in the book can be downloaded to print as transparencies or accessed by PowerPoint.

The website is password protected. Only lecturers will have access to the answers to the questions.

SUPPORT MATERIAL FOR

Principles of Economics, 2nd ed

by Turley & Maloney

Dynamic and easy to use, online support material for this book provides **lecturers** with:

- PowerPoint presentation slides
- Solutions to questions and case studies

To access lecturer support material on our secure site:

1) Go to *www.gillmacmillan.ie/lecturers*
2) Logon using your username and password. If you don't have a password, register online and we will email your password to you.

CHAPTER 1

INTRODUCTION TO ECONOMICS

'What is lacking [in economics] is any effective means of communication between abstract theory and concrete application.'[1]

Barbara Wootton

'If all economists were laid end to end, they could not reach a conclusion.'[2]

George Bernard Shaw

CHAPTER OBJECTIVES

Upon completing this chapter, the student should understand the:
- differences between the neoclassical, institutional and Marxian schools of economics;
- approaches used to develop economic theory;
- features of the production possibility frontier;
- concept of opportunity cost.

OUTLINE

1.1 Economic schools of thought
1.2 Economic models
1.3 Production possibility frontier

INTRODUCTION

This chapter is an introduction to some of the basic concepts that we will use throughout the book. We begin with an overview of three different approaches to the study of economics. Next, we will consider two methods used by economists to develop economic theory. Finally, we will examine the production possibility frontier that is the most basic model of an economy.

1.1 ECONOMIC SCHOOLS OF THOUGHT

There are three principal economic schools of thought: neoclassical, institutional and Marxian. Each of these schools approaches the study of economics from very different perspectives. In future chapters we will see how the differences in outlook lead to

1

disparate opinions about how to interpret economic events. Because they analyse problems differently, each school also advocates different types of policies to handle economic problems.

Neoclassical school

The neoclassical school emerged at the end of the nineteenth century and currently dominates economic thinking. Although economics is a social science, neoclassical economists use a method of study similar to that used in the natural sciences. The adoption of the deductive method (examined in greater detail in Section 1.2) separated neoclassical economists from the other social sciences and from other types of economists. This model begins with a theory that is either verified or refuted by data.

Neoclassical economists examine the choices made by individuals with limited resources and unlimited wants. They view consumers and producers, workers and employers as acting rationally and independently to promote their own self-interest. All participants in the market are able to calculate benefits and measure costs. Acting to promote their own self-interest, they promote the best interests of society. This is because society is viewed as a collection of individuals. Societal welfare is calculated by adding together the welfare gains made by individuals.

Exchange in markets is governed by contracts which are either formal (explicit) or informal (implicit). Parties enter into these contracts of their own free will. Milton Friedman (b. 1912) is an influential neoclassical economist who won a Nobel prize for economics. He describes the market exchange in the following way, 'So long as effective freedom of exchange is maintained, the central feature of the market organization of economic activity is that it prevents one person from interfering with another in respect of most of his activities. The consumer is protected from coercion by the seller because of the presence of other sellers with whom he can deal . . . The employee is protected from coercion by the employer because of other employers for whom he can work, and so on. And the market does this impersonally and without centralised authority.'[3]

Friedman acknowledges the link between the economic system and the political system. He argues that market capitalism is the economic system that best supports libertarian democracy. Libertarians believe that individual liberty is the foundation of democracy. 'One person, one vote' demonstrates the right of any citizen to express their preferences through their vote. Friedman views what happens in the political process as mirroring the market process. The consumer expresses his or her preferences in the way that s/he spends money. An employee expresses his or her preferences in the trade or occupation that s/he chooses. In terms of the economy, consumers and firms should only be restrained in their consumption and production decisions if their actions have unintended negative side effects which harm people who are 'outside' of the market. (See Section 8.3 for a discussion of market externalities.) Friedman believes that societies should rely on the market as much as possible because it is difficult to achieve consensus through the political process.[4]

As is typical of neoclassical economists, Friedman believes that government has an important, but limited, role. He states, 'The existence of a free market does not of course eliminate the need for government. On the contrary, government is essential both as a forum for determining the "rules of the game" and as an umpire to interpret and enforce the rules decided on. What the market does is to reduce greatly the range of issues that must be decided through political means, and thereby to minimize the extent to which government need participate directly in the game.'[5]

The goal of the neoclassical economic system is efficiency. Efficiency has three components:

i) *productive efficiency* means that all resources are employed using the best available technology;
ii) *economic efficiency* means that the economy is producing the quantity of goods and services preferred by its citizens; and
iii) *Pareto efficiency* means that there is no available alternative that keeps all individuals at least as well off, but makes at least one person better off.

Pareto efficiency combines productive efficiency and economic efficiency.

Pareto efficiency does not imply equity. An economy can be 'Pareto efficient' even if income is unevenly distributed. Neoclassical economists often argue against income redistribution in the form of taxation for the affluent and social welfare benefits for the poor. They believe that these policies diminish the market incentives that work best if people bear the fruits of their own efforts.

Institutional school

While the neoclassical school has a coherent political and economic ideology, the institutional school is a 'broad church'. Institutionalists view economics as the study of the ways in which institutions regulate the production of goods and services. They are united by the belief that the capitalist system requires periodic intervention to achieve social objectives. They are divided on the nature and frequency of that intervention.

The early institutionalists were also separated from the neoclassicals by the method that they used to study economic issues. While neoclassicals relied on the deductive model, institutionalists used the inductive model. They began with data and used them to build models to explain and predict economic phenomena. (See Section 1.2.)

A group of economists called the American Institutionalists emerged at the end of the nineteenth century as a reaction against the neoclassical school.[6] They attacked the neoclassical assumption that individuals in the market acted rationally and independently.

Thorstein Veblen (1857–1929) is one of the most famous of the American institutional economists. He believed that human behaviour was not motivated primarily by self-interest, but by an individual's association with important institutions like family, church, school system and workplace. These institutions evolved slowly.

Veblen believed that the choices made by individuals of all classes were shaped by the 'conspicuous consumption' of the 'leisure class'. With tongue in cheek, Veblen observed that it is the 'duty' of a 'gentleman' of this class to '. . . change his life of leisure into a more or less arduous application to the business of learning how to live a life of ostensible leisure in a becoming way. Closely related to the requirement that the gentleman must consume freely and of the right kind of goods, there is the requirement that he must know how to consume them in a seemly manner.'[7]

Veblen states that, 'The leisure class stands at the head of the social structure.' They set the standards that the lower classes imitate. Each class imitates the one above it with the result that '. . . the members of each stratum accept as their ideal of decency the scheme of life in vogue in the next higher stratum, and bend their energies to live up to that ideal.'[8]

Veblen was very critical of patterns of consumption that wasted time, effort and goods. It was at variance with an 'instinct for workmanship' which inspired men to seek 'effective work' which was serviceable and efficient. Unfortunately, the work of the productive classes was not valued by a society seeking to imitate the unproductive leisure class.

The market in the circumstances that Veblen describes could never produce an outcome that maximised society's welfare, because production was based on providing the goods and services needed for 'conspicuous consumption'. Veblen believed that government should intervene in the market by taxing the goods sought by the leisure class '. . . to compensate the persons who experience psychological losses in consequence of their display'.[9]

Unlike the neoclassical economists, some institutionalists were concerned about income distribution as well as efficiency. Uneven income distribution combined with technological improvements led to the production of surplus goods and services that the working class could not afford. Income redistribution could solve the chronic problem of over-production in the capitalist economy.

The criticism of the American institutionalists about the assumptions and methodology used by neoclassical economists may seem to be 'much ado about nothing'. It is an example of internal dissension that leads to change within academic disciplines. The Great Depression began at the end of the 1920s and continued into the next decade. This provided the external stimulus that led to the domination of economics by the institutionalists for the next few decades.

John Maynard Keynes (1883–1946) was the most important institutional economist. His attack on neoclassical economics is explained in detail in Chapter 11. For our purposes, he is important because he challenged the neoclassical belief that unregulated markets can be relied on to employ workers to produce the goods and services that maximise social welfare. Keynes explained how problems within the markets for goods and services led to unemployment which was involuntary. He argued that the neoclassical analysis of the labour market led to inappropriate policies which lengthened and deepened the depression.

Keynes saw government as an important and powerful institution that could intervene in the economy to resolve the problems inherent in the capitalist system. This central role for government, as a regulator of the economy, was far more powerful than advocated by the neoclassical economists.

Neoclassical economists have challenged the models developed by Keynes and his followers. During the 1970s, these models were not useful in explaining the problems of inflation and unemployment which plagued western economies. However, a legacy of Keynes is the increased involvement of government in the economy. In the US and the UK, neoclassical economists and their followers constantly challenge the involvement of government.

Other European countries, including Ireland, have followed a 'partnership model' where government is one of the 'social partners' along with other institutions including labour unions, business leaders, trade organisations and the voluntary sector (see Section 7.5). Advocates of this model recognise that problems in markets can have destabilising social effects. They discuss the ways in which government policy can be implemented to minimise the impact of market disruptions. Once a consensus emerges, government carries out the policies of the social partners.

Neoclassical economists are quick to point out that the interventions often blunt the incentives of the market. Institutional economists recognise the validity of this criticism. However, they argue that in small countries, labour and other factor inputs that become redundant may not be able to find employment, at least in the short-run. Social welfare payments help to support them during their transition from one job to another.

To summarise, both neoclassical and institutional economists support the capitalist system. Neoclassical economists have greater confidence in the ability of the market to provide outcomes that are 'socially' beneficial. The need for government intervention is the exception, rather than the rule. Institutional economists believe that capitalist economies are prone to instability that can be minimised through government intervention.

Marxian school

The writings of Karl Marx (1818–83) and his colleague Friedrich Engels (1820–95) form the basis of the most radical approach to economics.[10] They viewed economics as the study of the relations that people enter into in the course of production and of how these relations change over time. Marx's research approach was called historical materialism. He observed the complex relationships between a society's method of production and other social institutions under economic systems that included slavery, feudalism and capitalism.

Marx believed that different economic systems were based on different classes. A class shared a common interest. Economic systems also differed in the way in which they controlled the production process. Under capitalism, Marx identified two classes. The bourgeoisie were the owners of capital (property, plant and machinery). Labour owned the 'muscle power' needed to produce the economy's goods and services. Capitalism was defined as an economic system which produced for profit using privately owned capital goods and wage labour.

Neoclassical economists and most institutional economists view profit as the payment made to the capitalist for his or her efforts and risk. The capitalist deserves or has a right to earn profit in the same way that a worker is entitled to his or her wage. Marx did not agree. He believed that labour was the source of all value. It produced the machinery used in the production process. Labour produced enough goods and services to pay their own wages. Any surplus that remained was the profit appropriated by the bourgeoisie. Profit was used to increase the stock of capital that was the capitalist's source of future profit.

Marx also did not agree with the neoclassicals that the relationship between employees and employers was based on mutually agreed contracts. The bourgeoisie/labour relationship was characterised by conflict and exploitation. The way that the surplus was split was a source of conflict among the classes. The bourgeoisie was concerned with not only the amount of profit, but also the rate of profit. Increasing the rate of profit required lowering costs, relative to sales. Since wages were an important component of cost, there was a constant struggle against labour to cut the wage bill in order to increase the surplus paid as profit.

Unemployment was a tool used by the bourgeoisie to control labour. The threat of unemployment silenced the voice of labour asking for higher wages and allowed the capitalist to increase their share of the surplus.

Like the institutional economists, Marx saw the capitalist system as unstable. Internal contradictions within the capitalist system caused the instability. Increasing capital accumulation meant that the output of the economy was constantly expanding. The low wages paid to labour meant that demand for the output was stagnant or falling. During periods of overproduction, profits fell. This led to cuts in production and increased unemployment. Marx believed that contractions of economic activity would deepen, leading to depressions of increasing length and severity.

Unlike the institutional economists, Marx did not see government as an institution that eased the increasingly violent swings in the production cycle. Like the neoclassical economists, Marx saw the government as protecting the rights of private property. However, the enforcement of these rights protected the profits and capital gained at labour's expense. Government, therefore, was an institution that colluded with the bourgeoisie to exploit labour.

From this brief discussion, it is obvious that Marx did not see the capitalist system as a fair distributor of society's output. He did not attempt to find policies to improve its faults. He predicted its ultimate collapse, caused by labour rising against the bourgeoisie. This would lead to a new political and economic system based on a classless society.

At the end of the twentieth century, we observed the collapse of the Communist economies that were supposedly based on the principles of Marx. Former economies associated with the Soviet Union are converting to capitalism with an almost religious fervour. Can we forget about the radical critique of Karl Marx?

Some argue that the threat of communism and socialism put 'manners' on capitalism. Concern about the spread of socialism prompted Pope Leo XIII to write an encyclical in 1891. In it, he affirmed the church's belief that '. . . private property ought to be safeguarded by the sovereign power of the state . . .' In this statement, the church supports the legislative framework for the capitalist system. However, Leo XIII also argued in favour of associations (trade unions) for labour and outlined the ways in which living and working conditions for workers should be improved either voluntarily or through legislation.[11]

Others argue that it was concern about social stability, rather than the grinding poverty of the unemployed, that led to the enactment of national social welfare legislation in the US and western Europe during the Great Depression. According to this way of thinking, policies, which moved the capitalist system towards socialism, were not aimed at promoting social justice but at preserving the capitalist system.

Without the threat of socialism, the worst excesses of the capitalist system may resurface. Then the radical critique of Marx and Engels may gain new currency.

The characteristics of the different economic schools of thought are listed in Table 1.1.

Table 1.1: Characteristics of economic schools of thought

	Neoclassical	Institutional	Marxian
Economics defined	Study of how individuals choose to allocate scarce resources among alternative uses	Study of how institutions regulate the production of goods and services	Study of the social relations that people enter into in the course of production and how these relationships change over time
Focus of analysis	Consumers and firms	Institutions	Classes or groups who share common interests, particularly the ownership of the factors of production
Behaviours analysed	Choices made by consumers and producers	Regulation of the boundaries of individual choice	Struggle between the classes in the pursuit of economic interests
Relationship between actors	Harmonious; based on implicit or explicit contracts	Based on existing or new institutional relationships	Conflictual; disagreements about the distribution of resources among classes
Technology	Assumes harmonious implementation of new technology as it is developed	Institutional arrangements facilitate the development and adoption of new technologies	Implementation of technology may lead to class struggles
Political system	Libertarian democracy	Interventionist democracy	Communist/socialist

Source: Based on the work of Dr Terence McDonough from the National University of Ireland, Galway.

1.2 ECONOMIC MODELS

A model is an abstraction of reality. It represents the real thing, but with less detail. A map is a model of the road system. The amount of detail that you need depends on how you are travelling. If you are driving from Galway City to Carndonagh, Co. Donegal, an ordinary road map of Ireland will do. If you are travelling on a bicycle, a series of ordnance survey maps, which show the byroads and elevations is more appropriate.

Theories are developed using models that link the theory with the available empirical evidence. Like the road map, economic models attempt to simplify an issue, using only the necessary amount of detail. In this Section, we will discuss two types of model that are commonly used by economists: the inductive model and the deductive model.

Both types of model are borrowed from the branch of philosophy known as logic and are based on inference. An inference 'is a proposition that is perceived to be true because of its connection with some known fact'.[12] There are two forms of inference: deduction and induction.

Deductive model

A deductive model is based on a set of premises, and conclusions follow directly from them. The model is tested using available data to determine if it can be disproved. Because of this process, deductive inferences are always conservative.[13] Testing can prove a theory to be false but it cannot verify or confirm that it is true.

To summarise, the deductive model moves from general (the theory) to specific (the data). Figure 1.1 shows the process of developing and testing a deductive model.

Figure 1.1: The deductive model

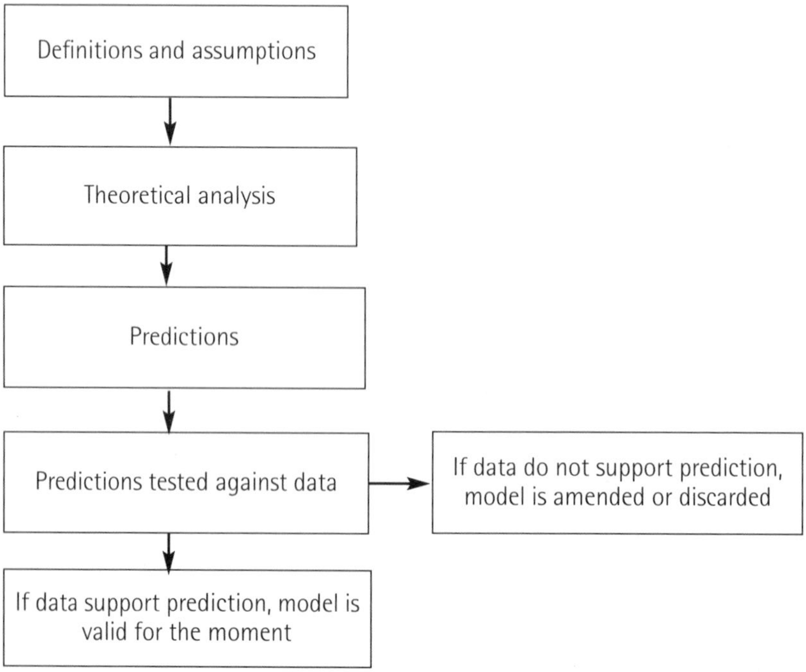

Definitions and assumptions   After the researcher identifies a problem of interest, s/he conducts a literature review to find any research that relates to the topic. Our knowledge about any subject increases incrementally. A researcher builds on the work of other people.

Suppose, for example, a researcher is interested in the relationship between income and education. She will search for any published or unpublished work on this topic.

Next she identifies and defines the variables that she intends to use to study the problem. For example, what is income? Does it include only the money received for paid employment, or does it also include transfer payments made by government? Does income include only wages and salaries or does it also include bonuses and stock options? We go through the same process for education. Is the researcher interested in the years spent in the educational system or the highest degree conferred? Will she include training? Does the training have to be certified by a governing body?

The researcher has to explain any assumptions that she is making. In this case, the researcher assumes that the years spent in the education system improve the knowledge, skills and ability of the individual.

Theoretical analysis   In this step, the researcher develops the model that she intends to test. She explains the relationship between the variables.

For example, the researcher may decide on the following model:

$$Income = f(education)$$

This model states that income is a function of education or income depends on education. In this model, education is the independent variable and income is the dependent variable.

Also, the researcher has to identify the way in which these variables interact. This is based on the assumptions. If years in education improve the knowledge, skills and ability of an individual, education and income should move in the same direction. This is called a 'positive' relationship.

Predictions   Based on the theoretical analysis, the researcher predicts the relationship that she will find when she tests her model with data. In this example, the researcher may predict that in Ireland, income increases with higher levels of educational attainment.

Predictions tested against data   Next the researcher must locate the data to test her model. This can be quite difficult. If she cannot find information on the entire population of the country, or if that amount of information is simply too great, she must identify a sample that represents the population. Then she must find two pieces of information for each individual in her sample: their educational attainment and their income. Our researcher may find some information available from published sources, but not exactly in the form that she needs. Sending a questionnaire to the sample is expensive and people may not want to answer questions concerning their income.

However, let us assume that she does find the data and tests her model. There are two possible outcomes.

Data support prediction   In this case the researcher finds a positive relationship between education and income. The data support the model's prediction. This means that although she or some other researcher may develop a better model in the future, in the meantime, this model is valid.

Data do not support prediction   In this case, the researcher makes the discovery that she has to amend or discard her model. There are two likely sources for this failure. First, she may have chosen the wrong independent variable. Perhaps experience is much more important than education as a predictor of income. In this case, she has to go 'back to the drawing board' to reconsider her variables, assumptions and relationships. Second, her data may not be sufficiently robust to test the model. In this case, she has to attempt to locate better data sources to retest the model. If she cannot amend the model, she has to discard it.

There are some benefits to the deductive model. First, the model is simple. It structures the research problem with a minimum of detail. Second, the model is transparent. This means that it is logical. Every step is clearly defined. Someone who follows the researcher using this method should be able to understand exactly what s/he did in order to criticise the results or to improve the model. Third, the model helps the researcher to think about cause and effect. This is useful, especially if policy can be used to change an independent variable. For example, in this situation, if the government wants to eliminate poverty, this model suggests that it should promote education. One policy could be to provide free third level education.

There are also problems associated with the deductive model. Institutional economists argue that deductive models are too simple. A cause and effect relationship using a small number of independent variables is unlikely to adequately explain the complicated events that occur in developed economies. This simplicity can lead to incorrect policy decisions. For example, in the model that we used above we assumed that

$$Income = f(education)$$

However, an equally defensible model is that

$$Education = f(income)$$

In other words, children from families with high incomes are more to likely avail of opportunities that extend their years in the educational system than children from low-income families. Indeed, there is probably a virtuous circle between the two variables which cannot be explained using the deductive model.

If the model cannot identify 'cause and effect', the policy prescriptions based on the model will be incorrect. People with low incomes may not take up educational opportunities. Free education may end up being of greatest benefit to people on higher incomes.

A second problem with this type of model is the availability of data. In some cases, the data exist but are inaccessible, usually for reasons of confidentiality. In other cases, the data are of poor quality or not specific enough to test the particular model.

Inductive model

Both deductive and inductive models are based on their connection with data. The deductive model uses data to verify the theory. For the inductive model, the researcher 'seeks to use factual data to discover empirical correlations that can then serve in the construction of theories, which will, hopefully be useful in prediction.'[14] The inductive model moves from the specific to the general, from the data to the theory.

The steps for the inductive model are outlined in Figure 1.2.

Figure 1.2: The inductive model

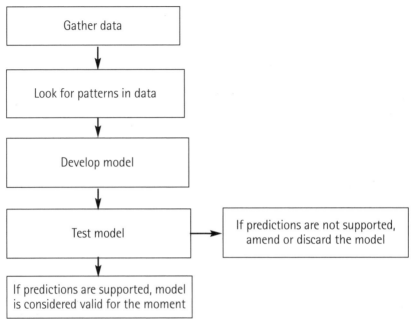

Gather data   After identifying the problem that is of interest, the researcher looks for data. For example, suppose the same researcher is still interested in investigating the relationship between education and income. She might check all of the available sources of information. The Census of Population, published by the Central Statistics Office (CSO) at five-year intervals, contains information about education and occupations for Irish households. Information concerning the hourly and weekly wage by industrial sector is published each month by the CSO. Information concerning unemployment and educational attainment is published annually by the OECD (Organisation for Economic Co-operation and Development). The Higher Education Authority (HEA) publishes information annually related to entry to third level education and the principal economic status of the student's family.

Look for patterns in data   Next the researcher looks for patterns in the data. For example, she might look to see if the children of farmers are more likely to attend third level education than the children of factory workers. She might look to see if people with less education are more likely to be unemployed.

Develop model   Based on patterns that she finds in the data, the researcher develops a model. The model may include a number of variables that the researcher found from various sources. It may involve observations about timing. Certain variables may lead changes in income while others may lag changes in income.

Test model   The researcher may develop the model using data from all but the most recent years. She will then test the model using the most current data available. Depending on the results of the test, she will accept, amend or discard the model.

The inductive model also has admirers and critics. The benefits include increased realism. The researcher is not limited by beginning with fixed theoretical relationships that she attempts to verify with inappropriate data. This research approach is more pragmatic in the sense that it is 'data led'. The researcher begins with whatever data are available, with all of their faults and limitations. Connections between the variables are discovered by observation. The researcher lets the information 'speak for itself' rather than prejudging links between different variables.

However, this form of modelling is criticised because it does not isolate causation. The past association between two variables may be extended coincidence. Also, the availability of new information may substantially alter the theory. If the general form changes with new information, it undermines confidence in the validity of the process.

The deductive model continues to be the preferred method of developing economic theory, particularly for neoclassical economists.

CASE STUDY
Extract from *The Irish Times*
Males make the grade in university exams
by Emmett Oliver

Top degrees at university continue to be the preserve of male students with 521 of them having achieved that distinction in the latest Higher Education Authority figures.

While 110 fewer female students reached this level, it should be borne in mind that the number of first-class honours degrees awarded per annum is small – about 7 per cent of all degrees.

However, the recovery by men between school and college is surprising, as there are sometimes only three to four years between the Leaving Cert and final exams at university.

Even more surprising is that males get more top degrees even though there are 5,588 of them in university compared to 6,737 females.

Males students seem to increase their performance greatly during this time, according to Higher Education Authority (HEA) figures, which form part of its annual report, due to be published later this year. It covers degrees awarded in the State's seven universities in 1997/98.

Experts traditionally use the number of top degrees awarded as the primary measurement of how the sexes are performing at third level. So while women are getting to university in larger numbers, they are not taking their share of the top degrees.

So what lies behind the performance of men at university when so many of them fail to shine in school exams? One salient factor is that males tend to do courses where high marks are available.

In engineering there are large numbers of first-class honours degrees awarded, mostly to male students because there are more of them than women engineers . . .

So one of the central reasons female students lag behind their male counterparts is they are not doing such courses as engineering where first class honours degrees tend to be awarded . . .

But even taking into account the dominance of men in engineering and information technology, there is no doubt there is an improvement in men's academic performance between school and university.

→

> The explanations behind the 'catch-up' effect are varied. The Union of Students of Ireland has pointed to the large number of male lecturers as the reason females get 'marked down' in university exams.
>
> It cited a report by Prof Catherine Belsey, an academic from University College, Cardiff, which showed that female students in its arts faculty were being under-marked before the introduction of anonymous marking . . .
>
> Other possible explanations are that female performance is lowered in a co-educational environment like a university. Research has supported this trend at school level, where girls in single-sex schools often do better than those who share with boys. It may be factor in university for those girls who leave their single-sex school and find their performance dropping . . .
>
> **Source:** *The Irish Times*, 18 September 2000.

Questions

1. Suppose you read this article and decide to develop a model to explain which students receive first class honours. Describe the deductive model. Begin with the deductive model using the following form:

$$\text{First class honours} = f(X_1, X_2)$$

Choose two independent variables for X_1 and X_2 and explain why you chose them.

2. Describe the inductive model. What kind of data might help you to explain how first class honours are awarded?

3. Which is the best type of model to study this issue?

Answers on Website

1.3 PRODUCTION POSSIBILITY FRONTIER

We will finish this chapter by introducing a neoclassical model of the economy called the production possibility frontier. This model demonstrates the limits of an economy's production caused by resources that are finite. We begin by defining relevant terms and stating the assumption of the model.

Definitions and assumptions

Definition

Factors of production are the resources of an economy. They include land, labour, capital and enterprise. They are sometimes referred to as the 'inputs'.

Land represents all of the natural resources available to an economy. Labour is the muscle power and the brainpower of workers. Capital represents the durable assets used during the production process including plant and machinery. Enterprise represents the co-ordination of skills of people who organise the other factors of production.

One of the assumptions of the model is that all resources are 'productive'. A second assumption is that while resources can be transferred from one type of production to another, they may not be equally productive in alternative employment. This is because some factors of production are specialised. For example, a person trained to be a chef would be more productive at organising a kitchen than organising a factory.

Theoretical analysis

The production function expresses the relationship between the factors of production and the output of the economy (Q).

$$Q = f \text{ (land, labour, capital and enterprise)}$$

This equation states that the output of the economy is a function of its resources (see Section 5.2). Because resources are productive, there is a positive relationship between the factors of production and output. Any increase in the quantity or quality of inputs will increase the output of the economy.

The production possibility frontier shows the limits of production at a point in time. For this simple model of the economy, we concentrate on the production of only two goods. However, the predictions that we make can be applied to a more complex economy.

Definition

The production possibility frontier (PPF) shows all possible combinations of two goods that can be produced using available technology and all available resources.

As an example, we will consider an economy where capital goods (machines) and consumer goods are produced. Table 1.2 records some of the possible combinations of the two goods that can be produced with the available resources and technology.

Table 1.2: Production possibilities for capital and consumer goods

Combination	Consumer goods	Capital goods
a	20	0
b	19	1
c	16	2
d	11	3
e	0	4

Points a and e reflect the extreme cases where the economy produces only one type of good. At point a, the economy produces only consumer goods and at point e, the economy produces only capital goods. At all other points, some of each good is produced.

We can show the same information on a diagram. Figure 1.3 shows the PPF. Consumer goods are shown on the vertical axis and capital goods are on the horizontal axis. Both axes are measured in units.

Figure 1.3: The production possibility frontier

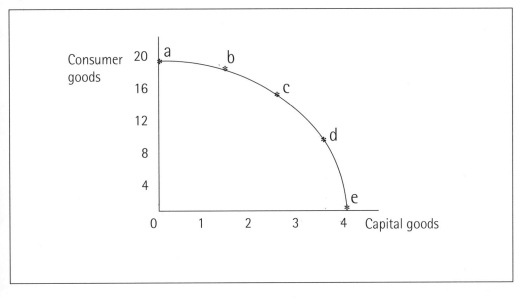

The production possibility frontier shows all of the combinations of consumer goods and capital goods which can be produced using the economy's limited resources. It is downward sloping. This means that there is a trade off. Producing more of one good requires producing less of another good. This trade off is an example of an opportunity cost.

Definition
The opportunity cost of an activity is measured in terms of the highest valued alternative foregone.

That is a rather laborious way of saying that if you spend €8 for a ticket to the cinema, you preferred that option to drinking a couple of pints at the pub or buying a book. These are alternative ways of spending €8. However, an opportunity cost is the 'best' opportunity foregone. Therefore, if on the day, the choice is between the cinema and the pub, the opportunity cost of your trip to the cinema is a visit to the pub.

In the case of the production possibility frontier, the opportunity cost of producing capital goods is consumer goods. Because the PPF is concave, we know that the opportunity cost is increasing. For example, the opportunity cost of producing the first unit of capital goods is one unit of consumer goods. To produce the second unit of capital goods, the opportunity cost is three units of consumer goods.

Why is the opportunity cost increasing? We stated in the assumptions that resources are not equally productive in alternative uses. Initially, the least productive resources are taken from the production of consumer goods and diverted to the production of capital goods. However, as more capital goods are produced, increasingly productive resources are taken from consumer good production. Therefore, the opportunity cost increases.

At every point along the PPF, all factors of production are employed. They are points of 'productive efficiency' as described in Section 1.1. Points inside the frontier, like point f, are attainable but not efficient. This is because some of the factors of production are unemployed. Point g represents a combination of goods that is unattainable. This combination of goods cannot be produced because it is beyond the limits of the economy's resources and technology.

Predictions

Based on the definitions, assumptions and theoretical analysis, what predictions can we make using this model?

First, we can use the model to predict the reasons for economic growth. Output depends on the quantity and quality of the factors of production. Any of the following 'events' will cause the PPF to expand:

i) an improvement of human capital through education and training;
ii) the discovery of oil off the west coast of Ireland; and
iii) the implementation of new work practices which makes labour more efficient.

Economic growth is shown in Figure 1.4.

Figure 1.4: Economic growth

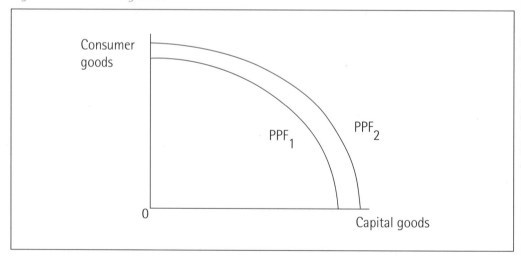

PPF$_1$ shows the original combinations of goods that the economy can produce. The improvement in the factors of production expands those combinations to the area bound by PPF$_2$.

Second, we can use the model to predict reasons for economic decline. Any of the following 'events' will cause the PPF to shrink:

i) emigration of Irish citizens;
ii) flooding which destroys the plant and machinery at an industrial estate; and
iii) deterioration of the national rail and road system.

Economic decline is shown in Figure 1.5.

Figure 1.5: Economic decline

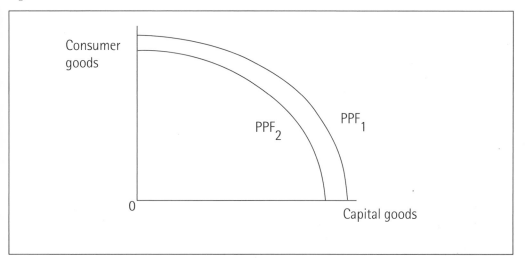

The original frontier shown by PPF$_1$, covers a broader area than the new frontier shown by PP$_2$. The 'events' listed above mean that the productive capabilities of the country have decreased.

Can we predict where on the frontier a country's production will lie? The answer to this question is no. This model deals with the productive capabilities of the economy, not the preferences of its citizens. We need more information to predict the amount of consumer goods and capital goods that this economy will produce.

SUMMARY

1. The neoclassical school is the dominant school in economics in the western world. Neoclassical economists believe that individuals, acting in their own self-interest, also promote the best interests of society. Therefore, they argue against government involvement in the market. The correct role of government is to establish and enforce the 'rules of the game'.
2. Both institutional and Marxian economists agree that the capitalist economy is prone to instability. Institutional economists see government as playing a key role in stabilising the economy. Marx believed that governments protected the rights of the bourgeoisie at labour's expense.

3. Economists develop models to link theory with data. The deductive model is used most often to conduct economic research. It begins with definitions and assumptions. The next step is the theoretical analysis that identifies independent and dependent variables and explains how they relate to each other. Then, the researcher makes predictions and tests those predictions using data. If the data support the theory, the model is considered valid for the moment.
4. An inductive model begins with data. The researcher looks for any data that relate to the research topic. S/he then examines the data to see if there are any relationships between variables. These relationships are used to develop a theory. While inductive models are considered more realistic than deductive models, they are criticised because the relationship between variables derived from data may be coincidental.
5. The production possibility frontier (PPF) is a model of an economy. It begins with the production function. The output of an economy is a function of the factors of production, which include land, labour, capital and enterprise. The PPF shows the maximum amount of two goods that can be produced, employing all of the factors of production and using the best available technology.
6. The opportunity cost of an activity is measured in terms of the highest valued alternative foregone. This concept has many applications in economics. In relation to the PPF, the opportunity cost of producing more of one good is the decrease in production of the alternate good.

KEYS TERMS

Neoclassical school	Marxian school
Milton Friedman	Karl Marx
Productive efficiency	Bourgeoisie
Economic efficiency	Deductive model
Pareto efficiency	Inductive model
Institutional school	Production possibility frontier
Thorstein Veblen	Factors of production
Conspicuous consumption	Production function
Leisure class	Opportunity cost
John Maynard Keynes	

REVIEW QUESTIONS

1. How do neoclassical economists define efficiency?
2. How do the neoclassical, institutional and Marxian views of government differ?
3. What is the connection between theories and models?
4. How does the deductive model differ from the inductive model?
5. Why is the production possibility frontier (PPF) concave?
6. Why do economies grow? Illustrate economic growth using the PPF.

WORKING PROBLEMS

1. Using the information in Table 1.3, answer the following questions:

Table 1.3: Production possibility frontier

Possibility	Units of butter	Units of guns
a	50	0
b	48	1
c	42	2
d	32	3
e	20	4
f	0	5

(a) Plot the PPF. (Put guns on the horizontal axis.)
(b) If the economy moves from combination c to combination d, what is the opportunity cost? (Hint: To produce the third unit of guns, the opportunity cost is 'X' units of butter.)
(c) If the economy moves from combination d to combination e, what is the opportunity cost?
(d) In general, what happens to the opportunity cost as the output of guns increases? Why?
(e) Suppose the PPF is a straight line. What does this imply about the opportunity cost and resources?

2. Show how each of the following 'events' will affect the PPF drawn for Question 1(a). Label the original frontier, PPF$_1$ and the new frontier PPF$_2$.
   (a) a new easily exploited energy source is discovered;
   (b) a large number of skilled workers emigrate from the country;
   (c) a new invention increases the output per worker in the butter industry;
   (d) a new law is passed compelling workers who could previously work as long as they wanted to retire at 60 years of age.

MULTI-CHOICE QUESTIONS

1. Which of the following statements describes the neoclassical view concerning the appropriate role of government?
   (a) Government should redistribute income through the income tax and social welfare system.
   (b) Government should intervene to stabilise economic fluctuations.
   (c) Government co-operates with the bourgeoisie to exploit labour.
   (d) The role of government is important but limited.
   (e) None of the above.

2. Marxian and institutional economists agree that:
   (a) government should intervene to stabilise economic fluctuations;
   (b) capitalist economies are inherently unstable;
   (c) capitalism should be replaced by a classless society;
   (d) the capitalist system ensures even distribution of goods and services;
   (e) none of the above.

3. Which of the following statements accurately describes the deductive model?
   (a) It begins with theory that is tested with data.
   (b) All definitions and assumptions are stated.
   (c) If the data do not support the theory, the model is amended or discarded.
   (d) It is transparent.
   (e) All of the statements above describe the deductive model.

4. The inductive model:
   (a) is unrealistic;
   (b) is the 'model of choice' for neoclassical economists;
   (c) moves from general to specific;
   (d) begins with data;
   (e) none of the statements above describe the inductive model.

5. When the government chooses to use resources to build a dam, those resources are no longer available to build a road. This illustrates the concept of:
   (a) a market mechanism;
   (b) an opportunity cost;
   (c) exploitation of the working class;
   (d) co-operation;
   (e) none of the above.

6. Consider the production possibility frontier shown in Figure 1.6.

Figure 1.6: Production possibility frontier

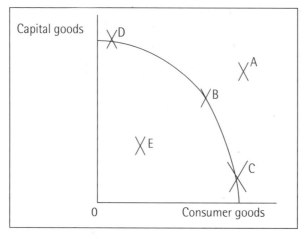

Which combination of goods and services may be produced *during a recession?*
- (a) A
- (b) B
- (c) C
- (d) D
- (e) E

TRUE OR FALSE (SUPPORT YOUR ANSWER)

1. According to Veblen, individuals make independent choices concerning the goods and services that they purchase. F

2. Data are an essential part of both the deductive and inductive models. T

3. Pareto efficiency means that the goods and services produced by an economy are evenly distributed. T

4. A problem with a deductive model is that the appropriate data are not always available. T

5. The opportunity cost of a cup of tea in the college canteen is a cup of coffee *and* a Mars Bar. T

6. An assumption of the PPF is that all resources are productive. F

CASE STUDY

Extract from *The Irish Times*
Harney tackles labour crisis
by Arthur Beesley

Failure to address the labour shortage could 'destroy' the Republic's economic growth, the Tánaiste has warned . . .

Stating that the booming economy would need 200,000 additional workers by the time the National Development Plan was completed in 2006, Ms Harney said such demand would require increased immigration by Irish people living abroad and by others within and outside of the European Economic Area (EEA).

The EEA comprises the 15 EU members – and Norway, Iceland and Liechtenstein.

Citizens of states in this zone do not need visas or permits to work in the Republic.

Such authorisations are required by non-EEA citizens. Ms Harney said about 18,000 work permits were issued this year, in addition to 1,000 work visas . . .

The Government intends infrastructure built in the plan to provide the foundation for the State's future economic development. In this context, Ms Harney said she would encourage Irish construction contractors to take foreign staff and to form partnerships with firms based outside of the state . . .

When asked whether the high cost of accommodation and property, in Dublin particularly, would deter people from coming to live in the Republic, Ms Harney said many Irish-based firms were offering relocation packages to workers with high qualifications. It was common also for groups of workers to share rented accommodation, she said.

In addition to labour from outside of the State, the Government saw employment opportunities from Irish women aged more than 35 years and among long-term unemployed . . .

Another element of Government policy was to provide training to upgrade the skills of the people already in the work-force. Certain multinationals with Irish operations have embarked on in-house 'upskilling' programmes . . .

Source: *The Irish Times,* 22 December 2000.

Questions

1. What is a production function? What are the factors of production and how are they related to an economy's output?
2. According to Mary Harney, what factor of production is limiting economic growth? What policies does she describe to overcome this problem? What effect will these policies have on the production possibility frontier?
3. Can you see other problems that may occur as a result of these policies? One is mentioned in the article but there may be others.

PART I

MICROECONOMICS

INTRODUCTION TO MICROECONOMICS

Microeconomics studies individual choice. Consumers and firms are the subjects of the analysis. Each is studied in isolation from the other before they interact in a particular product market. The purpose of the study is to develop an under-standing of the behaviour and actions of individual agents in the economy.

We begin our analysis of microeconomics in the market place characterised by voluntary exchange. The voluntary interaction between consumers and producers is the essence of the market system. The study of microeconomics will be divided into a number of topics.

Chapter 2 deals with consumers and producers interacting in a market for a particular product. The price mechanism, a central feature of the market system, is explained. A brief account of price controls concludes the chapter.

In Chapter 3 we examine the sensitivity of demand and supply to changes in price. This concept is called 'elasticity' and has important implications for the pricing strategy of firms seeking to maximise revenues.

Chapter 4 concentrates on the role of the consumer in the market place. We begin with the neoclassical assumption that each consumer acts as if s/he is attempting to maximise his or her utility or satisfaction. The negative relationship between price and quantity is explained in terms of utility. The demand curve for different categories of products is examined.

We begin a more intensive investigation of producer behaviour in Chapter 5. In traditional neoclassical economics, we assume that firms act as if they are attempting to maximise profit. We will see that both productivity and costs influence a firm's production decision.

In Chapter 6, we examine different types of market structures. The environment within which the firm operates determines a firm's behaviour. The pricing and output decision of the firm is largely influenced by the degree of competition facing the firm.

The initial chapters deal with the markets for final products. In Chapter 7, we focus on the market for factor inputs. Land, labour, capital and enterprise are all parts of the production process. This chapter includes sections on the Irish minimum wage and national wage agreements.

In the market system, market failures sometimes occur. Externalities or spillover effects can be positive or negative. To combat these effects, more extensive government intervention may be required. This aspect of microeconomics is discussed in Chapter 8. The provision of public goods by the government using taxpayers' contributions is also examined.

Part 1 of the textbook concludes with applied microeconomic policy. Chapter 9 includes two topics that are particularly relevant to Ireland in the first few years of the new millennium, namely taxation policy and competition policy.

CHAPTER 2

DEMAND, SUPPLY AND THE MARKET

'The price of ability does not depend on merit, but on supply and demand.'[1]

George Bernard Shaw

'When the demand price is equal to the supply price, the amount produced has no tendency either to be increased or to be diminished; it is in equilibrium.'[2]

Alfred Marshall (1842–1924)

CHAPTER OBJECTIVES

Upon completing this chapter, the student should understand:

- demand and the demand curve;
- supply and the supply curve;
- factors influencing demand and supply;
- price mechanism and market equilibrium;
- price controls.

OUTLINE

2.1 Demand and consumers
2.2 Supply and producers
2.3 Market equilibrium and the price mechanism
2.4 Price controls

INTRODUCTION

Why do consumers pay €7.50 for a kilogram of Irish beef and €25 for a haircut? The answer lies in the analysis of 'the market'. We begin our analysis by looking at the market for a particular good or service like beef or haircuts. The willingness of consumers to purchase a particular good or service is the basis of market demand. The willingness of producers to provide a particular good or service is the basis of market supply. The interaction of consumers and producers determines the market price for a good or service.

After considering the components of a market and the way in which price is determined, we will look at price controls. These are actions taken by government, to promote the interests of either the producer or the consumer.

27

2.1 DEMAND AND CONSUMERS

If you were asked to describe a 'market' your description might vary from the stock exchange, to a website, to a corner shop. In an economic context, we usually discuss the market for a particular good or service like a chocolate bar or a haircut. In this case, the 'market' is not a place, but a theoretical concept or model.

Definition
The market is any arrangement that facilitates the buying and selling of a good, service, factor of production or future commitment.

Generally, there is a time dimension. This recognises that market conditions of demand and supply for a particular product only last for a limited period of time.

The appropriate length of time varies with the particular good or service. Upheavals in oil-producing countries mean that the price of a barrel of oil on the world market is constantly changing. We may want to look at the market for oil on a daily basis. The market for candy bars is more stable. It may be possible to look at a market for this product over a longer period of time like a month or year.

The point is that whenever we look at a market for a particular good or service, the time dimension will always be identified within the model.

The model of the market shows the interaction of consumers and producers. Consumers generate the demand for a good or service.

Definition
Demand is the quantity of a good or service that consumers purchase at each conceivable price during a particular time period.

Demand relates not only to what consumers want, but what they can afford. Sometimes this is called 'effective' demand or purchasing power. It is the desire for a product backed up by an ability to pay.

Demand does not refer to a particular quantity, but to a whole range of quantities. The reason we associate a commodity with a particular price is because in a market system, price is determined by the interaction of the consumers and the suppliers. If we observe consumers in isolation, we are then faced with a range of prices, and subsequently, with a range of quantities.

What determines the level of demand? Why do consumers demand a small or large quantity of a product? One of the key factors which determines demand is the price of the good. We can write this relationship in mathematical form:

$$Qd = f(P)$$ [2.1]

where: Qd = Quantity demanded; P = Price.

This relationship can be expressed in a number of different ways. For example,

> Quantity demanded is a function of price
>
> *or*
>
> Quantity demanded depends on price
>
> *or*

Each level of quantity demanded is associated with its own price

Equation 2.1 is called the demand function. It involves two variables where a variable is defined as a symbol that can represent any unspecified number or value. Price is the explanatory variable in that it serves to explain the specific level of quantity demanded. It is autonomous or independent. Quantity demanded is the dependent variable. It is conditional on the level of price.

We can examine the relationship between price and quantity for a good by considering a demand schedule.

Definition

A demand schedule is a table which indicates the quantity of a particular good which consumers are willing to purchase at various prices during a specified time period.

In this definition, we implicitly assume that any other factors which could conceivably influence the quantity demanded do not change during the relevant time period. Using the terminology of the economist, we say that a demand schedule examines the relationship between price and quantity demanded, *ceteris paribus*.

Definition

=>(all being equal.)

Ceteris paribus is a Latin phrase which means 'other things being equal'. In economics this phrase is used to mean that the relationship between two variables can be examined, assuming that other factors are not changing.

The factors which are held constant when we consider the demand schedule include the prices of related goods, consumers' income and their tastes.

Table 2.1 shows the demand schedule for beef measured in kilograms for a one-month period. For each price, there is a corresponding level of quantity demanded.

Table 2.1: The demand schedule for beef (per month)

Price, P (Euros)	Quantity demanded, Qd (thousands of kilograms)	Price, P (Euros)	Quantity demanded, Qd (thousands of kilograms)
5.00	2,625	7.50	2,000
5.50	2,500	8.00	1,875
6.00	2,375	8.50	1,750
6.50	2,250	9.00	1,625
7.00	2,125	9.50	1,500

We can see from this schedule that when price increases from €7.00 per kilogram to €7.50 per kilogram, the quantity demanded falls from 2,125,000 kilograms to 2,000,000 kilograms.

This demand schedule is a specific example of a general relationship. With few exceptions, as the price of a good falls, the quantity demanded of that good rises. This relationship is observed so frequently that we call it the law of demand.

Definition

The law of demand refers to the inverse or negative relationship between price and quantity demanded, *ceteris paribus.*

Generally, we illustrate this relationship using a two dimensional graph. It is customary to represent price on the vertical axis and quantity on the horizontal axis. We plot the points from the demand schedule and join them together to form the demand curve.

Figure 2.1 illustrates the demand curve for beef described by the demand schedule. Because the relationship between price and quantity is negative, the demand curve is downward sloping.

Figure 2.1: The demand curve for beef

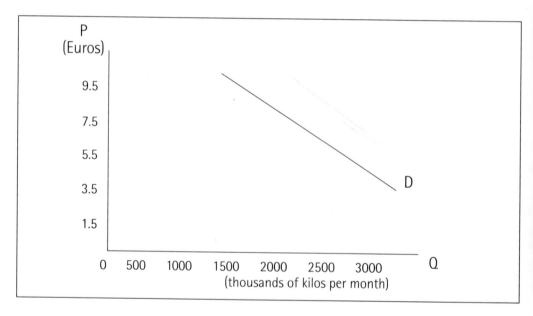

The demand curve cannot tell us the actual selling price or the quantity sold. This information is only determined when the consumers, represented by the demand curve interact with producers, represented by the supply curve to form a market.

At this stage we only offer an intuitive explanation as to why the demand curve is downward sloping. Recall that when we discussed the law of demand, we stated that other factors which affect demand are 'held constant'. Among those factors are the prices of related goods. A number of goods can be substituted for beef like chicken or lamb. As the price of beef increases, some consumers will purchase substitute goods in place of beef. Therefore, as the price of beef rises, the quantity of beef demanded falls. Alternatively, if the price of beef falls, it becomes cheaper relative to other types of meat. People will purchase more beef at a lower price instead of chicken or lamb. We offer a more detailed explanation of the downward sloping demand curve in Chapter 4.

When the demand curve is a straight line, it can be represented in a simple linear form, as follows:

$$Qd = a - bP \qquad\qquad \text{[2.2]}$$

where: Qd = Quantity demanded; P = Price; a and b = constants.

Equation 2.2 shows the general form of a linear relationship between price and quantity demanded. The negative relationship between the two variables is reflected in the minus sign before price, the independent variable. The demand schedule for beef, which we have been discussing, is based on a linear demand relationship. The equation for this specific relationship is:

$$Qd = 3,875,000 - 250,000P$$

A demand curve is not always a straight line. A convex demand curve which is bowed towards the origin is shown in Figure 2.2.

Figure 2.2: A convex demand curve

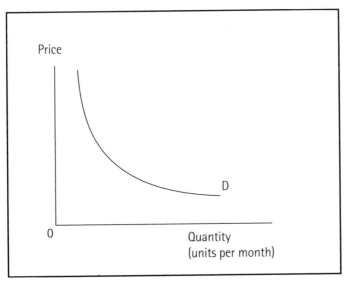

The exact shape of the demand curve depends on the nature of the relationship between the change in price and the subsequent change in quantity demanded. We will examine this in greater detail in Chapter 3.

Exceptions to the downward sloping demand curve

There are a few exceptional cases where the demand curve is not downward sloping. For a limited number of goods, the demand curve may be 'perverse' or upward sloping as shown in Figure 2.3.

Figure 2.3: A 'perverse' demand curve

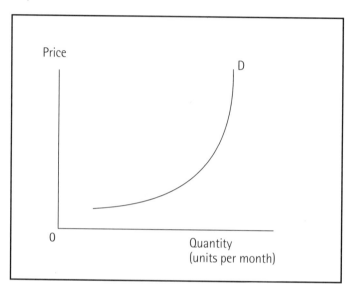

One exception is a snob or Veblen good. The demand curve of a Veblen good is upward sloping. The behaviour which underlies this demand curve was coined 'conspicuous consumption' by Thorstein Veblen, the American Institutional economist and author of *The Theory of the Leisure Class* (1899). He argued that certain sections of society, in particular the 'leisure' class, may not act like the consumers whom we have just described.

Veblen suggested that the ownership of goods which were expensive and frivolous conferred status on the owner because others realised that these 'ostentatious' goods could only be purchased by members of the upper economic class. Status increased when the price of the good increased. If the price of the good fell, the 'snob' value also fell, since it was now less expensive and more affordable to lower classes. In some circumstances the demand for the 'snob' good may actually fall when the price falls resulting in an upward sloping demand curve. Rolex watches and BMWs are possible examples.

Another exception is the Giffen good. The 'Giffen paradox' was described by Sir Robert Giffen (1837–1910) who, it is said, observed that an increase in the price of bread in nineteenth-century London, '. . . makes so large a drain on the resources of the poorer labouring families . . . that they are forced to curtail their consumption of meat and the more expensive farinaceous foods: and, bread being still the cheapest food which they can get and will take, they consume more, and not less of it'.[3]

This quotation suggests that the observation of a Giffen good requires a very specific set of circumstances. First, income levels must be low and the good must constitute a significant part of a consumer's purchases. Second, the good in question must have few affordable substitutes. Even so, an increase in demand in response to an increase in price will probably only occur over a very narrow range of prices. In western economies, characterised by relatively high levels of income and numerous substitutes, most economists believe that the Giffen paradox is no longer relevant.

In short, although a perverse demand curve is theoretically possible, this relationship is seldom observed. In general, we can rely on the negative relationship between price and quantity demanded described by the law of demand.

Other factors influencing demand

In reality there is a wide range of factors which determine the level of quantity demanded. Here we focus on the more important determinants or, as they are sometimes referred to, the underlying conditions of demand. Until now, these determinants were 'held constant' according to the *ceteris paribus* condition.

1. The price of related goods (Prelated goods)

If two goods are related, they are either substitutes for, or complements to, each other.

Definition
Two goods are substitutes if consumers consider one good as an alternative for the other good. If the price of one good falls, demand for the other good falls and vice versa.

Beef and lamb, butter and margarine, tea and coffee, cassette tapes and CDs, bus and rail transport and umbrellas and raincoats are examples of substitute goods and services. If the price of a return ticket on a bus between Galway and Dublin falls, we expect the demand for railway tickets for the same journey to fall. If we test this hypothesis and find that this relationship exists, we consider these services to be substitutes.

Definition
Goods which are complements are bought and consumed together. This implies that if the price of one good falls, demand for the other good increases and vice versa.

Examples of complementary goods include beef and horseradish sauce, CDs and CD players, personal computers and printers, airline tickets and hotel accommodation, automobiles and automobile insurance. Consider CDs and CD players. When they first appeared on the market, CD players were reasonably priced but CDs were expensive. Subsequently, the demand for CD players increased dramatically when the price of CDs fell, indicating that these goods are complements.

2. Consumers' income (Y)

Income was also 'held constant' when we considered the demand schedule. However, it is another explanatory variable. This means that if income changes, it will usually have an effect on demand. Normal and inferior goods are defined in terms of income.

Definition

For a normal good, there is a positive relationship between income and demand. Demand for a normal good increases as income increases or decreases as income decreases.

There are many types of beef. Round steak and sirloin are better cuts of beef. The demand for superior cuts or organic beef increases with income. Most goods from a walkman to an automobile are examples of normal goods.

Definition

For an inferior good, there is a negative relationship between income and demand. Demand for an inferior good decreases as income increases or increases as income decreases.

Minced beef, bus rides and 'yellow packs' are examples of inferior goods. Consider minced beef. If income increases, consumers substitute a better grade of meat for the minced beef. By establishing a negative relationship between demand for minced beef and income, we classify minced beef as an inferior good.

3. Consumers' tastes (T)

Tastes and preferences for the good also affect demand. Taste, in this context, is a broad concept. It is shaped by time, custom, tradition, fashion, location and social attitudes.

Economists generally believe that tastes change slowly over time. Therefore, they are comfortable with the assumption that consumers' preferences 'can be held constant' when the price/quantity relationship is examined. However, as the case study at the end of this section illustrates, the publicity surrounding Mad Cow Disease had an immediate impact on the demand for Irish beef.

4. Other factors (O)

Advertising, expectations about future market conditions and access to foreign markets are some additional factors which lead to changes in demand for a particular commodity. As a result of Mad Cow Disease, trade with Russia was curtailed and with Iran was discontinued. This led to a deterioration in the conditions of demand faced by the producers of Irish beef.

Hence, the quantity of a good demanded is determined by the price of the good itself and by the price of related goods, by the consumers' income, by the consumers' tastes and by a range of other factors. The complete mathematical representation for our demand function is in the form of:

$$\boxed{\text{Qd} = \text{f(P, Prelated goods, Y, T, O)}} \qquad \text{[2.3]}$$

where: Qd = Quantity demanded; P = Price; Y = Income; T = Tastes; O = Other factors.

In this demand function, as in the original demand function, quantity demanded is the dependent variable. The variables within the parentheses represent independent variables.

Suppose we want to examine the relationship between quantity demanded and price. We can show this using the demand function:

$$Qd = f (P, \overline{\text{Prelated goods}}, \overline{Y}, \overline{T}, \overline{O})$$

There is a line over all of the independent variables with the exception of price. The line indicates that underlying variables or the conditions of demand are held constant. We can interpret this function in the same way that we interpreted the original demand function. Quantity demanded depends on price, *ceteris paribus*.

We now examine the distinction between a movement along the demand curve and a shift of the demand curve.

A movement along the demand curve

A movement along the demand curve is caused by a change in price. Because of the *ceteris paribus* clause, all other factors influencing demand are held constant. For example, a move along the demand curve from A to B, as in Figure 2.4, is caused by a fall in price. As price falls from €7.50 to €6.00 per kilogram, the quantity demanded of Irish beef increases from 2,000,000 to 2,375,000 kilograms per month. Similarly, a movement from B to A is caused by an increase in price.

Figure 2.4: A movement along the demand curve

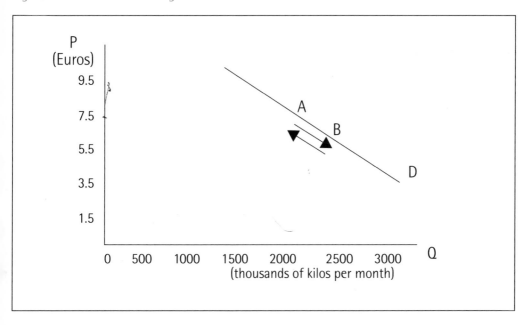

A shift of the demand curve

Suppose that one of the conditions of demand changes. For example, assume that income rises and beef is a normal good.

We can show this using the demand function:

$$Qd = f\,(\overline{P},\ \overline{Prelated\ goods},\ Y,\ \overline{T},\ \overline{O})$$

In this case, there is a line over all of the independent variables except for Y which represents income, the variable which is changing.

If one of the underlying variables changes, then each single point on the demand curve moves either out to the right or in to the left. Figure 2.5 shows the original demand curve, D. The second demand curve, D^1 reflects the increase in income. Every conceivable price corresponds to a higher level of demand. For example, at price P^0, demand increases from Q to Q^1. An improvement in the conditions of demand leads to a rightward shift of the demand curve.

Figure 2.5: A rightward shift of the demand curve

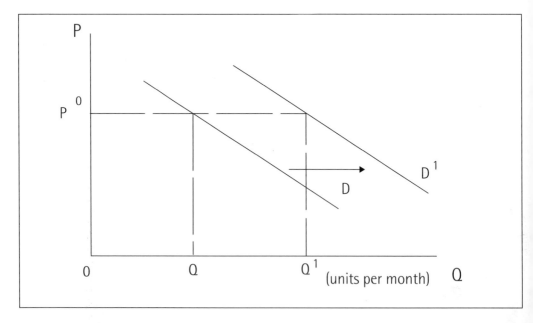

If income had fallen for a normal good the shift would have been to the left. A deterioration in the conditions of demand leads to a leftward shift of the demand curve. This is shown in Figure 2.6.

Figure 2.6: A leftward shift of the demand curve

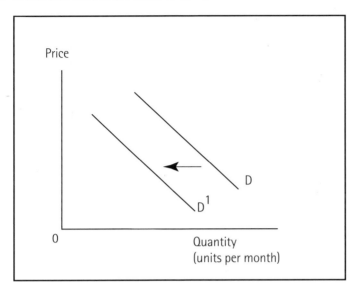

Table 2.2 contains a number of possible changes in underlying factors which would result in either a rightward or a leftward shift of the demand curve. Draw these for yourself.

Table 2.2: Changes in independent variables that cause shifts of the demand curve

Independent variable	Rightward shift of demand curve	Leftward shift of demand curve
↑ substitute good	√	
↓P substitute good		√
↑P complement good		√
↓P complement good	√	
↑Y (normal good)	√	
↓Y (normal good)		√
↑Y (inferior good)		√
↓Y (inferior good)	√	
Preference improves	√	
Preference disimproves		√

CASE STUDY

Mad Cow Disease and demand for Irish beef

Mad Cow Disease is the name given by journalists to bovine spongiform encephalopathy (BSE). BSE was first identified by British scientists in 1986. It is a disease which attacks the central nervous system of cows turning their brains to sponge. Cows who are infected with BSE lose co-ordination and weight and eventually die.

It is thought that this disease is caused by feeding practices. Transmissible spongiform encephalopathy (TSE) infects sheep and other animals, both wild and domestic. It is commonly known as scrapie in sheep. Before BSE was identified, the remains of sheep (both meat and bone) were rendered into meal and used as a protein supplement for cattle. The highest concentrations of BSE occurred in Britain, where the supplement was prepared differently than in other parts of Europe. It was through the protein supplement that TSE moved from one species (sheep) to another (cattle).

For years it was not known if humans could 'catch' mad cow disease. At the beginning of the twentieth century, a disease to the human central nervous system called Creutzfeldt-Jakob disease (CJD) was identified. However, no one knew if humans could become ill by eating the meat of BSE-infected cattle. At first, British scientists said 'NO!' British cattle had a much higher level of infection than any other country in the world. A link between BSE and CJD would devastate the British beef trade.

In March 1996, British scientists changed their opinion to 'maybe'. A variant of CJD was the cause of death of ten people during a two-year period. Eight of these people were between the ages of 18 and 41 which was far younger than most victims of this disease. A British advisory group which was studying the deaths believed that the most likely explanation of their infection was their consumption of the meat of BSE-infected cattle.

The first case of BSE was identified in Ireland in 1989. Although the number of cases reported here is tiny in relation to Britain and minute in comparison to the size of the national herd, the report of the British advisory group affected the market for Irish beef.

Extract from *The Irish Times*
BSE threat shows the customer is boss
by Audrey Magee

Over the past three weeks, food consumers have risen from being mere cogs in the massive food-producing machine to people with tremendous power in their pockets. The BSE crisis has shown producers, and meat producers in particular, that the consumer cannot be ignored.

'We have all realised a few things over the past few weeks. I don't think that the food business belongs to the farmer, the abattoir or the processor. The food business belongs to the consumer and she has proved that with the power of her closed purse when deciding she will not buy beef,' said Mr Eugene Kierans of the Irish Master Butchers' Association.

Sales of prime beef are again on the rise after falling by as much as 50 per cent in

⟶

some sectors after the British health minister, Mr Stephen Dorrell, announced a possible link between BSE and Creutzfeldt-Jakob Disease (CJD) in the Commons.

Mr Kierans said beef sales at butchers fell by about 20 per cent . . . Superquinn said sales fell between 20 and 30 per cent . . . who re

Dunnes Stores reported a 40 per cent drop in beef sales. The dip was most noticeable in urban areas, where sales were halved, while the fall was less dramatic in rural areas at about 35 per cent . . .

Fish Sales in Killybegs, Co Donegal, said there had been a huge rise in its business. 'It is very hard to tell how much of this is the result of BSE because it came right in the middle of Holy Week when there are high demands on fish. But I must say it has done us no harm. It has helped especially in the North . . .'

Pork prices, meanwhile, have risen by about 1 per cent as demand for the meat increases. One pork butcher reported a 5 per cent increase in sales while chicken is seen as the best alternative to beef by shoppers at Dunnes Stores . . .

Source: *The Irish Times,* 13 April 1996.

QUESTIONS

1. On one diagram, draw the demand curve for Irish beef before the announcement of the British health minister and immediately after the announcement.
2. What variable caused the 'change in demand'?
3. Does the change in the market for Irish beef have 'knock-on' effects in any other markets?
4. Consider the market for fish. Using the demand function, identify changes to underlying conditions which affected demand for this product. Show these changes on a diagram.

Answers on website

2.2 SUPPLY AND PRODUCERS

Supply and the quantity supplied can be analysed in a similar fashion to that of demand and the quantity demanded.

Definition

Supply is the quantity of the good or service that sellers offer at each conceivable price during a particular period of time.

It is not a particular quantity, but a whole set of quantities. Whereas demand is related to wants, supply is related to resources. The time period may be hours, weeks, months or years.

Resources are 'inputs' which are used to produce goods and services. These inputs or factors of production are land (the natural resource), capital (the manufactured resource) and labour and enterprise (the human resources). It is the cost of the factors of production which underlie the supply curve. This will be discussed in greater detail in Chapters 5 and 7.

Again, we begin with price as the main explanatory variable. Quantity supplied is the dependent variable. This relationship can be written in a mathematical form, as follows:

$$Qs = f(P)$$
[2.4]

where: Qs = Quantity supplied; P = Price.

This equation states that the quantity supplied depends on price. It is a function of price. There is a positive relationship between price and quantity supplied. We can examine the relationship between these two variables by looking at a supply schedule for beef.

Definition

A supply schedule is a table which indicates the quantity of a particular good which producers are willing to supply at various prices, over a particular period of time.

In this case, the factors which we are 'holding constant' include the wage of labour, the price of materials, the state of technology and government regulations. Table 2.3 shows the supply schedule for beef.

Table 2.3:   The supply schedule for beef (per month)

Price, P (Euros)	Quantity supplied, Qs (thousands of kilograms)	Price, P (Euros)	Quantity supplied, Qs (thousands of kilograms)
5.00	1,000	7.50	2,000
5.50	1,200	8.00	2,200
6.00	1,400	8.50	2,400
6.50	1,600	9.00	2,600
7.00	1,800	9.50	2,800

From the table, we can see that there is a positive relationship between price and quantity supplied. At €6.00 per kilogram, 1,400,000 kilograms of beef are supplied to the market. If the price increases to €7.50, producers are willing to supply 2,000,000 kilograms of beef to the market.

Again, we illustrate this relationship by plotting a supply curve on a two-dimensional graph.

By plotting the range of prices on the vertical axis and the levels of quantity supplied on the horizontal axis, we can derive the upward sloping supply curve. Figure 2.7 illustrates the positive relationship between the two variables.

Figure 2.7: The supply curve of beef

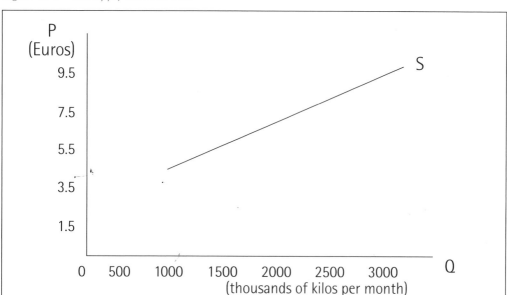

At this point, we will only offer an intuitive explanation about why the supply curve is upward sloping. A more rigorous explanation will be advanced in Chapter 6.

Notice that the supply curve starts above the origin. We can interpret this as meaning that if price is less than €2.50 per kilogram, beef will not be supplied to the market. Producers must pay for their inputs which include feeding stuffs for cattle, fertiliser and machinery. At a price below €2.50, even the most efficient producer cannot cover his or her costs and make a profit. Applying a concept we discussed in Chapter 1, the opportunity cost of producing beef is too high. Since we assume that producers attempt to maximise profits, we expect them to divert their resources whenever possible to markets where they can do this. Farmers may move into tillage or sheep production until market conditions for beef improve.

At a price above €2.50, beef manufacturers begin production. As price increases, production expands. In doing so, resources may have to be diverted from the production of other goods to produce beef.

The supply curve can be represented in a linear form, as follows:

$$Qs = c + dP \qquad [2.5]$$

where: Qs = Quantity supplied; P = Price; c and d = constants.

Equation 2.5 is the general form of a linear relationship between price and quantity. The plus sign before the price variable reflects the positive relationship between the price and the quantity supplied. As price increases, so does the quantity supplied. The supply schedule for beef which we have been discussing is based on a linear relationship. The specific equation for this example is:

$$Qs = -1,000,000 + 400,000P$$

A supply curve may not be a straight line, depending on the nature of the manufacturers' costs. A non-linear upward sloping supply curve is shown in Figure 2.8.

Figure 2.8: A non-linear upward sloping supply curve

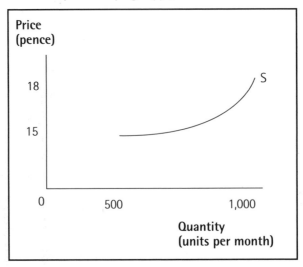

Exceptions to the upward sloping supply curve

The positive relationship between price and quantity supplied holds true for most goods produced in competitive markets. There are, however, exceptions to this rule. One example is illustrated below.

Figure 2.9: An exception to the upward sloping supply curve

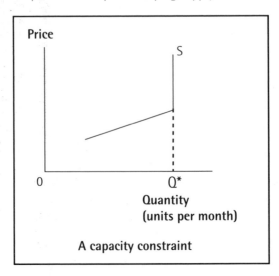

Figure 2.9 depicts a 'kinked' supply curve. The supply curve is upward sloping over a range of production. Then the supply curve changes and is vertical. Beyond Q*, firms operating in this market cannot respond to an increase in price because of plant size, access to raw materials or the availability of skilled labour. The vertical part of the supply curve reflects maximum production capacity. It is impossible to produce beyond output level Q* because of this capacity constraint.

Factors such as the level of technology, the price of inputs or raw materials and the extent of government regulations will affect the position and shape of the supply curve.

Other factors influencing supply

1. Technology (T)

A supply curve is drawn for a particular technological process. A technological improvement means that suppliers can use inputs more efficiently, and the cost of producing a unit of output falls.

A technological improvement can result from improved machinery, like the introduction of robots to the milking parlour. It can also result from different work practices which make labour more efficient. Often, a technological improvement involves both new machinery and changing work practices.

2. Input prices (I)

Output is produced by using a certain combination of inputs, including labour, raw materials and machinery. A supply curve is drawn for a particular price level of these factors of production. A reduction in input prices (e.g. lower wages, lower fertiliser costs, lower rental prices for machinery) induces farmers to supply more output at each price. Higher input prices, making production less profitable at each conceivable price, results in less output.

3. Government regulations (G)

Government regulations can positively or negatively affect producers' costs. Safety regulations which reduce accidents and safeguard the health of workers may be cost reducing. Compliance with restrictions and regulations legislated by government can also increase the costs of firms operating in particular markets. Depending on the nature of the regulation, supply can be either positively or negatively affected.

4. Taxes (Tx)

Taxes on wages, property, utilities or other inputs increase the costs of production. A reduction in taxes decreases the costs of production.

5. Subsidies (Sy)

Government subsidies to producers decrease the cost per unit of output. Farmers have received extensive subsidies from the Irish government and the European Union. These are designed to supplement farm income to encourage people to remain in farming.

'Premium' payments, an amount paid annually on certain types of cattle, has led to the overproduction of beef. In order to decrease the number of cattle in the European Union, there is now a limit or quota on the number of units which are subsidised.

6. Other factors (O)

Other factors influencing the level of quantity supplied include the price of other commodities, expectations of the future, climatic conditions and other unpredictable events. The extended supply function is of the form:

$$\boxed{Qs = f(P, T, I, G, Tx, Sy, O)} \qquad [2.6]$$

where: Qs = Quantity supplied; P = Price; T = Technology; I = Input costs;
         G = Government regulations; Tx = Taxes; Sy = Subsidies; O = Other Factors.

Suppose we want to examine the relationship between quantity supplied and price. We can show this using the supply function:

$$Qs = f\,(P,\ \overline{T},\ \ \overline{I},\ \overline{G},\ \overline{Tx},\ \overline{Sy},\ \overline{O})$$

There is a line over all of the independent variables with the exception of price. The line indicates that underlying variables or the conditions of supply are held constant. We can interpret this function in the same way that we interpreted the original supply function. Quantity supplied depends on price, *ceteris paribus*.

We now examine the distinction between a movement along the supply curve and a shift of the supply curve.

A movement along the supply curve

A movement along the supply curve is caused by a change in price. This is illustrated in Figure 2.10 below. The move along the supply curve from A to B is caused by an increase in price. As price rises from €5.00 to €6.50 quantity supplied rises from 1,000,000 to 1,600,000 units. Similarly, a decrease in price from €6.50 to €5.00 results in a fall in the level of quantity supplied. This is represented by a movement from B to A.

Figure 2.10: A movement along the supply curve

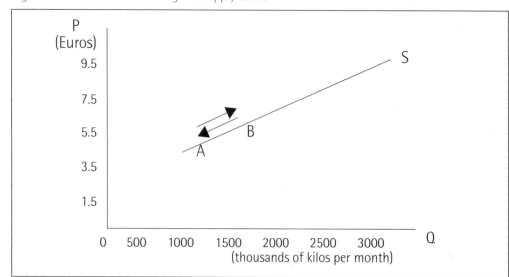

A shift of the supply curve

Figure 2.11: A rightward shift of the supply curve

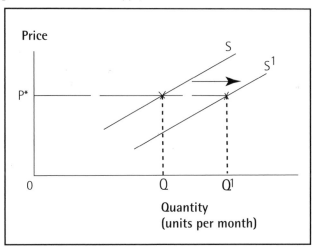

Suppose that one of the conditions of supply changes. For example, suppose the price of hay, which is used to feed cattle in the winter falls. Hay is one input used in the production of beef. We can show this change using the supply function.

$$Qs = f (\overline{P}, \overline{T}, I, \overline{G}, \overline{Tx}, \overline{Sy}, \overline{O})$$

In this case, there is a line above all of the variables with the exception of I which represents the price of an input which is changing.

Because the price of the input falls, farmers can produce cows, which are used for beef at a lower cost.

We can illustrate this improvement by a rightward shift of the supply curve, as shown in Figure 2.11. Because of the change in an underlying variable, the supply curve shifts from S to S^1. If we hold the quantity constant, we observe that Q units of beef can be produced at a lower cost per kilogram.

This rightward shift indicates an increase in supply. For example, at price P*, the quantity of beef supplied increases from Q to Q^1. At every price, a larger number of kilos of beef is produced.

Alternatively, suppose that the European Union decides to eliminate the 'premium' payment on cattle. We can show this change using the supply function:

$$Qs = f (\overline{P}, \overline{T}, \overline{I}, \overline{G}, \overline{Tx}, Sy, \overline{O})$$

In this case, the line is above all of the variables with the exception of Sy which represents the subsidy which is changing.

Figure 2.12 shows the original supply curve (S) which reflects beef production under the condition of the subsidy. Supply curve S^1 illustrates the new supply curve reflecting the elimination of the subsidy. This model predicts that if the subsidy on cattle is eliminated, it will lead to a reduction in the supply of beef.

Figure 2.12:   A leftward shift of the supply curve

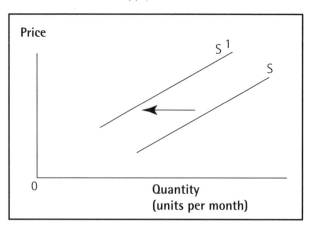

Table 2.4 contains a number of possible changes in the underlying factors which result in either a rightward or a leftward shift of the supply curve. Draw the supply curves for yourself.

Table 2.4:   Changes in underlying factors that cause shifts of the supply curve

Independent variable	Rightward shift of supply curve	Leftward shift of supply curve
Technological improvement	√	
↓ I	√	
↑ I		√
G (cost saving)	√	
G (cost increasing)		√
↓ Tx	√	
↑ Tx		√ .
↓ Sy		√ .
↑ Sy	√	

2.3 MARKET EQUILIBRIUM AND THE PRICE MECHANISM

So far, we have looked at consumers and producers in isolation. In a market, the demand curve, which represents the collective purchasing decisions of all consumers for a particular good, interacts with the supply curve which shows how much of the same good firms produce. When consumers and firms interact, as reflected in the intersection of the demand curve and the supply curve, price is established, as we will soon discover.

Market equilibrium

Alfred Marshall (1842–1924), the economist most noted for bringing demand and supply to the forefront of economic thinking, compared demand and supply to the blades of a pair of scissors (see Appendix 2.1).[4] The demand curve shows the negative relationship between price and quantity demanded. The supply curve shows the positive relationship between price and quantity supplied.

In a market economy, price is determined by both sides of the market.

Definition
Price can be defined as that which is given in exchange for a good or service.

It is impossible to say whether it is demand or supply which determines the market price just as it is impossible to say which blade of Marshall's scissors does the actual cutting. Price is determined by the interactions of consumers and producers. Theoretically, the consumer and the producer are equally important participants in the market.

It is the interaction of the demand curve and the supply curve which determines the quantity which will be traded in the market and the price that will be charged. There is one price and one quantity where the actions of the buyers and sellers coincide. We call this point equilibrium, a concept used frequently by economists.

Definition
Equilibrium implies a state of balance, a position from which there is no tendency to change.

At equilibrium, the market 'clears' in the sense that the quantity demanded equals the quantity supplied. At all other prices, either quantity demanded is greater than quantity supplied (excess demand) or quantity supplied is greater than quantity demanded (excess supply).

The equilibrium price does not reflect equity or fairness or any other moral concept. It simply reflects the positions of the demand and supply curves which, in turn, represent the interaction of the two basic economic agents in the marketplace.

The role of price

The role of price in a market economy is very important. Price can signal, allocate and motivate. Think of how much information is conveyed by this single piece of information. In most cases, we do not have to conduct a market survey to see if consumers like a product or if they value it in comparison to other products. Similarly, we do not have to contact all possible producers to examine their production methods. Instead, price is the information link between buyers and sellers. Buyers indicate that a price is too high if they do not purchase a good, causing inventories to accumulate.

Similarly, producers may deduce that a price is too low if inventories are depleted and consumers are left waiting for a product. Price is the signal used to communicate information between buyers and sellers.

Price also has an important role in allocating society's resources. Figure 2.13 illustrates the price mechanism at work in the market. By observing a change in consumer preferences from good X to good Y, we can clearly see the important role of price.

Figure 2.13: The role of price in the allocation of resources

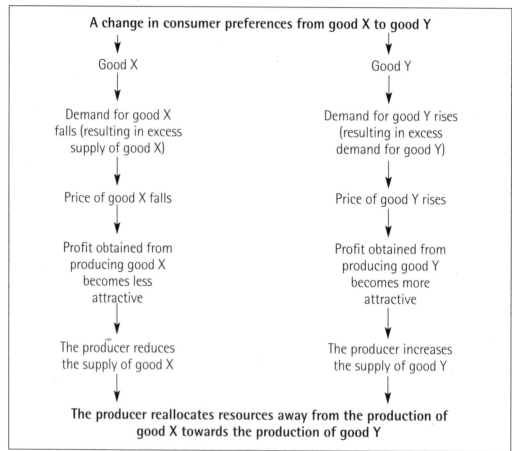

The falling price for good X and the higher price paid for good Y signals a change in the market which is communicated from the consumers to current and potential producers. The potential for higher profits causes a reallocation of resources away from the production of good X towards good Y. It is profit, in the absence of government intervention, which is assumed to act as the motivating force in a market economy. This means that more of the scarce resources of society are being allocated to the production of good Y, the good preferred by consumers.

In all economies, some form of mechanism must exist in order to allocate resources. In a market economy, it is the price mechanism which solves the three basic questions in economics: what is produced, how it is produced and for whom it is produced. The price mechanism is an automatic process. No central agency is required to signal, allocate or motivate. The market, through adjustments in prices, carries out these functions.

This does not mean that we can rely on the price mechanism to ensure that all of the goods and services which we value as a society are produced. Also, in some cases, the demand curve and the supply curve do not convey all of the important information needed to allocate society's resources. We will discuss the provision of public goods and market failures in Chapter 8.

Figure 2.14 illustrates a market for beef. The demand curve is represented by D and the supply curve is represented by S. It is the intersection of the consumers' demand curve D with the producers' supply curve S which determines the equilibrium price and quantity E in this market. The intersection is at a price of €7.50. This is the only price where quantity demanded (2,000,000 kilograms) is equal to quantity supplied (2,000,000 kilograms). In equilibrium, there is neither excess demand nor excess supply.

Figure 2.14: The market for beef

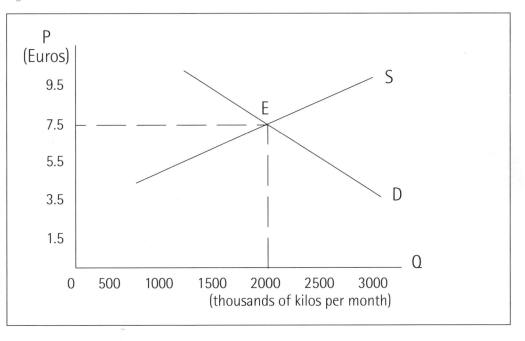

The equilibrium price and quantity (P, Q) can also be derived mathematically from a pair of linear equations. The general format of the two-variable demand and supply equations is as follows:

$$Qd = a - bP$$ [2.2]

$$Qs = c + dP$$ [2.5]

We can solve for price and quantity using these equations. In general, the equilibrium condition is as follows:

$$Qd = Qe = Qs$$ [2.7]

where: Qe = equilibrium quantity.

The demand curve for beef was given by the equation Qd = 3,875,000 – 250,000P, whereas the supply curve was given by Qs = –1,000,000 + 400,000P. Solve for price and quantity using these simultaneous equations as follows:

$$3,875,000 - 250,000P = Qe = -1,000,000 + 400,000P$$

Solving for the unknown P, we get:

$$3,875,000 - 250,000P = -1,000,000 + 400,000P$$
$$4,875,000 = 650,000P$$
$$P = 7.50$$

If P = 7.50, then we can solve for the unknown Qe. This is solved by substituting P = 7.50 into either the demand or the supply equation since, in equilibrium, the quantity demanded equals the quantity supplied.

$$Qe = 3,875,000 - 250,000(7.50) = 3,875,000 - 1,875,000 = 2,000,000$$

The equilibrium price and quantity is (7.50, 2,000,000). This is the same equilibrium which is illustrated using the demand curve and the supply curve in Figure 2.14.

Tending towards market equilibrium

At all prices above the equilibrium price, quantity supplied is greater than quantity demanded. This is illustrated in Figure 2.15.

Figure 2.15: Excess supply in the market for beef

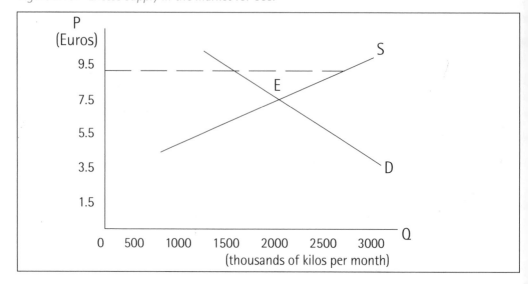

At €9.00, suppliers are willing to supply 2,600,000 kilos, whereas consumers demand only 1,625,000 kilos. At this price there exists excess supply or surplus. We can actually estimate the amount of excess supply. At a price of €9.00 there is an excess supply of 975,000 kilos of beef (2,600,000 – 1,625,000).

In order for the market to clear, quantity demanded must equal quantity supplied. In this particular case, suppliers cut price in order to eliminate the excess inventory or surplus. Price continues to fall. As price falls quantity supplied falls whereas quantity demanded rises. Thus, as price adjusts downwards, the excess is eliminated.

Remember, in a market economy, prices are allowed to adjust in order for markets to clear. Prices are continually cut until the excess is eliminated. In this particular market, price must fall to €7.50 before the excess is completely eliminated. At €7.50 the beef market returns to equilibrium.

At all prices below the equilibrium price, quantity demanded is greater than quantity supplied. This is illustrated in Figure 2.16.

Figure 2.16: Excess demand in the market for beef

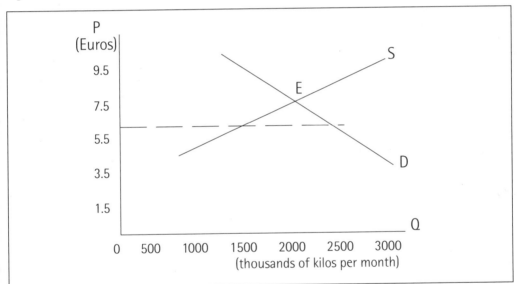

At €6.00, consumers demand 2,375,000 units but suppliers are only willing to supply 1,400,000 units. In this example there exists excess demand or a shortage. We can estimate the actual amount of excess demand. At a price of €6.00 there is excess demand of 975,000 kilos of beef (2,375,000 – 1,400,000).

In order for the market to clear, quantity demanded must equal quantity supplied. Suppliers increase price, and by doing so the excess demand or shortage is eliminated. As price rises, quantity supplied rises and quantity demanded falls. Price continues to rise until quantity demanded is equal to quantity supplied. At €7.50 the market returns to equilibrium.

These two cases illustrate how market pressures or market forces, operating through the price mechanism, lead to equilibrium. The speed of the adjustment in prices depends on a number of factors. The size of transaction costs, the number of competitors in the market and the availability of information can determine the speed of adjustment. The equilibrium level of price and quantity remains constant unless there is a change in either the conditions of demand or supply or a combination of both.

A change in the conditions of demand

Figure 2.17 illustrates an equilibrium position, E, with quantity demanded equal to quantity supplied.

Figure 2.17: A change in the conditions of demand

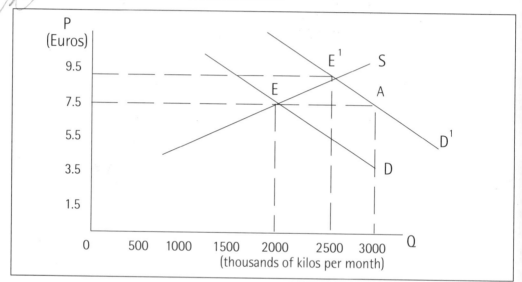

Suppose income rises. For a normal good, an increase in income shifts the demand curve out and to the right from D to D^1. Equilibrium is no longer at E. A new equilibrium is reached at E^1. The diagram indicates an increase in equilibrium price and an increase in equilibrium quantity. We need to explain the adjustment process by which we move from E to E^1.

At the old equilibrium price of €7.50, quantity demanded is equal to quantity supplied. However, as income increases the quantity demanded increases at that particular price (and at all other price levels). At €7.50, the new level of quantity demanded is 3,000,000 kilos. Quantity supplied is still at the old level of 2,000,000 units. At the old equilibrium price there is excess demand. This is shown by the segment marked |EA| in Figure 2.17. The actual amount of excess demand is 3,000,000 − 2,000,000 = 1,000,000 kilos.

In a market economy, excess demand signals disequilibrium. Price adjusts in order for equilibrium to be restored. Suppliers respond to excess demand by increasing price. As price rises from €7.50, quantity demanded falls and quantity supplied rises. Price continues to be pushed up until all the excess demand disappears. As price approaches €9.00 the excess demand is eliminated. At €9.00 the market clears. The new equilibrium quantity is 2,600,000 kilos. Due to an increase in income, both equilibrium price and equilibrium quantity increase.

A change in any factor which results in a rightward shift of the demand curve leads to an increase in the equilibrium price and quantity. Similarly, a change in any factor which results in a leftward shift of the demand curve leads to a decrease in both equilibrium price and quantity.

A change in the conditions of supply

Figure 2.18 illustrates an equilibrium position E.

Figure 2.18: A change in the conditions of supply

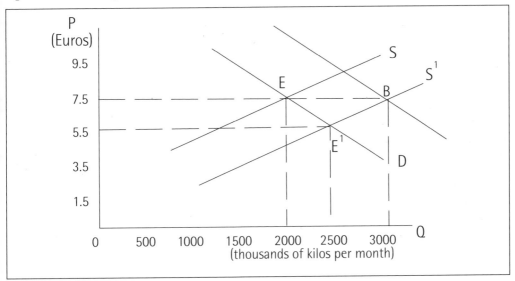

Suppose that technology improves. This means that, in theory, the same amount of inputs can now produce more output. In graphic terms an improvement in technology shifts our supply curve to the right. Equilibrium is no longer at E. A new equilibrium is reached at E^1. The diagram indicates a decrease in equilibrium price and an increase in equilibrium quantity. What is the adjustment process?

At the old equilibrium price of €7.50, the equilibrium quantity is 2,000,000 kilos. However, due to the technological improvement the quantity supplied increases at that particular price (and at all other price levels). The new level of quantity supplied is 3,000,000 kilos. Quantity demanded is still at the old level of 2,000,000 kilos. At the old equilibrium price there exists excess supply. This is shown by the segment marked |EB| in Figure 2.18. The actual amount of excess supply is 3,000,000 − 2,000,000 = 1,000,000 kilos.

Price adjusts in order to restore equilibrium. Suppliers respond to excess supply by reducing prices. As price falls from €7.50, the quantity demanded rises and the quantity supplied falls. Price continues to be pushed down until all the excess is eliminated. At €5.50 the market clears.

E^1 represents the new equilibrium. Equilibrium price is €5.50 and the equilibrium quantity is 2,375,000 kilos. Due to the improvement in technology, the equilibrium price falls and the equilibrium quantity rises. Any factor which results in a rightward shift of the supply curve leads to a decrease in the equilibrium price and an increase in equilibrium quantity. Similarly, any factor which causes a leftward shift of the supply curve results in an increase in equilibrium price and a decrease in equilibrium quantity.

A change in the conditions of demand and supply

In the market for beef, the conditions of demand and supply are constantly changing. Consider the following scenario. Suppose there is decrease in the price of lamb, a substitute product for beef. The demand function for beef shows that the quantity of beef demanded is a function of the price of a related good, *ceteris paribus*. This variable is changing while all of the other variables are remaining constant.

$$Qd = f\,(\overline{P},\ \text{Prelated goods},\ \overline{Y},\ \overline{T},\ \overline{O})$$

A decrease in the price of the substitute good shifts the demand curve for beef to the left.

As the same time, an outbreak in tuberculosis requires that a significant percentage of the national herd be destroyed. This extraordinary event is shown by a change in 'other factors'.

$$Qs = f(\overline{P},\ \overline{T},\ \overline{I},\ \overline{G},\ \overline{Tx},\ \overline{Sy},\ O)$$

This calamity leads to a leftward shift of the supply curve for beef.

What can we deduce about the new equilibrium? We can say, unambiguously, that the equilibrium quantity will decrease. The shift of either curve to the left will lead to that result. But can we be as certain about price? Consider Figure 2.19.

Figure 2.19: Alternative scenarios for demand and supply curve shifts in the market for beef

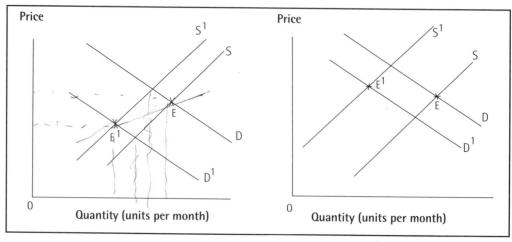

The left panel of Figure 2.19 is drawn to show a demand curve shift which is far greater than the supply curve shift. As a result, equilibrium price falls. The right panel of Figure 2.19 is drawn to show a relatively small demand curve shift and a relatively large supply curve shift. In this case, equilibrium price has risen.

We cannot predict the direction of change of the equilibrium price unless we have more information about the magnitude of the changes in both demand and supply.

This simple example exposes one of the serious limitations of this type of analysis. We can confidently predict the direction of change of the market equilibrium, if – and only if – one change occurs.

2.4   PRICE CONTROLS

In a market economy, price is determined by demand and supply. In a planned economy, this is not the case. It is government, through a particular department or pricing authority, that decides not only which goods to produce, but what price to charge.

Involvement by the state in the market is not restricted to planned economies. Authorities in the European Union and the United States have regularly intervened in agricultural markets with a variety of mechanisms designed to maintain domestic production levels and to supplement farm income. Tax incentives and grants are frequently used by the Irish government to promote certain kinds of activities (such as training and research and development) or to attract certain types of industry (such as multinational manufacturing subsidiaries). Many types of intervention are quite complex and at times it is difficult to disentangle their effects on the market for a particular good or service.

One of the easiest and most transparent forms of market intervention is price controls.

Definition
Price controls are government regulations which limit the ability of the market to determine price.

This price level may not equate demand with supply. An adjustment towards equilibrium will not result because prices are rigid.

Two common types of price controls are price ceilings and price floors.

Price ceilings

Definition
A price ceiling is a maximum price on a good or service legislated by the government.

When implemented, the supplier cannot charge above this 'maximum' price. Its purpose is to help consumers. It is usually imposed in times of scarcity. Without the imposition of a price ceiling, scarce supply would usually result in a high equilibrium price. The government may regard this high price level as undesirable, particularly in a market for basic commodities such as food and fuel.

In order to make these products more affordable, the government sets a price below this high equilibrium price. It does so by imposing a price ceiling, which is legislated

by the authorities at a price below the market clearing level. We know from the previous section that any price level below the equilibrium results in excess demand. However, prices will not adjust upwards in order for the market to clear. Prices are fixed at this level. It is illegal for suppliers to increase price in order to eliminate excess demand. This excess demand, or shortage, can become a permanent feature of the market.

Figure 2.20: Imposition of a price ceiling

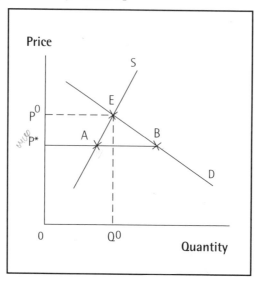

Price controls are particularly common during periods of crisis like wars or natural disasters. During the Emergency (World War II) price controls were placed on many products including tea.

Figure 2.20 shows the market for tea. In the absence of price controls, the price of tea would have been unaffordable to many Irish households. This price is represented by P^0. The government intervened and legislated that the price of tea could not exceed 3 shillings and sixpence per pound weight. This was approximately one sixth of a pound before decimilisation, or 17p. This is represented by P^* on Figure 2.20.

However, because of the lower price, quantity demanded increases whereas quantity supplied decreases. The net result is excess demand at this new price level. The shortage caused by the price ceiling is indicated on the diagram as the distance between point A and point B.

To mitigate the problems caused by the scarcity of tea, the government imposed a price control which caused a shortage. To reduce the problems caused by the shortage, the government opted for a system of rationing. Rationing means that the government restricts the amount of a commodity that consumers are allowed to buy. During the Emergency, every man, woman and child was entitled to purchase 1.5 ounces of tea per week from their grocer.

A system of price controls and rationing often leads to the emergence of a 'black market'. In this instance, the black market refers to illegal activities of buyers and sellers who trade for prices which are above the legislated price ceiling. The 'black market' price of tea during the Emergency was 'a pound for a pound'. This price was approximately six times higher than the price ceiling which was imposed by the government. At today's prices (2000), a pound of tea on the black market would cost €22.88!

To summarise, although there may be compelling reasons to impose price controls in conditions of scarcity of essential commodities, there are a number of negative side effects. Organising the price control and a system of rationing is expensive particularly if there are large numbers of consumers and suppliers. Shortages and the desire to distribute the commodity evenly lead to black market activities. If the controls are to be taken seriously, the government must police the market and prosecute offenders. Also, the control on price serves as a disincentive for producers to supply goods or services to the market. All of these costs, both explicit and implicit, must be added together and matched against the benefits which consumers will receive. Unless the need is very compelling, the opportunity cost may be too high. For this reason, governments in developed countries rarely impose price controls.

Price floors

Definition
A price floor is a minimum price legislated by government on a good or service.

When implemented, the consumer is not legally permitted to purchase the good or service below this price. The purpose of a price floor is to help producers. In order for the supplier to attain a price higher than the market price, the government can impose a price floor above the market level. Any price level above the market price results in excess supply. However, since prices are fixed they cannot adjust downwards in order for the market to clear. The resulting excess supply or surplus can become a permanent feature of the market. The surplus is purchased by a government agency or exported.

An example of a price floor is the intervention price within the Common Agricultural Policy (CAP). This price floor is imposed by the EU in agricultural markets. In theory, if price falls below a particular price, EU agencies 'intervene' and buy the surplus stocks of agricultural products.

Figure 2.21 illustrates the beef market and the imposition of intervention prices.

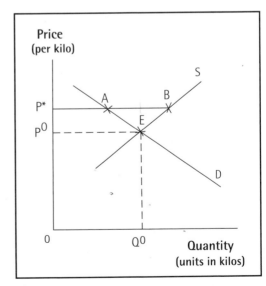

Figure 2.21: CAP and intervention prices

With no price controls the market price would be P^0. However, because of CAP, suppliers (farmers) are guaranteed fixed prices which are above the market price. This is operated by setting a price floor at P^*. This minimum price results in excess supply and is represented by the distance between points A and B. The surplus, however, is not eliminated through a downward adjustment of prices. The producers know that the surplus will be purchased by EU intervention agencies and put into storage. It is the imposition of price floors which explains the existence of the famous 'wine lakes' and 'butter mountains', as well as the beef surplus. Up to 3.7 billion ECU-worth of food stocks were, at one time, in intervention.[5]

In the example above, we can see that the benefits received by farmers impose a cost on other sectors of society. First, the consumers are paying P^* for a product which is higher than the equilibrium price. Second, the intervention bureaucracy is expensive to operate. Various EU and national government agencies are involved in the inspection of produce and the payment of subsidies. Also, any surplus must be stored.

The higher price of food is absorbed by EU consumers. The cost of administering the programme is paid for by EU taxpayers. When we look at it this way, we can see that a price floor is really a method of income redistribution from one section of society (consumers and taxpayers) to another (producers).

SUMMARY

1. Demand is a specific term used by economists to explain the consumers' desire for a commodity. This desire is supported by an ability to pay. The demand curve illustrates the negative relationship between price and quantity demanded. It is drawn on the assumption that all other factors are held constant. There is an important distinction between a change in quantity demanded (a movement along the demand curve) and a change in demand (a shift of the demand curve).
2. Supply is a specific term used by economists to explain the amount of a commodity produced and supplied to the market. The implicit assumption is that the motivating force behind production is profit. There is a positive relationship between price and quantity supplied and this is represented by an upward sloping supply curve. All other factors are assumed to be held constant. There is a distinction between a movement along the supply curve (change in quantity supplied) and a shift of the supply curve (change in supply).
3. Consumers and producers interact in the market and, in doing so, determine a market-clearing price. This market price, in graphic terms, occurs at the intersection of the demand curve and the supply curve. Adjustment to equilibrium is an automatic process in the market system. Any excess demand results in a price rise whereas excess supply leads to a price fall.
4. Central to the market economy is the price mechanism. Prices play many key roles: they allocate resources, provide incentives, signal changes and reward economic agents.
5. Demand and supply analysis is a very useful tool in the study of economics. Changes in demand and supply conditions and intervention by the state affect the market price and can be analysed using basic demand and supply diagrams.

6. Even in market economies, some prices are legislated by government in the form of price controls. Price ceilings (maximum) and price floors (minimum) are two types. Some examples of price controls can be found in market economies, particularly in agricultural markets.

KEY TERMS

Market
Demand
Purchasing power
Quantity demanded
Demand schedule
Ceteris paribus
Law of demand
Demand curve
Veblen good
Giffen good
Substitutes
Complements
Normal good
Inferior good
Supply

Factors of production
Quantity supplied
Supply schedule
Supply curve
Price
Equilibrium
Price mechanism
Surplus
Shortage
Price controls
Price ceilings
Price floors

REVIEW QUESTIONS

1. Explain the law of demand. What are the exceptions to the downward sloping demand curve? Explain your answer.
2. Explain why the supply curve has a positive slope. Describe a possible exception to this norm.
3. What does the concept 'equilibrium' mean? How do markets which exhibit excess demand and excess supply 'clear' or return to equilibrium?
4. Explain the following economic terms:
   (a) substitute
   (b) complement
   (c) normal good
   (d) inferior good
   (e) Veblen good.
5. (a) Explain what effect an improvement in preferences would have on the equilibrium price and quantity of a good.
   (b) Explain what effect an increase in the price of inputs would have on the equilibrium price and quantity of a good.
6 How does the price mechanism within a market economy differ from that which would operate in a planned economy? In what way does a price ceiling or a price floor interfere with the price mechanism? Why are they imposed?

WORKING PROBLEMS

1. Consider the following equations:

$$Qd = -P + 20$$
$$Qs = 3P - 10$$

  (a) Find the equilibrium using simultaneous equations.
  (b) On a diagram, sketch the demand curve and the supply curve.
  (c) Suppose P = 10. Calculate the shortage or surplus.
  (d) Suppose P = 4. Calculate the shortage or surplus.

2. Consider the market for bread shown in Figure 2.22.

Figure 2.22: Market for bread

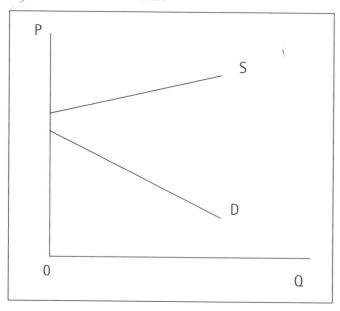

  (a) If the government does not intervene in this market, will bread be supplied to the market?
  (b) Will a form of price control be effective in this situation?
  (c) Will a subsidy to suppliers be effective in this situation?
  (d) Why would a government intervene in this type of market?

MULTI-CHOICE QUESTIONS

1. Which of the following 'events' will cause a rightward shift in the demand curve for wine (a normal good)?
  (a) an increase in the price of beer;
  (b) a decrease in income;

(c) a decrease in the price of cheese (a complement);
(d) none of the above;
(e) both (a) and (c) above.

2. Which of the following 'events' will cause the supply curve for wine to shift to the right?
(a) a frost kills half of the grape crop;
(b) there is an improvement in technology;
(c) there is an increase in the wage paid to labour;
(d) a study is produced which states that drinking wine improves your health;
(e) none of the above.

3. The price of wine will tend to fall if:
(a) there is a surplus at the current price;
(b) the current price is above equilibrium;
(c) the quantity supplied exceeds the quantity demanded at the current price;
(d) all of the above;
(e) none of the above.

4. A technological improvement lowers the cost of producing coffee. At the same time, a study is published which states that drinking coffee causes heart disease. In response to these 'events', the new equilibrium quantity of coffee will:
(a) rise;
(b) fall;
(c) remain the same;
(d) rise or fall, depending on the relative shifts of the demand and supply curves;
(e) none of the above.

5. Suppose the market for milk is described by the following equations:
$$Qd = 150 - P$$
$$Qs = -50 + P$$

Q = quantity (litres of milk per day)
P = price (cents)

Further, suppose the government implements a price floor at P = 120. What can we predict will happen in this market?

(a) there will be shortage of 70 litres;
(b) the market will clear;
(c) there will be a surplus of 70 litres;
(d) there will be a surplus of 40 litres;
(e) it is impossible to say with the information given.

6. Which of the following statements accurately describes a price ceiling?
   (a) it is generally designed to help producers;
   (b) it is generally designed to help consumers;
   (c) a surplus may be a permanent feature of this market;
   (d) a shortage may be a permanent feature of this market;
   (e) both statements (b) and (d) accurately describe a price ceiling.

TRUE OR FALSE (SUPPORT YOUR ANSWER)

F 1. The demand curve for a Veblen good slopes down from left to right.

T 2. Maximum revenue is the motivating force behind production and supply.

3. An increase in the costs of production reduces supply and, in turn, forces up the market price.

4. Excess demand in a market economy would force prices down towards the equilibrium level.

5. A price floor is a form of price control designed to help the consumer.

6. A price ceiling is set below equilibrium.

CASE STUDY

In this case study, we will examine the impact of a change in an excise duty on the market for wine. Aside from raising revenue, excise duties are imposed on specific goods and services to discourage consumption and production of goods and services which have detrimental effects on individuals other than direct consumers or producers.

Extract from *The Irish Times*

Wine prices set to drop as Brussels orders cut in duty
by Patrick Smyth

Ireland's wine drinkers will shortly be lifting a glass to Brussels with the news that the Government is being forced by the European Commission to reduce excise duty on wine to the level of that on beer.

The total excise duty on a litre of still table wine is €2.15, one of the highest levels in Europe, while that on beer (4 per cent proof) is 62p. So the expected reduction in excise duty should cut prices by as much as €1.53 a litre . . .

The Commission argues that the Government is in breach of the Excise Duties Directive which bans tax discrimination between comparable, and hence competing, products – the wine and beer markets are regarded essentially as one . . .

More than 37 million bottles were consumed in the Republic in 1997, a 47 per cent increase on 1990. Last year we drank an estimated nine litres a head, but still have one of the lowest rates of wine drinking in the EU . . .

Source: The Irish Times, 11 October 1999.

Questions

1. Will the change in excise duty affect the demand curve or the supply curve? Show this with a function and a diagram.
2. What will happen to equilibrium price and quantity in the wine market as a result of this change? Show this using a diagram.
3. What will happen to the market for beer? Show the change to the beer market with a function and a diagram.

APPENDIX 2.1: THE HISTORY OF DEMAND AND SUPPLY ANALYSIS

Most textbooks today explain the price mechanism with the aid of demand and supply analysis. Changes in the market price are explained by changes in the conditions of demand and supply. This analysis is simplified further by the use of the two-dimensional demand/supply diagram. However, this was not always the case.

At certain times throughout history different theories of price and value have been espoused. Some economists focused primarily on the demand side of the market. These include W. Stanley Jevons (1835–82) and Leon Walras (1834–1910) of the neoclassical school of economic thought. In contrast, the classical school led by David Ricardo (1772–1823) and John Stuart Mill (1806–73) concentrated on the supply side and the costs of production. The economist primarily responsible for bringing consumers and producers together, for studying the interaction of demand and supply and for, ultimately, pushing this analysis to the forefront of economic thinking was the Professor of Political Economy at the University of Cambridge, Alfred Marshall. The familiar demand and supply diagram appeared in Marshall's book *Principles of Economics* in 1890. The actual drawing is reproduced below in Figure 2.23.

Figure 2.23:   Alfred Marshall's original demand and supply diagram

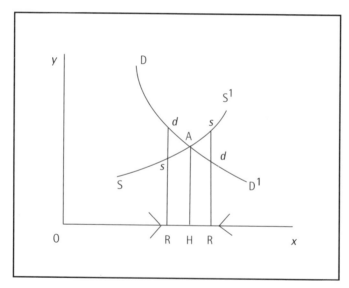

Source: Alfred Marshall, *Principles of Economics*, 8th edition.

CHAPTER 3

ELASTICITY OF DEMAND AND SUPPLY

elastic: – *adj.* **1** able to resume its normal bulk or shape spontaneously after contraction, dilatation, or distortion. **2** springy. **3** (of a person or feelings) buoyant. **4** flexible, adaptable (*elastic conscience*). **5** *Econ.* (of demand) variable according to price. **6** *Physics* (of a collision) involving no decrease of kinetic energy.[1]

'It is clear that economics, if it is to be a science at all, must be a mathematical science.'[2]

W. Stanley Jevons (1835–82)

CHAPTER OBJECTIVES

Upon completing this chapter, the student should understand:

- the concept of price elasticity of demand;
- determinants of price elasticity;
- the relationship between elasticity and total revenue;
- cross-price and income elasticity;
- price elasticity of supply.

OUTLINE

3.1 Price elasticity of demand
3.2 Cross-price elasticity of demand
3.3 Income elasticity of demand
3.4 Elasticity of supply

INTRODUCTION

The demand curve illustrates the negative relationship between price and quantity demanded. Therefore, if price increases, we can confidently predict that the quantity demanded will fall, *ceteris paribus*. In Chapter 2, we described this relationship as the law of demand. Although the law is useful, from a producer's point of view, it is not enough. The producer would like to know the sensitivity or responsiveness of quantity demanded to changes in price. Why? Total revenue depends not only on price, but also on the quantity sold. The producer would like to know if the additional revenue generated from the price increase will more than offset the revenue lost arising from the fall in sales.

The relevant economic concept is elasticity. This term was first used in an economic context by the British economist, Alfred Marshall.

Definition
Elasticity measures the change in one variable in response to a change in another variable.

A producer is interested in the change in quantity demanded which will result from a change in price. This is one of three forms of elasticity of demand. Specifically, they include:

- Price elasticity of demand, η, which measures the sensitivity of quantity demanded to changes in price.
- Cross-price elasticity of demand, $\eta_{A,B}$, which measures the sensitivity of quantity demanded of good A to changes in the price of good B.
- Income elasticity of demand, η_Y, which measures the sensitivity of quantity demanded to changes in income.

The first three sections of this chapter examine the three elasticities of demand. The final section is a brief explanation of the price elasticity of supply. This considers the degree of responsiveness of quantity supplied to changes in price.

3.1 PRICE ELASTICITY OF DEMAND

Definition
Price elasticity of demand measures the responsiveness of quantity demanded to changes in the price of the same good or service.

It is sometimes referred to as own-price elasticity. The additional term 'own' distinguishes it from cross-price elasticity.

The formula for calculating the price elasticity of demand is as follows:

$$\eta = \frac{\%\text{ Change in Quantity Demanded}}{\%\text{ Change in Price}} = \frac{\dfrac{Q_2 - Q_1}{Q_1} \times 100}{\dfrac{P_2 - P_1}{P_1} \times 100} = \frac{\dfrac{\Delta Q}{Q} \times 100}{\dfrac{\Delta P}{P} \times 100} \qquad [3.1]$$

where Q_1 = original quantity demanded; Q_2 = new quantity demanded; ΔQ = change in quantity demanded; P_1 = original price; P_2 = new price and ΔP = change in price.

We can make sense of this formula by way of example.

The Cake Shoppe in Clifden is the only location in town which sells locally baked bread. The owner checks his records and notices that he sells 250 loaves per week at a price of €1. He increases the price to €1.10. The level of demand falls to 200 loaves.

What is the price elasticity of demand, the single numeric value which describes the responsiveness of quantity demanded to changes in price for this particular example? It is explained in the following few steps:

Step 1

Calculate the percentage change in price.

$$\frac{P_2 - P_1}{P_1} \times 100 = \frac{1.10 - 1.00}{1.00} \times 100 = \frac{.10}{1.00} \times 100 = 10\%$$

There is a 10% change (increase) in price.

Step 2

Calculate the percentage change in quantity demanded.

$$\frac{Q_2 - Q_1}{Q_1} \times 100 = \frac{200 - 250}{250} \times 100 = \frac{-50}{250} \times 100 = -20\%$$

There is a 20% change (decrease) in quantity demanded.

Step 3

Calculate the price elasticity of demand.

$$\eta = \frac{\% \text{ Change in Quantity Demanded}}{\% \text{ Change in Price}} = \frac{\frac{\Delta Q}{Q} \times 100}{\frac{\Delta P}{P} \times 100} = \frac{-20\%}{10\%} = -2$$

A 10% increase in price results in a 20% decrease in quantity demanded. The percentage change in quantity demanded is twice as large as the percentage change in price. The single numeric value which explains the sensitivity of quantity demanded to a change in price in this example is −2 (or 2 if, for the sake of simplicity we omit the minus sign and work with absolute values).

Because we measure elasticity as a percentage divided by a percentage, we eliminate the problem of different units of measurement. For example, the demand for milk, at retail, is measured in terms of price (in cents) per litre. Fabric, on the other hand, is measured in terms of price (in euros) per metre. If we calculate elasticities, we can directly compare the price elasticity of demand for milk with the price elasticity of demand for fabric. It is for this reason that we refer to elasticity as a 'unit free' measure of response. The numeric value, in this case −2, is called the coefficient of elasticity. Another example is illustrated in Table 3.1.

Table 3.1: The demand for cinema tickets

Price, P (€)	Quantity, Q (thousands)
15.00	0
12.00	15
9.00	30
6.00	45
3.00	60
0.00	75

Consider two price levels and their respective quantity levels.

Suppose price falls from €12 to €9. As a result quantity demanded rises from 15,000 to 30,000 units. For calculation purposes, let

$P_1 = €12.00$ and $Q_1 = 15,000$
$P_2 = €9.00$ and $Q_2 = 30,000$

We now derive the coefficient of elasticity for this particular example.

$$\eta = \frac{\dfrac{Q_2 - Q_1}{Q_1} \times 100}{\dfrac{P_2 - P_1}{P_1} \times 100} = \frac{\dfrac{30,000 - 15,000}{15,000} \times 100}{\dfrac{9 - 12}{12} \times 100} = \frac{\dfrac{15,000}{15,000} \times 100}{\dfrac{-3}{12} \times 100} = \frac{100\%}{-25\%} = -4$$

In this example a 25% change in price results in a 100% change in quantity demanded. The percentage change in quantity demanded is four times greater than the percentage change in price. The elasticity coefficient is –4.

The six points which form the demand curve have their own respective measures of elasticity. Table 3.2 shows the various elasticity measures at each price.

Table 3.2: Elasticity measures for cinema tickets

Price, P (€)	Quantity, Q (thousands)	Elasticity measures (numeric values)
15.00	0	–infinity
12.00	15	–4.0
9.00	30	–1.5
6.00	45	–0.67
3.00	60	–0.25
0.00	75	–0.00

The demand curve, with the respective elasticity measures, is shown in Figure 3.1.

Figure 3.1: The demand curve for cinema tickets

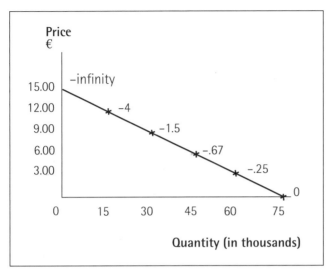

As we move down the demand curve the absolute values for the price elasticities decline. This applies in the specific case, as shown above, and in the general case, as shown in Figure 3.2. Why? Each successive fall in the price level, down along the vertical axis, represents a larger percentage fall in price. Therefore, the denominator in the formula for price elasticity of demand increases in size. Likewise, each successive rise in the quantity level, from left to right along the horizontal axis, represents a smaller percentage rise in quantity. The numerator in the formula for price elasticity of demand reduces in size. Hence, as we move down the demand curve the fractional measure of elasticity approaches zero.

Figure 3.2: Elasticity values and the demand curve

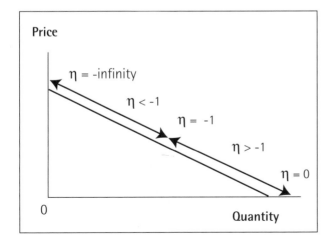

It is important to note that each point on the demand curve has its own unique elasticity measure. It may appear odd that a straight line, with a constant slope in mathematical terms, can have a set of elasticity measures. The answer lies in the fact that we measure elasticity at different prices and subsequently examine the proportionate change in demand. This gives us a different elasticity measure at each price level on the demand curve (see Appendix 3.1 for an explanation of arc elasticity).

However, there are a small number of exceptions. Three of these exceptions are shown in Figure 3.3. In each of these cases, price elasticity is the same at each point along the demand curve.

Figure 3.3: Three special cases of price elasticity

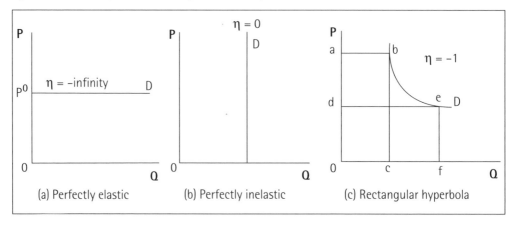

(a) Perfectly elastic   (b) Perfectly inelastic   (c) Rectangular hyperbola

(a) A horizontal demand curve is perfectly (infinitely) elastic and has an elasticity coefficient equal to minus infinity. Demand is infinite at price P^0. The demand for an individual farmer's wheat in the US is an example of a perfectly elastic demand curve. If the farmer charges a price above P^0, there will be no demand for his product. Demand is perfectly responsive to a change in price. The market for agricultural commodities features perfectly elastic demand curves and is a good example of what economists call a 'perfectly competitive' market. We will discuss the different market structures in greater detail in Chapter 6.

(b) A vertical demand curve is perfectly inelastic and has an elasticity coefficient equal to zero. Price has no effect on the quantity demanded. For example, the demand for insulin by diabetics is perfectly inelastic over a certain price range. A certain quantity is required regardless of the price. Demand is unresponsive to a change in price.

(c) A demand curve in the shape of a rectangular hyperbola has an elasticity coefficient equal to minus one. In this case, any percentage change in price is matched by an equal percentage change in quantity demanded. It is drawn so that the areas of all rectangles under the demand curve are equal. For example, the area of rectangle [ab0c] is equal to the area of rectangle [de0f].

Categories of price elasticity

There are three categories of price elasticity: elastic, inelastic and unit elastic.

Definition

The demand for a good is price elastic if the percentage change in quantity demanded is greater than the percentage change in price.

Numerically, the coefficient of elasticity is less than –1. The demand for a good with an elasticity coefficient equal to minus infinity is defined as perfectly elastic.

Definition

The demand for a good is price inelastic if the percentage change in quantity demanded is less than the percentage change in price.

The coefficient of elasticity falls between 0 and –1. The demand for a good with an elasticity coefficient equal to zero is defined as perfectly inelastic.

Definition

The demand for a good is unit elastic if the percentage change in quantity demanded is equal to the percentage change in price.

Numerically, the coefficient of elasticity is equal to –1.

A summary of the different categories of price elasticity is presented in Table 3.3 below.

Table 3.3 Summary of price elasticities

Category	ΔP compared to ΔQ (in percentage terms)	Elasticity Coefficient
Perfectly Elastic	ΔP < ΔQ	η = –infinity
Elastic	ΔP < ΔQ	η < –1
Unit Elastic	ΔP = ΔQ	η = –1
Inelastic	ΔP > ΔQ	η > –1
Perfectly Inelastic	ΔP > ΔQ	η = 0

The number line provides us with another opportunity to examine the different price elasticities. This is presented in Figure 3.4 below.

Note

Figure 3.4: Using the number line to distinguish between the categories of price elasticities

Figure 3.4: *Using the number line to distinguish between the categories of price elasticities*

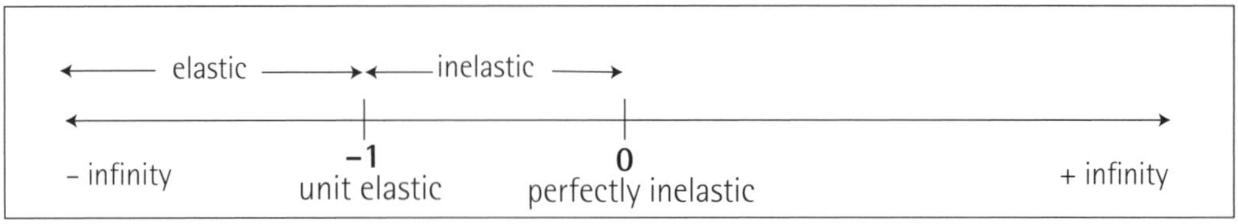

The determinants of price elasticity

The price elasticity of demand for any commodity is influenced by a number of different factors which are examined below.

1. The number and availability of substitutes

The demand for commodities which have a large number of readily available and close substitutes is likely to be highly elastic. For example, the owner of the Cake Shoppe in Clifden found that the demand for his bread was elastic. Why? Numerous, acceptable substitutes are available from Irish Pride, Pat the Baker, etc.

Similarly, if few substitutes are available for a good, demand is likely to be inelastic. For example, a commodity whose demand had, in the past, a low elasticity measure because of the scarcity of readily available substitutes was oil. The Organization of Petroleum-Exporting Countries (OPEC), being aware that many consumers were heavily dependent on oil as their major energy source, took the opportunity to increase the price of oil by over 300% in 1973–74. The inelastic nature of the demand for oil meant that the fall in demand was not excessive.

2. The width of the definition

The narrower the definition of the good, the higher its elasticity measure. The broader the definition of the good, the lower its elasticity measure. For example, the demand for Guinness has a higher elasticity measure than the demand for alcohol whereas the demand for trousers has a lower elasticity measure than the demand for Levi 501s. In general, the demand for a particular brand of a commodity is more elastic than the demand for the commodity as a whole.

3. The time dimension

In certain circumstances, demand is inelastic over a short time period and is elastic over a long period of time. In many cases it takes time for consumers to adjust their patterns of consumption to changes in price. Again, oil is a good example. The initial response to the increase in the price of oil was conservation. Consumers turned down the thermostat to use less oil. However, they could not immediately switch from oil to other fuels because that required a change in their heating systems. Over time, consumers did adapt or change their heating systems, often to combinations of oil, gas, electric and solid fuels. They were better able to switch from oil to other heating substitutes and their demand for oil became more price elastic.

4. *Proportion of income spent on the commodity*

If the price of a good is inexpensive, relative to income, demand is likely to be inelastic. For example, consumers are unlikely to change their demand for paperclips even if the price increases.

On the other hand, demand is likely to be elastic if the price of an item requires a large percentage of the consumer's income. For example, if a consumer wishes to purchase a personal computer, she might watch the advertisements for Dell on the first page of *The Irish Times*. Although some people may purchase the latest model at the highest price because it is 'state of the art', others will wait a few months until the price falls. Demand for this expensive product is 'elastic' because consumer demand is responsive to a change of price.

Other factors influencing the price elasticity of demand include the durability of the good and the habit-forming or addictive nature of the good.

Although the measurement of price elasticity of demand seems to be quite straightforward, in reality it is not. Table 3.4 shows a sample of price elasticities for consumer goods in Ireland. These were calculated by different researchers over a seventeen-year period. Notice the variations in the estimations for each classification.

Table 3.4: Price elasticities in Ireland

Good	elasticity estimation by		
	O'Riordan (1976)	Conniffe & Hegarty (1980)	Madden (1993)
Food	−0.43	−0.42	−0.57
Alcohol	−0.48	−0.56	−0.65
Tobacco	−	−	−0.35
Clothing and footwear	−1.01	−0.70	−0.69
Petrol	−	−	−0.19
Fuel and power	0.11	−0.06	−0.17
Durables	−0.48	−0.84	−1.05
Transport and equipment	−1.59	−1.02	−1.06
Other goods	−0.76	−0.35	−0.69
Services			−1.01

Source: 'A New Set of Consumer Demand Estimates for Ireland' by David Madden, *The Economic and Social Review*, 24 January 1993.

Although in certain classifications such as food and alcohol, the elasticity estimates are quite consistent, other classifications such as transport and equipment and durables show considerable variation.

Part of this variation may be caused by actual changes in consumer behaviour over time. However, most of the variation is probably due to differences in data and techniques. The earlier studies covered shorter estimation periods and the goods included in each classification have changed over time. Also, the mathematical techniques used to measure elasticity changed with each new study. Madden, the author of the article, actually calculated fifteen different sets of estimates.

This shows us that we cannot simply accept that numbers, such as elasticities, are anything more than an estimate. If we want to use the elasticities for taxation policy or revenue projections, we must be quite certain that we understand the method by which the elasticities were calculated.

Elasticity and total revenue

There is an important relationship between price elasticity and total revenue (TR). Total revenue is simply defined as price (P) multiplied by quantity (Q) and can be written as follows:

$$\boxed{\text{TR} = \text{P} \times \text{Q}}$$ [3.2]

Total revenue is normally represented by a shaded area, as shown in Figure 3.5. Continuing with the example of cinema tickets, if price is €6, quantity demand is 45,000 tickets and total revenue is €6.00 × 45,000 = €270,000. This is represented by the shaded area in Figure 3.5.

Figure 3.5: The demand curve and total revenue

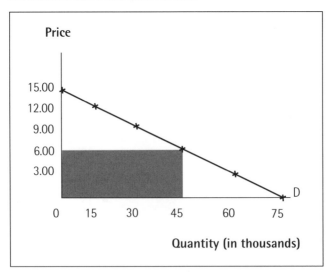

A change in price results in a change in quantity demanded which may result in a change in total revenue.

The price elasticity of the demand for the good determines the extent to which a change in price affects total revenue. This information can be used by the firm to decide if price should be changed. We can say pricing policy depends largely on the elasticity of demand. Two alternative cases are discussed below.

Case 1: A price increase

A producer is considering an increase in the price of a commodity. The producer knows that if she increases price, the consumers will respond by reducing the level of quantity demanded. However, it is the magnitude of the change in quantity which determines whether total revenue rises or falls.

If demand for the commodity is elastic (or at least elastic between two particular prices), the subsequent drop in demand in percentage terms is large relative to the price change in percentage terms. This is illustrated in Figure 3.6(a).

Figure 3.6:   Case 1: A price increase

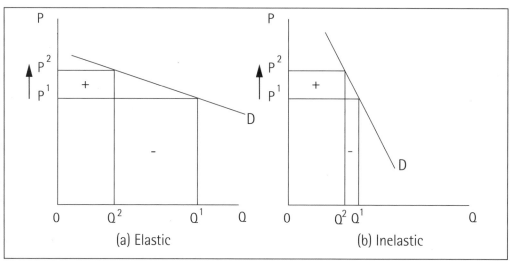

(a) Elastic   (b) Inelastic

The small box denoted by (+), represents the revenue gained from the increase in price. The large box, denoted by (–), represents the revenue lost from the subsequent fall in demand. The revenue lost due to the fall in demand is greater than the revenue gained from the price increase. If demand is elastic, total revenue falls as a result of the price increase.

If demand for the commodity is inelastic (or at least inelastic between the two prices involved), the subsequent fall in demand in percentage terms is small relative to the price change in percentage terms. This is shown in Figure 3.6(b). The magnitude of the price change is the same as for the elastic demand curve. However, the revenue gained from the increase in price (+) outweighs the revenue lost from the subsequent fall in demand (–). If demand is inelastic, total revenue rises as a result of the price increase.

To summarise, when revenue maximisation is the objective, the producer will increase price if the demand for the commodity is price inelastic over the relevant price range, *ceteris paribus*.

Case 2: A price cut

A producer considers a cut in price. The producer knows that if she decreases price, consumers will respond by increasing the level of quantity demanded. However, will revenue increase or decrease as a result of this price cut? Again, the answer depends on the elasticity of demand. Figure 3.7(a) shows a price cut for a good represented by an 'elastic' demand curve.

Figure 3.7: Case 2: A price cut

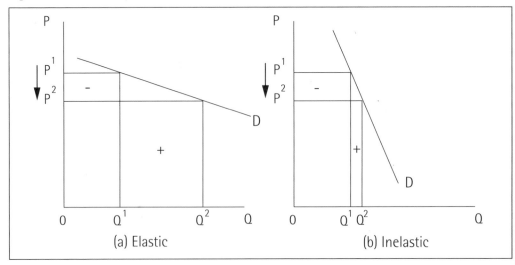

The additional revenue gained from the increase in demand (+) outweighs the revenue lost from the fall in price (–). By cutting price, the producer increases total revenue.

Figure 3.7(b) is the demand curve for a good represented by an 'inelastic' demand curve. The size of the price cut is the same as with the elastic demand curve. However the revenue gained due to the increase in demand (+) is less than the revenue lost due to the decrease in price (–). Total revenue falls as a result of the price cut.

If revenue maximisation is the objective, the producer should cut price if demand is elastic.

Table 3.5 presents the change in total revenue in response to price changes. Different demand elasticities are considered.

Table 3.5: Summary table of elasticity and total revenue

Price elasticity of demand	Price change	Total revenue change
Elastic	Increase Decrease	Fall Rise
Inelastic	Increase Decrease	Rise Fall

Price elasticity and maximum total revenue

The upper part of Figure 3.8 shows that demand is elastic along the upper segment of the demand curve and inelastic along the lower segment of the demand curve. The point of unit elastic demand ($\eta = -1$) separates the elastic and inelastic segments.

The lower part of Figure 3.8 shows the change in total revenue as price falls. Along the elastic portion of the demand curve, if price falls, total revenue increases. Along the inelastic portion of the demand curve, if price falls, total revenue falls. Total revenue reaches the maximum at the point of unit elastic demand.

Figure 3.8: Price elasticity and maximum total revenue

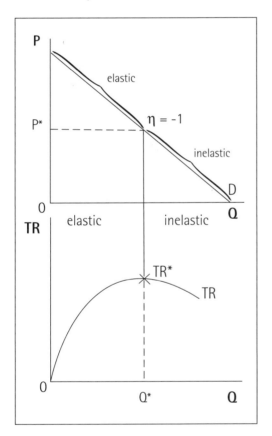

At the point of unit elastic demand, where $\eta = -1$, the total revenue curve is at its highest point. This indicates the specific price level, P* and corresponding quantity level, Q* where total revenue is maximised. If revenue maximisation is the producer's objective, (P*,Q*) is the desired price and output combination.

Government revenue and price elasticity

CASE STUDY

Governments as well as producers are interested in price elasticity of demand. Much government revenue is generated through levying taxes on goods and services. In 1998, value added tax (VAT) and excise duties accounted for 41% of the tax revenue collected by the state.

Definition
Value added tax (VAT) is an integrated sales tax levied at each stage of production and distribution.

Definition
Excise duties are imposed to discourage the production and consumption of goods and services which have detrimental effects on individuals other than direct consumers or producers.

Table 3.6 shows the amount of tax levied on twenty cigarettes between the years 1990 and 1998.

Table 3.6: Incidence of excise duty and VAT per packet of twenty cigarettes (all prices in £)

Year	Excise duty	VAT	Total tax content	Retail Price
1990	1.08	0.36	1.44	1.95
1991	1.17	0.34	1.51	1.95
1992	1.33	0.40	1.73	2.28
1993	1.42	0.42	1.84	2.43
1994	1.50	0.44	1.94	2.56
1995	1.60	0.47	2.07	2.70
1996	1.69	0.49	2.18	2.84
1997	1.76	0.51	2.27	2.95
1998	1.84	0.54	2.38	3.09

Source: Revenue Commissioners (1998) Statistical Report.

In 1998, the retail price of cigarettes was £3.09. Excise duty and VAT accounted for £2.38 which was 77% of the retail price.

What happens to tax revenue when the price of cigarettes increases? The answer depends on elasticity as we will see in the case study below.

Extract from *The Irish Times*
Higher tax 'would cut tobacco deaths'
by Dr Muiris Houston

Higher taxes are the key to cutting cigarette consumption, especially among the poor, the young and the relatively uneducated, according to a major new publication.

A 10 per cent rise in cigarette prices would motivate about 42 million people worldwide to stop smoking. The World Bank researchers estimate that raising taxes could prevent about 10 million tobacco-related deaths.

The 512-page publication is the outcome of a three-year research project by a team of economists, epidemiologists, public health specialists and lawyers from 13 countries.

Cigarette-tax increases have the greatest impact on consumption in low- and middle-income countries. Conversely, high-income countries see a greater positive impact on cigarette-tax revenues. The Republic could expect a 6.7 per cent rise in revenue and a 3 per cent reduction in tobacco consumption if a 10 per cent rise in prices was implemented, according to the World Bank.

The report also addresses the cost of healthcare. Despite their shorter lifespan, smokers incur higher medical costs than non-smokers. In high-income countries, the treatment of tobacco-related diseases consumes up to 15 per cent of annual health spending . . .

Source: *The Irish Times*, 9 August 2000.

Questions

1. From the information given in the article, why is it appropriate that cigarettes are the subject of an excise duty?
2. Is demand for cigarettes in Ireland elastic or inelastic? Explain using information from the article. Show this information on a diagram.
3. The article infers that demand in low- and middle-income countries may be elastic. What accounts for the difference between high-income countries and low- and middle-income countries?

Answers on website

The next section deals with cross-price elasticity of demand and the difference between substitutes and complements.

3.2   CROSS-PRICE ELASTICITY OF DEMAND

Definition
Cross-price elasticity measures the sensitivity of quantity demanded of one good or service to a change in the price of another good or service.

If two goods are related, they are either substitutes for or complements to each other.

The formula for cross-price elasticity is very similar to the one used for own-price elasticity. It is the percentage change in quantity demanded of one good divided by the percentage change in price of the other related good. For two goods, A and B, cross-price elasticity $\eta_{A,B}$, can be expressed as follows:

$$\eta_{A,B} = \frac{\% \text{ Change in Quantity Demanded of Good A}}{\% \text{ Change in Price of Good B}} \qquad [3.3]$$

$$\eta_{A,B} = \frac{\frac{\Delta Q}{Q} \times 100 \text{ of Good A}}{\frac{\Delta P}{P} \times 100 \text{ of Good B}}$$

If two goods are related to each other, the relationship is in either of two forms.

One possibility is for goods A and B to be substitutes for each other. Examples include beef and pork, apples and oranges, electricity and natural gas. Let us suppose the price of apples increases. The percentage change in the price of apples is positive. As apples and oranges can be used as substitutes for each other, consumers consequently consume less apples and more oranges. The percentage change in the quantity demanded of oranges is also positive. If both the numerator and the denominator are positive, then the quotient is also positive.

A positive numeric value also results if the price of apples falls. In this situation, the percentage change in the price of apples and the percentage change in the quantity demanded of oranges are both negative. In brief, if goods are substitutes for each other, their cross-price elasticity is positive.

A second possibility is for goods A and B to be complements to each other. Examples include petrol and cars; pencils and erasers; cigarettes and lighters. Let us suppose the price of pencils increases. The percentage change in the price of pencils is positive. As pencils and erasers are consumed together, consumers subsequently demand fewer pencils and, in turn, fewer erasers. The percentage change in the quantity demanded of erasers is negative. If the numerator is negative and the denominator is positive then the quotient is negative.

A negative value also results if the price of pencils falls. In this situation, the percentage change in the price of pencils is negative but the percentage change in the quantity demanded of erasers is positive. In brief, if goods are complements to each other, their cross-price elasticity is negative.

The above analysis can be clearly illustrated by means of a number line, as Figure 3.9 shows.

Figure 3.9: Using the number line to distinguish between different cross-price elasticities

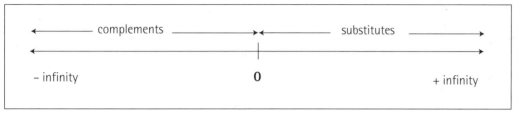

If cross-price elasticity of demand is close to zero, the two goods are not related. For example, an increase in the price of apples is unlikely to affect the demand for flowers.

As the magnitude of the number increases, so does the strength of the relationship between the two goods. For example, blocks of ice cream and wafers are often bought together. We expect a large percentage increase in the price of the ice cream block to result in a large percentage decrease in the demand for wafers, *ceteris paribus*. This large negative number indicates that the two goods are 'strong' complements.

3.3 INCOME ELASTICITY OF DEMAND

Definition
Income elasticity of demand measures the responsiveness of quantity demanded to changes in income.

When discussing the role of the consumer and demand in Chapter 2 we distinguished between a normal and an inferior good. Both goods were defined, not in terms of price, but in terms of income.

Economists attempt to determine whether a good is normal or inferior using the following formula for income elasticity of demand:

$$\eta_Y = \frac{\text{\% Change in Quantity Demanded}}{\text{\% Change in Income}} = \frac{\frac{\Delta Q}{Q} \times 100}{\frac{\Delta Y}{Y} \times 100}$$ [3.4]

For a normal good, η_Y is a positive number. This is because income and demand are moving in the same direction.

Suppose we want to test to see if a good is normal. We could consider a range of increasing incomes. In this case, the denominator is a positive number. We then check to see if demand for a particular good or service is increasing over this range of incomes. If so, the numerator is a positive number. The quotient of a positive number divided by a positive number is a positive number.

If income is falling, the denominator is a negative number. If demand for a good or service is decreasing over this range of incomes, the numerator is also a negative number. Both the numerator and denominator are negative which means that the quotient, representing η_Y is positive. As long as income and demand are moving in the same direction, income elasticity is positive and the good is normal.

Alternatively, for an inferior good, η_Y is a negative number. As income changes, demand for the inferior good changes in the opposite direction.

The relationship between income and quantity demanded can be shown diagrammatically. It is called the Engel curve, after the German statistician Ernst Engel (1821–96) who carried out extensive research on the effect of changes in household budgets on household expenditures. Figure 3.11 illustrates the Engel curve for normal goods and inferior goods.

Figure 3.10: Engel curves

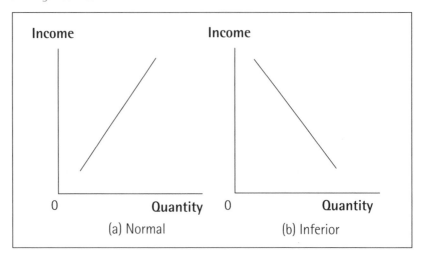

(a) Normal   (b) Inferior

Figure 3.10(a) shows the positive relationship between income and quantity demanded which we associate with a normal good. By definition, as income increases, the demand for the normal good increases. The Engel curve for the normal good is upward sloping. Figure 3.10(b) illustrates the Engel curve for an inferior good. When income increases, we expect consumers to substitute goods of higher quality for the inferior good. The relationship between income and quantity demanded for the inferior good is negative. Hence, the Engel curve for the inferior good is downward sloping.

As with all elasticities, the above analysis can be illustrated by the use of the number line as shown in Figure 3.11.

Figure 3.11: Using the number line to distinguish between normal and inferior goods

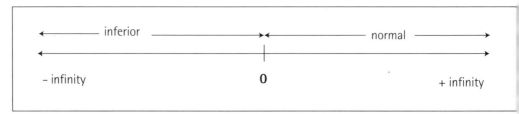

The number line shows that negative numbers ($\eta_Y < 0$) are associated with income elasticities for inferior goods and positive numbers ($\eta_Y > 0$) are associated with income elasticities for normal goods. However, a further distinction can be made within the 'normal' classification.

All normal goods have a positive income elasticity. Further, a good is a 'luxury' or superior good if the percentage change in quantity demanded is greater than the percentage change in income. It has an elasticity coefficient greater than one. Examples include yachts, expensive cars and jewellery.

A good is a 'necessity' if the percentage change in quantity demanded is less than the percentage change in income. The elasticity coefficient is between zero and one. Examples include soap and eggs.

Figure 3.12 shows the numerical values of necessities ($0 < \eta_y < 1$) and luxuries ($\eta_y > 1$), the two categories of 'normal' goods.

Figure 3.12: Using the number line to distinguish between different income elasticities

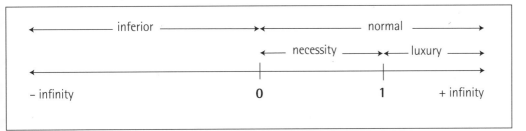

A sample of income elasticities is listed in Table 3.7.

Table 3.7: Income elasticities in Ireland

	Income elasticity estimation by		
Good	**O'Riordan (1976)**	**Conniffe & Hegarty (1980)**	**Madden (1993)**
Food	0.58	0.68	0.50
Alcohol	1.15	1.51	0.65
Tobacco	–	–	0.03
Clothing and footwear	1.75	1.37	1.74
Petrol	–	–	1.10
Fuel and power	1.61	1.66	0.29
Durables	1.67	1.72	1.95
Transport and equipment	2.12	3.52	2.31
Other goods	0.92	0.67	2.03
Services			0.90

Source: 'A New Set of Consumer Demand Estimates for Ireland' by David Madden, *The Economic and Social Review*, 24 January 1993.

Again, we observe considerable variation between the three sets of income elasticities. We notice that in looking at these broad classifications, there are no inferior goods. Only food and tobacco can be classified as necessities. According to the findings, clothing and footwear, durables, and transport and equipment are unambiguously luxuries. The other categories of goods vary between necessities and luxuries, depending on the study.

This reinforces the point that we made earlier. If anything, there is greater variation in the estimation of income elasticities than there was for price elasticities. This variation may be due to differences in consumer behaviour over time, differences in the data collection procedures and/or differences in technique.

3.4 ELASTICITY OF SUPPLY

The analysis of the relationship between price and quantity applies equally as well to supply as it does to demand.

Definition
The price elasticity of supply measures the responsiveness of quantity supplied to changes in price.

The elasticity coefficient is positive, reflecting the conventional upward sloping supply curve. Terms such as elastic and inelastic are used to describe the degree of sensitivity between changes in price and the corresponding changes in quantity supplied.

Factors such as the availability of inputs, the state of technology and the level of excess capacity affect the price elasticity of supply. Time is also an important factor. We can distinguish between three different periods of supply. They are illustrated in Figure 3.13 and we will discuss the periods using the example of The Tea Cozy, a local cafe owned by Josephine Joyce.

Figure 3.13: Periods of supply

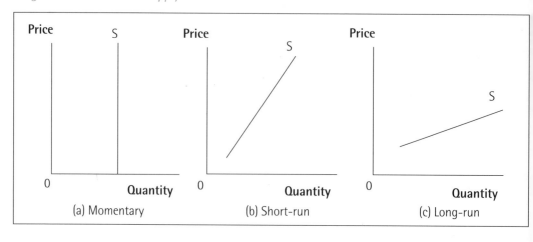

Momentary (market) supply

This period is so short that the firm does not have time to respond to price changes. In effect, the supply is fixed and this is reflected in a vertical supply curve. The momentary supply curve, shown in Figure 3.13(a) is perfectly inelastic with an elasticity coefficient equal to zero.

For example, consider the situation which confronts Josephine Joyce. She owns a small cafe located in the Inagh Valley at the crossroad to Maamaen. This is a popular spot in the summer for hikers. Josephine works alone and her business is generally scattered throughout the opening hours.

One day, a bus stops outside of her door and forty hikers, ready to begin their excursion pour into her tiny cafe. What can she do? Her husband Sean, who stopped for a cup of tea gives her a hand, but there are only two of them. The cafe has a limited number of tables and the stock of food is finite. With the resources at her disposal, she is simply unable to cater for the tourists' needs. 'On the day', the number of meals that Josephine can serve from her cafe is perfectly inelastic, limited by the resources that are immediately at hand.

Short-run supply

This period of time allows for some inputs to be varied while others remain unchanged. The short-run supply curve, as represented in Figure 3.13(b), illustrates how quantity supplied responds to changes in price with the possibility that some alterations in the production process can be made. It has a positive elasticity coefficient.

Returning to the Tea Cozy, Michael Gibbons, the local archaeologist tells Josephine that he is scheduling a tour for hikers to Maamaen for each weekday throughout the summer. Josephine, always looking for new opportunities, organises the family that very night. They clean out the stock room and gather extra tables, chairs and cutlery from their friends and relations. Josephine convinces two neighbours, Francie and Mary to work for a few hours each day to prepare food and to serve the hikers. Josephine calls her suppliers to increase the food order, to be delivered the following morning.

These inputs can be varied in the short-run, but Josephine is still limited by the size of her cafe and the capacity of her appliances. These inputs require planning permission and financing and cannot be changed in the short-run.

Long-run supply

This period of time is long enough to allow for the full adjustment of the inputs involved in the production process. The long-run supply curve, as represented in Figure 3.13(c), shows how quantity supplied responds to price changes allowing for the possibility of adjustments of all inputs used in the production of the commodity. It also has a positive elasticity coefficient. The long-run supply curve is flatter than the short-run supply curve because more adjustments can be made in response to price changes in the long run.

At the end of the summer, Josephine applies for planning permission and borrows money from the Cashel Credit Union to finance construction to expand her cafe and to upgrade her appliances. By the beginning of the next tourist season, she has adjusted all of the inputs to cope with the changes in demand.

The length of these time periods varies from market to market. For Josephine, 'momentary' was a day and the 'long-run' was a year. For the automobile industry, momentary may be a week, since it is more difficult to schedule labour and organise the other necessary inputs. The long-run may be five years, the time that it takes to design and construct a new manufacturing facility.

Only a brief discussion on the price elasticity of supply is given here. Supply and its price elasticity is largely influenced by costs and their responsiveness to output changes. This is analysed in greater detail in Chapter 5.

SUMMARY

1. Elasticity of demand explores the direction and the magnitude of changes in quantity arising out of changes in economic variables. There are three elasticities of demand: price, cross-price and income.
2. Price elasticity of demand measures the responsiveness of quantity demanded to changes in price. This sensitivity can be expressed in the form of a numeric value. The coefficient of elasticity is usually negative. Each point on the demand curve has an elasticity measure. There are three categories of price elasticity: elastic, inelastic or unit elastic. Factors which influence price elasticity include the time period, the number of substitutes available and the width of the definition and the proportion of income spent on the good or service.
3. The price elasticity of demand determines the extent to which a change in price affects total revenue where total revenue is simply price times quantity. In order to maximise total revenue, a producer will only increase price if demand is inelastic and, likewise, will only cut price if demand is elastic. Total revenue is maximised at the point of unit elastic demand.
4. Cross-price elasticity measures the sensitivity of quantity demanded of one good to changes in the price of another good. Substitute goods have a positive cross-price elasticity. Complementary goods have a negative cross-price elasticity.
5. Income elasticity of demand measures the sensitivity of quantity demanded to changes in income. A positive income elasticity reflects a normal good. An inferior good has a negative income elasticity. We also use income elasticities to classify goods as either necessities or luxuries, depending on the magnitude of the response to a change in income.
6. Price elasticity of supply measures the responsiveness of quantity supplied to changes in price. The elasticity coefficient is usually positive. Its magnitude depends on the availability of inputs.

KEY TERMS

Elasticity	Unit elastic
Elasticity of demand	Perfectly inelastic
Price elasticity	Perfectly elastic
Cross-price elasticity	Total revenue
Income elasticity	Engel curve
Coefficient of elasticity	Luxury
Elastic	Necessity
Inelastic	Elasticity of supply

REVIEW QUESTIONS

1. Explain the term 'elasticity'. How is this term related to the theory of demand and supply?
2. What is the connection between the three different measures of elasticity of demand? What are the differences between each measure?
3. Explain the difference between point elasticity of demand and arc elasticity of demand.
4. What factors influence the price elasticity of demand for a good?
5. How is elasticity useful when analysing the effect of price changes on total revenue?
6. Explain why both cross-price elasticity and income elasticity can result in either positive or negative coefficient values whereas price elasticity is usually limited to negative values.

Working problems

1. The demand for Solero Ice, a popular ice cream is shown in Table 3.8.

Table 3.8: Demand for Solero Ice

Price (€)	Quantity (thousands per year)
1.80	20
1.50	30
1.20	40
0.90	50
0.60	60

(a) Sketch the demand curve for Solero Ice.
(b) Estimate a measure of price elasticity at all five points on the demand curve.
(c) Explain why these values (in absolute terms) decline as the demand curve slopes down from left to right.
(d) At which price is total revenue maximised?

2. The set of data in Table 3.9 below was processed over a five-year period. It has been confirmed that there was no change in the preferences of the family in question. Also, there were no changes recorded in the price of any other good.

Table 3.9

Year	1	2	3	4	5
Price of A (€)	72	60	60	66	72
Price of B (€)	36	28	22	28	36
Family income (€000 per year)	170	250	250	250	265
Quantity of A demanded (per year)	60	75	85	70	65
Quantity of B demanded (per year)	130	150	180	170	160

From the above data, calculate:
    (a) the price elasticity of demand for A;
    (b) the price elasticity of demand for B;
    (c) the income elasticity of demand for A;
    (d) the cross-price elasticity of demand for B.

Interpret your answers.

MULTI-CHOICE QUESTIONS

1. The demand curve for a product is elastic when:
    (a) the amount of income spent on the product is small;
    (b) there are many substitutes;
    (c) quantity demanded is unresponsive to a change in price;
    (d) consumers have insufficient time to adjust to changes in price;
    (e) none of the above.

2. Price elasticity of demand for a particular service is $\eta = -1$. At this point:
    (a) demand is elastic;
    (b) demand is inelastic;
    (c) demand is unit elastic;
    (d) total revenue is maximised;
    (e) both (c) and (d) are correct.

3. Suppose price elasticity of demand for a CD player is $\eta = -1.5$. We can interpret this number as meaning that:
    (a) if price increases by 10%, quantity demanded decreases by 15%;
    (b) this is an inferior good;
    (c) this good is a complement;
    (d) this good is a substitute;
    (e) revenue is maximised at this price.

4. Mars bars and Kit Kats are substitutes. This means that:
   (a) as the price of Mars bars increases, the demand for Kit Kats decreases;
   (b) as the price of Mars bars increases, the demand for Kit Kats increases;
   (c) as the price of Mars bars decreases, the demand for Kit Kats decreases;
   (d) as the price of Mars bars decreases, the demand for Kit Kats increases;
   (e) both statements (b) and (c) are true.

5. Suppose income increases by 10% and demand for wine increases by 12%. Wine is:
   (a) an inferior good;
   (b) a normal luxury;
   (c) a normal necessity;
   (d) price inelastic;
   (e) none of the above.

6. The momentary supply curve is:
   (a) perfectly inelastic;
   (b) inelastic;
   (c) elastic;
   (d) perfectly elastic;
   (e) none of the above.

TRUE OR FALSE (SUPPORT YOUR ANSWER)

1. Price elasticity of demand measures the responsiveness of price to changes in quantity demanded.

2. A 15% rise in price with a subsequent 5% fall in quantity demanded results in a price elasticity coefficient of −3.

3. A good which has few or no substitutes is likely to have a relatively steep demand curve.

4. The cross-price elasticity of demand for white tennis balls and yellow tennis balls is likely to be high and positive.

5. All necessities are normal goods but not all normal goods are necessities.

6. The longer the time period, the more elastic is supply and the flatter the supply curve.

CASE STUDY

Extract from *The Irish Times*
Ahern blames labour shortages for social housing shortfall
by Joe Humphreys

The Taoiseach, Mr Ahern, has blamed labour shortages in the construction industry for undermining Government plans to expand its social housing stock. Speaking at the publication of the National Economic and Social Forum report on the housing crisis, he said the Government had committed €800 million this year to housing, including social and affordable homes. However, he said, the industry was already at full capacity and was unable to build units quickly enough. 'It is not just a financial issue. It is the capacity – that we can turn out, not just housing but quality housing. He said: 'The industry presently finds it almost impossible to build any more than there are . . . Much of the industry is working six days already. No unemployment in the industry, and then how do you build more on that? That is the capacity problem. . . . '

However, the NESF's chairwoman, Ms Maureen Gaffney, criticised the three Bacon reports on the housing sector, which had formed the basis of Government policy, for marginalising social and affordable housing. She said the report had concentrated on the private sector but 'whatever about not being able to buy in a suburb of your choice it's another thing not being able to buy in any other area. Introducing the report, Ms Gaffney said the needs of the 55,000 families would be met in the period of the partnership agreement. But this was only 'the tip of the iceberg . . . we are standing still when we should be running,' she said. . . .

'A major and justified criticism of Government policy to date is that it has failed to address housing as a system consisting of a number of inter-related tenures,'* said the commission in a statement. 'The sectoral nature of the terms of reference in recent studies has led to policy fragmentation and sets of recommendations for one sector that have potential negative implications for the other housing tenures.' The commission added that the failure to tackle the current crisis, particularly in the social housing area, was deepening the division in Irish society . . .

* Tenure is the title under which property is held. The housing tenures include the private, rented, local authority and voluntary sector. The National Economic and Social Forum report states that social housing accounts for only 8% of all houses built.

Source: *The Irish Times,* 13 September 2000.

Questions

1. The article does not define 'social' housing. What do you think that it is?
2. According to the Taoiseach, is the supply curve for social housing elastic or inelastic? Why?

3. Does Maureen Gaffney think that the supply of social housing is elastic or inelastic? Why?
4. From Ms Gaffney's comments, which part of the housing market appears to be attracting most of the resources? What problems are caused by this imbalance?

APPENDIX 3.1: ARC ELASTICITY

The definition for price elasticity used in this chapter is often referred to as point elasticity. It measures the elasticity at every point along the demand curve. Each elasticity coefficient is calculated from an initial point or base. This base reflects the starting price and the corresponding quantity level. Consequently, the result varies as the initial price changes.

Arc elasticity measures the elasticity of demand over a price range using the midpoint or average price as the base. In graphic terms, it is the elasticity over the length of a segment or arc of the demand curve. Hence, it is called arc elasticity. The formula for arc elasticity is expressed as follows:

$$[3.5]$$

$$\frac{\dfrac{\Delta Q}{.5(Q_1 + Q_2)} \times 100}{\dfrac{\Delta P}{.5(P_1 + P_2)} \times 100} = \frac{\dfrac{\Delta Q}{Q_1 + Q_2} \times 100}{\dfrac{\Delta P}{P_1 + P_2} \times 100}$$

where Q_1 = original quantity demanded; Q_2 = new quantity demanded; ΔQ = change in quantity demanded; P_1 = original price; P_2 = new price and ΔP = change in price.

An example is shown below using the same price levels and quantity levels as in the earlier example of cinema tickets.

Price, P (€)	Quantity (thousands)
12.00	15
9.00	30

Let P_1 = €12.00
Q_1 = 15,000
P_2 = €9.00
Q_2 = 30,000

Thus,

$$\frac{\dfrac{Q_2 - Q_1}{.5(Q_1 + Q_2)}}{\dfrac{P_2 - P_1}{.5(P_1 + P_2)}} = \frac{\dfrac{30,000 - 15,000}{.5(15,000 + 30,000)}}{\dfrac{9 - 12}{.5(12 + 9)}} = \frac{\dfrac{15,000}{22,500}}{\dfrac{-3}{10.5}} = -2.33$$

The elasticity coefficient using the arc formula is –2.33. As expected, it is between the coefficient of –4 (this is the point elasticity with a base of P_1 = €12.00 and Q_1 = 15,000) and the coefficient of –1.5 (this is the point elasticity with a base of P_1 = €9.00 and Q_1 = 30,000).

   The arc elasticity method provides a measure at neither the start nor the end price but at an average price. Thus, the elasticity coefficient using the arc method lies between the two relevant point elasticity measures.

CHAPTER 4

THE CONSUMER AND DEMAND

'Value in use cannot be measured by any known standard; it is differently estimated by different persons.'[1]

David Ricardo (1772–1823)

'Value depends entirely on utility.'[2]

W. Stanley Jevons (1835–82)

CHAPTER OBJECTIVES

Upon completing this chapter, the student should understand:

- marginal utility and the principle of diminishing marginal utility;
- the equi-marginal principle;
- indifference curves and budget lines;
- substitution and income effects;
- differences in the demand curves for normal, inferior and Giffen goods;
- the differences between the two main theories of demand.

OUTLINE

4.1 An historical perspective
4.2 The marginal utility analysis
4.3 The indifference-preference analysis
4.4 Consumer surplus

INTRODUCTION

In Chapter 2 we gave an intuitive explanation as to why the demand curve slopes down from left to right. This chapter provides us with a more rigorous explanation of the theory of demand. It examines the behaviour of consumers in the market and how they react to price changes. Its purpose is to explain the downward sloping demand curve as described in Chapter 2.

We begin with an historical account of the theory of demand. This is followed by an analysis of the two main theories of consumer behaviour. The concept of consumer surplus is also explained.

4.1 AN HISTORICAL PERSPECTIVE

Marginal utility analysis

There are two main theories of demand. The first is the marginal utility or cardinalist analysis. Central to this approach is the assumption that satisfaction can be measured in absolute terms like weight or height.

This approach was instrumental in elucidating the paradox of value which remained unresolved for many centuries and left scholars from Plato to Adam Smith baffled. The paradox of value means that some goods, for example, water and salt, have a high value in use but a low value in exchange while others, such as diamonds and gold, have a low value in use but a high value in exchange.

In the 1770s Adam Smith asked the question, 'How is it that water, which is so essential to human life, has a low market value whereas diamonds, which are relatively trivial, have a high market value?'[3] This paradox remained unanswered until the marginal utility revolution of the 1870s. Economists including W. Stanley Jevons in England, Carl Menger (1840–1921) in Austria and Leon Walras in Switzerland were independently responsible for bringing the marginal utility approach to the forefront of economic thinking.

The 'marginalists', as they were later identified, claimed that the market value of a good is determined by its utility to the consumer. The marginalists' contribution was to distinguish between total utility and marginal utility. Total utility is the pleasure or satisfaction which an individual receives from consuming a particular good or service. Marginal utility is the additional utility which a person receives if she consumes one more unit of a particular good or service. While total utility increases with consumption, the addition to utility (or marginal utility) diminishes as more units are consumed.

The distinction between total and marginal utility was central to the solution to the water-diamond paradox. Water is essential. Therefore, the total utility that we receive from consuming it is high. But, the extra amount of satisfaction obtained by consuming an additional unit of water (or its marginal utility) is low because we consume such a large volume. On the other hand, because we consume such a small amount of diamonds, we obtain a high amount of satisfaction at the margin. The few units of diamonds which we do consume have a high marginal utility. The application of marginal utility was the first step in explaining the paradox of value.

Indifference-preference analysis

The marginalists, particularly Jevons, believed that a method for measuring utility would ultimately be discovered. So far an absolute measure of happiness has not been found and this deficiency limits the usefulness of this approach. A second approach, called the indifference-preference or ordinalist analysis relies on ranking or ordering preferences, rather than assigning absolute values to the level of utility gained from consumption. This approach entered the mainstream of economic theory through the efforts of John R. Hicks (1904–89) and Roy G. Allen (1906–83).

Although the second approach dominates consumer theory, it is a modification rather than a replacement of the utility approach. Hence, we will begin our examination of consumer theory with the marginal utility analysis and then discuss the indifference-preference analysis.

4.2 THE MARGINAL UTILITY ANALYSIS

An outline of utility theory

Classical economists, particularly David Ricardo, believed that the value of a good was determined by the wages paid to labour. This is called the labour theory of value. This explanation focuses on the supply side of the market. The marginalists, on the other hand, argued that utility was the basis of value. Their discussion focused on the consumer, or the demand side of the market. In terms of the theory of price determination as we know it today (and as explained in Chapter 2), each of the groups mentioned above was looking at only one half of the story. We will now look at the marginalists' contribution to our understanding of the demand side of the market. We begin by defining a few of the relevant terms.

Definition
Utility is the satisfaction or pleasure that is derived from consuming a good or service.

Definition
Total utility (TU) is the total satisfaction that a consumer gains from the consumption of a given quantity of a good or service.

Definition
Marginal utility (MU) is the extra or additional satisfaction that the consumer gains from consuming one extra unit of a good or service.

The difficulty with this approach is the measurement of utility which is both abstract and subjective. This problem can be overcome by defining a unit of measure called a 'util'. A util is an imaginary unit which measures satisfaction or utility. If a person consumes a particular commodity, the satisfaction which she receives is measured in utils.

Using the util as a unit of measure, we can examine the relationship between total utility and marginal utility. Table 4.1 shows the total utility and marginal utility derived by an individual from eating packets of crisps.

Table 4.1: Consumer's utility from consuming crisps

Quantity (packets)	TU (utils)	MU (utils)
0	0	
		7
1	7	
		4
2	11	
		2
3	13	
		1
4	14	
		0
5	14	
		−2
6	12	

To calculate total utility, we add the utils for each unit consumed. Marginal utility is the utility gained from consuming one more unit. The marginal utility gained from consuming the first unit is 7 utils. The marginal utility gained by consuming the second unit is 4 utils (11 utils–7 utils), and so on.

This information is shown in Figure 4.1. Satisfaction, measured in utils, is the variable on the vertical axis. The number of packets of crisps consumed (Q) is the variable on the horizontal axis.

Figure 4.1: Total and marginal utility

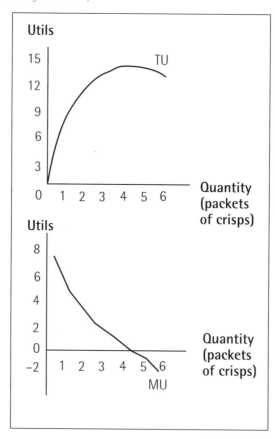

Typically, total utility curves are in the shape of a reverse U (our example only illustrates the first six units consumed). For the first few units total utility increases but at a decreasing rate. It is rising but at a slower and slower rate. Total utility then reaches a maximum. The level of satisfaction derived from consuming the particular commodity is at its highest. After this it declines and slopes down. The consumption of more units of the good has a negative impact on total utility. In fact, these extra units yield dissatisfaction or what economists call disutility.

The marginal utility curve slopes downwards. The first unit consumed gives the greatest satisfaction or the highest number of utils. The consumer gains less utility from each additional packet of crisps consumed. This example shows behaviour that we observe so frequently that we call it the principle of diminishing marginal utility.

Definition
The principle of diminishing marginal utility means that the greatest number of utils is gained from the first unit of a commodity that is consumed. Each additional unit yields less utility.

This extra satisfaction is the marginal utility. So the marginal utility for each additional unit consumed decreases. In other words, the marginal utility curve declines as consumption increases.

Initially the total utility curve increases at a decreasing rate and the marginal utility curve slopes downwards but the values are still positive. The marginal utility curve intersects the quantity axis when total utility is at a maximum. Finally, as the total utility curve slopes downwards reflecting disutility, the marginal utility curve is below the quantity axis reflecting both negative and declining values. We now turn to the consumer's objective which economists assume to be utility maximisation.

Utility maximisation and consumer equilibrium

We begin with the assumption that the consumer aims to maximise utility subject to constraints. The two constraints which limit the choices of the consumer are income and prices.

The utility-maximisation equilibrium condition is best illustrated with an example.

Jimmy Keenan, a bachelor farmer, drives to Dundalk every Saturday to do his weekly shopping. He has €48 which he spends on three items: bread, meat and cigarettes. Bread costs €2, meat costs €4 per kilogram and cigarettes cost €6 per package of 20. Table 4.2 presents the total utils which Jimmy gains by consuming each of these commodities.

Table 4.2: Utility saved by Jimmy Keenan

Bread		Meat		Cigarettes	
Q	TU	Q	TU	Q	TU
0	0	0	0	0	0
1	24	1	48	1	60
2	46	2	92	2	114
3	66	3	132	3	162
4	84	4	168	4	204
5	100	5	200	5	240
6	114	6	228	6	270

The marginal utilities are presented in Table 4.3. They are constructed for differently priced goods. For the purpose of comparison we divide the marginal utility for a unit of good by its price to calculate the marginal utility per euro (MU/€).

Table 4.3: *Maximising utility by equalising MUs per euro spent*

Bread				Meat				Cigarettes			
Q	TU	MU	MU/E	Q	TU	MU	MU/E	Q	TU	MU	MU/E
0	0			0	0			0	0		
		24	12			48	12			60	10
1	24			1	48			1	60		
		22	11			44	11			54	9
2	46			2	92			2	114		
		20	10			40	10			48	8
3	66			3	132			3	162		
		18	9			36	9			42	7
4	84			4	168			4	204		
		16	8			32	8			36	6
5	100			5	200			5	240		
		14	7			28	7			30	5
6	114			6	228			6	270		

We will find the best bundle which Jimmy Keenan can afford by applying the equi-marginal principle.

Definition

The equi-marginal principle states that utility is maximised when the utility for the last euro spent on each good is the same.

Assuming that all of the consumer's income is spent, this principle ensures that the consumer will not find it possible to increase utility by switching a euro's worth of expenditure from one good to another.

For two goods X and Y, the equi-marginal principle can be expressed in algebraic terms, as shown in Equation 4.1.

$$\frac{MU_X}{P_X} = \frac{MU_Y}{P_Y}$$ [4.1]

In the example above, the utility-maximising rule holds for four different combinations;

Combination 1 = (3 bread, 3 meat and 1 cigarettes)
Combination 2 = (4 bread, 4 meat and 2 cigarettes)

Combination 3 = (5 bread, 5 meat and 3 cigarettes)
Combination 4 = (6 bread, 6 meat and 4 cigarettes)

Total cost and total utility for these four combinations are calculated in Table 4.4.

Table 4.4: Four possible combinations

	Combination 1	Combination 2	Combination 3	Combination 4
Bread at €2 ea.	€ 6	€ 8	€10	€12
Meat at €4 ea.	€12	€16	€20	€24
Cigarettes at €6 ea.	€ 6	€12	€18	€24
Total cost	€24	€36	€48	€60
Total utility	258	366	462	546

Combinations 1 and 2 do not satisfy the condition that all income is used. Thus, the consumer is not maximising utility with either of these combinations. The income limit of €48 is exceeded in the choice of combination 4. The consumer maximises utility when he chooses combination 3. All income is spent and total utility is equal to 462 units.

The following is the utility-maximising combination subject to the €48 budget constraint,

$$\frac{16}{2} = \frac{32}{4} = \frac{48}{6}$$

Similarly, we can consider other combinations which will use all of Jimmy's available income, but do not satisfy the principle that the utility for the last euro spent is equal for all available goods. We will compare combination 3 (the utility-maximising combination of bread, meat and cigarettes) with two other affordable combinations:

Combination 3 = (5 bread, 5 meat and 3 cigarettes)
Combination 5 = (4 bread, 4 meat and 4 cigarettes)
Combination 6 = (5 bread, 2 meat and 5 cigarettes)

Total cost and total utility for these three combinations are calculated in Table 4.5.

Table 4.5: Three affordable combinations

	Combination 3	Combination 5	Combination 6
Bread at €2 each	€10	€ 8	€10
Meat at €4 each	€20	€16	€ 8
Cigarettes at €6 each	€18	€24	€30
Total cost	€48	€48	€48
Total utility	462	456	432

All of these combinations are affordable, but only combination 3 maximises utility. This is the only one of the three combinations where marginal utility divided by price is equal for the last unit of each good consumed.

Combination 3 is the best combination that Jimmy can afford. He cannot increase utility by switching a euro's worth of expenditure from one good to another. Since there is no tendency to change, it is an equilibrium position.

This analysis can be used to explain why the demand curve is negatively sloped. For example, let us concentrate on the utility derived from the consumption of meat. At the existing price level of €6 the utility-maximising rule indicates that the Jimmy will purchase three kilos of meat. Suppose that the butcher cuts the price of beef. As a result Jimmy will switch consumption away from both bread and cigarettes to the lower-priced meat. The utility-maximising rule will yield a new combination in equilibrium. The new combination will include a higher quantity of meat at the lower price. This suggests a negative relationship between the price and the quantity demanded which is reflected in a downward sloping demand curve for this commodity.

Synopsis of the marginal utility approach

The assumptions

1. The consumer can measure satisfaction by utils.
2. Consumer choices are limited by income and prices.
3. The principle of diminishing marginal utility.

The theory

The consumer wishes to maximise utility, given her income and price constraints.

The predictions

Consumer equilibrium is achieved with the combination of goods which satisfy the equi-marginal principle. In other words, the consumer will maximise utility where the utilities for the last euro spent are equal for all commodities, and all income is spent.

The weaknesses

1. There is no 'satisfactory' way of measuring utility.
2. Interpersonal utility comparisons are not possible.

We now turn to the second approach.

4.3   THE INDIFFERENCE-PREFERENCE ANALYSIS

The problem of measuring utility led to the development of the indifference-preference approach. This approach acknowledges the difficulties involved in attempting to measure utility. These difficulties can be overcome by an ordinal approach which merely requires that the consumer rank or order different alternatives according to his or her preference. It does not depend on allocating specific numerical values to different levels of satisfaction.

A number of assumptions apply to the consumer's preferences.

1. The consumer ranks alternatives according to tastes and preferences which do not depend on income or prices. A consumer's tastes and preferences change slowly over time and therefore we can consider them as 'constant' at a particular moment in time.
2. Preferences must satisfy the law of transitivity, i.e. if a consumer chooses combination A over combination B and also chooses the same combination B over combination C then the consumer must be consistent by choosing combination A over combination C.
3. The consumer prefers more to less. This observation excludes what we call 'bads', e.g. pollution, garbage, where the consumer prefers less to more.
4. Any two consumption bundles can be compared. This is known as the axiom of completeness. A consumer can state that he prefers combination A to combination B or that he prefers combination B to combination A or that he is indifferent between combination A and combination B.

The first assumption makes reference to the two constraints, income and prices. These constraints are represented by a budget line which we will discuss later. We begin our analysis with a look at another new concept – an indifference curve.

The indifference curve

Definition

An indifference curve shows all the bundles of two goods that give the same level of utility to the consumer.

Although these points represent different combinations of goods, the consumer is indifferent between the combinations. We say that utility is constant along any given indifference curve. Indifference curves reflect the consumer's tastes and preferences for the good.

There are a number of properties of indifference curves. These are listed here and discussed in greater detail in Appendix 4.1.

1. Indifference curves slope down from left to right.
2. The slope of the indifference curve is determined by tastes and preferences and is called the marginal rate of substitution (MRS).
3. Indifference curves are normally convex to the origin.
4. Indifference curves do not intersect.
5. There is a multiple set of indifference curves, called a preference map.
6. The higher the indifference curve, the higher the level of utility.

An indifference curve is illustrated in Figure 4.2.

Figure 4.2: An indifference curve

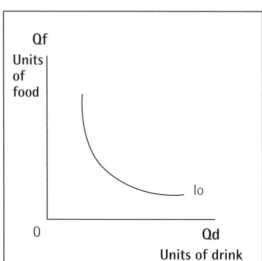

The horizontal and vertical axes represent physical units of drink and food.

Indifference curves reflect individual tastes and preferences. For example, a consumer may consume both food and drink but prefer drink. This set of preferences is shown in Figure 4.3(a). The indifference curve is relatively steep. To gain an additional unit of drink, the consumer is willing to give up several units of food. Alternatively, Figure 4.3(b) shows a relatively flat indifference curve. In this case, the consumer is willing to give up several units of drink in order to gain an additional unit of food. This particular indifference curve indicates that the consumer prefers food to drink.

Figure 4.3: Indifference curves and preferences between two goods

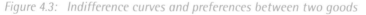

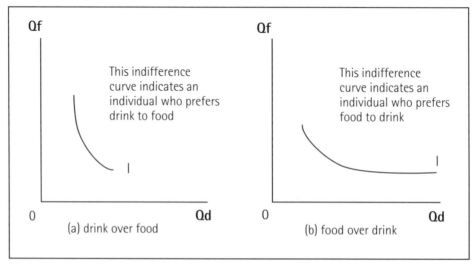

The income of the consumer and the prices of the goods limit the endless wants of the consumer. These constraints are reflected in our second new concept, the budget line.

The budget line

Definition
The budget line illustrates the maximum combination of two goods that the consumer can purchase, given her level of income and prices.

It constrains the consumer's choices. In effect, it splits the two-dimensional space into two parts, the affordable and the unaffordable. The feasible alternatives are located on or inside the budget line whereas the much larger range of infeasible alternatives is found outside the budget line. The two constraints, income and prices, determine the position and the slope of the budget line. A change in either or both of the constraints results in a new budget line.

The position of the budget line is determined by the level of income, as illustrated in Figure 4.4. As income increases, the budget line moves away from the origin and, as a result, the affordable space increases. At a higher income, the consumer can afford more units of food and more units of drink. If income falls, the budget line moves closer to the origin and the affordable space contracts.

Figure 4.4: The budget line and changes in income

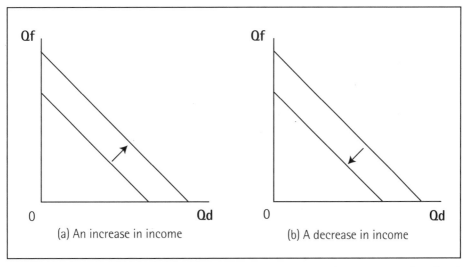

(a) An increase in income   (b) A decrease in income

The slope of the budget line is determined by relative prices of the two goods. The slope measures the opportunity cost of one good, food, in terms of another good, drink. For example, suppose that drink costs €2 per unit and food costs €1 per unit. In order to consume a unit of drink, the consumer must forgo two units of food. The opportunity cost of a drink is two units of food. To put this another way, the budget line indicates the trade-off between the two goods. Formally, the slope of the budget line is equal to the negative of the ratio of the two prices. Equation 4.2 states this in mathematical form.

$$\text{Slope of the budget line} = \frac{-Pd}{Pf}$$

[4.2]

where: Pd = price of drink; Pf = price of food.

If the good on the vertical axis is expensive in relation to the good on the horizontal axis, the budget line is relatively flat. Conversely, if the good on the horizontal axis is expensive in relation to the good on the vertical axis the budget line is relatively steep. This is shown in Figure 4.5.

Figure 4.5:   Relative prices and the slope of the budget line

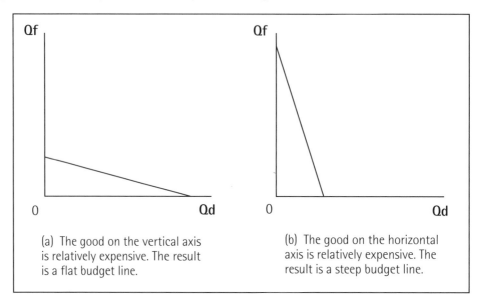

(a) The good on the vertical axis is relatively expensive. The result is a flat budget line.

(b) The good on the horizontal axis is relatively expensive. The result is a steep budget line.

CASE STUDY

Inflation and the purchasing power of people on 'fixed incomes'

Inflation is a rise in the general price level. It will be discussed in greater detail in Chapter 17. However, in this case study, we will look at the effect of inflation for people on 'fixed incomes'. These are people who receive unemployment benefits, social welfare payments or old age pensions. Their budget is 'fixed' in the sense that often, their total income consists of the money which they receive from the state in the form of a weekly payment which changes only annually.

Increases to dole payments and old age pensions are announced by the Minister of Finance on budget day. The change to the payments happens a few months later. Table 4.6 shows the payments made for unemployment assistance and old age pensions in the past two budgets and compares them with the anticipated inflation rate. This is the rate which the Minister expects price levels to rise in the next year.

Table 4.6:   Inflation, pensions and social welfare

	1999	2000	%Δ
Inflation rate	2%[a]	2.5%[b]	
Old age pension (weekly)			
Contributory			
– under 80	€89.00	€96.00	7.9%
– over 80	€94.00	€101.00	7.4%
Non-contributory			
– under 80	€78.50	€85.50	8.9%
– over 80	€83.50	€90.50	8.4%
Unemployment assistance (weekly)			
Short-term	€72.00	€76.00	5.6%
Long-term	€73.50	€77.50	5.4%

[a] actual
[b] estimate

We can see from the table that the actual inflation rate for 1999 was 2%. The estimate for the inflation rate in 2000 is 2.5%.

Consider the pensioner who is under eighty years of age and receiving a contributory pension. 'Contributory' means that this person was employed and paid PRSI which is 'pay related social insurance'. In effect, the state collected this money when the person was working and it gives it back after the person retires. In 1999, this pensioner received £89.00 per week. This amount increased by 8% to £96.00 in 2000. This is shown in the %Δ column.

For the year 2000, the government expected an increase in the price level of 2.5%. If the estimate was correct, the real pension increase would be 5.5%. This is the pension increase of 8% less the increase in the general price level of 2.5%. To express this in a different way, if Charlie McCreevy's inflation estimate was correct, the pensioner could purchase 5.5% more goods and services in 2000 than in 1999.

The case study shows what happened to the purchasing power of people on fixed incomes when the actual inflation rate was higher than anticipated.

Extract from *The Irish Times*
McCreevy could yet pay for disregarding inflation threat
by Denis Coghlan

Nothing is more likely to galvanise voters to rebel against the status quo than a fall in their living standards. If the present rates of inflation persist, pensioners and social welfare recipients are likely to be worse off at the end of this year than they were in 1999 in spite of the roar from the Celtic Tiger . . .

It wasn't supposed to be like this. When the social partners sat down to negotiate the terms of the Programme for Prosperity and Fairness last year, the rising economic tide was predicted to lift all boats, but that was before Charlie McCreevy did a solo run in his December budget and gave the most expensive breaks to the well-heeled in society.

There was a 2 per cent cut in the top and standard rates of income tax, along with reductions in corporation, capital gains and capital acquisition taxes. Down the list came the little people. Old age pensioners got €7 a week and those on the dole received an extra €4.

Since then, inflation has soared to 6.2 per cent and welfare recipients and the unemployed became poorer as their 5 per cent budgetary rise was wiped out . . .

Source: *The Irish Times*, 19 August, 2000.

Questions

1. What is the difference between the 'estimated' inflation rate and the 'actual' inflation rate for 2000? How does this affect the 'real' increases for pensioners and social welfare recipients?
2. The article states that welfare recipients and the unemployed are poorer in 2000 than they were in 1999. Is this true? Is it true for pensioners?
3. Sketch the budget line, for 1999 for a person receiving short-term unemployment assistance. Draw a new budget line for 2000. Describe why the new budget line differs from the 1999 budget line.

Answers on website

Consumer equilibrium

Consider a student, Eileen, who can choose between only two goods, food and drink. In Figure 4.6 the quantity of food, Qf, is depicted on the vertical axis and the quantity of drink, Qd, is depicted on the horizontal axis. A set of indifference curves and a budget line are drawn.

Figure 4.6: Maximising consumer utility constrained by income and prices

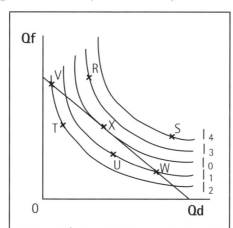

Eileen chooses the combination of food and drink that maximises her utility and uses all her income. Graphically, this is where the budget line, reflecting the budget constraint, is tangent to the highest possible indifference curve, reflecting the consumer's preferences. Alternatively, this is the point where the slope of the budget line is equal to the slope of the indifference curve.

Point X is the optimal consumption bundle. Recall (see property two in Appendix 4.1) that the slope of the indifference curve is the marginal rate of substitution (MRS) whereas the negative of the ratio of prices is the slope of the budget line. Equation 4.3 states that they are equal at X, the point of tangency, which is the optimum bundle which the consumer can afford.

[4.3]

$$\textbf{MRS} = \frac{\textbf{--P}_d}{\textbf{P}_f}$$

Let us examine other consumption bundles. Bundles R and S are desirable but unattainable. They are desirable because they are on higher indifference curves: they are unattainable because they are outside the budget line. Eileen does not have sufficient income to purchase either of these combinations. In contrast, bundles T and U are attainable but undesirable. Eileen can afford them because they are inside the budget line. They are undesirable because it is possible for Eileen to reach a higher level of utility if she spends all of her income. Neither V nor W is the optimal consumption bundle because it is possible to reach a higher indifference curve and still remain on the budget line.

Point X, and only point X, is the optimal consumption bundle. This point is called consumer equilibrium. Like any equilibrium, when the consumer is at this point, there is no tendency to change. Eileen is at the highest level of satisfaction possible given her income and the prevailing prices. This is the best bundle that Eileen can afford.

Income change analysis

In the analysis above, income and prices were held constant. Now we will consider a change in equilibrium arising out of a change in income with prices held constant. We will observe that the changes in the equilibrium positions will differ, depending on whether the goods are normal or inferior.

Two scenarios are illustrated in Figure 4.7. Figure 4.7a shows a budget line for two normal goods, food and drink. Figure 4.7(b) shows a budget line drawn for food (a normal good) on the vertical axis. Bus rides, an inferior good, is represented on the horizontal axis. In both cases income increases and the budget line shifts out and to the right. Since prices do not change, the new budget line is parallel to the original budget line.

Figure 4.7: A change in income

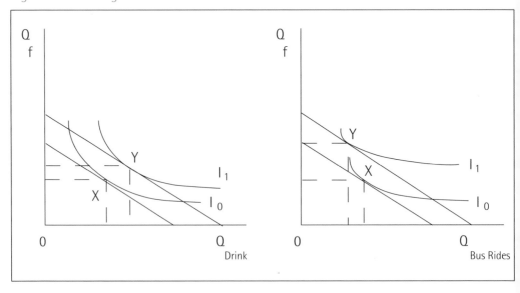

Consider Figure 4.7(a). Before the income change, the consumer was in equilibrium at point X. The consumer is now in equilibrium at the optimal consumption bundle Y. This bundle contains more units of both food and drink. If both goods are classified as normal, an increase in income results in an increase in the consumption of both goods.

Now consider Figure 4.7(b). Again, the point of consumer equilibrium, after income increases, is represented by point Y. In this case, an increase in income results in the consumption of more of the normal good, food, but less of the inferior good, bus rides.

We can now see that an increase in income affects consumer equilibrium differently, depending on whether a good is normal or inferior. If a good is normal, more of that good will be consumed if income increases. On the other hand, if a good is inferior, less is consumed if income increases. We will now turn our attention to the effect of a change in price on consumer equilibrium.

Price change analysis and the demand curve

A change in price alters the equilibrium position. We begin by examining the effect of a change of price on the budget line. Different price adjustments are illustrated in Figure 4.8.

Figure 4.8: A change in price

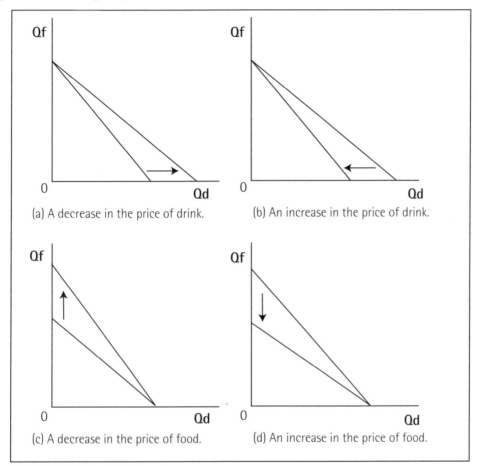

(a) A decrease in the price of drink.

(b) An increase in the price of drink.

(c) A decrease in the price of food.

(d) An increase in the price of food.

The slope of a budget line is equal to the negative of the ratio of prices. A change in the price of one commodity alters the slope of the budget line. When this happens the budget line pivots around one or other of the intercept points, outwards or inwards depending on whether there is a price decrease or price increase. All four possible cases are presented above.

Suppose the price of drink decreases. What happens to the consumption of drink? Any change in consumption arising out of a change in price can be split into two separate changes. The first is called the substitution effect, and the second, the income effect.

Definition
The substitution effect is the change in consumption that is caused by the change in the relative prices of the two goods, holding utility constant.

If the price of drink falls, food becomes relatively more expensive in comparison to drink. The consumer reacts to the change in relative prices by consuming more drink and less food.

Definition
The income effect is the adjustment of demand to the change in real income alone.

When price falls, the consumer is wealthier in the sense that the decrease in the price of drink has increased her real income. From Figure 4.8(a), we can see that the affordable space is larger as a result of the decrease in price. The purchasing power of the consumer has increased.

From the previous section, we know that the consumer does not respond uniformly to a change in income. The consumer's response depends on whether the good, as defined in economic terms, is normal or inferior.

Therefore, when price decreases, two separate effects are evident. The substitution effect results in an increase in quantity demanded. The consumer will purchase more of the good which is relatively cheaper. The income effect varies depending on whether the good is normal or inferior.

The addition of these two effects amounts to the total change in quantity and is called the total price effect. This is expressed in Equation 4.4.

$$\boxed{\textbf{Total price effect = substitution effect + income effect}} \qquad \textbf{[4.4]}$$

First, we consider the case of a normal good.

A case of a normal good

Figure 4.9 shows the price change and its effect on the consumption of food and drink. Both food and drink are normal goods. X is the original equilibrium bundle. As the price of drink decreases the budget line rotates around the vertical intercept and moves out to the right along the horizontal axis. The new budget line reflects the change in price and, as a result, has a different slope. The new equilibrium is at bundle Z, the point of tangency between the new budget line and the highest possible indifference curve. More units of drink are consumed at bundle Z than at bundle X. This suggests that there is a negative relationship between price and quantity demanded.

Figure 4.9: The substitution and income effect for a normal good

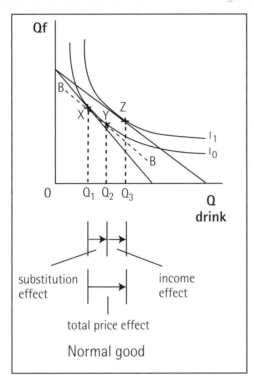

How do we know that bundle Z lies to the right of bundle X and thus reflects a higher level of quantity demanded? The move from X to Z can be divided into two separate parts. First, there is the substitution effect. This can be illustrated by drawing a hypothetical budget line, BB, which is parallel to the new budget line but is tangent to the original indifference curve, at point Y. Recall that the level of utility is constant along a particular indifference curve. The move from X to Y is the substitution effect. The consumer is changing her consumption bundle in response to the change in relative prices and at the same time keeping utility constant. Consumption of drink is higher at Y than at X.

Second, there is the income effect. As the price of drink decreases the purchasing power of the consumer increases. Since drink is a normal good, as income increases the consumer demands more drink. The income effect is the move from Y to the new bundle Z which must lie to the right of Y in order to reflect that drink is a normal good.

The total price effect is the move from X to Z with Z lying to the right and thus reflecting higher units of drink consumed. As price decreases, quantity demanded increases.

Figure 4.10 shows how this analysis combined with a price consumption curve can help in the graphical derivation of a demand curve. The upper figure shows three budget lines which correspond to decreasing prices of drink. Each new budget line pivots to the right. There is a unique equilibrium (X,Z and U) associated with each budget line. As the affordable space increases, the consumer can move to higher indifference curves.

There is a line called the 'price consumption curve' which joins these three equilibria. This curve shows the consumer's preferred combinations given her income and the change in relative prices.

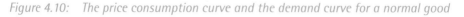

Figure 4.10:   The price consumption curve and the demand curve for a normal good

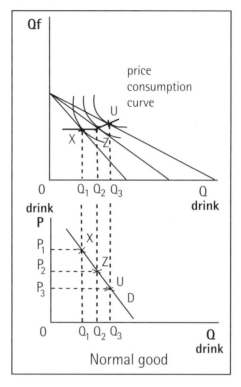

The lower diagram shows the consumer's demand curve for drink. We are looking at the 'price consumption' relationship for a single good. The three price levels, shown on the vertical axis, correspond to the falling price of drink which caused the budget line to pivot to the right. The horizontal axis shows the units of drink consumed at each price level. The consumer responds to the change in the price of drink by increasing her consumption of drink. The demand curve slopes downward from left to right.

The analysis above applies to a normal good. We now turn our attention towards inferior goods.

A case of an inferior good

Now we will consider a decrease in the price of an inferior good, bus rides. The substitution effect is always the same, regardless of whether a good is normal, inferior or Giffen; when the price of a good falls, the demand for that good increases. In this case, when the price of bus rides falls, we expect the consumer to react to the change in relative prices by using buses more often as a means of transport.

The income effect is the change in consumption which arises from a change in real income. For a normal good, as price decreases real income increases and, consequently, consumption increases. However, for an inferior good, as real income increases consumption decreases. In this case, as a response to the increase in real income, we expect that the consumer will demand fewer bus rides, an inferior good.

We now have an increase in consumption arising from the substitution effect and a decrease in consumption arising from the income effect. One appears to offset the other and since the total price effect is the addition of the two, it is unclear whether consumption increases or decreases.

In fact, the decrease in quantity due to the increase in income is relatively small so that it does not outweigh the increase in quantity which arises from the substitution effect. The substitution effect outweighs the income effect for an inferior good (with the exception of the Giffen good which is explained later). The increase in quantity arising from the substitution effect (reflected in the move from X to Y) is greater than the decrease in quantity arising from the income effect (reflected in the move from Y to Z). The total price effect (shown by the move from X to Z), which is the addition of the substitution and the income effect, is still an increase in quantity. This is shown in Figure 4.11.

Figure 4.11: The substitution and income effect for an inferior good

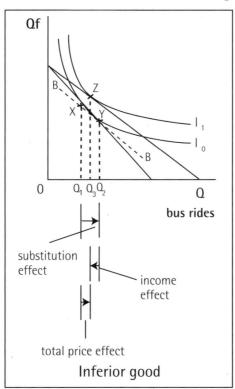

As price decreases for an inferior good the quantity consumed increases but not by as much as it would for a normal good. The demand curve for an inferior good is downward sloping but, on account of the smaller change in quantity consumed, the demand curve is relatively steep. The price consumption curve for the inferior good is shown in Figure 4.12.

Figure 4.12: The price consumption curve and the demand curve for an inferior good

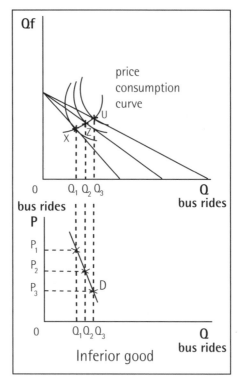

The difference between the normal good and the inferior good is reflected in the respective slopes of the demand curves. The demand curve for the inferior good is steeper than the demand curve for the normal good *ceteris paribus*.

A case of a Giffen good

Definition

A Giffen good is a very inferior good with an upward sloping demand curve.

We need to consider the effect of a price change on a Giffen good. The Giffen good received its name from Sir Robert Giffen who, it is believed, claimed that during the Irish famine of the 1840s, the consumption of potatoes increased even though the price increased.[4] Theoretically, this strange phenomenon can be explained using substitution and income effects.

The substitution effect is always the same. However, in the case of a strongly inferior or Giffen good, the income effect not only offsets the substitution effect, it actually outweighs it. In the case of a Giffen good a rise in the price results in a negative substitution effect, but a stronger, positive income effect. As price increases, demand increases. The demand curve for the Giffen good is upward sloping.

Figure 4.13 shows the substitution and income effects for a price fall of a Giffen good. The increase in quantity arising from the substitution effect (X to Y) is smaller than the decrease in quantity arising from the income effect (Y to Z). At the new consumer equilibrium, point Z, the consumer is consuming less of the Giffen good than before.

Figure 4.13: The substitution and income effect for a Giffen good

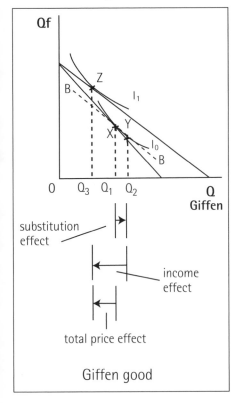

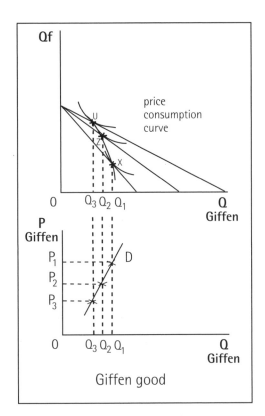

Figure 4.14: The price consumption curve and the demand curve for a Giffen good

Figure 4.14 shows the backward bending price consumption curve. As price falls, the quantity consumed decreases. The price-quantity relationship is positive and this is reflected in an upward sloping demand curve.

A complete summary of the price changes and the subsequent quantity changes for all three categories of goods is presented in Table 4.7.

Table 4.7:   Summary of price changes and quantity changes

Price change	Type of good	Substitution effect	Income effect	Total effect
Decrease	Normal	Qd increases	Qd increases	Qd increases
	Inferior	Qd increases	Qd decreases	Qd increases
	Giffen	Qd increases	Qd decreases	Qd decreases
Increase	Normal	Qd decreases	Qd decreases	Qd decreases
	Inferior	Qd decreases	Qd increases	Qd decreases
	Giffen	Qd decreases	Qd increases	Qd increases

Synopsis of the indifference-preference approach

The assumptions

1. The consumer ranks alternative combinations of goods according to her preferences.
2. The consumer's choices are limited by income and prices.
3. The principle of diminishing marginal utility.

The theory

The consumer wishes to maximise her satisfaction subject to income and price constraints.

The predictions

The optimal consumption bundle is found where the budget line is tangent to the highest possible indifference curve. At this tangency point, the respective slopes are equal.

The weaknesses

1. Indifference curves are difficult, if not impossible, to derive in the real world.
2. The assumptions which underlie the theory are restrictive and ignore the effects of common practices e.g. advertising.

4.4   CONSUMER SURPLUS

In *Principles of Economics* Alfred Marshall defined consumer surplus as the '. . . excess of the price which he would be willing to pay rather than go without the thing, over that which he actually does pay . . .'[5]

Definition

Consumer surplus is the excess of what a person is prepared to pay for a good over what the person actually pays.

Sometimes this concept is referred to as the social benefit accruing to the consumer who purchases the good. This term is used to describe the operation of the price mechanism which allows consumers to acquire goods at a lower price than they are willing to pay.

Before we look at a market consisting of many consumers, we begin with the consumption decision of a single consumer. Consider Anthony, a hat lover. Figure 4.15 shows Anthony's demand curve for hats.

Figure 4.15: Anthony's demand curve for hats

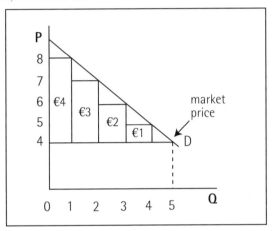

We can see that Anthony is willing to pay €8 for the first hat that he purchases. This is the hat from which he derives the highest marginal utility, therefore, he is willing to pay the most for it. However, the market price is only €4 per hat. Therefore, although Anthony is prepared to pay €8 for this hat, he only has to pay €4. His consumer surplus is €4 for the first unit. Because of diminishing marginal utility, Anthony is willing to pay only €7 for the second hat. For this unit, his consumer surplus is €3. Anthony continues to consume until the consumer surplus on the last unit purchased equals zero. In this example, the market price of €4 equals the price that Anthony is willing to pay for his fifth hat.

From Figure 4.15, we can see that Anthony is willing to pay €30 for five hats (=€8+€7+€6+€5+€4). To put this in another way, we can say that Anthony is gaining €30 worth of pleasure or benefit from his purchase of hats. Anthony's total expenditure is €20. Anthony's total consumer surplus for hats is the amount that he is willing to pay less the amount that he has to pay (the total expenditure). The consumer surplus in this example is €10 (the sum of €4+€3+€2+€1).

The market demand curve is derived by adding individual demand curves. We can think of the market demand curve for hats as representing the amount that consumers collectively are willing to pay for a particular quantity of that good. Consider Figure 4.16.

Figure 4.16: Market demand curve for hats

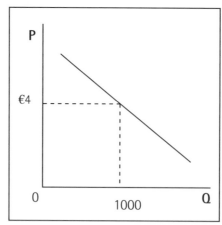

If 1,000 hats are available for sale, consumers are willing to pay €4 per hat. This is the market price. However, there are some consumers who are willing to pay more for those hats. Since they only have to pay €4 per hat, some consumers pay less than they are willing to pay. In other words, just as with Anthony, we can identify consumer surplus for the market. It is the difference between the market price and the price that consumers are willing to pay.

Figure 4.17 shows consumer surplus for the market.

Figure 4.17: Consumer surplus

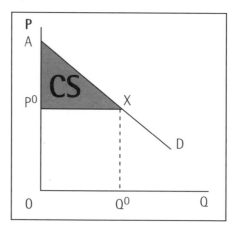

Suppose that the market price for hats is P^0 and at this price, the market demands Q^0 hats. The total benefit or satisfaction received by the market is represented by the area [OAXQ^0]. This is the total amount that consumers are willing to pay for Q^0 hats. The total expenditure on hats is represented by the area [OP^{0}XQ^0]. The difference between the total benefit and the total expenditure is represented by the shaded triangle P^{0}AX. This is the area of consumer surplus.

Consumer surplus is a very important concept in economics and has many worth-while applications. These include cost-benefit analysis and the efficiency and distribution effects of tax changes and subsidies.

SUMMARY

1. There are two main approaches to the theory of consumer behaviour and demand. The first is the marginal utility theory. It is based on the assumption that utility is measurable. A marginal utility curve is derived which slopes downward and reflects the principle of diminishing marginal utility. The consumer maximises utility if the utility for the first euro spent on each good is the same. This is called the equi-marginal principle.
2. The second approach is the indifference-preference theory. It requires the ordering of different alternatives according to the consumer's preferences. The preferences of the consumer are reflected in indifference curves whereas the constraints are reflected in the budget line.
3. The consumer maximises satisfaction where the budget line is tangent to the highest possible indifference curve. At this point, called consumer equilibrium, the negative of the ratio of prices is equal to the marginal rate of substitution.
4. The demand curve for a good can be derived by splitting the quantity change into two separate components. The substitution effect is the change in demand arising out of the change in relative prices. It is the same for all categories of goods. The income effect is the change in demand arising out of the change in real income. It varies depending on whether the good is normal or inferior.
5. The substitution and income effect analysis is useful when deriving the demand curve for the three categories of goods. The demand curve for a normal good conforms to the law of demand by sloping downwards from left to right. The demand curve for an inferior good also slopes down but it is steeper on account of an income effect which partially offsets the substitution effect. The exception is the Giffen good whose demand curve has a positive slope.
6. Consumer surplus arises from the difference between the price consumers pay for the good and the price they are willing to pay. In effect, it is a benefit to consumers. It has many useful applications in economics.

KEY TERMS

Marginalists	Marginal rate of substitution	Indifference curve
Utility	Relative prices	Budget line
Total utility	Optimal consumption bundle	Preference map
Marginal utility	Substitution effect	
Util	Income effect	
Diminishing marginal utility	Price consumption curve	
Equi-marginal principle	Giffen good	
Preferences	Consumer surplus	

REVIEW QUESTIONS

1. Briefly explain the main differences between the marginal utility approach and the indifference-preference approach in the context of consumer choice theory.
2. Using the marginal utility approach explain how the consumer maximises utility. Show how this approach and, in particular, the concept of marginal utility is related to the law of demand and the conventional downward sloping demand curve.
3. List and briefly explain the assumptions of consumers' preferences and the properties of both the budget line and indifference curves.
4. Using the indifference-preference approach, explain how the optimal consumption bundle is derived.
5. Suppose we have a two-good model with both goods classified as normal. The price of the good, whose quantity is represented on the horizontal axis, increases. Use the substitution and income effect analysis to explain why consumption is likely to decrease in response to this price increase.
6. Suppose the good, whose quantity is represented on the horizontal axis, is a Giffen good. Consider a price increase. Derive the price consumption curve which is associated with this change in price. How does this vary from the price consumption curve for a normal or inferior good? Explain the reason for the difference.

WORKING PROBLEMS

1. Monica spends a day on the beach. She has an income of €22 and can spend this budget on some combination of mineral water, ice cream and soft drinks. Mineral water sells for €4, ice cream for €2 and soft drinks for €1. The hypothetical marginal utility values are presented in Table 4.8.
   What combination yields Monica maximum utility?

Table 4.8: Monica's three alternatives: mineral water, ice cream and soft drinks

Mineral water		Ice cream		Soft drinks	
Q	MU	Q	MU	Q	MU
	36		30		32
1		1		1	
	24		22		28
2		2		2	
	20		16		20
3		3		3	
	18		12		14
4		4		4	
	16		10		8
5		5		5	
	10		4		6
6		6		6	
	6		2		4
7		7		7	

2. Both Annie and Ellie each receive €150 per week for their old age pension. They purchase two goods, bread and tea. Bread costs €1.50 per loaf and tea costs €3.00 per 250g weight. On two separate diagrams, draw a budget line for Annie and Ellie. Annie prefers bread and Ellie prefers tea. Draw an indifference curve for each budget line which reflects the difference in preferences for these two women.

MULTI-CHOICE QUESTIONS

1. According to the marginal utility approach:
    (a) the substitution effect and the income effect confirm that consumption responds negatively to price changes;
    (b) real income changes allow for the possibility of an upward sloping demand curve;
    (c) the consumer maximises utility where the utility for the last euro spent on each good is the same;
    (d) indifference curves slope downwards from left to right;
    (e) none of the above.

2. The substitution effect of a price change:
    (a) is the same for all goods;
    (b) is the change in demand due solely to the change in relative prices;
    (c) is the change in demand which results from a change in income;
    (d) differs depending on whether a good is normal, inferior or a Giffen good;
    (e) both (a) and (b) above.

3. Which of the following is not a property of indifference curves?
    (a) Combinations of goods on the one indifference curve yield the same level of satisfaction to the consumer.
    (b) Indifference curves reflect the income and price constraints.
    (c) The slope of an indifference curve is the marginal rate of substitution.
    (d) Indifference curves usually slope downwards from left to right.
    (e) Indifference curves do not intersect.

4. Suppose Ellie Lyden, an old age pensioner, received an increase of €10 per week immediately following the budget announcement. *Ceteris paribus*, her new budget line for tea and bread will:
    (a) be parallel to her old budget line;
    (b) show an increase in the amount of tea that she can buy but a decrease in the amount of bread;
    (c) show that her 'affordable space' has decreased;
    (d) be the same as her old budget line;
    (e) none of the above.

5. Figure 4.18 shows consumer equilibrium for Jack whose income is €300 per week. From this diagram we know that:

Figure 4.18

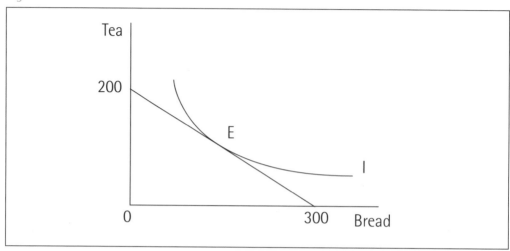

(a) the price of tea is €1.50;
(b) the price of bread is €1.00;
(c) the slope of the budget line is –0.67;
(d) the marginal rate of substitution is –0.67;
(e) all of the above.

6. The difference between the price consumers pay for the good and the price they are willing to pay for the good is called:
(a) substitution effect;
(b) marginal utility;
(c) marginal rate of substitution;
(d) consumer surplus;
(e) none of the above.

TRUE OR FALSE (SUPPORT YOUR ANSWER)

1. Diminishing marginal utility means that the second Mars Bar tastes better than the first.

2. The marginal utility approach states that utility is maximised when utility for the last euro spent is equal on each good.

3. The consumer surplus is the difference between the market price of a commodity and the price that suppliers are willing to supply the goods.

4. The optimal consumption bundle is the intersection point between the highest possible indifference curve and the given budget line.

5. The demand curve for an inferior good is positively sloped.

6. For a Giffen good the income effect is stronger than the substitution effect and this produces an upward sloping demand curve.

CASE STUDY

Read the following quotations. Each quotation challenges at least one of the assumptions underlying consumer theory. Which assumptions are challenged? Do you think that the challenge is serious? In other words, does the challenge make you question the validity of the model?

'Young Dubliners from affluent areas are up to 15 times more likely to go to university than their counterparts from disadvantaged parts of the city, according to a new analysis of third-level admissions.'

Source: 'Huge disparities in access to third-level colleges in Dublin, new analysis shows' by Paul Cullen in *The Irish Times*, October 7, 1994.

'It is not wrong to want to live better; what is wrong is a style of life which is presumed to be better when it is directed towards 'having' rather than 'being', and which wants to have more, not in order to be more but in order to spend life in enjoyment as an end in itself.'

Source: John Paul II. (1991) *On the Hundredth Anniversary of Rerum Novarum.* Washington DC: Office for Publishing and Promotion Services United States Catholic Conference.

'With the ghost of Guinness Light still haunting St James' Gate, Guinness Ireland group took the brave step of launching yet another world first. Breo White Beer, the company tells us, is a completely new type of beer . . . The company plans to spend (five million pounds) on the brand and its marketing activities.'

Source: 'Breo World First for Guinness' compiled by Gabi Thesing in *Business and Finance*, 30th April–6th May 1998.

APPENDIX 4.1:   THE PROPERTIES OF INDIFFERENCE CURVES

The properties of indifference curves were listed in Section 4.3. A more detailed explanation is provided below.

1. Indifference curves slope down from left to right

Figure 4.19:   Indifference curves slope down from left to right

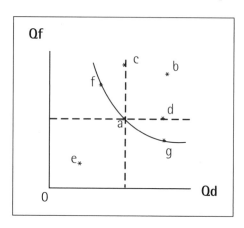

Consider bundle a in Figure 4.19. Now compare this bundle with other possible bundles. Let us begin with the quadrant to the northeast of a. Compared to bundle a, bundle b offers more of both goods, bundle c offers more food and the same amount of drink whereas bundle d offers more drink and the same amount of food. All of these bundles are preferred to bundle a because the consumer prefers more to less. Hence, these cannot form a locus of points with bundle a which maintains constant utility. This rules out all the possible bundles in the northeast quadrant.

A similar analysis can be applied to the southwest quadrant. All bundles in this quadrant contain less food and/or less drink than are included in bundle a. Since more is preferred to less, the consumer prefers bundle a to any bundle in the southwest quadrant. Bundle e and similar bundles do not lie on the same indifference curve as bundle a.

The only options left are areas to the northwest and southeast of bundle a. Bundles like f and g could possibly be on the same indifference curve. In comparison to bundle a, bundle f contains more food but less drink. Bundle g, on the other hand, contains more drink and less food. It is possible that the consumer is indifferent between bundles a, f and g. Therefore, they form an indifference curve which slopes downwards from left to right.

2. The slope of the indifference curve is determined by tastes and preferences and is called the marginal rate of substitution (MRS)

The MRS indicates the willingness of the consumer to give up a certain amount of one good in order to obtain one unit of the other good without changing utility. If the two goods are food and drink then the MRS is given by the amount of food that the consumer is willing to sacrifice in order to gain an extra unit of drink. This is expressed in Equation 4.5.

[4.5]

$$\text{MRS} = \frac{-\Delta Qf}{\Delta Qd}$$

3. Indifference curves are normally convex to the origin

Figure 4.20 indicates that as we move down and to the right along the indifference curve the MRS declines or diminishes. The indifference curve is said to exhibit a diminishing marginal rate of substitution. As we move down the indifference curve, less food and more drink is consumed. A rational consumer is now willing to give up less and less food in order to obtain an extra unit of drink. The MRS diminishes. In the example below, the MRS declines from 3 units to 1 unit.

Figure 4.20: The slope of the indifference curve and the marginal rate of substitution

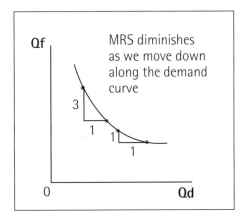

Diminishing marginal rate of substitution means that indifference curves are usually convex to the origin. However, there are many exceptions to the rule of convexity. Three exceptions are shown in Figure 4.21.

Figure 4.21: A sample of indifference curves

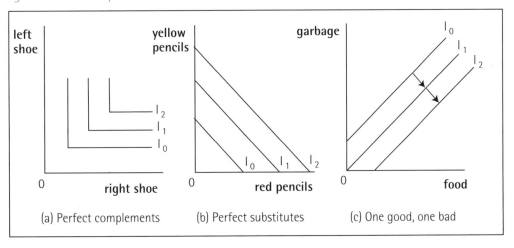

Case (a) represents perfect complements; two goods which are consumed together. The indifference curves for such goods are L-shaped. An example of perfect complements are left shoes and right shoes. An individual with one left shoe is no better off if she has two right shoes or three or four. Additional right shoes will leave her at the same level of utility (I_0) as the original pair. To move the consumer to a higher level of utility (I_1) she must have a second pair of shoes.

Perfect substitutes, such as red pencils and yellow pencils, are represented by case (b). Here the indifference curves are straight lines with negative slopes equal to –1. The consumer is willing to exchange one red pencil for one yellow pencil. In this case, the marginal rate of substitution is constant, rather than diminishing.

Case (c) shows the indifference curve for a good and a 'bad'. A 'bad' is a commodity that the consumer does not like. In order to accept more of the 'bad' which leads to increasing disutility, the consumer must be compensated with more of the 'good' which increases utility. Therefore, the indifference curve has a positive slope. Higher utility is achieved as the curves move from garbage towards food.

4. Indifference curves do not intersect

To establish the validity of this property we use the 'proof by contradiction' method which is used frequently in mathematics. In this particular case there are only two possible alternatives; the indifference curves either intersect or they do not intersect. These are mutually exclusive outcomes. Let us presuppose that they do intersect (the idea is to end up with a contradiction which then implies that the only other alternative must be true).

Figure 4.22: Indifference curves do not intersect

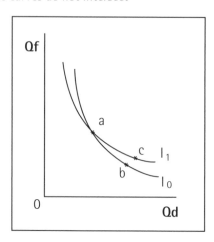

Two indifference curves are drawn, intersecting at point a, as in Figure 4.22. Consider I_0. The consumer is indifferent between bundle a and bundle b as both lie on I_0. Consider I_1. The consumer is also indifferent between bundle a and bundle c as both lie on I_1. If she is indifferent between bundles a and b, and also indifferent between bundles a and c then the law of transitivity implies that she is also indifferent between bundle b and bundle c. However, Figure 4.22 clearly shows that bundle c offers more of both goods than bundle b. The consumer is not indifferent between these two bundles and opts for bundle c over bundle b. Thus, we have a contradiction which implies that the original proposition was incorrect. The alternative must be true. Indifference curves do not intersect.

5. *There is a multiple set of indifference curves, called a preference map*

Figure 4.23: A preference map

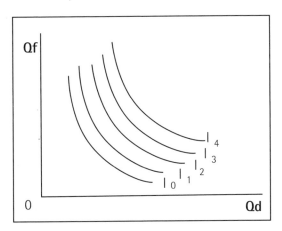

Every bundle represents some level of satisfaction to the consumer. Hence, every point is on an indifference curve. There is a set of indifference curves. This set is called a preference or indifference map and is drawn in Figure 4.23. For every two consumption bundles there is a third between them. Consequently, for every two indifference curves there is a third between them. Therefore, there is a multiple set of indifference curves.

6. *The higher the indifference curve, the higher the level of utility*

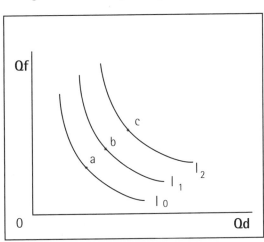

Figure 4.24: A set of indifference curves, each reflecting a higher level of utility than the previous (lower) one

Figure 4.24 illustrates three indifference curves. Consider bundles a, b and c. Bundle c offers more of both goods compared to bundle b. Consequently, bundle c is preferred to bundle b. Likewise, bundle b is preferred to bundle a. The same applies to indifference curves. Indifference curves which are further from the origin are preferred to indifference curves which are closer to the origin. For example, I_2 is preferred to I_1 which, in turn, is preferred to I_0.

CHAPTER 5

THE FIRM AND PRODUCTION

'Whatever may be the abundance of the source of production, the producer will always stop when the increase in expense exceeds the increase in receipts.'[1]

Augustin Cournot (1801–77)

'Normal profits are simply the supply price of entrepreneurship to a particular industry.'[2]

Joan Robinson (1903–83)

CHAPTER OBJECTIVES

Upon completing this chapter, the student should understand:

- short-run production and the law of diminishing returns;
- long-run production and returns to scale;
- opportunity cost and normal profit;
- short-run and long-run costs; fixed and variable costs;
- the output decision for the profit-maximising firm.

OUTLINE

5.1 The objectives of the firm
5.2 Production
5.3 Costs
5.4 Profit-maximising output level
5.5 Economies of scale and implications for Ireland

INTRODUCTION

Whereas the theory of demand is primarily concerned with the consumer and utility, the theory of supply is related to the producer and the costs of production. Costs are the main determinants used by producers to decide what amount of output is to be supplied at the different price levels. We begin the chapter by examining the traditional, neoclassical objective of profit maximisation. Other objectives are briefly mentioned. The theory of production and an analysis of costs follow. This is followed by a description of the output decision for profit-maximising firms. A brief discussion concerning economies of scale in the Irish context concludes the chapter.

5.1 THE OBJECTIVES OF THE FIRM

A firm's behaviour depends largely on its aims. By this we mean that the output produced and the price charged by the firm depend largely on the objective of the firm. For example, the price and output decision of a profit-maximising firm is likely to be different than that of a revenue-maximising firm because of the different objectives. A few of these objectives and their associated models are discussed below.

The traditional, neoclassical theory is based on the assumption that the objective of the firm is to maximise profits. It differs from the 'managerial' model which emphasises the differences between ownership and control in modern corporations. Firms are owned by shareholders. Decisions on the operation of the firm are made by managers. Although the shareholders want to maximise profits, managers may choose to maximise other objectives such as sales revenue, market share or their own salaries.

Another alternative to the neoclassical model is the behavioural model developed by Simon (1955) and Cyert and March (1963). The behavioural model is based on the idea that a firm is comprised of groups or coalitions who have their own objectives. Workers demand better pay, job security and improved working conditions. Shareholders, seeking maximum return for their investment, demand higher profits. There are other demands made from outside the firm by the government, consumers' associations and other interest groups. This model is very different from the neoclassical model which sees the firm as an individual entity with only one objective, profit maximisation.

The managerial and behavioural models are important contributions to the theory of the firm. However, the neoclassical model, based on profit maximisation, continues to dominate microeconomic theory. We will explain this traditional model in detail.

5.2 PRODUCTION

Any production process involves the transformation of inputs into units of output. Inputs, or factors of production, are usually classified into four categories: labour, land, capital and enterprise. The relationship between these inputs and the output which they generate can be presented in the form of a production function for an economy as demonstrated in Chapter 1. It can also refer to the inputs employed and the outputs produced by the firm.

Definition

The production function shows the relationship between the amounts of inputs used and the maximum amount of output generated.

The production function can be expressed in algebraic form as follows:

$$\text{TP} = f(\text{L, Land, K, Enterprise})$$ [5.1]

where: TP = total product or output; L = number of workers employed; K = capital including plant and machinery.

Literally, this expression means that the amount of a product which a firm can produce, depends on the amount of inputs which are used in the production process. Land, labour, capital and enterprise are the independent variables and total product is the dependent variable. In the examination of production which follows, we distinguish between the short run and the long run.

Production in the short run

To begin our discussion, we must explain a few relevant terms.

Definition
The short run is a period of time where there is at least one factor of production which does not change.

The quantity of a 'fixed' factor does not vary as the level of output varies. The fixed factor is generally land or machinery, the latter falling into the general classification of capital.

In order to discuss production, we will consider a business developed by Sean McHale, an entrepreneur from County Mayo. Sean owns a small firm called Key Chains Ltd. He began producing key chains and selling them from the boot of his car. As his business expands, Sean finds that he cannot produce enough key chains to meet all of his orders. Therefore, he hires one employee, then a second and a third. We will consider how each additional worker affects Sean's output.

For this example, we will use a simple, short-run production function with only two inputs: capital and labour. To produce key chains, Sean uses two machines. These machines represent capital and this factor is fixed in the short run. Labour is a variable input. Table 5.1 presents the changes in output which result from increasing the number of employees.

Table 5.1: Key chain production per week

(1) Number of workers	(2) K	(3) Total product (TP)	(4) Average product (AP)	(5) Marginal product (MP)
0	2	0	0	
				100
1	2	100	100	
				220
2	2	320	160	
				310
3	2	630	210	
				410
4	2	1040	260	
				360
5	2	1400	280	
				340
6	2	1740	290	
				220
7	2	1960	280	
				−120
8	2	1840	230	

We can see by looking at the total product column, that production begins with the addition of labour. In this case, Sean is the first labourer and, working on his own, he can produce 100 key chains per week. The total product continues to increase as Sean hires more staff. However, with the addition of the eighth worker, total product falls.

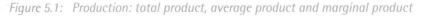

Figure 5.1:   Production: total product, average product and marginal product

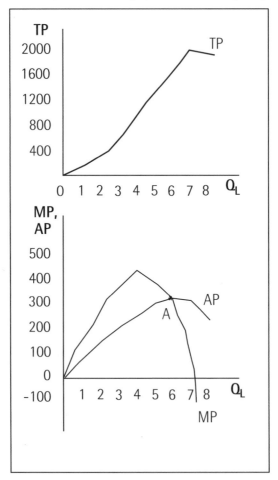

The same information is shown in Figure 5.1. The upper diagram shows the total product curve. It shows the relationship between the variable input, labour and output or total product. Labour is represented on the horizontal axis and total product is represented on the vertical axis. The total product curve shows the same relationship that we described above. Production begins with the addition of the first labourer. The upward sloping line indicates that output increases until we add the eighth worker. Then the total product curve slopes downward.

The total product curve separates space into attainable output and unattainable output. Levels of output which are above the curve are unattainable using the available labour. For example, three labourers could not produce 700 key chains. All output possibilities inside and on the curve are attainable. Those on the curve reflect the maximum attainable output levels. In this example, three labourers could produce 630 key chains (on the curve) or fewer (inside the curve).

It is more obvious from the diagram that the production level changes by a different amount with each additional worker because the total product curve is not a straight line. Variations in the total product curve are explained using the concept of marginal product.

Definition

The marginal product is the change in total output obtained from an additional unit of a variable input, holding other inputs constant.

In this example, the marginal product of labour is the extra output derived from the addition of one extra worker while capital is held constant. This relationship is described in Equation 5.2:

$$MP = \frac{\Delta TP}{\Delta Qv}$$

[5.2]

where: Δ = change; MP = marginal product; TP = total product; Qv = quantity of variable input.

Column 5 of Table 5.1 presents the data for the marginal product of labour. Output begins with the addition of the first unit of labour. The marginal product of the first worker is 100 key chains, the number of units which Sean can produce if he works on his own. To find the marginal product of the second employee, we subtract the total product of two workers from the total product of one worker (320 – 100 = 220). Since the change in labour is one, we divide 220 by 1 which equals 220 key chains. This means that the addition of the second worker has increased total product by 220 key chains.

The bottom diagram of Figure 5.1 shows the marginal product of labour curve. We can see that the marginal product curve rises sharply with the addition of each labourer until four individuals are hired. In other words, each additional labourer is adding more to total output than the last. With the addition of the fifth worker, the marginal product of labour begins to fall. After the fourth worker, the marginal product curve is downward sloping.

To understand why the marginal product of labour rises and falls, we will return to Key Chains Ltd and look specifically at Sean's production process. Initially, Sean did everything himself. Before he hired his first employee, Sean made a list of all the tasks required to produce and sell key chains. He broke the process into seven stages:

1. order and receive materials;
2. cut design (machine 1);
3. laminate design (machine 2);
4. cut chain;
5. assemble ring, chain and laminated design;
6. inspect finished product;
7. sell.

Each of these tasks can possibly be completed by a different person who specialises at that task. The division of labour usually increases productivity. This is called increasing marginal returns.

Definition

Increasing marginal returns means that an additional unit of a variable factor adds more to total product than the previous unit.

In other words, if labour is the variable factor, the additional worker adds more to the total product than the previous worker. This is what happens when Sean hires Maeve who worked as a machine operator in Dublin for a few years before returning home to Mayo. He trains her to use the machines, to cut the chain and to assemble the key chains. Sean continues to order materials, to inspect and to sell the key chains.

The addition of Maeve causes output per week to more than double, from 100 key chains to 320 key chains per week. The marginal product, caused by adding another worker, is 220 units. Maeve concentrates on the production of key chains while Sean specialises in ordering and selling.

A few months later, Sean decides to hire another person. Tom, a former assembly line worker, has recently been made redundant. Because of his previous experience, Sean divides the manufacturing process between Maeve and Tom. Maeve continues to work on the machines, while Tom cuts the chain and assembles the pieces. Total product almost doubles. The marginal product attributed to the addition of the third worker is 310 units.

Well pleased with the increases in output, Sean hires a fourth worker. Taragh assumes the tasks of ordering materials and inspecting the finished product. The addition of this worker results in an increase of 410 units per week.

Sean adds a fifth, sixth and seventh worker. He continues to divide the tasks. However, he finds that while total product continues to rise, the marginal product is falling. Increasing marginal returns ends with the addition of the fourth worker.

Perplexed by this development, Sean decides to take a day off from selling, to observe the operation. He notices that the two machine operators are constantly working. However, they do not produce enough of the laminated design to keep the other members of the staff constantly occupied. Sean can see that the problem is with the machines, not the operators. The odd breakdown of machinery suggests that the machines are being used to capacity.

The problem that Sean observes occurs so regularly, that it is called the law of diminishing returns.

Definition

The law of diminishing returns means that if at least one factor is fixed, a point is reached when an additional unit of a variable factor adds less to total product than the previous unit.

In other words, if labour is the variable factor, an additional worker adds less to total product than the previous worker. In this case, Sean's capital is limited to two machines. With the addition of the fifth worker, marginal product diminishes.

Sean decides that given the limitations imposed on the production process by the machinery, he will not hire any additional workers in the short run. Indeed, we can see from Table 5.1 that the addition of the eighth worker would cause the total product to fall!

The 'law of diminishing returns' was identified by the classical economists. John Stuart Mill (1806–73), when describing agricultural production said, '. . . the state of the art being given, doubling the labour does not double the produce'.[3] The law of diminishing returns is widely observed in practice and characterises many production activities.

We can come to a further understanding of the total product curve by comparing it to the marginal product curve. When the marginal product curve is rising, the total product curve is becoming steeper. This means that marginal returns are increasing; each worker is contributing more to total product than the last.

When the marginal product curve begins to fall, the total product curve becomes flatter. In other words, when the marginal product is falling, the total product curve is increasing at a decreasing rate. This means that marginal returns are decreasing; each worker is adding to total product, but by less than the previous worker.

When the marginal product curve cuts the horizontal axis, the marginal product of labour becomes negative. The additional worker is causing the total product to fall. At this point, the total product curve begins to slope downward.

Next we will consider the average product and its relationship with the marginal product.

Definition
The average product is the total output divided by the number of units of the variable input employed.

For example, the average product of labour is the total output divided by the total units of labour. Equation 5.3 states this relationship in algebraic form.

$$AP = \frac{TP}{Qv} \qquad \text{[5.3]}$$

where: AP = average product; TP = total product; Qv = quantity of variable input.

Column 4 of Table 5.1 presents the data for the average product of labour. If three workers produce 630 key chains, the average product of labour is 630/3 which equals 210. Notice that the average product of labour also rises and then falls. Both the average product of labour and the marginal product of labour are derived by looking at the relationship between total product and labour. But is there a particular relationship between the AP and the MP?

A simple example may clarify this relationship. Suppose that a footballer has an average score over three games of 1 goal per match. Consider two possibilities for the fourth match.

First, suppose that the footballer scores 2 goals in the fourth game. The 'marginal' score is 2. This is the number of goals that he adds to his total by playing in the fourth game. The footballer's average increases to 1.25 goals per game. We can think of the marginal goals as dragging up the average. Now consider the possibility that the footballer fails to score in the fourth game. The 'marginal' score is 0 which is below the average score of 1. This drags down the average to 0.75. If the marginal score is above the average score, the average score is dragged up. Conversely, if the marginal score is below the average score, the average score is dragged down.

We can see this same relationship in the bottom frame of Figure 5.1. When the marginal product of labour is above the average product of labour, the average product of labour is rising. However, when the additional labourer fails to add more to total product than the previous worker, the marginal product of labour falls. When the marginal product of labour is below the average, the average product of labour falls. Hence, the marginal product curve must cut the average product curve at its highest point, labelled point A.

We will end this discussion with one final comment on the short run. The short run is not a particular length of time: it varies from market to market. For example, the short run may only last for a few months in the catering business. If Bewleys wants to expand, the management must find a new location, arrange for financing and prepare the site before they can open. This period of time will be far shorter than the time which it will take for Bord na Móna to open a new production site. Finding a suitable location, applying for planning permission, arranging for financing, and determining the technological processes might take years, rather than months.

Production in the long run

We observed that at Key Chains Ltd, the level of output was limited by the machinery. In the short run, Sean's capital was fixed. In the long run, it is possible for Sean to increase the number of machines, the size of the plant and the production process. In the long run, all inputs can be varied.

Definition
The long run is a period of time when all the factors of production can be varied in quantity.

The long-run production function shows combinations of inputs and the quantities of output produced. There are three possible relationships between inputs and outputs. The long-run production function may exhibit all three relationships over the range of production.

1. Increasing returns to scale mean that the increase in output is proportionately greater than the increase in inputs. For example, if we double the amount of inputs, the level of output will more than double.
2. In the case of constant returns to scale, the increase in output matches the increase in inputs. In this situation, a doubling of inputs is matched by a doubling of output.
3. Decreasing returns to scale mean that the increase in output is proportionately smaller than the increase in inputs. Therefore, if inputs double, output will increase but by less than a factor of two.

These cases relate to the scale of production which requires further discussion.

Increasing returns to scale are closely related to the concept of economies of scale where an increase in the scale of production leads to lower costs per unit produced. Where there are constant returns to scale, changing the level of output over a range of production does not affect the cost per unit. Decreasing returns to scale are closely related to the concept of diseconomies of scale where an increase in the scale of production results in higher unit costs.

There are a number of reasons why a firm experiences increasing returns to scale over a range of production. As firms produce large numbers of units of output, more labour is hired and employees become increasingly specialised in the tasks which they perform. In the long run, large firms can purchase dedicated machinery and train their workers to operate it efficiently.

Firms which produce high levels of output can purchase inputs at a discounted price. Large firms put intense pressure on their suppliers to reduce the cost of inputs, particularly if they are a major customer.

Another source of increasing returns to scale is indivisibilities. Some capital investments are only suitable for high levels of output and when used in those circumstances, are very efficient. A combine harvester can be used to reap and thresh thousands of acres of wheat or corn. However, this type of machinery is 'indivisible'. It is impossible to purchase anything less than a whole combine harvester and it is very expensive to operate one at low levels of output.

Finally, there are a group of costs incurred by the firm which are called 'overheads'. These are some of the operating expenses of a firm which do not arise from the production of the good or service. They include the costs of advertising, marketing and research and development. The cost of overheads decreases as they are spread over more units.

It is believed that firms experience decreasing returns to scale beyond a certain range of production. When a firm grows beyond a certain size, the cost of managing the firm may increase disproportionately. The decision-making process may become slower and more complex. Staff morale problems, which in turn lead to production problems, are more likely to occur. Firms may experience problems in co-ordinating production activities. All of these factors may cause the cost per unit of production to increase.

The relationship between the scale of production and the long-run cost of production will be discussed further in the next section.

5.3 COSTS

Costs are payments for the use of factors of production. Labour receives wages. Rent is paid for the use of land. Interest is the cost of capital. Profit is the payment for enterprise.

At this point, a student of accounting as well as others may be confused. Why does the economist consider profit as a cost while the accountant considers profit as the difference between revenues and costs? The answer is that accountants and economists define costs differently.

Economists are interested in economic costs which include both the explicit costs like wages, rent and interest recognised by accountants and the opportunity cost discussed in Chapter 1. The opportunity cost is the economist's way of acknowledging that all factors of production, including enterprise, can be used in alternative ways.

Consider Sean, the owner of Key Chains Ltd. Sean could use his talents in a number of different ways. He could produce something else besides key chains or he could work for another firm. Economists believe that Sean will continue to produce and sell key chains, if and only if he makes a 'normal' profit.

Definition
Normal profit is the amount or percentage of profit which the entrepreneur requires to supply his or her expertise.

It is the amount of profit that the entrepreneur could earn in the next best alternative business. A normal profit is the opportunity cost of the entrepreneur. It is a cost to the firm in the sense that production will cease if the normal profit is not earned by the entrepreneur.

It is possible that the entrepreneur will earn more than a normal profit. Economists refer to this as economic profit or supernormal profit.

Definition
Economic or supernormal profit is the difference between revenue and economic costs.

'Economic costs' refer to the explicit costs which are found in the Profit and Loss Account like cost of sales, operating costs, interest charges and taxation. It also includes a 'normal profit', for the entrepreneur.

An example showing the difference between accounting profit and economic profit is shown in Table 5.2.

Table 5.2: Accounting versus economic profit

The accountant's interpretation		
Total revenue		600,000
Total cost		380,000
Profit		220,000
The economist's interpretation		
Total revenue		600,000
Economic costs		570,000
of which:	Explicit costs	380,000
	Opportunity cost	190,000
Supernormal or economic profit		30,000

We will now consider costs in greater detail. As with inputs, we will distinguish between the short run and the long run.

Short-run costs

You will recall from our discussion of factor inputs that the short run is the length of time when some inputs are fixed and other inputs are variable. Factors of production must be paid. If the factor of production is fixed in the short run, we consider the cost to be fixed as well. Fixed costs are the payments to fixed factors of production. They remain constant as output varies.

We will return to the example of Key Chains Ltd. Recall that Sean uses two machines to manufacture key chains. The machines are Sean's fixed input. If we were considering a more complex production function, fixed costs might include rent, insurance premiums and the price of the phone connection.

You will also recall that other inputs, such as labour and raw materials, vary with the level of production. Variable costs are the payments to variable factors of production. They are incurred with the first unit of production and generally increase as production increases.

For Key Chains Ltd, labour is the only variable input and therefore, wage is the variable cost. Other variable costs for Sean might include monies paid for the materials used to produce the key chains and the charge for telephone calls. Like wages, these costs will change with the level of production.

The short-run total cost is equal to the sum of the fixed costs and the variable costs. This relationship is expressed in the following equation:

$$\boxed{\textbf{STC} = \textbf{SFC} + \textbf{SVC}}$$ [5.4]

where: STC = short-run total cost; SFC = short-run fixed cost; SVC = short-run variable cost.

Table 5.3 shows the details of the short-run costs for Key Chains Ltd.

Table 5.3: Short-run costs (per week) for Key Chains Ltd

(1) Labour	(2) Q	(3) SFC	(4) SVC	(5) STC	(6) SMC	(7) SAFC	(8) SAVC	(9) SATC
0	0	100	0	100		–	–	–
					2.00			
1	100	100	200	300		1.00	2.00	3.00
					0.91			
2	320	100	400	500		0.31	1.25	1.56
					0.65			
3	630	100	600	700		0.16	0.95	1.11
					0.49			
4	1040	100	800	900		0.10	0.77	0.87
					0.56			
5	1400	100	1000	1100		0.07	0.71	0.79
					0.59			
6	1740	100	1200	1300		0.06	0.69	0.75
					0.91			
7	1960	100	1400	1500		0.05	0.71	0.76

Column 3 shows the fixed costs which are constant regardless of the level of output. The variable costs, shown in column 4, increase with the level of production. Column 5 shows the total costs. Since total costs include both fixed and variable costs, they increase as the quantity of output increases. The curves drawn in the left-hand panel of Figure 5.2 are based on the short-run fixed, variable and total costs.

Figure 5.2:   Short-run cost curves for Key Chains Ltd

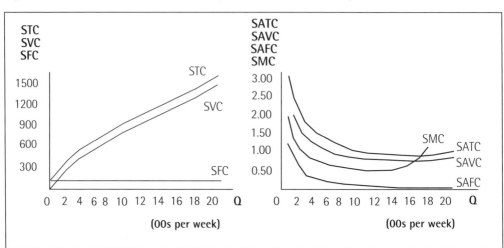

Fixed costs are independent of the level of production. These costs are incurred even if no output is produced. Therefore, the short-run fixed cost curve (SFC) is a horizontal line, at €100 (the cost of the machinery). Variable costs are incurred when production begins and increase as production increases. In this example the wage per worker equals €200. Therefore, the short-run variable cost curve (SVC) begins at the origin and is upward sloping.

The short-run total cost curve (STC) is the vertical summation of the other two curves: it begins at €100. The fixed costs are the only costs incurred before production begins. The STC curve is upward sloping and is always above the SVC curve by an amount equal to the value of the fixed costs. In the short run, fixed costs always separate the STC curve from the SVC curve.

We can examine other important economic concepts more conveniently by looking at the cost per unit. We will begin by defining the average cost and the marginal cost.

Definition

Average total cost is total cost divided by the number of units produced.

We can calculate average variable costs and average fixed costs. The addition of average fixed cost and average variable cost is average total cost.

$$\boxed{\textbf{SATC = SAFC + SAVC}}$$ **[5.5]**

where: SATC = short-run average total cost; SAFC = short-run average fixed cost; SAVC = short-run average variable cost.

The key to understanding how much a firm will produce and sell is its marginal cost which is the most important of all cost concepts.

Definition

The marginal cost is the extra cost incurred from producing an additional unit of output.

In the short run it is expressed as follows:

$$SMC = \frac{\Delta STC}{\Delta Q} \qquad [5.6]$$

where: Δ = change; SMC = short-run marginal cost; STC = short-run total cost; Q = level of output.

The marginal and average costs for this example are calculated in columns 6 through 9 of Table 5.3. We notice immediately that the short-run average fixed costs are falling as the costs are spread over more units. All of the other short-run costs fall initially and then rise again. These relationships can be examined more easily by looking at a diagram.

The right-sided frame of Figure 5.2 shows the short-run average fixed cost curve (SAFC), the short-run average variable cost curve (SAVC), the short-run average total cost curve (SATC) and finally the short-run marginal cost curve (SMC). Notice that the SAFC curve is downward sloping. As production expands, the average fixed costs fall. Both the SAVC and the SATC curves fall initially and then rise. The SMC curve also falls and rises again.

We can relate the changes in the marginal cost to our discussion about marginal product in Section 5.2. Remember that in the simplified production function for Key Chains Ltd, labour is the only variable input. Therefore, wage is the only variable cost. With the addition of each of the first four workers, the marginal product increases. Assuming that all workers are employed at the same wage, if the marginal product of labour is increasing, the marginal cost to produce key chains falls. With the addition of the fifth worker at Key Chains Ltd, labour is less productive. Therefore, the marginal cost of producing a unit of output increases.

To summarise this relationship, if the marginal product of labour is rising, its marginal cost is falling; if the marginal product of labour is falling, its marginal cost is rising.

The relationship between 'average' and 'marginal' described in Section 5.2 also applies to costs. Both the short-run average total cost and variable cost 'follow' the marginal cost. When the marginal cost is below the average, the average costs fall. When the marginal cost is above the average, the average costs rise. In terms of the diagram, the SMC curve intersects both the SATC curve and the SAVC curve at their lowest points.

CASE STUDY

Extract from *The Sunday Business Post*
Controls needed to cut costs in claims culture

The extent to which many small and budding businesses are affected by the claims culture in Irish society has increased in recent years, according to Tony Briscoe, IBEC's assistant director for social policy.

The problem of insurance claims is not lost on small business entrepreneurs during the set up phase when they go shopping for insurance cover. They are frequently shocked to learn that the third and fourth more costly element of their list of . . . costs (including wages, materials and premises) is the cost of indemnity cover; to provide for potential claims by the public or by future employees.

This is a cost which has no direct or proportional relationship to their levels of production, sales or profit. Additionally, it is money which has to be paid over often before the business receives any sales revenue. In some areas of work, because of their level of exposure to claims, the initial premiums many small firms have to pay can be as much as equivalent of four months payroll cost.

'The potential for somebody suing them, particularly for business involved in the services area where they deal with the public is quite considerable,' said Briscoe.

Among the measures proposed by IBEC and the SFA (Small Firms Association) to . . . bring about some realism in the cost of insurance are:

- Greater account being taken by the legal system for contributory negligence by persons bringing claims.
- A book of quantum, providing realistic values for general damages awards.
- A reduction in the period within which a claim for personal injuries may be brought, to six months (currently three years).
- Severe penalties for fraudulent, spurious and exaggerated claims.

Source: *The Sunday Business Post.*

Questions

1. What is the difference between 'variable' costs and 'fixed' costs?
2. What are the four largest costs for a new enterprise? Which are variable and which are fixed?
3. How would the proposed changes help the entrepreneur? Explain your answer in the context of fixed and variable costs.

Answers on website

Long-run costs

The long run is a period of time which is long enough to vary all factors of production. Since inputs can be used with greater flexibility, we do not differentiate between variable and fixed costs. We will begin by discussing the shape of the long-run average cost curve (LAC).

The LAC curve shows the relationship between the lowest attainable average cost and output when all inputs are variable. In theory, the LAC curve can be in any of three forms or some combination of all three. A downward sloping LAC curve reflects declining unit costs as production increases. This is known as economies of scale. The straight line LAC curve reflects constant returns to scale. An upward sloping LAC curve reflects diseconomies of scale where the cost per unit of production increases as the level of output increases. Figure 5.3 shows all three cases.

Figure 5.3: The slope of the long-run average cost curve

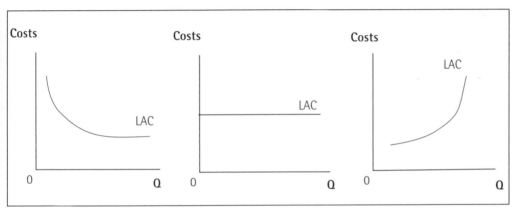

The typical long-run average cost curve is thought to be a combination of these three curves. The U-shaped LAC curve supposedly captures realistic trends in costs relative to output levels. It is shown in Figure 5.4.

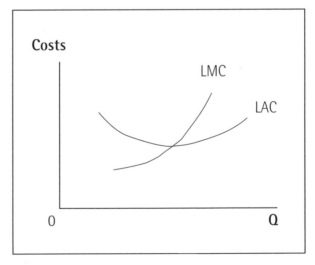

Figure 5.4: The U-shaped long-run average cost curve

Initially, the LAC curve is downward sloping which means that the average cost per unit is falling over a range of production. Economies of scale are associated with the use of specialised labour and machinery. Large firms can decrease their cost per unit because of their ability to negotiate for discounts for the purchase of inputs, to efficiently use 'indivisible' capital assets and to spread 'overhead' costs over a large number of units.

The LAC curve is relatively flat over a range of production. This means that the firm can expand production with little change in the cost per output. Over this range of production, the firm experiences constant returns to scale.

Eventually the LAC curve is upward sloping which means that the average cost per unit increases with output. Diseconomies of scale are associated with managerial problems which firms experience when they increase in size. The LMC curve is also shown in Figure 5.4.

At the bottom of the LAC curve, costs per unit of production are at their lowest. This level is called the minimum cost production level. It is of great significance and is explained in greater detail in the next chapter when we discuss different market structures.

The relationship between average costs and marginal costs also applies in the long run. In other words, when the marginal cost is below the average cost, the average costs fall. When the marginal cost is above the average cost, the average costs rise. As in the short run, the long-run marginal cost curve (LMC) cuts the LAC curve at the lowest point.

The envelope curve

The long-run average cost curve can be explained in terms of short-run average total cost curves. This is shown in Figure 5.5.

Figure 5.5:   The envelope curve

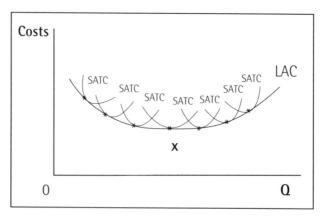

A set of SATC curves is reproduced in Figure 5.5. Each short-run average total cost curve is U-shaped because of the law of diminishing returns. The LAC curve is said to 'envelope' the SATC curves. Each point on the LAC curve is a point of tangency with respective points on corresponding SATC curves. There is a tendency to match the points on the LAC curve with minimum points on the SATC curves. This is incorrect.[4]

Point x is the minimum point of the LAC curve. Each point to the left is a tangency point with a point on the falling part of the respective SATC curves. Each point to the right is a tangency point with a point on the rising part of the respective SATC curves. Only at the minimum point x on the LAC curve is the corresponding SATC curve also at a minimum. This suggests that to the left of point x the plants are not working to full capacity whereas to the right of point x the plants are overworked. At point x the plant is optimally employed, in the sense that it is producing at the lowest possible cost per unit.

This completes the discussion of the derivation of short-run and long-run cost curves. We will now discuss the way that we use these cost curves to identify the firm's profit-maximising level of output.

5.4   PROFIT-MAXIMISING OUTPUT LEVEL

The sole objective of the firm in the neoclassical model is profit maximisation. In this section we will derive the profit-maximising output level using two methods. These methods are essentially the same, though each looks at revenues and costs from a slightly different perspective.

The first approach requires values for total revenue (TR) and total cost (TC) for each level of production. The output level where the difference between total revenue and total cost is the largest is the profit-maximising output level. The second approach is based on marginal revenue (MR) and marginal cost (MC) values. By comparing marginal revenue and marginal cost we can derive the same profit-maximising output level as above.

We will use another example to illustrate the relevant concepts. Liam from County Meath produces potatoes. Again, we will consider only two inputs for the short-run production function. Land is a fixed factor of production and rent is a fixed cost. Labour is the variable input and wage is the variable cost. Column 4 of Table 5.4 shows the total cost (fixed cost plus variable cost) associated with the different levels of output for potatoes.

Table 5.4:   Total revenue, total cost and profit for the production of potatoes

(1) Q (tons)	(2) P (€00)	(3) TR (€00)	(4) TC (€00)	(5) Profit (€00)
0	–	0	36	–36
1	33.0	33	50	–17
2	31.5	63	62	1
3	30.0	90	73	17
4	28.5	114	82	32
5	27.0	135	92	43
6	25.5	153	105	48
7	24.0	168	119	49
8	22.5	180	144	36
9	21.0	189	171	18

Although Liam is always conscious of his costs, that is only half of the story. Over the years, he notices that to sell more potatoes, he must sell his potatoes at a lower price per ton. In other words, the demand curve for his product is downward sloping.

There is a particular price associated with each level of output. The price per ton of output is shown in column 2 of Table 5.4. Farmer Liam is interested in the total revenue which he will receive at each level of production. We know from Chapter 3 that total revenue is the price of the good times the quantity of output sold.

Total revenue is calculated in column 3 of Table 5.4.

Profit is the difference between total revenue and total cost. Recall that a normal profit is included in the calculations for cost. Therefore, if profit is zero, the firm (or in this case the farmer) is making a normal profit. Any profit which is greater than zero is called economic or supernormal profit. Profit is calculated in column 5 of Table 5.4. In this example, the difference between total revenue and total cost is maximised when seven tons are produced. At this level of output, profit is €4,900.

As we mentioned earlier, this profit-maximising level of output can also be identified by comparing the marginal revenue and the marginal cost.

Definition

Marginal revenue is the change in total revenue resulting from a one unit change in output.

Algebraically, we can describe this relationship in the following way:

$$MR = \frac{\Delta TR}{\Delta Q}$$

[5.7]

where: Δ = change; MR = marginal revenue; TR = total revenue; Q = level of output.

Marginal revenue is calculated in column 3 of Table 5.5. Consider the additional revenue which Liam gains by producing and selling the seventh ton. When he produces and sells six tons, he earns €15,300 in revenue. For the production and sale of seven tons, Liam earns €16,800. The difference between the two is €1,500. Since one additional ton is produced, we divide this total by one. In this example, the marginal revenue gained from the production and sale of the seventh ton is €1,500.

We have already defined the marginal cost as the additional charge incurred from producing and selling one unit of output. The marginal cost is calculated in column 5 of Table 5.5.

The total cost of producing seven units is €11,900. However, producing the first six units costs the farmer €10,500. Therefore, the marginal cost of the seventh unit is (11,900 − 10,500)/1 which is €1,400.

Table 5.5:   Total revenue, marginal revenue, total cost and marginal cost

(1) Q (tons)	(2) TR (€00)	(3) MR (€00)	(4) TC (€00)	(5) MC (€00)	(6) MR–MC (€00)	(7) Output decision
0	0		36			
		33		14	19	Increase
1	33		50			
		30		12	18	Increase
2	63		62			
		27		11	16	Increase
3	90		73			
		24		9	15	Increase
4	114		82			
		21		10	11	Increase
5	135		92			
		18		13	5	Increase
6	153		105			
		15		14	1	Increase
7	168		119			
		12		25	–13	Decrease
8	180		144			
		9		27	–18	Decrease
9	189		171			

The last two columns of Table 5.5 help us to determine the profit-maximising output level for Liam. Marginal revenue is greater than marginal cost from the first unit of production to the seventh unit of production. As output increases by one unit the additional revenue is greater than the additional cost incurred. This means that he can earn additional profits by increasing production. Since we assume that Liam wants to maximise profits, output should be increased.

Marginal revenue is less than marginal cost beyond the seventh unit of production. The extra revenue is not large enough to cover the extra cost incurred. Production should not be increased beyond seven units. A profit-maximising firm (farmer) will continue to produce as long as the difference between the marginal revenue and marginal cost is positive. The difference is calculated in column 6 above. In this example the difference is positive up to seven units of production.

In brief, when marginal revenue is greater than marginal cost, the level of output should be increased. When marginal revenue is less than marginal cost, output should be reduced. Consequently, a firm produces at the profit-maximising output level when marginal revenue is equal to marginal cost.

This is a necessary, but not sufficient condition for profit maximisation. An examination of the second condition will be covered after we compare the profit-maximising output level using total revenue and total cost with the level of output determined using marginal revenue and marginal cost. Figure 5.6 shows the relationship between the two approaches.

Figure 5.6: Profit maximisation with total revenue and total cost, marginal revenue and marginal cost

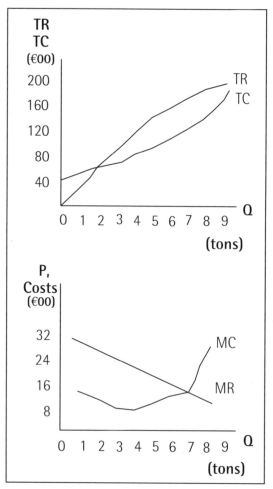

In the top frame of Figure 5.6, we have drawn the curves for total revenue (TR) and total cost (TC). When the gap between the TR and TC curves is the greatest, profits are maximised. As we saw in the table, this occurs at a production level of seven units.

In the bottom frame, we can see the relationship between marginal revenue (MR) and marginal cost (MC). Consider a production level of six units. From the diagram, we can clearly see that the MR curve is above the MC curve. Therefore, the firm can increase profits by producing and selling more units. Now consider the production level of eight units. On the diagram, we can see that the MC curve is above the MR curve. If the firm produces at this level, total profits will fall. Therefore, the profit-maximising level of production is between six and eight units of production. The profit-maximising firm will produce seven units. This is where the MR curve intersects the MC curve. Refer to Appendix 5.1 to see how this is related to cost minimisation and the least-cost production technique.

Using either approach, the profit-maximising level of output is the same.

In the example of the potato-producing farmer, the profit-maximising decision was to produce. This is not always the case. In some situations, firms operate at a loss, at least in the short run. The owner of the firm may decide that he can minimise his losses by producing where marginal revenue equals the marginal cost. Alternatively, he may decide that it is better to shut down, and pay only the fixed costs. In other words, it is costing him more to produce than it would to shut down. We will extend our analysis to show how the owner of a profit-maximising firm makes that choice both in the short run and in the long run.

The output decision of the firm in the short run

There are two conditions for short-run equilibrium. First, we have already discussed the marginal condition. A profit-maximising firm which is going to produce will choose a production level where marginal revenue equals short-run marginal cost (MR = SMC). However, there is a second condition which must also be met: it is the average condition. A firm will produce this level of output if, and only if, average revenue or price is no less than short-run average variable cost (P ≥ SAVC).

Definition
Average revenue is a firm's total revenue divided by the quantity sold.

It is simply the price of the good.[5]

This second condition implies that in order to produce the firm must at least cover its variable costs. This equilibrium position is illustrated in Figure 5.7.

Figure 5.7: Output decision in the short run

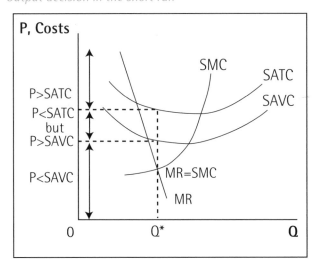

The marginal condition, where MR = SMC, is met at output level Q* in Figure 5.7. Given the present market conditions and the short-run costs, the profit-maximising output level is Q*. However, this condition alone is not enough to determine the firm's production decision as it does not provide for the possibility of not producing at all. This requires the second condition. The average condition involves comparing average revenue with average cost, at Q*. Given the nature of costs in the short run, three distinct possibilities arise.

If average revenue or price exceeds the short-run average total cost resulting in an economic profit, the firm will continue to produce at this output level. If the price level falls between the SATC and the SAVC curves, the firm is operating at a loss. It is covering its variable costs and making some contribution to the fixed costs which must be paid even if production is temporarily halted. Under this condition, the firm will continue to produce because it will lose even more if it closes. Instead of maximising profits, the firm is minimising losses. A favourable change in market conditions could turn short-run losses into profits.

If price is lower than the short-run average variable cost the situation is more serious. In this case the firm is not covering its variable costs. The day-to-day expenses such as labour costs, tax bills, social insurance and so on are not met. At Q* the variable cost per unit of production exceeds the price received for each unit. The firm minimises losses by shutting down. A shutdown is preferred to continued production at Q*.

In brief, a firm that is not making profits will attempt to limit their short-run losses. The decision to produce in the short run requires that both the marginal and average conditions are met. Ultimately any profit-maximising firm produces in the short run as long as it covers its variable costs.

In the short run, we have seen that a firm may continue production, even if it is not making a normal profit. In the long run, the owner of the firm can make a number of choices, which include switching his resources to another form of enterprise where he can make at least a normal profit. We now explore the output decision for a profit-maximising firm in the long run.

The output decision of the firm in the long run

There are two conditions for long-run equilibrium. The first condition states that the profit-maximising firm will produce where marginal revenue equals the long-run marginal cost (MR = LMC). The marginal condition is met at the output level of Q* as illustrated in Figure 5.8.

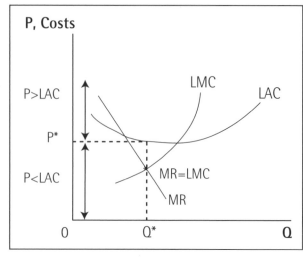

Figure 5.8: Output decision in the long run

As before, this condition is not sufficient as it does not cover the alternative of not producing at all. The second condition states that a firm will produce in the long run if price is greater than or equal to the long-run average cost ($P \geq LAC$). This condition implies that the firm will only produce in the long run if it can cover all of its costs. In the long run, two cases arise.

If price equals or exceeds the long-run average cost, the firm will continue to produce where marginal revenue equals marginal cost. If the price obtained for the product is P^*, shown in Figure 5.8, the firm is covering its costs and making a normal profit. If price is greater than P^*, the firm is making supernormal profits. In either situation, the firm will continue to produce in the long run.

Alternatively, if price is lower than P^*, then losses result. Since a firm must cover all of its costs in the long run, it will have no choice but to stop production and close down. In this case, we would expect the factors of production to be released for use in activities which will earn at least a normal profit.

In brief, the long-run output decision requires that both the marginal and the average conditions are met. Ultimately all costs must be covered in the long run.

We will conclude this chapter by returning to economies of scale and discussing the important ramifications of this concept in the Irish context.

5.5 ECONOMIES OF SCALE AND IMPLICATIONS FOR IRELAND

Although economies of scale appear to be simply a technical relationship, its relevance for a small country like Ireland is quite profound.

When Fianna Fáil came into power in 1932, it attempted and succeeded in increasing industrial production by imposing tariffs on imports. This protected the domestic manufacturers since the tariffs made imported goods more expensive than goods which were manufactured in Ireland. One consequence of this protectionist policy was that it raised problems with our main trading partner, Britain, leading to the 'Economic War'.

What is more relevant to this discussion is that the small size of the domestic market meant that in most industries, production was not very efficient. Why? Although consumer products like clothing and shoes were being produced here, the inputs and machinery needed for production were largely imported. The domestic industries were not large enough to support the development of other domestic firms who could supply the inputs. Increasing returns to scale in the production process meant that inputs could be produced far more cheaply by foreign-based firms who were producing initially for larger domestic markets and then exporting.

Unfortunately, the cost of the foreign inputs made Irish products expensive relative to the goods produced in other countries. The small size of the Irish market meant that Irish manufacturers were producing at a high cost per unit and were unable to benefit from scale economies which would have lowered their costs and ultimately made the price of Irish goods more competitive in the international market.

For a number of reasons, the protectionist policies of the 1930s and 1940s were abandoned. One of the main reasons was the deterioration of the 'terms of trade'. This means that the price of imports increased faster than the price of exports. Ireland was importing more than she was exporting, a situation which cannot persist indefinitely for a small country. One of the main goals of policy-makers in the 1950s, a period of reorientation towards free trade, was to promote export growth. In 1965, Ireland joined Britain to sign the Anglo-Irish Free Trade Agreement (AIFTA) and began to dismantle trade barriers. In 1973, Ireland joined the European Economic Community (EEC) under an agreement that they would implement free-trade policies for all manufacturers by 1978.

By entering these trade agreements, Ireland was attempting to increase the size of potential markets. Only by expanding demand could Ireland hope to compete in the increasing number of markets that were characterised by 'scale' economies.

Ireland's concerns about producing for larger markets was mirrored by other member countries of the EEC. Because of different types of trade barriers, many industries were unable to produce at the lowest cost per unit. Some of these barriers were easily recognised, like the physical barriers at the entry of various European countries which delayed the movement of both goods and people. This added to the transportation cost of delivering goods to the market.

However, other non-tariff barriers are less transparent. To protect their domestic industries, governments often impose regulations and standards which favour indigenous firms. If foreign firms want to produce for the same market, they must comply with these regulations which are often different than the standards in their own country. Therefore, a firm must produce a different good for each market, and in doing so misses out on the economies of scale that would result from producing the same good for the two markets.

This problem was so pervasive that European policy-makers and firms felt that it was causing European firms to lose competitiveness to firms which were producing for larger markets. US and Japanese firms, many of whom produce for the US market, are able to manufacture goods for the entire market of over two hundred million people. Generally, regulations are established nationally. Goods move freely from New York to San Francisco. The situation in Europe was far different because regulations changed from country to country and goods were stopped at every national border.

This concern of the Commission to the European Council is clearly outlined in the White Paper entitled 'Completing the Internal Market', published in 1985. It states,

> 'Until such barriers are removed, Community manufacturers are forced to focus on national rather than continental markets and are unable to benefit from the economies of scale which a truly unified internal market offers. Failure to achieve a genuine industrial common market becomes increasingly serious since the research, development and commercialisation costs of the new technologies, in order to have a realistic prospect of being internationally competitive, require the background of a home market of continental proportions.'[6]

As we can see, economies of scale is far more than a technical relationship between the cost of production and the quantity produced. It is a concept which has helped to shape industrial policy, particularly since the 1950s, and has moved Ireland into closer relations with other European countries.

SUMMARY

1. The production process involves the transformation of inputs or factors of production into output. The production function shows the maximum amount of output that can be produced employing different amounts of land, labour, capital and enterprise.

2. The short run is a period of time when at least one input is 'fixed' or does not change. The marginal product is the change to total output from an additional unit of a variable input, holding other inputs constant. Increasing marginal returns means that an additional unit of a variable input adds more to total output than the previous unit, *ceteris paribus*. The law of diminishing returns means that if at least one factor is fixed, a point is reached when an additional unit of a variable factor adds less to total product than the previous unit.

3. In the long run, all inputs can be changed. We consider the relationship between inputs and outputs in the long run in terms of 'returns to scale'. Increasing returns to scale means that if factor inputs double, outputs increase by a factor of more than two. Constant returns to scale means that doubling inputs doubles outputs. Decreasing returns to scale means that doubling inputs leads to an increase of inputs, but by a factor of less than two.

4. Economists include a 'normal' profit as a cost of production. This is the opportunity cost of the entrepreneur. Variable costs are the costs associated with employing variable factors of production. They begin with production and increase as production increases. Fixed costs are the costs associated with employing fixed factors of production. They are constant in the short run, regardless of whether or not a firm produces. Economic or supernormal profit is the difference between total revenue and economic costs which include variable costs, fixed costs and a normal profit.

5. Marginal cost is the additional cost incurred if output is increased by one extra unit. Marginal revenue is the change in total revenue arising from a one unit change in output. In the short run, a profit-maximising firm produces where marginal revenue equals marginal cost if it has covered all of its variable costs. If a firm does not cover its variable costs, it minimises its loss in the short run by temporarily shutting down.

6. In the long run, a firm must make at least a normal profit. A profit-maximising firm produces where MR = LMC, if it covers its long-run average cost. If the firm does not cover its long-run average costs, it exits the industry.

KEY TERMS

Profit maximisation	Economies of scale
Factors of production	Diseconomies of scale
Production function	Specialisation of labour
Short-run production	Indivisibilities
Fixed input	Normal profit
Variable input	Opportunity cost
Total product	Economic profit
Marginal product	Total cost

Increasing marginal returns	Fixed costs
Law of diminishing returns	Variable costs
Average product	Average cost
Long-run production	Marginal cost
Increasing returns to scale	Envelope curve
Constant returns to scale	Marginal revenue
Decreasing returns to scale	Average revenue

REVIEW QUESTIONS

1. What are the objectives of a firm? What is the objective of the firm in the traditional neoclassical theory?
2. Explain the difference between short-run production and long-run production. What is the difference between the 'law of diminishing returns' and 'returns to scale'?
3. List the three possibilities that production can exhibit in the long run. What are the sources of economies of scale?
4. How is the economist's interpretation of costs different from the accountant's? What is the difference between accounting profit and economic profit?
5. What two conditions must be met in order for a profit-maximising firm to produce? How is the output decision in the short run different from the long run?
6. Explain the relationship between the diminishing returns of the variable factor and the short-run marginal cost curve. What does this suggest about the theory of production and the theory of costs?

WORKING PROBLEMS

1. This is a weekly production schedule for mushrooms.

Table 5.6

Land	Labour	Output	Average	Marginal
20	0	0		
20	1	1		
20	2	3		
20	3	6		
20	4	10		
20	5	16		
20	6	20		
20	7	21		
20	8	20		
20	9	18		

(a) What are the inputs used in this production process?
(b) How do you know that this is a short-run production function? Which inputs are fixed and which are variable?

(c) Sketch the total product curve.
(d) Complete the table for the AP and MP of labour.
(e) Explain why the MP of labour declines.
(f) Where does the MP of labour curve cut the AP of labour curve? Explain why.

2. The cost of land is €50 per acre and the cost of labour is €100 per worker per week.

Table 5.7

Land	Labour	Output	SFC	SVC	STC	SMC	SAFC	SAVC	SATC
2	0	0							
2	1	1							
2	2	3							
2	3	6							
2	4	10							
2	5	16							
2	6	20							
2	7	23							
2	8	25							
2	9	26							
2	10	24							

(a) Complete the table.
(b) Draw the respective cost curves.
(c) Will the SATC curve and the SAVC curve ever intersect?
(d) Where will the SMC curve cut the SAVC and the SATC curves? Why?

MULTI-CHOICE QUESTIONS

1. Diseconomies of scale:
    (a) arise due to indivisibilities and the division of labour;
    (b) exist when the cost per unit of production rises as the level of output rises;
    (c) exist when the LAC curve falls as output rises;
    (d) arise due to increasing layers of bureaucracy and problems with management-staff relations;
    (e) both (b) and (d) above.

2. The law of diminishing returns:
    (a) is reflected in the slope of the total product curve;
    (b) is a short-run concept;
    (c) sets in when the marginal product of the variable factor begins to decline;
    (d) occurs when production is constrained by fixed factors of production;
    (e) all of the above.

3. The short-run marginal cost curve:
    (a) reflects the law of diminishing returns;
    (b) cuts the SATC and SAVC curves at their lowest points;
    (c) is a mirror image of the marginal product curve;
    (d) both (a) and (c) above;
    (e) (a), (b) and (c) above.

4. The profit-maximising output level in the short run is given by:
    (a) TR = TC and AR = SAVC;
    (b) MR = SMC and AR ≥ SAVC;
    (c) TR > TC and MR > SMC;
    (d) MR = SMC and AR < SATC;
    (e) none of the above.

5. Economic costs:
    (a) are no different than accounting costs;
    (b) include the opportunity cost of the entrepreneur;
    (c) are equal to the explicit costs of production;
    (d) guarantee that normal profit and economic profit are equal;
    (e) none of the above.

6. The mainstream orthodox treatment of the firm is based on the assumption of:
    (a) sales maximisation;
    (b) revenue maximisation;
    (c) growth maximisation;
    (d) profit maximisation;
    (e) none of the above.

TRUE OR FALSE (SUPPORT YOUR ANSWER)

1. When the total product curve is upward sloping and increasing at a decreasing rate the marginal product of the variable input is declining.

2. One reason for decreasing returns to scale are discounts which large firms receive for purchasing large quantities of inputs.

3. The two conditions for a profit-maximising firm are the average and marginal conditions.

4. Normal profit is a cost of production.

5. A firm will only continue to produce in the long run if the market price covers both fixed and variable costs.

6. The LAC curve is formed by the minimum points of the SATC curves.

CASE STUDY

Extract from *The Irish Times*
Short screen breaks are key to reducing injuries
in HEALTH MATTERS
by Joe Armstrong

Short, strategically spaced rest breaks can reduce eye-strain and musculoskeletal discomforts for video display terminal operators without decreasing productivity, according to a recent official study.

The report was conducted by the US National Institute for Occupational Safety and Health and is published in the scientific journal *Ergonomics* . . .

A Field Study of Supplementary Rest Breaks for Data-entry Operators by Dr Traci Galinsky compared results under two rest-break schedules for a group of 42 data-entry operators employed by the Inland Revenue Service.

Under one schedule, the operators worked their regular daily schedule, including two 15-minutes rest breaks, one in each half of the work shift.

In the other schedule, the conventional breaks were supplemented with four five-minute breaks spaced throughout the day, giving 20 extra minutes of break time . . .

Under the supplementary schedule, the workers constantly reported less eye soreness, visual blurring and upper-body discomfort.

Moreover, 'increases in the discomfort of the right forearm, wrist and hand over the course of the work week under the conventional schedule were eliminated under the supplementary schedule. These beneficial effects were obtained without reductions in data-entry performance,' says the report.

In short, the quantity and quality of work were comparable under both schedules, measured by numbers of keystrokes and accuracy in typing data from paper forms into the computer.

In a comment equally pertinent to the Irish workplace, institute director Dr Linda Rosenstock said that, with the move to a service economy, increasing numbers of workers were employed in visual display terminal-intensive jobs. 'It is encouraging that practical steps exist for improving job quality and perhaps reducing the risk of musculoskeletal injuries from these growing numbers of workers . . .'

Source: *The Irish Times.*

Questions

1. Describe the difference in the work practices of the two groups. What impact did the change in work practices discussed in this article have on the participants in the study?
2. What impact did the change in work practices have on worker productivity?
3. What impact might these new work practices have on variable costs?

APPENDIX 5.1: COST MINIMISATION USING ISOQUANTS AND ISOCOST LINES

A more detailed analysis of the theory of production requires the use of concepts and techniques similar to those used in the theory of consumer choice. By the use and application of these new concepts we can derive the least-cost technique of producing a certain level of output.

An isoquant is a locus of points, showing the various combinations of two inputs that can be used to produce a given level of output. The most common combination of inputs discussed in neoclassical theory is labour and capital. Therefore, the isoquant is drawn on a diagram with capital on the vertical axis and labour on the horizontal axis. A single isoquant is shown in Figure 5.9.

Figure 5.9: An isoquant

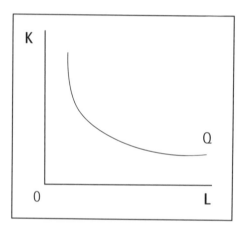

The slope of an isoquant is called the marginal rate of technical substitution (MRTS) which is equal to the amount of an input that can be replaced by one unit of another factor without changing the level of output. It measures the trade-off between two factors of production. Equation 5.8 states this in algebraic terms.

$$\text{MRTS} = -\frac{\Delta K}{\Delta L} \qquad \text{[5.8]}$$

An isoquant has similar properties to an indifference curve. Isoquants slope down from left to right; they are usually drawn convex to the origin; there is an isoquant map with each isoquant representing a different level of output; the higher the isoquant, the higher the level of output. The slope is the MRTS. It diminishes as we move down the isoquant from left to right.

The isocost line reflects the cost of the inputs. The isocost line shows all the combinations of the two factors that can be employed for a certain amount of money. Figure 5.10 illustrates an example of an isocost line.

Figure 5.10: An isocost line

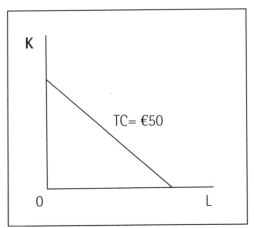

Higher isocost lines are associated with higher costs. Likewise, lower costs are reflected in isocost lines closer to the origin. The slope of an isocost line is equal to the negative of the factor price ratio, $-\frac{P_L}{P_K}$, the price of labour over the price of capital. A change in relative prices results in a change in the slope of the isocost line.

A profit-maximising firm chooses the particular combination of inputs that minimises cost. The least-cost technique of production is the combination of inputs that minimises the total cost of producing a given level of output. It is determined by superimposing a set of isocost lines onto a given isoquant. This is shown in Figure 5.11.

Figure 5.11: The least-cost input combination

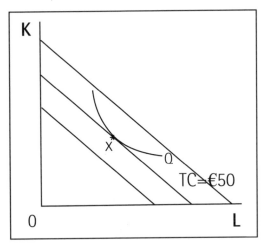

The optimal level, where the profit-maximising firm will minimise costs, is given by the tangency point between the isoquant and the lowest possible isocost line. At this point x the respective slopes are equal. This is expressed in algebraic form in Equation 5.9.

$$\text{slope of isoquant} = \text{MRTS} = \frac{-\Delta K}{\Delta L} = \frac{-P_L}{P_K} = \text{slope of isocost line} \qquad [5.9]$$

This approach is similar to the analysis used in consumer choice theory. The similarities are outlined in Table 5.8.

Table 5.8: Duality between consumer choice theory and production theory

Consumer theory	Production theory
Each indifference curve reflects a different level of utility.	Each isoquant represents a different level of output.
Constraints reflected by budget lines.	Costs reflected by isocost lines.
The consumer maximises utility subject to the price and income constraints.	The producer produces a certain level of output by using the least-costly combination of inputs available.
Utility maximisation occurs where $$\text{MRS} = -\frac{P_d}{P_f}$$	Cost minimisation occurs where $$\text{MRTS} = -\frac{P_L}{P_K}$$

CHAPTER 6

MARKET STRUCTURES

'By perfect competition I propose to mean a state of affairs in which the demand for the output of an individual seller is perfectly elastic.'[1]

Joan Robinson (1903–83)

'People of the same trade seldom meet together, even for merriment and diversion, but the conversation ends in a conspiracy against the public, or in some contrivance to raise prices.'[2]

Adam Smith (1723–90)

CHAPTER OBJECTIVES

Upon completing this chapter, the student should understand:

- the supply curve of the perfectly competitive firm;
- efficiency;
- monopoly power;
- product differentiation and monopolistic competition;
- mutual interdependency between oligopolistic firms;
- the differences between the market structures.

OUTLINE

6.1 Perfect competition
6.2 Monopoly
6.3 Monopolistic competition
6.4 Oligopoly
6.5 Market structure spectrum

INTRODUCTION

The theory of the firm was explained in Chapter 5. However, there are many aspects of a firm's behaviour which remain unanswered. Will the profits be high or low? Will the price charged to the consumer be high or low, relative to costs? Will the firm produce efficiently? Will the level of output be small or large? Many of these questions depend on the environment within which the firm operates and, in particular, the degree of competition facing the firm. There may be only one firm in the market. If so, the firm will behave differently than a firm in a market where there are a large number of competitors.

It is traditional at this stage of our analysis to divide markets into categories according to the degree of competition and market power. Market power signifies the degree of control that a firm or a group of firms have over price. The market structure ultimately determines a firm's behaviour. There are four broad categories: perfect competition, monopolistic competition, oligopoly and monopoly. The differences between each case depend on a number of key characteristics. They are:

- the number of firms in the market;
- the nature of the product, whether it is differentiated or undifferentiated;
- the availability of information;
- the freedom of entry and exit, depending largely on the existence of barriers to entry.

Throughout the discussion of market structures, we assume that there are a large number of consumers whose actions are unco-ordinated, except through the market. In other words, consumers are not grouping together to exert pressure on firms in the market. Also, we assume that the objective of all firms is profit maximisation. The profit-maximising level of output for firms is explained in terms of the marginal condition and the average condition. These concepts were explained in the previous chapter.

We begin in Section 6.1 by explaining perfect competition. Monopoly, monopolistic competition, and oligopoly are discussed in Sections 6.2, 6.3 and 6.4 respectively. An overall summary of the complete market structure spectrum is explained in Section 6.5.

6.1 PERFECT COMPETITION

Perfect competition lies at one end of the market spectrum. The model of the perfectly competitive market is based on strict and unrealistic assumptions, which we will discuss below. This means that it is difficult to find examples of perfectly competitive markets. The markets for certain raw materials, agricultural products and the stock exchange are usually cited as examples of perfectly competitive markets.

With so few examples, a student might be forgiven for asking why she is required to spend so much time and energy in understanding this market structure. Perfect competition and monopoly are located at the two ends of the market spectrum. If we understand the extreme cases, we can use them as a basis of comparison for other commonly observable market structures which lie between the extremes. Also, at the end of this section, we will define and discuss efficiency. We examine perfect competition as the benchmark of efficiency and later discuss how other market structures compare.

Perfect competition is one form of market structure with a number of identifying characteristics:

1. There is a large number of firms and the output of any firm is small relative to the market output. Because its output is small, each firm is a price taker and cannot influence price.
2. The market product is homogeneous. The commodity produced by one firm is identical to the product produced by any other firm in the market.

3. There is perfect information. Consumers are aware of market prices and firms are aware of the actions of their competitors.
4. There is complete freedom of entry to and exit from the market.

The fact that the firm is a price taker has very important implications for the demand curve facing the firm.

Let us consider an example. Molly is a street trader on Moore Street. The price of apples is 25 cents each. Molly can sell as many apples as she likes at this market price; hence, there is no incentive to cut price. Likewise, there is no incentive to increase price. Her three sisters Margie, Annie and Bridie along with the other street traders are all selling apples for the same price. If Molly increases her price she will not be able to sell, as customers will go elsewhere. In summary, her individual actions will have no effect on the market price of apples which is determined by the total market demand and supply on any given day.

In terms of price, the demand for Molly's apples is perfectly elastic. The demand curve that Molly and other street traders face for their product is horizontal. This is illustrated in Figure 6.1.

Figure 6.1: The perfectly competitive market

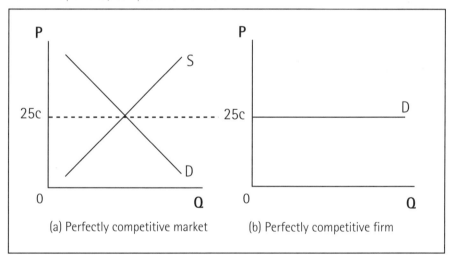

(a) Perfectly competitive market   (b) Perfectly competitive firm

The left-hand panel of Figure 6.1 illustrates the market for apples on any given day on Moore Street. The equilibrium price is 25 cents. It is determined by market demand and market supply. The market demand is the aggregate of all the individual consumers' demand curves whereas the supply curve is the sum of all the street traders' supply curves. Any change in market demand or market supply will affect the equilibrium price. For example, an influx of tourists into Dublin will increase the demand for apples. Hence, the market demand is pushed right resulting in an increase in the price.

The right-hand panel illustrates the demand curve of the perfectly competitive firm; in this case, Molly. Molly is a price taker. She sells her apples for 25 cents. On this day, all other things being equal, she will neither increase price nor cut price. The demand curve is horizontal. We say it is perfectly elastic at a price level of 25 cents.[3]

A horizontal demand curve has important implications for the relationship between price and marginal revenue. Before we consider a numerical example for a firm operating in a perfectly competitive market, we will briefly recall some of the definitions discussed in detail in Chapter 5.

Total revenue is the amount which a firm receives for selling its goods and services. It is calculated by multiplying price times quantity (TR = P × Q). Marginal revenue is the change in revenue which a firm receives if it produces and sells one more unit $(MR = \frac{\Delta TR}{\Delta Q})$. Average revenue equals total revenue divided by the quantity sold $(AR = \frac{TR}{Q})$. If we multiply both sides of this equation by Q, we are left with another equation for total revenue (TR = AR × Q). Comparing this with the first equation, we see that P = AR. This result will hold regardless of whether a firm's demand curve is horizontal or downward sloping.

However, if a firm is operating in a perfectly competitive market, marginal revenue is also equal to price and to average revenue. We will illustrate this with an example. Table 6.1 shows a firm's demand schedule.

Table 6.1: Price, marginal revenue and average revenue

Q	P	TR	MR	AR
0	10	–		
			10	
1	10	10		10
			10	
2	10	20		10
			10	
3	10	30		10
			10	
4	10	40		10

It is obvious from the table that this firm is operating in a perfectly competitive market because it does not have to lower its price in order to sell more output. Regardless of the quantity which the perfectly competitive firm chooses to sell, the last unit will be sold at the market price of P = 10. Hence, the marginal revenue received from selling additional output is equal to the price received, i.e. MR = P.

In terms of a diagram, the marginal revenue curve and the demand curve are one and the same for a firm in a perfectly competitive market. This is shown in Figure 6.2.

The output decision in the short run

How much will a firm in a perfectly competitive industry produce in the short run? From our discussion in Chapter 5, we know that if a firm is going to produce, the profit-maximising level of output is where marginal revenue equals marginal cost. This is also illustrated in Figure 6.2.

Figure 6.2: Marginal revenue and marginal cost

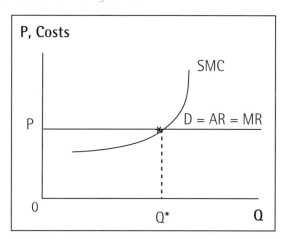

We can see from Figure 6.2 that the profit-maximising level of output is at Q* where MR = SMC. Moreover, at Q*, MR = SMC = P for a firm in a perfectly competitive market. We will see in the next sections that this result differs for firms which operate in other, less competitive market structures.

We know from Chapter 5 that MR = MC is a necessary but not sufficient condition for producing at the profit-maximising output level. The second condition relates to average revenue and average cost. The short-run cost curves which we derived in Chapter 5 are reproduced below. Four possible cases are presented in Figure 6.3.

Figure 6.3: Four scenarios for a perfectly competitive firm

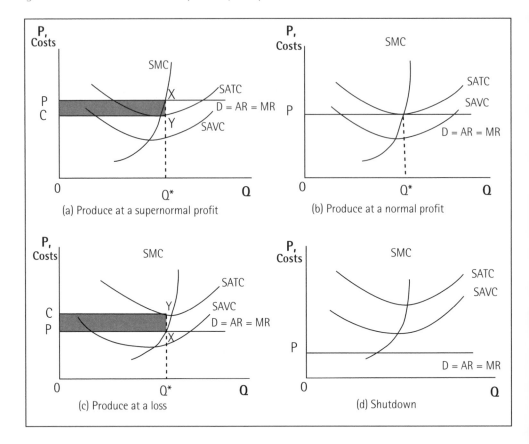

In panel (a), price is above the short-run average total cost. This is presented by drawing the demand curve above the short-run average total cost curve. The first condition is met at Q* where MR = SMC.

Secondly, at this output level, price is greater than average total cost. From our discussion in the previous chapter, we know that a 'normal' profit is included as a cost of production. Since the AR curve is above the SATC curve, at the profit-maximising level of production, this firm is making a supernormal profit. The supernormal profit per unit is measured by the distance between the SATC curve and the AR curve at Q*. This is shown on the diagram by line segment |XY|.

The shaded area on the diagram is the area of supernormal profits. We identify this area by subtracting the area of total cost from the area of total revenue. On the diagram, total revenue is defined by the area of the rectangle [PXQ*0]. Total cost is shown by the rectangle [CYQ*0]. The difference between the two areas is the shaded rectangle [PXYC] which represents the total supernormal profits received by the firm.

In panel (b) the profit maximising output is Q*, where the marginal revenue equals the short-run marginal cost. The AR curve is tangent to the SATC curve. At this point, the firm is making a normal profit.

In panel (c) price is below the short-run average total cost but above the short-run average variable cost. This is presented by drawing the AR curve above the SAVC curve but below the SATC curve. Because we assume that firms will maximise profits (or alternatively minimise losses), we conclude that a firm that faces this situation will produce at Q*. The alternative is to cease production and pay all of the fixed costs. At Q*, the firm is covering its variable costs and making some contribution to its fixed costs. The loss per unit is shown by the line segment |YX| which represents the difference between average total cost and price. The area of economic loss is shown by the shaded rectangle [CYXP]. This is the area which remains when total revenue, represented by the area [PXQ*0] is subtracted from total cost, represented by the rectangle [CYQ*0].

In panel (d) price is below the short-run average variable cost. This is presented by drawing the AR curve below the SAVC curve. The market price does not cover the variable costs of the firm. The firm in this situation minimises losses by discontinuing production.

Deriving the short-run supply curve

The above analysis can be used to derive the short-run supply curve for a firm in a perfectly competitive market. Let us begin with a market price of P_0. At P_0 the firm will produce at Q_0 where MR = SMC. Both the marginal condition and the average condition are met. This gives us point X, the first point on the supply curve.

Figure 6.4: Derivation of the short-run supply curve

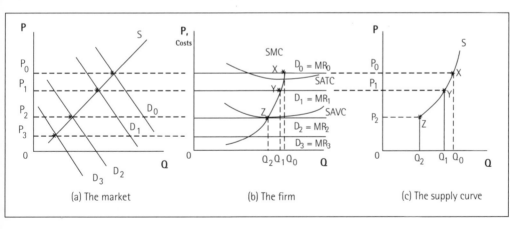

Suppose there is a change in market conditions. In panel (a) the demand curve shifts down to the left (from D_0 to D_1). The firm reacts to the lower price by cutting production to Q_1 where MR_1 = SMC. Point Y is another point on the supply curve. As price falls, less is produced.

Suppose the fall in demand reduces the market price to P_3. For the firm, this price level is below both the average total cost and the average variable cost. The firm minimises its losses by discontinuing production and paying its fixed costs. There is no corresponding output level for this price, or any price below P_2.

At P_2, price is equal to average variable cost. The AR curve is tangent to the SAVC curve. A price just below P_2 is the shutdown price.

Definition
The shutdown price is less than the short-run average variable cost of producing a unit of output.

At P_2, the firm will produce Q_2 units of output, shown as point Z on Figure 6.4, panel (b). Below this price, the firm will not supply output.

We can see from panel (c) of Figure 6.4 that the SMC curve beginning at point Z is the supply curve for the firm in the short run. All profit-maximising firms produce where MR = SMC. For a firm in a perfectly competitive market, marginal revenue is equal to the price. Therefore, a firm in this market will produce where P = SMC, as long as the average variable costs are covered.

What can be implied from the above? Under perfect competition, the firm's supply curve in the short run is its marginal cost curve above the shutdown price. Hence, the amount the firm supplies to the market depends primarily on its costs of production.

The short-run supply curve for the competitive market is simply the horizontal sum of the supply curves of all individual firms. It shows the sum of all the quantities produced by all firms at each given price in the short run. This is the same supply curve which we discussed in Chapter 2.

The output decision in the long run

The analysis in the long run is a little different. It is based on the assumption that firms are free to enter and exit the market. Let us begin by looking at two possibilities: the long-run equilibrium following short-run losses and the long-run equilibrium following short-run supernormal profits.

Figure 6.5 depicts the long-run equilibria following short-run losses. Panel (a) illustrates the market demand and supply conditions whereas the firm's position is depicted in panel (b).

We assume that all firms maximise profits. However, we have seen that in the short run, a firm may operate at a loss, or temporarily shut down and pay its fixed costs. From our discussion in the last chapter, we know that in the short run, some inputs to the production process are fixed. In the long run, all inputs are variable. Therefore, a firm can exit a market in the long run, and channel its assets into another market where it can earn at least a normal profit. If losses are incurred by firms in a perfectly competitive market in the long run, we confidently predict, based on this model, that those firms will exit the market.

As the number of suppliers in the market falls, the supply curve shifts to the left. This is reflected in panel (a). As a result of this shift, price is driven up. The price continues to rise until market equilibrium is restored.

Panel (b) depicts the position for the individual firm. At P_0 losses result (the difference between average revenue and long-run average cost). In a perfectly competitive market all individual firms are price takers. Hence, as price rises due to the change in market conditions, the price which the individual firm can charge also rises. The AR curve continues to shift upwards until it cuts the LAC curve at a tangency point, A. The firms which remain in the perfectly competitive market will earn a normal profit in the long run.

Figure 6.5: The long-run position following short-run losses

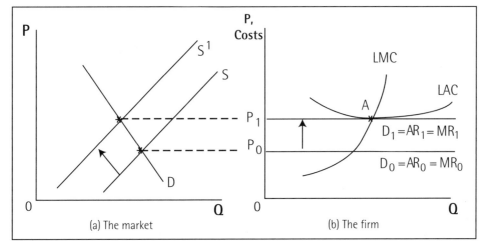

Figure 6.6 depicts the long-run equilibria following short-run supernormal profits. Panel (a) illustrates the market demand and supply whereas the firm's equilibrium position is depicted in panel (b).

In the short run, firms in the perfectly competitive market can earn supernormal profits. However, because of the assumption of perfect information, other firms are aware of the supernormal profits in the market. Also, we assume that firms are free to enter the market. An increase in the number of firms shifts the market supply curve to the right from S to S^1, as shown in panel (a). Price falls until a new equilibrium is reached.

Figure 6.6: The long-run position following short-run profits

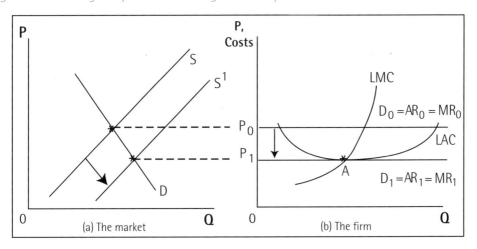

Panel (b) depicts the position for the individual firm. Supernormal profits are made at P_0. As market price falls, the price which the individual firm can charge also falls. In this case, prices will continue to fall until all supernormal profits are 'competed' away. The AR curve continues to shift downwards until it cuts the LAC curve at a tangency point, A. The result is normal profit. The inflow of new firms stops as supernormal profits diminish.

Panel (b) in Figure 6.5 and Figure 6.6 illustrates long-run equilibrium for a firm in a perfectly competitive market. At point A, the firm is producing at the minimum point of the long-run average cost curve. The firm is said to be making optimum use of its resources since it is producing at the least possible cost per unit. Also, at equilibrium, the firm is only making a normal profit.

This is very desirable from the point of view of the consumer and society as a whole. The firm is producing in its most efficient manner while at the same time the consumer is being charged no more than the marginal cost of production. This is an example of efficiency, a concept which requires further explanation.

When markets are perfectly competitive, the amount of a good produced is socially optimal. Another way to say this is that equilibrium in a perfectly competitive market is Pareto efficient. By Pareto efficient, we mean that no other level of output can make one individual better off without making another individual worse off (see Chapter 1.1).

Figure 6.7 shows long-run equilibrium in a perfectly competitive market. The supply curve is derived by adding together the marginal cost curves of all firms producing for this market. In long-run equilibrium, all firms in a perfectly competitive market are covering their costs and making a normal profit. We can think of the supply curve as showing the amount that producers are willing to supply at each price.

The market demand curve is derived by adding together individual demand curves based on the marginal utility that a consumer gains from the consumption of this product. The demand curve represents the amount that consumers are willing to pay for different amounts of this product. They are willing to pay for a product, as long as the marginal benefit which they receive from consuming it, is greater than or equal to the price of the product.

In Figure 6.7, the market equilibrium level of output is Q^* and the market clearing price is P^*. Suppose the amount of output is Q^{**}. This amount of output is not efficient. Suppliers are willing to accept P_s for Q^{**} units of output and consumers are willing to pay P_d. As long as one consumer is willing to pay more than the marginal cost, a producer benefits from increasing production. Both parties are better off.

By contrast, at an output level which is greater than Q^*, consumers are not willing to pay the producers' marginal cost. Additional output will only make a consumer better off at the expense of a producer. This is not efficient.

We therefore conclude that Q^* is the socially optimal and efficient amount of output. At Q^*, consumers are willing to pay the marginal cost to the producers. All gains from trade are exhausted. (For further discussion of efficiency in perfectly competitive markets, see Sections 8.1 and 9.2.)

Figure 6.7:   Perfectly competitive markets and efficiency

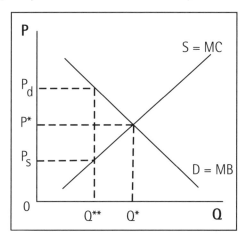

CASE STUDY
Extract from *The Irish Times*
Oil price bites at haulage companies
by John Cradden

Small Irish firms in the transportation sector are especially likely to feel the pinch from the continuing increase in oil prices, which have reached a 10-year high.

The average price of a litre of petrol is currently 76.8 pence, while diesel averages 67.6 pence, according to the Automobile Association. The AA estimates that petrol prices have increased by 32 per cent since January 1999, when oil prices were at their lowest, while the price of diesel has risen by 26.7 per cent in the same period.

Many small transport firms have closed over the past 18 months, according to Mr Pat Delaney, director of the Small Firms Association. He says that the sector has contracted and become more competitive during the period.

'Rising oil prices are likely to exacerbate difficulties in the sector and will only lead to more closures,' he said, 'It's a cut-throat market and any increase is going to have a huge impact.

The concern over rising fuel prices is especially acute among small road haulage companies, which are already finding times very difficult according to Mr Jimmy Quinn, spokesman for the Irish Road Haulage Association. 'There is a huge cloud over the sector at the moment. Companies are having to postpone the purchase of new equipment, instead of spending their money on keeping older vehicles on the road,' he said . . .

Source: *The Irish Times*, 16 August 2000.

Questions

1. The article mentions two factors which are increasing the variable costs of the haulage companies. What are they? On a diagram, show the change to a firm's short-run average variable and average total costs.
2. Is there any evidence that the market for transport services is perfectly competitive?
3. What are 'normal profits'? Are all of the firms in this sector making normal profits in the short-run? Why or why not?
4. How will the closure of haulage companies affect the long-run equilibrium in this market? Show this change on a diagram for the industry and for a firm that survives the current changes.

Answers on website

6.2 MONOPOLY

Monopoly is another form of market structure which is also identified by a number of characteristics:

1. There is only one firm in the market. In effect, the firm is the market.
2. A unique product is sold. There are no close substitutes.
3. There are barriers to entry which preclude the possibility of new firms entering the market, even if the monopolist is making supernormal profits.

Most Irish monopolies are state-owned and they are declining in number. They include Aer Lingus, Aer Rianta, Dublin Bus and Iarnrod Eireann. Most of the remaining monopolies are preparing for privatisation. Previously protected markets will be open to competition. Irish-owned companies may become take-over targets or enter into joint ventures with foreign-owned firms.

Barriers to entry are the main source of market power. There are barriers to entry for monopolists and oligopolists. The various types of barriers and the factors which account for their strength are detailed in Table 6.2.

Table 6.2: Barriers to entry

Type	Description	Low barrier	High barrier
Type of asset	*Specific assets* have more value in their current use than in the next best alternative. *General assets* can be shifted to alternative activities.	general	specific
Excess capacity	Incumbents are able to produce more output at an equal or lower price. Can be caused by cyclical demand or adopted as a strategy to deter new entrants.	insignificant excess capacity	substantial excess capacity
Reputational effects	Based on history of retaliation against new entrants and/or the resources available to incumbents to retaliate.	no retaliation anticipated	retaliation expected
Precommitment contracts	Long term contracts with suppliers to purchase inputs at favourable rates; with distributors to give their product a favourable location; with consumers to provide and maintain their product.	none or few	extensive
Pioneering brand advantage	Customer loyalty given to first entrant into an industry.	quality of product can be judged prior to purchase	product must be purchased before testing
Cost of entry	Set-up costs required for a firm to enter a market.	low	high
Economies of scale	*Minimum efficient scale* is the amount of output required to produce a product at the lowest cost per unit.	MES at low % of industry output	MES at high % of industry output
Government regulations	Licensing agreements are required before a firm can enter some markets. *Patents* legally restrict firms from copy-ing an innovation for 17 years. Other regulations are designed to ensure product quality and/or consumer safety.	unregulated	regulated
Learning curve effects	Incumbents operating in an industry benefit from knowledge which allows them to produce at a lower cost per unit.	small cost advantage	large cost advantage
Cost of exit	*Exit barriers* are factors that keep firms competing in an industry. Sources of barriers include labour agreements, government intervention and emotional attachment to an industry, location or employees.	low	high

Single-price monopolist

Since the monopolist is the only firm in the market, its demand curve is the downward sloping market demand curve. If the demand curve is downward sloping, marginal revenue is less than price. This point is best illustrated with an example. In this example, we are considering the behaviour of à 'single-price' monopolist. All of the monopolist's customers are charged the same price. Table 6.3 is the demand schedule for the monopolist.

Table 6.3:   Price, marginal revenue and average revenue

Q	P	TR	MR	AR
0	10	–		
			9	
1	9	9		9
			7	
2	8	16		8
			5	
3	7	21		7
			3	
4	6	24		6

In order to sell more of its product, the monopolist must lower price. In this example, to increase sales from two units to three units, the monopolist cuts its price from €8 to €7. Let us consider what happens to the marginal revenue. At P = €8, the monopolist sells two units, collecting total revenues of €16. The total revenue increases to €21 when the monopolist charges €7 per unit. However, the marginal revenue falls to €5 per unit. Why? Because to sell the extra unit, the single-price monopolist must cut the price for all units. The monopolist has gained revenue by selling more units, but has lost revenue because the price per unit is lower. For this reason, marginal revenue is always less than price if the demand curve is downward sloping. Notice, however, that the average revenue equals price, for reasons which were explained in the previous section.

On a two-dimensional graph, the marginal revenue curve is drawn below the demand curve. Since price equals average revenue, the demand curve and the average revenue curve overlap. The revenue curves are illustrated in Figure 6.8.

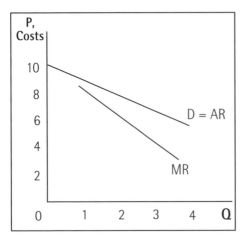

Figure 6.8: The demand curve and the marginal revenue curve

We will now examine the equilibrium for the monopolist.

Short-run equilibrium

Figure 6.9 illustrates the equilibrium position for the monopolist.

Figure 6.9: Monopoly equilibrium

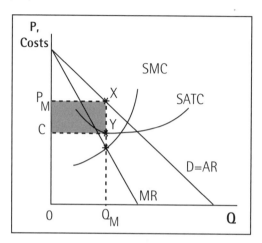

The demand curve, D is downward sloping with the marginal revenue curve drawn below it. The cost structure of the firm is given by the average total cost curve, SATC and the marginal cost curve, SMC. The two profit-maximising conditions are the marginal condition and the average condition. These two conditions must be met in order for the monopolist to produce in the short run.

The marginal condition is met at output level Q_M. At this level of production, marginal revenue is equal to marginal cost. The second condition requires that the average revenue is no less than the average variable cost at this output level.

In Figure 6.9 the difference between price and SATC is profit and is given by the vertical distance $|XY|$. The total profit made by the monopolist is the profit per unit multiplied by the total quantity sold. In Figure 6.9 it is given by the area $[P_M XYC]$, the difference between the total revenue area $[P_M XQ_M 0]$ and the total cost area $[CYQ_M 0]$. This shaded area represents supernormal profits.

The distinction between the long run and the short run is less important for the monopolist who is making supernormal profits. Unlike the firm in a perfectly competitive market, competition will not drive down price and profit. Supernormal profits, as shown in Figure 6.9 can persist in the long run.

However, there is no guarantee that a monopolist will make supernormal profits. Profits depend on cost conditions and demand conditions, regardless of market structure. Panel (a) of Figure 6.10 shows a monopolist who is making normal profits. In panel (b), the monopolist is operating at a loss.

Figure 6.10: *Monopolist earning a normal profit; sustaining a loss*

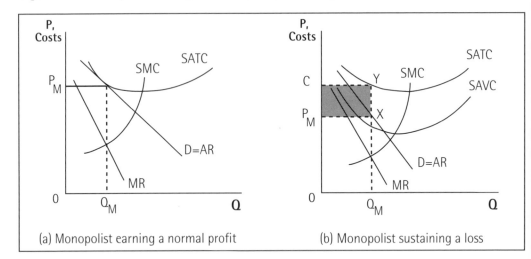

(a) Monopolist earning a normal profit   (b) Monopolist sustaining a loss

In panel (a) the marginal condition is fulfilled when Q_M units of output are produced. However, at this level of output, the average revenue curve is tangent to the average total cost curve. Therefore, the monopolist is making a normal profit.

The monopolist in panel (b) is sustaining a loss (maybe due to weak demand or high costs). The level of output is Q_M, determined by the intersection of the marginal revenue curve and the marginal cost curve. In this situation, the monopolist will produce at a loss because the price is greater than the average variable cost. In other words, the monopolist minimises her losses by producing, rather than closing down and paying her fixed costs. The loss per unit is shown by the segment |YX|. The total loss is shown by the shaded rectangle [CYXP$_M$].

If a monopolist is operating at a loss in the short run, we expect the owner to close if she is not covering her variable costs. In the long run, we expect a monopolist who cannot make a normal profit to exit. The only exception to this is the state-owned or semi-state monopoly. Aer Rianta, which runs the airports in Ireland, could operate if price were less than short-run average variable cost, if it were subsidised by the government. The 'loss-minimising' strategy will be followed by any private sector monopolist.

It is evident from Figure 6.9 and Figure 6.10 that the monopolist does not produce at the lowest point of its average cost curve. In addition, price always exceeds marginal cost. This is due to the existence of monopoly power which is reflected in the downward sloping demand curve. With price exceeding marginal cost, the consumer pays more for the good than the marginal cost to produce it.

Price discriminating monopolist

In the discussion above, the monopolist charged the same price to all consumers. Under some circumstances, a monopolist may charge different prices for the same product.

Definition

A price discriminating monopoly occurs when a monopolist charges different prices to different customers for the same product for reasons other than differences in costs.

There are two conditions necessary for price discrimination:

1. Submarkets featuring demand curves with different price elasticities must be identified. In other words, the producer must be able to classify consumers into separate groups.
2. The markets must be separated so that the products cannot be resold.

Submarkets can be identified by classification of customer, geographically or by time. Iarnrod Eireann, for example, offers cheaper train tickets to students than to other travellers. A traveller who purchases a return ticket from Galway to Dublin pays less than one who purchases a return ticket from Dublin to Galway. It is cheaper to purchase a daily return ticket on Tuesday, Wednesday or Thursday than the other days of the week.

The monopolist is attempting to charge as close as possible to the maximum price which the consumer is willing to pay. A monopolist who can practise price discrimination can increase profits, beyond what is earned by a single-price monopolist.

There are different methods of price discrimination. The most common forms are called third degree and first degree price discrimination.

Definition

Third degree price discrimination occurs when a firm separates consumers into classes and establishes a different price for each class.

ESB charges two rates for electricity. One is for their commercial customers and the other is for households. Eircom charges different rates at different times. The highest charge per minute occurs during 'business' hours. In the evenings and on weekends, when people are more likely to make discretionary calls, the charge per minute decreases. Cinemas offer cheaper tickets for their matinee performances to attract senior citizens and other people who are not working or studying. In the evenings, when most people are free to attend the cinema, the price increases. These are all forms of third degree price discrimination.

The supplier who practises first degree price discrimination must have detailed knowledge of the preferences of the consumer.

Definition

First degree price discrimination occurs when every buyer is charged the maximum price that he or she is willing to pay.

Customised financial or legal services are examples where the seller of the service may be able to charge the maximum price. The consumer must believe that the good or service offered by the monopolist is unique in order to purchase under these circumstances. Either form of price discrimination results in higher profits because the monopolist is capturing all or part of the consumer surplus. (See Section 4.4 to revise consumer surplus.)

We will consider an example involving first degree price discrimination. Table 6.4 is a demand schedule for the price discriminating monopolist.

Table 6.4: Demand schedule for the price discriminating monopolist

Q	P	TR	MR
0	10	–	
			9
1	9	9	
			8
2	8	17	
			7
3	7	24	
			6
4	6	30	

This table is similar to the table which we used for the single-price monopolist with one important difference. To sell the second unit, the producer does not have to cut the price on the first unit. The monopolist sells the first unit for €9, the second unit for €8.

This leads to the collection of higher total revenue with the marginal revenue per unit sold higher for the price discriminating monopolist than it was for the single-price monopolist. In this case, the marginal revenue is equal to price. (Review Table 6.3 to see that the marginal revenue is lower than price for the single-price monopolist.) Therefore, the demand curve and the marginal revenue curve overlap for the price discriminating monopolist.

Now, we will consider the difference in the quantity produced between the two types of monopolists. Consider Figure 6.11.

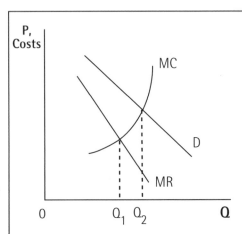

Figure 6.11: Profit-maximising levels of output for the single-price monopolist and the price discriminating monopolist

If the monopolist is charging a single price, its marginal revenue curve is below the demand curve. Profit maximisation requires that it produce where marginal revenue equals marginal cost. This is indicated by the level of output Q_1.

For the monopolist practising first degree price discrimination, the demand curve and the marginal revenue curve overlap. The profit-maximising level of output is Q_2. You can see from the diagram that the level of output increases if the monopolist practises price discrimination.

The absence of a supply curve

One important characteristic of a monopoly is the absence of a supply curve. For a perfectly competitive firm, the marginal cost curve is its supply curve. For a monopoly, supply is affected by cost considerations and also by demand conditions. Hence, it is impossible to draw a supply curve which is determined independently of demand. This is illustrated in Figure 6.12.

Figure 6.12:   The absence of a supply curve

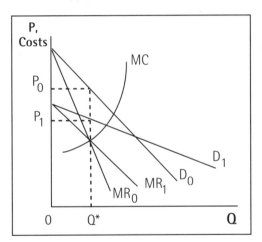

Figure 6.12 is similar to Figure 6.9 above. The demand curve, D_0 is drawn downward sloping with the marginal revenue curve, MR_0 drawn inside it. The marginal cost curve, MC, is upward sloping.

Let us now superimpose another set of demand and marginal revenue curves onto the diagram. The marginal cost curve cuts both sets of marginal revenue curves at the same point. At output level Q^*, price can either be P_0 or P_1 depending on the conditions of demand. Q^* is sold at P_0 when the demand curve is D_0, and at P_1 when the demand curve is D_1. Hence, for a given level of output different demand conditions give rise to different prices. There is no unique relationship between price and quantity supplied. In conclusion, there is no identifiable supply curve for the monopolist.

Students tend to think that a monopolist can charge any price and produce any quantity of output that she wants. In other words, she has an unlimited ability to extract supernormal profits. From the discussion above, we can see that this is not true. Like the perfectly competitive firm, the monopolist will maximise profit by producing where MR = MC. The maximum price which she can charge is limited by the demand curve which the monopolist faces for her product.

Comparing the perfectly competitive market with the single-price monopolist

It is a useful exercise to compare the equilibrium position of the perfectly competitive market with that of the monopolist. To do this, we join all the firms in the perfectly competitive market together to form one single firm. Further, we assume that the demand and cost conditions remain the same although the market structure changes. We then compare the price and output decision of the perfectly competitive market with that of the single-price monopolist. This is illustrated in Figure 6.13.

Figure 6.13:   Perfect competition and monopoly compared

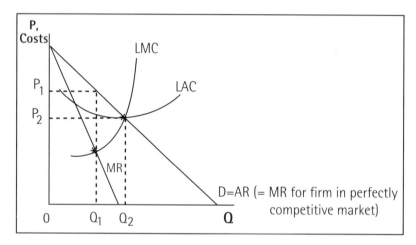

For the perfectly competitive market, the equilibrium in the long run is given by the equation MR = MC = AC = AR. In this case, the output level is Q_2 and the price charged is P_2. The single-price monopolist produces where MR = MC. The output level is Q_1 and the price is P_1. Since barriers to entry preclude the entry of new firms to the market, this equilibrium can persist into the long run. The single-price monopolist is producing less output and charging a higher price than the perfectly competitive market.

With regard to efficiency, when the market structure is characterised by monopoly, the level of output produced in this market is not efficient. The level of output will be below its socially optimal level and the price charged for that output will be above the socially optimal level.

Figure 6.14 shows market equilibrium for a single-price monopolist. At market equilibrium, the additional cost of producing the last unit of output (MC_1) is less than what consumers are willing to pay (P_1). Since the price that consumers are willing to pay must reflect the utility to them of the good, then increasing output beyond Q_1 adds more to consumer utility than it adds to producers' cost. However, since the monopolist is charging only one price, P_1 and Q_1 are the profit-maximising combination. If she drops her price for one customer, the price she will get for all other units sold will fall as a result.

So the potential gain to the monopolist from increasing output beyond Q_1 is wiped out by the loss in earnings on the existing level of output Q_1, as a result of the fall in market price. This is still socially inefficient as the value of the gain to consumers exceeds the cost of producing the extra output. In fact, if it were possible for consumers to share some of their gains (from higher output and lower prices) with the producer, both could be made better off.

If the market structure were perfectly competitive, then output would be at its socially efficient level Q_2. The area BCE represents the net gain to society from increasing output to the level that would occur in a perfectly competitive market.

Figure 6.14:   Monopoly equilibrium and efficiency

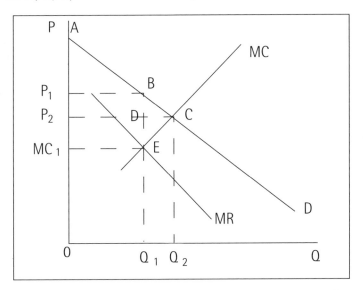

There are also distributional effects. Recall that the consumer surplus is the amount which a consumer is willing to pay, over and above what she actually has to pay. In a perfectly competitive market, the area of consumer surplus is the greatest. It is shown by the triangle ACP_2 in Figure 6.14. With a single-price monopolist, the area of this triangle shrinks to ABP_1. Part of the area of original surplus is appropriated by the monopolist as revenue (P_1BDP_2). The rest of the consumer surplus (BCD) along with the triangle DCE, is lost to both parties because of the pricing strategy followed by the monopolist.

Comparing the single-price monopolist with the monopolist practising first degree price discrimination

A monopolist practising first degree price discrimination charges every customer exactly what s/he is willing to pay. We saw in Table 6.4 that marginal revenue equals price which means that the demand curve and the marginal revenue curve are the same (as they are in a perfectly competitive market).

This monopolist will produce at Q_2, (on Figure 6.14) the same level of output as the perfectly competitive market. There is no unique price level because price changes with every unit of output that is sold. The level of output is socially optimal. The net gains to society occur in the market for the monopolist practising first degree price discrimination, just as they did in the perfectly competitive market.

However, the gains from trade are distributed differently. Because each consumer pays exactly what she is willing to pay, there is no consumer surplus. The entire area under the demand curve (ACQ_20) is appropriated by the monopolist as revenue. The consumer is worse off since all of the gains from trade are appropriated by the monopolist.

6.3 MONOPOLISTIC COMPETITION

The model of monopolistic competition was independently developed in the 1930s by the American economist Edward Chamberlin (1899–1967) and the English economist, Joan Robinson. Some credit must also go to Piero Sraffa (1898–1983) who was unhappy with the existing market set-up in the 1920s and who subsequently began the search for alternative market structures.[4]

Monopolistic competition incorporates features of both perfect competition and monopoly. It is similar to perfect competition in that there are a large number of firms in the market. There is also freedom to enter and exit. However, it differs from perfect competition in that the product is differentiated rather than homogeneous. Product differentiation means that in the short run, firms have a degree of market power resulting in supernormal profits.

Definition

Product differentiation means that the good produced by one firm is different from the good produced by the firm's competitor.

There are close, but not perfect substitutes available.

Differentiation is achieved through various strategies which include product design, customer service, packaging and advertising. Examples of monopolistically competitive markets include book publishers, filling stations, retail outlets and restaurants.

Product differentiation has implications for the demand curve which the firm faces. Recall that the demand curve for the firm in the perfectly competitive market is perfectly elastic because there are perfect substitutes. The demand curve for the monopolist is inelastic because there are no substitutes. A firm in a market classified as monopolistically competitive faces competitors who are producing similar, but not identical products. Therefore, the demand curve faced by this firm is downward sloping, but more elastic than the demand curve of the monopolist.

The short-run equilibrium position for the monopolistically competitive firm is illustrated in Figure 6.15.

Figure 6.15:   *A monopolistic competitor's short-run equilibrium*

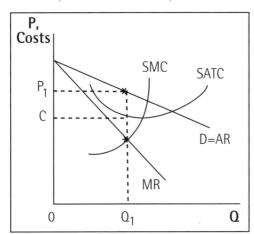

The firm's demand curve is downward sloping with the marginal revenue curve drawn below it. The average cost curve and the marginal cost curve are superimposed onto Figure 6.15. The profit-maximising firm in a monopolistically competitive market must meet the same conditions as firms in other markets.

The firm will produce at output level Q_1, where marginal revenue is equal to marginal cost, (MR = SMC). It will charge a price based on its demand or average revenue curve. In this case, the price is P_1. At this price, average revenue exceeds average cost. The difference, given by the distance between P_1 and C, is profit per unit. This profit per unit multiplied by the quantity sold gives us the total profit earned by the firm.

In the short run, the firm in the monopolistically competitive market can earn supernormal profits. However, it cannot maintain this equilibrium position or continue to earn supernormal profits in the long run.

The long-run equilibrium position is illustrated in Figure 6.16.

Figure 6.16:   *A monopolistic competitor's long-run equilibrium*

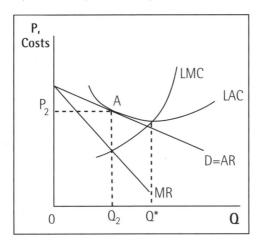

In the long run, because of the absence of entry barriers, new entrants will enter the market, attracted by supernormal profits. The overall market supply rises, causing the market price to fall. The demand for the existing firm's product subsequently falls as its share of the market demand declines. The existing firm's demand curve also becomes more elastic because new firms produce similar products.

Supernormal profits are 'competed away' with the influx of new firms. Equilibrium in the long run is achieved when participating firms are making normal profits only. There is no further incentive for potential firms to enter the market. In graphic terms, this occurs when the firm's average revenue curve is tangent to its average cost curve. Long-run equilibrium is achieved at point A in Figure 6.16. Hence, the monopolistic competitor is not producing at the point of full productive capacity. The difference between Q_2 and Q^* represents excess capacity.

The long-run equilibrium condition for a monopolistic competitor is MR = MC and AR = LAC. It is evident from Figure 6.16 that the firm under conditions of monopolistic competition does not produce at the lowest point on its average cost curve. In this regard, monopolistically competitive markets compare unfavourably to perfectly competitive markets. Furthermore, on account of product differentiation and the subsequent monopoly power that exists, price exceeds marginal cost. This market structure does not exhibit efficiency.

Part of the explanation for such inefficiencies lies in the fact that advertising, branding and other forms of product differentiation constitute additional costs to the firm. The positive aspect of monopolistic competition is the wider product choice it offers to the consumer. Benefits such as improved quality and service may also result from non-price competition. Unfortunately we gain variety at the expense of efficiency.

6.4 OLIGOPOLY

Another commonly observed market structure is oligopoly. It is another form of imperfect competition. An oligopolistic market consists of a small number of firms, each with some ability to affect the market price. The most important feature of this market structure is the recognition of interdependence between firms.

Firms in other market structures act independently of each other when choosing market strategies. In oligopoly, the reaction of competitors to a change in price or some other market strategy is critical. Firms are said to be mutually dependent. If oligopolistic firms decide to compete with each other, they effectively act under conditions similar to perfect competition. In contrast, if they decide to collude, they act in the market as a monopolist. In either case, the level of price for this market structure is generally higher than the perfectly competitive market, and the level of output is lower.

Products are either homogeneous or differentiated. In some oligopolistic markets, products are identical. Examples include the oil market and basic commodity markets e.g. tin, copper, steel etc. In others, products are differentiated. The automobile, newspaper and the beer markets are examples.

The most common method of measuring the degree of market power is the use of concentration ratios, which are defined as the percentage of total output that is accounted for by the largest producers in the market. The most common concentration ratios are the four-firm and the eight-firm concentration ratios. The four-firm ratio, for example, tells us the percentage of market output which is produced by the four largest firms. The larger the percentage, the more concentrated the market. (For other ways of defining market power, see Section 9.2.)

Table 6.5: Concentration ratios for two markets in Ireland

Motor fuel market   CR4 in 1994 was 74%   *Source:* Statoil and Conoco   (In the 1996 Report of Investigation by The Competition Authority)
Tea market   CR4 in 1995 was 83.7%   *Source:* Taylor Nelson AGB plc, supplied by Unilever   (In the 1996 Report of Investigation by The Competition Authority)
Note: CR4 = four-firm concentration ratio

Unlike the other market structures, there is no single theory of oligopolistic behaviour. This is because oligopolies exhibit a wide variety of behaviour. The most important models, however, are briefly explained below. They differ because of the assumptions made about a firm's behaviour and its reaction to its rivals' strategies.

The collusion model

One option available to firms in oligopoly is that of collusion. This occurs when firms get together and collude over price and output strategies. In such cases, the equilibrium position regarding price and output is similar to the monopoly. The equilibrium position is illustrated in Figure 6.17.

Figure 6.17:   Collusive oligopoly

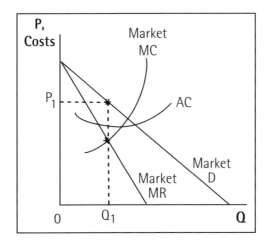

The market demand curve is drawn downward sloping with the market marginal revenue curve drawn below it. Profits are maximised at the output level where MR = MC. The total market output Q_1 is shared out in a number of different ways. For example, a quota system may be in place where each respective firm is allotted a sales quota. The results of collusion are higher prices, higher profits and lower output than would otherwise be the case. The name given to these formal groupings is a cartel.

Definition

A cartel is a group of firms in a particular market who collude on price and output decisions in an effort to earn monopoly profits.

Cartels are outlawed in many countries to protect consumers and society. However, the illegal actions of cartels are difficult to investigate and prosecute.

In November 2000 the director of the Irish Competition Authority, Mr Pat Massey, estimated that price-fixing by cartels costs Irish consumers about €635 million per year. Mr Massey recommended that the government implement a 'leniency' programme. An individual who discloses the price-fixing arrangements of a cartel will be granted immunity from prosecution. This type of legislation was passed in the United States and has proven effective, along with other types of investigations, in combating this form of 'white collar' crime.

As difficult as it is to uncover and prosecute national cartels, international cartels, like the Organisation of Petroleum Exporting Countries (OPEC) act without fear of reprisal. See Information Box 6.1 for more information concerning OPEC.

INFORMATION BOX 6.1

The Organisation of Petroleum Exporting Countries

The Organisation of Petroleum Exporting Countries, or OPEC as it is commonly known, was set up in 1960. There were five original member states: Saudi Arabia, Iran, Iraq, Kuwait and Venezuela. Currently there are eleven members of the cartel. It emerged out of the growing conflict at the time between the oil-exporting countries and the major oil companies. Its impact on world markets was not felt until 1973 when oil production was curtailed after the Arab-Israeli Yom Kippur war. The price of oil rose from $2.91 per barrel in 1973 to over $11 per barrel in 1974. Because of the close co-operation between member states, among other factors, prices were steady during the 1970s.

All this changed in 1978 with the second oil crisis, triggered by the revolution in Iran. The result was an increase in the price of oil from $20 per barrel in 1979 to over $30 in 1980. A decline in demand in the early 1980s persuaded OPEC members to curtail production. A production ceiling of 16 million barrels per day was agreed in 1984. However, increasing production from non-member states and falling consumption led to gradually falling prices.

The 1990s brought with it an upturn in the world economy and the Gulf War of 1990. The effect of both these events was an increase in the price of oil. This was not to last,

$\longrightarrow$

however. Divisions between members within the cartel and competition from non-OPEC members resulted in the decline of OPEC's influence. By December 1998, the price of oil fell below $10 per barrel. The cartel was unable to curtail the supply because members were not adhering to their quotas.

In 1999, OPEC's fortunes changed again. The president of Venezuela, Hugo Chavez, breathed new life into OPEC. Although Venezuela was one of the founding members of OPEC, it was also one of the biggest 'cheaters'. Because oil is Venezuela's most important source of foreign revenue, the country regularly negotiated a quota and then produced and sold more onto the world market. As the price of a barrel of oil fell below $10 per barrel, this source of revenue decreased.

In March, 1999, Venezuela's oil minister announced that Venezuela would cut back oil production by 4%. This was the beginning of a new discipline within the cartel. Chavez is now president of OPEC. Through his efforts, OPEC members agreed in September 2000 to stabilise the price of oil at $25 per barrel. The depletion of world reserves, problems in the Middle East, the continued robust growth of the US economy and the recovery of the European and Japanese economies have made this benchmark price difficult to attain. From the middle of 2000, the price of oil fluctuated at close to $30 per barrel.

Brent crude oil is the standard or benchmark crude oil. Other types of crude oil are priced relative to it. Figure 6.18 shows the price of a barrel of Brent crude oil between January 1998 and October 2000.

Figure 6.18: Price per barrel of Brent crude oil

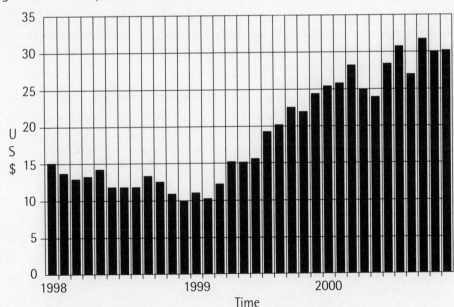

Source: For 2000, TradingCharts.com Inc. (http://futures.tradingchart.com)
For 1998–99, (http://Public/Reports/reports.cfm)

It may seem that OPEC should continue to push up the price of oil. However, this strategy is risky for a number of reasons. First, increasing the price of oil makes it worthwhile for countries which are not members of OPEC, but have oil reserves, to begin exploration for new oil sources. An increase in the supply of oil will cause the price per barrel to fall. Second, if the price of oil is too high, it could have a destabilising effect on the world economy, triggering a world-wide recession. This demand-side shock to the oil market would cause the price of oil to fall. Third, some members of the cartel, most notably Saudi Arabia, are influenced by the US. Pressing for exorbitant price increases could cause the Saudis, who control massive oil reserves, to discontinue their co-operation with the cartel. Finally, the European Union has called for the creation of a world competition authority to prosecute international cartels. Although the effectiveness of such a body is uncertain, maintaining price stability at a reasonable level in the oil market makes its creation much less likely.

In general, once a cartel is formed, there is an incentive to cheat. The benefits of cheating on a collusive agreement as compared to adherence to the agreement (when joint profits are maximised) come in the form of higher output levels and higher profits for the cheating firm at the expense of rivals. Furthermore, cartels face competition from non-members who are not bound by any formal agreement.

The price leadership model

The price leadership model demonstrates a tacit form of collusion compared to the explicit collusion of the cartel. It is based on the existence of a dominant supplier. One producer sets price and others follow. Although other firms in the market are technically free to choose whether or not to 'follow the leader', their freedom is limited by the ability of the dominant firm to retaliate. Examples of dominant firms include Kellogg's (breakfast cereals), Goodyear (tyres), Intel (semiconductors) and Coca Cola (soft drinks).

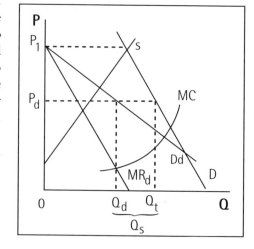

Figure 6.19 illustrates the equilibrium position for the price leadership model with a dominant firm.

Figure 6.19: The price leadership model with a dominant firm

Market demand is represented by the demand curve, D. The quantity supplied by the smaller firms is given by the supply curve, s. The dominant firm's demand curve is the difference between these two curves. In graphic terms, we subtract the quantity supplied by the smaller firms at each price from the total quantity demanded in the market. The difference at each price is the dominant firm's demand curve and is labelled Dd. Take, for example, the price P_1. At P_1 the smaller firms' supply curve intersects the market demand curve. This means that at this price the total market demand is met entirely by the smaller firms. As a result, the quantity demanded of the dominant firm is zero. Hence, at P_1 the dominant firm's demand curve intersects the price axis.

Knowing the demand curve for the dominant firm, we can now derive its marginal revenue curve. If a firm's demand curve is drawn downward sloping, its marginal revenue curve is drawn below it. The dominant firm's marginal revenue curve is labelled MR_d.

The profit-maximisation output level for the dominant firm is attained by producing where its marginal revenue is equal to its marginal cost. The output level is Q_d and the price charged by all firms is P_d. The total quantity demanded in the market at P_d is given by the output level Q_t. This comprises Q_d which is the amount supplied by the dominant firm, and Q_s, the amount supplied by the other smaller firms.

The dominance of the price leader depends on its costs, its financial assets and its excess capacity. If its marginal costs are substantially lower than its competitors, it can temporarily charge a price which is lower than the average variable costs of its competitors, forcing them to temporarily shut down. Although the collusion is 'tacit', under certain circumstances the dominant firm can be quite persuasive.

The kinked demand curve model

This model was developed by Paul Sweezy in the US and R. Hall and C. Hitch in the UK in the 1930s.[5] The model is used to explain why the price in an oligopolistic market, once established, tends to remain the same, even though demand and cost conditions change. It assumes asymmetrical reactions by competitors in a market to a change in price by one firm. For example, if one firm increases price, the others will not respond. The action of increasing price results in a sharp decrease in demand for the initiating firm. In contrast, if the firm cuts price, the others will follow. Only a small increase in the quantity demanded for its product will result for the firm who initiated the price cut. The kinked demand curve outlined in Figure 6.20 results from the asymmetrical responses of market competitors.

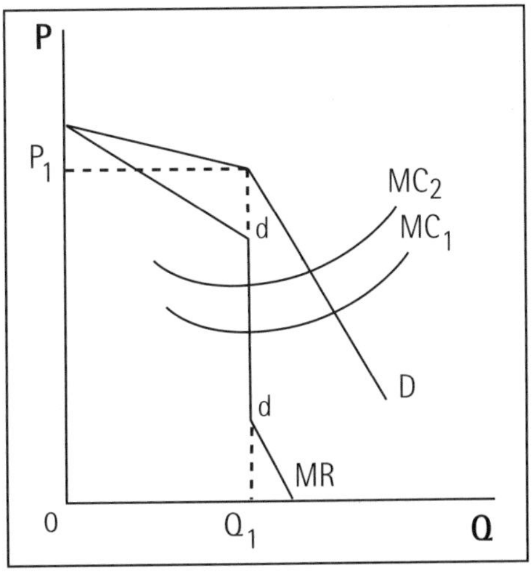

Figure 6.20: The kinked demand curve

The oligopolistic firm's kinked demand curve is drawn in Figure 6.20. Suppose that the market price for the product supplied by the market is P_1. If one firm increases price above P_1, the other firms will not follow. As a result, the firm loses its market share. Consumers purchase the product at a lower price from the firm's competitors. The demand curve for the firm is elastic above the price of P_1.

Alternatively, suppose that the firm cuts price so that it is below P_1. Its competitors react by cutting their prices. The price change does not significantly increase demand for the firm's product. The demand curve for the firm is inelastic below the price of P_1.

Above P_1 the demand curve is relatively flat. Below P_1 the demand curve is relatively steep. At P_1, the demand curve is said to be 'kinked'. A kinked demand curve will result in a discontinuous marginal revenue curve. At Q_1, there is said to be a 'jump' in the marginal revenue curve.

This model of oligopoly is used to explain price rigidity and the absence of price wars in oligopolies even when there is no explicit collusion. In particular, the discontinuous part of the MR curve (the segment dd) provides an explanation for price rigidity. Along this segment, marginal cost could increase significantly without affecting the profit-maximising output or price level. In effect, the oligopolist absorbs the increase in costs and, by doing so, maintains the existing price level. This partly explains the price stickiness or inflexibility which is sometimes associated with oligopolies.

This model is based on the assumption made about the reactions of firms to changes in price by a competing firm. Although it is the most famous of all oligopolistic models, it omits a whole range of other possible reactions and consequently results in a rather restrictive model. It fails to explain how the initial price is reached. In explaining the reason behind price rigidity, it fails to account for other possible explanations such as the administrative expenses involved in changing prices. Finally, the model has not stood up well to empirical tests.

To address the criticisms directed at these models and their assumptions regarding firms' behaviour and pricing strategies, economists began to use a particular branch of mathematics called 'game theory' which focuses on the interdependent decision-making of firms in a market. It is applied to firms operating under conditions of oligopoly and in particular those firms which anticipate rivals' reactions. See Information Box 6.2 for more on game theory.

INFORMATION BOX 6.2

Game theory

Game theory is a mathematical technique used to analyse strategic interaction. It was first developed in the 1940s by the mathematician and physicist John von Neumann and the economist Oskar Morgenstern to analyse the behaviour of firms in oligopolistic markets.[1]

A game consists of rules, players (decision-makers), strategies (actions) and payoffs (scores). In any single game, the players are allowed to make certain moves, as defined by the rules of the game. The player tries to maximise his or her own payoff.

One of the most famous games in game theory is the prisoners' dilemma.   ⟶

The prisoners' dilemma

Michael and Jean are charged for committing a lewd act in public. They are remanded in custody, each facing a possible sentence of up to one year in jail. On meeting the two prisoners, the sergeant immediately suspects them of involvement in another crime committed recently in the locality: the robbing of local church funds.

He places the prisoners in separate rooms. Each prisoner is made aware of the sergeant's suspicion of their involvement in the more serious crime of robbery. They are told that if both confess to the crime, the jail sentence will be four years. Each is also told that if only one of them confesses to the crime, the confessor's sentence will be squashed while the accomplice will receive an eight-year jail sentence. If neither confesses, both prisoners will spend only one year in jail for the lesser offence.

This can be presented as a game with two players, each player having two strategies – to deny the charge or to confess to the crime. With two players and two strategies, there are four possible outcomes:

- neither Michael nor Jean confess to the more serious crime;
- both Michael and Jean confess to the more serious crime;
- Michael confesses, Jean denies involvement;
- Jean confesses, Michael denies involvement.

We use a payoff matrix to tabulate the possible alternative strategies of both players. Table 6.6 shows the payoff matrix for Michael and Jean.

Table 6.6: The prisoners' dilemma payoff matrix

		Michael's strategies	
		Confess	Deny
Jean's strategies	Confess	M. 4 years J. 4 years	M. 8 years J. Free
	Deny	M. Free J. 8 years	M. 1 year J. 1 year

Each square shows the payoffs for the two players (M for Michael and J for Jean) for each possible strategy. We begin with the top left-hand box. If both confess, they each get a four-year jail sentence. In contrast, if both deny the charge, they each get a one-year jail sentence. This strategy is recorded in the bottom right-hand box. The more interesting payoffs are to be found in the two remaining boxes. If Michael confesses and Jean denies, the court will free Michael but will hand down an eight-year jail sentence to Jean. This possibility is presented in the bottom left-hand box. The other possibility is for Jean to confess and for Michael to deny. This combination will involve freedom for Jean but the much longer sentence of eight years for Michael. →

It is evident from the above analysis that the two players are faced with a dilemma. Neither player knows what the other's decision will be. Should Michael confess in the hope that Jean denies the charge? Likewise, should Jean confess hoping to minimise the amount of time she spends behind bars? The answers to these and other questions are to be found in the 'equilibrium' for the game. The equilibrium for this particular type of game is called the Nash equilibrium. This is the result of all participating players playing their best strategy given the actions of their competitors. It is named after John Nash, the American mathematician who introduced this concept in 1951.

In the case of the prisoners' dilemma, the equilibrium occurs when Michael makes his best choice given Jean's choice and, likewise, when Jean makes her best choice given Michael's choice. However, the Nash equilibrium for the prisoners' dilemma is a special case. No matter what Jean does, Michael's best choice is to confess. Likewise, no matter what Michael does, Jean's best choice is to confess. Hence, the equilibrium of the prisoners' dilemma is that both players confess. This equilibrium where there is a unique best action regardless of what the other player does is called the dominant strategy equilibrium.

From the prisoners' viewpoint, however, this is a bad outcome. If both denied the charges, they would receive only a one-year jail sentence. Unfortunately, they have no way of communicating to each other. Yet, they do know that despite the action of the other individual, their best choice is to confess. On confessing, a bad outcome is delivered.

Similar techniques can be applied to firms in oligopolistic markets. Such firms may decide to alter output levels or prices, depending on the actions of others. Assumptions are made about the behaviour of their rivals. All possible strategies can then be analysed in the same way as above.

The application of game theory to the study of a firm's behaviour in oligopolistic markets has been one of the most outstanding recent developments in the field of economics. In recognition of this, the 1994 Nobel prize in Economics was awarded to three economists for their work in this field. The recipients were John Nash (of Nash equilibrium fame), John Harsanyi and Reinhard Selten who introduced time and uncertainty to game theory models.

[1] J. von Neumann and O. Morgenstern, *The Theory of Games and Economic Behaviour*, Princeton University Press, 1944.

6.5   MARKET STRUCTURE SPECTRUM

We have now completed our analysis of the different market structures. One useful way of comparing one structure with another is by examining the market structure spectrum. The market structure spectrum is similar to any other spectrum such as the spectrum of light or colour. The different market structures are presented in a line from left to right. It is primarily the degree of competition which explains the differences between the market structures.

On one extreme of the spectrum we have 'perfect' competition. Monopoly is the other extreme where there is no competition. Most markets, in reality, lie somewhere in between these two extreme cases. It is monopolistic competition and oligopoly that lie between these two polar extremes, with the former being known as 'competition among the many' and the latter being referred to as 'competition among the few'. In these two cases there are varying degrees of competition between the respective firms.

Figure 6.21:   The market structure spectrum

Figure 6.21 illustrates the market structure spectrum. The various market structures include perfect competition, monopolistic competition, oligopoly and monopoly. The last three structures are sometimes grouped together and referred to as 'imperfect competition' because in each of these structures, an individual firm has some ability to control price. A summary of the different market structures and their characteristics is included in Table 6.7.

Table 6.7:   The characteristic differences between market structures

	Perfect competition	**Monopolistic competition**	**Oligopoly**	**Monopoly**
No. of firms	Many	Many	Few	One
Type of product	Identical	Differentiated	Identical or differentiated	Unique
Barriers to entry	No	No	Yes	Yes
Pricing strategy	Price taker	Price maker	Interdependent	Price maker
Long-run profits	Normal	Normal	Possibility of Supernormal	Possibility of Supernormal
Examples	Agricultural markets Capital markets	Service stations Restaurants	Automobile fuel Cement	Rail-transport Airport management

It is often difficult to classify firms into a specific market structure. Also, the framework which we have discussed is often criticised because the models are simple and static while the actual behaviour of firms is complex and dynamic. However, the more realistic and dynamic models developed by Joan Robinson, Herbert Simon, Michael Porter and others are reactions against these comparative static models. A thorough knowledge of these models is essential to understand and appreciate the models of the critics!

The next step in our analysis of microeconomics involves taking a closer look at the factors of production which are used in the production process. Chapter 7 examines, in detail, the four basic factors of production.

SUMMARY

1. A firm's behaviour depends largely on the degree of competition and market power. We examined four market structures in detail: perfect competition, monopolistic competition, oligopoly and monopoly. They differ in relation to the number of firms in the market, the nature of the product sold, the entry to and exit from the market and, finally, the availability of information.
2. Perfect competition is a model which describes idealised economic conditions that are rarely met in practice. It consists of a large number of small firms with no single firm large enough to influence price. Each firm is a price taker. There is freedom of entry and exit on account of the absence of entry barriers. A standardised product is sold. Perfect knowledge exists with consumers and firms accurately informed about prices, profits and quality. As a result, perfectly competitive firms cannot make supernormal profits in the long run.
3. A monopolist is the sole producer in the market. It is a price maker. There are barriers to entry. A unique product is sold with no close substitutes readily available. As a result, the monopolist can make supernormal profits. The single-price monopolist charges a higher price, produces less output and can earn supernormal profits in the long run. There is no well-defined supply curve for the monopolist. A monopolist can also practise price discrimination.
4. Monopolistic competition is similar to perfect competition, with one important exception: it assumes product differentiation. Goods are close rather than perfect substitutes for each other. This allows for some market power. The short-run equilibrium in monopolistic competition is similar to the monopoly equilibrium. A firm in this industry can earn supernormal profits in the short run, but freedom of entry ensures that only normal profits are earned in the long run. A firm in this industry does not produce at the lowest possible cost per unit. Its failure to exhibit efficiency is partly offset by the wider choice it offers to the consumer.
5. Oligopoly is another example of imperfect competition. In oligopoly, the actions of firms are interdependent. Each firm tries to anticipate the action and reactions of its competitors when formulating and implementing its own strategy. The models are broadly divided into two: those that assume collusion and those that assume competition. Collusion may be open or tacit.
6. The market structure spectrum highlights the differences between the market structures. The amount of competition varies from 'pure' in a perfectly competitive market to a complete absence of any competition in a monopoly. The other cases exhibit varying degrees of competition. Monopolistic competition, oligopoly and

monopoly are sometimes called 'imperfect competition' to distinguish them from perfect competition. One characteristic common to all imperfectly competitive markets is a degree of market power, reflected in a downward sloping demand curve.

KEY TERMS

Market power	Third degree price discrimination
Perfect competition	First degree price discrimination
Monopolistic competition	Product differentiation
Oligopoly	Interdependency
Monopoly	Concentration ratios
Price taker	Collusive oligopoly
Barriers to entry	Cartels
Short-run supply curve	Dominant firm
Shutdown price	Kinked demand curve
Efficiency	Game theory
Single-price monopolist	Nash equilibrium
Price discriminating monopolist	Imperfect competition

REVIEW QUESTIONS

1. Derive the short-run supply curve under conditions of perfect competition.
2. Explain why the perfectly competitive firm produces at the minimum point of the average cost curve in the long run. What does this suggest about perfect competition?
3. Outline the short-run equilibrium position for a monopoly. Why is it not possible to draw a well-defined supply curve for the monopolist?
4. (a) Outline the differences and the similarities between perfect competition and monopolistic competition.
   (b) Sketch the short-run and long-run equilibrium positions of the monopolistic competitor.
5. Using the kinked demand curve model, explain the rationale for price rigidity.
6. Explain the main differences between perfect and imperfect competition. Give examples of each.

WORKING PROBLEMS

1. Figure 6.22 shows the cost curves of a firm competing in a perfectly competitive industry. Complete Table 6.8.

Figure 6.22

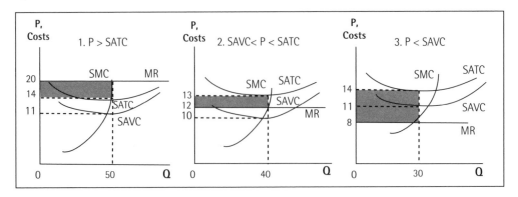

Table 6.8

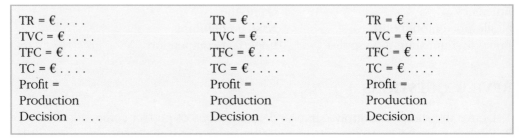

TR = €	TR = €	TR = € . . . .
TVC = €	TVC = €	TVC = € . . . .
TFC = €	TFC = €	TFC = € . . . .
TC = €	TC = €	TC = € . . . .
Profit =	Profit =	Profit =
Production	Production	Production
Decision	Decision	Decision . . . .

2. Figure 6.23 shows two equilibrium positions in the long run. Which equilibrium is for a perfectly competitive firm and which is for a monopolistically competitive firm? Explain. What are the main differences between the two market structures at equilibrium? What are the similarities at equilibrium?

Figure 6.23: Long-run equilibrium

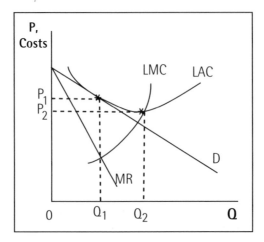

MULTI-CHOICE QUESTIONS

1. Firms act independently of each other in the following market structures:
   (a) perfect competition and imperfect competition;
   (b) perfect competition, oligopoly and monopolistic competition;
   (c) monopolistic competition and oligopoly;
   (d) perfect competition and oligopoly;
   (e) perfect competition and monopolistic competition.

2. Figure 6.24 illustrates a short-run equilibrium position for a perfectly competitive firm where price is less than average total cost.

Figure 6.24

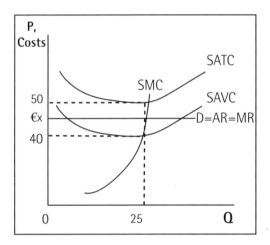

If the loss is equal to €75, the market price x must be equal to:
   (a) 48;
   (b) 46;
   (c) 45;
   (d) 47;
   (e) none of the above.

3. The special identity for a firm in a perfectly competitive industry is:
   (a) MR = MC;
   (b) AR = D;
   (c) P = MC;
   (d) ATC = AVC;
   (e) none of the above.

4. Assuming identical demand and cost conditions, a monopolist, compared to a perfectly competitive market, charges:
   (a) a higher price for a higher output;
   (b) a higher price for a lower output;

(c) a lower price for a lower output;
(d) a lower price for a higher output;
(e) none of the above.

5. Figure 6.25 illustrates the equilibrium position for the profit-maximising single-price monopolist.

Figure 6.25

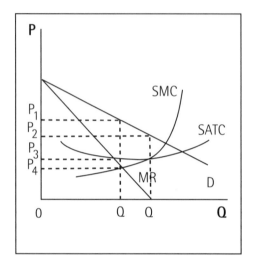

The single-price monopolist charges price equal to:
(a) P4;
(b) P3;
(c) P2;
(d) P1;
(e) none of the above.

6. Which model in oligopoly is useful in explaining price rigidity?
(a) price leadership model;
(b) single-price monopolist;
(c) collusion model;
(d) kinked demand curve model;
(e) none of the above.

TRUE OR FALSE (SUPPORT YOUR ANSWER)

1. The market demand curve in perfect competition is downward sloping from left to right.

2. The supply curve for the perfectly competitive firm in the short run is its marginal cost curve above the shutdown price.

3. Price discrimination involves charging different prices for different goods to different consumers.

4. The demand curve for the monopolistic competitor is more elastic than the demand curve for the monopolist because of the absence of available substitutes.

5. At equilibrium in the long run, the firm under conditions of monopolistic competition produces at the output level where MR = MC = AR = AC.

6. Once a cartel is formed, there is no incentive to cheat.

CASE STUDY

The shortage of taxis, particularly in Dublin, has been an ongoing source of aggravation for passengers and business interests represented by IBEC and the Dublin City Chamber of Commerce. Even union representatives of the taxi drivers acknowledge that the number of taxis has to increase. The question is, 'How should these increases be implemented?'

Before November 2000, the number of taxi plates was regulated. Taxi licences were issued by Dublin City Council. The Council approved 200 new licenses per year in 1997 and 1998. Most commentators agreed increases in demand far outstripped these small increases in supply. The long queues for taxi passengers bore witness to the shortage.

Increases in demand and inelastic supply meant that the value of the taxi plate increased. Drivers saw the plate as an investment asset, like a house, which increased in value.

In November 2000, new legislation was introduced by the Minister of State for the Environment, Mr Robert Molloy. Under the terms of that legislation, new licences are granted to anyone as long as s/he is a licensed driver, insured and driving a car which passes a vehicle test. The initial fee is £5000 for a taxi license and £100 for a wheelchair-accessible taxi license.

The taxi drivers will be affected in two ways. First, there will be increased competition for fares as the number of taxis on the road increases. Second, since supply is unrestricted, the asset value of their taxi plate will be completely lost.

To partially offset this loss in the value of the taxi plate, tax legislation was proposed by the Minister of Finance to allow the holders of taxi licenses to write off capital losses over a number of years.

Was this the correct course of action? Who gains and who loses by the changes to the taxi industry? Two items appeared on the editorial page of *The Irish Times* on Thursday 23 November 2000. One argues in favour of the changes and the other argues against them. Read them, answer the following questions and decide for yourself!

$\longrightarrow$

Extract from *The Irish Times*
The End of the Taxi Monopoly
(an editorial)

The bully-boy tactics engaged by taxi drivers should not dissuade the Government from breaking up the cartel and putting in place a licensing system that will provide an efficient and cost-effective transport service. The nettle should have been grasped years ago. There was a string of reports urging reform of the sector. But political pressure, particularly within Fianna Fáil, ensured that the taxi cartel flourished while the travelling public endured a down-at-heel and desperately inadequate service . . .

Blockading Dublin airport and the Dáil, along with the major roads around the cities of Dublin, Cork, Galway and Waterford, caused huge disruption yesterday and the travelling public was seriously inconvenienced. It was not the kind of behaviour designed to attract public sympathy. Rather, it was a crude threat against the Government and the economy. And there was an open-ended promise of more disruption to follow. Yesterday's disruption was predictable. Individuals who enjoy a privileged position rarely surrender without a struggle. And taximen were so successful in defending their monopoly and financial advantage in recent years, that they came to see themselves as being exempt from the rules of competition . . .

Letters to the Editor
by David Quigley

Sir,— It is an appalling injustice that ordinary working people who have put their homes up for licences will now face financial ruin. My father is a taxi-driver in Waterford who has recently put the house up as collateral against a loan of £80,000 for a taxi plate after many years of driving for other owners.

The tax relief proposed by the Minister may help to bring my father's earnings closer to those of someone who has less than a tenth the financial burden to bear weekly; but it will not compensate for the fact that he is left with something worthless at the end. He is now paying back about £100,000, including interest, while the man who sold him the plate can buy another for £5000. This is clearly wrong. My father is an honest man who has worked harder than most all his life.

There is a need for a better taxi service, but to suggest that this move will encourage that is [sic] an indication of the limited capacity of the Minister to see reason. What will happen is that the people who have been (in) this industry for years will be forced out and lose their homes as well as their investment. Most taxi-drivers don't have a pension; the value of their plate is their retirement fund and their legacy to their children. I would suggest that the Minister should deduct the license fee of £5000 from whatever the existing plate-owners owe on their plates and settle the rest. This would ensure that the all-new taxi industry would begin with everyone on a level playing-field . . . If this

$\longrightarrow$

does not happen, protesting drivers will ensure that there will be chaos on the streets this Christmas.

I would like to remind the Minister that the taxi-drivers and their extended families may make up more than 10,000 votes in the next election and the Minister can be assured that these votes will be cast against his party. I will personally organise the campaign to ensure this happens.

—Yours, etc.,

Source: *The Irish Times*, 23 November 2000.

Questions

1. The editorial refers to the taxi industry as both a 'monopoly' and an 'oligopoly'. What is the difference between the two market structures? Does the taxi industry fit the characteristics of these two market structures? Why or why not?
2. Under the old system, what were the barriers to enter the taxi industry? Does the new system affect the barriers?
3. According to the editorial, who gains from a taxi 'cartel' and who loses?
4. According to Quigley, who gains if the new system is implemented and who loses?

CHAPTER 7

FACTOR MARKETS

'*Wages* are determined by the bitter struggle between capitalist and worker.'[1]

Karl Marx (1818–83)

'Profit is the result of risks wisely selected.'[2]

Frederick B. Hawley (1843–1929)

CHAPTER OBJECTIVES

Upon completing this chapter, the student should understand:

* derived demand;
* marginal productivity theory;
* wage determination;
* the capital market and the cost of capital;
* economic rent;
* the sources of profits.

OUTLINE

7.1 Labour and wages
7.2 Capital and interest
7.3 Land and rent
7.4 Entrepreneurship and profit
7.5 National partnership agreements

INTRODUCTION

Until now, our analysis of markets focused on the final output of goods and services. We mentioned that land, labour, capital and entrepreneurship are combined in the production process. Further, rent, wages, interest and profit constitute the costs of the firm. However, when we mentioned the price of these factors, we took them as 'given'.

We will now look at each of the factor markets individually. We will attempt to explain how the rental rate, the wage rate, the interest rate and the profit rate are determined within their respective factor markets.

According to the traditional or neoclassical theory of distribution, factor prices can be explained in terms of demand and supply analysis. In the resource market, however, the roles of firms and households are reversed. The firms that supply the goods and services in the product markets are now the source of the demand for the factor inputs. The householders, who demand final goods and services are now the suppliers of the resources. In short, firms are the buyers of resources and households are the sellers of the same resources. We will use marginal productivity theory to provide us with an understanding of the demand for the various factor inputs.

In this chapter we discuss each of the four factor markets. We begin, in Section 7.1, with the labour market. Capital, land and enterprise and their respective factor prices are discussed in Sections 7.2, 7.3 and 7.4 respectively. Although each market is explained separately, they are inter-related in practice; developments in one resource market can affect other resource markets. Section 7.5 looks at the national partnership agreements and national wage agreements, implemented in Ireland since 1987. The partnership model brings the representatives of the market for labour, capital, land and enterprise together with the government and other social partners to plan the future and negotiate change.

7.1 LABOUR AND WAGES

The labour market is comprised of a demand for and supply of labour. We begin by studying the demand for labour.

The demand for labour

A firm's demand for labour is a derived demand.

Definition

A derived demand means that an input is not demanded for its own sake but for its use in the production of goods and services.

A farmer requires labourers in order to produce foodstuffs; a car manufacturer requires workers to help on the production line; an insurance sales company requires staff to put together saleable products and to sell them to potential customers. The demand for this resource stems from what the employment of labour can produce.

In order to understand the demand for labour we need to return to production theory in general (Section 5.2) and to marginal productivity theory in particular. This was developed by several economists including E. von Bohm-Bawerk (1851–1914) and J. Bates Clark (1847–1938) in the late nineteenth century.[3] This theory postulates that wages, as well as other factor payments, depend largely on the productivity of the factor input. The existence of perfectly competitive markets is an underlying assumption of this theory.

Before we consider an example, recall a few of the terms which were defined in Chapter 5. We are considering the production function of a firm in the short run, which means that some inputs are fixed and some inputs are variable. Total product (TP) is the total output produced during a specified time period, using particular amounts of inputs. Marginal product (MP) is the additional units of output generated by the addition of a variable input. The declining productivity of labour reflects the law of diminishing returns. The law states that in the short run, when capital is fixed, an additional worker will eventually produce less output than the previous worker.

We can also look at the contribution of an additional worker in monetary terms.

Definition
The marginal revenue product (MRP) of labour is the addition to revenue from the employment of an extra worker.

Equation 7.1 states this in algebraic form:

$$MRP = \frac{\Delta TR}{\Delta Q_L}$$

[7.1]

where: Δ = change; MRP = marginal revenue product;
TR = total revenue; Q_L = number of workers.

The MRP of labour measures the monetary value of the extra output generated from the employment of an additional worker. The MRP of labour can also be calculated by multiplying the marginal product by the marginal revenue earned per unit. In simple terms:

$$MRP = MP \times MR$$

[7.2]

where: MRP = marginal revenue product;
MP = marginal product; MR = marginal revenue.

Table 7.1: Daily production schedule for Hibs (Ireland) Ltd

(1) Labour (wkrs)	(2) TP (units)	(3) MP (units)	(4) MR = P (€)	(5) MRP (€)	(6) Wage (€)	(7) Contribution (€)	(8) Wage (€)	(9) Contribution (€)
0	0							
		55	4	220	100	120	48	172
1	55							
		43	4	172	100	72	48	124
2	98							
		33	4	132	100	32	48	84
3	131							
		25	4	100	100	0	48	52
4	156							
		18	4	72	100	−28	48	24
5	174							
		12	4	48	100	−52	48	0
6	186							
		5	4	20	100	−80	48	−28
7	191							
		1	4	4	100	−96	48	−44
8	192							

We will now apply these concepts using an example in an effort to understand the hiring decision of the firm. Hibs (Ireland) Ltd is a manufacturing company. The relationship between the number of workers employed and the total output generated by the workforce is recorded in Table 7.1. Because Hibs is producing a good for a perfectly competitive market, MR = P.

How many workers will Hibs Ltd employ? Column 5 records the extra revenue that each additional worker contributes to the business. The cost to the firm of hiring each worker is recorded in column 6. Because the labour market is perfectly competitive, all labourers can be hired for the same wage. The difference (column 7) between the two is simply the net contribution that each additional worker makes to the firm. In other words, this is what the labourer produces, in excess of her or his wage.

For example, if the wage rate is €100 and the marginal revenue product of the first worker is €220, the net contribution of the first worker must be €120 (€220 – €100). The contribution from the second worker is €72 (€172 – €100) and so on. In this example the first four workers each make a positive net contribution, i.e. MRP ≥ W. The contributions from the employment of a fifth worker, a sixth worker, a seventh and so on are all negative (MRP < W). Hence, Hibs Ltd employs until MRP = W. In this example, if the wage rate is €100, Hibs Ltd employs four workers.

If the wage rate falls from €100 to €48, will Hibs Ltd increase or decrease the size of its workforce? This scenario is shown in columns 8 and 9 of Table 7.1. For a wage rate of €48, the first six workers contribute positively to the firm. In this case, MRP = W when six workers are employed. Thus, if the wage rate falls, this model predicts that the profit-maximising firm will employ more workers. The opposite is true if the wage rate rises.

In general, the lower the wage rate the more workers will be employed.

Derivation of the demand curve for labour

Hibs Ltd employs workers up to the point where the MRP = W. In other words, the profit-maximising firm will employ an additional labourer if the amount that he produces is sufficient to pay his wage.

Figure 7.1 plots the relationship between the marginal revenue product of labour and the number of workers employed as described in columns 1 and 5 of Table 7.1.

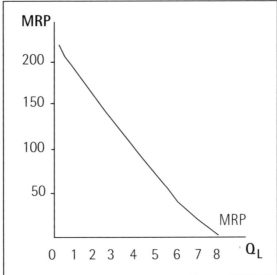

Figure 7.1: Marginal revenue product curve for Hibs Ltd

We can see from the figure that the MRP of the fourth worker is €100 while the MRP of the sixth worker falls to €48. However, we can interpret this diagram in another way. We can ask, 'If the wage is €100, how many employees will Hibs Ltd employ?' At a wage rate of €100, we predict, using this model, that Hibs Ltd will hire four workers. If the wage rate falls to €48, the firm will hire six employees. At a lower wage rate, firms can hire additional workers.

For Hibs Ltd and for all other profit-maximising firms, workers will be employed up to the point where the marginal revenue product equals the wage paid to labour i.e. MRP=W. Therefore, the MRP curve is the firm's demand curve for labour. Figure 7.2 depicts the same curve as Figure 7.1. However, we have substituted wage for the marginal revenue product on the vertical axis. The horizontal axis continues to represent the number of workers employed.

Figure 7.2: The demand curve for labour for Hibs Ltd

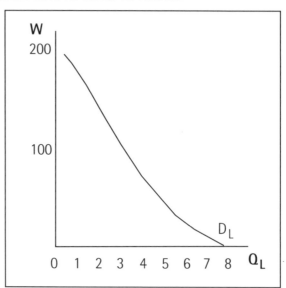

Figure 7.2 shows the amount of labour that Hibs Ltd will hire at each wage rate. It is downward sloping, depicting the negative relationship between the wage rate and the number of workers employed. It is drawn holding other variables constant, including the technological process and the training of the labour force. Also, because the demand for labour is 'derived', factors which affect the product market will also affects the labour demand curve. A change in any of the underlying variables which affects the price of a product, will also cause the position and/or the slope of the demand curve for labour to change.

In summary, we have used the marginal productivity theory to derive the marginal revenue product for labour. For a profit-maximising firm, workers will be hired up to the point where W = MRP of labour. Hence, the marginal revenue product curve for labour is the demand curve for labour. It is derived from the productivity of labour, the wage paid to labour and the price of the product.

Derivation of the market demand curve for labour

In order to obtain the market demand curve for labour we need to sum all the individual firms' demand curves for labour. The market demand curve for labour shows the quantity of labour demanded at each wage rate by all firms in the market. In graphic terms this market demand curve can be derived by 'adding' or aggregating the firms' individual demand curves. This exercise is illustrated in Figure 7.3.

Figure 7.3: Derivation of the market demand curve for labour

Two individual demand curves, D_L^1 and D_L^2, are drawn. The market demand curve, D_L^{1+2}, can be derived by summing up the separate levels of labour demanded at each wage rate. If, for example, the wage rate is €5, the total number of workers demanded would be 95 (40 + 55). At a wage level of €8, the total number demanded would be 70 (25 + 45). This exercise is repeated for each wage level. The result is a downward sloping market demand curve for labour.

We now turn our attention to the supply of labour.

The supply of labour

An individual's decision regarding the supply of labour is related to the wage rate. All other things being equal, an increase in the wage rate increases the incentive to work. As a result, the quantity of hours worked increases. Hence, the supply curve for labour for an individual is upward sloping. This is depicted in Figure 7.4.

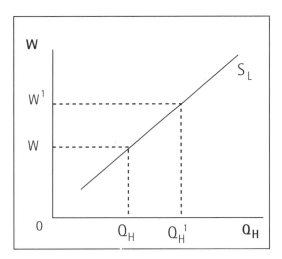

Figure 7.4: The individual supply curve for labour

The individual supply curve for labour shows the number of hours offered for work at any given wage rate. At a wage rate of W, the quantity of hours worked is Q_H. At the higher wage rate of W^1, the number of hours worked increases to Q_H^1. As the wage rate increases, the number of hours worked increases.

An interesting aspect of an individual's labour supply is the possibility that the supply curve could be backward bending. This can be explained by examining the trade-off between work and leisure for an individual. According to this theory, individuals work to earn the money to purchase goods and services. At lower wage levels, any increase in the wage rate is likely to elicit an increase in the number of hours worked. At lower levels of wages, the labour supply curve is upward sloping.

However, the opportunity cost of labour is to forgo leisure activities. As wages continue to increase, individuals may resist a further increase in the number of hours worked, preferring leisure to labour. Hence, as wages increase, the number of hours worked declines. This is reflected in the backward bending labour supply curve depicted in Figure 7.5.

Figure 7.5: A backward bending labour supply curve

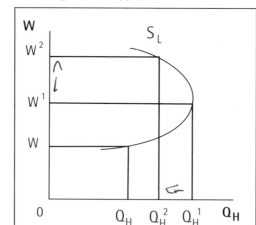

If the wage rate increases from W to W^1, the individual is prepared to increase the number of hours worked from Q_H to Q_H^1. Beyond this wage level, however, the individual is not prepared to work longer hours. If wage levels increase beyond W^1, the individual will sacrifice work in return for more leisure. For example, if wages increase from W^1 to W^2, the number of hours worked declines from Q_H^1 to Q_H^2.

The backward bending supply curve can be explained using substitution and income effects. The substitution effect is caused by a change in the relative prices of work and leisure. At higher wages, more goods and services can be purchased. The opportunity cost of leisure time increases with the wage rate. The substitution effect suggests that labour will be substituted for leisure under these conditions.

The income of the worker increases with the wage rate. Leisure activities are considered to be 'normal' goods (or services). Therefore, the demand for these goods increases with income. More time allocated to leisure activities means that less time is available for work. The income effect suggests that more time will be allocated to leisure (and less to labour) as income increases.

Initially, the substitution effect outweighs the income effect and the first portion of the labour supply curve is upward sloping. However, beyond a certain wage, the income effect is stronger than the substitution effect. This part of the labour supply curve is backward bending.

In this instance, we cannot conclude that what is possibly true for an individual can be applied to the market. Empirical evidence suggests that the labour supply curve for the market is upward sloping, even over the wide range of incomes that we observe in modern, developed economies. As wages increase, the extra workers who enter the labour market more than offset the effects of the backward bending individual supply curve.

Therefore, while admitting that the backward bending supply curve of labour is a theoretical possibility which may one day be observed, we will assume that the market labour supply curve is upward sloping in line with the empirical evidence. This is drawn in Figure 7.6.

Figure 7.6: Market supply curve for labour

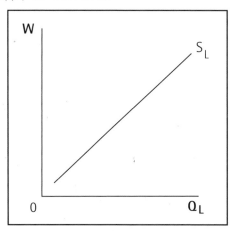

This positive relationship is depicted in an upward sloping market supply curve for labour. The supply curve for labour considers the relationship between wages and the number of people working, *ceteris paribus*. The variables which are held constant include the tax and social welfare system, educational policies, the degree of unionisation (see Information Box 7.1) and the size of the labour force. If any of these underlying variables change, the position and/or the slope of the labour supply curve will change.

210

Principles of Economics: An Irish Textbook

INFORMATION BOX 7.1

The trade union movement in Ireland

The purpose of a trade union is to represent workers and to maximise their power in the workplace. They also play a wider role in the social and political arena. Trade union power is based largely on the solidarity between workers.

Although trade unions existed in Ireland in the eighteenth century, they were first legalised in 1871 when the first Trade Union Act was passed. Almost twenty-five years later, in April 1894 the Irish Trade Union Congress (ITUC) was founded. 119 delegates from different labour organisations were present, representing 21,000 trade unionists directly and a further 39,000 indirectly through the trade councils. The first President of Congress was Thomas O'Connell. Other famous trade unionists included William O'Brien, James Larkin and Louie Bennett.

The Irish Transport and General Workers Union (ITGWU) was founded in 1909 by James Larkin. On his return from the US in 1910, James Connolly joined and worked as a full-time official in Belfast. The next few years were both eventful and traumatic for the labour movement in Ireland.

The Irish Labour party was formed in 1912. In its infancy, membership was restricted to trade unionists. Two years later, the great Dublin lock-out occurred. Even with the massive publicity which surrounded the lock-out, it had a detrimental impact on the union movement in the short term. Less than two years later, James Connolly was executed after the 1916 Easter Rising. Connolly had been the chief organiser of the ITGWU in Ulster as well as one of the founding members of the Irish Labour Party. His loss to the trade union movement was immense.

Although membership of the ITGWU had increased to 100,000 in 1922, it subsequently fell to below 16,000 by the end of the decade. The ITUC membership also fell, from 189,000 in 1922 to 92,000 in 1929. The economic conditions during the Depression, in addition to government policy, were contributing factors to the decline in union membership.

The last seventy years have witnessed great changes in the trade union movement in Ireland. In 1959, the Irish Congress of Trade Unions (ICTU), the co-ordinating body for trade unions in Ireland, was established. In 1990, the country's two largest unions – the ITGWU and the FWUI (Federated Workers' Union of Ireland) – were amalgamated to form the Services, Industrial, Professional and Technical Union (SIPTU).

A number of other smaller unions also merged. However, there are currently over seventy unions listed on the Registrar of Friendly Societies.

The 1980s was a particularly difficult decade for the trade union movement. Spiralling inflation led to increased wage demands. Union members voted with their feet. Between 1981 and 1987, an average of over 350,000 workdays per year were lost due to industrial disputes.

At the end of that decade, ICTU, under the leadership of Peter Cassells, entered into negotiations with the social partners for the first national partnership agreement. This was the beginning of a new era of industrial relations. Although there will always be issues that separate labour and management, the national and local partnership

→

agreements provide a framework for discussing those issues in a forum which is less combative than other industrial relations models.

Trade union membership rose to over 500,000 members in 1999. About 40% of trade union members are public sector employees. The remaining 60% are employed in the private sector. Many multinational firms, particularly in telecommunications and computer-related industries, have resisted unionisation. Because of this, trade union density (trade union membership/employed members of the labour force) is falling. The numbers employed in the labour force are growing more rapidly than trade union membership.

Using the demand and the supply curve, we now consider the labour market.

Labour market equilibrium

Figure 7.7 depicts the labour market with a downward sloping demand curve and an upward sloping supply curve. The intersection of the demand curve and the supply curve determines the equilibrium wage rate and the equilibrium quantity of labour. At W*, the quantity demanded of labour is equal to the quantity supplied. W* is the wage rate that clears the labour market.

Figure 7.7: Labour market equilibrium

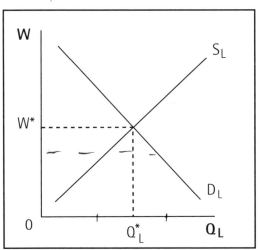

At all other wage levels, there is either a shortage or a surplus of labour. At wage rates above the equilibrium level, an excess supply of labour exists. This surplus labour results in downward pressure on wages. At wage rates below the equilibrium level, an excess demand for labour results. Such a shortage of workers puts upward pressure on wage levels. W* is the equilibrium wage rate. At W* the quantity demanded and quantity supplied of labour are equal.

As we discussed previously, the labour demand curve and supply curve are drawn holding other variables constant. A change in one of the underlying variables will cause the demand curve or the supply curve to shift. Any shift of the demand curve or the supply curve of labour results in a change in the equilibrium wage rate and the quantity of labour.

For example, suppose we examine demand and supply conditions for labour in the construction industry. In the winter months severe weather conditions can adversely affect the construction industry. In response to worsening weather conditions, construction companies reduce their demand for labourers. The effects of such a change are shown in Figure 7.8.

Figure 7.8: A change in labour demand

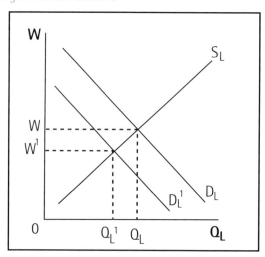

Equilibrium is initially at (W, Q_L). The adverse weather conditions force the construction companies to cut their workforce. Fewer labourers are required to work on the construction sites. This reduction in demand is illustrated in graphic terms as a leftward shift of the demand curve for labour. The excess supply of labour arising from the fall in demand forces wage levels downwards. As wage levels fall, fewer workers are willing to supply their services. Equilibrium is restored at (W^1, Q_L^1), the intersection of the old supply curve, S_L and the new demand curve, D_L^1. The net result is a lower equilibrium wage level combined with a lower quantity of labour. An improvement in demand conditions will result in higher wages and a higher quantity of labour.

The neoclassical model of the labour market and minimum wage legislation

In Section 2.4, we discussed price controls. Minimum wage legislation is a form of price control for the labour market. It is legislated by governments to ensure that wages will not fall below a certain level. Proponents of the minimum wage argue that it is the single most effective policy to decrease the range of income distribution and to lift workers out of poverty. By putting a floor under wages, it moves those in employment into higher income brackets. They argue that the enforcement of minimum wage legislation reduces the exploitation of labour by those employers who refuse to pay a wage which will allow an adequate living standard.

Many economists take a very different view. Figure 7.9 shows the model of the labour market after the imposition of a minimum wage.

Figure 7.9: Labour market with a minimum wage

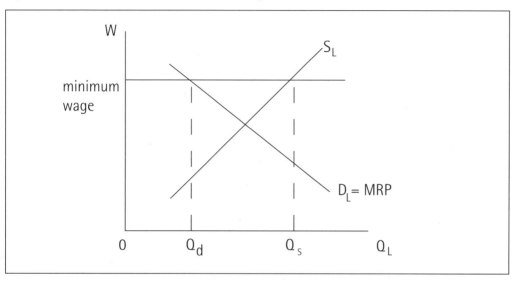

Generally, the minimum wage is set above the labour market equilibrium. This model predicts that, as a result of the minimum wage legislation, there will be a surplus of labour or unemployment in the labour market. The supply of labour, or the number of people who are willing to work at the minimum wage, is greater than the demand for labour. Unemployment will persist because the wage rate cannot adjust to 'clear' the market.

The economic profession has been almost united in their condemnation of minimum wage legislation.[4] Rather than improving the living standards of the working poor, who are supposed to benefit from this legislation, they argue that it benefits those who can find employment at the expense of those who are 'involuntarily' unemployed. These are individuals who are willing to work for less than the minimum wage. Profit-maximising employers cannot hire these workers because the amount that they are producing (as measured by the marginal revenue product) is less than the minimum wage.

In spite of the opposition of the economics profession, minimum wage legislation has been implemented. The United States passed the Fair Labour Standards Act in 1938. France enacted its first minimum wage legislation over fifty years ago. The Irish government adopted a minimum wage on April 1, 2000.

Minimum wage legislation in Ireland

The positive merits of minimum wage legislation have been discussed in Ireland for many years, particularly by trade unions and organisations attempting to combat poverty. Employers' organisations and the government were less enthusiastic. Their attitudes were shaped by economists' predictions that the imposition of a minimum wage would lead to higher levels of unemployment. Until the late 1990s, the rate of unemployment in Ireland was above the EU average. Policy makers were unwilling to risk enacting a policy that could make a bad situation worse.

By the end of the 1990s, the labour market situation had changed. Instead of unemployed labour, there were labour market shortages in many sectors. The Fianna Fáil and Progressive Democrats coalition included a commitment to implement a national minimum hourly wage as one of the objectives of the Government's Action Programme for the New Millennium. They appointed a National Minimum Wage Commission. Their terms of reference were:[5]

1. to advise the best way to implement minimum wage legislation with regard to improving the situation of the low paid;
2. to examine existing mechanisms to recommend changes to ensure compliance with minimum wage legislation by employers;
3. to examine any adverse impact on competitiveness, particularly with regard to small and medium-sized enterprises; and
4. to consult with the social partners before the finalisation of the report.

Based on the work of the Commission, the Inter-Departmental Group was formed with representatives from various government departments. The Group's task was to find ways to implement the Commission's recommendations. For a policy which is theoretically simple, the implementation of a minimum wage is complex.

For example, the Commission was concerned about the effect of the minimum wage on people who are under 18 years of age. Research pointed to two possible effects. First, students, attracted by jobs paying the minimum wage might discontinue their studies. From the point of view of the teenager and society, the Commission did not consider this to be a beneficial outcome. An individual's future earning capacity is far greater if they complete their second level education and proceed to training or third level. Second, employers might not be willing to pay the minimum wage to employ teenagers. Generally, unemployment among teenagers is high relative to other age groups.

The rate was another contentious issue. The Commission recommended a rate of £4.40 per hour. The Irish Congress of Trade Unions (ICTU) and the Irish National Organisation of the Unemployed (INOU) argued that a rate of £5 per hour was the minimum required to improve the quality of life of the low paid. They stated that market conditions already made £4.40 lower than the wage rate paid for cleaning staff and fast food operators, particularly in urban areas. In response to this, the Small Firms Association (SFA) conducted a survey of its members.[6] If a minimum wage of £5 per hour were imposed, the survey showed that one in three firms would let staff go and half of the respondents would place expansion plans on hold. The director of the SFA stated that employers would replace unskilled workers with more highly skilled workers, implying that those without skills were not productive enough to earn £5 per hour. He concluded that unskilled workers would be 'permanently locked out of jobs'.

In April 2000, the minimum wage was finally implemented under the terms shown in Table 7.2. Notice that the government established rates for workers under 18 years of age and for those in training which are lower than the rate set for 'experienced' adults. The minimum wage of £4.40 for experienced adults pleased employers rather than unions. On the other hand, labour unions and other organisations that had lobbied for years for this legislation were pleased that the principle was adopted.

Table 7.2: Minimum wage rates in Ireland (2000–02)

	Rates of pay		
	2000	2001	2002
Employee	**(1 April)**	**(1 July)**	**(1 October)**
Adult experienced (£)	£4.40	£4.70	£5.00
Adult experienced (€)	€5.59	€5.97	€6.35
Under 18	70% of adult hourly rate		
Over 18 in structured training or study:*			
1st period	75% of adult hourly rate		
2nd period	80% of adult hourly rate		
3rd period	90% of adult hourly rate		

* Each period is one-third of the training period. A period must be at least one month and no longer than 12 months.

Source: Department of Enterprise, Trade and Employment

The government, in negotiations with the social partners for the Programme for Prosperity and Fairness, agreed that workers who are being paid the minimum wage should not pay income tax after 2002.

The question remains, what should we expect from the minimum wage? The case study below suggests that the effects will not be as good as its advocates expect or (thankfully) as bad as economists predict!

CASE STUDY

Extract from *The Irish Times*
French paradox casts long shadow on minimum wage
by Lara Marlowe

As the Republic prepares to adopt a minimum wage for the first time on April 1st, France celebrated the 30th anniversary of the Minimum Guaranteed Interprofessional Growth Salary (SMIC) on January 2nd.

Its precursor, the Minimum Guaranteed Interprofessional Salary (SMIG) came into effect 50 years ago on February 12th.

The half-century gap between France's adoption of a minimum salary and the

———→

imposition of a £4.40 hourly wage in the Republic is the result of a long difference of opinion between continental economists and politicians and their counterparts among *les Anglo-Saxons*, as the French refer to the English-speaking world.

The French insisted that by increasing demand, the guaranteed minimum wage stimulated economic growth. Furthermore, it was an instrument of social justice, and therefore an untouchable sacred cow.

British and US economists saw the minimum wage as artificial interference in the law of supply and demand and a deterrent to hiring that could only aggravate unemployment. The challenge was to find a compromise between the 'unemployment' created by French-style policies and the 'poverty trap' in Britain and the US.

Over the past decade, the French and Anglo-American points of view have drawn closer.

Two US economics professors introduced a comparative study of the New Jersey and Pennsylvania fast food industries in 1992. To widespread amazement, it proved that in New Jersey – where the minimum wage was higher – employment increased, while jobs were lost in Pennsylvania.

Two years later, the British economists Dickens, Machin and Manning concluded that a reasonable minimum wage provided an incentive to work where there had been none, without making a company less competitive . . .

Ironically, while others are coming around to the French view, the minimum wage has lost some of its lustre here. It has not fulfilled the goal of establishing a social safety net for all employees. More than 15 per cent of the French workforce – 2.8 million people – earns less than the minimum monthly wage . . . and this often in accordance with the law . . .

By establishing part-time, minimum wage 'Employment Solidarity Contracts' (CES), the French government has undermined its own objectives of financial equality.

Another government measure that allows apprentices to be paid as little as 25 per cent of the SMIC contradicts the idea that the minimum wage ends the exploitation of young workers . . .

Source: *The Irish Times*, 28 January 2000

Questions

1. Using the model of the labour market, explain why the British and American economists believed that minimum wage legislation 'could only aggravate unemployment'.
2. The belief of French economists that a minimum wage stimulates economic growth can also be explained using the model of the labour market. However, it requires reconsidering the concept of 'derived' demand. Using diagrams for a goods market and the labour market, show how the two markets are interacting.
3. The French experience was not a complete success. Why? What lessons can the Irish government learn from the French experience?

Answers on website

Conclusions and criticisms of the neoclassical model of the labour market

The neoclassical model of the labour market continues to influence the thinking of economists and policy-makers. The student, when reading this section, should recognise the similarities between the model of the product market and the model of the labour market. We have essentially adapted the 'tools of the trade' and used them to analyse a different market.

While one may question many of the assumptions of the product market, applying them to the labour market seems to be inappropriate. We speak of a labour market as if labour is homogeneous. We discuss workers as if they were interchangeable. While wheat may be homogeneous, labourers are not: workers differ in their training and their ability. There are huge differences in the education and training required for various occupations and professions. However, we lump everyone together to discuss the 'labour market'.

The labour demand curve is based on marginal productivity. Workers are not uniformly productive, either when compared to each other, or in comparison with themselves! Changes in health and personal circumstances cause the productivity of even the most stable workers to vary.

Also, although firms may be willing to vary their output decision fairly quickly, they are unlikely to change their employment levels, particularly if their workers are skilled. 'Derived demand' for labour suggests that if demand for a product increases, firms will demand more labour. Workers with sufficient skills may not be available. Similarly, if demand for a product falls, management may be reluctant to make labour redundant. Recognising the hardship caused by unemployment and the problems in reassembling a skilled group of employees, they may prefer to maintain their labour force in the hope that the demand for their product will increase. In other words, the labour market may not respond as quickly, or as predictably as the product market to a change in demand or supply.

In product markets, we expect a single price, except in cases of imperfect competition. Wage differentials in sectors of the labour market occur for many different reasons. These include working conditions in certain sectors, trade union power, workers' qualifications and skills, geographic immobility and discrimination. Even in a given industry, in a particular firm, one employee may be paid more than another to do the same job, simply because the employer values that employee more.

Alternative labour market models have been offered by Barbara Bergmann, Gary Becker, Victor Fuchs and others. Students who are interested in the criticisms above are encouraged to read more about this complex and important topic.

7.2 CAPITAL AND INTEREST

We will now look at the market for capital. In this instance, we are looking at the relationship between the interest rate, the payment for capital and the amount of capital goods which are demanded and supplied by households and firms. We will begin by defining some relevant terms.

Definition
Capital goods are durable assets used during the production process.

Durable means that the assets are useful for longer than one time period. They include plant, machinery, tools and factories.

Definition
The capital stock includes all of the capital goods controlled by a firm.

We measure the capital stock of a firm or of a country at a point in time.
The capital stock of a firm loses value over time. This is called depreciation.

Definition
Depreciation refers to the decline in value of the capital stock due to its use in production or its age.

In order to maintain its capital stock, a firm must replace the machinery as it wears out. Investment changes the capital stock.

Definition
Investment refers to additions to the capital stock purchased or leased over a particular time period.

Investment is a flow. Gross investment is the total increase to the capital stock over a period of time, including the additions necessary to replace depreciating assets. Net investment constitutes an increase over and above the replacements needed to maintain the capital stock.

Demand for capital goods

As in the labour market, the demand for capital goods is a derived demand. Firms invest in capital assets based on current demand and anticipated future demand for their product. Unlike the labour demand curve, the relevant time span for investment decisions may be considerably longer than a single period.
Marginal productivity theory can be used to derive the demand curve for capital goods.

Definition
The marginal revenue product of capital is the extra revenue generated by additions to the capital stock.

In this case, if the size and training of the labour force is held constant and capital is added, additional units of capital are less productive than previous units.
For a profit-maximising firm, the addition to revenue which results from buying or leasing the capital asset must be greater than or equal to the cost of the asset. The process of determining when the two are equal is more difficult than in the labour

market because a capital good is durable. The benefits accrue over a number of years. Therefore, we have to estimate the revenue stream generated over the life of the asset and compare that with the cost of the asset.

Present value and future value

We will try to clarify the process by looking at an example. We return to the owner of Hibs Ltd who is thinking of purchasing a new piece of machinery valued at €10,000. Ms Hibs anticipates that the asset will last for two years and will have no salvage value. She expects the asset to generate the following revenue stream:

Year	Revenue
1	6,000
2	7,000

She begins by estimating the present value of this revenue stream.

Definition
Present value is the estimate of what the revenue stream of a capital asset is worth today.

To grasp this concept, we can consider an alternative decision which Ms Hibs could make. Instead of purchasing a new piece of machinery, she could buy bonds which would earn a rate of interest of 10% per annum, compounded annually. In this case, we are considering the future value of the €10,000. If she invests this money today, what will it be worth in one year, in two years? We can use the future value formula to calculate the value of €10,000 in one year.

$$FV = PV\,(1+i) \qquad (7.3)$$

where PV represents the present value and FV represents the future value of this sum at the interest rate of i. In this example, with a 10% rate of interest, the future value of €10,000 at the end of the first year will be €11,000.

Since the interest is compounded annually, the interest from year one is added to the principal. In year two, Ms Hibs will earn 10% interest on €11,000. At the end of two periods, Ms Hibs would receive a sum of €12,100.

The general form if there is more than one period is:

$$FV = PV(1+i)^t \qquad (7.4)$$

where t represents the number of time periods over which the sum is invested.

Suppose that Ms Hibs discovers that she will receive €12,100 in two years. She wants to know how much that sum is worth today, in other words, what is the present value of the €12,100? The general form of the equation used to solve this problem is derived from the future value formula. We simply solve for the present value.

$$PV = \frac{FV}{(1+i)^t} \qquad (7.5)$$

If the market rate of interest is 10%, the present value is €12,100 or €10,000. In this case we are discounting the future value. $\frac{}{(1 + 0.1)^2}$

Definition
Discounting is the process of reducing the future value of a sum of money or a flow of revenues to the present value.

The problem which confronts us with the revenue stream of the capital asset is slightly more complicated because the revenues for each year must be considered separately. To calculate the present value, we will use the following equation:

$$PV = \sum \frac{R_t}{(1 + i)^t} \tag{7.6}$$

where R represents the additional revenue earned by the asset in period t. The expression $\sum$ means that we add together the discounted revenue for each of the t periods. We can use this equation to calculate the present value of the revenue stream which the new piece of machinery will generate.

$$PV = \frac{6,000}{(1 + 0.1)} + \frac{7,000}{(1 + 0.1)^2} = €11,240$$

Now, we compare this amount with the cost of the machinery. Obviously, €11,240 is significantly greater than €10,000. In this case, Ms Hibs will clearly benefit from purchasing this asset. However, she would still purchase the asset if the present value was €11,000 or €10,500. Indeed, we would expect Ms Hibs to invest in capital goods up to the point where the present value of the revenue generated by the asset is equal to the cost of buying the asset.

Rate of return on capital and the interest rate

We will now look at this problem from a slightly different perspective. We will try to determine the minimum rate of return which Ms Hibs must earn in order for her to decide to acquire an additional capital asset.

Definition
The rate of return on capital is a measure of the productivity of a particular capital asset.

We can calculate the rate of return using the following formula:

$$C = \frac{R_1}{(1 + r)} + \frac{R_2}{(1 + r)^2} \tag{7.7}$$

where C is the cost of the asset, R_1 and R_2 are the revenues earned in periods 1 and 2 respectively and r is the rate of return on the asset. Substitute the figures for the asset purchased by Hibs Ltd into Equation 7.7 and solve for r.

$$10,000 = \frac{6,000}{(1 + r)} + \frac{7,000}{(1 + r)^2}$$

The rate of return equals 0.19 or 19% for this asset. By comparing the cost of the asset to the present value of the anticipated revenue stream, we realised that Ms Hibs, as the owner of a profit-maximising firm, will purchase this asset. We reach the same conclusion by comparing the rate of return on capital to the interest rate. Using this form of analysis, we can see that Ms Hibs will buy or lease the asset because the rate of return on capital is greater than the 10% interest rate. Further, as long as the rate of return on capital is greater than the interest rate, we assume that a profit-maximising firm will continue to invest in capital assets.

Interest rates and the demand for capital goods

Finally, we can consider the relationship between the interest rate and the demand for capital goods. From our discussion above, we assume that capital becomes less productive as more capital is employed, *ceteris paribus*. We also know that a profit-maximising firm will acquire additional capital goods if the rate of return on capital is greater than or equal to the interest rate. What happens if the interest rate falls?

As interest rates fall, *ceteris paribus*, firms will acquire more capital goods. Although the new acquisitions are less productive than previous capital goods, the lower interest rate means that money invested in bonds will earn lower returns. Even less productive capital assets will earn more than the market rate of interest. The relationship between interest rates and the demand for capital goods is negative. As interest rates fall, the demand for capital goods increases. Figure 7.10 shows a downward sloping demand curve for capital goods.

Figure 7.10: The demand curve for capital goods

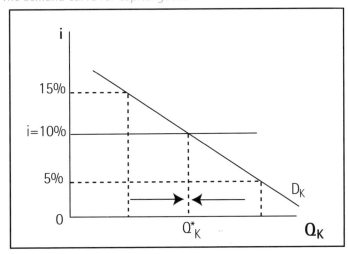

D_K represents the demand curve for capital goods. It is downward sloping: the lower the interest rate, the larger the amount of capital goods demanded. We can think of this curve as representing, for any interest rate, the amount of capital goods demanded by profit-maximising firms, *ceteris paribus*. What variables are held constant? Among others, they include the size and training of the labour force, the taxation system and firms' expectations about the future.

The supply curve for capital goods

Funds are needed to finance capital goods. Whereas the labour supply curve is influenced by the labour/leisure trade-off, the supply curve for capital goods is influenced by the trade-off between consumption and savings. Households provide the funds for capital goods. As interest rates increase, the supply of capital increases. At higher rates of interest, households are willing to forgo present consumption in favour of future consumption. The supply curve for capital (S_K) is upward sloping as depicted in Figure 7.11.

Figure 7.11: The supply curve for capital goods

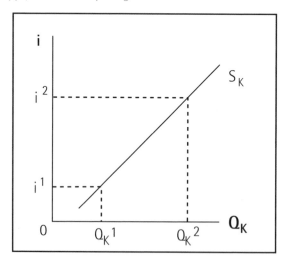

At an interest rate of i^1, Q_K^1 is supplied. As interest rates rise, the supply of capital increases. With a higher interest rate of i^2, Q_K^2 is supplied.

Equilibrium in the capital market

The demand curve D_K is derived from the demand for final output produced in the goods market. It is downward sloping. The supply curve shows the quantity of capital at any given interest rate. It is upward sloping. The equilibrium interest rate is determined by the demand for and supply of capital. In graphic terms, equilibrium occurs at the intersection of the demand curve D_K and the supply curve S_K. The interest rate represented by i^* is the return on capital that clears the market for capital goods. This is shown in Figure 7.12.

Figure 7.12:   Capital market equilibrium

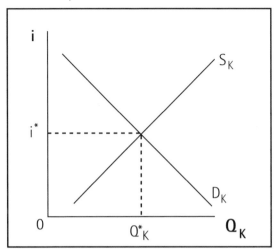

Adjustment to equilibrium is an automatic process in the market for capital goods. For example, suppose the market interest rate is above i*. At any rate above the equilibrium interest rate there exists an excess supply. The actions of savers and investors in the capital market will eventually push interest rates downwards. The interest rate continues to fall until it reaches i* where the market is in equilibrium. The inverse is true for interest rates below equilibrium where adjustments will occur upwards from positions of excess demand.

Conclusions and criticisms of the neoclassical model of the capital market

In this analysis, we assume that firms have perfect knowledge of their present and future revenue streams. This assumption is questionable in the short run. In the long run, over the lifetime of a durable asset, it is unrealistic. Today, all companies are concerned that new technologies will make capital goods obsolete before they are fully depreciated. Firms must begin the decision-making process concerning the acquisition of capital goods based on an estimate of the additional revenue that each asset will generate. Although firms face considerable uncertainty, economists rationalise this by saying that firms act 'as if' they have perfect knowledge.

Also, the analysis of the capital market presents a single interest rate established through market competition. In reality, interest rates offered to firms differ for a number of reasons. One of the main reasons why interest rates differ is risk. If the lender is concerned that the loan may not be repaid, s/he will charge a higher rate of interest as a premium against that risk. Interest rates also vary depending on the duration of the loan. Also, small loans generally pay higher rates of interest than large loans. The costs of administering the loan are high relative to the size of the loan and these costs are paid for by the borrower.

7.3 LAND AND RENT

Rent is the return on land. The term 'rent' can be quite misleading as it means different things to different people.[7] In particular, it is often confused with another term frequently used by economists. The term is 'economic rent'.

Definition
Economic rent is a payment in excess of the opportunity cost.

It is a surplus payment to any factor in excess of the minimum payment needed to keep a factor in its present use (see Appendix 7.1). This minimum payment is known as transfer earnings because if earnings fall below this level, the factor input would be withdrawn, i.e. it would be transferred to some other activity.

Definition
Transfer earnings is what a resource could earn in its best alternative use. It is the opportunity cost of employing a factor.

The essential feature of economic rent is that it is a surplus. Hence, its payment is not necessary to guarantee the supply of a particular factor.[8]

The terms 'economic rent' and 'transfer earnings' can be applied to all factor resource markets. We will attempt to clarify these terms in the context of the labour market shown in Figure 7.13.

Figure 7.13: Economic rent and transfer earnings

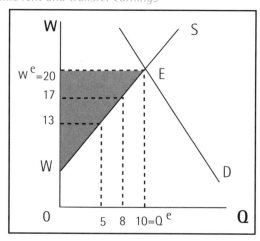

Let us suppose that the actual market wage is €20. In the above market, the fifth worker is willing to work for a wage of €13. This amount is equal to her transfer earnings and her economic rent is the surplus, i.e. €7. If the eighth worker is willing to work only at the higher wage of €17, her economic rent is only €3 (€20 – €17). The tenth worker is the final addition to the workforce. Her transfer earnings amount to €20 with no surplus or economic rent.

In Figure 7.13 transfer earnings is given by the area under the supply curve [0WEQ^e]. The shaded area between the supply curve and the factor price [WW^{e}E], is equal to economic rent.

In reality, most factor earnings are a composite of transfer earnings and economic rent. It is the elasticity of supply of the factor input that determines the relative size of each component of total income. If the supply curve for a factor input is perfectly elastic, all of factor earnings will be transfer earnings. Continuing with the labour market, for example, each worker will earn exactly the amount necessary to persuade them to remain in the industry. As the supply curve becomes increasingly inelastic, the area of economic rent increases. Many of the individuals working in the market would remain in their position for a wage which is far less than the equilibrium wage.

In terms of land, economic rent is specifically the price paid for the use of land and other fixed resources. It is this fixed supply which distinguishes rental payments from other factor payments.

As with all other economic resources, rent can be explained in terms of demand and supply analysis. The demand for fixed resources is a derived demand: it stems from the products produced on the land. Figure 7.14 shows the market for land. In this market, we are looking at the relationship between rent, the price of land, and the quantity of land that is demanded and supplied.

Figure 7.14:   The market for land

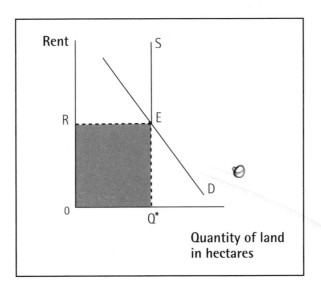

Quantity of land
in hectares

The downward sloping demand curve for land is derived from the marginal revenue product of land. In turn, the marginal revenue product of land is determined by the physical productivity of the land and the marginal revenue of the product produced on the land.

The demand curve is downward sloping because land exhibits diminishing marginal returns. The first units of land that are employed are the most productive.

Referring again to Figure 7.14, we observe that the supply curve for land is perfectly inelastic. This is because the supply of land is virtually fixed.[9]

The equilibrium rent R is determined by the intersection of the demand curve D and the supply curve S. With a fixed supply of land at Q*, the amount of economic rent is given by the shaded area [0REQ*].

In the market for land, the entire rental price is an economic rent. Why? Since land is a natural resource, fixed in supply and provided free by nature, the cost of production or supply cost is zero. Hence, the opportunity cost of supplying a fixed amount of this resource is zero. Since there are no transfer earnings, the entire price of land is an economic rent. If the economic rent is reduced or even removed, the supply of land remains the same.[10]

Given that the supply of land is fixed, demand becomes the sole 'active' determination of rent. A change in demand will cause a change in the rental price. For example, agricultural land along the west coast of Ireland is being bought by developers to build holiday homes. This constitutes a 'change in demand'. The marginal revenue product of land used for development is higher than the marginal revenue product of land devoted to agriculture. The demand curve for land shifts out to the right and rental prices increase. The subsequent higher rental prices do not induce landlords to increase supply. The only effect of the increase in demand is a rent increase.

The inverse is true for a decline in the demand for land. Changes in population, economic prosperity and property tax are examples of the factors which influence the demand for land and natural resources.

7.4 ENTREPRENEURSHIP AND PROFIT

A fourth category of factor inputs is entrepreneurship. It is distinct from other resources in the economy in the sense that it is difficult to define and impossible to measure. The entrepreneur receives profit as a payment.[11]

Profit is different from other factor prices because it is a residual; it is paid out to the entrepreneur after all other factor payments are made. Also, profit is not guaranteed. In fact, it may be negative in the short run.

As we mentioned in Chapter 5, the use of the term 'profit' can be quite misleading (see Section 5.3 for a more complete discussion). In particular, accountants and economists define the word differently. Profit as defined by the accountant, is simply the difference between total revenue and total cost. The economist includes normal profit as an economic cost. A normal profit is the opportunity cost of the entrepreneur. Therefore, if total revenues equal total economic costs, the firm has made a 'normal' profit. For the economist, if total revenues exceed economic costs, the firm makes a 'supernormal' or economic profit. In terms of the difference between normal profit and supernormal profit, the former can be regarded as the entrepreneur's transfer earnings and the latter as the entrepreneur's economic rent.

There are several explanations for the existence of economic profits. We will consider three. Economic profits can be considered as:

1. a reward for uninsured risk;
2. a reward for innovation;
3. the result of a monopolistic market structure.

A brief explanation follows.

A reward for uninsured risk

For Frank Knight and other economists, profit is the reward entrepreneurs receive for taking risks in times of uncertainty.[12] Uncertainty arises from dynamic changes in the economy. Profit is the reward for a risk successfully taken. Knight distinguished between insurable and uninsurable risks. Insurable risk is covered by insurance premiums, he argued. Uninsurable risks are the source of profit. 'Business ability' was also a factor in the determination of profit.

A reward for innovation

Others define profit as a payment for innovation which can be defined as the application of invention to industry. The great Austrian economist Joseph Schumpeter was the main exponent of this theory (see Information Box 7.2). The act of innovation as described by Schumpeter was to be distinguished from the act of invention. Schumpeter's innovator, called the 'entrepreneur', was responsible for the dynamic characteristic of the capitalist system.

For Schumpeter, successful innovation depended on leadership rather than intelligence. The result of successful innovation was profit which was a central feature of the capitalist system.

INFORMATION BOX 7.2

Joseph Schumpeter (1883–1950)

Joseph Schumpeter was born and educated in Austria. While at the University of Vienna he studied under Bohm-Bawerk (refer to Section 7.1 and marginal productivity theory). He began teaching economics at the University of Czernowitz and later at the University of Graz. He was also the Austrian Minister of Finance for a brief period after World War 1. Between 1925 and 1932 he held the Chair of Public Finance at Bonn. After emigrating to the US in 1932 he became a Professor at Harvard University where he remained until his retirement in 1950.

One of Schumpeter's greatest contributions to economics was his economic character, the 'entrepreneur'. The entrepreneur played a central role in the capitalist system, argued Schumpeter. He was the agent largely responsible for change and for economic development. For Schumpeter, the entrepreneur's role was vastly different from that of the labourer, landowner, capitalist and so on. The entrepreneur was the person who innovates, the person who creates 'new combinations' in production.

$\longrightarrow$

Schumpeter identified several types of innovation. They include the creation of a new product, the creation of a new method of production, the opening of new markets, the discovery of a new source of supply and new organisations of industry.

Schumpeter was a strong supporter of enterprise, capitalism and the *laissez-faire* doctrine. Within a capitalist system, economic development is both a dynamic and erratic process, he argued. He openly acknowledged the dangers (arising not from its weaknesses but rather from its strengths) that inherently exist in a capitalist system. He discussed 'creative destruction', i.e. the implementation of new combinations that perpetuate economic change. He recognised that this was a disruptive process which required limited government intervention to reduce inequalities, control monopolies, smooth out the business cycle and so on. However, he believed that continuous intervention by the state would eventually undermine the role of the entrepreneur. The performance of the economy would begin to falter, he argued. In the long run, Schumpeter predicted that capitalism would decay and be replaced with socialism.

Schumpeter's major works include *Theory of Economic Development* (1912) written when he was 28 years old. *Business Cycles* (1939) has been rediscovered in recent years, and recognised as an important work concerning an economic phenomenon which is constantly discussed but poorly understood. The entrepreneur plays a central role in Schumpeter's model of the business cycle. *History of Economic Analysis* (1954) was published posthumously. In it, Schumpeter critically reviews the work of economic scholars including Smith and Marshall.

Schumpeter is not as widely known as Keynes nor did he hold Keynes in high esteem. His economic works are even further removed than Keynes' from the neoclassical tradition. Still, both economists are undoubtedly among the greatest economists of the twentieth century. Many current writers, particularly in the area of business economics, owe an intellectual debt to Schumpeter. He recognised that the individual contributed more than her marginal revenue product. The entrepreneur was the central figure in economic development.

A more recent account of innovation has been given by Michael Porter (see Information Box 7.3).

INFORMATION BOX 7.3

Michael Porter and Innovation

Michael Porter is regarded as the world's leading authority on competitive advantage. By competitive advantage, he is referring to the ability of certain firms to create and sustain a dominant position in particular industries for a significant period of time. Central to this theory is the importance of innovation.[1]

The factor conditions referred to by Porter move beyond the traditional endowments of land, labour and capital emphasised by the classical economists. Factors vital to economic growth are created, not inherited. The stock of factors is less important than the rate at which they are upgraded.

$\longrightarrow$

Porter groups factors into broad categories including human resources, physical resources, knowledge resources, capital resources and infrastructure. Competitive advantage is based on the efficient employment of factors which may be basic or advanced. Basic factors are internationally mobile and are attracted to where they are most efficiently employed. Advanced factors require sustained investment and are necessary to achieve higher-order competitive advantages which are difficult for other firms to duplicate.

For Porter, innovation is the key to achieving and maintaining competitive advantage. He defines innovation as 'improvements in technology and better methods or ways of doing things' that are 'commercialised'. He goes on to say that innovation can manifest itself in many different ways. They include product changes, process changes, new approaches to marketing, new forms of distribution and new conceptions of scope (notice the similarity to Schumpeter's 'new combinations'). Innovation grows out of pressure, challenges and change. Whereas many view change as unwelcome, Porter sees it as both necessary and desirable. Innovation and change are inextricably linked.[2]

Once innovation is achieved (more likely in a mundane manner rather than in any radical fashion), continuous improving must follow so that the advantage is not lost to competitors who attempt to imitate any improvement.

Finally, 'innovation is the result of unusual effort' which ultimately must lead to unnatural acts by firms if the advantage achieved from innovation is to be sustained. This behaviour is inherent in 'leaders', i.e. in firms or individuals that recognise the dynamics of an industry and the importance of embracing and institutionalising change rather than avoiding it. Of course, sixty years ago Schumpeter said the same thing!

1 For a short summary of the book (*The Competitive Advantage of Nations*), read the article 'The Competitive Advantage of Nations' by M. Porter, *Harvard Business Review*, Mar.–Apr. 1990.
2 A leading guru on innovation and entrepreneurship is Peter Drucker. To understand why he views entrepreneurship as a practice which can be successfully managed, read his 1985 bestseller *Innovation and Entrepreneurship*.

The result of a monopolistic market structure

Until now, we have discussed factor markets under conditions of perfect competition. Consider the case of a monopoly. A monopoly is a sole producer in an industry. Its ability to restrict output, control price and deter entry allow supernormal profits to persist. If the demand for the monopolist's product or service is high, profits will also remain high. Profits arising from a monopoly position are viewed as socially less desirable than profits sourced from risk and from innovation. And unlike the other two sources, government action may be taken in order to restrict monopoly profits.

7.5 NATIONAL PARTNERSHIP AGREEMENTS (NPAs)

In the previous sections, we considered the factors of production separately, as if the decisions made by the entrepreneur were independent of the decisions made by labour.

The neoclassical approach suggests that each factor acts independently and receives what it deserves based on its own marginal productivity. Government never constructively enters into the factor market. When it does 'interfere' with the labour market, as with the imposition of the minimum wage, unemployment is the result.

This model of the factor markets is of some use in explaining and predicting events in large economies such as the United States. Ergas (1984) suggests that in the US, market changes which lead to the reallocation of the factors of production are perceived as legitimate. There is a strong 'exit' mechanism, where resources 'vote with their feet'.[13] For example, if steel cannot be produced cheaply enough in Pittsburgh to compete on the world markets, the owners of the mills can move to another state or another country where it can produce steel cost effectively. The unemployed steelworkers can move to a new industry in Pittsburgh, or leave the area to find employment. Because the country is large and the economy is diversified, there is scope for movement of the factors of production as well as a strong belief in the efficiency and fairness of the market.

Ergas points out that western European economies rely on 'voice' rather than 'exit'. He states that 'change is induced through consensus and through the conscious societal weighting of interests and options, buttressed by mechanisms for redistributing income between winners and losers'.[14] He believes that Europeans do not have the same 'faith' in the legitimacy of market outcomes. He states, '. . . it can be argued that the Western European economies, being considerably smaller, could not smoothly absorb the levels of social conflict tolerable in large, geographically mobile and diverse societies like the United States'.[15]

The Irish economy is both 'small' and 'open'. Its economic activity is very small compared to the US or Japan. Ireland is also relatively small in comparison to the other EU economies. Because of this, it must accept many policies that are implemented to benefit larger member states. It is open in the sense that Ireland is a 'trading' nation. Both imports and exports are very large in relation to national income. This means that the Irish economy is vulnerable to disruptions in international markets.

Because the Irish economy is both small and open, problems in the national and international economy can have destabilising consequences, which are unacceptable to its citizens. The neoclassical model, therefore, is a poor starting point to discuss the Irish factor markets, particularly since 1987. The factor markets in Ireland do not act independently. Government is actively involved with representatives of business, labour unions, the farming community and the voluntary sector to establish an economic and social framework called the national partnership agreement. Five agreements have been negotiated since 1987. A brief history of the national partnership agreements follows, with details of the five national wage agreements and a concluding section wherein we consider the future of the agreements.

History of the national partnership agreements (NPAs)

In the 1980s, the Irish economy was in crisis. During a prolonged recession, the unemployment rate approached 18% in spite of massive emigration. The spectre of national insolvency loomed as the debt to GNP ratio approached 130%. This meant that the national debt was 30% higher than national income. To pay for government spending and to service the debt, rates of tax increased. The high tax rate combined with a high inflation rate meant that the living standard of workers was falling. Many emigrated to the UK and the US. Workers that remained 'took to the streets' for higher pay, disrupting the production of goods and the provision of services.

In 1986, the National Economic and Social Council (NESC), an advisory board comprised of organisations representing employers, trade unions and farming organisations, together with civil servants published the *Strategy for Development*. This formed the basis of the first of five successive national partnership agreements (NPAs).

The NPAs are negotiated between the social partners. The composition of the social partners for the first three agreements included the government and organisations representing trade unions, employers and farming interests. Beginning with the second partnership agreement, submissions were considered from organisations representing children, parents, women, religious denominations, various trade interests and the unemployed. In the fourth and fifth partnership agreements, the composition of the social partners expanded to include the community and voluntary sector.

As the membership expanded, so has the number of topics included in the agreement. One of the principal reasons for entering into the agreement was to break the 'wage/price' spiral that caused labour unrest and contributed to inflation in the 1980s. Periodic increases in wages are negotiated as part of the agreement. The social partners also outline the broad parameters of tax reform, social welfare payments and government spending. They 'rowed in' to support the government in the preparations for the single currency. They agreed to changes to improve the industrial relations machinery and to modernise the public sector.

The NPAs survived changes in government and were negotiated with various coalitions. This demonstrates the depth of commitment to consensus that bridged narrow organisational self-interest and political divides.

Of particular interest to us in this chapter, because it is related to the labour market, is the national wage agreement (NWA) which has been a cornerstone of each of the NPAs to date. Generally, this is the part of the agreement that receives the most coverage in the national press. Unfortunately, an NPA is deemed a success if the provisions of the pay agreement are negotiated and maintained. This is an unfair assessment because even the most cursory examination of an NPA reveals that it is more than just a wage agreement. It is a general framework for economic and social progress.

The national wage agreements (NWAs)

The general thrust of the NWAs has been to increase 'take-home pay' while restraining 'nominal pay'. In other words, gross pay, or the amount paid by firms increased by small amounts each year. At the same time, the government implemented changes to personal taxation so that the net pay of workers increased. The social partners hoped that by keeping wage increases low, Irish firms could attain international competitiveness and hire more workers.

Maintaining moderate increases in gross wages meant that firms could retain profits. This provided the source of funds needed to increase investment. Particularly in 1987, when the first agreement was negotiated, the lack of growth in investment for machinery was a cause of great concern. The social partners agreed that this had to change to support higher levels of employment in the future.

Table 7.3 shows the parameters of the five NWAs.

Table 7.3: National wage agreements (1987–2000)

Agreement	Programme for National Recovery (PNR)	Programme for Economic and Social Progress (PESP)	Programme for Competitiveness and Work (PCW)	Partnership 2000 for Inclusion, Employment and Competitiveness (Partnership 2000)	Programme for Prosperity and Fairness (PPF)
Basic wage increase	1988 2.5% 1989 2.5% 1990 2.5%	1991 4% 1992 3% 1993 3.75% Jul–Dec 1996 1%	1994 2% 1995 2.5% Jan–Jun 1996 2.5% Oct 99–Mar 2000 1%	1997 2.5% 1998 2.25% Jan–Sep 1999 1.5% (once-off lump sum)	Apr 2000–Mar 01 5.5% Apr 01–Mar 02 5.5%+2% Apr 02–Dec 02 4% + 1%
Considerations for the low paid	none	If change to basic wage results in an increase of less than: 1991 £5.00 per week 1992 £4.25 pw 1993 £5.75 pw a higher % increase can be agreed through local negotiations.	If change to basic wage results in an increase of less than: 1995 £3.50 pw Jan–Jun 96 £3.50 pw a higher % increase can be agreed through local negotiations.	If change to basic wage results in an increase of less than: 1998 £3.50 pw Jan–Sep 99 £2.40 pw Oct 99–Mar 00 £1.60 pw a higher % increase can be agreed through local negotiations. Applies on pro-rata basis to part-time employees.	If change to basic wage results in an increase of less than: Apr 00–Mar 01 £12 pw Apr 01–Mar 02 £11 pw Apr 02–Dec 02 £9 pw a higher % increase can be agreed through local negotiations. Applies on pro-rata basis to part-time employees.
Local bargaining	none	Exceptionally, an additional 3% can be added over the period of the agreement.	none	• Beginning in 1999, an additional 2% can be added over the rest of the agreement. • Financial participation linked to local partnership agreements.	• Financial participation linked to local partnership agreements.

Source: Department of Enterprise, Trade and Employment.

The duration of each programme is approximately three years. Annual percentage increases to the basic wage varied between 2% and 7.5% for the fifteen-year period. Compliance with the terms of the national agreements is voluntary. An 'inability to pay' clause was introduced in the second agreement. It states that increases should be negotiated through industrial relations machinery, considering the competitive circumstances of the firm.

Also beginning with the second agreement, there were special considerations designed to increase the basic wage of the low paid. It should be noted that these considerations only apply to people on very low wages.[16] ICTU (Irish Congress of Trade Unions) expressed a desire to implement a minimum wage in the PESP published in 1991. This became a reality in 2000 as discussed in Section 7.1.

A local bargaining clause that allowed for a small additional increase in the basic wage was a feature of the second and fourth agreements.

The fourth agreement, Partnership 2000, promoted the development of 'enterprise partnership'. One of the topics discussed was 'financial involvement'. The ambiguity of language allowed business and labour to interpret this as a local bargaining clause. An enterprise, in compliance with the national wage agreement, could increase the basic wage by the amount specified in the NWA and implement an employee participation scheme in the form of gainsharing, profit sharing and employee share ownership schemes. Trade unions published local partnership agreements featuring employee participation schemes, providing models for other firms to follow.

One might wonder why the social partners did not object to this interpretation of the agreement. During Partnership 2000 (1997–2000), the unemployment rate was falling and skills shortages were developing in many industries. It is likely that the social partners believed that the NWA would unravel if enterprises did not have a way of increasing employee remuneration to attract and maintain their staff. The most recent agreement maintains the ambiguity.

What are these schemes? How do they differ from the more traditional forms of payment that we discussed earlier in the chapter? These issues are briefly explained in Information Box 7.4.

INFORMATION BOX 7.4

Employee Participation Schemes

Employee participation scheme is an umbrella term that includes gainsharing, profit sharing and employee share ownership plans. These are variable wage approaches. Virtually all enterprises pay a fixed basic wage. An increasing number of enterprises are also including a variable wage component in their remuneration packet. The size of the payment changes from period to period according to the performance of the enterprise. It is never negative, but in some periods, there may be no variable payment.

In their purest form, all employees of an enterprise participate in the scheme for an equal share. Research suggests that employee participation schemes work best when they incorporate mechanisms for employee involvement in enterprise decision making.

→

Gainsharing is an incentive system that rewards employees for improved performance. The gain is accrued through either productivity improvements or cost-cutting measures. The amount of the gain is calculated using a previously agreed formula and shared between employees and the organisation. Gainsharing is not necessarily linked to profit. Theoretically, employees can share a 'gain' even in years when an enterprise is unprofitable. In practice, this is unlikely. Non-profit organisations and government departments can implement gainsharing schemes.

Profit sharing is an arrangement whereby employees receive some portion of a firm's profit. Generally, the payments are distributed in cash or company shares.

An *Employee Share Ownership Plan* (ESOP) is a legally established method by which a company distributes shares to its employees. Such plans are often, but not always, linked to profit. An ESOP is designed to give employees a long-term, concentrated holding in shares. Both profit sharing schemes and ESOPs are only appropriate for firms in the private sector.

Employee participation schemes are supported by important European and Irish institutions. These institutions attempt to influence enterprises to implement these forms of remuneration in conjunction with local partnership agreements. They believe that linking pay to productivity and profit will encourage labour to 'think like owners'.

These schemes are obviously different from the model of wage determination described in Section 7.1. For one thing, profit sharing and share ownership schemes reward labour with part of the income generally awarded to the owners of capital and entrepreneurs. Second, if these schemes are properly implemented, the role of labour changes. It is not simply reacting to changes imposed by the manager or entrepreneur. Labour is actually proposing and implementing change.

Negotiations for the PPF, published in 1999 were particularly difficult. Labour market shortages meant the firms in some sectors, particularly those dominated by multinational corporations, were offering wage increases at the end of Partnership 2000 which were above the agreed limits to attract and retain staff. These increases were in excess of what other sectors, often dominated by indigenous firms, could afford to pay.

Workers were concerned that they were not benefiting sufficiently from the economic 'boom'. The wage increases for the PPF were higher than for any other agreement. However, when the inflation rate increased to 6% during 2000, it completely wiped out the value of the 5.5% increase negotiated for that year. ICTU used the review clause that was part of the agreement to insist that the pay increase be renegotiated. After another round of intensive negotiations, unions and employers' organisations agreed to an additional 2% increase to be paid from April 2001 and a 1%, once-off lump sum to be paid from April 2002. The government had already signalled significant tax cuts to 'copperfasten' the agreement.

Do the national wage agreements work?

This question is difficult to answer. In other chapters we will discuss the spectacular performance of the Irish economy during the 1990s. Most commentators believe that the national partnership agreements helped to establish the conditions for the recovery of the Irish economy.

In this section we will approach this question from the point of view of the labour market. Did NWAs improve the situation of Irish labour? One important labour market indicator is the unemployment rate. This is the number of unemployed people divided by the number of people in the labour force (see Section 17.2 for more information). Table 7.4 shows the numbers unemployed and the corresponding unemployment rates between 1988 and 2000.

Table 7.4: Unemployment in Ireland (1988–2000)

Year	Numbers Unemployed (thousands)	Unemployment rate (%)
1988	217.0	16.3
1989	196.8	15.0
1990	172.4	12.9
1991	198.5	14.7
1992	206.6	15.1
1993	220.1	15.7
1994	211.0	14.7
1995	177.4	12.2
1996	179.0	11.9
1997	159.0	10.3
1998	126.6	7.8
1999	96.9	5.7
2000	74.9	4.3

Source: Central Statistics Office.

As can be seen from Table 7.4, the unemployment rate remained persistently high until 1993. The years between 1990 and 1993 were particularly disappointing because the growth in national income as measured by GNP (see Table 7.5) coincided with an increase in the unemployment rate.

The unemployment rate dropped steadily after 1994. The drop in the unemployment rate is even more impressive because the size of labour force was increasing as emigrants returned home. Also, the percentage of 'long-term' unemployed (unemployed for more than one year) fell from 10.4% of the labour force in 1988 to 1.6% in 2000. The policy of the social partners to award low wage increases and to spread the benefits of employment throughout the labour force appears to have worked.

A second issue concerns the adherence of firms to wage increases negotiated under the partnership agreements. One can legitimately ask the question, if firms or the public sector do not adhere to the terms of the agreement, should they be negotiated? For one thing, the opportunity cost of negotiations is high. It takes months to conclude a deal. More importantly, the process loses credibility if participants do not 'follow the rules'. Further, the sectors (often unionised) that maintain the wage increases negotiated under the NWA, lose ground to sectors that do not.

Table 7.5 shows three series of annual data. The second column shows the increase negotiated for the private sector under the various NWAs. The third column shows the percentage increase in the hourly average manufacturing wage. The sectors covered by the manufacturing wage are mainly in the private sector.

Table 7.5: Comparison between the percentage increases negotiated under various NWAs, the average manufacturing wage and nominal GNP

Year	National wage agreement, base wage (% change)	Average manufacturing wage (% change)	Nominal GNP (% change)
1988	2.5%	4.7%	5.8%
1989	2.5%	4.0%	10.6%
1990	2.5%	3.9%	8.4%
1991	4.0%	4.4%	4.4%
1992	3.0%	4.0%	5.8%
1993	3.75%	5.4%	8.5%
1994	2.0%	2.9%	8.3%
1995	2.5%	2.2%	11.6%
1996	3.5%	2.5%	10.2%
1997	2.5%	3.3%	14.7%
1998	2.25%	4.1%	14.6%
1999	2.0%	5.8%	11.0%

Source: National Partnership Agreements; CSO, *Statistical Bulletins* various years.

During the first agreement (1988–90), the average increase in the manufacturing wage was consistently higher than the negotiated wage. During this period, the partnership process was gaining credibility. For the duration of the PESP (1991–93), the gap between the two narrowed. Also, for this agreement there was a local bargaining clause and special provision for additional increases for the low paid. Both of these clauses could legitimately widen the gap between the negotiated base wage and the actual manufacturing wage. Between 1994 and 1997, the negotiated increase and the actual increase were within 1% of each other.

The largest gap emerges at the end of Partnership 2000 (1998–99). It is too wide to be explained by the local bargaining clause and provisions for the low paid. During this period, there were shortages in many sectors of the labour market. It appears that compliance with the terms of the national wage agreement broke down as firms increased wages to attract and retain staff.

Another statistic, which helps to shed light on the 'mood' of the labour market, is the number of days lost due to industrial disputes. When workers 'vote with their feet', it shows their dissatisfaction with pay and working conditions. Table 7.6 shows the 'total days lost' due to industrial disputes between 1981 and 1999.

Table 7.6: Total days lost due to industrial disputes (1981–99)

Year	Total days lost	Year	Total days lost
1981	433,979	1991	85,513
1982	434,530	1992	190,609
1983	319,015	1993	61,312
1984	386,421	1994	25,550
1985	417,726	1995	130,300
1986	309,178	1996	114,584
1987	264,339	1997	54,508
1988	143,393	1998	37,374
1989	50,358	1999	215,157
1990	222,916		

Source: CSO, *Statistical Bulletin*, various years

The number of days lost because of industrial disputes was highest during the early and mid 1980s. This period preceded the first agreement, the Programme for National Recovery (1988–90). However, even during the period of the national agreements, there are some years where the number of days lost is quite high like 1990 and 1999. The figures for 2000 were not available for the publication of this book. However, at the end of 2000, the country experienced a 'winter of discontent' where teachers, taxi drivers, train and airline personnel 'took to the streets'. The increase in labour disputes in 1999 and 2000 may indicate that the limitations placed on wage increases, negotiated as part of the national partnership agreements, are no longer acceptable to labour. Time will tell if industrial disputes triggered both the beginning and the end of the national wage agreements.

Why is labour dissatisfied? Two reasons come to mind. First, the percentage increases in wages are much lower than the percentage increases in national income. This is shown in Table 7.5. The fourth column reports the percentage change in nominal Gross National Product (GNP) (see Section 10.3 for more information on GNP). GNP is considered to be a good measure of Irish national income. During the 1990s, the gap between the increase in GNP and the average manufacturing wage widened. If labour was not receiving what it believed to be a 'fair share' of national income, what was getting it?

Research conducted by Phillip Lane suggests that between the years of 1987 and 1996, the share of business income going to the owners of business in the form of profit was increasing, while the share paid to workers in the form of wages was falling. This is shown in Table 7.7.

Table 7.7: Share of business income paid as wages and profits

Year	Wage share (%)	Profit share (%)
1987	74.9	25.1
1988	72.2	27.8
1989	72.2	27.8
1990	69.6	30.4
1991	69.6	30.4
1992	71.2	28.8
1993	69.6	30.1
1994	69.3	30.7
1995	66.3	33.8
1996	65.2	34.8

Source: P. Lane. Profits and wages in Ireland, 1987–1996, *Journal of Statistical and Social Inquiry Society of Ireland*. Vol. XXVII, Part V, 1998.

The social partners realised that limiting wages would increase the share of profits. They followed this policy to promote investment. Retained earnings are one of the primary sources of funds used by firms to finance the purchase of machinery. The social partners believed that increased investment would lead to employment growth. Indeed, they were right. Investment did grow during the period of the NWAs. This is a factor that contributed to Irish employment growth during the 1990s.

However, a policy that made a great deal of sense initially, when business confidence was low, may not be quite as necessary when the economy is booming. The discontent by Irish labour may be a sign that they want a larger share of business income.

Second, at the end of 1999, the inflation rate started to increase. The inflation rate is a measure of changes in the price level (see Section 17.1). If prices increase more rapidly than income, the real purchasing power of consumers falls. This is exactly what happened during 2000, the first year of the Programme for Prosperity and Fairness.

The negotiated wage increase of 5.5% for the first year of the PPF was completely eroded by an estimated inflation rate of 6%. Employees were slightly better off than they were in the previous year in terms of 'take-home pay' because of tax reductions. However, many sectors clearly felt that they were not benefiting enough from the 'Celtic Tiger' economy. This led the unions to renegotiate wage increases in the PPF. Time will tell if the increases are large enough to satisfy workers, and if the unions can deliver industrial peace.

The future of national partnership agreements

Do 'one size fits all' wage increases suit the current economic situation in Ireland? The answer is probably no. Competition for labour in some sectors is so intense that the wage increases offered by firms far exceed the terms of the PPF. If the terms of the NWAs are not heeded by the private sector, it undermines the integrity of the partnership process.

Shortages of nurses in Dublin and Cork have led to the closure of wards and curtailment of health services. Teachers' unions warn that promising students are not entering the profession because they can receive significantly better wages in the private sector. If the public sector cannot attract nurses or teachers, their wages and salaries have to increase. Anything saved on their wages and salaries will be lost in the future because of deteriorating standards in health care and education.

Will the national partnership agreements survive without the national wage agreements?[17] Hopefully they will. They provide a framework for economic and social progress. The composition of the social partners mirrors Irish society. As a model of negotiating change it has served Ireland well. However, the survival of the NPAs will require an honest assessment of what they helped to achieve. This assessment must go beyond wage stability. Otherwise, if the NWAs become redundant, we may lose the NPAs as well. If that happens, we may indeed be guilty of 'throwing out the baby with the bath water'.

SUMMARY

1. The factors of production are the inputs used in the production process which result in final output. There are four factor inputs – labour, capital, land and entrepreneurship. The return to labour is the wage; interest is the reward to capital; rent is the return on land, and profit is the reward to entrepreneurship. According to the neoclassical theory of distribution, factor prices can be explained by demand and supply analysis.
2. The demand curve for labour is derived using marginal productivity theory. Profit-maximising firms will employ workers up to the point where MRP of labour = W. The MRP curve is the demand curve for labour, showing the number of workers employed at any given wage rate. It is downward sloping, showing that the lower the wage rate, the larger the number of workers who will be employed. The supply curve for labour shows the number of hours offered for work at given wage rates. It depends on the trade-off between work and leisure. It is normally upward sloping. The demand for and supply of labour simultaneously determine the equilibrium wage rate and quantity of labour.
3. The interest rate is the opportunity cost of capital. In deciding whether to purchase new capital, the firm must weigh the future benefits accruing from the investment against the cost of the investment. The demand curve for capital goods is downward sloping. The supply curve for capital goods is influenced by the trade-off between consumption and savings. The equilibrium interest rate is the cost of capital that clears the market for capital goods.
4. Transfer earnings is the portion of total earnings that is required to keep a factor in its present use. Economic rent is the portion of earnings in excess of transfer payments. Economic rent is paid on any factor of production that is in fixed supply. In terms of land, rent is the price paid for the use of land and other fixed resources. It is this fixed supply of land which distinguishes rental payments from other factor payments. The entire rental price is an economic rent.
5. Entrepreneurship is difficult to define and to measure. The reward to enterprise is profit. Unlike other factor payments, profit is a residual. It is received after all other

factor payments are made. There are several different sources of economic profit. One, it is the reward for uninsurable risk in the face of uncertainty. Two, it arises from acts of innovation carried out by the entrepreneur. Three, monopoly profits arise from output restriction, high prices and barriers to entry.

6. Five national partnership agreements (NPAs) have been negotiated between the social partners since 1987. They provide an economic and social framework, built by consensus, to help the country to meet the challenges of a rapidly changing environment. One important part of each NPA is the national wage agreement. The social partners agree the parameters of annual wage increases for a three-year period. This part of the NPA is coming under increasing pressure because of inflation, labour discontent and a general concern that a 'one size fits all' policy is no longer appropriate for a rapidly growing economy.

KEY TERMS

Labour	Discounting
Wage rate	Rate of return
Derived demand	Interest rate
Marginal productivity theory	Land
Marginal revenue product	Economic rent
Demand curve for labour	Transfer earnings
Supply curve of labour	Entrepreneurship
Backward bending supply curve	Profit
Wage differentials	Uninsurable risk
Capital goods	Innovation
Capital stock	Entrepreneur
Depreciation	National Partnership Agreement
Investment	National Wage Agreement
Present value	

REVIEW QUESTIONS

1. Explain the term 'the factors of production'. What are the rewards to each respective factor input?
2. Explain the derivation of the downward sloping labour demand curve.
3. What effect would an increase in labour supply have on the equilibrium price and quantity in the labour market?
4. (a) 'An investment is worthwhile if the present value of the future benefits exceeds the cost of the investment.' Explain.
   (b) 'The equilibrium interest rate clears the market for capital goods.' Explain.
5. (a) Explain the three sources of economic profit.
   (b) Outline the contributions of Frank Knight and Joseph Schumpeter to the theory of profit.
6. What are the national partnership agreements? Discuss their contribution to the Irish economy.

WORKING PROBLEMS

1. A number of entries in Table 7.8 have been deliberately omitted. Using marginal productivity theory, answer the questions below.

Table 7.8

Labour (wkrs)	TP (units)	MP (units)	P (€)	MRP (€)	Wage (€)
0	0				
		–	5	60	40
1	–				
		–	5	–	40
2	27				
		13	5	–	40
3	–				
		–	5	50	40
4	–				
		9	5	–	40
5	–				
		–	5	–	40
6	65		5		40

(a) Complete the table.
(b) According to the marginal productivity theory, how many workers will be employed if the wage rate is €40?
(c) If the wage rate rises to €50, how many workers will be employed?

2. A hypothetical labour market is depicted in Figure 7.15.

Figure 7.15: The labour market

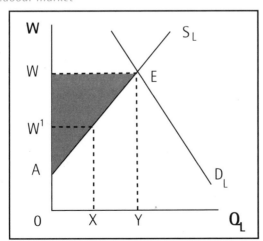

With respect to Figure 7.15 fill in the blanks below

    (a) total earnings is given by the area [ ]
    (b) transfer earnings is given by the area [ ]
    (c) economic rent is given by the area [ ]
    (d) transfer earnings for worker X is equal to _____ .
    (e) economic rent for worker X is equal to _____ .

MULTI-CHOICE QUESTIONS

1. Under conditions of perfect competition, the MRP of labour:
    (a) is equal to the MP of labour multiplied by the marginal revenue of the good;
    (b) is the additional revenue due to employing an extra unit of labour;
    (c) curve falls because of the short-run law of diminishing returns;
    (d) curve is the demand curve for labour;
    (e) all of the above.

2. A derived demand for labour:
    (a) can be explained using the marginal productivity theory;
    (b) is derived from the demand for the product which labour produces;
    (c) can be represented by a downward sloping demand curve;
    (d) all of the above;
    (e) none of the above.

3. The present value of €5,000 two years from now at an interest rate of 6% is:
    (a) €5,618;
    (b) €5,600;
    (c) €4,450;
    (d) higher than €5,000;
    (e) both (a) and (d) above.

4. Figure 7.16 shows the labour market for university postgraduates.

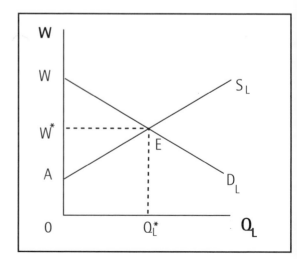

Figure 7.16: The labour market for university postgraduates

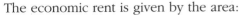

The economic rent is given by the area:
  (a) $[AEQ_L*0]$;
  (b) $[W*EQ_L*0]$;
  (c) $[W*EA]$;
  (d) $[WEQ_L*0]$;
  (e) none of the above.

5. The more inelastic the supply curve becomes:
  (a) the more transfer earnings is paid;
  (b) the more economic rent is paid;
  (c) the less economic rent is paid;
  (d) both (a) and (c) above;
  (e) none of the above.

6. Profit is different from the other resource prices because:
  (a) it is a residual;
  (b) it can be negative;
  (c) it is a category of factor income;
  (d) both (a) and (b) above;
  (e) both (a) and (c) above.

TRUE OR FALSE (SUPPORT YOUR ANSWER)

1. Resource prices serve as an allocative mechanism.

2. The declining MRP of labour reflects the law of diminishing returns: an additional labourer produces more output than the previous labourer.

3. The higher the interest rate, the lower is the present discounted value of the future MRPs and the smaller the number of capital goods demanded.

4. Transfer earnings is the opportunity cost of employing a factor.

5. A factor of production does not earn economic rent if its supply curve is perfectly elastic.

6. Profit is the return to the entrepreneur.

CASE STUDY

As discussed in Section 7.5, the *Programme for Prosperity and Fairness (PPF)* was negotiated with great difficulty. It came under pressure when the inflation rate in 2000 outstripped the wage increase negotiated as part of the agreement. The extract below was leaked from a 'confidential memorandum' sent from Jack O'Connor, the recently elected vice-president of SIPTU to Des Geraghty and John McDonnell, the union's president and general secretary respectively. It was written on 8 September 2000. Padraig Yeates reported on its content in an article in *The Irish Times* on 13 September. Readers are advised to visit *The Irish Times* website to see the text of the memo. Parts of it are reprinted below.

Extract from an Internal SIPTU memo

From: Jack O'Connor, Vice President
Subject: PPF/Pay/Inflation
Date: 8 September 2000.

OVERVIEW
The PPF is predicated on, and dependent upon, achieving strong non-inflationary economic growth . . . GNP was envisaged as averaging growth of 5.6% per annum . . . Clause 1 committed the parties to improving living standards through pay increases and significant tax reform. All commentators now confidently predict growth rates in excess of 10%, i.e. double the rate envisaged under PPF . . .

Inflation, which was expected to average 3 to 3.5% during the PPF ballot, is now running at 6.2%, and most commentators expect it to exceed 7% . . . The rate of inflation has now surpassed the first phase of the PPF increase by 1 to 1.5% . . .

Moreover, essentials like food, petrol and fuel absorb a greater proportion of the incomes of the middle and lower paid. Acute labour shortage in all sectors is driving up the market rate. Accordingly, the relative and absolute position of thousands of our members who are restricted to the minimum 5.5% increase is actually deteriorating . . .

The position has become untenable.

Many Union members are not experiencing any improvement in living standards . . . Indeed, in many cases their position relative to their non Union peers is deteriorating . . . We are rapidly approaching the point at which our industrial policy is at variance with our members' interests. Further pay increases may exacerbate the inflation crisis, but we cannot manage the economy and we cannot allow Union members to suffer the burden of maintaining economic competitiveness for the benefit of others.

RECOMMENDATIONS
We must immediately launch an imaginative initiative . . . promoting a combination of measures . . . designed to achieve the improvement in living standards envisaged in the PPF whilst maintaining the consensus approach (if possible) and sustaining competitiveness . . .

$\longrightarrow$

In light of the current rate of inflation, labour shortages and levels of expenditure we will also have to seek to negotiate a pay increase above the terms envisaged in PPF. Assuming a net pay increase of 10.5% and an inflation rate of 3 to 3.5%, living standards should have already risen by approximately 7%. Instead, inflation now at almost 7% means that 4% of the expected improvement has been wiped out. We should immediately submit a claim for a 5% increase.

CONCLUDING OBSERVATIONS
This strategy may well result in the collapse of consensus and adverse economic consequences, but the game is up. The alternatives are a renovated PPF supported by a range of Budgetary measures, or a reversion of pre collective bargaining. The present position is no longer tenable.

Source: Padraig Yeates. 13 September 2000. Unions press for new deal under PPF pact. *The Irish Times.* website (http://www.ireland.com/ newspaper/special/2000/siptumemo/)

Questions

1. Why do you think that Mr O'Connor is concerned about the payment of union members relative to their non-union peers?
2. This memo was written before the review of the PPF. Do you think that Mr O'Connor was satisfied with the wage increase obtained by ICTU as a result of the review? Why or why not?
3. Does Mr O'Connor think that the NWA should be negotiated at any cost? What is the alternative?
4. Why do you think that the memo was leaked?

APPENDIX 7.1: DAVID RICARDO AND ECONOMIC RENT

The theory of economic rent was developed in the nineteenth century by the British economist, stockbroker and MP David Ricardo (1772–1823) in his book *The Principles of Political Economy and Taxation* (1817). His theory arose from the Napoleonic wars and the rising corn (grain) prices which occurred at the same time as the rise in land rents. It was argued at the time that the high corn prices were a direct result of the landlords' policy of high land rents. Ricardo disagreed strongly with such an analysis. He saw the cause and effect in reverse. High rents were an effect and not a cause of high corn prices, he argued. In his own words 'Corn is not high because a rent is paid, but a rent is paid because corn is high.'[18]

The Napoleonic wars were directly responsible for a shortage of corn. The subsequent rise in the price of corn, he argued, forced landlords to seek out more land in order to take advantage of profitable corn production. Subsequent high demand for land in turn forced up the land rents. For Ricardo, rent was price determined and not price determining.

The above analysis can be described in the context of the demand for and supply of land. The supply of land is fixed, with land having only one use: to grow corn. The demand for land is a derived demand, stemming from the demand for corn. The payment to land is a surplus. This surplus payment is rent, according to Ricardo.

CHAPTER 8

MARKET FAILURE

by Eithne Murphy

'There are only two qualities in the world: efficiency and inefficiency, and only two sorts of people: the efficient and the inefficient.'[1]

George Bernard Shaw

'Good men are a publick good.'[2]

Proverb

CHAPTER OBJECTIVES

Upon completing this chapter, the student should understand:

- perfectly competitive markets and efficiency;
- externalities, public goods and market inefficiency;
- educational, economic and legal remedies for market failures.

Outline

8.1 Markets and efficiency
8.2 Markets and inefficient outcomes
8.3 The market failure of externalities
8.4 Remedies for external effects
8.5 Public goods
8.6 Public good provision

8.1 MARKETS AND EFFICIENCY

The principal, though not the only, ideological defence of the market system is that it represents a form of economic organisation that is efficient. By efficiency, we mean that the market system ensures that human wants and desires are satisfied without waste of resources. It is a system that validates self-interest. The efficiency outcome of the market system is predicated upon a number of behavioural, ethical and environmental assumptions.

The *behavioural assumptions* are that individuals know their own desires and wants, and that they attempt to satisfy these wants in a rational manner.

The *ethical assumptions* are that human want satisfaction adds to individual welfare, and that societal welfare is simply an aggregate of individual welfares.

247

The *environmental assumptions* are that markets are perfectly competitive in the sense of all economic agents being price takers, and that private benefit/cost is the same as social benefit/cost.

All market transactions are assumed to take place within a legal framework that recognises the right to private property and that provides for the enforcement of contracts.

The system ensures that not only are the right goods produced but that correct quantities of the goods are produced.[3] The correct quantity of a good is one that ensures that all mutually beneficial trades have been exhausted. Let us consider the market represented in Figure 8.1.

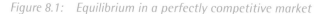
Figure 8.1: Equilibrium in a perfectly competitive market

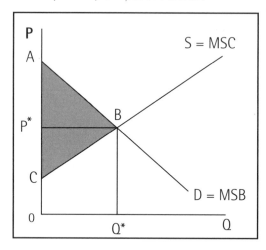

The market clearing price and output are P* and Q* respectively. The price P* is also the value of the utility that the last consumer received by consuming that good. Obviously, if she was willing to pay a price P*, she would not be rational unless the good yielded her a utility that was greater than or equal to the price that she paid. As long as there is net utility to be gained from consuming more of a good, it is rational for her to consume more of that good. By net utility we mean the monetary value of the satisfaction that she gets from consuming the good less the cost of the good.

The profit-maximising level of output is one where marginal cost equals price. Any other level of output would not be profit-maximising, which would not be rational behaviour for a self-interested producer. At price P* and output Q*, all mutually beneficial trades between the seller and the buyer of the good have been exhausted. If output sold on the market was less than Q*, then there is a potential buyer and a potential seller who can agree to trade at a price that would make both of them better off. Not to do so would be irrational if both are motivated by self-interest. Output will never exceed Q*, since there is no price for more output that will make a potential supplier and a potential buyer better off.

If we equate the private with the social, then the marginal cost to a producer of increasing output is the same as the marginal cost to society of increasing output.

Likewise, the marginal benefit to a consumer of consuming extra output equals the marginal benefit to society of that extra consumption. In other words, the market supply curve, which is the private marginal cost curve (MC), is the same as the marginal social cost of production (MSC). Similarly, the demand curve, which is the private marginal benefit curve (MB), is the same as the marginal social benefit of consumption (MSB). Market equilibrium therefore occurs at Q*, where MSC of production equals MSB from consumption.

The shaded area ABC (in Figure 8.1) between the demand and supply curves represents the combined net gain (in monetary terms) to buyers and sellers from participating in the market. Equating the private and the social, we can say that the area ABC is the net value to society as a result of producing a quantity Q* of the good and selling it at a price P*.

8.2 MARKETS AND INEFFICIENT OUTCOMES

By pursuing his own interests in a rational way, the individual is assumed to maximise his own welfare, and the social effects of such behaviour (when it occurs within the context of perfectly competitive markets) is an economic system without waste. As the eighteenth-century doctor and writer Bernard Mandeville claimed, 'Private vices are public virtues.'[4] Pushing this argument to its logical limit, one could in fact claim that if individuals did directly take the well-being of others into account in their behaviour, the social consequences would be less benign. Likewise, if individuals are not *rational* in the pursuit of their own interests, the market outcome will exhibit waste.

The efficiency of markets only holds if no economic agent has enough power to influence prices in the market and if markets actually exist for all goods and services. *Monopolistic competition*, *oligopoly* and *monopoly* are all forms of market structure where sellers have some power, which can be manifested in an ability to set prices. The market outcome in these instances is inefficient, usually because too little of the good is produced and the market price of the good is too high. When markets deviate from perfect competition in the ways just mentioned, the price at which the good is sold will exceed marginal cost. In other words, the marginal social benefit of the last unit sold exceeds the marginal social cost of production. There would be net utility gains to society if more of the good were produced.

There are goods and bads that are not traded in the market, yet they still affect human welfare. When these goods/bads are a by-product of production or consumption decisions – that is to say, when they are associated with private goods in some way – we call them *externalities*. These externalities have effects that are external to those effects captured by market exchange. These external effects may positively enhance human welfare or may reduce human welfare. Either way, the synonymity between individual private welfare and social welfare no longer exists. This results in either too much or too little production of certain goods.

An extreme form of externality are *public goods*. These goods have the characteristics that everybody must consume them in the same amount and that no one can be excluded from consumption. These are goods for which no private market exists, which is obviously inefficient if people derive utility from the existence of public goods.

8.3   THE MARKET FAILURE OF EXTERNALITIES

Externalities can be classified according to their causes and according to their effects. The general classification of causes are production activity and consumption activity. The general classification of effects are negative welfare effects and positive welfare effects. We will look at examples of each type of externality.

Negative production externalities

A negative production externality occurs when the act of producing a good or service has a side-effect that reduces the welfare of others not involved in that market.

An example of a negative externality in an Irish context is the water polluting effect of agricultural practices. Farmers, in their rational pursuit of profits, responded to the incentives of the Common Agricultural Policy by intensifying their agricultural production. A common practice has been the use of animal manures (in particular slurry) as a fertiliser. A by-product of this activity has been the run-off of this highly toxic and polluting substance into waterways. The subsequent pollution and fish-kills have had repercussions for bathers, fishermen, those in the tourist trade (who depend on Ireland's pollution-free image) and for anyone who values the environment. We can say that the social costs of farmer behaviour exceed the private costs. Since farmers presumably only care about private costs, this results in too much of the polluting activity taking place.

Figure 8.2 demonstrates how the market outcome differs from the socially efficient outcome. In the presence of a negative production externality, the private supply curve (which is the private marginal cost of production) is below the true marginal social cost of production (MSC), bearing in mind the negative external effects of that activity. The socially optimal level of output is where the demand schedule intersects with the MSC curve, which is the level of output Q_2. P_2 would be the market clearing price associated with this output level.

Figure 8.2:   Market with negative production externality

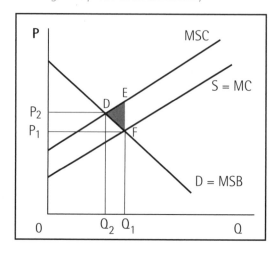

The actual market outcome is an output/price combination Q_1P_1. P_1, which is also the marginal social benefit (MSB) from the last unit of output produced, is less than the MSC of producing that last unit. Increasing output from Q_2 to Q_1 adds more to social cost than it does to social benefit; that is to say it imposes a net loss on society. The area DEF is the net loss in societal welfare as a result of overproduction of the good which produces the negative externality.

It is interesting to note that the existence of negative externalities merely allows us to conclude that the level of an activity is too high. It does not necessarily imply that the optimal level of that activity is zero. For the latter to occur, there would have to be no intersection between the MSC and the MSB curves, as shown in Figure 8.3. It is possible that for an activity like nuclear power, which has the potential to impose devastatingly high costs on our environment, the socially optimal level of output is as depicted in Figure 8.3; that is to say, it is zero.

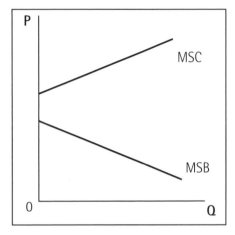

Figure 8.3:   Market where no output is socially optimal

Positive production externalities

A positive production externality exists when the act of production improves the welfare of those not involved in that market. An example of a positive production externality in an Irish context is the effect of the decisions of firms to locate in a certain area, say for example Galway. The individual firm will weigh up the private benefits and costs of locating in an area and only if, on the basis of such calculations, the benefits exceed the costs, will they proceed with the location decision.

However when many firms locate in an area costs can fall. This is because their respective economic existences may be inter-dependent. A computer firm will prefer to locate where it has access to skilled labour, developed financial services and firms who produce inputs that it requires. Likewise, the decisions of related industries, who will be selling to or buying from the computer company, will be in part determined by whether or not the computer company locates in the area. These production externalities are also called *economies of agglomeration*. The net effect of each firm producing in a certain area is to reduce the cost of production to related firms.

Individual producers are not interested in the spillover effects of their decisions: their decisions are made on the basis of their own costs and benefits. As a result, the MC per unit which they calculate is above the MSC per unit which includes the positive production externalities.

As shown in Figure 8.4, when positive production externalities exist, the market level of output (Q_1), which occurs where MC equals price, is below the socially optimal level of output (Q_2), which occurs where MSC equals MSB. The area GHQ is the net loss in societal welfare which results from the underproduction of the good, whose production causes positive externalities.

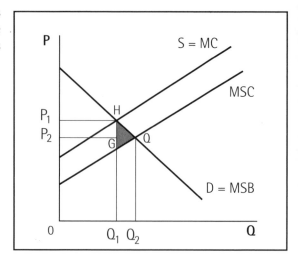

Figure 8.4: Market with positive production externality

Negative consumption externalities

As a rational self-interested individual, I will purchase and consume a good if the value of the utility I derive from its consumption is greater than or equal to the cost of the good. For some goods, private consumption reduces the welfare of others as a by-product of the consumption activity. Notwithstanding the high cost of cars in Ireland, many Irish people drive cars or aspire to driving them as soon as their personal financial circumstances make driving a feasible option. A by-product of individuals' desire to drive is major traffic congestion, air pollution, noise pollution and increased danger to pedestrians, cyclists and other motorists. Undoubtedly, the marginal social benefit (MSB) of every additional car on the road is much less than the private benefit to its owner.

Since at each level of output the marginal social benefit is less than the marginal private benefit, the MSB curve is below the market demand curve. As shown in Figure 8.5, the market equilibrium results in too much consumption of that good. The market level of consumption (Q_1) is given by the intersection of the market demand and market supply curves. The socially efficient level of output is lower and occurs at Q_2, where the MSB and MSC curves intersect. The area MNO is the inefficiency (or the loss in net societal welfare) associated with overconsumption of goods that produce negative externalities.

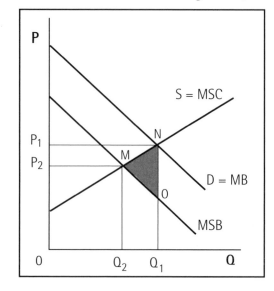

Figure 8.5: Market with a negative consumption externality

Positive consumption externalities

Some consumption activities confer utility, not just on those individuals who consume the good, but also on others as a by-product of their consumption. An example could be education. Individuals (and their families) make many sacrifices to ensure that they get a good education. Presumably, their motives are fairly self-interested. Education confers direct and indirect benefits on the individual: direct benefits in terms of the value of education in itself and indirect benefits in terms of its effect on one's prospects in the labour market.

However, it could be claimed that a highly educated population has positive social repercussions that are not confined to the individual. The marginal social benefit per unit of education which includes the positive externality, exceeds the marginal private benefit. Therefore, the MSB curve is above the market demand curve.

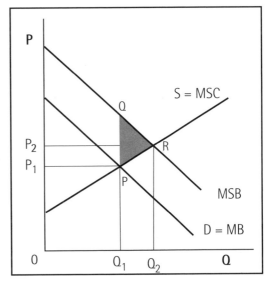

If left to the market, too little of the good will be consumed, since the market level of consumption (Q_1) (see Figure 8.6), is below the socially optimal level of consumption (Q_2), where MSB equals MSC. The efficiency loss, that is a consequence of the underconsumption of a good with positive external effects, is denoted by the area PQR in Figure 8.6.

Figure 8.6: Market with a positive consumption externality

8.4 REMEDIES FOR EXTERNAL EFFECTS

Our use of language is very value laden. The fact that we refer to market imperfections or market failures seems to imply that perfection or success is achievable, if appropriate remedies are applied. Indeed the response of many economists to market failure is not to reject the market mechanism as an allocater of resources and wealth, but to identify the source of the market failure and to correct it with appropriate policy instruments.

Other economists are wary of any policies that entail government intervention, on the grounds that the remedy may be worse than the disease. Their thesis is that political failures will only compound market failures. The market system, notwithstanding its failings, is still the most efficient social and economic organisation for the allocation of goods and resources. In the rest of this section we are going to look at a variety of private and public responses to the market failures that are externalities.

Spontaneous market remedies

A socially inefficient level of production or consumption takes place precisely because those causing the external effect are only concerned with their individual welfare. External costs or benefits do not form part of their calculations and do not inform their decisions. If they did, then the market outcome would be efficient. Expansion of firms sometimes results in the internalisation of the externality.

For example, if a farmer is also in the tourist trade, then he will bear in mind the effect of his agricultural activities on his tourist business, since he is hoping to derive profit from both activities. He will weigh up the benefits of fertilising his land with animal slurry (in terms of its potential contribution to agricultural profits) with the potential costs to his tourist trade if water pollution occurs. If he can predict both accurately, then the level of animal fertiliser that he applies to his land will be efficient. (This does of course presuppose that nobody else is affected by his activity.)

Educational remedies

These are often recommended in the context of activities that create negative externalities. Can the farmer be persuaded to exercise better control over the dangerous animal wastes that his farming practices produce? Can the general public be persuaded to abandon their cars and use more environmentally friendly methods of locomotion? Can firms be persuaded to locate in certain areas because it will be good for the local economy and for the social fabric of the community where they locate?

The answer depends on how one perceives the individual. If one accepts that individuals are inherently self-interested, then the answer is negative, unless of course there is some way that doing the socially appropriate thing is in one's own private interest. Yet there are many educational initiatives that are designed to inform people of the negative social consequences of many of their activities and to persuade them to act differently.

Such initiatives (which are usually publicly funded) are either naïvely motivated and a waste of public finances or they have some effect because to say that individuals are only self-interested is an oversimplification of a more complex reality. To the extent that individuals are social beings and that their identity is also associated with something beyond themselves (for example their community, their class or their country), then education has a role to play in reducing activities that generate negative externalities and increasing activities that generate positive externalities.

Economic remedies

Economic remedies are those that operate through the market mechanism. The market environment is summarised in the prices that individual economic agents (be they consumers or producers) face. If prices change because of government policies, then economic agents will adjust their consumption and production behaviour in a rational way in response to the new set of price signals.

Recall the market with negative production externalities that was depicted in Figure 8.2. The market equilibrium output was too high and the market price was too low. The socially optimal level of output was output level Q_2, where the marginal benefit to society of the last unit of the good sold equals the marginal cost to society of producing that good. However at output level Q_2, the producer's actual private costs are less than price, so he has an incentive to produce more of the good.

The only way that the producer (who is a rational economic agent) can be persuaded not to produce more than Q_2, would be if it were not in his private interest to produce a higher level of output. This will only be the case if at output level Q_2 the private marginal cost to the producer is equal to the price P_2. The government can make this happen if it levies a unit tax equal to the difference between marginal social cost and marginal private cost; in other words a unit tax equal to the vertical distance $|EF|$. This is the same as increasing the marginal private cost of production; that is to say, it shifts the MC curve upwards. The socially efficient tax will shift the MC curve upwards until it is the same as the MSC curve.

The revenue from this tax could then be used to compensate those who are negatively affected by the production activity. There would be a net gain to society as the true social cost savings of lowering output from Q_1 to Q_2 would exceed the loss in consumer welfare caused by lowering output from Q_1 to Q_2.

Conversely, when a production activity yields positive production externalities, the optimal government strategy is to subsidise production of the good so as to increase production from Q_1 to Q_2 (see Figure 8.4). This can be achieved by offering a subsidy per unit of output equal to the difference between the higher private marginal costs and the lower social marginal costs of production. If the unit subsidy is equal to the vertical distance between the market supply curve and the marginal social cost curve; that is to say $|GH|$ then the producer will rationally respond to this change in his economic environment by expanding production to its socially optimal level Q_2. The producer's MC of production is now the same as the MSC of production, thanks to the producer subsidy that they receive.

The revenue required to pay for the subsidy could be collected from those reaping the external benefit from the externality. There would be a net gain to society as the increase in social cost from increasing output from Q_1 to Q_2 is less than the increase in consumer welfare.

Where economic interventions are concerned, it does not matter whether the cause of the externality is production or consumption, since market clearing (equilibrium) means that production equals consumption in a closed economy. Hence, when there is a negative consumption externality, such as depicted in Figure 8.5, the appropriate economic strategy is to tax production (or consumption) of the good in order to reduce consumption to socially efficient levels. In terms of Figure 8.5, the appropriate unit production tax is the difference between marginal private benefit and marginal social benefit (the vertical distance $|NO|$), and the optimal level of output is where marginal social benefit equals marginal social cost; that is to say output level Q_2.

Conversely, when the consumption externality is positive, as shown in Figure 8.6, the appropriate policy is to subsidise production (or consumption) of the good in order to increase consumption of the good to its socially efficient level. The appropriate unit subsidy is the difference between marginal social benefit and marginal private benefit (the vertical distance $|PQ|$).

Government taxes and subsidies that are designed to indirectly influence the level of production and consumption are known as Pigouvian taxes/subsidies after the British economist Pigou.[5] The main drawback of this approach is information. When negative or positive externalities occur, it is very difficult to know the precise extent of the inflicted damage or conferred benefit. Thus such measures may adjust output in the correct direction (assuming that external effects from an activity are either positive or negative but not both) but it seems highly unlikely that the post tax/subsidy level of output will be exactly where marginal social benefit equals marginal social cost.

Legal remedies

There is a variety of legal possibilities. Where negative externalities occur, these remedies could incorporate any of the following:

1. a ban on the activity that is generating the negative externality;
2. legally compelling the creator of the externality to engage in activities that eliminate or reduce the external effects that arise from his/her activities;
3. legally defining property rights, either to engage in an activity or to prevent an activity taking place, and allowing that property right to be traded.

Banning an activity is beneficial to those suffering the negative externality from the activity in question but such measures hurt those whose livelihood may depend on the activity that inadvertently causes the externality. We all know that certain farming practices damage the environment, as do too many cars in our cities! Yet very few individuals suggest abandoning totally these agricultural practices or propose a car-free environment. Why is this? It is a recognition of competing rights and the complex interaction between certain activities and their external effects. Farmers have a right to make a livelihood. Banning certain practices outright may make it more difficult for them to carry on farming successfully. Cars represented an amazing technological advance over previous means of transportation. In many ways, possession of a private car can greatly enhance the quality of the owner's lifestyle.

Unless the marginal social cost of an activity exceeds the marginal social benefit for all positive levels of that activity, then a complete ban on the same activity is an inefficient response, since it inflicts a greater hurt than benefit. It is only an appropriate response to activities that are deemed to have very large (or potentially large) negative external effects such as, for example, nuclear energy.

The second legal response allows the creator of the negative externality to continue to engage in their original production or consumption activities but obliges him to modify these activities in some way in order to minimise the external effects. This response usually has negative financial repercussions for the individual subject to the new laws governing their activities. Farmers may be required to build better storage facilities for animal wastes or all cars may have to have catalytic converters.

For legal measures to have the desired effect, there has to be some degree of monitoring combined with sanctions in the event of breaches of the law. The appropriateness of financially penalising the creators of negative externalities by obliging them to modify their behaviour is an ethical question. All laws, just like all economic policies, inevitably have redistribution effects. Sometimes governments give financial assistance to parties to help them to comply with new standards and legal obligations.

A third potential legal response owes its origin to Ronald Coase, who wrote a paper entitled 'The Problem of Social Cost'.[6] This paper affected the way economists, lawyers, philosophers and others think about externalities. Returning to our farmer example, the farmer's activity is harming fishermen and those in the tourist trade. Should the farmer be restrained? If the farmer is banned from spreading animal wastes on his land, then water pollution will not occur and fishermen and those in the tourist industry will be better off. However the farmer will be worse off. *Either way some party is hurt.*

Traditionally, laws tended to penalise the creator of the negative externality. What Coase pointed out was that it was not the farmer's explicit intention to harm those engaged in other activities; the harm inflicted is merely a by-product of an activity, the purpose of which is to maximise farm income. For Coase, the optimal solution is one that maximises net welfare; that is to say it is an empirical issue. If the gain to the farmer from polluting the environment outweighs the losses to those who are harmed by the pollution, then it is socially more efficient if the pollution is allowed to take place. Conversely, if the gain to the farmer is less than the costs imposed on others, then it is socially efficient if the activity causing the pollution does not take place.

Coase went on to argue that, if property rights are clearly defined, then the parties affected by the externality will bargain their way to an efficient solution. (This does of course pre-suppose that bargaining is not a costly activity.)

Let us suppose that the gain to the farmer from his pollution activities outweighs the costs to others adversely affected by his pollution activities. In addition, let us suppose that the law gives precedence to fishermen and those in the tourist trade. In other words, they have the right to a clean environment, which is so important to their livelihoods. In this situation, it pays the farmer to compensate fishermen etc. in order to be allowed to continue the activity that is so profitable to him. The farmer is still better off than he would be if he did not engage in the polluting activity. Fishermen and those in the tourist trade are adequately compensated in order to allow this polluting activity. Otherwise, they would not have waived their rights to a clean environment. The outcome is an efficient one, since it maximises joint net welfare.

If the law gives precedence to the farmer's right to a livelihood, then the parties will bargain to the same socially efficient outcome. The fishermen etc. will have to pay the farmer to produce less, and therefore pollute less. The process continues until there is no compensation that the fisherman can offer the farmer that will leave them better off. That is because the value of the damage inflicted on them is less than the value of the gain to the farmer from inflicting that damage. So regardless of who has the property rights, if bargaining is possible the outcome will be socially efficient.

From an efficiency perspective, it is a matter of indifference how the legal regime allocates property rights (be it the right to a clean environment or the right to pursue one's livelihood). From a distribution point of view, the allocation of property rights is fundamental to the welfare of the parties whose interests are at stake. Whichever party is given the property right, they are in possession of a valuable asset that has a market value and that can be traded. Hence, if the property right is to a clean environment, then the law favours those who need and value a clean environment and the farmer will have to pay for the right to pollute it. The converse is the case if the law favours the farmer and gives him the legal protection to pursue his livelihood as he sees fit. He is then in possession of a valuable income-earning asset which he can trade.

Solving the efficiency problems of externalities is not as straightforward as it might appear in theory. Again, one of the biggest problems is information; information as to the source or sources of the externality, information as to the size of the external effects and information of the value to the various parties of the continuance or non-continuance of the externality inducing activity.

For example, in Ireland there have been many cases of water pollution and fish-kills as a result of slurry run-off from land. It is not always easy to identify the individuals responsible, just as it is very difficult to put a value on unpolluted waters. An additional aspect to the problem is the number of individuals or parties affected. Unpolluted water is valued by anglers. It is valued by those in the tourist industry, who trade on Ireland's image as an unspoilt environment. It is valued by bathers. It is valued by all those who value the environment for its own sake. There are so many individuals involved that bargaining is no longer a costless activity (a necessary condition for the Coase theorem to hold).

An additional problem (and one that commonly afflicts groups) is the incentive(s) that individuals have to free ride on the efforts of others. I might value a clean environment but if others fight the battle for me, then I might achieve my objective at little personal cost in terms of time and effort. This tendency to free ride on the efforts of others makes it difficult for individuals, who are affected by the externality in different ways, to organise their efforts in order to bargain their way to an efficient solution.

Even when there are few parties involved, another barrier to the efficient resolution of the problem of externalities is the existence of asymmetric information. If the law guarantees the right to unpolluted waters and a farmer wishes to negotiate that right with me, then I have an incentive to overstate the value that I place on a clean environment, especially if that increases my compensation when I trade that right. There are many examples where it is possible that this form of overstatement is taking place.

Many companies when they are legally required to take measures to prevent pollution will overstate the cost to them of the new measures and the potential cost to the economy in terms of lost jobs. This is rational behaviour if it allows them to gain a waiver from the restrictive measures.

A very contentious, contemporary issue is the proposed new light rail (LUAS) development in Dublin. While everyone agrees that something needs to be done to alleviate traffic problems in the city, the LUAS appears to be arousing strong negative feelings as well as positive feelings. Among the groups opposed to the scheme are some traders, who feel that their businesses will be adversely affected by the development, as well as those who represent the motor car trade. Most of the arguments centre on the disruption that the development will cause during the construction phase and a suggestion that going underground is a better alternative. While not claiming to know the motivation of all the groups opposed to the scheme, it would be naïve not to presume that there is some degree of overstatement (on the part of the groups opposed to LUAS) of potential economic losses that will ensue if LUAS goes ahead, and of the expected disruption during the construction phase.

So far we have looked at legal remedies to negative externalities but the law also has a role to play where positive externalities are involved. Many firms, in their pursuit of profit, develop new products and processes. The development of new products and processes is never a costless process. The problem arises because information is an extreme form of positive externality. It is in fact a public good (a category of good that will be looked at in more detail in the next section). This is a problem because firms would obviously be reluctant to invest in research and development if the product of that investment could be costlessly copied by competitors. Yet the positive social benefits which result from the development of new products and processes make these activities very desirable from an efficiency perspective.

The legal response is usually to give a patent to the inventor for a specific but finite period of time, that allows him or her to internalise the external effects of the invention. Eventually, patent rights expire and others can exploit the knowledge that was previously protected by patent. The law is therefore designed to encourage activities that give rise to positive external activities in the first place and, eventually, to ensure that the external effect is widespread.

8.5 PUBLIC GOODS

The classic reference for the pure theory of public goods is Paul Samuelson (1954, 1955).[7] A characteristic of private goods is *rivalry* in consumption. If individual 1 consumes a good, then individual 2 cannot consume the same good: the good has finite properties. A public good, by contrast, is *non-rival* in consumption. Street lighting is a public good: its existence gives me utility by enabling me to see at night. However my consumption of street lighting does not reduce the amount of street lighting available for anybody else.

Another feature of private goods is their *excludability*. When a good is in my possession, I can exclude others from consuming that good. This capacity for exclusion is what enables me to sell my good for a positive price. If someone is not willing to pay me the price for the good that I demand, then I can prevent them from consuming the good in my possession.

By contrast many public goods have the characteristic of *non-excludability* or they are excludable at prohibitively high costs. It is not possible to prevent someone from consuming street lighting if they fail to pay for it. It is precisely this feature of non-excludability that renders the private market unsuitable for public good provision. No potential producer has any incentive to incur the costs necessary to provide public goods if a price cannot be charged for consuming the same goods. To the extent that public good consumption improves the utility of individuals and that the increase in aggregate utility for all concerned exceeds the cost of providing the public good, then on efficiency grounds it should be provided. If the market does not provide the good, then the market is not an efficient mechanism for maximising human welfare.

A feature of private goods is that individuals consume them in different quantities according to their preferences. A feature of public goods is that all individuals have to consume the public good in the same quantity regardless of their preferences. The marginal utility of the last unit consumed of a private good is the same for everyone, since all individuals face the same price and all maximise utility by consuming a good in such quantities that marginal utility equals price. By contrast, the marginal utility from consuming the last unit of a public good will differ among individuals. The market demand curve for a private good is derived by *horizontally* summing together individual demand curves. For each potential price, market demand is calculated from individual demands.

This procedure does not make sense for a public good since all individuals have to consume the same amount. Yet individuals value the public good differently. Some are willing to pay a high price as a reflection of the utility that they derive from it. Others are only willing to pay a low price for the good. In order to estimate the benefit that the public good yields to the public, we have to *vertically* sum together individual demand curves.

An individual demand curve can be interpreted in two ways. On the one hand, it shows us the quantity that a utility-maximising individual will consume at different prices. On the other hand, it shows us how much individuals are willing to pay for each successive unit of the good. Marginal willingness to pay must be a reflection of marginal utility from consumption, if individuals are rational utility maximisers. Vertically summing individual demand curves gives us group marginal willingness to pay for different levels of the public good. The efficient level of output of a public good is where the group marginal willingness to pay equals the marginal cost of providing the last unit of the public good.

Figure 8.7 illustrates how the market demand curve is derived when the market consists of only two individuals, individual 1 and individual 2, both of whom value the public good differently. When the marginal cost of providing the good is given by the supply curve S, then the optimal level of output of the public good is Q*, where marginal cost equals the combined marginal benefits to both individuals.

Many public goods have the characteristic that the marginal cost of provision is zero, since most of the cost of providing the good is a fixed cost. In this instance, the optimal level of output is Q** and the optimal price that should be charged at this level of output is zero, the same as marginal cost.

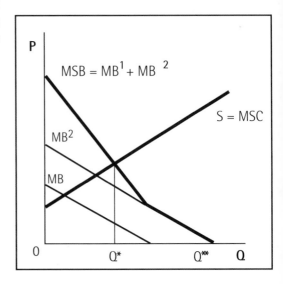

Figure 8.7:   Constructing a demand curve for a public good

In reality, it is hard to find genuine examples of pure public goods. Coole National Park is an example of a public good; my enjoyment of what it has to offer should not diminish the enjoyment that others get from this unique environment. Yet if enough individuals decide that they want to experience Coole, this will affect my utility. Congestion will occur and consumption is no longer non-rival.

Likewise, there are ways and means of excluding individuals from consuming what is essentially a public good. The capacity to exclude depends on legal arrangements and on the state of technology. A law could be passed allowing Coole National Park to be fenced off and only those willing to pay would be permitted to enjoy what it has to offer.

Technological advances can also mean that the cost of excluding non-subscribers or non-payers is dramatically reduced. Excluding those who do not pay their television licences from watching RTE 1 and Network 2 is a difficult task, since all you need is an aerial to view these channels. Excluding non-subscribers to cable television from watching cable television is now a relatively inexpensive procedure, thanks to the technological advance that is cable.

Once exclusion is possible, then a price can be charged for use and private provision becomes a viable option. Private beaches and toll bridges are but two examples of public goods that have been made inaccessible to non-payers thanks to the possibility of exclusion.

8.6 PUBLIC GOOD PROVISION

The inability to exclude individuals from benefiting from a public good would appear to indicate that self-interested individuals would not be willing to pay for that good. The logic of self-interest implies that individuals would free ride; that is to say they would hope to benefit from the provision of the good without having to pay for it. If all individuals behave in a rational self-interested fashion, then the good will not be provided, unless it is possible to finance provision in some compulsory fashion, such as taxation. Yet private provision of public goods does exist and not just where exclusion is possible.

Private donations

Many individuals give of their resources in order to provide public goods. For example, it is quite normal for individuals to donate money to support their local church, community centre, library etc. Money is not the only resource; many people give of their time in order to improve the quality of their local community. (Think of all the voluntary clubs or of the tidy towns competition.)

Why don't individuals free ride and let others make the donations and let others put in the effort to provide goods from which all can benefit? Presumably some individuals do free ride. However, it is interesting that many do not behave in what is deemed to be a rational, self-interested fashion.

Of course it may be that individuals perceive that their private contributions make a difference to the level of public-good provision and that the private utility that they get from the increase in the public good outweighs the value of their donation. This would be rational, utility-maximising behaviour. It may be that giving of one's time to the local community brings non-pecuniary rewards in the form of social approval. This could also be deemed rational utility-maximising behaviour.

This still does not explain why individuals make donations when the marginal effect of their donation is negligible and when, as is often the case, the donation is anonymous. Either their behaviour is not governed by narrow self-interest or they have a concept of rational behaviour that differs from that of narrowly self-interested man. If one's sense of identity is not completely individualistic, for example one may identify with their local community, then there is no conflict between what is in one's own interest and what is in the interest of the local community.

This could explain donations to help maintain the local community centre. But what about individuals who pay their TV licence or honestly declare all their income to the Revenue Commissioners (when they could get away with doing otherwise) or who make a contribution to help bone marrow research? Is this due to a broader sense of identity? It certainly could be (although one would expect the social identity to be stronger at local level) but it could also be due to a different concept of rationality. This individual could rationalise as follows: I could potentially derive utility from medical research, I would prefer if I did not have to pay but then if everybody reasoned in a like-minded fashion, there would be no research and no potential future benefits to me or to anyone else. Therefore in order to be consistent, I must behave as I would wish others to behave, which prompts me to ignore narrow self-interest and to contribute to the broader community.

Club membership is another example of a private market response to the demand for public goods. Usually the marginal cost of using the public good may be negligible but the cost of providing the good in the first place may be quite high. (Think of golf clubs.) The response is for a number of individuals to form a club and to make donations to the club in order to finance the provision of the good. Obviously a good such as a golf club is not a pure public good, in the sense that it is feasible to exclude non-members from benefiting from the good. The success or otherwise of private club provision of public goods usually depends on the size of their membership and on the size of the contribution necessary in order to provide the public good. Free-riding behaviour is more difficult, the smaller the club membership, as identification of the free-rider is more likely.

Government provision

Traditionally pure public goods such as national defence, street lighting, roads, clean water supply etc. were provided by central or local government and paid for by taxation. This is one way around the free-rider problem, to the extent that taxation is compulsory and universal. It does not, of course, ensure that the level of public good provision is optimal. As shown in Figure 8.7, the optimal level of that public good is Q^{**}, when the marginal cost of providing the good is zero. It is rational to provide that level of the good provided that the value of the utility to all individuals who consume the good exceeds the total cost of providing the good. Let us assume that this is the case.

How then should the tax burden be distributed among individuals? In an ideal world, taxation should be proportional to private benefit gained from the provision of that good. This does not work in reality because, firstly, it would involve a very complex taxation system; and, secondly, each individual would have an incentive to understate the value to them of the public good in order to minimise their tax burden. The net effect would be the under-provision of the public good.

An alternative approach is to decide in advance that, if a public project goes ahead, then everyone will have to pay a pre-determined amount towards its construction. Everyone is then asked the value they place on the public good, in order to determine whether the summation of individual benefits exceeds the cost of providing the good.

The problem with this approach is that everyone has an incentive to overstate the value to them of the good, if they value the good more highly than their pre-determined individual contribution. There is no cost to such behaviour and it could involve getting more of the good, which would be welfare enhancing to the individual concerned. Alternatively, if they value the good less than their pre-determined contribution, they have an incentive to state that the value they place on the good is zero, since that will increase the probability that the good will not be provided, which would be welfare-maximising for this individual. Either way, individuals do not have an incentive to truly reveal their preferences.

Demand revelation mechanisms

It is almost impossible to determine precisely the optimal level of public good provision. This is because of asymmetric information; only the individual knows the value he or she places on public goods such as, for example, a clean or a safe environment. This is information that they may not be willing to share with others, if dissemination of that knowledge reduces their consumer surplus by increasing their fee/donation/tax burden as a consequence. There are different mechanisms designed to extract this information from individuals.

Majority voting

There is a well-established literature on the efficiency of voting as a mechanism to determine the optimal mix of publicly provided goods and the optimal level of public good provision. It is also well established in the literature that such mechanisms do not work well. Crafty politicians are adept at manipulating the electoral agenda in order to get the outcomes that they most desire.

Also, when individuals are voting on the level of provision of a public good, the outcome will always be determined by the median voter. That is not necessarily efficient, since it does not guarantee an outcome where the optimal level of the public good is determined by the value of the good to the average individual (unless of course the median voter is also the average voter). If the value of the good to the median voter is less than the value of the good to the average voter, then the good will be under-provided. The converse is the case when the value of the good to the median voter is greater than the value of the good on average. This result occurs because each individual has one vote and each vote has equal weight, regardless of how strongly each individual feels about the provision or non-provision of the public good in question.

Revealed preference methods

One may not be able to get individuals to honestly declare their preferences, but in some instances the value they place on certain public goods can be inferred from their behaviour, if their consumption of that good is linked to private market behaviour.

For example, the time and cost that individuals spend in travelling to a national park or beach or nature reserve can give some indication of the value to them of that public good, so travel cost can be treated as a proxy for price.

Why do two identical houses located in different areas sell for different prices? Why do individuals pay a premium to live in a safe neighbourhood, in a neighbourhood with public amenities, near a park, or near the sea? The premium that they are willing to pay for an identical house must reflect the value to them of safety, public amenities, the park, and the sea.

Methods of indirectly inferring the value that individuals place on existing public goods are not without their flaws. These methods are dependent upon the existence of complementary markets for private goods. The cost that one is willing to incur to travel to a natural amenity or the premium that one pays to live in a certain location could very easily (and probably does) understate the value to the individual of the public good that they are consuming. Also, such methods are not suitable for all public goods, since not all public-good consumption has a related and complementary private-good consumption. The advantage of revealed preference methods is that they focus on what people actually do (as opposed to what people claim they do) and use behaviour to infer preferences.

SUMMARY

1. Perfectly competitive markets ensure that there is no waste in the allocation of resources and goods. This presupposes that everyone is a price taker and that the private benefit/cost from an activity equals the social benefit/cost.
2. Externalities occur when the activities of a firm or individual inadvertently affect the welfare of others. Externalities are not transmitted through the market. When externalities are present, the market outcome is not efficient; that is to say, there is waste.
3. Positive externalities occur when the production or consumption of a good enhances the welfare of others. When externalities are positive, then the market outcome will result in either under-production or under-consumption of the good generating the externality. Negative externalities occur when the production or consumption of a good reduces the welfare of others. When externalities are negative, then the market outcome will result in either over-production or over-consumption of the good generating the externality. Inefficient levels of production or consumption occur when externalities are present because the firms or individuals causing the externality do not take into account the effect of their activities on other parties.
4. Government intervention can improve the efficiency of markets that generate externalities. The principal forms of intervention are the use of economic and/or legal instruments. Interfering with the price mechanism through indirect taxation or

subsidisation is an economic response to the problem of externalities. The law can either defend the rights of those generating the externality, or defend the rights of those affected by the externality. If the law, as well as assigning property rights, also allows the parties involved to trade their legal rights, then the parties involved could bargain their way to an efficient solution. Parties will bargain their way to an efficient solution, provided that property rights are clearly assigned and that the transactions costs involved in bargaining are negligible. This result is known as the Coase theorem.

5. Public goods are an extreme form of externality. They are goods that are non-rival in consumption, in the sense that consumption by one individual does not reduce potential consumption by other individuals. They are also non-excludable, in the sense that it is impossible or prohibitively expensive to prevent someone from consuming a public good. Private markets will either not produce the public good or will under-produce the good. Either way, the private-market outcome is inefficient, which is why most public goods are provided by government and paid for via taxation.

6. A major difficulty in correcting market failures, such as externalities and public goods, is insufficient information about the effects of such market failures on the welfare of individuals. This problem is not easy to overcome since individuals often have an economic incentive not to be honest in such instances.

KEY TERMS

Market efficiency
Marginal social benefit
Marginal social cost
Negative production externalities
Positive production externalities
Negative consumption externalities
Positive consumption externalities
Pigouvian taxes/subsidies
Coase theorem
Public goods
Non-rivalry
Non-excludability
Demand revelation mechanisms

REVIEW QUESTIONS

1. Explain what is meant by externalities and why it is that the market, if left to its own devices, will not be efficient when externalities are present.
2. Discuss and assess the different remedies designed to correct the market failure of externalities.
3. When the marginal cost of producing a public good is zero, why is it inefficient to exclude anyone from access to that good?

CHAPTER 9

MICROECONOMIC POLICY ISSUES IN IRELAND

by Francis O'Toole

'The hardest thing in the world to understand is the income tax.'

Albert Einstein (1879–1955)

'The Supreme Power who conceived gravity, supply and demand, and the double helix must have been absorbed elsewhere when public utility regulation was invented.'

F.M. Scherer

CHAPTER OBJECTIVES

Upon completing this chapter, the student should understand:

- the reasons for, and the canons of, taxation;
- the scale and sources of taxation;
- the structure of different types of taxes and the political and social importance of taxation;
- the process of competition and the concept and indicators of market power;
- the framework of competition policy in Ireland;
- the natural monopoly problem and possible solutions.

OUTLINE

9.1 Taxation policy
9.2 Competition policy

INTRODUCTION

There has been a growing awareness within Ireland of the importance of microeconomic policy issues in recent years. For example, recent changes in what may be termed microeconomic tax policy have had large economic, as well as political and social, effects (e.g. the tax treatment of housing or of married couples). Similarly, the decisions to allow competition within Irish telecommunications and to privatise Eircom (previously known as Telecom Eireann) have had a significant impact upon almost every Irish household.

It is also true, however, that the increased awareness of the importance of microeconomic policy issues has been driven to some extent by the realisation that the scope for macroeconomic policy decision-making has been reduced significantly by the increased role of the European Union in monetary policy and fiscal policy. For example, Irish authorities now only contribute in a relatively small way to the determination of Irish interest rates. Of course, microeconomic policy issues and macroeconomic policy issues should never be viewed as completely separate matters. Microeconomic policy decisions (e.g. lower taxes on income) have always had macroeconomic consequences (e.g. higher inflation).

This chapter covers two broadly defined microeconomic policy issues: taxation and competition. The chapter begins by reviewing taxation policy. The interested reader is directed to recent budgets and to the business press for more up-to-date information. The second part of the chapter deals with competition policy. The related policy issues of the regulation of specific markets or sectors of the economy and privatisation are also discussed.

9.1 TAXATION POLICY

Reasons

There are at least three reasons for the existence of significant levels of taxation within Ireland. First, the state needs to finance the provision of public services (e.g. roads, education and health). Second, the state needs to generate funds in order to redistribute income (e.g. unemployment assistance payments). Third, the state may use taxes in order to alter behaviour (e.g. taxes on energy consumption). If successful (unsuccessful), this latter motive may lead to the collection of little (much) taxation revenue; in this regard, the reader should consider the taxation of alcohol, hydrocarbon oils and tobacco products.

Canons

Adam Smith developed his so-called canons of taxation in *An Inquiry into the Nature and Causes of the Wealth of Nations* (1776). Given that the significance of taxation has increased dramatically in the intervening two centuries, Smith's canons of equity, certainty, convenience of payment and economy of collection are even more important today. Smith's canons are often referred to under the headings of equity, efficiency and effective administration.

1. *Equity* The ability-to-pay principle, which underlies the majority of tax systems, relates an individual's tax payment to the individual's ability to pay, which in practice is taken as the individual's level of income. This principle generally suggests the adoption of a progressive tax system. A progressive (regressive) tax structure implies that an individual's average tax payment – the individual's tax payment as a proportion of the individual's income – should increase (decrease) with income. For example, the Irish income tax system's basic structure appears progressive; the individual is confronted with brackets of increasing magnitude as the individual's income increases.

In contrast, the basic structure of the Irish social insurance (Pay Related Social Insurance) system appears regressive and the basic structure of Value Added Taxation (VAT) appears proportional (i.e. neither progressive nor regressive).

2. *Efficiency* Taxes place a wedge between the price received by the seller and the price paid by the buyer. As such, taxes distort market transactions by distorting market signals (i.e. prices). For example, income tax contributes to the wedge between the buying price of labour (the total cost of labour to the employer) and the selling price of labour (the net wage received by the employee). It is likely that many potentially beneficial economic transactions do not take place because of the existence of this so-called tax wedge. Efficiency requires that the distortions that are inevitably caused by the existence of taxation should be as small as possible, subject to meeting the government's revenue requirement.

More technically, the presence of a tax causes an income effect and a substitution effect. The income effect is unavoidable as it relates to the reduction in purchasing power caused by the existence of the tax. For example, if the government collects an extra €100m in excise duties on tobacco products then there is an extra cost of €100m imposed on consumers of tobacco products. As such, the income effect can be viewed as arising from a financial transfer from taxpayers to the relevant tax authority (e.g. the Office of the Revenue Commissioners). The substitution effect measures the response by consumers to the change in relative prices (i.e. market signals) caused by the tax. For example, smokers react to the presence of excise duties on tobacco products by reducing their consumption of tobacco products. Tax efficiency requires that substitution effects be minimised, subject to meeting the government's revenue requirement. As a general principle, tax efficiency requires that low (high) taxes be placed where economic responses are large (small). For example, it is often argued that low taxes on corporate profits are justified from an efficiency perspective as corporations, especially when foreign-owned, are rather mobile. Conversely, it is sometimes argued that high excise duties on alcohol, hydrocarbon oils and tobacco products are justified from an efficiency perspective, as consumers of these products do not appear to be particularly responsive to the high taxes. It should be apparent to the reader that the demands of tax efficiency and tax equity may not work in the same direction.

3. *Effective administration* The effective administration of a tax system requires that the compliance costs of the tax authorities and taxpayers be minimised, subject to meeting the government's revenue requirement. Effective administration also requires the minimisation of tax code uncertainty. Ineffective administration is characterised by the presence of widespread tax evasion and tax avoidance. Tax evasion refers to the illegal non-declaration of taxable monies whereas tax avoidance refers to the legal circumvention of the tax system.

Scale and sources

It is important to have some knowledge of the scale of taxation and the relative importance of different types of taxation within Ireland. In the absence of such knowledge, media discussion may give a false impression about the significance of a proposed tax change. Expressing total taxation revenue as a proportion of a country's Gross Domestic Product (GDP) is a frequently used measure of the overall scale of taxation within a country. Of the twenty-nine members of the Organisation for Economic Co-operation and Development (OECD), only six countries rank below Ireland in terms of this measure; Ireland's figure of approximately 32% is the lowest within the European Union (EU) and is lower than all other OECD countries apart from Turkey, the United States of America, Australia, Japan, South Korea and Mexico. It should be noted that the use of GDP, as opposed to Gross National Product (GNP), underestimates the overall scale of taxation in Ireland. However, notwithstanding this and other comparison difficulties, Ireland cannot overall be classified as a high tax country.

Figures on the overall scale of taxation, however, can mask important differences between countries with respect to the composition of taxation revenue. Income tax accounts for approximately 31% of Irish tax revenue. The equivalent EU (unweighted) average figure is approximately 26%. In addition, social security contributions by employees, which some view as very similar to personal income tax, account for approximately 4% of Irish tax revenue; the equivalent EU figure is approximately 8%. Social security contributions by employers account for approximately 8% of Irish tax revenue; the equivalent EU figure is approximately 16%. Taxes on goods and services, which include VAT and excise duties, account for approximately 39% of Irish tax revenue with the equivalent EU figure being approximately 30%. Corporation tax accounts for approximately 11% of Irish tax revenue and approximately 9% of EU tax revenue. (Other taxes account for approximately 7% of Irish tax revenue and approximately 11% of EU tax revenue.) Differences between Ireland and other EU members reflect different national features (e.g. age profiles) and priorities (e.g. treatment of foreign investment). However, in an increasingly integrated European market, at least some of these differences may be expected to decline (e.g. taxes on goods and services).

Types of taxes

Income tax

Income tax is charged on income accruing to all residents within the Irish state, whether arising within or outside the state, and on the income of non-residents generated within the Irish state, to an extent which depends on the double taxation agreements between Ireland and the home country of the non-resident. Income is taxed according to two main schedules in Ireland. Income from an office, employment or pension (Schedule E) is taxed on a Pay As You Earn (PAYE) basis with the employer typically deducting tax from the employee's gross income. Profits from trade, professions, etc., rental income, interest income and income from abroad is taxed according to Schedule D; this category encompasses the income of the self-employed.

Income taxes are imposed according to a given table, which is typically subjected to change in the annual budget. The present system in Ireland, as of 6 April 2001, has two tax rates: a standard rate of 20% and a higher rate of 42%. The standard rate applies as soon as the individual's tax-free allowances are used up. The automatic personal allowance in 2001 is £5,500 (€6,983.56) for an individual and £11,000 (€13,967.12) for a married couple; there is also an extra PAYE allowance of £2,000 (€2,539.48) available to those individuals taxed under Schedule E.[1] The width of the standard rate tax band is £20,000 (€25,394.76) for an individual, £40,000 (€50,789.52) for a two-income married couple and £29,000 (€36,822.40) for a one-income married couple. The introduction of a distinction between two-income and one-income married couples represents a movement towards the so-called individualisation of the standard rate band; the introduction of this policy caused significant political controversy and led to the bringing forward of changes in related policy areas.[2]

A number of important discretionary (i.e. not automatically available to all) allowances are also available and these can significantly reduce the individual's income tax payment and affect the progressiveness of the income tax code. Perhaps the most important of these are the allowances against tax of contributions to pension funds and superannuation schemes, which are intended to encourage individuals to provide for retirement. Another important discretionary allowance is relief against tax on the interest component of mortgage repayments. An individual (married couple) can claim this annual allowance on interest payments up to a ceiling of £2,000/€2,539.48 (£4,000/(€5,078.95).[3] This allowance can only be claimed at the standard rate of tax.

Pay Related Social Insurance

Social insurance contributions by both employees and employers are used to support so-called social provisions (e.g. dental care and state pensions). These contributions do not cover fully the associated social provisions, especially state pensions. Employee contributions are referred to in Ireland as Pay Related Social Insurance (PRSI). The PRSI system is complex, with a variety of rates and conditions applying to different classes of insured individuals. Most employees contribute 4% of gross income, with a weekly (non-cumulative) allowance of £100 (€126.97), up to an income ceiling of £28,250 (€35,870.10), above which there is no contribution due. Employees earning less than £226 (€286.96) are exempt. The standard rate of employer contribution is 12% on all incomes. However, the employer rate for incomes at or below £280 (€355.53) per week is reduced to 8.5%, with the rate jumping to 12% on all income once income rises above this threshold.[4]

Value Added Tax and excise duties

The Value Added Tax (VAT) system is a highly integrated sales tax, where the tax is levied at each stage of production and distribution and where companies at each stage are required to account for the tax. VAT is imposed upon a large range of goods and services in Ireland at rates up to the standard rate of 20%. Food and children's clothing and footwear are among a small number of goods and services that are zero-rated or exempt from VAT. The allocation of goods and services between the 12.5% lower rate and the 20% standard rate appears somewhat arbitrary but was influenced by employment considerations. For example, the lower rate was probably imposed in garage services and hairdressing so as to encourage employment in these areas.

Excise duties are imposed across a small range of products in Ireland. The major excisable goods are alcohol, hydrocarbon oils, motor vehicles and tobacco products. These goods have in the past been collectively referred to as 'sin' goods. Perhaps this partially explains why approximately 77% of the price of a packet of cigarettes is accounted for by a combination of VAT and excise duties. Equivalent figures for a litre of (unleaded) petrol and a pint of beer are approximately 67% and 36% respectively.

Corporation tax

A key feature of the Irish corporate tax system has been its dual rate structure. There is a standard rate of 20% and a preferential rate on profits in manufacturing and certain internationally traded service activities of 10%. There is also a 12.5% rate that applies to the profits of a company whose profits do not exceed £200,000 (€253,947.62) in a year. The government has committed itself to unifying all of these rates at 12.5% from the beginning of 2003. The original rationale for the lower rate of 10% in manufacturing was so as to encourage the expansion of employment, particularly by the influx of foreign investment. The rationale for unifying the various rates at 12.5% is twofold. First, it is unlikely that the EU would have allowed a lower rate to apply only to internationally mobile sectors in the future; other EU countries would be likely to lose out in such a scenario. This factor supports the unification of rates across sectors. Second, there appears to have been a consensus within Irish society that capital, relative to labour, had become increasingly mobile. This factor supported a low tax being imposed on capital, relative to labour. Given the recent tightening of the Irish labour market, it will be interesting to see if this consensus, with respect to the relative tax treatment of labour and capital, remains.

Policy Areas

Income tax and social welfare

Although taxation and social welfare may warrant separate administrative units in Ireland, it is not possible to evaluate separately the effects of the social welfare and taxation systems on equity and efficiency. For the unemployed, the social welfare safety net takes the form of unemployment assistance/benefits together with other allowances such as differential rent and medical cards (which entitle the holder to free medical care). For the employed with low income, the social welfare safety net may take the form of family income supplement (FIS) for those with children, together with other allowances such as differential rent and medical cards. Interactions between the tax and social welfare systems almost inevitably lead to the existence of unemployment and poverty traps. An unemployment trap is said to exist when an individual or household is as well off, in monetary terms, unemployed as employed. A poverty trap is said to exist when an individual or household faces a marginal tax and benefit withdrawal rate of at least 100%, i.e. an increase in gross income gives rise to a decrease in net income.[5] Although there has been much improvement in recent years, it is still the case in Ireland that interactions between the tax and social welfare systems can result in the existence of unemployment and poverty traps, particularly for households with a relatively large number of children. Significant improvements in this area have been made by relating family income supplement payments more closely to net, as opposed to gross, income. Reductions in the standard rate of tax, which has fallen from 27% to 20% in the past six years, have also facilitated improvements in this area.

Tax harmonisation

With the increased openness of world economies many taxes are under pressure to follow patterns established elsewhere. Within the context of the EU, for example, rather strict tax harmonisation guidelines have been issued with respect to VAT. Looser guidelines have also been issued in the area of corporation tax and these guidelines, together with other considerations, have led the Irish government to equalise corporation tax rates across the different sectors of the Irish economy. Even when there is an absence of formal guidelines, arbitrage opportunities place some limits on the extent of tax differences between countries. Indeed, variations in the levels of excise duties imposed on alcohol, hydrocarbon oils and tobacco products across countries within the EU have decreased considerably in the past ten years. For example, all readers will be aware of differential tax treatment of certain products giving rise to cross-border trade between Northern Ireland and the Republic of Ireland; somewhat older readers will be aware that the direction of this trade has changed dramatically over the past twenty years.

Property and wealth taxes

Ireland is rather unusual in that it collects a very small proportion of its taxes from what can be broadly termed property and wealth taxes. Up until 1977 Ireland had a very broad based system of property taxes or rates that financed local authorities' expenditures; in that year those taxes attaching to residential property were abolished. Not only did this result in a significant reduction in revenue, it also removed the economic underpinnings of local government in Ireland. The re-introduction of a residential property tax in the 1980s was very controversial despite the tax rate being very low and applying only above a very high threshold (at the time). The residential tax was abolished in 1997. The possible re-introduction of the property tax in more recent years has been made more difficult, at least in administrative terms, by soaring house prices.

There have been no taxes imposed on wealth *per se* in Ireland since 1977. However, some revenue is collected from the taxation of capital transfer between individuals, in particular, the capital acquisitions tax. The capital acquisitions tax is a tax levied on the recipient of the transfer of assets belonging to a recently deceased individual. The tax is supported by the taxation of transfers (gifts) between living individuals.

CASE STUDY

Extract from *The Irish Times*
Government rejects ESRI call on tax cuts
by Mark Brennock and Miriam Donohoe

The Government has rejected a call from the ESRI [Economic and Social Research Institute] to abolish mortgage interest relief and to postpone the tax cuts promised under the Programme for Prosperity and Fairness (PPF) to reduce the risk of a property price collapse.

. . .

Responding to the publication of the ESRI's quarterly economic report, which suggested economic growth should be slowed, Mr Ahern said: 'It's only a short time ago I would have been here explaining how we need to do something about the 18 per cent unemployment. We didn't panic during those bad times; there is no reason why we should do so in the good times.'

. . .

Mr Ahern said that if the State continued to build houses at the rate of 50,000 per annum, the pressures in the housing market identified in the ESRI report would be eased. Speaking to reporters at the end of the Lisbon EU Summit, Mr Ahern said the National Development Plan was geared towards providing the State with the infrastructure necessary to sustain growth. Meanwhile, the Minister for Finance, Mr McCreevy, and the Tánaiste, Ms Harney, also rejected the ESRI report findings.

In an interview with INN, Mr McCreevy said he would not be abolishing mortgage interest relief. 'People have subsidised mortgages and it is not politically on to do away with this.' Mr McCreevy also made it clear that the tax benefits under the PPF would not be held back. 'We have set out in the PPF how we intend to introduce these tax cuts. It is a judgment call to get right the balance between pay and tax.'

In the last year or so, the Minister said, a number of economists disagreed as to what was the correct formula for the Irish economy. 'The Irish economy is the most successful in all of Europe for the last number of years and that must be borne in mind.'

Ms Harney said cuts in personal taxation were a key element of the anti-inflationary strategy which was being pursued by the Government. 'The wide-ranging reductions in personal taxation conceded in budget 2000 will be of significant benefit to all taxpayers. Those tax reductions helped to secure the new partnership deal which paves the way for continued stability and prosperity over the next three years.'

. . .

Source: The Irish Times, 25 March 2000.

Questions

1. Outline some of the economic, and other, effects of abolishing mortgage interest relief.

2. Outline some of the possible contributions of taxation policy to an anti-inflationary strategy.
3. How might cuts in personal taxation be structured so as not to conflict with an anti-inflationary strategy? Explain your answer.

Answers on website

9.2 COMPETITION POLICY

Competition

Other sections of this textbook address in detail the issue of the importance of market structure; the reader should review these sections as appropriate. In these other sections, the market characteristics and outcomes associated with perfect competition are contrasted with the market characteristics and outcomes associated with monopoly; perfect competitive markets are seen to generally perform well relative to monopolistic markets.

Allocative Efficiency

In particular, perfectly competitive markets have the characteristic of being allocatively efficient, as firms are forced by their own self-interests to price at marginal cost, i.e. $P = MC$.[6] This equality between price and marginal cost is regarded as highly desirable by economists as price represents the value placed by society on the marginal unit of the product while marginal cost represents the cost to society of producing that marginal unit. Consider the two alternatives: (i) price is greater than marginal cost (i.e. $P > MC$); and (ii) price is less than marginal cost (i.e. $P < MC$). If price is greater than marginal cost, then the marginal value (or benefit) to society of an extra unit is greater than the marginal cost to society of producing that extra unit. In short, society should have more of the product; resources are being allocated inefficiently. Indeed, the primary disadvantage associated with a monopolistic market structure is that the monopolist produces a level of output at which price is greater than marginal cost (i.e. $P > MC$). Alternatively, if price is less than marginal cost, then the marginal value (or benefit) to society of the last unit produced is less than the marginal cost to society of producing that last unit. In short, society should have less of the product; resources are being allocated inefficiently. However, if price is equal to marginal cost (i.e. $P = MC$), society requires neither more nor less of the product; resources are being allocated efficiently.

    The state is seldom given a stark choice between choosing a perfectly competitive structure or a monopolist structure for a particular market. However, the state can attempt to facilitate the conditions or characteristics that encourage outcomes associated with perfectly competitive markets. In short, the state can encourage the competitive process. Broadly defined, competition policy attempts to protect and enhance the process of competition. The process of competition, although difficult to define, is facilitated by the presence of effective competition and/or potential competition. Effective competition focuses particular attention on the degree of interbrand, and intrabrand, competition between firms within a particular market. Interbrand competition refers to competition between sellers of different brands within a given market; for example, Coca-Cola Enterprises Inc. and PepsiCo, Inc. may be said to compete within the cola market and/or the soft drinks market. Intrabrand competition refers to competition between sellers of the same brand; for example, Superquinn and Dunne Stores compete to sell Coca-Cola to consumers. Potential competition focuses particular attention on the ability of potential entrants to dissuade incumbent firms from abusing their market position.

The presence of market power does not support the process of competition. An individual firm is said to have market power when it has the ability to price above marginal cost. A perfectly competitive firm does not have market power, as it cannot (profitably) price above marginal cost; a monopolist has market power as it can (profitably) price above marginal cost. As noted above, pricing above marginal cost is inefficient (from society's perspective) as such pricing implies that too little of the product is being produced. In practice, almost all firms have some degree of market power. As such, it is generally accepted that the process of competition is only threatened when a firm (or a small number of firms acting collectively) has substantial market power, i.e. the firm has the ability to price significantly above marginal cost.

Market power

Ideally the existence, or otherwise, of substantial market power could be identified by a close inspection of data on a firm's own-price elasticity of demand. As described in detail in Chapter 3, a firm's own-price elasticity of demand measures the percentage decrease (increase) in demand that would follow from a percentage increase (decrease) in the price of the firm's product. A low own-price elasticity (in absolute terms) signals the possession of substantial market power as the firm has the ability to significantly increase price without losing significant market share.[7] The general non-availability of data on own-price elasticities of demand, however, leads to the need for indirect indicators of the existence, or otherwise, of substantial market power. Typical indicators include data and information on market shares and market concentration, entry barriers and the competitive environment within the market. These indicators attempt to identify the presence, or otherwise, of substantial market power in the context of a previously well defined market. The first step, therefore, is the defining of the relevant market. As an example, the reader should consider whether cola constitutes a relevant market for the purposes of competition policy or should the relevant market be broader and encompass (at least) other soft drinks.

Market definition and market power

The relevant market, for competition policy purposes, has been thought of as representing the minimum set of products over which a (perhaps hypothetical) firm would have to have monopoly control before it could be sure of exercising a given degree of market power. In practice, this 'given degree of market power' is perceived of as the ability to profitably raise prices (above competitive levels) by 5% for a significant period of time (say, a year). Profits would fall if the price increase resulted in a large fall in volume demand.[8]

The European Commission and the Irish Competition Authority have, in the past, adopted the following somewhat simpler approach to market definition and market power. A market is said to be composed of those products that are regarded as interchangeable or substitutable by the consumer, by reason of the products' characteristics and their intended use. Market power, in turn, is defined as a position of economic strength enjoyed by a firm that enables it to hinder the maintenance of effective competition on the relevant market by allowing it to behave to an appreciable extent independently of competitors and ultimately of consumers.

Market power and market concentration

Once the market has been established the market shares of the market participants and overall market concentration should be estimated. Regulatory authorities have commonly adopted two alternative approaches for this purpose – concentration ratios and the Herfindahl-Hirschman Index (HHI).

Definition

A concentration ratio measures the total market share of a given number of the largest firms.

For example, the C_4 ratio measures the total market share of the four largest firms in a market.

Definition

The Herfindahl-Hirschman Index is defined as the sum of the squared percentage shares of all firms of the relevant variable (sales, assets . . .) in the market.

As such, the HHI varies between 0 (corresponding to a market with an infinite number of infinitesimally small firms) and 10,000 (corresponding to a market with a single firm, i.e. a pure monopoly). For example, a market consisting of only two equally sized firms would have a HHI of 5,000 (= $50^2 + 50^2$) whereas a market consisting of five equally sized firms would have a HHI of 2,000. A market with a HHI below 1,000 is generally regarded as a non-concentrated market and as a market in which market power issues are unlikely to arise. A market with a HHI above 1,800 is generally regarded as a concentrated market and as a market in which market power issues may arise.

Market power and barriers to entry

Market power is only likely to exist when there is both high market concentration and high entry barriers. Without entry barriers, any attempt by an incumbent firm or incumbent firms to abuse an apparent position of market power is likely to attract entry by other firms. The definition of entry barriers, however, provokes the greatest degree of disharmony between protagonists of the so-called Chicago and Harvard Schools. The Chicago School tends to view entry barriers as being restricted to '. . . costs that must be borne by an entrant that were not incurred by established firms.'[9] In the extreme, so-called Chicago economists only accept restrictive licensing schemes as valid examples of entry barriers. Within an Irish context, licenses for entry into transport (e.g. taxis) would be regarded as an example of an entry barrier. Harvard and the vast majority of other economists have a broader definition of entry barriers in mind. The Harvard School tends to define entry barriers as any '. . . factors that enable established firms to earn supra-competitive profits without threat of entry'.[10] Economies of scale, excess capacity, lower average costs as a result of experience (learning-by-doing), brand proliferation, restrictive distributional agreements and product differentiation (perhaps as a result of excessive advertising) represent some of the major examples of entry barriers as justified by this broader definition of entry barriers.

Market power and competitive environment

The overly mechanical reliance on summary statistics on market concentration (and entry barriers, where available) is fraught with some danger. The existence or otherwise of a non-competitive environment within a market should also be considered. By non-competitive environment it is meant the market conditions that would facilitate tacit or explicit price co-ordination between competitors. The presence of a trade association may, for example, be indicative of conditions that would facilitate tacit or explicit price co-ordination between competitors. Although difficult to quantify precisely, a non-competitive market structure that facilitated the altering of pricing (and other dimensions of competition, say advertising) strategies at exactly the same point in time, in the same direction and by the same magnitude is not conducive to the restraint of market power.

Example: The Irish Competition Authority's *Interim Report of the Study on the Newspaper Industry* (1995) provided a number of interesting details on the pricing policies of market participants within the newspaper market(s): 'The Irish Times and Irish Independent have repeatedly increased prices on the same day and by the same amount while constantly maintaining a price differential of 5p between them.' and '. . . prices of the Evening Herald and Evening Press have repeatedly changed simultaneously over the period since 1984. Throughout this period the retail price of both titles were identical.'

Competition policy in Ireland

Legislation to prohibit restrictive business practices in Ireland was first enacted in 1953 with the Restrictive Trade Practices Act that established the Fair Trade Commission. Legislation was based on the 'control of abuse' principle with restrictive practices considered on a case-by-case basis. The Minister (Industry and Commerce), on the advice of the Commission, could issue a Restrictive Practice Order to cover a particular trade. A failing of competition policy in Ireland over past decades was that it was Order-led; for sectors of the economy not covered by an Order, it remained legal to engage in price-fixing and market-sharing. Repeated enquiries were carried out into the behaviour of several trades as new anti-competitive practices emerged. Policy towards mergers and monopolies was, and to a large extent is, dictated by a separate piece of legislation – the Mergers, Take-overs and Monopolies (Control) Act 1978. The Minister of Enterprise, Trade and Employment had, and to a large extent has, sole jurisdiction over acquisitions and mergers. Although this Act could also have been used to impose severe sanctions on monopolies no such sanctions have been imposed.

The Competition Acts 1991 and 1996 The Competition Act 1991 introduced a prohibition-based system of competition law to Ireland. Anti-competitive agreements between undertakings (firms) and restrictive trade practices are prohibited under Section 4 and the abuse of a dominant position is prohibited under Section 5. The Competition Authority was established under the Act to play a supportive and advisory role; it had no enforcement powers. The passing into legislation of the Competition (Amendment) Bill 1996 represented a significant change in emphasis. The primary aim of this legislation was to provide more effective enforcement of competition policy. It is now a criminal offence not to comply with the conditions of a licence granted by the Authority. This Act criminalises anti-competitive behaviour and allows for prison sentences of up to two years and fines of up to 10% of a firm's world-wide turnover. New powers of search and greater rights of discovery, including the right to conduct a 'dawn raid', have been granted to the Director of Competition Enforcement (a member of the Competition Authority) and the ability to initiate prosecutions, both civil and criminal, now resides with the Authority. Furthermore, it can now carry out studies without being requested to do so by the Minister.

Regulation policy

Competition policy is complementary to the process of competition as it attempts to facilitate the market conditions that give rise to market outcomes associated with perfectly competitive markets. For example, competition policy attempts to facilitate ease of entry into (and exit from) a market and attempts to create the conditions generally associated with a competitive environment. Competition policy does not replace, or substitute itself for, the process of competition. More specifically, competition policy does not dictate the number of firms within a market nor the price (output) that individual firms can charge (produce). In contrast, regulation policy often substitutes for the process of competition. Regulation policy tends to dictate the number of firms within a market and/or the price (output) that individual firms can charge (produce). Agriculture, cable and satellite TV, electricity, gas, telecommunications, transportation and water represent just some examples of the many markets that are, or have been, regulated in many countries.

From an economic perspective, the major justification for the use of regulation policy, as opposed to competition policy, is the existence of so-called natural monopolies. However, regulation policy may also be used for other purposes; the 'public interest' has been used to justify the use of regulation policy in many contexts. For example, the state has asserted a public interest in the existence of a concentrated transportation market in Ireland in the past.

Definition

A market is said to be a natural monopoly if its total output can be produced more cheaply by a single firm than by two or more firms.

Technically, a natural monopoly exists if $C(Q) = C(Q_1 + \ldots + Q_N) < C(Q_1) + \ldots + C(Q_N)$, where Q represents total output, C(Q) represents the total cost of producing Q and N represents the relevant number of firms.[11] A natural monopoly exists if there are very significant economies of scale. In such a case, an individual firm's marginal cost (MC) and average cost (AC) curves decline continuously and the firm's marginal cost (MC) curve will be below its average cost (AC) curve. From an economics perspective, the existence of a natural monopoly gives rise to serious concerns. The natural monopolist, being a monopolist, has an incentive to maximise profits by producing a level of output at which price is greater than marginal cost, i.e. resources are allocated inefficiently. The natural monopolist can be regulated in a number of ways.

Marginal cost pricing

The regulator can apparently achieve allocative efficiency by insisting that the natural monopolist produce a level of output at which price is equal to marginal cost. There are at least two problems with this apparent solution. First, the regulator may not have enough information to be able to determine the output level at which price is equal to marginal cost; it may not be in the natural monopolist's interest to help in this regard. Second, if the natural monopolist produces the allocatively efficient level of output, it will sustain losses. Pricing at marginal cost implies pricing below average cost as the marginal cost curve of the monopolist lies below the average cost curve of the natural monopolist. One possible solution to this latter problem is for the regulator to provide the natural monopolist with a subsidy to offset the losses associated with achieving allocative efficiency. However, these subsidies must be financed by increased taxes elsewhere; these increased taxes, of course, also lead to inefficiencies. It may also be difficult politically to provide a natural monopolist with a subsidy.

Average cost pricing

The problems associated with implementing marginal cost pricing have tended to lead regulators towards the adoption of some form of average cost pricing. Setting price at average cost avoids the problem of having to subsidise the natural monopolist but at the expense of sacrificing allocative efficiency. Pricing at average cost ensures that the natural monopolist makes neither economic profits nor economic losses; pricing at average cost also ensures that the natural monopolist prices above marginal cost. Average cost pricing regulation also suffers from the problem of dampening cost-reducing incentives. For example, if the natural monopolist succeeds in reducing costs by 10%, the regulator may respond by insisting that prices also be reduced by 10%. Indeed, the natural monopolist has no obvious reason not to allow costs to actually increase.[12] In practice, average cost pricing is often adapted so as to encourage innovation by allowing for some profits. This type of regulation – adjusted average cost pricing – is referred to as rate-of-return regulation.

Franchise bidding

Rather than regulating the natural monopolist on an on-going basis, it may be preferable to auction the (franchise) rights to be the natural monopolist in the first place. If the auction is done on the basis of the highest bid winning, the outcome is likely to be equivalent to a standard monopoly outcome. However, the monopoly profits are transferred to the state as a result of the bidding process as the bidders would find themselves forced to bid higher and higher amounts until almost no net profits could be gained. A possible alternative is for the auction to be done on the basis of bidders committing to charging a certain price to customers in the future. The results of this process are likely to be close to the results obtained by average cost pricing regulation, as bidders would find themselves forced to offer lower and lower prices until almost no net profits could be expected. A further possibility is for the 'auction' to be done on the basis of a number of criteria; 'bidders' would then compete on the basis of quality as well as price considerations. This latter possibility is often referred to as a 'beauty contest'. The interested reader is directed to the second case study for an example and further discussion.

Public enterprise and privatisation

Rather than the state attempting to regulate the natural monopolist, many governments, particularly within Europe, have in the past elected to actually become the natural monopolist. The distinctive feature (and advantage or disadvantage depending on one's perspective) of this approach is that the objective of the natural monopolist is no longer necessarily the maximisation of private profits. The management of a public enterprise must ultimately be somewhat accountable to voters as opposed to shareholders and, as such, it is possible that the management's goal will be the maximisation of public welfare as opposed to private profit. Within an Irish context, airport management, electricity, telecommunications and transportation provide just four of the many possible examples of state ownership and enterprise. However, a sustained movement away from public ownership and enterprise and towards privatisation began in the early 1980s. Within a European context, the UK government led by Margaret Thatcher was at the forefront of this movement; the privatisation of British Telecom (1984) and British Gas (1986) represented very significant economic and political events. Many of the large privatisations within the UK were accompanied by the setting up of specialist independent regulatory agencies (e.g. Oftel and Ofgas). The lesson from the UK privatisation experience appears to be that the creation of market conditions suitable for facilitating the process of competition or the continued or renewed regulation of a natural monopoly is as important as the ownership structure (i.e. public or private enterprise).

Ireland has only recently started the process of privatisation. After successfully selling its stake in Irish Life, the state recently privatised Eircom (previously known as Telecom Eireann). Initially, the privatisation proved to be a political success as Eircom's share price increased by over 20% above its floatation price. However, Eircom's share price has since fallen considerably below its floatation price. The evolution of Eircom's share price may well have serious repercussions for future proposed privatisations in Ireland (e.g. Aer Rianta). However, from an economics perspective, the success, or otherwise, of the privatisation of Eircom will be judged primarily by the effect of the privatisation on the process of competition within the Irish telecommunications market(s).

SUMMARY

1. Taxation finances the provision of public services, facilitates the redistribution of income and alters economic behaviour. A tax can be judged according to its contribution to equity, efficiency and effective administration. Ireland is not a high tax country. The size of the tax rate and the width of the tax base determine tax revenue. Relative to other members of the European Union, Ireland places high taxes on consumption and low taxes on property and wealth. Ireland's corporate tax structure has been, and will continue to be, unusual by international standards.
2. Competition policy and regulation policy attempt to facilitate allocative efficiency. Competition policy attempts to facilitate the conditions necessary for the creation of effective and potential competition. Competition policy does not attempt to set the number of firms or the prices (quantities) that individual firms can charge (produce). Regulation policy attempts to address the natural monopoly problem. Regulation policy attempts to set the number of firms and/or the prices (outputs) that individual firms can charge (produce). Privatisation alters the ownership structure of a firm; it does not necessarily alter the market's competitive environment.

KEY TERMS

Taxation Policy
Equity
Ability-to-pay principle
Progressive tax
Regressive tax
Proportional tax
Efficiency
Income effect
Substitution effect
Effective administration
Tax evasion
Tax avoidance
Pay As You Earn
Pay Related Social Insurance
Value Added Tax
Excise duties
Corporation tax
Unemployment trap
Poverty trap
Tax harmonisation
Rates
Residential property tax
Capital acquisitions tax

Competition Policy
Perfect competition
Monopoly
Allocative efficiency
Market power
Own-price elasticity of demand
Market definition
Concentration ratio
Herfindahl-Hirschman Index
Entry barriers
Competitive environment
Competition Authority
Natural monopoly
Economies of scale
Marginal cost pricing
Average cost pricing
Franchise bidding
Public enterprise
Privatisation

REVIEW QUESTIONS

1. Discuss the progressiveness, or otherwise, of the Irish tax system. Discuss the progressiveness, or otherwise, of at least two individual components of the Irish tax system. How important are these components? How has the progressiveness of the Irish tax system been affected in recent budgets?

2. Describe some general aspects of the Irish tax system that are shaped by the European Union. Describe some individual components of the Irish tax system that are shaped by the European Union. How important are these aspects and components?

3. Describe possible advantages and disadvantages associated with using the Herfindahl-Hirschman index for assessing market concentration.

4. Consider a number of concentrated markets in Ireland. Is there scope for improved competition within these markets? Is regulation of these markets necessary? Explain your answers.

TRUE OR FALSE (SUPPORT YOUR ANSWER)

1. Irish taxation revenue as a proportion of Ireland's GNP is higher than Irish taxation revenue as a proportion of Ireland's GDP.

2. Efficiency requires that high taxes be placed on products with high price elasticities of demand.

3. Expenditure taxes (i.e. VAT and excise duties) in Ireland are low compared to other members of the European Union.

4. Allocative efficiency requires that price be equal to marginal cost.

5. A Herfindahl-Hirschman Index (HHI) of 500 implies the existence of a highly concentrated market.

6. The major justification for the existence of regulation policy, as opposed to competition policy, is the existence of natural monopolies.

CASE STUDY

Extract from *The Irish Independent*
Doyle opts for beauty contest on 3G licences
by Pat Boyle

The telecoms regulator has ruled against an auction and decided to award four third generation mobile phone licences on the basis of a 'beauty contest' in a move which is expected to restrict the price of a new licence to between £70m and £150m. Third generation mobile phones are expected to revolutionise mobile usage and will work 200 times faster than existing models, carrying more data faster and allowing for quick internet access.

One licence is being retained for a new entrant to the Irish mobile phone market and analysts are predicting plenty of interest from overseas groups including the likes of Orange and Vodafone from the UK. Other bidders are expected to include existing operators Eircell and Esat as well as Meteor and Irish Multichannel. Irish Multichannel director Willie Fagan welcomed the decision to opt for a beauty contest, but said his group had yet to decide how it would get involved, whether in a consortium or on its own.

During a briefing to announce how the licences would be awarded, the regulator Etain Doyle said 'supply side considerations' would be the deciding factor in making the licence awards. Before deciding on the beauty contest approach, the regulator had sought the views of the industry. The decision was made with a 'clear reference to the consumer', Ms Doyle said. 'I believe that the beauty contest will best secure competitive prices, choice and quality in the Irish market,' she said. While an auction would yield a big windfall for the Exchequer, the operators would then have less to spend on developing the network, and Ms Doyle pointed to the impact this would have on prices. Given the small size of the Irish market, its lower population and consequent higher per capita costs, it was felt that an auction system would reduce the feasibility of lower prices being achieved. The regulator will be looking for new licence holders to provide for an effective and speedy 'roll-out' of their services around the country, as well as 'roaming' facilities to allow subscribers use other networks.

Ms Doyle will also be anxious to ensure that successful applicants allow other service providers access to their new networks to establish 'virtual' networks and allow for greater competition. Now that the regulator has opted to bypass the auction system, analyst Jemma Houlihan of ABN Amro believes that euro 200m represents a 'cap' on the cost of an Irish third generation licence.

. . .

The beauty contest will involve a preliminary round after which companies will be invited to tender their bids. It is anticipated that the first licences will be awarded in May next year with the first networks up and running by 2002.

Source: *Irish Independent*, 27 July 2000.

QUESTIONS

1. Describe possible advantages and disadvantages associated with using a beauty contest to award third generation mobile phone licences in Ireland.
2. Describe possible advantages and disadvantages associated with using an auction to award third generation mobile phone licences in Ireland.
3. What method do you think is most appropriate for the awarding of third generation mobile phone licences in Ireland? Why?

PART II

MACROECONOMICS

INTRODUCTION TO MACROECONOMICS

Macroeconomics is concerned with the operation of the economy as a whole. In this branch of economics, we deal with aggregate variables such as national output, the general price level and total employment. Arising out of our study of macroeconomics is an appreciation of policy issues.

Our starting point in macroeconomics is the measurement of economic activity. Chapter 10 examines the different ways of measuring economic activity. The problems associated with the National Accounts are also discussed.

The two main doctrines of economic thought are outlined in Chapter 11. The classical school of economics dates back to Adam Smith. The Keynesian revolution challenged the existing economic orthodoxy of the time.

In Chapter 12, the Keynesian model of income determination is explained. The policy implications arising out of the Keynesian model are also discussed. The chapter ends with an account of the Irish experience with Keynesian economics.

In a non-barter economy, transactions are facilitated by money. The money stock and interest rates are important variables in any modern economy. Monetary policy is a policy instrument used by government to achieve various economic objectives. Chapter 13 examines the role of money in the economy, both in the context of the Irish economy and in the euro area.

A model of the macroeconomy is presented in Chapter 14. The IS/LM model is a useful framework to explain fiscal and monetary policies and to examine the divergent views of Keynesians and monetarists.

Chapter 15 introduces open economy macroeconomics. Our examination of macroeconomics until now has been largely within the confines of a closed economy. This chapter analyses the effect which factors such as external trade, foreign interest rates and flexible exchange rates have on the economy. It also examines Ireland's experience and performance within the European Monetary System. Economic and Monetary Union, the European Central Bank and the euro are all discussed.

A more complex model of the macroeconomy is examined in Chapter 16. Prices and output are determined in the AD/AS model. This framework can be used to analyse macroeconomic problems and policy options.

Chapter 17 examines a number of important macroeconomic issues. Unemployment, inflation and international trade are discussed in the context of a small open economy on the periphery of Europe. Some policy options are also examined.

Our final chapter examines the issue of economic growth and long-run changes in both economic activity and the living standards of a nation. A simple model explaining economic growth is presented. Factors that might explain an economy's growth, both in an international and domestic context, are outlined. The chapter ends with a brief account of the 'Celtic Tiger' phenomenon.

CHAPTER 10

MEASURING THE MACROECONOMY

'Among the most effective measures of the economic performance of a nation is its total net product, or national income – the sum of all goods produced during a given period . . .'[1]

Simon Kuznets (1901–85)

'For, unlike many measurements in the physical sciences, there is no unique way of measuring either the size of an economy at a particular point in time, or its growth over time.'[2]

Paul Ormerod

CHAPTER OBJECTIVES

Upon completing this chapter, the student should understand:

- the circular flow model of economic activity;
- the different ways of measuring economic activity;
- the meaning of gross domestic product (GDP) and other similar measures of economic activity;
- the shortcomings of GDP as a measure of economic activity;
- the Irish National Accounts.

OUTLINE

10.1 **The circular flow of economic activity**
10.2 **The three methods for measuring economic activity**
10.3 **The National Accounts**
10.4 **Limitations of GDP as a measure of economic activity**
10.5 **The Irish experience**

INTRODUCTION

This chapter begins with the circular flow model of economic activity. Although it is a very simple model, it introduces all of the principal agents in the economy: households, firms, financial institutions, the state and foreign markets. The model also explains how these sectors interact.

We use this model to introduce the three ways by which economic activity is measured. Gross domestic product (GDP), the most common measure of economic activity, is explained in detail. GDP is often used as a measure of national economic activity and as a basis of international comparisons. Its defects as a measure of prosperity are also discussed.

The chapter ends with an analysis of the Irish National Accounts as published by the Central Statistics Office (CSO).

10.1   THE CIRCULAR FLOW OF ECONOMIC ACTIVITY

The circular flow is a simplified model of the economy showing the movement of resources between consumers and producers. The French economist François Quesnay (1694–1774) is credited with its discovery.[3] It is believed that he modelled it on William Harvey's famous circulation of blood diagram.

A modern economy is very complex. There are many different sectors (households, firms, government, financial, foreign) with each sector comprised of many interacting individual units. In order to understand this sophisticated system we need to begin with a simple model.

We begin with a model of the private sector: households and firms. These are identifiable not by who they are but by what they do: households consume whereas firms produce. In a simple, closed economy the only transactions are between households and firms. The result is a model of the economy which shows the transactions between households and firms. This model is called the circular flow and is illustrated in Figure 10.1.

Figure 10.1:   The circular flow between households and firms

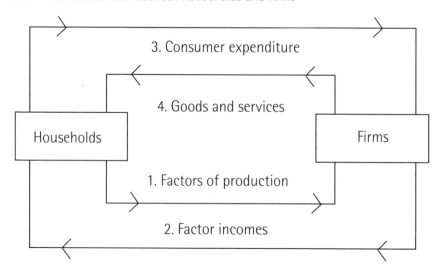

It is the households who own the basic factors of production. These inputs are supplied to the firms (1) in order to produce goods and services. The firms pay the households factor incomes for the use of these inputs (2). There is a special term given to each return on the different factors of production: wages are the return on labour, interest on capital, rent on land and profit on enterprise. Households receive the factor incomes and use them to buy goods and services from the firms (3). These goods and services are supplied by the firms to the households (4).

The transactions between households and firms are reflected in the loops drawn above. There is a distinction between the inner loop and the outer loop. Flows 1 and 4 (the inner loop) reflect the transfer of real or non-monetary resources. Flows 2 and 3 (the outer loop) reflect the transfer of money or monetary payments.

In this simple model all output is sold (output = expenditure) and all income is spent (income = expenditure). Thus, output must equal income (output = income). These equalities are discussed again in the next section of this chapter.

The transactions, in terms of the agent involved, are summarised in Table 10.1.

Table 10.1: Summary of transactions between households and firms

Households	Firms
Supply factors of production to firms.	Use factors of production to produce goods and services.
Receive factor income in return for inputs.	Pay households for use of inputs.
Spend income on goods and services.	Sell goods and services to households.

The simple circular flow can be modified to include the banking sector. In the above analysis, the households spend all of their factor incomes on goods and services. In Figure 10.2 the households are faced with two options: to spend on goods and services or to save. One of the functions of the banking system in the circular flow is to facilitate savings. However, savings is a leakage or a withdrawal from the circular flow. A leakage is simply a movement of funds out of the circular flow. This can diminish the level of economic activity in the economy. A simple example is illustrated below.

Let us suppose income is equal to €10,000 and households save 20% of their income. Spending is now limited to €8,000 (80% of €10,000). In these circumstances there are no economic incentives for firms to continue producing €10,000 worth of goods since their sales on the domestic market (no foreign sector exists so there is no possibility of exporting goods to foreign markets) are limited to the €8,000 which households are prepared to spend. The value of output produced is limited to €8,000. Consequently the income generated is limited to €8,000. If we assume that households still save 20% of their income, spending in the next round is reduced to €6,400 (80% of €8,000). This process continues with the level of economic activity diminishing further with every round. This appears quite alarming and we might question whether there is any escape from this vicious circle. An escape exists in the form of 'investment expenditure' which is an injection into the circular flow. An injection is a movement of funds into the circular flow: it is an addition to economic activity. The term 'investment' was defined in Chapter 7. It is corporate or business expenditure on machinery, fixtures and fittings, vehicles and buildings. It also includes inventory build-ups of raw materials, semi-finished and finished goods. Firms may finance investment expenditure by borrowing from the very same financial institutions which facilitated those households who had surplus funds and decided to save a percentage of their income. The borrowing facility is the other main function of the banking system. Financial institutions serve as intermediaries to bring together those who have excess funds (households) and those who are in need of funds (firms).

Figure 10.2: The circular flow, savings and investment

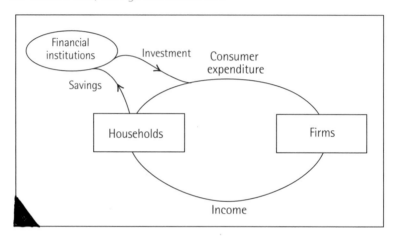

If savings are greater than investment in money terms the level of economic activity diminishes. However, if investment is greater than savings the level of economic activity increases. The level of economic activity remains unchanged if savings are matched by investment: the economy is said to be in equilibrium. See Appendix 10.1 for more material on this subject.

The circular flow with savings and investment is now adjusted to include the government or the public sector. The government is involved in spending large amounts of money on defence, security, education, health services and so on. It also spends money on transfer payments.

Definition

Transfer payments redistribute wealth rather than provide a unique good or service. They include pensions, unemployment benefits, disability allowances and other payments.

All of these forms of expenditure are injections into the circular flow. However, these expenditures need to be financed. It is government revenue, primarily in the form of taxation, which finances such expenditure. Taxes are usually divided into two categories, direct and indirect. The former is a tax on income. Examples include personal income tax and corporate tax. Indirect tax is a tax on expenditure. Excise duties and VAT are examples. Taxation, both direct and indirect, is a leakage from the circular flow. Direct taxes are a leakage from the income loop; indirect taxes are a leakage from the expenditure loop. The adjusted circular flow is illustrated in Figure 10.3. Government spending and taxation is incorporated in the circular flow model.

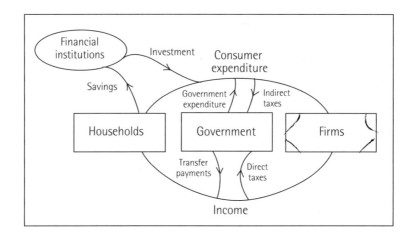

Figure 10.3:
The circular flow
including the
government

There is one final adjustment to be made to the circular flow model. International trade between countries is a very important part of total expenditure. The analysis to date was applied to a closed economy. We now adjust the model to include foreign markets. Exports are Irish goods and services purchased by non-residents. Export earnings are a monetary flow from the foreign market into the domestic market. Hence, it is an injection into the circular flow. Imports are goods and services purchased by Irish households and firms from foreign-based firms. Payment for imports is a monetary flow from the domestic market into the foreign market: it is a leakage out of the circular flow. The difference between exports and imports is referred to as net exports. Its value is positive if the value of exports exceeds the value of imports. It is negative if the value of imports exceeds the value of exports.

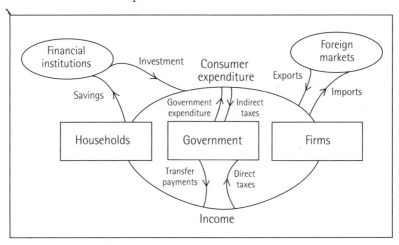

Figure 10.4:
The complete
circular flow

Figure 10.4 is the complete version of the circular flow diagram. All agents and their transactions with each other are included. A more complete explanation is now required.

On receipt of the factors of production from the households, the firms engage in the production of goods and services. The income which the firms pay out for the use of the factor inputs is reflected in the lower loop of the diagram.

In a simple model without government intervention or a banking sector, as represented in Figure 10.1, the households receive and, in turn, spend all of the national income. However, the introduction of the government sector ensures that the households do not receive all of the national income. The amount which the households actually receive is referred to as disposable income. This is national income supplemented by transfer payments but excluding taxes. On receipt of this income, the households allocate a certain amount to savings. The rest is allocated to consumer expenditure.

The upper loop shows that consumer expenditure is only one form of expenditure. Others include investment expenditure by the corporate sector, public expenditure by the government, expenditure on domestic goods and services by non-residents and expenditure on foreign goods and services.

There were no leakages or injections in our simple model. The analysis is a little more complicated when we extend the model to include other sectors. In Figure 10.4 savings, taxation and imports constitute the leakages whereas investment, government expenditure, transfer payments and exports constitute the injections. Economic activity depends largely on the relative size of these injections and leakages.

National income is one measure of economic activity. An important difference between the leakages and the injections is their respective relationship with national income. Leakages are endogenous variables. This means that they vary with one of the other components of the model. In this particular case, savings, taxation and imports will all increase when national income increases. There is a functional relationship between these variables and national income.

In contrast, all four injections are independent of the income level. They are exogenous. They are part of the model in that they affect the level of national income. However, their values are determined by variables which are outside the model. For example, investment depends on expectations about the future and the interest rate. Government spending and transfer payments are determined within the political process. Exports increase or decrease with foreign income. These variables are not a function of national income. This subtle difference between leakages and injections is fundamental to the stability of the economy. This issue will be discussed in greater detail in Chapter 12.

In relation to the leakages and injections in the economy three possibilities arise and are summarised in Table 10.2.

Table 10.2: Injections, leakages and their effect on economic activity

	Injections		Leakages
Effect on			
economic activity			
	Injections	<	leakages

If the leakages are greater than the injections, in money terms, the level of economic activity diminishes. If the injections are greater than the leakages the level of economic activity increases. The level of economic activity remains unchanged if the leakages and the injections are equal. The economy is said to be in equilibrium.

This completes our study of the circular flow model. We will now examine the ways in which economic activity is actually measured.

10.2 THE THREE METHODS FOR MEASURING ECONOMIC ACTIVITY

There are three approaches to measuring the economic activity of a country. These are portrayed in Figure 10.5.

Figure 10.5: A simplified version of the circular flow

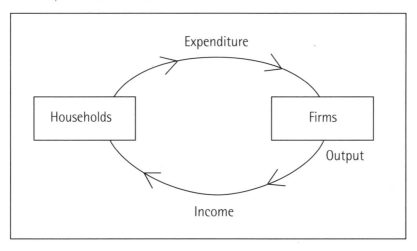

Figure 10.5 is a simplified version of the circular flow. It highlights the three approaches for measuring national economic activity. It indicates that the factors of production are combined to produce *output*. In turn, the factors of production are paid *income* which then becomes *expenditure*. These are the three methods for measuring a nation's economic activity. As we will see later they are defined in such a way that they should yield the same result. In practice they usually give slightly different results due to measurement errors which arise from the difficulty in collecting and tabulating all of the data involved.

Explanations for all three are provided below. In Ireland, the income and expenditure methods are widely used. Estimates for the two methods will differ as they arise from different data sources. In order to reconcile the two estimates, an adjustment is made to personal expenditure. The income and expenditure approaches are published annually by the CSO in the publication entitled *National Income and Expenditure*. For our purpose the most important is the expenditure approach because many subsequent chapters in this textbook incorporate material which is largely based on this method of calculation.

Expenditure method

National expenditure is the sum of the expenditures of consumers, firms, government and the foreign sector on domestically produced goods and services. More specifically, we add household spending on consumer goods and services, spending by firms and households on capital goods, government purchases of goods and services and finally, net exports. Imports are substituted because consumption, investment and government spending cover both domestically produced goods and foreign-produced goods. Exports are added in order to get a value for total expenditure on domestic production.

Table 10.3 shows the calculation of national income using the expenditure approach for the calendar year 1999. The numbers in the column on the left-hand side are the item numbers used by the CSO.

Table 10.3: Measuring economic activity in Ireland using the expenditure method

	Description	£m
55	Personal consumption of goods and services	34,743
56	Net expenditure by central and local government on current goods and services	8,753
57	Gross domestic fixed capital formation	16,175
58	Value of physical changes in stocks	−57
59	Exports of goods and services	60,457
60	less Imports of goods and services	−50,978
12a	Statistical discrepancy	−41
61	Gross domestic product at market prices	69,052
14	Net factor income from the rest of the world	−9,984
63	Gross national product at current market prices	59,068
24	less Provision for depreciation	−7,114
	Net national product at market prices	51,954
26	less Taxes on expenditure	−9,577
27	plus Subsidies	1,788
15	Net national product at factor cost = National income	44,166

Source: CSO, *National Income and Expenditure 1999*, August 2000.

Income method

Alternately, national income is derived by adding the different incomes of the factors of production: remuneration of employees, income from the self-employed, profit of companies and rent of dwellings (imputed in the case of owner-occupied). In Ireland it is based on data collected by the Revenue Commissioners for the purpose of income tax assessment. The calculation of national income for the year 1999 as published by the CSO is shown in Table 10.4.

Table 10.4: Measuring economic activity in Ireland using the income method

	Description	£m
	Income from agriculture, forestry and fishing:	
1	Income from self-employment and other trading income	1,810
2/3	Wages/contribution to social insurance	261
	Non-agricultural Income:	
4/6	Trading profits	23,131
7	Adjustment for stock appreciation	–562
8/9	Rent	3,679
10	Wages, salaries and pensions	26,304
11	Employers' contribution to social insurance	1,782
	Adjustments	–2,255
13	Net domestic product at factor cost	54,149
14	Net factor income from the rest of the world	–9,984
15	Net national product at factor cost = National income	44,166

Source: CSO, *National Income and Expenditure 1999*, August 2000.

Output method

To arrive at a figure for national output, we add together the money value of the output produced from the various sectors of the economy. There is the danger of double or multiple counting when adopting this approach.

Definition

Double counting occurs if the expenditure on intermediate goods is included in the calculation of national output.

National output does not consist of the full value of every single item produced in the economy since the output of one good may be the input for another.

For example, a farmer may sell his cow at the market to a retail outlet for €800. The cow is slaughtered, packaged and sold for the retail value of €1,000. A straight summation of transactions suggests that national output has increased by €1,800. In this case, national output would be overstated because the value of the cow has been double counted. The cow is the input for the retail meat trade. The addition to national output is actually €1,000.

In order to avoid double counting one of two methods can be used. Firstly, we can sum the value added at each stage of production. Secondly, the final value of all finished goods can be calculated with the value of all intermediate goods excluded. Since the sum of all the value added at each stage of production must equal the value of the final output produced, these two methods yield the same figure.

Table 10.5 shows economic activity in Ireland in 1999, by sector of origin.

Table 10.5:　Measuring economic activity in Ireland using the output method

	Description	£m
16	Agriculture, forestry and fishing	2,072
17	Industry (including building)	21,904
18	Distribution, transport and communication	9,448
19	Public administration and defence	2,333
20	Other services	21,211
21	Adjustment for stock appreciation	−562
	Adjustments	−2,255
23	Net domestic product at factor cost	54,149
29	Net factor income from the rest of the world	−9,984
15	Net national product at factor cost = National income	44,166

Source: CSO, *National Income and Expenditure 1999*, August 2000.

Figure 10.6 summarises graphically the three ways of measuring the level of national economic activity.

Figure 10.6:　The three methods of measuring economic activity

INCOME	OUTPUT	EXPENDITURE

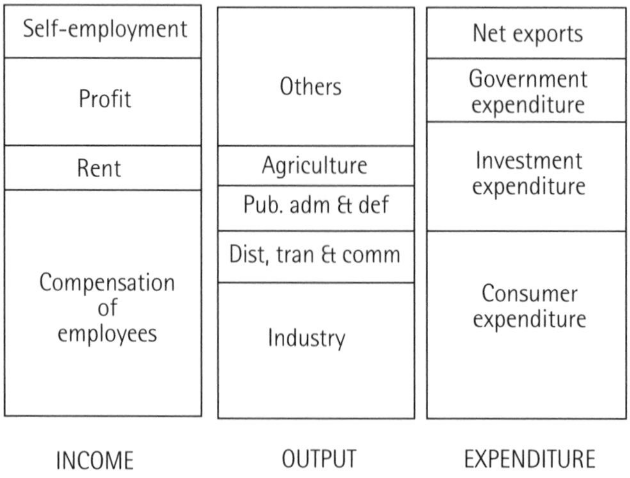

We will now define the various measures of economic activity which appear in the National Accounts.

10.3   THE NATIONAL ACCOUNTS

Simon Kuznets of Harvard University developed the national income accounting system which provided the basic framework for measuring economic activity.[4] The key concept in the national income accounts and the most common measure of a country's economic performance is gross domestic product.

Definition

Gross domestic product (GDP) is the value of all goods and services produced domestically in the economy, regardless of the nationality of the owners of the factors of production.

GDP for Ireland includes the value of output produced by subsidiaries of foreign multinationals operating in Ireland. The output of Irish multinationals operating outside the country is excluded. GDP is a flow concept, i.e. it is the value of goods and services produced over a particular time period. In Ireland it is measured on a yearly basis. In 1999 the CSO estimate for GDP was £69,052m (€87,677m).

There are many different variations to GDP, outlined in Figure 10.7. The figure also highlights the differences between the calculation of GDP and disposable income, another economic measure which is frequently used. An explanation of Figure 10.7 follows.

Figure 10.7:   From GDP to disposable income

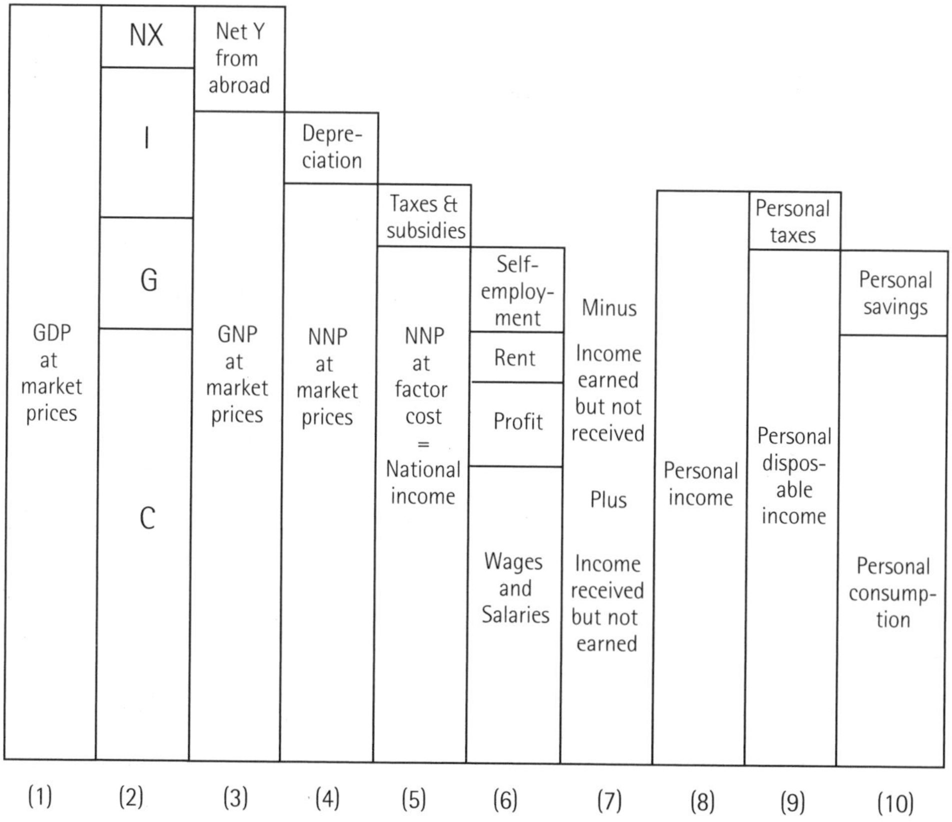

Composition of GDP

GDP is comprised of consumer expenditure, investment expenditure, government expenditure on goods and services and net exports (exports less imports), as shown in columns 1 and 2 in Figure 10.7.

- Consumer expenditure, or simply consumption (C) is spending by the household sector on durable (e.g. furniture, cars, etc.) and non-durable (e.g. food, drink, etc.) goods and services. The CSO estimates that consumer expenditure for 1999 was £34,743m, accounting for just over 50% of GDP. It is by far the largest component of GDP. However, in comparison to other western economies, the percentage of total expenditure devoted to consumption in Ireland is not high. Table 10.6 shows comparable percentages for other countries.

Table 10.6:   Consumption as a percentage of GDP, 1999 (US$bn)

Country	GDP	Consumption/GDP
US	8,709	68
UK	1,374	64
Belgium	246	63
France	1,410	60
Germany	2,081	58
Ireland	85	49
Norway	145	48
Singapore	85	39

Source: World Bank, *World Development Report 2000/2001.*

Consumer expenditure is dependent on a range of factors including income, wealth, advertising, prices and expectations. These factors and their relationship with consumer expenditure are discussed in greater detail in Chapter 12.
- Investment expenditure (I), or to use its full title gross domestic fixed capital formation, is the total outlay on all capital goods. This category of goods includes machinery, factories, vehicles and so on. All new buildings and all construction work on roads, harbours, airports, forestry development and so on is included. It also includes new home spending. Although the contribution to a single year's GDP is small relative to consumption, investment expenditure is viewed as the key to long-run economic activity. In 1999 investment expenditure was £16,175m, accounting for 23.4% of GDP. This component of GDP is more volatile than any other and therefore more difficult to predict. Its volatility is primarily due to the factors which influence it. These include expectations and interest rates, two factors which are known to fluctuate wildly.
- Government expenditure, denoted by G, measures spending by the state on current goods and services. The CSO estimate for 1999 was £8,753m. This accounts for almost 12.7% of GDP. It is important to note that transfer payments are excluded from this component as they do not involve payment in exchange for production.

Government expenditure as a percentage of GDP varies significantly from economy to economy. For example, welfare states tend to have a high government expenditure share of GDP. Examples include Sweden and Denmark where the respective ratios were 26% and 25%, in 1999. In contrast, the US and Japan have low government spending/GDP ratios. The relevant figures for 1999 were 15% and 10% respectively.

• Net exports, denoted by NX, is the difference between the exports and the imports of goods and services. Net exports can be positive, reflecting a trade surplus where the value of exports exceeds the value of imports; or negative, reflecting a trade deficit where the value of imports exceeds the value of exports. In Ireland the ratio of exports or imports to GDP is very high. In 1999 the ratio of exports to GDP was 87.6% whereas the ratio of imports to GDP was 73.8%. This reflects the extreme openness of the Irish economy. As a result, Ireland is an economy which is very susceptible to changes in the international economic climate. This component of GDP is determined by a wide range of factors including the level of domestic and foreign income, exchange rates and relative inflation rates.

GDP is the sum of consumer expenditure, investment expenditure, government expenditure and net exports and can be expressed as follows:

$$\text{GDP} \equiv \text{C} + \text{I} + \text{G} + \text{NX} \qquad \text{[10.1]}$$

where the symbol $\equiv$ denotes an identity. An identity is something that is true by definition.

Variations of GDP

One variant of GDP is gross national product.

Definition

Gross national product (GNP) is the value of all goods and services produced by a country's productive factors regardless of their geographical location.

In 1999, Ireland's GNP was valued at £59,068m (€75,001m).

Values for GNP and for GDP in Ireland for the period 1975–99 are recorded in Appendix 10.2.

Although GDP is used for comparison with other EU countries, GNP is probably a better measure of Irish economic activity. GNP reflects only the part of economic activity that is produced and shared by Irish nationals.

Column 3 of Figure 10.7 indicates that the difference between gross domestic product and gross national product is net factor income from the rest of the world.

Definition

Net factor income from the rest of the world is the outflows of income earned by foreigners operating in Ireland minus the inflows of income earned by foreign subsidiaries of Irish companies.

There are more foreign multinationals operating in Ireland sending profits abroad than there are Irish multinationals sending profits home.[5] The net repatriation of profits and the interest payments on the national debt to non-residents are both outflows. In 1999, net factor income from abroad amounted to an outflow of £9,984m. Hence, GDP is consistently larger than GNP in Ireland. This was not always the case. About a quarter of a century ago, emigrants' remittances and interest on the country's external assets meant that the net factor income from abroad was positive. This resulted in GNP greater than GDP (see Appendix 10.2).

Gross national disposable income GNDI (not included in Figure 10.7) is GNP plus net current transfers from the rest of the world. These payments are not in exchange for goods or services and they include, among others, emigrants' remittances and net current transfers from the EU. These should be included in any accurate measure of Irish economic activity. In 1999, current transfers accounted for an inflow of £951m. Taking this into account, GNDI for 1999 was £60,019m.

Columns 3 and 4 show that the difference between gross national product and net national product (NNP) is a provision for depreciation. We defined depreciation in Chapter 7 as the value of capital which has been used up during the production process. Whereas GNP does not account for the capital depleted in the production process, NNP does. The CSO estimated that depreciation for 1999 amounted to £7,114m. Deducting depreciation from GNP meant that NNP at market prices was valued at almost £52bn in 1999.

Columns 4 and 5 illustrate the difference between NNP measured at market prices and NNP at factor cost. The difference is accounted for by indirect taxes and subsidies, or net taxes. To calculate NNP at factor cost we deduct indirect taxes from and add subsidy payments to NNP at market prices. In 1999, £9,577m of indirect taxes were deducted from NNP at market prices and £1,788m of subsidies were added, giving us a figure of £44,166m which represents NNP at factor cost.

NNP at factor cost, or national income as it is commonly known, is represented in Columns 5 and 6. It is simply the addition of payments to the factors of production. These factor payments are wages, profits, interest and rent.

Column 7 of Figure 10.7 shows that the difference between national income and personal income is accounted for by what economists call 'income earned-but-not-received' and its counterpart 'income received-but-not-earned'. An example of the former is retained earnings of companies. Transfer payments are an example of the latter. In 1998 (latest figures available) personal income was £43,114m.

The last term to be explained is personal disposable income which is sometimes referred to as take-home or after-tax income. Personal disposable income is defined as personal income minus personal taxes, as shown in columns 8 and 9 of Figure 10.7. An individual or household divides disposable income between personal consumption and personal savings. This is shown in column 10 of Figure 10.7. In 1998, disposable income was £34,544m. Of this amount, over £31,219m was spent on personal consumption while £3,325m was reserved for personal savings.

The differences between national income and personal consumption for 1998 are shown in Table 10.7.

Table 10.7: *From national income to personal consumption*

	Description	£m
84	National income before adjustment for stock appreciation	40,365
85	less Government trading and investment income	−575
86	plus National debt interest	2,066
87	plus Transfer income	7,031
89	less Undistributed profits of companies before tax	−5,773
90	Personal income	43,114
92	less Personal taxes	−8,570
	Personal disposable income	34,544
	of which	
91	Personal consumption of goods and services	31,219
94	Personal savings	3,325

Source: CSO, *National Income and Expenditure 1999*, August 2000.

GDP can be measured in two ways.

Definition
Nominal GDP or GDP at current prices is a measure of economic activity based on the current prices of the goods and services produced.

Definition
Real GDP or GDP at constant prices measures economic activity in the prices of a fixed or base year.

Increases in nominal GDP can arise for two different reasons: an increase in the quantity of goods and services produced, or an increase in the price of these goods and services. Increases in real GDP arise from only one source: an increase in the quantity of goods and services produced. By measuring production in constant terms, we separate the actual changes in the quantity of goods and services produced from the change in the price level. In effect, we isolate the production change from the price change.

Two conclusions apply here. One, GDP at constant prices is a better measure of a country's economic performance. Two, in terms of the source of higher income and output levels, an increase in the quantity of goods and services produced is preferred to an increase in their price.

GDP at current prices can be converted to GDP at constant prices by means of a price index called the GDP deflator.

Definition
The GDP deflator is the ratio of nominal GDP to real GDP expressed as an index.

Price indices and their construction are discussed in Chapter 17.

Let us take an example to highlight the difference between the two measures. It is estimated that between 1979 and 1986 the Irish economy, measured in terms of increases in nominal GNP, grew by 130%. However, the increase over the same period measured in real GNP terms was only 3%. This suggests that the increase recorded in nominal GNP during this period was due to changes in the price level with no significant increase in production recorded.

In order to take into account the size of or changes in the population of a country, GNP or GDP per capita is used. This measure is expressed in Equation 10.2.

$$\boxed{\textbf{GDP per capita = GDP/population}} \qquad \textbf{[10.2]}$$

This is a better measure of a country's standard of living than GDP itself. For example, two countries with similar values for GDP may have very different standards of living because of variations in the size of their respective populations. In this case, GDP per capita is a more suitable measure.

Table 10.8 depicts GNP and GNP per capita for a small sample of countries. It is evident that GNP can be quite misleading at times. In Table 10.8, this is particularly true in the case of India whose GNP appears relatively high but because of its vast population its GNP per capita is relatively small.

Table 10.8:　GNP, population and GNP per capita, 1999 (US$)

Country	GNP 1999 (bn)[1]	Population 1999 (m)	GNP per capita[1] 1999
Ethiopia	6.6	63	100
Bangladesh	47.0	128	370
India	442.2	998	450
China	980.2	1,250	780
Czech Rep.	19.4	5	3,590
Greece	124.0	11	11,770
Ireland	71.4	4	19,160
US	8,351.0	273	30,600
Switzerland	273.1	7	38,350

Source: World Bank, *World Development Report 2000/2001.*

[1] Preliminary World Bank Estimates.

Furthermore, any increase in GNP recorded may be offset by an increase in the size of the population. In this case, as above, GNP per capita is a more suitable measure. We now consider the following case study in order to highlight some of the issues which we have already explained.

CASE STUDY

Extract from *OECD Economic Surveys: Ireland*
Continuing strong growth in a virtuous circle

The Irish economy is still growing very fast as the benefits of inward direct investment propagate through the rest of the economy. Real GDP, having risen more than 11 per cent in 1995, moderated only slightly in 1996, before bouncing back to about a 10 per cent rate in 1997 and 1998. This growth record has been the best in the OECD for four consecutive years. Although GNP is a more appropriate measure of the performance of the economy in such a small, open economy as Ireland's, the overall picture remains unchanged, because its growth rate has been only $1^1/_2$ percentage points lower than its GDP counterpart in this period. Net exports accounted for about 4 percentage points on average of the strong real GDP growth in 1997 and 1998. The rest, about 6 percentage points, is attributable to domestic demand. The same pattern was observed in the 1994 to 1996 period, in contrast to the early 1990s when net exports accounted for the larger part of output growth. This indicates that a virtuous circle continues to work: initial favourable supply shocks, in the form of start-ups of high-productivity operations of multinational companies, lead to increased income and thus domestic demand, which then brings about an increase in production in indigenous industries, especially in services.

. . .

Source: OECD *Economic Surveys: Ireland*, 1999, pp. 63–65.

Questions

1. What are the components of domestic demand? How have these components fared in the period 1995–98?
2. What accounts for the difference between GDP and GNP? Why is the distinction between GDP and GNP important in the context of the Irish economy and its growth performance?
3. Using GDP data, compare Ireland's growth record in the period 1995–98 with a selection of other OECD countries. What do the data indicate?

[NB: For this exercise, international sources of data include the IMF and the OECD. Irish sources include the ESRI and the CSO.]

Answers on website

In brief, the national accounts do more than just describe the overall level of economic activity in the economy. Economists, policy-makers, interest groups and others are concerned with a whole range of issues such as the level of consumer spending, taxes, savings and other important components of the circular flow model. Notwithstanding the importance of these individual aspects of the national accounts, its overall contribution to economics is in its ability to measure a country's economic performance, either from year to year or in comparison to other economies. The collection of this data has greatly facilitated research into macroeconomic issues.

Any measure of economic activity is subject to criticism for what it includes or what it fails to include. We will now examine some of the shortcomings of GDP.

10.4 LIMITATIONS OF GDP AS A MEASURE OF ECONOMIC ACTIVITY

GDP is not a perfect measure of a country's economic performance: it has many weaknesses. Listed below is a comprehensive, although not exhaustive, record of transactions which are omitted from GDP. In addition, GDP does not measure or account for many aspects of a modern economy. A list of these is also included below.

Omissions

- *Transactions within the 'shadow' economy*   These include illegal activities such as drug-trafficking and prostitution and legal activities which are not reported to avoid tax payment. It is very difficult to estimate the value of such transactions. Estimates vary significantly from country to country. For example, in the US estimates of the unofficial economy share in GDP range from 10–15%, while in Italy the range is 20–25%. In contrast, estimates for the UK and Switzerland, for example, are usually less than 10%. Using a currency–demand approach where it is assumed that shadow transactions take place in the form of cash, one estimate of the share of the unofficial economy in Ireland gives a figure of 7.8%.[6] It is common for a large shadow or hidden economy to exist in developing and transition countries. While this suggests that their national income statistics significantly underestimate the value of economic activity in these regions, their standard of living is still far below the average for western European countries.[7]
- *Externalities*   These are side-effects generated in the production or consumption of commodities (see Chapter 8). They can be either positive, generating an external benefit, or negative, generating an external cost. Positive examples include education, inventions and attractive lawns. Pollution, congestion and waste disposal are examples of negative externalities. It is very difficult to calculate accurate values for these 'spillover' items. The omission of positive externalities from the National Accounts results in a GDP figure which underestimates the level of economic activity. Likewise, the exclusion of negative externalities results in an overestimated value of GDP.
- *Non-monetary transactions*   These are activities which, although economically beneficial, are undertaken by individuals primarily for their own benefit and not sold to the market. They include household work, gardening and DIY. Another example is the work done by voluntary, community or charity organisations. The reason for the omission of such activities is the difficulty in obtaining accurate figures for the value of the product or service involved. The omission of these non-monetary transactions results in a value of GDP which underestimates the level of economic activity.

- *Non-marketable goods and services* Examples include state education and health care, defence and justice. These contribute to economic activity but, by their very nature, are not priced by market forces. These economic activities are included in the calculations for GDP but are done so at cost price whereas if a private body undertook the same service it would be included at market price. These activities are particularly important when making international comparisons.

GDP is neither a measure of, nor accounts for, the following:

- It is not a measure of economic wellbeing or welfare.[8] Arthur Pigou (1877–1959) argued that there is a close correlation between the level of national income and the level of economic welfare. In recent years, many would argue that the relationship is not very close. By definition, GDP measures only the value of goods and services produced. In preference to GDP, the United Nations (UN) uses a measure called the human development index (HDI). Its constituents are GDP per capita, education attainment and life expectancy at birth. Table 10.9 shows the HDI for a small sample of countries.

Table 10.9: The human development index, 1998

Country	HDI	HDI Rank	GDP Rank
Canada	0.935	1	9
US	0.929	3	2
UK	0.918	10	23
Switzerland	0.915	13	4
Denmark	0.911	15	7
Ireland	0.907	18	16
Portugal	0.864	28	31
Romania	0.770	64	70
India	0.563	128	121
Mozambique	0.341	168	162
Sierra Leone	0.252	174	174

Source: UNDP, *Human Development Report 2000.*

[1] on the basis of GDP per capita (PPP US$) 1998.

- It is not a measure of the competitiveness of an economy or its workforce. Competitiveness is measured annually by the International Institute for Management Development (IMD), which publishes the World Competitiveness Survey. The survey looks at 290 criteria, of which forty-one are background information and are not used in the calculations of the overall rankings. Of the remainder, about two-thirds is 'hard' data. This is information collected from international, regional and national sources, like the *National Income and Expenditure* report. The rest of the information comes from survey data collected from a panel of experts. The categories of criteria include an assessment of a country's macroeconomic performance; participation in international trade; government policies relating to competitiveness; capital markets and financial services; natural, technical and communication resources; corporate management practices; scientific and technological capacity; and the quality and quantity of human resources. Ireland was ranked seventh in 2000. This is considerably higher than Ireland's GDP per capita ranking for the same year.

- Per capita GDP does not reflect disparities in income distribution. Although per capita income is increasing, distribution of that income is becoming more skewed. A number of relevant studies have been conducted by the Economic and Social Research Institute (ESRI) over the past two decades. In a recent publication, the ESRI considers changes in 'relative poverty' among Irish households. Measures of relative poverty differ from measures of absolute poverty. For example, one measure of absolute poverty is the minimum amount of income required to pay for the food, clothing and shelter necessary to keep a person alive. In 'real' terms, this amount changes very little over time. Measures of relative poverty are 'moving targets'. As an economy develops, the basic requirements to participate socially and economically change. Items that were considered luxuries twenty years ago, like telephones and televisions, are found in almost every household in Ireland today. Households that cannot afford these goods and services are relatively deprived, though strictly speaking, they can live without them. The ESRI classifies a household as living below the 'poverty line' if its disposable income (income from all sources, after tax is deducted) is less than 50% of the mean (average) income for all Irish households. Information was gathered from surveys taken in 1994 and 1997. The surveys revealed that there was an increase of about three percentage points in the number of households living below the poverty line, from 18.8% in 1994 to 21.9% in 1997.[9] The rising tide of the Celtic Tiger economy did not lift all boats. Increasing per capita GDP masks increasing inequality in the distribution of Irish income.

  A measure of income inequality is the Gini coefficient. Its range, as it is normally expressed, is between zero and one. Zero reflects no inequality. One reflects perfect inequality (all of the nation's income received by a single household). Two different sources give Ireland a Gini coefficient of between 0.330 and 0.320.[10] While acknowledging the difficulties in measuring income inequality (cross-country comparison, in particular) it would appear that income inequality in Ireland, as measured by the Gini coefficient, did not change all that much between the years 1987 and 1993. According to Callan and Nolan (1999), '. . . the level of inequality was stable between the mid-1980s and the mid-1990s . . .'[11]

- It does not take into account differences in the composition of GDP. A common example compares countries with similar values for GDP. One nation is engaged in the production of weapons while the other is involved in the production of food. There is a very large difference in terms of relative economic wellbeing yet the relative data for GDP would not detect this difference. Let us take one further example.

  Consider the relative importance of consumption and investment in terms of their respective contributions to the long-term prosperity of an economy. Some would argue that an increase in economic activity which arises out of greater expenditure on investment is more desirable than a similar increase in economic activity that arises out of greater expenditure on consumption. It is not coincidental that the countries which have achieved the fastest growth rates in recent times, the newly industrialised countries (NICs) for example, have proportionately more expenditure on investment relative to other countries. For example, investment expenditure accounted for 37% and 35% of GDP in 1997 in Singapore and Korea respectively. This compares to approximately 15% for both the UK and Ireland.[12]

Unfortunately a straightforward comparison of the respective GDPs would not detect these and other subtle but important differences.

- It does not take into account the quality of the goods produced or improvements in quality over time. For example, a calculator purchased in 1970 was both more expensive and less sophisticated than a calculator purchased today.

In response to the criticisms which the economics profession faced on account of these omissions a number of alternatives to GDP as a measure of a country's economic performance have emerged. For example, in 1972 Professors James Tobin (b. 1918) of Yale University and William Nordhaus (b. 1941) estimated a value of net economic welfare (NEW).[13] They argued from the outset that GNP, which measures production, is not the ideal measure and should be replaced with some measure of consumption. They adjusted the GNP figure by subtracting the following set of activities: health and educational spending which were considered capital expenditure, 'disamenities' and 'regrettable necessities'. A value of non-market activities and leisure were added to give us the NEW. Between 1929 and 1965 in the US it was estimated that the NEW grew at an annual rate of 1.1% per capita whereas an annual 1.7% per capita was recorded for the more conventional measure, NNP.

Notwithstanding the deficiencies listed above, GDP is still the most common measure used by the economics profession today. It is reasonably accurate given the complexities of a modern economy. Moreover, it is consistent from year to year and this facilitates yearly comparisons. It is likely to remain as the measure of economic activity for the foreseeable future.

This chapter concludes with a brief account of certain aspects of the Irish National Accounts.

10.5 THE IRISH EXPERIENCE

Although the National Accounts appear to be quite technical and tedious, the controversies which arise from them are lively.

Most of the tables in this section are taken from the annual CSO publication entitled *National Income and Expenditure*. Reports of this kind provide the 'raw materials' of economic research and are the sources of data used in most studies. The annual editions of these publications are always reported by the media.

In this section, we want to show how an economist uses these reports to understand what is happening in the national economy. First, we examine in some detail the difference between GDP and GNP. We will then discuss the difference between GNP and GNDI. We conclude by examining the components of GNDI, and personal consumption in particular.

GDP vs GNP

As we stated earlier, for Ireland, GDP is greater than GNP. The two figures are separated by net factor income from abroad. Table 10.10 shows the relevant data from the report *National Income and Expenditure 1999*.

Table 10.10:   Difference between GDP and GNP (at current market prices), £m

	1990	1991	1992	1993	1994	1995	1996	1997	1998	1999*
GDP	28598	29675	31529	34054	36624	41409	45634	52760	60582	69052
Net factor Income from abroad	–3258	–3215	–3537	–3671	–3716	–4685	–5147	–6332	–7389	–9984
GNP	25339	26460	27992	30383	32908	36725	40487	46428	53193	59068

* Preliminary
Source: CSO, *National Income and Expenditure 1999*, August 2000.

From this table we can see that net factor income from the rest of the world has increased in magnitude every year, with the exception of 1991. Since 1990, over 10% of GDP has left the country.

Obviously, Irish nationals benefit more from the portion of GDP that remains in the country than from the portion that leaves. Therefore, GNP is generally considered to be a better measure of Irish economic activity than GDP.

However, most international comparisons are based on GDP. More importantly, most comparisons within the EU are based on GDP. The reason is that for most developed countries, there is not much of a difference between GNP and GDP.

Table 10.11 shows the ratio of GNP to GDP for fourteen member states of the EU. If the ratio is one, the two measures are essentially the same. This means that the outflows of interest and profits equal the inflows. A number greater than one indicates that the inflows are greater than the outflows. This could happen if a country is the home base for many multinationals who are sending their profits home or if the country lends more to other countries than it borrows. These inflows are added to the income of the nation. If the ratio is less than one, then the outflows exceed the inflows.

Table 10.11:   Ratio of GNP/GDP for 1999

Country	GNP/GDP
Austria	1.005
Belgium	1.020
Denmark	0.977
Finland	0.974
France	1.012
Germany	0.999
Greece	1.001
Ireland	0.841
Italy	0.988
Netherlands	0.999
Portugal	0.983
Spain	0.981
Sweden	0.980
UK	0.974

Source: World Bank, *World Development Report 2000/2001.*

Most of the countries exhibit a ratio which is very close to one, with the exception of Ireland. Ireland has the dubious distinction of exhibiting the most disproportionate outflows.

Ultimately, this means that while Ireland appears to be catching up to (and possibly surpassing) her European partners, in terms of GDP, the standard of living is not catching up as fast.

In the Irish context, a better measure of the trend in living standards than either GNP or GDP is Gross National Disposable Income (GNDI). As we explained in Section 10.3, GNDI is GNP plus net current transfers from abroad. Table 10.12 reports GNDI for the period 1990–99. The gap between GNP and GNDI will continue to narrow as EU transfers to Ireland decline.

Table 10.12:   GNP and GNDI, 1990–99, £m

	1990	1991	1992	1993	1994	1995	1996	1997	1998	1999*
GNP	25339	26460	27992	30383	32908	36725	40487	46428	53193	59068
Net current transfers from abroad	1412	1608	1245	1309	1156	1110	1355	1290	1038	951
GNDI	26752	28068	29237	31691	34064	37835	41842	47718	54231	60019

* Preliminary
Source: CSO, *National Income and Expenditure 1999*, August 2000.

Another advantage of this measure is that it can be decomposed into total consumption expenditure and total savings. In turn, total consumption expenditure can be either private (C) or public (G), as in Table 10.3. The decomposition of disposable income and of consumption expenditure in Ireland for the period 1990–99 is in Table 10.13.

Table 10.13:   GNDI and its use, 1990–99, £m

	1990	1991	1992	1993	1994	1995	1996	1997	1998	1999*
GNDI	26752	28068	29237	31691	34064	37835	41842	47718	54231	60019
Savings	5151	5242	4922	6034	6605	8466	10017	12544	15035	16524
Expenditure	21601	22826	24316	25657	27459	29369	31825	35174	39196	43495
of which										
Personal consumption of goods and services	17293	18085	19161	20162	21621	23192	25311	27900	31219	34743
Government consumption of goods and services	4308	4741	5155	5495	5838	6177	6514	7274	7978	8753

* Preliminary
Source: CSO, *National Income and Expenditure 1999*, August 2000.

We began this investigation of the Irish National Accounts with GDP, the international standard measure of economic activity. Table 10.14 reports a 10.3% annual increase in nominal GDP for the period 1990–99. In this section, we noted that both GNP and GNDI are better measures of Ireland's economic activity. Interestingly, for the same period, the annual percentage increases in GNP and GNDI, of 9.9% and 9.4% respectively, are smaller than the GDP annual increase.

Table 10.14:   Annual percentage increases in main aggregates

	1990–99
Gross Domestic Product (GDP)	10.3
Gross National Product (GNP)	9.9
Gross National Disposable Income (GNDI)	9.4
Total consumption expenditure	8.1
of which	
Government consumption of goods and services	8.2
Personal consumption of goods and services	8.1

Source: CSO, *National Income and Expenditure 1999*, August 2000.

Yet another measure of a nation's economic success is the level of private consumption by its residents. The annual percentage increase in the personal consumption of goods and services was 8.1%, the same percentage increase recorded for total consumption expenditure. While this average annual growth rate is excellent, it is below the GDP average annual growth rate and still leaves Ireland, in terms of private consumption levels, behind many of its EU partners. This is shown in Table 10.15.

Table 10.15: Private consumption expenditure

	IRL	UK	DK	I	D	EU-15
1974	76.6	109.8	99.2	96.8	106.2	100
1979	77.3	102.9	102.3	98.3	114.1	100
1984	70.9	101.7	101.0	102.4	114.6	100
1989	75.0	110.9	93.8	104.6	108.2	100
1994	85.9	107.9	102.2	104.1	107.1	100
1999	95.5	114.7	102.3	100.9	106.3	100

Source: European Commission, 2000.
Note: IRL = Ireland; UK = United Kingdom; DK = Denmark; I = Italy; D = Germany.

Table 10.15 shows private final consumption expenditure at current prices per capita for a selection of EU countries, where EU-15 = 100. Despite the phenomenal growth rates of recent years, Ireland still, but only just, lags behind the average for the EU-15 member states.

The point of this short exercise was to use the National Accounts to assess a country's economic wellbeing. In addition, we have shown that measures of economic activity other than GDP are worth considering and monitoring. This is particularly true in the case of Ireland.

SUMMARY

1. The circular flow diagram depicts the workings of a modern economy where transactions between households, firms, government, the banking system and the foreign markets are described. These transactions are real or monetary.
2. The three methods for measuring a country's economic activity are the income, output and expenditure approaches. They are defined so that each should yield the same result. In Ireland the data are published by the CSO in the annual *National Income and Expenditure* publication.
3. National income accounting is the system economists use to measure the economic activity of a country. The most common measure used is gross domestic product. All other terms used are simply a variation of this measure.
4. Nominal GDP is a measure of goods and services at current prices. Real GDP is measured at constant prices, by the use of a fixed or base year. Changes in GDP can come from two sources: price changes or production changes. Real GDP is a better measure because it isolates the production changes.

5. Although GDP is the most common measure of economic activity, it has a number of significant shortcomings. Both its omissions and its failure to capture changes in other economic variables have forced economists to look for alternative measures. The human development index (HDI) and the net economic welfare (NEW) are two of the more common alternatives.

6. The *National Income and Expenditure*, published by the CSO, is the main source of data for economists who are studying changes in Ireland's national income. More importantly, it reports on GDP, the measure of national income which is used for international comparisons.

KEY TERMS

Circular flow
Leakages
Injections
Investment
Transfer payments
Expenditure method
Income method
Output method
Double counting
Value added
National Accounts
Gross domestic product
Gross national product
Net factor income from abroad
Gross national disposable income
Net economic welfare

Net national product
Depreciation
Market prices
Factor cost
National income
Personal income
Disposable income
Nominal GDP
Real GDP
GDP deflator
GDP per capita
Shadow economy
Externalities
Human development index
Gini coefficient

REVIEW QUESTIONS

1. Explain, with the aid of a diagram, the complete circular flow model. List the injections and the leakages. Explain how these movements into and out of the circular flow can influence the level of economic activity.

2. Describe the transactions that occur between the following sets of agents: households and firms; households and government; firms and financial institutions; firms and government; firms and foreign markets.

3. List and briefly explain the three approaches to measuring economic activity. Using the circular flow diagram, explain why, in principle, they yield the same result.

4. Outline the differences between gross domestic product and national income. Explain all relevant terms used.

5. Do you think GDP is an underestimate or an overestimate of the level of economic activity in Ireland? Support your answer.

6. For Ireland, does GDP or GNP provide a more accurate measure of economic activity? Support your answer.

WORKING PROBLEMS

1. On the basis of the data below determine national income using:
   - (a) income method;
   - (b) output method;
   - (c) expenditure method.

Table 10.16

Item	€bn	Item	€bn
Rent	450	Personal consumption	4,000
Interest	300	Transport and communication	1,500
Agriculture	100	Profits	300
Investment	600	Depreciation	300
Indirect taxes	800	Subsidies	400
Net income from abroad	250	Government expenditure	700
Exports	3,050	Industry	3,000
Public administration	650	Imports	2,400
Compensation of employees	4,200		

2. The following information has been gathered for an imaginary economy:

Table 10.17

Item	€bn
Consumer expenditure (C)	250
Government expenditure (G)	500
Investment (I)	150
Taxes (TX)	350
Transfer payments (TR)	200
Exports (X)	360
Imports (M)	340

Using the above data calculate the following:
   - (a) GDP;
   - (b) disposable income;
   - (c) savings;
   - (d) net exports;
   - (e) injections and leakages. Comment on their relative sizes.

MULTI-CHOICE QUESTIONS

1. Within the circular flow model:
    (a) transactions are either real or monetary;
    (b) transfer payments are an injection and reflect current production;
    (c) economic activity will increase if injections exceed withdrawals;
    (d) both (a) and (c) above;
    (e) (a), (b) and (c) above.

2. Which of the following set of variables is an injection into the circular flow diagram?
    (a) exports, taxes and investment;
    (b) government expenditure, exports and investment;
    (c) investment, imports and subsidies;
    (d) imports, savings and taxes;
    (e) none of the above.

3. Which of the following is an example of a real flow from firms to households?
    (a) factors of production;
    (b) payments for goods and services;
    (c) goods and services;
    (d) payments for factors of production;
    (e) none of the above.

4. The three broad methods of measuring economic activity are:
    (a) GNP, GDP and NNP;
    (b) income, expenditure and output;
    (c) national income, personal income and disposable income;
    (d) budget, balance of payments and expenditure estimates;
    (e) none of the above.

5. The difference between gross national product and gross domestic product is accounted for by:
    (a) depreciation;
    (b) indirect taxes;
    (c) transfer payments;
    (d) net factor income from abroad;
    (e) personal taxes.

6. Which of the following is a better measure of the standard of living?
    (a) GDP per employee;
    (b) investment expenditure;
    (c) GDP per capita;
    (d) personal savings;
    (e) GDP.

TRUE OR FALSE (SUPPORT YOUR ANSWER)

1. The circular flow model implies that the value of exports, a leakage, must be equal to the value of imports, an injection, in order for economic activity to remain unchanged.

2. The four factors of production are wages, interest, rent and profit. Workers are paid rent, lenders earn profit, landowners earn wages and interest is the residual.

3. The values for GNP and national income would be equal if depreciation, indirect taxes and subsidies were all valued at zero.

4. If two countries have the same GNP, then the standard of living is the same in both countries.

5. If over some period of time prices have doubled and real GDP has doubled, then nominal GDP has doubled.

6. The Irish GDP figure exceeds the GNP figure because outflows of factor income exceed inflows of factor income.

CASE STUDY

Extract from *The Irish Examiner*
Economy continues on high
by Brian O'Mahony

Central Statistics figures confirmed yesterday the extraordinary growth rate of the economy, showing it grew 57% at constant market prices in the past six years. In 1999 Gross National Product rose 7.8%, while the internal economy, measured by Gross Domestic Product, showed an increase of 9.8%. The CSO's figures are slightly below the Central Bank's assessment for 1999, which put GNP at 8.5% for the year. Nevertheless, they confirm the sixth successive year of strong growth by the economy and raise fears about the final destination of the rate of inflation. At 5.5%, the record high figure is destined to go even higher putting pressure on wages and on the Programme for Prosperity and Fairness. Alan McQuaid, of Bloxham Stockbrokers, said the figures simply confirm everything we know about the economy.

CSO figures confirm the boom in consumer spending, which sustained its strong growth trend. According to the CSO, consumer spending grew by 11.3% in 1999, while government spending was slightly lower at 9.7%. Again economists point out the figures confirm the Irish economy outpacing the rest of Europe, with an expansion rate almost three times the EU average. The rapid economic growth has

→

fuelled fierce debate over the inflation rate and its impact on wages and salaries. The Irish Congress of Trade Unions has demanded a review of a new national pay deal. Jim Power, Bank of Ireland, said we have moved to a wage spiral and forecasts an overall wage bill hike of 14% for the current year.

Source: *The Irish Examiner*, 21 July 2000.

Questions

1. Using the CSO National Income and Expenditure (NIE) 1999, show, on a graph, the annual percentage change in nominal GNP and GDP, for the period 1994–99.
2. Explain what is meant by 'constant' market prices. Using the NIE figures for 1993 and 1999, show how the figure of 57% is calculated.
3. Aside from consumer and government spending, what are the other constituents of GNP? Use the CSO data for 1998 and 1999 to calculate the percentage increase in these other constituents of GNP.

[NB: The relevant data can be found in the *National Income and Expenditure 1999* publication.]

APPENDIX 10.1: SAVINGS AND INVESTMENT

The classical doctrine of economics argued that the equality of savings and investment was an automatic process with the rate of interest playing the key role. This equality between savings and investment can be explained in mathematical form. Suppose there is no government and no foreign sector. The expenditure approach measures GDP as the sum of consumer expenditure and investment expenditure. This identity can be expressed as follows:

$$Y \equiv C + I \tag{1}$$

However, we can also view GDP as national income which is equal, in the absence of government, to disposable income. Disposable income in turn is either spent or saved. This can be written as follows:

$$Y \equiv C + S \tag{2}$$

Combine Identity 1 and 2

$$C + I \equiv Y \equiv C + S \tag{3}$$

The left-hand side of [3] shows the components of expenditure whereas the right-hand side shows the allocation of income. Subtracting consumption from both sides yields:

$$I \equiv S \qquad \qquad [4]$$

Identity [4] shows that in a simple model of the economy investment and savings are equal. This was one of the basic tenets of the classical school which dominated economic thinking in the nineteenth century.

However, in the *Treatise on Money* Keynes argued that savings and investment were very different activities, carried out by two very different sets of people and, moreover, were not necessarily identical. In the next two chapters we will examine in greater detail Keynes' views on these activities.

APPENDIX 10.2: GNP AND GDP FOR IRELAND, 1975–99

Table 10.18: GNP and GDP for Ireland, 1975–99, £m

Year	GDP (current)	GDP[1] (constant)	GNP (current)	GNP[1] (constant)
1975	3816	17688	3821	18505
1976	4681	18098	4645	18772
1977	5735	19356	5627	19857
1978	6801	20776	6573	20981
1979	7976	21470	7693	21617
1980	9433	21928	9075	21985
1981	11448	22535	10943	22436
1982	13489	22833	12562	22053
1983	14916	22863	13732	21790
1984	16556	23708	14917	22146
1985	17969	24285	16003	22357
1985[2]	18577	25106	16611	23206
1986	19703	25194	17686	23037
1987	21075	26310	18963	24061
1988	22718	27488	20056	24675
1989	25418	29201	22185	26000
1990	27188	31265	24056	27898
1990[3]	28598	32986	25339	29512
1991	29675	33622	26460	30186
1992	31529	34746	27992	30890
1993	34054	35682	30383	31935
1994	36624	37736	32908	33950
1995	41409	41409	36725	36725
1996	45634	44594	40487	39431
1997	52760	49382	46428	43105
1998	60582	53609	53193	46484
1999[4]	69052	58876	59068	50123

Source: Central Statistics Office.
Notes: 1. In 1995 prices.
2. Discontinuity in 1985. 1985 figures are approximate estimates.
3. 1990 to 1999 based on ESA95 methodology. Earlier years' data based on ESA79. The main difference between the two accounting systems is that ESA95 includes more accruals information.
4. Preliminary

CHAPTER 11

THE KEYNESIAN REVOLUTION

'The General Theory of Employment is the Economics of Depression.'[1]

John R. Hicks (1904–89)

'Whenever I ask England's six leading economists a question, I get seven answers – two from Mr Keynes.'[2]

Winston Churchill

CHAPTER OBJECTIVES

Upon completing this chapter, the student should understand:

- the pre-Keynesian economic doctrine;
- the economic turbulence caused by the Great Depression;
- the contribution of Keynes to modern macroeconomics.

OUTLINE

INTRODUCTION

This chapter deals with the background to Keynesian economics. We begin with a description of the classical doctrine of economics. This is followed by a discussion on Keynes and his life, his ideas and his contribution to macroeconomics. The last section deals with the Great Depression of the 1930s and the emergence of the economics of Keynes.

11.1 THE CLASSICAL DOCTRINE OF ECONOMICS

Disagreement among economists is not new. In the seventeenth century, prior to the emergence of the classical doctrine, economics was not considered to be a distinct academic discipline. Even then, two groups, the mercantilists and the physiocrats, held radically different views about the way that the economy operates. Economic disagreements to this day, particularly about the appropriate role of government, date back to the mercantilist/physiocrat debate. These two groups helped to lay the groundwork for the discussion of economic issues.

The actual word 'mercantilism' had different meanings but was generally understood to mean 'the economics of nationalism'. According to followers of mercantilism the key to national economic prosperity was the accumulation of gold and silver. All policies were aimed towards building a positive balance of trade. Economic thinking was dominated by this policy concern.

Mercantilism was particularly strong in France. Jean Baptiste Colbert (1619–83) served as the Minister of Finance during the reign of Louis XIV. Under his guidance, every aspect of French production was state controlled. Manufactured products were promoted at the expense of agricultural products. All imports and exports were closely monitored.

Many of the writers of the day were merchant businessmen. Critics of mercantilism were quick to point out that the businessmen themselves were often the main beneficiaries of the policies which they advocated. At the time, many felt that the excessive regulations by government led to production inefficiencies. It is often said that the burden of taxation, unevenly spread, ultimately led to the French Revolution.

Not surprisingly, the main reaction against mercantilism also came from the French. While not advocating the overthrow of the monarchy, the physiocrats argued for a radical departure from the policy of state regulation. Physiocracy is derived from the French word 'Physiocrate' which means the 'rule of nature'. The physiocrats, and later the classical economists believed that there was natural order in the economic system which was analogous to the laws of nature. The massive state intervention of the mercantilists was at best ineffective, and at worst served as a deterrent to economic growth.

François Quesnay was a prominent physiocrat. He attempted to explain and identify the general laws which govern economic behaviour. Quesnay and the physiocrats believed that the agricultural sector was the only productive sector of the economy. The export duties placed on grain by the mercantilists were both unnecessary and served as a disincentive to production. In this sense, the rule of government violated natural law. It is from the physiocrats that we inherit the ideological basis for *laissez-faire* which generally refers to an economic system which is characterised by free trade and low levels of state intervention.

Adam Smith (1723–90) is considered to be the father of economics and the founder of the classical school. His book, *An Enquiry into the Nature and Causes of the Wealth of Nations* was at one level a reaction against mercantilism. His thinking was obviously influenced by his acquaintance with François Quesnay. Like Quesnay, Smith attempted to understand the general principles which underlay economic growth.

For Smith, the basis of wealth was the division of labour. Production expands significantly as labour becomes more specialised. It is within this context that Smith adopted the free-trade doctrine of the physiocrats. A larger market expands the opportunities for specialised labour.

Smith also advanced the physiocrats' argument concerning 'deregulation'. He attempted to explain the economic forces which cause individuals, motivated by self-interest, to achieve objectives which are socially beneficial. The 'invisible hand' is often interpreted as the forces of competition. Consumers, acting independently of each other, nevertheless communicate their needs to producers. Producers, who are striving to make a living, attempt to satisfy consumer needs. This is the basis of the perfectly competitive market structure.

Smith observed that the mercantilist system promoted collusive agreements between merchants and politicians, often at the expense of the ordinary citizen. He argued that unregulated competition would ensure that goods were produced more efficiently and distributed more evenly among the population. Competition, in short, was a system that militated against a concentration of wealth and in favour of a more equitable distribution of resources.

Smith was one of a group of economists who came to be known as the classical school. Others include David Ricardo (1772–1823), Thomas Malthus (1766–1834) and John Stuart Mill (1806–73). They dominated economic thought in the hundred years following the publication of *The Wealth of Nations*. They were academics, with the exception of David Ricardo, who was a stockbroker by profession. This raised the tenor of the economic debate since they could no longer be accused of advocating particular policies which advanced their self-interest.

Although they ultimately became known as economists, their writings span many of the classical subjects including history, politics, physics, philosophy and juris-prudence. Political economy was originally taught under the chair of moral philosophy by Smith at the University of Glasgow. Needless to say, Smith's economic perspective was influenced by his study of philosophy.

The classical economists focused on the issues of growth, value and distribution. Unlike their successors, the classical economists never saw growth as an automatic process. Discussions focused not only on attempting to understand the conditions which promoted economic growth, but also on the type of policies which would foster these conditions. In this sense, *laissez-faire* should not be construed as the lack of government policy, but as a positive initiative to support competition.

The end of the nineteenth century was a period of transition. It was during this period that economics was firmly established as a distinct academic discipline. Many within the discipline attempted to align it with the natural sciences rather than with what were considered to be the less rigorous social sciences. A deductive methodology was adopted. Models were developed, based on restrictive assumptions, which are logical within their own framework. This approach may be traced back to Ricardo, but it is very different from the descriptive, historic approach which was more common to the other classical economists.

The 'Marginalists' were a group of economists who included W. Stanley Jevons (1835–82), Carl Menger (1840–1921) and Leon Walras (1834–1910). The work of these economists represented the transition between the classical and neoclassical schools. One of the unresolved issues of the classical school was the theory of value. This was partly because the classical economists concentrated on the supply side. They assumed that goods had some utility, otherwise nobody would want them. However, the value of goods was determined by the amount of labour which it took to produce them.

The contribution of the marginalists was to develop the downward sloping demand curve which was based on diminishing marginal utility. Goods had utility, as suggested by the classicals, but that marginal utility diminished as more of the good was consumed. Only falling prices could entice an individual to consume more of the same good.

This idea was later applied by neoclassical economists to the supply side. The upward sloping supply curve is based on the idea of diminishing marginal productivity which causes marginal costs to increase when more is produced. Part of the marginal cost curve is the supply curve for the perfectly competitive firm. The two curves combine to form a model of price determination. When price is set in the competitive market, based solely on the forces of demand and supply, it means that resources are efficiently diverted to the uses which achieve the highest possible utility for the consumer. The 'market' is the neoclassical model which conceptualises Adam Smith's 'invisible hand'.

In the decades which preceded the Great Depression, the neoclassical economists developed general equilibrium and partial equilibrium models which were mathematically difficult and aimed at a narrow range of consumption and production problems. They followed the thinking of the physiocrats and the classical economists, recommending a circumscribed range of government activity. Their emphasis on individual choice meant that they saw government as limiting the range of individual actions. Government spending meant that less money was available for private investment. It had to be paid for by taxation which limited the disposable income of consumers. Specific policy recommendations of the neoclassicals will be contrasted with Keynesian alternatives in Section 11.3.

11.2 THE LIFE AND WORKS OF JOHN MAYNARD KEYNES

Keynes is to economics what Freud is to psychoanalysis, Einstein is to Physics and Darwin is to biology.[3] Mark Blaug in his recent work *John Maynard Keynes: Life, Ideas, Legacy* referred to the three great revolutions in modern economics: Adam Smith's support for unregulated markets, the 'marginal revolution' and finally the emergence of a new orthodoxy – Keynesian economics.

John Maynard Keynes was born in Cambridge, England in 1883. His parents were middle-class intellectuals. His father John Neville was a well-respected philosopher and economist who worked with Alfred Marshall in Cambridge. Keynes, with the help of scholarships, was educated in Eton and then in King's College, Cambridge where he studied classics and mathematics, winning many college prizes in the process. At the time his other academic interests included philosophy and literature but noticeably, not economics.

He graduated in 1905 at the age of 22 and opted for a career in the civil service. In order to prepare himself for the entry examinations he attended economics lectures in Cambridge. His lecturer was Alfred Marshall who taught Keynes the basic tenets of neoclassical economics. Little did he know that this son of a former colleague would question the very essence of what he and his contemporaries represented.

After briefly studying economics Keynes disappointed Marshall and others by joining the civil service. On completing his exams, it is said that he remarked, 'I evidently knew more about Economics than my examiners.'[4] This was not the last time that Keynes expressed self-belief, verging on arrogance.

His two-year experience in the India Office was the inspiration behind his first book on economics, *Indian Currency and Finance*. While working for the civil service, Keynes made significant progress with his thesis on probability. On the basis of this work, Keynes was offered a Fellowship at King's in 1909. He began teaching economics and within two years had become the editor of *Economic Journal*, the most respected economics journal in the UK at the time. His *Treatise on Probability*, published in a revised form in 1921, was well received by his peers and particularly by philosophers.

Keynes' talents were also recognised outside academic circles. During World War I he had re-entered the civil service and by 1919 he had become the senior British Treasury representative at the Versailles Peace Conference. However, he became very disillusioned with the Allied treatment of the Germans and when the figure of £24bn in reparations was demanded, he resigned. On returning to England he wrote *The Economic Consequences of the Peace* for which he received international acclaim. In the book Keynes was highly critical of the harsh economic terms agreed by the Allies and he predicted serious consequences for the future including the possibility of 'vengeance' in the form of a 'final civil war . . . before which the horrors of the late German war will fade into nothing . . .'

Keynes spent the next few years teaching, writing and speculating in financial markets. This latest interest made Keynes a millionaire although he was to lose heavily during the Wall Street crash of 1929. By 1936 he had recovered his losses and was worth approximately half a million pounds.

In 1923 *A Tract on Monetary Reform* was published. This marked a change in Keynes' view on economics and, particularly, on the role of government. Prior to its publication Keynes was regarded as a supporter of the classical doctrine of economic liberalism. He had advocated the reliance on market forces in preference to active government intervention. He was also a strong supporter of international free trade which he saw as a necessary condition for economic prosperity.

In this publication Keynes advocated the active use of monetary policy in order to determine the price level. This was to be done within the context of a managed monetary system which was to replace the Gold Standard. This support for managing the economy, both in a positive and active fashion, was a shift away from the *laissez-faire* policies of the nineteenth century. However it was not until 1936, with the publication of *The General Theory*, that the economics profession acknowledged the beginning of a revolution.

A Tract on Monetary Reform did make a significant impact but for a very different reason. In it Keynes argued against returning to the Gold Standard at the pre-war fixed exchange rate. He believed that price stability was more important than exchange rate stability with exchange rate policy ideally being subordinate to the needs of the domestic economy. In advocating this policy, Keynes argued against the conventional wisdom advocated by the economic and financial establishment of the day. The Treasury, bankers and business people, for various reasons supported the reinstitution of the Gold Standard. Unlike Keynes, they applauded the decision by the Chancellor of the Exchequer, Winston Churchill, to rejoin in 1925 at the pre-war exchange rate.

Keynes wrote a number of pamphlets prior to 1936 which indicated his growing mistrust of the market system and his belief in tackling unemployment with the aid of government policies. By this time he was involved with the Liberal Party and had the job of advising its leader, Lloyd George. It was widely known that Keynes supported public works programmes in order to provide employment. As usual Keynes presented his argument in a graphical and emotive way: 'If the Treasury were to fill old bottles with bank-notes, bury them at suitable depths in disused coal mines which are then filled up to the surface with town rubbish, and leave to private enterprise . . . to dig the notes up again . . . there need be no more unemployment . . .'[5]

Some of Keynes' early work was criticised within the economics profession because it was not grounded in theory. Whereas the *Tract* was written for a general audience, the *Treatise on Money* (1930) was pitched at a more professional level. Nonetheless, it was severely criticised. Friedrich von Hayek (1899–1992) and D. H. Robertson (1890–1963), two contemporaries of Keynes, wrote less than favourable reviews of the book.

Yet many elements of this book re-appeared in *The General Theory* which Keynes started shortly after the publication of the *Treatise* and took four years to complete. Valuable contributions were made by his Cambridge followers, including Richard Kahn (1905–89), Joan Robinson (1903–83), Piero Sraffa (1898–1983), Roy Harrod (1900–78) and James Meade (1907–95). His letter to George Bernard Shaw in 1935, in anticipation of the book's publication, is another example of Keynes' self-belief. He wrote '. . . I believe myself to be writing a book on economic theory which will largely revolutionise – not, I suppose, at once but in the course of the next ten years – the way the world thinks about economic problems.'[6]

The General Theory of Employment, Interest and Money of 1936 is generally agreed to be a very difficult book to read and understand. As the title suggests it is concerned almost exclusively with theory; this differentiates it from the *Treatise*. To this day, almost sixty-five years later, economists and commentators argue over the precise meaning of many elements in the book. Essentially it is a book on unemployment, with the causes and solutions analysed in very obscure language. Terms such as the consumption function, the marginal propensity to consume and the multiplier confused many a reader. Yet most students of economics today are familiar with these and other Keynesian concepts. This illustrates the influence that *The General Theory* and more particularly Keynes has had on economics.

The pattern of his life was disturbed yet again by World War II. In 1939, he re-entered the Treasury as an adviser to the Chancellor of the Exchequer. *How to Pay for the War*, which was published in 1940, dealt not with the problems of deficiencies in demand as *The General Theory* did, but with the problems arising out of excess demand. His influence was evident in both the British budget of 1941 and the UK White Paper on *Employment Policy* of 1944. The latter is of historical importance as it marks the first time in modern economic history that there was a government commitment to securing 'a high and stable level of employment'.[7]

In the same year Keynes was the head of the British delegation at the Bretton Woods Conference. Just prior to that, he put forward a plan, known as the Keynes Plan, which aimed to restore stability to the international economy and, in particular, to international trade which had been decimated by the break-up of the Gold Standard and the outbreak of World War II. The establishment once again rejected his ideas and opted instead for the less radical approach proposed by the American delegation. This led to the establishment of the International Monetary Fund (IMF).

On Easter Sunday, April 1946, at the age of 62, he died at his Sussex farmhouse in Tilton. After such a fulfilling life his only regret was the wish that he had drunk more champagne.

11.3 THE KEYNESIAN REVOLUTION

Though educated by neoclassical economists, Keynes diverged from them both theoretically and in terms of his policy prescriptions. The catalyst for this change was the Great Depression.

Thursday, 24 October 1929 will always be remembered as Black Thursday, the day that the stock market on Wall Street crashed.[8] Panic and confusion reigned. It was reported that eleven speculators committed suicide during the crash. Wall Street did not recover in the subsequent months or years. By November 1929, the average price of fifty leading stocks had fallen to 50% of their September levels. In July 1932, the Dow Jones index of industrial companies was 90% below its value of September 1929.[9]

The Great Depression followed the Wall Street crash in both the US and the UK. After a prosperous decade in the 1920s, aggregate economic activity in the US reached a peak in August 1929. Real GNP fell by nearly 30% between the 1929 peak and the 1933 trough. The unemployment rate rose from about 3% or 1.5 million people to close to 25% or 12 million people. Investment expenditure fell by 75% during this period while consumer expenditure dropped by 20%. The UK suffered a similar fate. Unemployment reached over 22% in the winter of 1932 which meant that 3 million people were out of work.

Economists, politicians and journalists could not agree on the cause of the crash or on the preferred policy response.[10] The classical school of economics advanced policies based on their belief in the ultimate stability of the market and its ability to return to full employment. Keynes argued against this non-interventionist approach and proposed radical changes in economic policy. He suggested an urgent need for active and extensive government intervention. To understand the differences between the policy recommendations, we must first consider some of the theoretical distinctions which separate the classical and Keynesian schools.

Often, when we discuss the upheaval in the study of economics which we attribute to Keynes, we call it the 'Keynesian revolution'. To understand why Keynes was revolutionary, we will look at how his point of view differed from the classical position. We will begin with the theoretical differences and then discuss how these translated to differing policy recommendations.

Classical economists built on the foundation laid by the physiocrats. Their belief in the stability of the market led them to advocate minimum government intervention. Keynes, however, followed the mercantilists. He not only adopted some of their ideas, he advocated a much more prominent and active role for government. Keynes believed that the market was inherently unstable. Government policy could counter instability in the market.

Keynes began his theoretical attack by looking at the classical model of the labour market. For classical economists, this was the source of unemployment. Labour was demanded by firms and supplied by households. At the equilibrium wage rate, all labour that wanted to work could work: there was no involuntary unemployment.

When confronted with the high unemployment which existed during the Great Depression, classical economists argued in favour of a cut in the wage rate to alleviate the excess supply of labour. Keynes had the advantage of learning from the US experience. In 1932–33, the wage rate fell but this did not lead to increased employment as classical theory predicts.

This led Keynes to look for a different explanation for unemployment. He thought that the cause of unemployment was a deficiency in the demand for goods. He argued that a cut in the wage rate would reduce consumer expenditure and lead to a deficiency in demand. This would create uncertainty among investors who would be less likely to undertake investment expenditure. As the demand for consumer and capital goods fell, so would the demand for labour. In short, the decrease of the wage rate actually exacerbated the problem of unemployment.

Moreover, there was little agreement between the classical school and Keynes on the flexibility of wages. Wage flexibility was an intrinsic part of the classical doctrine. In contrast, Keynes argued that wages may not respond quickly to changing market conditions. Institutional arrangements like labour contracts and unions keep wages rigid. In fact, he disputed the desirability of flexible wages. Since consumption is one source of demand, falling wages led to a decrease in consumer expenditure. Inflexible wages helped to maintain the level of demand in an economy.

Keynes continued his theoretical attack with a discussion of Say's Law which states that 'Supply brings forth its own demand.' This is an idea which is often depicted through the circular flow. Households provide the factors of production which are used by firms to produce goods. The households are paid income by the firms which they use to purchase the goods which the firms produced. To take this one step further, households can either consume or save their income. However, in the classical model, based on Say's Law, savings will always re-enter the circular flow in the form of investment. In other words, savings, a leakage from the circular flow, always equals investment, an injection into the circular flow. The classical economists advocated thrift. A high savings rate released labour and capital from producing consumer goods to producing investment goods. This increased the productive capacity of the economy.

Keynes disagreed with the classical analysis of savings and investment. He argued that savings and investment were very different activities, carried out by different people and influenced by different factors. There was nothing automatic about the process. Savings might sit as idle balances if investors were not inclined to use them. A high rate of savings reduced consumer expenditure which led to a reduction of national income. In this case, savings, the leakage from the circular flow, is greater than investment, the injection. The result is a slowdown of economic activity.

For classical economists, investment depends on the interest rate. The interest rate is determined in the market for loanable funds. The source of the supply of loanable funds is savings. Investors demand loanable funds for investment. The interest rate, which can be thought of as the price of borrowing money, adjusts to bring the demand and supply into equilibrium.

Keynes believed that interest rates were determined in the money market. Money supply was determined by the monetary authorities. Money demand depended on income and the households' preference for holding money rather than interest-bearing assets. The interest rate was determined by the interaction of the demand for and supply of money.

Keynes did not deny that interest rates influenced firms' investment decisions. However, he argued that investment decisions depended mainly on their expectations for future profits. Even at very low rates of interest, firms would not invest if they did not feel that their revenues would cover the cost of borrowing money. From Keynes' perspective, investment was not simply a mathematical decision based on anticipated costs and revenues. The revenue prediction depended on the investors' belief of future business conditions. In his own words, 'Thus if the animal spirits are dimmed and the spontaneous optimism falters, leaving us to depend on nothing but a mathematical expectation, enterprise will fade and die; – though fears of loss may have a basis no more reasonable than hopes of profit had before.'[11]

Differences in theory naturally led to differing policy recommendations. The policy recommendations of the British Committee on National Expenditure which was set up in 1931 to address the problems of the Great Depression offered policy prescriptions which were neoclassical. The preoccupation over the balanced budget led the Committee, under the chairmanship of Sir George May, to recommend cuts in government expenditure and increases in taxation. They were concerned that government spending would 'crowd out' private investment.

Keynes argued against this non-interventionist approach. Unemployment, according to Keynes, resulted from a failure of demand. The policy recommendations of the Committee would aggravate this situation in two ways. Increased taxation decreases disposable income. With less income, households will spend less and consumer expenditure falls. A decrease in government expenditure directly decreases the demand in the economy.

According to Keynes, government spending was not a diversion of funds from the private sector. The public sector compensated for deficient demand which originated in the private sector. Keynes advocated fiscal policy measures, primarily government spending on public works projects, in order to generate employment. He said, 'I expect to see the State . . . taking an even greater responsibility for directly organising investment.'[12] As a consequence of this higher expenditure, the neoclassical rule of balancing the budget each year was abandoned. Adam Smith's advice that 'The only good budget is a balanced budget' became redundant. Keynes' ideas were adopted by Lloyd George, leader of the Liberal party who proposed an increase in the amount spent on public works programmes.

In addition, Keynes advocated using monetary policy to stimulate demand. This would translate into low interest rates which would induce new investment expenditure. However, he was sceptical of relying solely on monetary policy because, as was mentioned earlier, reduced interest rates alone might not be enough to entice investment. The use of both fiscal and monetary policy to stimulate demand and increase employment, is in sharp contrast to the *laissez-faire* policies advocated by neoclassical economists.

Figure 11.1 illustrates the relationship between the economic variables which were mentioned in *The General Theory*.

Figure 11.1: The relationship between the variables in the Keynesian model

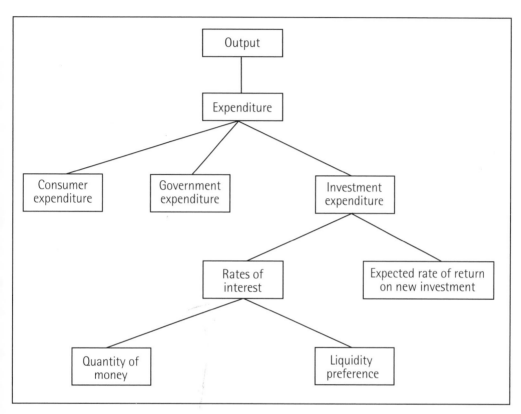

Output depends on total expenditure which is comprised of consumer, government and investment expenditure. Consumer expenditure is explained by the consumption function which is described in the next chapter. Investment expenditure depends on the rate of interest and the expected rate of return on new investment. Finally, the rate of interest is determined by the quantity of money and what Keynes called the liquidity preference, i.e. the demand for money.

The Keynesian model which is outlined in the next chapter and the policy recommendations which follow are ultimately short-term in duration. Keynes' dismissive nature of the long run explains the absence of any long-term analysis. Such a view is epitomised in his famous line '*In the long run* we are all dead.'[13]

SUMMARY

1. The pre-Keynesian or classical school of economics believed that markets were inherently stable and would automatically tend towards full-employment. Unemployment arose out of imperfections in the market system which over time would disappear. Hence, government intervention was unnecessary and, in some cases, counterproductive.

2. Keynes' early grounding in economics was of a neoclassical origin. One of his first teachers in economics at Cambridge was Alfred Marshall. On returning to Cambridge, Keynes began to question the economic orthodoxy of the time. This was evident in many of his great works and in particular *The General Theory*. Outside England, he is probably best remembered for his attack on the Versailles treaty and, later, for his contribution to the setting up of the international organisations after World War II.

3. The Keynesian revolution emerged out of the Great Depression of the 1930s and challenged the orthodox classical economic doctrine of the time. For Keynes, an economy could be at an equilibrium which is below the full-employment level. Insufficient demand was the primary cause of low output and high unemployment. There was a role for government in ensuring sufficient demand.

KEY TERMS

Mercantilists
Physiocrats
Classical economics
Laissez-faire
Invisible hand
Marginalists
Keynesian revolution
Say's Law

REVIEW QUESTIONS

1. Briefly outline the main differences between the classical and the Keynesian schools of economic thought.
2. Assess J. M. Keynes' contribution to modern macroeconomics.
3. Why did the Keynesian revolution occur in the 1930s? What were the different explanations given to explain the Great Depression?

CHAPTER 12

THE DETERMINATION OF NATIONAL INCOME

'After several years of plunging production, followed by a sluggish recovery, his decision to examine the forces that determined output made sense, but after even more decades of regarding prices as the proper object of enquiry for economists, the shift was not easy.'[1]

Lorie Tarshis (b.1911)

'. . . if I were an Irishman, I should find much to attract me in the economic outlook of your present government towards greater self-sufficiency'.[2]

John Maynard Keynes (1883–1946)

CHAPTER OBJECTIVES

Upon completing this chapter, the student should understand:

- the assumptions of the Keynesian income determination model;
- aggregate expenditure and the equilibrium level of national income;
- the expenditure multiplier;
- the policy implications arising out of the Keynesian model;
- the experience with Keynesian economics.

OUTLINE

INTRODUCTION

Over sixty years after its inception, the Keynesian model of income determination is still considered to be at the core of modern macroeconomics. This chapter deals with the Keynesian model. We begin with the income determination model for a closed economy. The framework is then extended to an open economy model. The last two sections deal with the major policy implications arising out of the Keynesian model and the Irish experience.

12.1 THE MODEL OF INCOME DETERMINATION

We begin our analysis by constructing a simple model of the economy. We work with a two-sector economy with two primary sources of demand – households and firms. Households are engaged in consumption, denoted as C whereas firms are engaged in investment, denoted as I. Initially, there is no government or foreign trade sector. Furthermore, we ignore the differences between the different measures of national income. Henceforth, we use national income, total output and GNP interchangeably.

A number of basic assumptions concerning the Keynesian income determination model are made. First, wages and prices are inflexible. Second, since price does not adjust to changes in demand, all of the adjustment is made by the quantity produced. In other words, suppliers produce what is demanded at the going price. Third, the economy can operate at less than full capacity: this means that there are unemployed resources. Because of this excess capacity, an increase in demand will increase output and employment but it will have no effect on price. Fourth, the monetary system is omitted from the model.

In order to fully understand the workings of the model we need to examine both consumer and investment expenditure in detail. We do so by introducing two new concepts – the consumption function and the investment function.

Consumption and the consumption function

Consumption is defined as household spending on consumer goods and services which include food, clothes, videos, washing machines and so on. In the pre-Keynesian era, the predominant view was that the interest rate determined savings and, in turn, consumption. In contrast, Keynes believed that the level of income was the main explanatory variable. The relationship between consumption and income is described by the consumption function.

Definition
The consumption function shows consumer expenditure at different levels of income.

It can be written as an equation in the following form:

[12.1]

$$C = f(Y_d)$$

where C is planned household consumption and Y_d is aggregate disposable income. Disposable income was defined in Chapter 10 as national income plus transfer payments minus personal taxes. In terms of explaining changes in consumer expenditure, it is a better explanatory variable than national income. Equation 12.1 simply states that consumption depends on disposable income. It is a positive relationship.

Keynes argued this was a stable relationship and as current income increased, expenditure on consumer goods increased. However, the increase in consumer spending is not as great as the increase in income because some of the extra income is saved. Keynes explained this tendency to consume in the following way: 'Our normal psychological law that, when the real income of the community increases or decreases, its consumption will increase or decrease but not so fast . . .'.[3] He called this the marginal propensity to consume.

Definition
The marginal propensity to consume (MPC) is the fraction of each additional unit of disposable income that is spent on consumer goods and services.

The consumption function can now be defined more specifically:

[12.2]

$$C = bY_d$$

where

$$b = \frac{\Delta C}{\Delta Y_d} = MPC$$

Furthermore,

$$0 < b < 1$$

b is less than one because only a portion of disposable income is spent on goods and services. The remainder is saved.

Let us consider an example. Table 12.1 provides a set of disposable income and consumption levels.

Table 12.1: The consumption function

Disposable income, Y_d	Consumption, C
0	0
100	75
200	150
300	225
400	300
500	375
600	450
700	525
800	600

As disposable income rises in increments of €100 consumption rises in increments of €75. The MPC is equal to the change in consumption divided by the corresponding change in disposable income. Hence, in this example,

$$b = \frac{\Delta C}{\Delta Y_d} = \frac{75}{100} = 0.75$$

If disposable income increases, households will plan additional consumption equal to three-quarters of any increase in disposable income.

This particular consumption function is represented by the following equation,

$$C = .75Y_d$$

For example, if disposable income increases by €100, planned consumption increases by the b × €100 which in this example is equal to 0.75 × €100 = €75.

This consumption function is represented in Figure 12.1.

Figure 12.1: The consumption function, $C = .75Y_d$

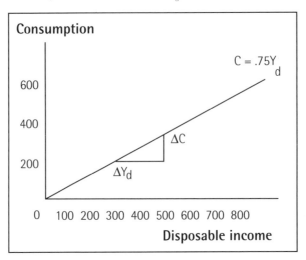

Figure 12.1 shows the specific consumption function $C = .75Y_d$ in diagrammatic form. This diagram can be drawn by substituting values for disposable income (Y_d) and solving for consumption (C). Alternatively, the points can be plotted directly from Table 12.1. By convention consumption, the dependent variable, is positioned on the vertical axis. Disposable income, the independent variable, is on the horizontal axis. The line shows the positive relationship between consumption and disposable income; as disposable income increases, so does consumption. The slope of any line shows how the variable on the vertical axis changes in response to a change in the variable on the horizontal axis. The slope of the consumption function relates the change in consumption to the change in disposable income. This is the marginal propensity to consume.

The difference between disposable income and consumption is accounted for by savings. For example, at an income level of €100 consumption amounts to €75. The difference of €25 is accounted for by savings. As we will see, in every sense, the savings function is directly related to the consumption function.

Savings and the savings function

At a given level of income the household has two choices: either consume or save. This can be represented by the following identity:

$$Y_d \equiv C + S \qquad \text{[12.3]}$$

Rearranging the variables we can see that savings is, by definition, the difference between disposable income and consumption:

$$S \equiv Y_d - C \qquad \text{[12.4]}$$

The savings function, defined below, is usually written in the following format:

$$S = (1 - b) Y_d \qquad \text{[12.5]}$$

The derivation of the savings function is given in Appendix 12.1.

Definition
The savings function shows the relationship between savings and disposable income.

The relationship between the change in savings and the change in disposable income has a special name. It is called the marginal propensity to save.

Definition
The marginal propensity to save (MPS) is the proportion of a change in disposable income that is saved.

Since b represents the amount of additional disposable income that is spent on consumption, 1–b shows the amount of additional disposable income that is devoted to savings. Hence 1–b is the marginal propensity to save.

The consumption function reconsidered

In Table 12.1 and Figure 12.1 we assumed that consumption depended only on disposable income. Excluding all other factors is unrealistic as there are many others which affect the level of consumption. Expectations and aggregate wealth are examples of such factors. Thus, we must adjust our consumption function to allow for these other factors. An adjusted consumption function can be written in the following manner:

$$C = \bar{C} + bY_d \qquad \text{[12.6]}$$

This new consumption function has two separate parts.

$\bar{C}$ is called the autonomous component. This is the part of consumption which is independent of income levels: it changes as other factors vary.

bY_d is called the income-induced component. This is the part of consumption which is solely determined by the level of disposable income. It changes as disposable income varies. It corresponds to our simple consumption function which was described above.

Let us take an example. Table 12.2 provides a set of disposable income and consumption levels.

Table 12.2: The consumption function

Y_d	$\bar{C}$	bY_d	$C = \bar{C} + bY_d$
0	50	0	50
100	50	75	125
200	50	150	200
300	50	225	275
400	50	300	350
500	50	375	425
600	50	450	500
700	50	525	575
800	50	600	650

This particular consumption function is represented by the following equation:

$$C = 50 + .75Y_d$$

where €50 is the autonomous component and .75 is the marginal propensity to consume. We can use this equation to find the level of consumption at any level of disposable income.

For example, if the income level is €100, planned consumption is €50 + (b × €100) which is equal to €50 + (0.75 × €100) = €125.

This particular consumption function is graphically represented in Figure 12.2.

Figure 12.2: The consumption function, $C = 50 + .75Y_d$

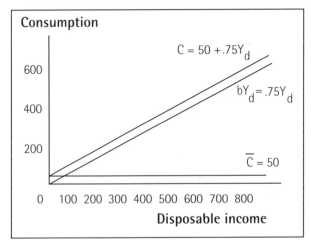

The position of the consumption function relative to the vertical axis depends on the value of $\bar{C}$. A change in the value of autonomous consumption will cause the consumption function to shift upwards or downwards. The slope of the consumption function depends on the value of b, the MPC. A small b results in a relatively flat consumption function whereas a large b results in a relatively steep consumption function.

Investment and the investment function

Investment expenditure is planned spending by firms on capital or producer goods such as tools and machinery, vehicles, premises, factories and so on. In simple terms it is the addition to the capital stock of the economy. This component of total spending, denoted as I, is far more volatile and unstable than consumer expenditure. This is predominantly because of the role of expectations, or what Keynes referred to as 'animal spirits', in determining the level of investment expenditure.

In the simple Keynesian model we treat investment as autonomous. It is independent of the current level of income, and can be represented by the following equation:

$$I = \bar{I}$$

[12.7]

The case where investment expenditure is equal to €100 is illustrated in Table 12.3.

Table 12.3: The investment function

Income, Y	Investment, $\bar{I}$
0	100
100	100
200	100
300	100
400	100
500	100
600	100
700	100
800	100

The equation for this particular investment function is as follows:

$$\bar{I} = 100$$

The corresponding diagram for investment expenditure is below.

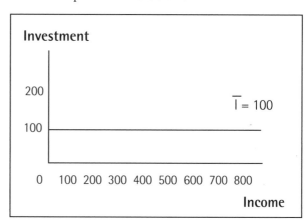

Figure 12.3: The investment function, $\bar{I} = 100$

Investment expenditure is constant relative to income levels. The diagram shows that investment is €100, regardless of the level of income. It changes, however, as other factors vary. One key factor which determines investment spending is the rate of interest, where the rate of interest is the cost of borrowed funds. This applies whether firms borrow funds to finance investment projects or forgo interest by financing investment with their own funds. Other factors include innovation and technical change, corporate taxes and, finally, expectations (of future earnings, inflation, interest rates and so on). Changes in any one or a combination of these factors cause the investment function to shift upwards or downwards.

Aggregate expenditure and the aggregate expenditure function

In our two-sector economy, total planned spending comprises planned consumer spending by households and planned investment spending by firms. In the Keynesian model total expenditure or total spending is termed aggregate expenditure, AE.

Definition

Aggregate expenditure is the amount that households and firms plan to spend on goods and services.

For a two-sector model, it is usually written in the following format:

$$AE \equiv C + \bar{I}$$

[12.8]

AE is simply the sum of planned consumer expenditure and investment expenditure. Table 12.4 shows a hypothetical example of an aggregate expenditure function which adds together the consumption and investment functions that were discussed above.[4]

We draw your attention to an important point. Disposable income, Y_d, was the explanatory variable used in the text up to this stage. With transfer payments and personal taxes accounting for the difference between disposable income and national income, it is reasonable to proxy 'Y_d' by Y, national income.

Table 12.4: Aggregate expenditure

Y	C	$\bar{I}$	AE ≡ C + $\bar{I}$
0	50	100	150
100	125	100	225
200	200	100	300
300	275	100	375
400	350	100	450
500	425	100	525
600	500	100	600
700	575	100	675
800	650	100	750

In algebraic form,

$$AE \equiv C + \overline{I}$$

where: $C = 50 + .75Y$ and $\overline{I} = 100$
Thus,

$$AE = (50 + .75Y) + 100$$
$$AE = 150 + .75Y$$

Figure 12.4 illustrates this particular aggregate expenditure function.

Figure 12.4: Aggregate expenditure, AE = 150 + .75Y

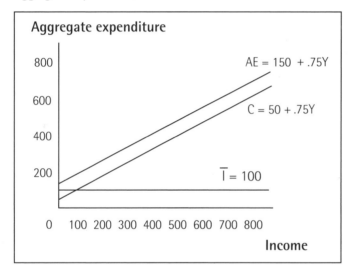

The diagram above clearly demonstrates that the AE function is simply the vertical summation of the consumption function and the investment function. It shows, at each level of income, the total planned expenditure by households and firms.

The equilibrium level of national income

Equilibrium is a state from which there is no tendency to change. In the context of the Keynesian model there is no tendency for income to either rise or fall at the equilibrium.

Keynes argued that the equilibrium level of income was determined by the planned level of expenditure in the economy. At the equilibrium level of income, households and firms are spending what they had planned to spend. At this level, there is no unplanned change in the level of inventories.

Table 12.5 illustrates that equilibrium is achieved through changes in the inventories of firms.

Table 12.5: Determining the equilibrium income level

Y	C	$\bar{I}$	AE	Unplanned Δ in inventories	Change in Y
0	50	100	150	Falling	Increase
100	125	100	225	Falling	Increase
200	200	100	300	Falling	Increase
300	275	100	375	Falling	Increase
400	350	100	450	Falling	Increase
500	425	100	525	Falling	Increase
600	500	100	600	Constant	No change
700	575	100	675	Rising	Decrease
800	650	100	750	Rising	Decrease

The equilibrium level of income (column 1) is determined by the level of planned aggregate expenditure (column 4). In this example, the equilibrium level of income is €600. We explain why by using a trial and error approach.

Suppose Y = €400. When income is €400 planned expenditure is €450. Aggregate expenditure exceeds output. Firms will experience an unplanned fall in their stocks, and they will respond by increasing output. An income level of €400 cannot be the equilibrium level of income because of this tendency to change.

Suppose Y = €700. When income is €700 planned expenditure is only €675. Aggregate expenditure is less than output. Firms will experience an unplanned rise in their stocks. They will respond by reducing output. Hence, an income level of €700 cannot be the equilibrium level of income.

Suppose Y = €600. Planned expenditure is also €600. Aggregate expenditure equals output. This is the equilibrium level of income as there is no tendency to change. Equilibrium occurs when income is equal to aggregate expenditure. This is the equilibrium condition and it is expressed in the following equation:

$$Y = AE$$

[12.9]

There are ways of showing the equilibrium level of income other than by tabular form. It can be depicted graphically or derived algebraically. We first consider the graphical presentation. The algebraic derivation will follow.

The equilibrium level of income: a graphical presentation

The equilibrium level of income can be derived with the aid of a 45° line. A 45° line divides our two-dimensional space into two equal halves. All points on the 45° line are equidistant from both axes. Therefore, at any point on the 45° line, the value on the vertical axis equals the value on the horizontal axis.

In this example, the 45° line shows where expenditure and income are equal. In Figure 12.5, the 45° line is drawn with the aggregate expenditure line in order to derive the equilibrium level of income. The equilibrium point is where the 45° line intersects the AE line. Figure 12.5 is sometimes referred to as the Keynesian cross diagram.

Figure 12.5: The equilibrium level of income

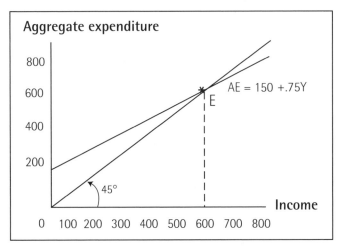

The 45° line and the AE line intersect at point E where Y = AE at an equilibrium level of €600. To the left of point E the AE line is above the 45° line. Aggregate expenditure exceeds output; excess demand results. There is an unplanned fall in inventories. As a result, the response of firms is to increase output.

The AE line is below the 45° line to the right of point E. Aggregate expenditure is less than output; excess supply exists. There is an unplanned rise in inventories. A reduction in output is the response of firms.

At point E, aggregate expenditure is equal to output and an equilibrium state exists. At the level of output where Y = €600 there is no tendency for change to occur.

The equilibrium level of income: an algebraic derivation

The equilibrium level of income can be determined algebraically using simultaneous equations. Although the solution is the same as the one obtained using the above two methods, this method is faster and more accurate. As previously stated:

$$AE \equiv C + \bar{I}$$ [12.8]

where consumption is defined as:

$$C = \bar{C} + bY$$ [12.6]

Substituting Equation 12.6 into 12.8, we get:

[12.10]

$$AE = \bar{C} + \bar{I} + bY$$

Group the autonomous components of expenditure together and substitute into Equation 12.10 above:

$$\bar{A} = \bar{C} + \bar{I}$$ [12.11]

$$AE = \bar{A} + bY$$ [12.12]

In equilibrium, income equals planned expenditure: [12.9]

$$Y = AE$$

Equation 12.9 is the equation for the 45° line. Using simultaneous equations, substitute the right-hand side of Equation 12.12 for the right-hand side of Equation 12.9. The solution is the intersection of the aggregate expenditure line and the 45° line or the 'Keynesian cross'.

$$Y = \bar{A} + bY$$

Solve for Y:

$$Y = \bar{A} \times \frac{1}{1-b}$$ [12.13]

This is the equation for the equilibrium level of income. The equilibrium level of income can be calculated by substituting values for $\bar{A}$, the total level of autonomous spending, and for b, the MPC. In the example above,

$$\bar{A} = \bar{C} + \bar{I} = 50 + 100 = 150$$
$$b = .75$$

Thus,

$$Y = \bar{A} \times \frac{1}{1-b} = 150 \times \frac{1}{1-.75} = 150 \times 4 = 600.$$

€600 is the equilibrium level of income. This corresponds with the income level which we derived from both the tabular form and the graphical approach.

There is an alternative way of presenting the equilibrium level of income. Rather than focus on the income-expenditure approach as above, we can use the savings-investment approach. This is explained in Appendix 12.2.

The government sector

We now extend our model in order to include the government sector. Since this model is concerned essentially with the short run, we can assume that government spending is autonomous and is independent of national income.[5]
Thus,

$$G = \bar{G}$$ [12.14]

Table 12.6 illustrates the equilibrium level of income (similar to Table 12.5) but incorporating government expenditure equal to €40.

Table 12.6: Determining the equilibrium income level with $\bar{G} = 40$

Y	C	$\bar{I}$	$\bar{G}$	AE	Unplanned Δ in inventories	Change in Y
0	50	100	40	190	Falling	Increase
100	125	100	40	265	Falling	Increase
200	200	100	40	340	Falling	Increase
300	275	100	40	415	Falling	Increase
400	350	100	40	490	Falling	Increase
500	425	100	40	565	Falling	Increase
600	500	100	40	640	Falling	Increase
700	575	100	40	715	Falling	Increase
760	620	100	40	760	Constant	No change
800	650	100	40	790	Rising	Decrease

The corresponding diagram is represented in Figure 12.6.

With the inclusion of government, aggregate expenditure now incorporates expenditure by the government on goods and services.

In algebraic form:

$$AE \equiv C + \bar{I} + \bar{G}$$

[12.15]

where C = 50 + .75Y, $\bar{I}$ = 100 and $\bar{G}$ = 40.

Thus,

$$AE = (50 + .75Y) + 100 + 40$$
$$AE = 190 + .75Y$$

Figure 12.6 shows the new aggregate expenditure function. The addition of government means that the intercept changes from 150 to 190. However, since government spending is autonomous, the slope of the line does not change. It is the marginal propensity to consume and still equal to .75.

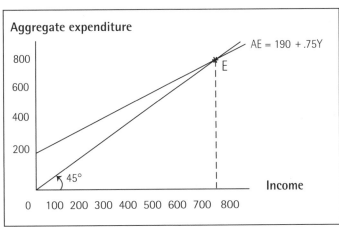

Figure 12.6: The equilibrium level of income with $\bar{G} = 40$

The inclusion of government expenditure has important implications. First, its inclusion results in a higher level of income. The equilibrium level of income was originally €600. Incorporating government expenditure into the model, where $\bar{G} = 40$, increases the equilibrium level of national income to €760. This can be confirmed by applying the algebra formula which was derived earlier. In this case,

$$\bar{A} = \bar{C} + \bar{I} + \bar{G} = 50 + 100 + 40 = 190$$
$$b = .75$$

Thus,

$$Y = \bar{A} \times \frac{1}{1-b} = 190 \times \frac{1}{1-.75} = 190 \times 4 = 760.$$

Second, any fall-off in consumer or investment expenditure can be offset by an increase in government expenditure. Government expenditure can replace investment expenditure as a source of demand. Likewise, if the economy is below full employment (an assumption of the Keynesian model) an injection of government spending will increase output closer to the full-employment level.

We now consider changes in expenditure and analyse their effect on the equilibrium level of income.

Changes in aggregate expenditure: the multiplier effect

According to the Keynesian model, a change in aggregate expenditure results in a change in national income. Furthermore, the change in income is usually a multiple of the change in spending. Keynes described this concept stating that a '. . . definite ratio, to be called the ×, can be established between income and investment . . .'[6]
 The concept of the multiplier was first developed by Richard Kahn (later Lord Kahn) and Colin Clark (1905–89) in 1931. Kahn was regarded as Keynes' 'favourite pupil' and later became a colleague. Clark was a lecturer in statistics in Cambridge at the same time as Keynes. The early theory dealt with an employment multiplier, which explained how a change in public investment brought about a multiple expansion of employment. In *The General Theory* of 1936 Keynes focused attention on an expenditure multiplier and explained how a change in spending causes a multiple change in income. This multiple is called the Keynesian expenditure multiplier.

Definition

The expenditure multiplier is the ratio of the change in income to the change in autonomous spending.

Any injection of spending causes a multiplier or domino effect. Why so? An initial increase in aggregate expenditure generates extra income. The increase in income induces an increase in consumption, according to our analysis of the consumption function. Next, the increase in consumption generates a further increase in income which, in turn, leads to a further increase in consumption. This process continues.

Let us consider a simple example to illustrate the multiplier effect. Suppose a tourist spends €1,000 in a hotel. As a result of this additional income the hotel management upgrades the restaurant facilities by spending €750 on the purchase of tables and chairs. The furniture suppliers decide to hire an additional worker for the month on account of the extra business. They pay their new employee €562.50 a month. This new member of staff is from the locality and spends over €420 on food and drink from the local supermarket. In turn, the supermarket decides to buy in more foodstuffs and beverages to meet the extra demand. They spend an additional €316. This process, with each person's expenditure becoming someone else's income, continues.

The initial injection of spending has led to a successive series with the increases becoming successively smaller:[7]

$$€1000 + €750 + €562.50 + €421.875 + €316.40625 + \ldots$$

This is illustrated in Figure 12.7.

Figure 12.7:   The multiplier with successive increases in consumption

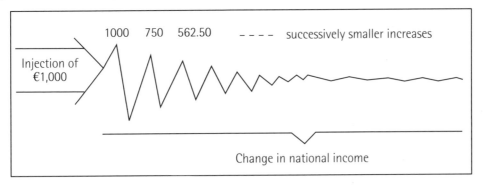

This is a convergent series which can be summed, in this case, to €4,000.[8] The initial €1,000 has now generated, in total, income of €4,000. The increase in income is four times greater than the increase in aggregate expenditure. The value of the multiplier is 4. This is an example of the Keynesian expenditure multiplier, or simply the multiplier, in action. This domino effect is illustrated in Figure 12.8.

Figure 12.8: The multiplier process

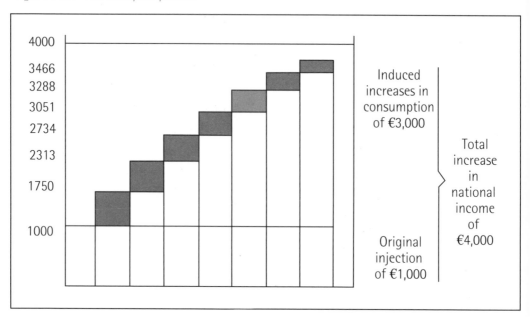

Figure 12.8 illustrates the effect of an initial injection of expenditure on both consumption and on national income. The increase in expenditure of €1,000 induces additional increases in consumer expenditure equal to €3,000. Thus, the overall increase in total income is €4,000.

Example: Using the data from above

Continuing with the previous example, suppose that government expenditure increases by €50, from €40 to €90. Table 12.7 shows the effect on the equilibrium level of income.

Table 12.7: Determining the new equilibrium income level

Y	C	$\bar{I}$	$\bar{G}$	AE	Change in Y
0	50	100	90	240	Increase
100	125	100	90	315	Increase
200	200	100	90	390	Increase
300	275	100	90	465	Increase
400	350	100	90	540	Increase
500	425	100	90	615	Increase
600	500	100	90	690	Increase
700	575	100	90	765	Increase
800	650	100	90	840	Increase
900	725	100	90	915	Increase
960	770	100	90	960	No change
1000	800	100	90	990	Decrease

The table indicates that the increase of €50 in government expenditure, from €40 to €90, increases the equilibrium level of income by €200, from €760 to €960.[9] This increase of €200 suggests a multiplier of 4 ($\frac{200}{50}$ = 4). This can be verified by tabular form, by the multiplier formula, and by means of a diagram.

By tabular form:

The example above is presented in Table 12.8.
    Example: $\Delta\bar{G}$ = 50 and b = .75

Table 12.8: The multiplier process in action

	$\Delta\bar{G}$	C	AE
Round 1	50		50
Round 2		50 × .75	50 × .75
Round 3		50 × .75²	50 × .75²
Round 4		50 × .75³	50 × .75³
,,		,,	,,
,,		,,	,,
,,		,,	,,
Totals	50	150	200

By the multiplier formula:

The multiplier formula is derived in Appendix 12.3. The multiplier is:

$$k = \frac{\Delta Y}{\Delta \bar{A}}$$

where $\bar{A}$ is autonomous spending. k is the symbol that Keynes used for the multiplier. k can also be calculated in the following manner:

$$k = \frac{1}{1 - b}$$

where b is the marginal propensity to consume. In terms of this example, the multiplier is:

$$k = \frac{\Delta Y}{\Delta A} = \frac{200}{50} = 4, \text{ or:}$$

$$k = \frac{1}{1 - b} = \frac{1}{1 - .75} = 4$$

We can use the multiplier to directly calculate the change in income using the following formula:

$$\Delta Y = k \times \Delta \bar{A}$$

In this example, k = 4 and $\Delta\bar{A}$ is the change in autonomous spending of €50.

$$\Delta Y = 4 \times 50 = €200.$$

Our familiar cross diagram can also illustrate the multiplier effect. We use the same example as above where government expenditure increases by €50.

By diagram:

Figure 12.9:   The new equilibrium level of income

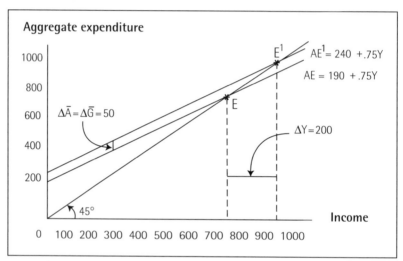

Figure 12.9 shows the multiplier effect on national income. The increase in government expenditure causes a shift of the aggregate expenditure line from AE to AE¹. The equilibrium level of income, as reflected in the intersection point between the 45° line and the AE line, increases from E to E¹. The vertical distance between the two AE lines, AE and AE¹, is equal to $\Delta\bar{A} = \Delta\bar{G} = 50$. The horizontal distance between the two income levels is equal to $\Delta Y = \Delta\bar{A} \times k = 50 \times 4 = 200$. In terms of length, the horizontal distance is four times the vertical distance. This reflects the multiplier which in this case is equal to 4.

The example above illustrates two important facts about the value of the multiplier. First, it depends on the size of the marginal propensity to consume. A large MPC results in a large multiplier; a small MPC results in a small multiplier. For example a MPC of .9 results in a multiplier of 10, a MPC of .75 results in a multiplier of 4 whereas a MPC of .6 results in a multiplier of 2.5.

Second, given that the MPC is less than one, the multiplier must be greater than one. This suggests than any increase in spending will lead to an increase in income of a greater amount. This has important implications for fiscal policy and its effectiveness in dealing with unemployment. This is discussed in greater detail in Section 12.2.

Most economists credit Keynes with the 'discovery' of the multiplier. However, its popularity, particulary in the United States, is due to the work of a Keynesian economist, Paul Samuelson (b.1915). Samuelson's textbook, *Economics* was first published in 1948. For the following thirty years, it was the principal text used at many universities in the US. For this and many other contributions to the discipline of economics, Paul Samuelson was awarded the Nobel prize in 1970.

It is important to note that the multiplier process is symmetric. Any decrease in expenditure causes a greater decline in national income because of the knock-on effect of lower induced expenditure. The failure of investment expenditure was the explanation given by Keynes to account for the Great Depression of the 1930s.[10]

Thus far, our analysis of the multiplier has been quite limited. First, the model has reflected a closed economy. Second, it has been expressed solely in terms of the MPC. We now redress these two shortcomings.

The foreign sector and a four-sector model

Our analysis so far has been almost entirely within the context of a closed economy. This is in line with Keynes' *The General Theory*. One reason for this was the major upheaval which was occurring in the international monetary system at the time *The General Theory* was written, after the collapse of the Gold Standard and before the Bretton Woods system was instituted. As a result, exchange rates floated freely on foreign exchange markets. Existing knowledge on flexible exchange rate regimes and how they influenced domestic economic variables was limited.

Another possible reason was the fact that foreign trade did not constitute a large percentage of GDP in either the US or the UK. Relative to the Irish situation, this position still remains. Moreover, given the open nature of the Irish economy (see Chapter 10 for a discussion on the relative openness of the Irish economy) the foreign sector is particularly vital to our analysis. We now adjust our model to incorporate the foreign sector.

The foreign sector is incorporated into the model by including a value for net exports, denoted by NX, the difference between exports, X and imports, M.

The level of exports from the domestic economy depends on a number of variables including foreign income, the competitiveness of domestic goods in relation to similar goods produced by firms in other countries and exchange rates. The most important variable is foreign income. Because exports are domestically produced goods and services purchased by foreigners, demand for these goods and services varies with the income of a country's main trading partners. As exports are not related to national income we can treat them as autonomous.

$$\boxed{X = \bar{X}}$$ [12.16]

In this example, take $\bar{X} = €90$.

The amount of goods and services which are imported into the domestic economy is affected by some of the same variables including the relative competitiveness of domestic goods and exchange rates. However, the ability of an economy to import goods depends on national income. Therefore, imports are a function of income. As income increases imports increase. The import function is of the form:

$$\boxed{M = mY}$$ [12.17]

where m represents the marginal propensity to import.

Definition
The marginal propensity to import (MPM) is the fraction of an increase in income that is spent on imports.

In this example, $M = .15Y$. This means that fifteen cents of each additional euro of national income is spent on imports. Table 12.9 shows hypothetical values for both exports and imports.

Table 12.9: *Exports, imports and net exports*

Y	$\overline{X}$	M	NX
0	90	0	90
100	90	15	75
200	90	30	60
300	90	45	45
400	90	60	30
500	90	75	15
600	90	90	0
700	90	105	−15
800	90	120	−30
900	90	135	−45
1000	90	150	−60

The net exports function is shown in Figure 12.10.

Figure 12.10: *Net exports function*

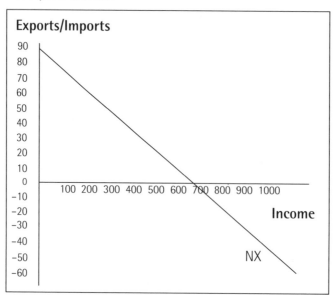

Table 12.10 illustrates the new equilibrium level of income with net exports varying as the level of income changes.

Table 12.10: *Determining the equilibrium income level with net exports*

Y	C	$\bar{I}$	$\bar{G}$	NX	AE	Unplanned Δ in inventories	Change in Y
0	50	100	40	90	280	Falling	Increase
100	125	100	40	75	340	Falling	Increase
200	200	100	40	60	400	Falling	Increase
300	275	100	40	45	460	Falling	Increase
400	350	100	40	30	520	Falling	Increase
500	425	100	40	15	580	Falling	Increase
600	500	100	40	0	640	Falling	Increase
700	575	100	40	−15	700	Constant	No change
800	650	100	40	−30	760	Rising	Decrease
900	725	100	40	−45	820	Rising	Decrease
1000	800	100	40	−60	880	Rising	Decrease

The corresponding diagram is represented in Figure 12.11.

Figure 12.11: *The equilibrium level of income with net exports*

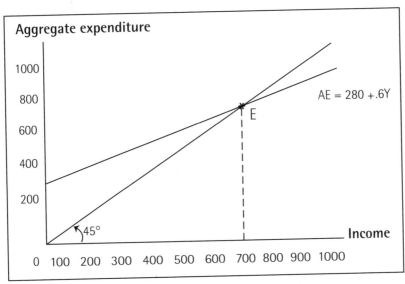

We can verify this equilibrium position algebraically. We begin with the expanded AE function, adding the foreign sector as follows:

$$AE \equiv C + \bar{I} + \bar{G} + \bar{X} - M \qquad \text{[12.18]}$$

where consumption and imports are defined as:

$$C = \bar{C} + bY \qquad [12.6]$$

$$M = mY \qquad [12.17]$$

Substitute Equations 12.6 and 12.17 into Equation 12.18 to get:

$$AE = \bar{C} + bY + \bar{I} + \bar{G} + \bar{X} - mY$$

Let $\bar{A} = \bar{C} + \bar{I} + \bar{G} + \bar{X}$, the autonomous components of AE, and substitute into the equation above:

$$AE = \bar{A} + bY - mY$$

Collect Y terms:

$$AE = \bar{A} + (b - m)Y \qquad [12.19]$$

In equilibrium:

$$Y = AE \qquad [12.9]$$

Substitute Y for AE in Equation 12.19 and solve for Y:

$$Y = \bar{A} \times \frac{1}{1 - b + m} \qquad [12.20]$$

This is the equation for the equilibrium level of income for the four-sector model of the economy. We can now use this derivation to find (a) the AE function and (b) the equilibrium level of income for our example.

(a) Equation 12.19 states that:

$$AE = \bar{A} + (b - m)Y$$

For our particular example:

$\bar{C} = 50$; $\bar{I} = 100$; $\bar{G} = 40$ (before the change in government expenditure); $\bar{X} = 90$; $b = MPC = .75$; $m = MPM = .15$. Substitute these values into Equation 12.19 to find the AE function:

$$AE = (50 + 100 + 40 + 90) + (.75 - .15)Y = 280 + 0.6Y$$

(b) Equation 12.20 states that:

$$Y = \bar{A} \times \frac{1}{1 - b + m}$$

where: $\bar{A} = 280$; $b = .75$; $m = .15$.

$$Y = 280 \times \frac{1}{1 - .75 + .15} = 280 \times 2.5 = €700$$

At this stage we need to examine the multiplier in an alternative form.

The multiplier reconsidered

It is possible to express the multiplier in terms of marginal propensity to save, MPS, rather than MPC. Since MPC = 1 − MPS, then the multiplier is the reciprocal of the MPS, or in equation form we can write it as follows:

$$\frac{1}{1-b} = \frac{1}{MPS}$$

[12.21]

This allows us to express the multiplier in terms of leakages. In the simple model of the economy the only leakage is savings. The higher the leakage, the smaller the multiplier. This is not surprising: a tendency to save limits the extent of consumer expenditure which, in turn, limits the final change in income. This format can be very useful when we extend the model to four sectors and when assessing the effectiveness of fiscal policy.

The extension of our model to include the foreign sector complicates not only the derivation of the equilibrium level of income but also the multiplier. Using the leakages format, the multiplier is equal to:

$$\frac{1}{MPS + MPM}$$

[12.22]

where MPS is the marginal propensity to save and MPM is the marginal propensity to import. This multiplier is derived in Appendix 12.4.

If taxes are considered and treated as a function of income, a further complication arises in the form of the marginal propensity to tax.

Definition

The marginal propensity to tax (MPT) is the proportion of any increment in income paid in taxes.

It is a leakage. Assuming consumer expenditure depends on gross income and on taxation, the multiplier is of the form:

$$\frac{1}{MPS + MPM + MPT}$$

[12.23]

The inclusion of the MPT, a leakage, further reduces the size of the multiplier.[11]

Approximations for these parameters in the Irish economy are MPS = 0.26, MPM = 0.4 and MPT = 0.24.[12] This gives us a multiplier of approximately unity which is relatively low by international standards.[13] This has important implications for the effectiveness of domestic fiscal policy. The Irish experience with Keynesian economics in general, and fiscal policy in particular, is discussed in Section 12.3.

One final concept which requires explanation is the paradox of thrift.

Thriftiness or savings is normally treated as desirable. The paradox of thrift suggests otherwise. How so? An increase in the planned level of savings results in a reduction in the equilibrium level of national income and because savings depends on income, the actual level of savings may even decline. This suggests that although savings can be viewed individually as a virtue it becomes a vice when the analysis is extended to society. It is, yet again, a fallacy of composition: the assumption that what is true for a part is true for the whole.

As a corollary to the above, the classical school and Keynes had very different views on the virtues of savings. The classical economists were in favour of high levels of savings which would lead to lower interest rates and higher investment levels. Keynes disagreed on the basis that too much savings had adverse effects on expenditure and output.

The Keynesian model, as presented above, is incomplete: it excludes money and interest rates, wages and prices, and finally, supply-side effects. These are dealt with in subsequent chapters. As for the criticisms, there are many. Some criticise the underlying assumptions of the model (fixed prices, cyclical tendencies, undesirable equilibrium). Others are critical of the policy implications (government action, budget deficits) while the empirical evidence (consumption function, multiplier) has been the subject of harsh review. Despite all this, the Keynesian model remains an important part of modern macroeconomics. For the moment we turn our attention to the policy implications arising out of the Keynesian model and the Western economies' experience with Keynesian economics.

12.2 THE POLICY IMPLICATIONS

A number of important policy implications arise out of the Keynesian model. With the possibility that the economy may settle at an income level below the full-employment level, Keynesians argued in favour of government intervention in order to narrow this deflationary gap between actual output and full-employment output. In *The General Theory* he called for public works programmes to provide jobs and to increase national income. He strongly supported demand management and, in particular, the active use of fiscal policy. There remains some controversy over his support for counter-cyclical policy.

The terms demand management, fiscal policy and counter-cyclical policy require explanations.

Definition
Demand management is the collective term used to explain various government policies which influence the level of aggregate expenditure in the economy.

These include fiscal and monetary policy. We will discuss monetary policy in the next chapter. Fiscal policy is described below.

Fiscal policy
Definition
Fiscal policy refers to the use of government expenditure and taxation in order to influence aggregate expenditure and, in turn, national output.

Irish fiscal policy was inherited from the British model and in both countries it is synonymous with budgetary policy. This is because fiscal policy in the UK is implemented primarily through the budget.[14] The budget is a record of what the government pays out in the form of expenditure and what it receives, usually in the form of tax revenue. It is the responsibility of the Minister for Finance.

In Ireland, each year's budget is divided into a current and a capital section. Current expenditure relates to spending on goods and services which are consumed during the fiscal year. For example, it includes wages and salaries of public servants and covers the operating expenses of public buildings. Current revenue is the income which accrues to the state from the day-to-day running of the economy. Examples include income tax, expenditure tax (e.g. VAT) and corporation tax.

Capital expenditure refers to spending on items which are not completely consumed during the fiscal year. Examples include expenditure on infrastructure and investment projects. The details of the government's capital spending are published each year in the Public Capital Programme (PCP). Capital revenue normally consists of interest on stocks owned by government, loan repayments and capital grants received from the EU.[15]

Measures of fiscal policy

Fiscal policy involves expenditure and the collection of tax and non-tax revenue. Within a single budget, expenditure can exceed revenue and if so, the government incurs a deficit. Alternately, if revenue exceeds expenditure, the budget is in surplus. If expenditure equals revenue, a balanced budget results.

There are two important measures of the relationship between revenue and expenditure. One measure is the Exchequer Borrowing Requirement (EBR) or Exchequer Surplus. This is the measure most frequently used by economists and politicians in Ireland to evaluate the cumulative effect of fiscal policy changes in the annual budget.

Definition
The Exchequer Borrowing Requirement (EBR) is the total amount of money that the central government borrows in any one fiscal year if current and capital expenditure exceeds current and capital revenue. If revenue exceeds expenditure, it is called an Exchequer Surplus.

A budget, in a given year, is expansionary if the government incurs a deficit as measured by the EBR or if the size of the EBR increases. The budget is contractionary if the government cuts the size of the EBR or if it moves from a deficit to an Exchequer Surplus.

A broader measure, called the General Government Deficit or Surplus, is used by the EU to compare the fiscal stance of EU member states.

Definition
The General Government Deficit (GGD) or Surplus (GGS) is calculated by adding the EBR or Exchequer Surplus to the borrowings of local authorities and non-commercial state-sponsored bodies.

A budget, in a given year, is expansionary if the government incurs a deficit as measured by the GGD or if the size of the GGD increases. The budget is contractionary if the government cuts the size of the GGD or if it moves from a deficit to surplus as measured by the GGS.

Table 12.11 presents figures for these measures over the twenty-year period 1980–99.

Table 12.11:   Measures of fiscal policy (£m)

Year	CBD[1]		EBR[2]		GGD[3]	
	£m	*%*	*£m*	*%*	*£m*	*%*
1980	−547	−6.0	−1218	−13.4	...	...
1981	−802	−7.3	−1721	−15.7	...	...
1982	−988	−7.9	−1945	−15.5	...	...
1983	−960	−7.0	−1756	−12.8	...	...
1984	−1039	−7.0	−1825	−12.2	...	...
1985	−1284	−8.0	−2015	−12.6	...	...
1986	−1395	−7.9	−2145	−12.1	...	...
1987	−1180	−6.2	−1786	−9.4	−1798	−8.5
1988	−317	−1.6	−619	−3.1	−1021	−4.5
1989	−263	−1.2	−479	−2.2	−449	−1.8
1990	−152	−0.6	−462	−1.8	−721	−2.5
1991	−298	−1.1	−499	−1.9	−773	−2.6
1992	−446	−1.6	−713	−2.5	−845	−2.7
1993	−379	−1.2	−690	−2.3	−867	−2.5
1994	15	–	−672	−2.0	−748	−2.0
1995	−362	−1.0	−627	−1.7	−1064	−2.6
1996	292	0.7	−437	−1.1	−279	−0.6
1997	604	1.3	−235	−0.5	406	0.8
1998	2091	3.9	747	1.4	1267	2.1
1999	3438	5.8	1192	2.0	1330	1.9

Source: Various Government publications.

1. CBD is the Current Budget Deficit. It is expressed as a percentage of GNP.
2. EBR is the Exchequer Borrowing Requirement. It is expressed as a percentage of GNP.
3. GGD is the General Government Deficit. In accordance with the requirements of the Maastricht treaty, the General Government Balance is calculated as a percentage of GDP estimated on the basis of ESA95.

Using the EBR as an indicator of fiscal policy, we can see that the budgets between the years 1982–90 were largely contractionary. The EBR as a percentage of GNP fell steadily and then stabilised.

Although the EBR is often cited, it is a less than perfect indicator of changes in active fiscal policy. This is because the size of the EBR is influenced by automatic stabilisers which respond to changes in the economic environment. Examples include taxes and transfer payments. They are 'automatic' in the sense that they are built into the economy and do not require discretionary action by government. Their purpose is to reduce the impact of shocks that arise from cyclical fluctuations in the economy. If, for example, an economy is going into a recession, unemployment rises. Transfer payments increase because more people are receiving social welfare payments. The decline in national income means that tax receipts are likely to fall. The combination of higher expenditure and lower tax receipts results in a higher EBR. By the same logic, a lower EBR is likely to result during a boom period because of higher tax receipts and lower expenditures on transfer payments.

Therefore, changes in the EBR may reflect changes in the automatic stabilisers rather than deliberate action taken by the administration. Changes in the EBR which arise out of direct action taken by the government in order to move the economy in a given direction are called discretionary changes. The budget deficit (or surplus) which results from these government decisions is called the structural or discretionary budget deficit (or surplus). An increase in the personal tax rate or an increase in the rate of old-age pensions are two such examples.

In brief, the structural or discretionary change in the EBR is a better measure of fiscal policy as it reflects active and deliberate changes by the government.

A second, more accurate measure of fiscal policy is the primary budget balance. Interest payments on the national debt are included as an expenditure item in the annual budget. However, the national debt and the subsequent interest payments do not reflect current policy but arise out of past government policy. Thus, in order to arrive at a correct measure for current fiscal policy it is necessary to exclude the debt service. This adjusted measure is known as the 'primary budget balance'.

Whereas the unadjusted-for-interest-payments current budget was in deficit every year between 1980 and 1993, the current primary budget had been in surplus continually since 1986. The difference is accounted for by the high level of interest payments on the national debt.[16] In 1999, for example, debt service payments on the debt amounted to over £2.5bn. More importantly, it suggests that fiscal policy since the mid-1980s was even more contractionary than originally suspected.

Some economists argue that fiscal policy should be counter-cyclical. This is a restrictive use of fiscal policy. It means that the government should use the fiscal instruments available to it to boost the economy in times of recession and to deflate the economy in times of overheating. The government should increase spending and/or cut taxes to counter deficiencies in demand. This is the origin of the phrase 'spending your way out of recession'. During boom periods, when there is excess demand, the government cuts spending and/or increases taxes and thereby incurs a surplus. Over the lifetime of the business cycle the government budget would, in effect, be balanced, as the classical school endorsed, but with deliberate imbalances running counter-cyclically.[17] Terms such as 'pump-priming' and 'fine-tuning' the economy are also used to describe such a policy.

The question of whether domestic fiscal policy has been counter-cyclical has caused great debate among the economics profession. Throughout the 1970s and the 1980s there are examples of periods when policies were strongly pro-cyclical, i.e. the fiscal changes implemented by the incumbent governments were either expansionary during the upturn or contractionary during the downturn of the business cycle.

One such period was the mid-1970s. The world economy experienced an upturn in activity after 1976. On the back of this favourable international climate it was expected that the Irish economy would grow without any further stimulus from the state sector. Moreover, this was an opportunity to reduce borrowing and counterbalance the budget deficits of previous years. Yet domestic fiscal policy during these years was highly expansionary and pro-cyclical. This occurred partly because of the promises made during the general election of 1977 and partly because of deliberate action taken by the government on the advice of some economists. The expansionary fiscal policy of those years was justified on the basis of the 'self-financing' claim (see The Irish Experience in Section 12.3).

A second period was the early to mid-1980s when the international economic climate was unfavourable. Most Western economies were either in the depths of recession or else slowly emerging from one. Financial markets were highly volatile with high interest rates and fluctuating exchange rates. As a result international trade suffered. Advocates of counter-cyclical fiscal policies would argue that such adverse economic conditions warrant expansionary fiscal policy at home in order to counter low demand and rising unemployment. Yet domestic fiscal policy during these years was highly contractionary and pro-cyclical.

The rationale behind this pro-cyclical policy was the attempt to restore order to the public finances. By 1982 the EBR was 15.5% of GNP. Borrowing to finance day-to-day spending was almost 8% of GNP. Fears grew both at home and abroad about the sustainability of the debt. A consensus was reached, among economists and politicians, to reduce borrowing and improve the national debt/GNP ratio. Other economic aims, including unemployment, were seen as subordinate to this primary objective.

Another aspect of fiscal policy which featured during this period is the concept of crowding out. Suppose the government increases expenditure. Furthermore, let us assume that it will be financed by borrowing rather than by tax increases. This induced borrowing creates a demand for funds in the financial markets, leaving less funds available for the private sector. This may lead to higher interest rates and in turn decreases in private sector spending. In effect, the initial injection of public sector spending crowds out both consumer and investment expenditure. It is obvious from this simple explanation that crowding out has very important implications for the effectiveness of fiscal policy. Moreover, it appears from the above description that the expansionary fiscal policy adopted by the government may be far less effective than previously believed.

Opinions vary on the extent of crowding out. Supporters of fiscal policy, Keynesians included, argue that only partial crowding out occurs. Government spending is compensating for insufficient private investment. Critics of fiscal policy, monetarists for example, argue that full and complete crowding out is the norm. Government spending replaces private investment. The economy suffers as a result because private investment is more efficient than public investment, it is argued.

This discussion on fiscal policy has been limited to the confines of a closed economy. Little or no reference has been made to economic variables such as capital flows, foreign interest rates and output levels, fixed or flexible exchange rates. Changes in fiscal policy affect and are affected by these variables which play an important role in an open economy. Chapter 15 explains these international effects.

The Western economies' experience with Keynesian economics

The active use of public works programmes dates as far back as the 1930s when economies like Sweden, the US and even Germany, under Adolf Hitler, were using public investment to stimulate the economy. Hitler's Four-year Plan to abolish unemployment, announced in 1933, depended largely on demand-side measures including the Reinhardt Programme of public works.[18]

In the UK, both the Labour and Conservative governments of the 1950s and 1960s advocated and implemented Keynesian demand-management policies. The government policies of that period appear to have had their desired effects on unemployment. However, on account of their tendency to influence the level of imports, they also led to periodic balance of payments crises. In the UK, the subsequent mix of contractionary and expansionary policies that followed became known as stop-go policies. Many economists were highly critical of such short-term policies and advocated strongly against the use of such policies in order to tackle rising unemployment.

Nineteen sixty-three is the year most often cited in the US as the high point of Keynesian economics. The Kennedy administration advocated the use of Keynesian economic policies. Investment tax credits were introduced in 1962 in order to stimulate private sector spending and reduce unemployment. Many of the top economic advisers of the day, including J. K. Galbraith (b. 1908), James Tobin (b. 1918), the late Arthur Okun (1928–80), Robert Solow (b. 1924), the late Walter Heller (1915–87) and Paul Samuelson were advocates of Keynesian economics.

Kennedy's successor, Lyndon Johnson, continued to adopt Keynesian-style policies early in his administration despite sufficient levels of demand and inflationary pressures arising from the US involvement in the Vietnam War. In 1964 Johnson persuaded Congress to enact personal tax cuts of 20% and a 10% cut for businesses. Notwithstanding the impact of the war, the results arising out of the Kennedy-Johnson experience with Keynesian economics were dramatic. Unemployment fell from 5.2% in 1962 to 4.8% in early 1965, and by 1966 it had fallen to 3.8%.

Support for Keynesian economics did not end with the Kennedy-Johnson administrations (1961–68). At the same time that the newly elected US President Richard Nixon was espousing the case for Keynesian economics with the infamous statement 'We are all Keynesians now', the UK Tory government under the leadership of Edward Heath was implementing similar Keynesian-style policies. The Chancellor, Anthony Barber, responding to the economic environment of the day which saw unemployment reach the one million figure for the first time in thirty years, increased public expenditure and cut taxes. What followed is commonly known as the 'Barber Boom' of the early 1970s. By the end of 1973 the unemployment figure was halved to 500,000. This dramatic improvement in the economy was attributed largely to the Keynesian-style policies adopted by the Chancellor.

However, things were to change in response to a number of factors. These included the economic environment of the time which was experiencing non-Keynesian trends of inflationary pressures in the face of deficient demand. Also, there was a growing dissatisfaction with Keynesian economics and the Phillips curve among the economics profession.[19] Finally, the ongoing economic research of the time focused less on the assumptions and conclusions of the Keynesian model and more on the microeconomic foundations of macroeconomics. Variables such as money, expectations and human capital were examined rather than the broad components of demand.

The economic environment of the 1970s was even more uncertain than the previous decade. The Bretton Woods system of regulating exchange rates broke down. There was an oil supply shock at the beginning and again at the end of the decade. There emerged a new phenomenon, called stagflation, which referred to rising unemployment accompanied by rising inflation. This phenomenon could not be explained within the framework of the basic Keynesian model.

In the UK, both the Tory government led by Edward Heath (in the later days of his administration) and, surprisingly, the Labour government of James Callaghan criticised the Keynesian economics of the past and adopted tough monetarist policies. Prime Minister Callaghan, addressing delegates at the 1976 Labour Party conference, said 'We used to think you could spend your way out of recession . . . I tell you in all candour that the option no longer exists and insofar as it did ever exist, it only worked by injecting demand into the economy.' However, it was the 1980s combination of Margaret Thatcher in the UK and Ronald Reagan in the US which was primarily responsible for the emergence of an alternative to Keynesian economics, i.e. supply-side policies. Supply-side economics and how it differs from demand management is explained in Chapter 16.

The revival of Keynesian economics in the 1990s was largely in response to the Anglo-American recession and the general dissatisfaction with the supply-side policies of the previous decade. This re-emergence was partly reflected in the election of a Democratic President in the US and the election of the Labour Party at home. Both parties in the past have supported and adopted Keynesian-style policies. It was believed that on the return to power they would re-introduce some demand-side policies.[20]

In brief, the adoption of Keynesian-style policies both in the US and in the UK in the 1960s and early 1970s coincided with a period of prosperity and low unemployment. This compared with the high unemployment rates of the inter-war period and likewise, the 1970s. Many attribute this success to the adoption of demand-management policies, but this is open to debate. What is probably less contentious is the significant contribution of a number of events other than the implementation of Keynesian economics. These include the decline in protectionism in favour of free trade, the importance of innovation, the adoption of new technologies and, finally, the stability of international financial markets.

Another contentious issue is the limits of Keynesian economics and the subsequent policy recommendations. Keynesian economics emerged out of the Great Depression, and the recommendations which followed were to apply to the economic environment of the time – one of mass unemployment, protectionism and floating exchange rates. The economic climate has changed dramatically over the past sixty-five years. Different periods with different problems require different solutions.[21] The adoption and success of Keynesian demand policies in the past does not necessarily require similar policies now or in the future.

This chapter concludes with a discussion on Keynesian economics within the context of Irish economic policy.

12.3 THE IRISH EXPERIENCE

Ireland was slow to adopt Keynesian economics. In the 1950s the authorities were more concerned with the substantial balance of payments deficits than with the unemployment trends. In the 1960s, policy was focused on attracting overseas industry and on building up the infrastructure in order to enhance the long-term development of the economy. Neither policy could be described as Keynesian which is in essence a short-term policy. However, if we lagged behind other European countries before the 1970s it is generally agreed that we surpassed these same countries in the twenty-five years that followed in our adoption of Keynesian demand management. The debate now centres on whether Keynesian policies were effective considering, in particular, the openness of the Irish economy.

The Irish experience with active use of fiscal policy began in earnest in the early 1970s.[22] Prior to this the Minister of Finance would balance his current budget every year, in accordance with sound accounting principles and, to a lesser extent, the classical economic doctrine. Nineteen seventy-two marks a watershed in Irish government policy. This was the year of the first planned current budget deficit in modern times. The Minister of Finance, Mr George Colley, admitted to taking a 'calculated risk' in opting for expansion in preference to stability. He went on to acknowledge '. . . a risk that I may be fuelling the fire of inflation rather than the engine of growth'.[23]

Unfortunately such a radical change in policy was overshadowed by the events of the following year when the world economy suffered an oil crisis which induced inflationary pressures throughout the Western world, including Ireland. Inflation was exacerbated even beyond what the Minister had feared. The difference, however, was in the cause and the extent of the rise in prices.

By 1975 the current budget deficit had increased to 6.8% of GNP. This was viewed by the incumbent government as being too high. According to the then Minister of Finance, Mr Richie Ryan, 'Borrowing for capital purposes is justifiable in the context of our long-term economic aims' but 'Borrowing to meet current deficits is not, no matter how desirable it may be by reference to immediately pursuing requirements.'[24] Taxes were raised and expenditure was curtailed in order to reduce the borrowing.

The general election of 1977 brought an abrupt end to this contractionary fiscal policy. Political parties promised tax cuts and expenditure increases although there was evidence of an economic recovery worldwide. The new government acted on its promises by abolishing rates on private dwellings, reducing motor tax, increasing tax allowances and creating over 11,000 new public-sector posts.

These and similar measures introduced by the government were justified on the basis that a fiscal stimulus would ensure a stable standard of living and a reduction in unemployment. In economic terms the policy was rationalised by reference to a self-financing fiscal boost. The then Minister of Finance, Mr Colley, aided by his economic advisers, argued that such a fiscal boost would ensure an increase in national income which, in turn, would generate sufficient taxes to self-finance the initial expansion. On account of these additional tax receipts, no substantial increase in borrowing would be necessary, it was argued. Unfortunately the results were somewhat different than the forecast.

Policy continued to be highly expansionary during a period when the economy, without any fiscal stimulus, was growing satisfactorily in real terms. Although this policy did manage to keep unemployment down and at the same time maintain a relatively high standard of living, it was also responsible for transforming the country into a net debtor, characterised by high annual budget deficits, external borrowing and a looming balance of payments crisis. This situation was exacerbated by the second oil crisis in 1979 and the subsequent world recession.

By 1981 the Exchequer Borrowing Requirement was 15.7% of GNP. Moreover, the government was borrowing over 7% of GNP to finance day-to-day expenditure. To make matters worse, the domestic political situation was far from stable with three elections within the space of eighteen months. Some commentators, unhappy with the domestic outlook, went so far as to call for assistance from the International Monetary Fund (IMF). This would have been a highly unusual and embarrassing move for a developed, Western economy.

The first step towards restoring some stability in the domestic economy was achieved when a consensus on the need for order in the public finances was reached among the main political parties. Fiscal rectitude, as it became known, took precedence over all other objectives, including a reduction in unemployment. The Coalition government of 1982–86 set about tackling the problem primarily by increasing taxes and, to a lesser extent, curtailing capital expenditure.

Some commentators were very critical of such a policy mix. They argued that the higher tax rates acted as a disincentive to work and only succeeded in siphoning off legitimate work to the shadow economy. Capital expenditure, they argued, was a key element in the long-term development of the economy and did not warrant cutbacks. In addition, they postulated that cutting capital expenditure was an 'easy target' on the basis that it was politically more difficult to cut current expenditure and, secondly, a number of key investment projects were coming to an end at this time. Notwithstanding these criticisms, some credit must be given to the Coalition partners for attempting to tackle the problem.

The highly deflationary policies which followed appeared to have more of an impact on unemployment than on the public finances. By 1986 the current budget deficit was 7.9% of GNP, the national debt/GNP ratio was 128% and the unemployment rate had increased to 17% of the labour force. On the positive side, inflation fell from 20% in 1981 to 3.8% in 1986. This was due to a combination of the deflationary policies of the administration and the international trend of lower prices.

The general election of 1987 and the subsequent change in government, with the support of the Tallaght Strategy, brought about another turn in policy and with it a dramatic improvement in both the public finances and the economy as a whole.[25] The cuts in current expenditure, the return to centralised wage bargaining with the Programme for National Recovery and the favourable international economic background all contributed to an economic performance over the period which surpassed even the most optimistic of forecasts.

In terms of the public finances, the austere measures introduced by the Minister of Finance, Mr Ray MacSharry, resulted in significant reductions in budget deficits and national debt/GNP ratios. Government expenditure was cut by 3.7% per annum on average between 1987 and 1989. The EBR was reduced from 12.1% of GNP in 1986 to 2.2% in 1989. Such draconian measures earned MacSharry the nickname of 'Mac the Knife'. What was even more extraordinary was the recorded growth rates in GNP during the same period. The increase was close to 3.6% per year on average, the highest growth rate recorded for any three-year period since the mid-1960s. Unfortunately, this did not translate into an equal growth in employment rates.

On reading the above account of the performance of the Irish economy during the period 1987–89 one might be led to believe that the remarkable transformation was due solely to the deflationary policies adopted by the government. However, the Keynesian model of income determination indicates that contractionary fiscal policy, as described above, deflates the economy and reduces national income. The Irish experience seems to suggest the opposite, that expenditure cuts can lead to increases in national income. This raised questions over the validity of the Keynesian model in the Irish context. It also gave rise to the phrase Expansionary Fiscal Contraction (EFC).[26] However, before we hastily disregard the work of Keynes, we need to look for possible explanations, other than the expenditure cuts, in order to explain the increases in GNP.

A detailed analysis of this period is beyond the scope of a basic textbook in economics. However, a number of possible, although not exhaustive, factors which contributed to the recovery are listed below. The occurrence of these raises doubts over the validity of EFC.

- The tax amnesty of 1987 which raised over £500 million in unpaid taxes. This extra source of income contributed to the reduction in the budget deficit which otherwise would have required further cuts in expenditure and/or hikes in tax rates. Furthermore, it is assumed the taxpayers who availed of the amnesty remained in the tax net and became an additional source of revenue in subsequent years.
- The 1980s was a boom period for the world economy. Higher income levels, lower inflation rates, stable exchange rates and lower interest rates all contributed to an environment which was conducive to external trade. Ireland, being a small open economy, availed of these conditions and recorded a strong export performance. The volume of Irish exports grew by 8.9% on average per annum between 1986 and 1989. Also, the recovery was export-led; improvements in domestic demand followed later.
- An increase in private sector confidence and more optimistic expectations for the future resulted in an increase in both consumer expenditure and investment expenditure. This new-found confidence was due, in part, to the credible economic policy adopted by the government, typified by the relatively low wage agreements contained in the Programme for National Recovery. Furthermore, financial markets at home and abroad and, likewise, foreign investment both at home and abroad reacted positively to the change in policy.
- In 1986 the Irish pound was devalued by 8% within the EMS exchange rate mechanism. This benefited Irish exporters by making Irish goods cheaper in foreign markets. Furthermore, interest rates declined as the domestic environment improved. The interest rate differential between Ireland and our UK and German counterparts narrowed significantly. For example, the three-month interest rate differential with the UK fell from –2.8% approximately at the end of 1986 to +4.8% approximately at

the end of 1988. Likewise, the interest rate differential with Germany fell, from 9% approximately to 3% approximately over the same period.

The period between 1987 and 1990 was followed by the Anglo-American recession of the early 1990s which slowed economic activity both at home and, in particular, in the UK and the US. The subsequent decline in economic growth on the European continent and in the Far East was less severe. However, by 1993–94 both the UK and Ireland had clearly emerged from the recession and were recording very satisfactory growth rates. As a result, the Irish authorities were able to reduce borrowing, particularly for current purposes. In terms of GDP, they were recording one of the lowest budget deficits in the EU.

However, the one area of economic policy which concerned private-sector economists was the growth of public expenditure. It is estimated that between 1989 and 1993 current government spending increased by 31% whereas the inflation rate over the same four-year period was only 11.5%. The period from 1995 onwards was one of rising tax revenues (on the back of record economic growth) and ever increasing budget surpluses. By 1999, the current budget was in surplus to the tune of 5.8% of GNP. By any standards, Ireland's public finances were in remarkable shape. The debt/GNP ratio, at 125% in 1987 was less than 55% in 1999. The turnabout was complete.

In brief, the consensus is that Keynesian-style policies were not very successful in Ireland in achieving their goals. On reflection, this is probably due more to the inappropriateness of fiscal policy in a small open economy like Ireland combined with the mismanagement by the authorities and institutional deficiencies relating to government decision-making rather than the ineffectiveness of Keynesian economics in general.

CASE STUDY

Extract from *The Economist*
An emotional budget

As the fastest growing economy in the European Union for the sixth year running, Ireland is flush. So is its government. With the fiscal surplus likely this year to be about 3.3% of GDP, Irish taxpayers were expecting a generous budget this month from Charlie McCreevy, the finance minister, and, brushing aside fears that the economy might start overheating, he duly gave it to them. Plaudits all round, then?

Far from it. By trying to change the tax system to assess married working couples individually (as in most of the rest of Europe) rather than as a household, he touched a raw political nerve. Traditionalists in his ruling centre-right Fianna Fail party have been up in arms, accusing Mr McCreevy of undermining the family by discriminating against mothers who stay at home to look after the children.

. . .

Even without the row about taxes and the family, the budget would have been controversial, especially abroad. The economy will probably have grown by over 8% in 1999, after growing by an annual average of 8.5% in the previous five years. Unemployment is only 5.1%, and members of the far-flung Irish diaspora are coming home for jobs. Real after-inflation interest rates are close to zero. Property prices are zooming. The middle class is growing richer.

Normally, Ireland's central bank would have raised interest rates to cool demand.

→

However, since joining the euro at the beginning of the year, Ireland has enjoyed the same low interest rates as stodgy Germany. In a boom like this, such worthy bodies as the OECD and the IMF have warned the Irish not to cut taxes. But Mr McCreevy and his friends retort that, given the size of the budget surplus, cuts would not necessarily overheat the economy. Besides, they say, the Irish economy is unlike others in the EU, partly because imports account for nearly three-quarters of GDP. Inflation, running at an annual rate of 2.8% in October, is not yet a worry, though labour shortages may yet make wages take off. In any event, Mr McCreevy plans – pretty uncontroversially – to pump a lot of money into a host of infrastructure projects, from roads, ports and telecoms to hospitals and schools.

The top rate of income tax, Mr McCreevy had proposed, should come down from 46% to 44% while the middle band, affecting average earners on some IR£17,000 ($22,100) a year, would drop from 24% to 22%.

. . .

Source: *The Economist*, 11 December 1999, pp. 44–46.

Questions

1. Explain the term 'fiscal surplus'. What options do the authorities have in dealing with a fiscal surplus?
2. Why are the 'worthy bodies as the OECD and the IMF' warning against tax cuts? Why is a high import propensity relevant? Alternately, why are the equally expansionary plans to increase expenditure uncontroversial?
3. How do personal income tax rates of 22% (standard rate) and 44% (top rate) compare to rates from the early 1990s? How does the take from personal income tax compare with the take from other sources of tax revenue?

Answers on website

SUMMARY

1. There are a number of assumptions to the Keynesian model of income determination. It is a fixed price model. It assumes that the economy is below full employment and that any increase in demand will increase output but will have no effect on prices.
2. The model incorporates many new concepts such as the consumption function, aggregate expenditure, the marginal propensity to consume and the multiplier. Output is determined by aggregate expenditure which is simply equal to total spending in the economy. Equilibrium exists at a point where aggregate expenditure equals output.
3. Any change in aggregate expenditure results in a greater change in output. This is explained by the multiplier process where the multiplier is simply the amount by which income changes as a result of an initial change in spending. The value of the Keynesian multiplier depends on the size of the leakages.

4. The Keynesian model can be extended to include both government and foreign sectors. If so, public expenditure and exports augment total spending by the private sector. Also, the value of the multiplier is affected by the marginal propensity to tax and import. As a result of these leakages, the multiplier in an open economy is smaller than the simple multiplier in the closed economy model.

5. Demand management is the collective term used to describe policies which aim to influence the level of demand and in turn the level of output in the economy. One example is fiscal policy which depends on the active use of government expenditure and taxes to influence demand. In Ireland, it centres around Budget day and the Book of Estimates. Measures of active fiscal policy include the discretionary budget surplus and the primary budget balance.

6. Keynesian economics was very popular among economists, policy-makers and politicians after World War II and particularly in the 1950s and the 1960s. However, Ireland was relatively slow, by international standards, to adopt short-term Keynesian-style policies. The success of such policy in Ireland, possibly due to the open nature of the economy, has been limited.

KEY TERMS

Consumption	Paradox of thrift
Consumption function	Deflationary gap
Marginal propensity to consume	Demand management
Savings function	Fiscal policy
Marginal propensity to save	Exchequer Borrowing Requirement
Autonomous expenditure	General Government Deficit
Investment function	Automatic stabilisers
Aggregate expenditure	Structural budget deficit
Equilibrium	Primary budget balance
Inventory changes	Counter-cyclical policy
Keynesian cross diagram	Crowding out
Expenditure multiplier	Fiscal rectitude
Marginal propensity to import	Expansionary Fiscal Contraction
Marginal propensity to tax	

REVIEW QUESTIONS

1. Explain the significance of the consumption function in the Keynesian model of income determination.
2. What determines the equilibrium level of income in the Keynesian model? Explain, in words, how this position is reached.
3. What is the Keynesian multiplier? What factors influence its size? Explain how it is related to:
   (a) consumption function;
   (b) leakages;
   (c) fiscal policy.

4. Briefly explain the differences between the income determination model as applied to a closed economy and the model as applied to an open economy.
5. What policy recommendations arise out of the Keynesian model? When did support for Keynesian economics emerge? Why did it lapse in the 1970s?
6. Critically assess the success or failure of Keynesian economics in the context of the Irish economy.

WORKING PROBLEMS

1. The following equations are from a simple model of the economy:

$$C = 110 + .8Y$$
$$\bar{I} = 300$$
$$\bar{G} = 150$$
$$\bar{X} = 250$$
$$M = .2Y$$

(a) Calculate the equilibrium level of income for this model.
(b) Suppose the government decides to double its expenditure on goods and services. What is the new equilibrium income level?
(c) Calculate, and interpret the size of, the multiplier for this particular model.

2. Prove, using algebra, that the sum of the marginal propensity to consume and the marginal propensity to save is equal to 1.

MULTI-CHOICE QUESTIONS

1. The classical school of economics held the view that:
    (a) the economy was at or close to full-employment;
    (b) large-scale government intervention was unnecessary;
    (c) large-scale government intervention was necessary;
    (d) both (a) and (b) above;
    (e) both (a) and (c) above.

2. If the marginal propensity to save increases from .2 to .25, then:
    (a) the slope of the consumption function steepens;
    (b) the marginal propensity to consume increases by the same proportion;
    (c) the expenditure multiplier increases from 4 to 5;
    (d) the savings function shifts downwards;
    (e) none of the above.

3. In the Keynesian cross diagram for the two-sector model:
    (a) investment is dependent on income levels;
    (b) when savings is less than investment output tends to decrease;
    (c) equilibrium is where $AE > \bar{I}$;

(d) income is determined by the level of expenditure;

(e) unplanned increases in stocks lead to an increase in output.

4. Due to a change in the pattern of consumption, the consumption function has flattened. This implies that the value of the multiplier has:
    (a) decreased since the marginal propensity to consume has increased;
    (b) decreased since the marginal propensity to consume has decreased;
    (c) increased since the marginal propensity to consume has increased;
    (d) increased since the marginal propensity to consume has decreased;
    (e) none of the above.

5. Suppose a model of the economy is represented by the following equations: $C = 120 + .8Y$, $\bar{I} = 280$, $\bar{G} = 300$. The equilibrium level of income is:
    (a) €700;
    (b) €3,500;
    (c) €560;
    (d) €140;
    (e) €584.

6. The government wants to increase national output by €300 million. Its economic advisers provide it with the following information: $S = .2Y$, $\bar{I} = 200$, $\bar{G} = 300$, $\bar{X} = 100$, $M = .2Y$. By how much should the government increase its spending on goods and services?
    (a) €120;
    (b) €300;
    (c) €750;
    (d) €1,500;
    (e) none of the above.

TRUE OR FALSE (SUPPORT YOUR ANSWER)

1. The classical school of economic thought argued that the self-adjusting mechanism of the market ensured the absence of any involuntary unemployment.

2. The autonomous component of the consumption function varies as income varies.

3. Unplanned decreases in inventories are a signal to firms to increase production.

4. The Keynesian multiplier is always greater than zero but less than one.

5. Adjusting the income determination model to include a value for exports and government expenditure (both autonomous) increases the equilibrium level of income.

6. Counter-cyclical fiscal policy implies the adoption of a budget deficit during a recession and a budget surplus during a recovery.

CASE STUDY

Extract from *Cara*
Tax Haven?
by Colm Rapple

While the tax burden has been getting heavier in most countries in the developed world of late, it has got significantly lighter in Ireland. Ireland ranks 22nd among the 29 countries of the Organisation of Economic Co-operation and Development (OECD) on a league table of tax as a percentage of national income. National income is defined as what the economists call gross domestic product or GDP. The main reason for Ireland's low ranking is the relatively low rates of social insurance contributions paid by both employees and employers.

All the other countries of the European Union rank higher than Ireland in the OECD listing. In 1997, taxes represented 32.8 per cent of gross domestic product in Ireland – well below the EU average of 41.5 per cent. Over the ten years to 1997, tax as a percentage of GDP rose in the OECD area as a whole by 2.1 percentage points. In Ireland, it dropped by 4.4 percentage points from 37.2 to 32.8 per cent. That's an 11 per cent decline in the tax burden. In only one other OECD country, Hungary, is the tax burden likely to have fallen more sharply over the decade, but the Hungarian statistics are only available back to 1991. These figures, recently published by the OECD in its annual 'Revenue Statistics' report gives the lie to the oft-quoted claim that Ireland is a high-tax country. As a matter of fact, the opposite is the truth. And the gap between the high tax countries and Ireland is actually widening. The OECD has yet to collect figures from all its members for 1998, but the Irish figure is in and it shows a further fall to 32.3 per cent of GDP. No doubt it fell even further last year and will fall again this year as a result of further substantial tax cuts announced in last December's budget.

. . .

So the notion that Ireland is a high tax country is a myth. So, too, is the belief that the Irish people would prefer tax cuts to better state services. A survey conducted by MRBI for the Irish Times revealed that almost half of the adult population (49 per cent) would prefer to see excess government revenue used to fund public services rather than given back in lower tax cuts. Another 15 per cent thought the money would be better spent on developing the country's infrastructure, while only 28 percent opted for cutting taxes.

Ireland has particularly low rates of social insurance contributions. Total contributions amount to 4.2 per cent of gross domestic product in 1997. That compared with an EU average of 11.8 per cent and an OECD average of 9.6 per cent. The EU average is actually understated because it included a low 1.6 per cent for Denmark which pays for social insurance from central funds, unlike Ireland, where the Government

$\longrightarrow$

makes no contribution to the social insurance fund except as an employer of public servants. Irish employers get off very lightly compared with their counterparts in other EU countries. At 2.7 per cent of GDP employers social insurance contributions in Ireland are well below the EU average of 6.7 per cent. The figure is 3.4 per cent in Britain, 7.8 per cent in Germany, 11.4 per cent in France, 5.0 per cent in Portugal and 10.5 per cent in Italy. The relatively low rates in Ireland reflect a policy of maintaining the competitiveness of labour-intensive firms competing against British counterparts at home and abroad. The benchmark had to be the British rates of social insurance contribution rather than the higher Continental rates.

The arguments in favour of such a policy are less convincing now that there are fewer labour-intensive industries and the strength of sterling has neutered British competition. But with the Irish exchequer awash with money, there is no pressure to increase Irish rates of social insurance contributions. The Irish tax burden will continue to lighten. The government has undertaken to reduce income taxes over the next three years so that the 15 per cent increase in gross pay negotiated as part of a new national agreement will translate into a 25 per cent increase in take-home pay.

Source: *Cara*, March/April 2000, p. 70.

Questions

1. The article reports that Ireland's tax/GDP ratio was 32.8% in 1997. What percentage of this is accounted for by (i) taxes on income and profits, (ii) taxes on goods and services, (iii) social security contributions?
2. Using OECD data, show the change in Ireland's tax/GDP ratio for the period 1988–97. How does this compare to the OECD average? What do the data indicate?
3. What was the government current expenditure/GDP ratio for Ireland in 1997? What was the breakdown of current expenditure in 1997?

[NB: The OECD website is www.oecd.org and the relevant publication is the OECD *Revenue Statistics 1965–1998*.]

APPENDIX 12.1: THE SAVINGS FUNCTION

The following is the derivation of the simple savings function:

$$Y_d \equiv C + S \qquad [12.3]$$

which can be rewritten as:

$$S \equiv Y_d - C \qquad [12.4]$$

The consumption function is defined as:

$$C = bY_d \qquad \text{[12.2]}$$

Substitute bY_d for C in Equation 12.4:

$$S = Y_d - bY_d$$

Since Y_d is common to the two components, we can rewrite the right-hand side of the equation as follows:

$$S = (1 - b)Y_d \qquad \text{[12.5]}$$

We know from the previous discussion about the consumption function that b, the marginal propensity to consume, is a positive number which is greater than zero but less than one. The marginal propensity to save (1–b) must therefore also be a positive number which is greater than zero but less than one. Equation 12.5 shows that there is a positive relationship between disposable income and savings. As disposable income increases, savings increases by a fraction of that amount.

Let us take an example. Table 12.12 provides a set of disposable income and savings levels.

Table 12.12: The savings function

Disposable income, Y_d	Savings, S
0	0
100	25
200	50
300	75
400	100
500	125
600	150
700	175
800	200

As disposable income increases by increments of €100, savings increase by increments of €25. The MPS is equal to the change in savings divided by the corresponding change in disposable income. Hence:

$$MPS = \frac{\Delta S}{\Delta Y_d} = \frac{25}{100} = 0.25$$

If disposable income increases households will plan additional savings equal to one-quarter of any increase in disposable income. This particular savings function is represented by the following equation:

$$S = .25Y_d$$

Proof:
If MPC = .75

then MPS = 1 – b = 1 – .75 = .25
If C = .75Y_d

then S = (1 – b)Y_d = (1 – .75)Y_d = .25Y_d

For example, an increase in disposable income of €100 leads to an increase in planned savings of (1 – b) × €100 which is equal to 0.25 × €100 = €25. This particular savings function is graphically represented in Figure 12.12.

Figure 12.12: The savings function, S = .25Y_d

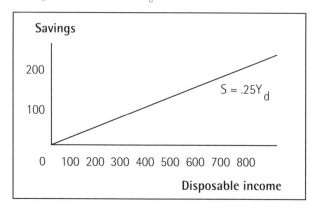

The upward sloping line shows that there is a positive relationship between savings and disposable income. The slope of the savings function is the marginal propensity to save.

The derivation for the more complicated savings function follows.

Beginning with Equation 12.4:

$$S \equiv Y_d - C$$ [12.4]

Recall that the consumption function is defined as:

$$C = \bar{C} + bY_d$$ [12.6]

Substitute into Equation 12.4:

$$S = Y_d - \bar{C} - bY_d$$

This can be written as:

$$S = -\bar{C} + Y_d - bY_d$$

Grouping the Y_d variables together, we obtain the equation of the savings function:

[12.24]

$$S = -\bar{C} + (1 - b)Y_d$$

The savings function, in the general case, with an intercept of $-\bar{C}$ and a slope equal to $(1 - b)$ is illustrated in Figure 12.13.

Figure 12.13: The savings function, $S = -\bar{C} + (1 - b)Y_d$

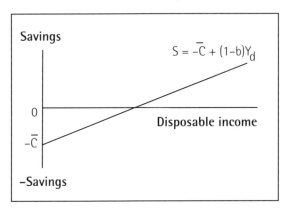

At low levels of disposable income savings are negative. This means that past savings are being used to finance expenditure. Dissavings is the reason why consumer expenditure can be larger than disposable income levels, as they are in Table 12.2. At the point where the savings function crosses the horizontal axis, savings is zero; all disposable income is spent. In the text the consumption function is $C = 50 + .75Y_d$. With a $\bar{C} = 50$ and a MPC $= .75$ the savings function is $S = -50 + .25Y_d$. This is drawn in the bottom frame of Figure 12.14 in Appendix 12.2.

APPENDIX 12.2: THE SAVINGS-INVESTMENT APPROACH

In the income-expenditure approach, equilibrium occurs when income, Y, is equal to expenditure, AE. However, using the two-sector model we can also express equilibrium in terms of savings and investment.

Table 12.13 continues the example which we have been using throughout the chapter. The information from this table is depicted graphically in the bottom frame of Figure 12.14.

Table 12.13:   The equilibrium level of income

Y	C	S	$\bar{I}$
0	50	−50	100
100	125	−25	100
200	200	0	100
300	275	25	100
400	350	50	100
500	425	75	100
600	500	100	100
700	575	125	100
800	650	150	100

By treating investment as autonomous, the investment function is drawn as a straight line. In our example it is equal to €100. The savings function is upward sloping. This reflects the positive relationship between savings and income. Savings equals €100 at an income level of €600. We can now compare the equilibrium levels of income from the income-expenditure approach and the savings-investment approach.

Figure 12.14 illustrates the equilibrium level of income. At €600, income equals expenditure (the top diagram) and savings equals investment (the bottom diagram).

Figure 12.14:   Deriving the equilibrium level of income

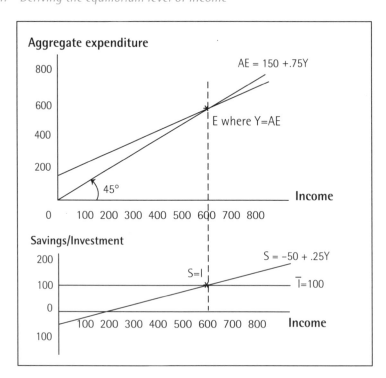

We confirm this as follows. Below €600 planned investment exceeds planned savings. Any excess of injections over leakages causes an unplanned reduction in inventories which leads to an increase in national income. Above €600 planned savings exceeds planned investment. The excess of leakages over injections causes unplanned increases in inventories which leads to a decrease in national income. National income is in equilibrium where planned savings equal planned investment.

APPENDIX 12.3: ALGEBRAIC DERIVATION OF THE TWO-SECTOR MODEL KEYNESIAN MULTIPLIER

We begin with Equation 12.13 from the text:

$$Y = \bar{A} \times \frac{1}{1-b} \qquad [12.13]$$

where:

$$\frac{1}{1-b} = k \qquad [12.25]$$

Substitute Equation 12.25 into Equation 12.13 above:

$$Y = \bar{A} \times k \qquad [12.26]$$

If there is a change in the autonomous component of expenditure, we can adapt this equation to calculate the resulting change in income:

$$\Delta Y = \Delta\bar{A} \times k$$

Solve for k:

$$\frac{\Delta Y}{\Delta \bar{A}} = k \qquad [12.27]$$

Therefore k represents the multiplier. We can see that in this simple model, the magnitude of the multiplier is directly related to the marginal propensity to consume.

APPENDIX 12.4: ALGEBRAIC DERIVATION OF THE KEYNESIAN MULTIPLIER INCLUDING THE FOREIGN SECTOR

Begin with Equation 12.20 from the text:

$$Y = \bar{A} \times \frac{1}{1-b+m} \qquad [12.20]$$

If there is a change in autonomous expenditure, what is the corresponding change in income?

$$\Delta Y = \Delta \bar{A} \times \frac{1}{1 - b + m}$$

Divide both sides by $\Delta \bar{A}$ to yield:

$$\boxed{\frac{\Delta Y}{\Delta \bar{A}} = \frac{1}{1 - b + m}}$$ [12.28]

In this situation the multiplier is:

$$\boxed{k = \frac{1}{1 - b + m}}$$ [12.29]

This multiplier is smaller than the simple multiplier $\frac{1}{1 - b}$. Imports are a leakage from the circular flow. The inclusion of the marginal propensity to import causes the multiplier to decrease in magnitude.

CHAPTER 13

MONEY, INTEREST RATES, THE CENTRAL BANK AND MONETARY POLICY

'Money is the most important thing in the world.'[1]

George Bernard Shaw

'How to have your cake and eat it too: lend it out at interest.'

Anonymous

CHAPTER OBJECTIVES

Upon completing this chapter, the student should understand:

- what money is, what money does;
- how the banking system creates money;
- the different theories of interest rate determination;
- the functions of a central bank;
- how monetary policy works;
- the Irish experience of monetary policy;
- monetary policy in the context of EMU.

OUTLINE

13.1 Money, money supply and money creation
13.2 Interest rate determination
13.3 The role of a central bank
13.4 Monetary policy
13.5 The Irish experience

INTRODUCTION

In the words of the economist Milton Friedman, 'Money matters'. Money is indeed a very important feature of any modern state: it facilitates the workings of the economy. Its importance, however, is not confined to the day-to-day operations of an economy. Money and monetary policy play an important role in the macroeconomic management of the country. It can influence such variables as expenditure, output, employment and prices.

We begin this chapter with a discussion on money: its definition, characteristics, functions and how it is created by the banking system. This is followed by the theory of interest rate determination. Two main theories are explained. A short history on the evolution of the Central Bank in Ireland follows. Monetary policy and its role is also discussed. The chapter finishes with a brief examination of monetary policy in Ireland, pre- and post-1999.

13.1 MONEY, MONEY SUPPLY AND MONEY CREATION

Over the centuries, money has taken many different forms. Examples include whales' teeth in Fiji, rats on Easter Island, dogs' teeth in the Admiralty Islands, silk and salt in China, sea-shells in Africa and cattle in ancient Ireland.

'Money', regardless of the form it takes, has a number of desirable attributes: it should be easily recognisable and acceptable, durable and divisible, convenient, uniform and relatively scarce.

Above all else, money is anything that is generally accepted as a means of payment. Any means of payment has a number of functions.

Functions of money

According to John R. Hicks, 'Money is as money does.'[2] This suggests that the functions of money are more important than its form (dollars vs euros, gold vs silver). The real power of money is in what it does, rather than what it is. We will now explain the most important functions of money.

1. *A medium of exchange*   Money is used in a monetary economy in order to allow for exchange between buyers and sellers. A non-monetary or barter economy is one where there is no accepted medium of exchange. There is a direct exchange of one good for another good. Consequently, there must exist a 'double coincidence of wants', i.e. each person must possess what the other person requires. Each person involved in a transaction must be a buyer and a seller simultaneously.

For example, if you have apples but want chocolate ideally you must find somebody who has chocolate and is willing to exchange chocolate for apples. This 'coincidence of wants' involves a number of problems. They include the high level of transaction costs incurred if intermediate trades are necessary, and the indivisibility and non-standardisation of some commodities.

Using money as a medium of exchange is more efficient. You can sell your apples to Dunnes Stores and buy chocolate bars at the corner shop.

2. *A unit of account*   Money is the common unit of measurement which allows for prices to be quoted. Hence, the exchange value of different commodities such as chickens, clothes and cars can be compared to one another. In the US, the prices of these and other goods are expressed in dollars. The pound sterling is the unit of account in the UK, and throughout the euro area the euro is the unit of account.

3. *A standard of deferred payment* This is the same as the function above but with a time dimension added. Obligations for future payments like leases and contracts are denominated in money.

4. *A store of value* Money, held rather than spent, can be used to make purchases in the future. Because of price inflation, money is not the best store of value. If it is not in an interest-bearing account, it is worth less in the future than it is worth today. Houses are the main store of value for most Irish families. In general, the value of a house appreciates with time.

In the modern world, there are many forms of money. Examples include coins, banknotes, cheques (drawn on current accounts), credit cards (plastic money) and balances in deposit accounts. There is, however, a need to define the money supply more strictly.

Definitions of money supply

In Section 13.3, we will discuss the functions of the Central Bank in detail. For now, we will briefly mention that the Central Bank is responsible for controlling the money supply. We continue the discussion of money by explaining the definitions of the money supply used by the Central Bank.

The 'narrow money supply' includes the most liquid forms of money.

Definition

The narrow money supply is defined as the notes and coins in circulation plus current (non-interest-bearing) account balances at credit institutions.

It is labelled M1 by the Central Bank.

The broad money supply or M3E adds the narrow money supply to other forms of money that can be readily converted into cash.

Definition

The broad money supply is defined as M1 plus deposit account balances.

Any definition of the money supply is somewhat arbitrary because it is very hard to draw a distinction between 'money' and 'non-money'. For example, although credit cards can be readily used to purchase things, they are not included in these definitions. Furthermore, defining monetary aggregates has been made more complicated by the introduction of the euro in January 1999 and Ireland's participation in the euro area. M1 is graphed in Figure 13.1.

Figure 13.1:   Money supply, M1 in Ireland 1981–98

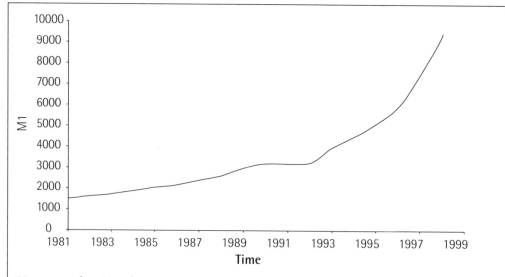

Note: In July 1997, there was a reclassification of credit institutions to include building societies, state-sponsored financial institutions and the TSB Bank.

Values for M1 and M3E at end year 1997 and 1998 are included in Table 13.1.

Table 13.1:   Monetary aggregates, end–December 1997 and 1998

	1997 (£m)	1998 (£m)	Year-to-year (change – %)
Currency	2,619	3,040	16.1
Current account balances	4,840	6,355	31.3
M1	7,459	9,395	26.0
Deposit account balances	34,832	40,220	15.5
M3E	42,291	49,615	17.3

Source: *Central Bank Bulletin*, Spring 1999.

Ireland's participation in stage three of EMU has resulted in some changes to these monetary aggregates. The series M1 and M3E as reported in Table 13.1 ceased in December 1998. From January 1999 onwards, it is customary to refer to the 'Irish contribution to euro area money supply'. This entails the Irish credit institutions' contribution to various euro area monetary aggregates, including narrow money supply (M1) and broad money (M3). The main differences between M3 and M3E are that the new series, M3, has a maturity cut-off point of up to two years for deposits or debt securities, and includes deposits of Irish credit institutions from residents of other monetary union member states. Values for M1 and M3 of Irish contribution, all in euros, are reported in Table 13.2.

Table 13.2: Monetary aggregates of Irish contribution, end-January 1999–2000

	1999 (€m)	2000 (€m)	Year-to-year (change – %)
Currency	3,536	4,321	
Overnight Deposits	8,628	12,053	
M1	12,164	16,374	34.6
Deposits	55,108	64,675	
Debt securities	10,698	12,215	
Repurchase agreements	297	680	
M3	78,266	93,943	20.0

Source: Various Central Bank of Ireland Bulletins.

One final term which requires an explanation is high-powered money or the monetary base.

Definition

High-powered money (H) is equal to currency plus reserves held by the Central Bank.

These reserves play an important role in the creation of money. We now explain 'money creation'.

Money creation

We know from the discussion of the circular flow that banks are financial intermediaries; they facilitate the transfer of purchasing power from lenders to borrowers. They are, however, also involved in other activities. In particular, banks can 'create' money. They do so by taking deposits, keeping a certain amount in reserve and lending out the remainder. This is known as the system of fractional reserves.[3] When they lend out these deposits, money is created. We will illustrate money creation with an example. In this particular example we assume that all the loans made by the bank are re-deposited.[4]

The Irish Bank (TIB) is the only financial institution on the island of Hibernia. A customer, Patricia O'Hara deposits €1,000 in her local branch. The balance sheet of TIB Bank is presented in Table 13.3.

Table 13.3: The balance sheet of TIB Bank

Assets		Liabilities	
Cash	1,000	Deposit	1,000

The deposit is a liability of the bank because it must return that money to Ms O'Hara if requested. The bank manager, with many years of experience, knows that it is unlikely that Ms O'Hara will withdraw all of her savings at once. Only a small percentage of this deposit is needed to meet the customer's demand for money. The remainder can be lent to other customers and firms who require funds.

The manager decides to keep 10% in reserves (€100) and lends out the residual (totalling in this case to €900) to another customer, Sean O'Shea.[5] The loan is an asset of the bank because it is owed to the bank by Mr O'Shea. The balance sheet reflects this transaction.

Table 13.4:   The balance sheet of TIB Bank

Assets		Liabilities	
Reserves	100	Deposit	1,000
Loan	900		
	1,000		1,000

A couple of days later, Patrick Murphy, the owner of the local furniture store, deposits the €900 which Sean O'Shea has spent on a suite of furniture. The bank manager proceeds to lend out 90% of this amount and retains 10% or €90. Mrs O'Brien, the local greengrocer, borrows the €810 in order to pay the builder for the extension to her shop. The builder, Niall Burke, who is also from the locality, decides to deposit this amount in order to guard against a 'rainy day'. With only one financial institution on the island the loan of €810 has found its way back to the bank. The bank holds €81 as reserves and advances the remaining €729 to another credible client. This process continues with the loan amount diminishing every time.

The final picture, in terms of the bank's assets and liabilities including all of the transactions described above is presented in Table 13.5.

Table 13.5:   The balance sheet of TIB Bank

	Assets		Liabilities	Customer
Reserves	100	Deposit	1,000	O'Hara
Loan	900			O'Shea
Reserves	90	Deposit	900	Murphy
Loan	810			O'Brien
Reserves	81	Deposit	810	Burke
Loan	729			
. . . .		. . . .		. . . .
Total reserves	1,000	Total deposits	10,000	
Total loans	9,000			

At the end of the process the liabilities equal the assets. An initial deposit of €1,000 with a required reserve ratio of 10% results in the bank's total deposits amounting to €10,000. The money creation process is depicted in Figure 13.2.

Figure 13.2: Money creation

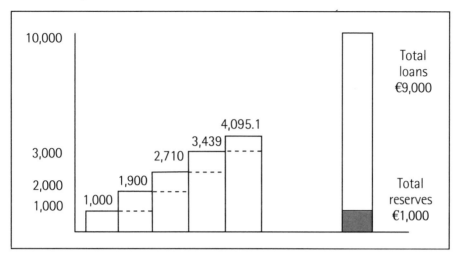

The deposits, loans and reserve amounts are recorded in Table 13.6.

Table 13.6: Money creation

Stages	Deposits (€)	Reserves (€)	Loans (€)
1	1,000	100	900
2	900	90	810
3	810	81	729
4	729	72.9	656.1
5	656.1	65.61	590.49
6 . . .			
7 . . .			
etc . . .			
Total	€10,000	€1,000	€9,000

In effect, there is a multiplier relationship at work. This multiplier is called the deposit multiplier.

Definition
The deposit multiplier is the multiple by which deposits will increase for every unit increase in reserves.

It can be expressed in equation form:[6]

$$\textbf{Deposit multiplier} = \frac{1}{r}$$ [13.1]

where r equals the percentage of deposits which are held in reserve or the reserve ratio.

In this example, where 10% of deposits are held in reserve, the deposit multiplier is 1/0.1 and equals 10. Therefore, an increase in reserves will ultimately lead to a tenfold increase in deposits. The relationship between the change in reserves and the subsequent change in deposits can also be expressed in equation form:

$$\Delta D = \frac{1}{r} \Delta R \qquad\qquad [13.2]$$

where D represents deposits and R represents reserves.

For this example, we substitute 10 for the deposit multiplier and €1,000 for the change in reserves caused by Ms O'Hara's initial deposit. Substituting these values into Equation 13.2, we find that the total change in deposits is 10 × €1000 or €10,000. This is the same amount which we calculated by adding the total deposits in Table 13.6.

In summary, a change in reserves leads to a multiple change in bank deposits. The value of the multiplier depends on the reserve ratio. The larger the reserve ratio, the smaller the deposit multiplier; the smaller the reserve ratio, the larger the deposit multiplier. A more complicated version of this multiplier is derived in Appendix 13.1.

The money creation process is neatly summed up below.

> Increase in reserves → increase in loans → increase in deposits
> → increase in money supply

The money creation process is also symmetric. Any withdrawal will lead to a decrease in reserves. As a result, banks reduce their lending, thus reducing the money supply. The reduction in the money supply will be a multiple of the fall in reserves.

This simplified analysis illustrates the power of a bank to create money. This analysis can also be extended to a two- or multi-bank system. Although the exercise is more difficult, the principle remains the same.

13.2 INTEREST RATE DETERMINATION

Again, we must begin this section by defining two important concepts.

Definition
Interest is the amount that is paid on a loan or the amount that is received on a deposit.

For example, Tomas borrows €2,000 from the bank to buy a second-hand car. At the end of the year his repayments to the bank equal €2,200. The principal is €2,000 and the interest is €200.

Definition
The rate of interest is the interest amount expressed as a percentage of the sum borrowed or lent.

In the example above, Tomas paid €200 in interest on a principal of €2,000. The interest rate is 10%.

In any economy there are many different rates of interest. They vary with time, risk, size and other factors.

There are two main theories of interest rate determination. The first is the classical approach where the interest rate is determined by the demand for and supply of loanable funds (or credit). This is called the loanable funds theory. The second is the Keynesian approach where the interest rate is determined by the demand for and supply of money. This is called the liquidity preference theory.

The loanable funds theory

For classical economists, interest was the 'price' paid for borrowing funds. According to this theory, if a firm is considering the purchase of a capital good, the total cost of that good increases with the interest rate. As the interest rate increases, fewer and fewer investment projects are considered because the revenue which they generate is not sufficient to cover the price of the investment. Alternatively, as the interest rate falls, more projects are viable. In short, there is a negative relationship between interest rates and investment.

Firms often finance the purchase or lease of capital goods by borrowing funds.[7] The relationship between the interest rate and the demand for loanable funds or credit is also negative. As interest rates rise, the price of capital goods rises and firms are less likely to borrow money to finance an investment project. Alternatively, as interest rates fall, the demand for loanable funds increases. Therefore, the demand curve for loanable funds, D is downward sloping as shown in Figure 13.3.

Figure 13.3: The demand curve for loanable funds

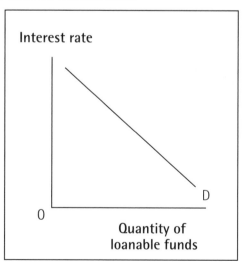

The supply of loanable funds is derived from the level of household savings. The classical economists argued that in order to persuade people to overcome the inclination to consume immediately, a reward in the form of interest had to be offered. The higher the rate of interest, the greater is the inducement to postpone current consumption, and so the greater is the supply of loanable funds. As the rate of interest rises, the supply of loanable funds increases.[8] Subsequently, the supply curve of loanable funds, S is upward sloping, as drawn in Figure 13.4.

Figure 13.4: The supply curve of loanable funds

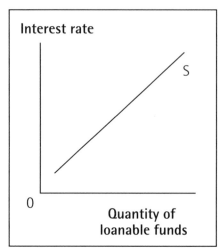

The rate of interest is determined by the demand for and supply of loanable funds. The function of the interest rate is to equate the demand for funds with the supply of funds in the same way that price adjusts to equate demand and supply in the goods market. The intersection of the demand and supply curves is the equilibrium rate of interest, i*. This is illustrated in Figure 13.5.

Figure 13.5: The market for loanable funds

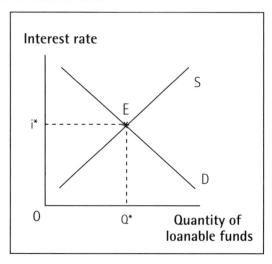

Changes in the demand for loanable funds occur for a number of reasons. Since firms carry out investment projects in anticipation of making a profit, it follows that anything which changes the expected profitability of investment projects will change the demand for loanable funds. An increase in demand causes a rightward shift of the demand curve whereas a decrease in demand causes a leftward shift of the demand curve.

Since the supply of funds is provided by household savings, any change in attitude towards savings will change the supply of loanable funds. An increase in supply causes a rightward shift of the supply curve whereas a decrease in supply causes a leftward shift of the supply curve.

In conclusion, the decision to save, or to hold cash balances, depends on one variable in the classical model: the interest rate. The decision of firms to invest depends on the same variable. The combination of the demand for and the supply of loanable funds determines the market rate of interest.

The liquidity preference theory

Keynes and his followers argued that the rate of interest was not determined by the demand for and supply of loanable funds but by the demand for money and the existing money supply.

The demand for money

The demand for money in the Keynesian model is more complex than in the classical model. We begin by defining liquidity preference.

Definition

Liquidity preference is the desire by households to hold assets in liquid form.

According to Keynes, it is based on three motives which we will now explain. We will discover that the demand for money depends not only on the interest rate but also on the income of the household. In other words, the demand for money depends on two variables rather than just one as we discussed in the classical model.

1.   *Transactions demand*   A certain amount of money is required as a medium of exchange so that people can undertake day-to-day transactions such as the purchase of groceries, public transport and entertainment. The level of transactions demand depends on a number of factors. They include institutional factors such as the length of time between pay-days, the price level and, more importantly, the income level. The rate of interest has little or no effect on the transactions demand for money.

2.   *Precautionary demand*   A certain amount of money is held as a precaution against unforeseen contingencies such as illness or accidents. This desire to hold cash balances is related primarily to income. Other factors include the availability of overdraft facilities and the age of the economic agent involved.

The transactions and precautionary motives are often combined. The addition of the two is sometimes referred to as the demand for 'active balances'; 'active' in the sense that these funds will be actively used to purchase goods and services. These two motives are directly related to the medium of exchange function of money.

The demand for 'active balances' is drawn as a vertical line. This is shown in Figure 13.6.

Figure 13.6: The demand for active balances curve

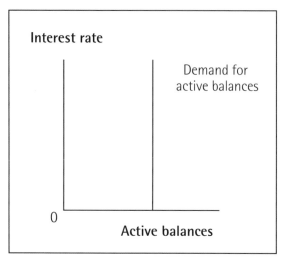

This means that it is interest rate inelastic; the demand for money balances does not change with the interest rate. Instead, the demand for money balances will change with income. An increase in income will shift the demand for active balances curve to the right. At higher income levels, more money is demanded for transactions and as a precaution against an uncertain future. If income levels fall, the demand curve will shift to the left.

3. *Speculative demand*   The final motive for holding money is to avoid losses from holding interest-bearing assets. For example, if investors had foreseen the Wall Street crash of 1987 they would have sold their interest-bearing assets and put the proceeds into bank accounts. This form of demand is sometimes called the demand for idle balances. It is related to the store of value function of money.

Suppose an individual holds a portfolio of assets. Assume there are only two types of assets – money and bonds.[9] Money has the advantage of instant spending power or complete liquidity. However, it earns little or no interest. In contrast, bonds earn a rate of interest but suffer from being relatively illiquid.

The individual must choose between holding money or holding bonds. The higher the rate of interest the more attractive it becomes to store wealth in bonds rather than money and with this the speculative demand for money declines. Hence, the speculative demand for money is inversely related to the rate of interest. If interest rates are high, the demand for bonds is relatively high whereas the demand for money is relatively low. A demand for 'idle balances' curve is drawn downward sloping, reflecting the inverse relationship between the speculative demand for money and the interest rate.

Figure 13.7: The demand for idle balances curve

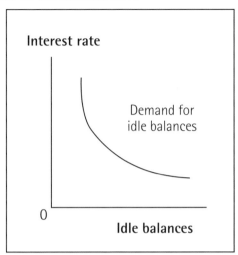

We can combine the demand for active balances curve with the demand for idle balances curve to yield the total demand for money curve. Keynes referred to this as the liquidity preference curve, denoted as L. It is the sum of the transactions demand, the precautionary demand and the speculative demand for money. The liquidity preference curve is downward sloping, reflecting the negative relationship between the total demand for money and the rate of interest. This inverse relationship arises largely from the speculative demand for money.

The liquidity preference curve, L is drawn in Figure 13.8.

Figure 13.8: The liquidity preference curve

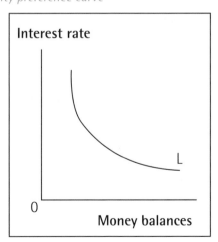

Money demand also depends on the level of income. As income increases, the demand for money increases; as income decreases, the demand for money decreases. A change in the level of income causes a shift of the demand for money curve. An increase in income shifts the money demand curve to the right. The opposite is true for a fall in the income level.

The supply of money

In the liquidity preference theory of interest rate determination, the money supply is assumed to be controlled by the Central Bank. Remember, because of the nature of the banking system, commercial banks have the power not just to transfer purchasing power but also to create it. In turn, if the Central Bank can regulate the amount that the commercial banks hold on reserve, it can regulate the amount of money which they can create, thus controlling the money supply. Hence, the money supply curve is vertical, independent of the rate of interest. We say it is interest rate inelastic, at least in the short run. The money supply curve, M_s is drawn in Figure 13.9.

Figure 13.9: The money supply curve

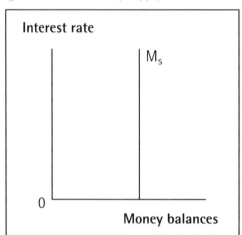

Money market equilibrium

Figure 13.10 shows a demand for money curve combined with a money supply curve. The interaction of the demand for and supply of money determines the interest rate. The rate of interest is the price of money and, like other prices it is determined by the forces of demand and supply. In the words of J. M. Keynes it is 'the reward for parting with liquidity for a specified period'.[10]

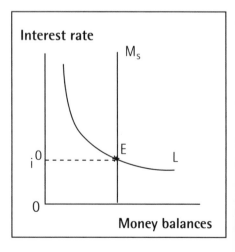

Figure 13.10: Money market equilibrium

In Figure 13.10 the equilibrium rate of interest is i^0. At an interest rate above the equilibrium there exists an excess supply of money which leads to a downward movement of the interest rate. At an interest rate below the equilibrium there exists an excess demand for money which results in an upward movement of the interest rate.

Figure 13.11 illustrates the effect of an increase in the money supply. The money supply curve shifts to the right, from M_s to M_s^1. This results in an excess supply at the old rate of interest, i^0. Interest rates fall and continue to do so until the excess supply is eliminated. This adjustment process ends when the demand equals supply at a new and lower equilibrium rate of interest, i^1. Alternatively, a decrease in the money supply results in a higher equilibrium rate of interest.

Figure 13.11: An increase in the money supply

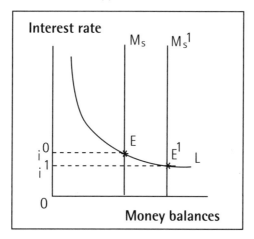

Figure 13.12 illustrates the effect of an increase in the demand for money (arising from an increase in income). The money demand curve shifts rightwards, resulting in excess demand at the old interest rate. Interest rates begin to rise and continue to do so until the excess demand is eliminated. Equilibrium returns to the money market at a higher interest rate, i^1, than before. Alternatively, a decrease in the demand for money results in a lower equilibrium rate of interest.

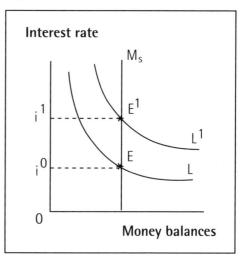

Figure 13.12: An increase in the demand for money

Finally, if interest rates are below 'normal', all market participants will expect a rise in interest rates. When explaining his liquidity preference theory, Keynes referred to the normal rate of interest, i.e. the rate of interest that is consistent with normal market conditions. If interest rates are low relative to the normal rate of interest, the market will expect an increase in the interest rate some time in the future. Due to the negative relationship that exists between interest rates and the price of bonds, we would expect a fall in the price of bonds.[11] In this case, investors would prefer to hold money to bonds because the holders of bonds will realise a capital loss.

Hence, at these 'low' interest rate levels, the demand for money may be perfectly elastic. This is illustrated by the horizontal part of the liquidity preference curve in Figure 13.8 above. Keynes referred to this as the liquidity trap. There is more discussion on the liquidity trap in the next chapter.

The two models suggest that the interest rate is determined in very different ways. In the loanable funds model, both the supply of funds and the demand for funds vary with the interest rate. In the liquidity preference theory, the interest rate is determined in the money market.

A more fundamental difference is that in the classical loanable funds theory, interest rate determination appears to be an automatic process. Funds become available from households as interest rates rise. Funds are demanded by firms as the interest rate falls. An adjustable interest rate clears the market. Keynes' speculative demand for money suggests that money is a 'safe' asset, preferred by investors, particularly in times of uncertainty. Equilibrium in the money market may be at very low rates of interest. Even at low rates of interest, firms are not enticed to put money to a productive use.

Finally Keynes suggests that in certain situations, the money supply can be used to affect the interest rate. Since the money supply is controlled by the government, policy-makers are able to adjust it to affect the interest rate and ultimately, private investment. We finish this section with a brief explanation of the term structure of interest rates.

The term structure of interest rates relates the yield or interest rate on a security to the length of time until the security matures. It is reflected in the yield curve.

Definition
The yield curve shows the way in which the yield on a security varies according to its maturity or expiry date.

It is customary to represent yields (interest rates on security) on the vertical axis and maturities (time period) on the horizontal axis. The slope of the yield curve can vary. Among other factors, inflation expectations can account for the differences in yield curve patterns.

The 'normal' shaped yield curve slopes up from left to right, as shown in Figure 13.13(a). This reflects the case where long-term interest rates are above short-term interest rates. This is viewed as the norm because the expectation of higher inflation over the long run will result in long-term securities offering higher yields than short-term securities.

Others types of yield curves are also shown in Figure 13.13.

In Figure 13.13(b) the yield curve is drawn as a straight line. A flat yield curve results when long-term and short-term interest rates are equal. When long-term interest rates are below short-term interest rates, a downward sloping yield curve is drawn, as in Figure 13.13(c).

Figure 13.13: Different yield curves

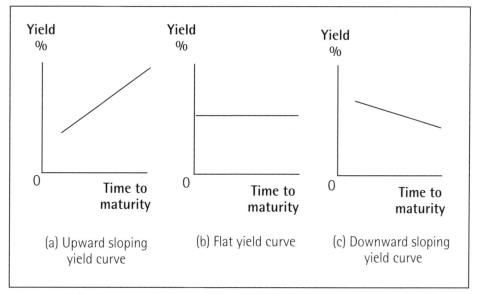

(a) Upward sloping yield curve   (b) Flat yield curve   (c) Downward sloping yield curve

Analysing the behaviour of the yield curve is quite common in financial markets. In particular, yield curves are used as a prediction tool. Market predictions about movements of short-term interest rates in the future are reflected in the slope of the yield curve. For example, a steep upward sloping yield curve means that short-term interest rates are expected to rise. In contrast, a flat or downward sloping yield curve means that short-term interest rates are expected to fall. Either way, yield curves reflect the prevailing expectations in the financial markets.

CASE STUDY

Extract from *The Irish Independent*
Central Bank sees rising credit trend as lending fuels spending
by Pat Boyle

A large slice of the current spending boom is being financed through credit, with figures from the Central Bank showing the annual growth in private sector credit at 34.7pc for March. While the March figure marks a slight decrease on the 34.8pc recorded in February, underlying figures reveal a rising trend over the two months.

According to an analysis from Bloxham Stockbrokers, the only thing which is likely to dampen the soaring credit growth is a sharp rise in interest rates. But while the

ECB is expected to continue with its policy of raising rates, the actual rate of increase is likely to be modest and not sufficient to affect demand for credit. According to Bloxham, one of the chief worries of the ECB is price stability in the eurozone.

In light of the high growth being experienced, this is a cause for some concern. However, while the ECB will continue to tighten rates this year and next, Irish private sector credit growth is likely to remain well above the eurozone average for the foreseeable future. Lending by credit institutions in February rose by €4.45bn to €100.6bn. Residential mortgages rose by €567m in March, some 20.2pc ahead of the figure for March 1999.

Source: *The Irish Independent*, 3 May 2000.

Questions

1. Using the two theories outlined in this chapter, explain the factors determining the demand for credit.
2. How do the Irish figures for money supply growth and credit growth compare to the euro area figures? What factors might account for the difference?
3. What changes regarding monetary aggregates have taken place as a result of Ireland's adoption of the single currency?

[NB: The Central Bank of Ireland Bulletin is a useful source.]

Answers on website

13.3 THE ROLE OF A CENTRAL BANK

The central bank is a very important component of any banking system. Yet, while some central banks are centuries old, others have been established quite recently.[12]

The first tentative step towards the establishment of a central bank in Ireland was taken in 1783 when Parliament established the Bank of Ireland. Its primary role was to issue banknotes. To a lesser extent, it acted as a bankers' bank and a lender of last resort.

The Bank of Ireland's role as central bank diminished following the Act of Union in 1801 when the Bank of England began to take on central bank activities in Ireland. However, the Bank of Ireland's role as a central bank effectively ended with the passage of the Bankers' Act of 1845. This Act promoted competition and relaxed restrictions concerning the issuing of banknotes. From this date on, the Bank of Ireland concentrated on commercial banking.

The most important financial event following political independence was the establishment of the Banking Commission called the Parker-Willis Commission, after its chairman Professor Henry Parker-Willis. It was established in 1926, in an environment which was hostile to the emergence of a central bank. In the following year, the Currency Act of 1927 introduced the Saorstat pound which was later renamed the Irish pound.[13] The Commission was also responsible for the regulation of the newly designed Irish notes and coins.

The Central Bank of Ireland was formally established in 1943, receiving its powers from the Central Bank Act of 1942. It was responsible for safeguarding the integrity of the currency and for controlling the amount of credit in the economy. New techniques and instruments for the purpose of implementing monetary policy were developed in the intervening decades. Notwithstanding these developments, the continuation of the sterling link confined the Central Bank of Ireland to a secondary role. All this changed in the 1970s.

In 1971 the Central Bank Act was passed. It was primarily concerned with the licensing and supervision of banks in the domestic market. This was to meet the structural changes which had occurred throughout the banking industry. Powers were further increased in 1989 when, among other things, building societies and all financial institutions in the International Financial Services Centre were placed under the regulation of the Central Bank. By 1993, the activities of the ICC Bank and the ACC Bank had also been brought under the supervision of the Central Bank. Since the early 1990s, events at home have been dominated by monetary developments in the EU, and in particular the establishment of the European Central Bank. Since the launch of the single currency in 1999, many of the functions of the Central Bank have been transformed from the Central Bank of Ireland to the European Central Bank.

Functions of a central bank

A central bank fulfils a number of functions. It issues and controls the currency, sometimes referred to as 'legal tender'. It acts as banker to the state.

A central bank is also the banker's bank. Reserves, required by law, are held for the commercial banking sector by the Central Bank. Since commercial banks operate with only a fraction of their deposits, the Central Bank ensures that they can obtain cash to meet any unexpected withdrawal of funds. Because of this role, the Central Bank is sometimes referred to as 'the lender of last resort'.

A central bank formulates and implements monetary policy which we will discuss in the next section. Adjusting the interest rate is the aspect of monetary policy which is most widely reported in the news.

Another function of the Central Bank is to manage the country's monetary system. It is responsible for the regulation and the supervision of all financial institutions.

We now examine one of its functions in more detail – the formulation and implementation of monetary policy.

13.4 MONETARY POLICY

Definition

Monetary policy refers to the use of money supply, credit and interest rates to achieve economic objectives.

We will discuss the use of credit guidelines and interest rates later. We begin, however, by looking at the supply of money in the economy.

In a closed economy, the supply of money can be controlled by the Central Bank which has a number of different options available. Three such options are described below. They are sometimes referred to as the tools or instruments of monetary policy.[14]

1. *Reserve requirements* All financial institutions are required to hold a certain amount of their deposits on reserve.

Definition
The reserve requirement is the percentage of deposits which banks are legally obligated to lodge at the Central Bank.

Changes in the rules that specify the amount of reserves a bank must hold to back up deposits can influence the money supply. For example, the higher the reserve requirement, the lower the deposit multiplier and subsequently the smaller the change in the money supply. Conversely, a decrease in the reserve requirement increases the amount of deposits that can be supported by a given level of reserves and will lead to an increase in the money supply.

2. *Open market operations*

Definition
Open market operations involve the buying and selling of government securities or bonds.

When the Central Bank buys securities, a cheque is drawn on the Central Bank as payment in favour of the client's commercial bank. When the cheque is presented for payment, bank deposits are transferred from the Central Bank to the commercial bank. Hence, the reserves of the commercial bank are increased. Moreover, its ability to create more deposits via the money multiplier process also increases. The end result is an increase in the money supply. In brief, an open market purchase expands the money supply; an open market sale reduces the money supply.

3. *Discount rate* As we discussed above, commercial banks must hold a percentage of their deposits as reserves. If their reserves fall below the legal limit, commercial banks borrow money from other banks, if possible, or from the Central Bank to make up the shortfall. The interest rate charged is called the discount rate.

Definition
The discount rate is the rate which the Central Bank charges financial institutions that borrow from it for purposes of maintaining the reserve requirement.

The lower the discount rate, the lower the cost of borrowing for reserves, the higher the amount of borrowing. As banks increase their borrowing from the Central Bank, the subsequent increase in bank reserves can support an increase in loans. We know from the money multiplier process that an increase in the money supply results. The opposite is true for a relatively high discount rate.

The discount rate is generally used as the base of all other interest rates. When the discount rate increases, all other interest rates on loans for firms and consumers generally follow. That is why announcements from the European Central Bank concerning their key interest rates are awaited with such interest by the financial markets.

One further possibility is for the Central Bank to make a formal request to the commercial banks to meet certain credit guidelines or to maintain a required reserve ratio. The request is sometimes accompanied with constraints. This practice of discouraging banks and other financial institutions is called moral suasion.

In conclusion, an increase in the money supply results from an open market purchase, a reduction in the discount rate and a reduction in the required reserve ratio. A sale of securities, an increase in the discount rate and a higher required reserve ratio lead to a reduction in the money supply.

This completes the operational aspect of monetary policy. We now examine the effects that monetary policy has on the macroeconomic variables of output and employment.

The effects of monetary policy

We will begin with an example which illustrates the relationship between the money supply, interest rates and national income.

Suppose the monetary authorities conduct an open market purchase. We know from our earlier discussion on the tools of monetary policy that the purchase of securities increases the money supply. This creates a disequilibrium (excess supply) in the money market which drives down the interest rate. The fall in the interest rate induces an increase in investment expenditure (and possibly consumer expenditure, particularly consumer goods bought on credit). Investment expenditure is one component of aggregate expenditure. The increase in aggregate expenditure will lead to an increase in national output, measured by GDP. If the link between economic growth and employment/unemployment is strong (see Okun's Law in Chapter 17), such increases in output will increase employment and reduce unemployment. In short,

Increase in M_s → decreases i → increases I → increases AE → increases GDP → decreases U

The effects of monetary policy are illustrated in Figure 13.14.

Figure 13.14: Monetary policy changes

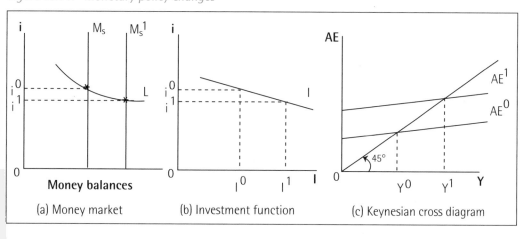

(a) Money market   (b) Investment function   (c) Keynesian cross diagram

The money market is represented in panel (a), the investment function in panel (b) and the Keynesian cross diagram in panel (c).[15] The increase in money supply shifts the money supply curve to the right. The equilibrium rate of interest falls from i^0 to i^1. Lower interest rates induce greater investment expenditure and this causes a movement down along the investment function (from I^0 to I^1). An increase in investment, one of the components of aggregate expenditure, shifts the AE curve upwards from AE^0 to AE^1, increasing the equilibrium income level.

We have shown that using a Keynesian model, an increase in the money supply expands national income. Conversely, a reduction in the money supply contracts national income. Using the IS/LM framework, changes in monetary policy are discussed in more detail in the next chapter.

This short discussion on monetary policy illustrates its effects on economic variables and its importance in the context of achieving macroeconomic objectives. A discussion on inflation and how changes in the money supply affect the general price level are omitted; these are explained in Chapter 17.

Monetary policy as a policy instrument

The use of monetary policy became fashionable in the 1970s because economists and governments were concerned that government spending was not having the desired effect on unemployment. Rather, it was increasing the percentage of national income which was controlled by the public sector. Further, high levels of government spending combined with interest payments led to spiralling government debts.

The main attraction of monetary policy is that it affects the spending patterns of the private sector. A change in the money supply affects the interest rate. Changes in the interest rate lead to changes in both investment and consumer spending. Therefore, everyone in the private sector can potentially benefit from the change in the price of capital funds. The economy is stimulated or deflated by lowering or raising the interest rate. The emphasis of this policy is on the private sector; it does not directly affect public sector spending or the national debt.

Monetary policy became the preferred macroeconomic policy in the US and the UK by the early 1980s. However, from the outset, the use of monetary policy to stabilise the economy was criticised by a group of economists called the 'monetarists'. Milton Friedman and Edmund Phelps were both early contributors to the debate.

They argued that the primary role of monetary policy is to maintain the price level which creates confidence in a national currency and ultimately in a national economy. They conceded that adjustments to the money supply might cause fluctuations in national output in the short run. However, they cautioned that the use of monetary policy to stabilise the economy leads to inflation and a weakening of the currency. Therefore, the use of monetary policy to stabilise the economy in the short run hinders the long-term growth of the economy.

We sometimes make the mistake of thinking that Keynesians advocate the use of fiscal policy, and monetarists advocate the use of monetary policy. In reality, particularly in the 1970s, Keynesians accepted and embraced the use of monetary policy.

In contrast, monetarists always believed in the importance of monetary policy but not in its use to stabilise the economy. Careful monitoring of the money supply ensures that inflation does not become entrenched in the national economy. For the monetarists, the role of monetary policy is to ensure price stability. This is much more limited than the role envisioned by the Keynesians.

Having discussed the two extreme positions on monetary policy, we will end with the observations of David Romer, who appears to be seeking the middle ground. He states that, 'The lesson I draw is that conducting monetary policy has always been difficult. The environment has been changing continually, the lags have been long, the uncertainty has been great. Thus, I would conclude that monetary policy should be conducted the way it always has been – using a mix of formal models, rules of thumb, shrewd observation, instinct, guesswork and prayer.'[16]

13.5 THE IRISH EXPERIENCE

The Irish experience pre-1999

From the comments above, we can see that for a closed economy, the role of monetary policy is debatable and even contentious. We will find that the scope of policy effectiveness is even narrower in a small open economy (SOE) such as Ireland.

Definition
A small open economy (SOE) refers to an economy that is so small relative to the world economy that domestic economic events have no effect on the rest of the world. The domestic economy is a price taker: it accepts world prices. Also, external trade (exports and imports) represents a high proportion of the country's GDP.

Ireland's economy exhibits these characteristics. Further, we find that Ireland, in common with other small open economies, exhibits particular behaviours which limit its ability to use monetary policy effectively. We will list these and then discuss their relevance in detail.

1. A SOE whose currency belongs to a fixed or semi-fixed exchange rate system does not control its money supply.
2. Domestic interest rates in the long term are determined primarily by external forces.
3. It may have some ability to manage the liquidity in the money market in the short term.

1. *Money supply*   The monetary authorities of a SOE cannot control its money supply to the same degree as other central banks.[17] Hence, there is little scope for an independent monetary policy. An example follows.

Independent of other central banks, suppose the Central Bank of Ireland decided (pre-1999) to increase the money supply in order to boost domestic spending. As the domestic money supply increases, interest rates fall. Because domestic interest rates are now lower than world interest rates, an outflow of capital results. In order to invest in other economies where interest rates are now relatively higher, the Irish pound is exchanged for foreign currencies. An excess supply of the Irish pound leads to a weakening of the Irish currency against foreign currencies which should cause a depreciation of the Irish pound. Because Ireland is a member of a semi-fixed exchange rate system, that is, the exchange rate mechanism of the European Monetary System, the Central Bank is obliged to maintain the value of the Irish pound between certain limits. The Central Bank intervenes by buying up and, in the process, eliminating the excess supply. On the purchase of the domestic currency, the money supply decreases and interest rates effectively revert to their original level. An independent monetary policy appears ineffective.

2.   *Interest rates*   Central banks in closed economies can 'set' their interest rate and adjust their money supply to support that interest rate. Interest rates in a SOE are determined largely by external factors, the most important of which is the level of foreign interest rates. As we explained above, investors will move capital to take advantage of higher interest rates in other economies. As a result, domestic interest rates cannot differ substantially from foreign interest rates if capital is mobile. Other external factors which affect the domestic interest rate work through the exchange rate. They include speculation and expectations concerning realignments of exchange rates.

This dependency on foreign interest rates is illustrated in the following example.

If the Bundesbank increased German interest rates, the Irish Central Bank was likely to follow. If it did not, an interest rate differential (a gap between German and Irish interest rates) would result. Given the absence of exchange controls, capital was likely to flow from Ireland to Germany where the return was now higher. As a consequence, the Irish pound would weaken against the German mark. This depreciation of the Irish pound would continue until the interest rate differential disappeared. This would happen only when the Irish Central Bank increased domestic interest rates or in the unlikely event of the Bundesbank rescinding its earlier decision.

3.   *Liquidity*   The above analysis seems to suggest the absence of any role for the Irish monetary authorities. This is not completely true. In the short term the Central Bank could influence liquidity levels by providing funds or withdrawing funds whenever necessary. Liquidity could be added to or drained from the domestic financial system by a number of different instruments. These are called liquidity management instruments. They included the following:

- *The short-term facility*   The STF was an overdraft facility which the Central Bank provided to those financial institutions that were short of reserves. Funds were drawn down on a quota basis overnight and this facility was available for up to seven days. Frequent use of the STF reflected a shortage of liquidity.
- *Secured advances*   The Central Bank provided a facility for banks to borrow funds on a longer term basis against the security of government bonds. It was an extension of the STF and was normally only used when a bank's quota was filled. This seldom happened and, hence, this instrument was rarely used.
- *Foreign exchange (FX) swaps*   A foreign exchange swap is a financial instrument whereby one party lends foreign currency to another party in exchange for domestic currency.[18] If the Central Bank wanted to add liquidity it could do so by swapping

Irish pounds for foreign currency. Conversely, liquidity could be removed by swapping foreign currency for Irish pounds. This particular instrument provided liquidity for periods of up to four weeks.

- *Sale and repurchase agreements (REPOs)* REPOs are financial instruments whereby one party agrees to buy a security on the condition that it will resell it to the other party at some future date. The Central Bank often bought securities from other financial institutions on the understanding that it would resell them back to the same banks on an agreed future date. Like swaps, REPOs provided liquidity for periods of up to one month.
- *Term deposits* At times of temporary surplus liquidity, the Central Bank quoted rates for overnight and term deposits. Although the Central Bank could not add liquidity through this method, it could discourage banks from holding surplus liquidity by quoting unattractive rates for term deposits.
- *Changes in the reserve ratio* Variations in the reserve ratio were used to add or withdraw liquidity. A reduction in the ratio allowed for greater liquidity; an increase permitted less liquidity. Variations in the reserve ratio were usually confined to periods where seasonal changes occur, e.g. Christmas.

In general, changes in one or more of these instruments allowed the Central Bank to add or remove liquidity from the domestic money market. Such action by the Central Bank aimed to avoid reductions in interest rates which would otherwise stem from excess market liquidity and, likewise, avoid increases in interest rates arising from shortages in liquidity in the market. In effect, the Central Bank attempted to smooth out changes in liquidity in order to prevent sharp movements in domestic interest rates.

The objective of monetary policy in Ireland

Pre-1999, monetary policy in Ireland was described in many different ways. Here is a small sample: '. . . the poor relation of economic policy in Ireland'; '. . . an unutilised instrument of public policy';[19] '. . . always there, exerting an influence, behind the scenes' and finally, the 'Hidden Stabiliser'.[20] The objective of Irish monetary policy was price stability, i.e. low inflation.[21]

Employing an exchange rate target strategy, the Central Bank tried to achieve price stability. By maintaining the value of the Irish pound within the Exchange Rate Mechanism (ERM), the Central Bank was able to sustain a low inflation rate. In order to maintain the exchange rate link with the German mark, it was, at times, necessary for the Central Bank to change interest rates. For example, a fall in the value of the Irish pound against the German mark might require a hike in interest rates, regardless of domestic economic conditions.

The 1992 Central Bank statement on monetary policy is a good summary of the aim of monetary policy at that time, 'The basic objective of monetary policy is to keep inflation as low as possible through the maintenance of a firm exchange rate for the Irish pound within the narrow band of the EMS.'[22]

The monetary policy experience in Ireland

An Irish financial system, independent from the UK, was established in the mid-1960s. In 1969 the Central Bank started a market for government securities. In the following year, a foreign exchange market was established. Assets which were owned by Irish commercial institutions but held in London were re-routed back to Ireland. The most significant change in the Irish monetary system occurred in 1979 when Ireland broke with sterling and joined the newly formed ERM of the European Monetary System. Prior to this, Irish interest rates were determined by factors such as UK interest rates, the value of sterling and the UK Treasury.

   The close relationship between Irish and UK interest rates in the period up to 1979 is highlighted in Figure 13.15.

Figure 13.15: Irish and UK interest rates 1971–79

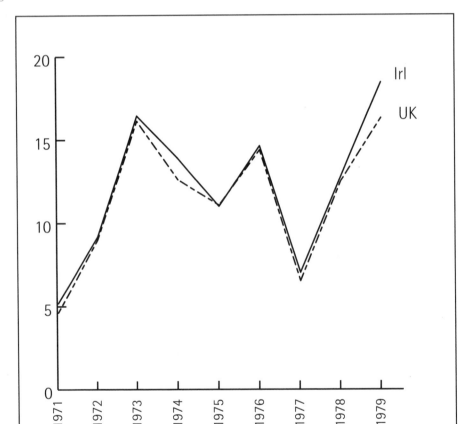

After 1979, UK interest rates and the value of sterling were no longer the dominant factors in the determination of Irish interest rates. This is not to suggest that the Irish monetary authorities were suddenly in charge of Irish interest rates: there was simply a change in the factors which determined Irish interest rates. Exchange rate and interest rate levels within the ERM became the most important factors in determining Irish monetary policy and, in particular, Irish interest rates. Moreover, it was the value of the German mark combined with German interest rates which became the dominant factor. This is because of the central role which Germany occupied within the exchange rate system. Irish, UK and German interest rates in the period 1980–99 are shown in Figure 13.16.

Figure 13.16:   Irish, UK and German interest rates 1980–99

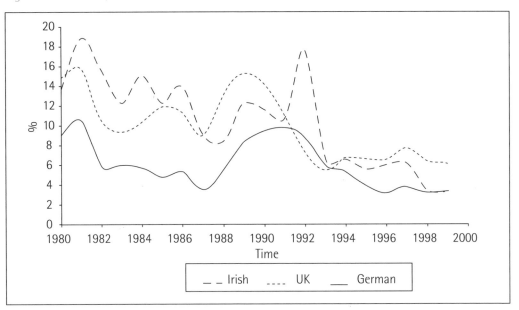

The large differential between Irish and German interest rates during the first few years of the EMS was unexpected and unwelcome. Fortunately in the later period of membership the differential narrowed substantially.

The Irish experience post-1999

The Treaty on European Union (see Chapter 15) and the new institutions that followed have changed the operation of monetary policy in Ireland and elsewhere. Since January 1999, the Irish exchange rate is fixed relative to other EU countries that have also adopted the euro. The Irish interest rate is set by the European Central Bank. The Central Bank of Ireland plays a secondary role in the formulation and implementation of monetary policy. We begin our analysis by identifying the new institutions that are responsible for the single monetary policy in the euro area.

We begin with the European System of Central Banks (ESCB). The ESCB is composed of the European Central Bank (ECB) and the national central banks of all fifteen EU member states. As not all EU member states adopted the euro on its launch in January 1999, the term Eurosystem has been used to describe the ECB and the central banks of the EU member states that participate in the euro area.[23]

The decision-making bodies of the ECB comprise the Governing Council and the six-member Executive Board. The Executive Board comprises the ECB president, the ECB vice-president and four other members who are appointed by the heads of the participating states. The appointment is for an eight-year non-renewable term. The Governing Council comprises the members of the executive board and the governors of the national central banks participating in the euro area. In the context of membership of the Governing Council, governors of the participating national central banks (including the governor of the Central Bank of Ireland) are required to act in a personal capacity and not as national representatives. This supra-national responsibility was designed to ensure that governors are not subject to any instructions and are required to act in the best interests of the euro area as a whole.[24]

It is the Governing Council that is the primary decision-making authority of the ECB. It formulates the single monetary policy for the euro area. Council decisions concerning monetary policy are made on the basis of a simple majority of votes, whereby each member has one vote. The role of the executive board is to manage the ECB and its primary function is to implement monetary policy in accordance with the guidelines and decisions laid down by the Governing Council. The national central banks take their instructions from the executive board and, by doing so, ensure a certain degree of co-ordination and decentralisation.

The provisions of the Maastricht Treaty attempt to ensure that the new ECB is independent from political interference. Article 107 states that neither the Community institutions nor national governments of the member states can interfere with or influence decisions of the ECB. The statutory powers of the ECB can only be altered by a revision of the Maastricht Treaty which, in itself, would require ratification by all EU member states. In theory, this makes the ECB even more independent than either the German Bundesbank or the US Federal Reserve (Fed). The purpose of this design or institutionalisation of Central Bank independence was to help establish the credibility and anti-inflation reputation of the new ECB. Despite the Treaty provisions regarding accountability (Article 109b), many view the new monetary institutions as undemocratic. Supporters of the ECB argue that the balance between independence and accountability is reasonable.

As stated in Article 105 of the Treaty, the primary objective of the single monetary policy in the euro area is price stability. In addition, the Treaty states that, 'Without prejudice to the objective of price stability, the ESCB shall support the general economic policies in the Community . . .'. For the euro area, price stability is defined as an annual increase in the Harmonised Index of Consumer Prices (HICP) of below 2% (see Chapter 17 for a description of the HICP). With respect to a time frame, there is explicit reference to price stability thus defined 'to be maintained over the medium term'. The aim of this is to ensure a forward looking, medium-term orientation for the single monetary policy. By any standards, including the admirable record of the Bundesbank and the Fed, achieving an inflation target of less than 2% over the medium term, albeit undefined, is a difficult task.

Monetary policy strategy

In choosing a monetary policy strategy that will yield price stability, the ECB had a number of options available to it. These include the following;

- exchange rate targeting (as used by the Central Bank of Ireland);
- interest rate targeting;
- monetary aggregate targeting (as used by the Bundesbank);
- inflation targeting (as used by the Bank of England).

In each of these cases, the ultimate target of price stability is achieved by means of an intermediate target, namely the exchange rate (pegged to an anchor country with a strong anti-inflation reputation), a short-term interest rate, broad money or forecasted inflation respectively. In its 1997 report on alternate monetary policy strategies, the European Monetary Institute (the predecessor to the ECB) came out in favour of two strategies, namely monetary aggregate targeting and inflation targeting. With this in mind, the ECB announced the Eurosystem's stability-oriented monetary policy strategy in October 1998, details of which can be found in the ECB *Monthly Bulletin* January 1999 issue. A short description follows.

As expected, the monetary policy strategy preferred by the Eurosystem did not opt for a single intermediate target. Instead two 'pillars' or key elements are used in the pursuit of price stability. The first pillar relates to a prominent role for money, in recognition of the monetary origins of inflation. It is in the form of a quantitative reference value (as opposed to a strict target) for broad money M3 growth, announced at 4.5% per annum.[25] In devising the strategy, cognisance was taken of the regime shift to EMU. In view of this regime change and the effect that it might have on the relationship between money and inflation, it was decided that deviations from the reference value would not automatically lead to a correction by the authorities. Also, the actual reference value of 4.5% could be changed in the future, if, for example, the trend growth in real GDP was to change. In view of this, a review of the reference value will take place on an annual basis. The second pillar is more broad-based, assessing the outlook for price developments and risks to price stability. A wide range of economic and financial indicators are used, including trends in wage levels, the exchange rate, bond prices and the yield curve. For example, if the inflation target was endangered by a sudden increase in wages arising from labour shortages, the ECB might respond by increasing short-term interest rates. A schematic presentation of the monetary policy strategy is given in Figure 13.17.

Figure 13.17: The ECB's monetary policy strategy

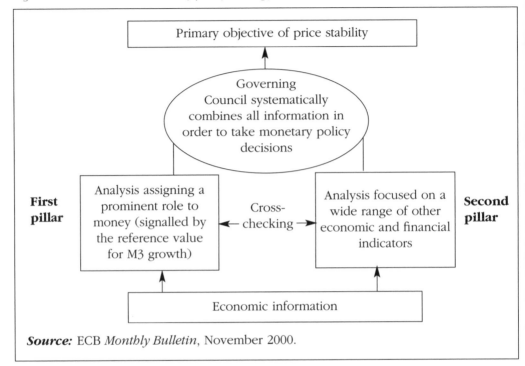

Source: ECB *Monthly Bulletin*, November 2000.

Since the announcement of the monetary policy strategy, the ECB has been criticised for the confusion arising from the twin pillar strategy. Many have called for the abandonment of the quasi money-supply 'target' in preference for a strict inflation target. Others have gone further and called for the ECB to 'target' not just inflation or money supply but asset prices and the level of the exchange rate. In response, the ECB reiterates that the two pillars are not targets but instruments which facilitate the achievement of its primary objective, namely, price stability. In addition, the ECB draws attention to the complexity of monetary policy and to the new and unfamiliar format of its monetary strategy.

The instruments of monetary policy

In the implementation of monetary policy in the euro area, there are a number of instruments available to the monetary authorities (see Section 13.4 for a general discussion on monetary policy instruments). The core elements of the operational framework are open market operations, standing facilities and minimum reserves.

Open market operations

As explained earlier, open market operations are the buying and selling of government securities. Although there are a number of instruments available to the Eurosystem for the conduct of open market operations, the main refinancing operations (MRO) is the most important.

Definition

Main refinancing operations are reverse transactions using tenders and are normally executed weekly, with a maturity of two weeks.

The procedure is as follows. The ECB sets the interest rate that will be applied on the main refinancing operations. This is followed by a tendering procedure, where the tender can either be at a fixed rate or a variable rate. Bids are made by Monetary Financial Institutions (MFIs), seeking liquidity in return for the delivery of collateral. Following this, the ECB decides on the total allotment and distributes *pro rata*.

The interest rate applied to the main refinancing operations is the Eurosystem's key interest rate. According to the ECB, the role of the MRO is to signal the monetary policy stance, steer short-term interest rates and provide the bulk of the liquidity to the banking system. By changing the interest rate and the size of allotments, the ECB can effect the market interest rate and the amount of liquidity. At the launch of the euro in January 1999, the refinancing rate was set by the ECB at 3%.

Standing facilities (credit lines)

The function of standing facilities is to provide or absorb liquidity with an overnight maturity. Two such facilities are available, namely a marginal lending facility and a deposit facility. The marginal lending facility may be used to obtain overnight liquidity from the national central banks. The deposit facility is used to make overnight deposits with the national central banks. The interest rate on the marginal lending facility provides a ceiling for the overnight market interest rate. The interest rate on the deposit facility provides a floor for the market rate. In January 1999, the lending rate and the deposit rate were set at 4.5% and 2% respectively. Money market interest rates, namely the overnight market interest rate (EONIA) and the euro interbank offered rates (EURIBOR) fluctuate around these levels.

Minimum reserve requirements

Reserve requirements allow MFIs to smooth out liquidity fluctuations. For example, a decrease in the reserve requirements reduces the liquidity shortage, tending to increase the money supply. Minimum reserves are applicable to all credit institutions in the euro area. The reserve requirement of each credit institution is calculated by applying a reserve ratio to selected liabilities of the balance sheet. The reserve ratio was set at 2% as from the start of stage three of EMU.

As for the operating target, namely the interest rate, there is some concern expressed over the sustainability of a 'one interest rate fits all' policy, especially in the context of the euro area where participating states are at different stages of the economic cycle. In the first couple of years of EMU, the biggest difference has been between the smaller, fast-growing economies of Ireland, Portugal and Finland and the bigger, sluggish economies of Germany and Italy. Given the economic and political realities of the euro area, the likelihood is that future monetary policy will reflect conditions in the bigger economies of France, Germany and Italy rather than in the peripheral economies of Ireland, Portugal and Finland.[26]

For exposition, a copy of an ECB press release relating to a monetary policy decision taken in March 2000 is reproduced here.

ECB PRESS RELEASE
Monetary policy decisions 16 March 2000

At today's meeting (which was also attended by the President of the European Commission, Mr. R. Prodi) the Governing Council of the ECB took the following monetary policy decisions:

1. The interest rate on the main refinancing operations of the Eurosystem will be raised by 0.25 percentage point to 3.5%, starting from the operation to be settled on 22 March 2000.
2. The interest rate on the marginal lending facility will be raised by 0.25 percentage point to 4.5%, with effect from 17 March 2000.
3. The interest rate on the deposit facility will be raised by 0.25 percentage point to 2.5%, with effect from 17 March 2000.

Following the regular examination of the outlook for price developments in the euro area on the basis of the latest information on monetary, financial and other economic developments, the Governing Council confirmed the assessment which was presented by the President of the ECB in his introductory statement at the press conference after the Governing Council meeting on 2 March 2000, as well as in the following issue of the ECB Monthly Bulletin. As noted there, economic conditions and prospects for the euro area appear to be better at present than at any time in the past decade. At the same time, upside risks to price stability were seen as a reason for vigilance. Today's decision addresses these upside risks, thereby contributing to maintaining the favourable outlook for the euro area economy.

With regard to the first pillar of the monetary policy strategy of the Eurosystem, the prolonged deviation of M3 growth from the reference value of 4.5% points to the existence of ample liquidity in the euro area, especially when seen in conjunction with the continued strong growth of credit granted to the private sector.

Considering the second pillar, most indicators and forecasts point to increasing upward pressures on consumer price inflation over the medium term. The strong rise in oil prices and the downward movement of the exchange rate of the euro in the past are putting upward pressure on import costs and producer prices. In the context of a strong cyclical upswing, there is a risk that these developments could, via second round effects, have lasting effects on consumer price inflation.

Today's increase in ECB interest rates follows the interest rate decisions taken on 4 November 1999 and 3 February 2000 and continues the policy of countering these emerging upside risks to price stability in a timely and pre-emptive manner. By ensuring a non-inflationary environment, this move will contribute to ensuring sustainable economic growth in the euro area.

Source: ECB website, http://www.ecb.int, March 2000

SUMMARY

1. Money is anything that is accepted as a medium of exchange. It is also a unit of account, a standard of deferred payment and a store of value. Narrow money supply

is defined as notes and coins and balances on current accounts. Broad money supply is defined as the narrow money supply plus balances on deposit accounts.

2. The banking system can create money. This phenomenon can be explained by the multiplier process. The deposit multiplier relates a change in reserves to the change in deposits. It depends inversely on the reserve ratio.

3. The classical loanable funds theory and the Keynesian liquidity preference theory are the two main models of interest rate determination. In the former, the interest rate is derived from the demand for and supply of funds. In the latter, it is the demand for and supply of money which determine the interest rate. For Keynes, the demand for money depends on the interest rate and the level of income.

4. The functions of the Central Bank are many and diverse. It is the government's and the banker's bank. It issues notes and coins. It regulates the financial institutions. It formulates monetary policy. The Central Bank of Ireland was formally established in 1943. Its powers were increased in 1971 and again in the late 1980s. The European Central Bank was established in 1998.

5. There are a number of ways by which the Central Bank can control the level of reserves and, in turn, the money supply. They include open market operations, changes in the discount rate and changes in the reserve requirements. Changes in these instruments affect the money supply and, in turn, other macroeconomic variables such as interest rates, output and employment.

6. The aim of monetary policy is price stability. Pre-1999, the Central Bank of Ireland employed an exchange rate targeting strategy. Since January 1999, there has been a single monetary policy in the euro area. The European System of Central Banks (ESCB), comprising the European Central Bank (ECB) and the national central banks, is responsible for the formulation and implementation of monetary policy.

KEY TERMS

Money	Lender of last resort
Medium of exchange	Monetary policy
Double coincidence of wants	Open market operations
Unit of account	Discount rate
Standard of deferred payment	Moral suasion
Store of value	Monetarists
Narrow money supply	Small open economy
Broad money supply	Liquidity
High-powered money	Short-term facility rate
Reserve ratio	Secured advances
Deposit multiplier	Foreign exchange swaps
Interest	Sale and repurchase agreements
Interest rate	Term deposits
Loanable funds theory	Price stability
Liquidity preference	European System of Central Banks
Transactions demand	European Central Bank
Precautionary demand	Yield curve

Active and idle balances   Eurosystem
Speculative demand   Main refinancing operations
Liquidity trap   Standing facilities

REVIEW QUESTIONS

1. What is 'money'? What are its functions? What are the different definitions of money supply in Ireland?
2. Explain how the banking system creates money.
3. Explain Keynes' three motives for holding money.
4. What are the functions of a central bank? How can a central bank influence the money supply?
5. Explain what effect an increase in the money supply has on the rate of interest and the level of output.
6. Explain the monetary policy strategy of the Eurosystem.

WORKING PROBLEMS

1. Patrick O'Hara deposits €5,000 with ABC Bank. The reserve requirement is 20%.
   (a) What is the value of the deposit multiplier?
   (b) What will be the increase in deposits?
   (c) Fill in the blanks in Table 13.7.

Table 13.7: Money creation

Stages	Deposits (€)	Reserves (€)	Loans (€)
1	5,000	____	____
2	4,000	800	____
3	____	____	2,560
4	2,560	____	____
5			
6 . . .			
etc. . .			
Total	€ ____	€ ____	€ ____

2. Suppose €400 falls from Milton's helicopter into the hands of Maria, a student. What is the minimum increase in the money supply that can result? What is the maximum increase that can result? (Assume the reserve ratio is 5%.)

MULTI-CHOICE QUESTIONS

1. Money:
    (a) is broadly defined as coins in circulation;
    (b) can be created by the banking system;
    (c) is equal to income;
    (d) both (a) and (c) above;
    (e) (a), (b) and (c) above.

2. A customer deposits €800 in AOB Bank. The required reserve ratio is 12.5%. What is the potential increase in the money supply?
    (a) €6,400;
    (b) €5,600;
    (c) €10,000;
    (d) € 8,750;
    (e) none of the above.

3. In the liquidity preference theory of money:
    (a) there are three motives for holding money; ✓
    (b) the money supply is interest rate inelastic; ✓
    (c) the interest rate is the price of money;
    (d) the demand for money is positively related to income;
    (e) all of the above.

4. An increase in the money supply results from:
    (a) an open market sale and a reduction in the reserve ratio;
    (b) a reduction in the discount rate and an increase in the reserve ratio;
    (c) an open market purchase and an increase in the reserve ratio;
    (d) an open market purchase and a reduction in the discount rate; ✓
    (e) none of the above.

5. In a SOE:
    (a) interest rates are largely influenced by external factors; ✓
    (b) an independent monetary policy is ineffective; ✓
    (c) the monetary authorities control the money stock;
    (d) both (a) and (b) above; ✓
    (e) both (b) and (c) above.

6. The primary objective of monetary policy in the euro area is:
    (a) price stability;
    (b) low interest rates;
    (c) a strong euro;
    (d) stable money supply growth;
    (e) none of the above.

TRUE OR FALSE (SUPPORT YOUR ANSWER)

1. There is no generally accepted means of payment in a barter economy.

2. Broad money supply is defined as notes and coins and current account balances.

3. The higher the reserve ratio, the greater the bank's ability to create money.

4. The liquidity preference is positively related to income and negatively related to interest rates.

5. A lowering of the discount rate increases the money supply.

6. The national central banks are responsible for the formulation of monetary policy in the euro area.

CASE STUDY

Extract from *The Irish Independent*
Loan rates up but the euro slide continues
by David Murphy

Europe pushed up interest rates again yesterday – but the euro continued to fall. This dealt a double blow to Ireland, bringing increased costs for home owners and further inflationary worries for the Government. The quarter per cent increase also erodes benefits workers had been expecting from the new national pay deal. The rise was intended to support the beleagured [sic] euro which has recently been falling rapidly against the dollar. But immediately after the authorities in Frankfurt made their announcement, the currency fell to fresh lows, pushing the Irish pound down to its weakest level ever against sterling, at 73.3p. The European Central Bank said the rise was due to rising inflation across the 11 eurozone countries. But economists said it did little to help Ireland's economic situation.

Home owners will now be faced with higher mortgage costs which will feed into inflation, causing further headaches for the Government, which has been warned by the Irish Congress of Trade Unions that rising costs could collapse the new national pay agreement. The rise in cost of home loans over the first four months of the year will nearly wipe out the basic 5.5pc minimum pay increase for lower paid employees who

⟶

have mortgages under £100,000. When inflation – currently at 4.6pc is included, the rate rise will knock out any real increase for a household with a £30,000 income, even if their mortgage was just £60,000.

Analysts were last night warning that the euro was in freefall. Two per cent was yesterday wiped off the euro's value in spite of Frankfurt's latest attempt to shore up the currency with a rates rise. The new increase means that the monthly cost of a £100,000 mortgage will go up by £13.75 to £651 and a £50,000 home loan will rise by £6.88 to £325. The bank's move is the third rate increase in as many months and has done nothing to revive the euro.

John Beggs, an economist with AIB, said inflation could rise from its current level of 4.6pc to 4.8pc before it begins to decline. On Tuesday, the Department of Finance predicted it would fall to 3pc by the year's end, but Mr Beggs predicted it would be 3.5pc by December. He warned that there was a growing risk that the Irish pound could fall as low as 70p sterling. Although this will make exports by Irish companies cheaper it will push up the costs of imports which may stoke up inflation.

Source: *The Irish Independent*, 28 April 2000.

Questions

1. What were the reasons given for the increase in euro interest rates? Explain your answer.
2. The article refers to a number of adverse effects arising from an increase in interest rates. What are these effects?
3. What is the main interest rate set by the ECB? Using the ECB *Monthly Bulletin*, report this interest rate, on a monthly basis, for the period January 1999–January 2000. What other interest rates are set by the ECB? Do the same exercise for these interest rates.

[NB: The ECB *Monthly Bulletins* can be found on the ECB website, www.ecb.int.]

APPENDIX 13.1: DERIVATION OF MONEY MULTIPLIER

In Section 13.1 we explained the deposit multiplier. The analysis was based on the assumption that no cash was held by the public and no excess reserves were held by banks. We now adjust our analysis to account for such possibilities. The result is a money multiplier which relates a change in the money supply to a change in high-powered money.

The broad money supply, M is defined as current and deposit account balances, D plus currency, C.

$$M = D + C \qquad [1]$$

High-powered money, H is defined as currency, C plus bank reserves, R.

$$H = C + R \qquad [2]$$

Dividing Equation [1] by Equation [2], we get the ratio of money supply to high-powered money:

$$\frac{M}{H} = \frac{D + C}{C + R} \qquad [3]$$

Dividing the numerator and the denominator by D, we get:

$$\frac{M}{H} = \frac{1 + \dfrac{C}{D}}{\dfrac{C}{D} + \dfrac{R}{D}} \qquad [4]$$

Multiplying both sides by H results in:

$$M = \frac{1 + \dfrac{C}{D}}{\dfrac{C}{D} + \dfrac{R}{D}} H \qquad [5]$$

If there is a change in the reserves component of H, we can adopt this equation to calculate the resulting change in money supply:

$$\Delta M = \frac{1 + \dfrac{C}{D}}{\dfrac{C}{D} + \dfrac{R}{D}} \Delta H \qquad [6]$$

Divide both sides by ΔH to get:

$$\frac{\Delta M}{\Delta H} = \frac{1 + \dfrac{C}{D}}{\dfrac{C}{D} + \dfrac{R}{D}} \qquad [13.3]$$

The left-hand side of Equation 13.3 is the change in money supply arising out of a given change in the reserves component of high-powered money. The right-hand side of Equation 13.3 is the money multiplier. Any change in the reserves leads to a multiple change in the money supply. Its value depends on the currency deposit ratio, $\frac{C}{D}$ and the reserve deposit ratio $\frac{R}{D}$. If $\frac{C}{D} = 0$, the money multiplier is equal to the simple deposit multiplier defined in the text.

Table 13.8: Central bank balance sheet December 1998

Assets	(£m)	Liabilities	(£m)
External Reserves	6,448	Currency	3,040
Others	1,931	Bank deposits	2,258
		Government deposits	1,674
		Others	1,405
	8,379		8,379

Source: *Central Bank Bulletin*, Spring 1999.

By using the data presented in Table 13.1 and Table 13.8, we can calculate the value for the money multiplier in Ireland for December 1998 as follows:

$$\frac{C}{D} = \frac{3,040}{46,575} = 0.065$$

and

$$\frac{R}{D} = \frac{2,258}{46,575} = 0.048$$

Hence,

$$\frac{\Delta M}{\Delta H} = \frac{1 + \dfrac{C}{D}}{\dfrac{C}{D} + \dfrac{R}{D}} = \frac{1 + 0.065}{0.065 + 0.048} = \frac{1.065}{0.113} = 9.42$$

In December 1998, the money multiplier in Ireland was 9.42 approximately. Hence, a £100 increase in high-powered money would lead to an increase in the money supply of £942.

CHAPTER 14

A BASIC FRAMEWORK FOR MACROECONOMIC ANALYSIS – THE IS/LM MODEL

'[The IS/LM diagram is] to macroeconomic textbooks what the benzene ring diagram is to textbooks of organic chemistry.'[1]

Christopher Bliss

'A basic version of that model [IS/LM] remains the core of many introductory textbooks, which use it throughout to analyse the effects of changes in some exogenous macroeconomic variables and, in particular, the impact of alternative monetary and fiscal policies.'[2]

Jordi Gali

CHAPTER OBJECTIVES

Upon completing this chapter, the student should understand:

- the purpose, derivation, position and slope of the IS curve;
- the purpose, derivation, position and slope of the LM curve;
- how interest rates and national income are determined in the IS/LM model;
- fiscal and monetary policy in the context of the IS/LM model;
- the policy differences between Keynesians and monetarists.

OUTLINE

14.1 The goods market and the IS curve
14.2 The money market and the LM curve
14.3 Equilibrium in the IS/LM model
14.4 Fiscal and monetary policy
14.5 The Keynesian-monetarist debate

INTRODUCTION

Sir John R. Hicks, the 1972 Nobel prize winner in economics, is credited with bringing the IS/LM model to the forefront of economic thinking. His famous article 'Mr Keynes and the Classics: a suggested interpretation', which first described a SI-LL (now commonly referred to as the IS-LM) framework, was published in the journal

Econometrica in 1937. With the help of refinements from economists such as Hansen (1887–1975), Klein (b. 1920), Modigliani (b. 1918) and Patinkin (b. 1922), the IS/LM model became the accepted framework for analysing macroeconomic concepts and policies.[3] It was the model which popularised many Keynesian ideas and, moreover, dominated macroeconomic theory until the 1970s. Notwithstanding the achievements of others, it was Hicks who converted many of his contemporaries to the Keynesian doctrine – a doctrine which many had failed to comprehend given the revolutionary nature of the ideas and the obscurity of the language used.

The IS/LM framework is an extension of the Keynesian income determination model which we introduced in Chapter 12. Many assumptions underlie both models. First, both are demand-side models with aggregate expenditure determining output and employment. Linked to this is the assumption that the economy is operating at less than full capacity, i.e. equilibrium is at less than full employment in both models. Second, prices are assumed to be exogenous, i.e. they are assumed 'fixed'.[4] Third, both models are developed for a closed economy.

These assumptions can also be viewed as inherent weaknesses of the model. Other criticisms might include the absence of any reference to expectations and the supply-side of the economy where supply bottlenecks may exist. Notwithstanding these omissions, the IS/LM model has been described as the most successful textbook model in the history of macroeconomics.

The IS/LM framework differs in a number of ways from the simple Keynesian model. First, investment is now treated as a function of interest rates. Second, the money market is included. Moreover, it analyses the interaction between two markets: the goods market and the money market. Because both markets are included, the effects of fiscal and monetary policy on interest rates and income can be examined.

The outline to this chapter is as follows. We begin by analysing the goods market. A goods market equilibrium curve is derived. An analysis of the money market follows. Central to this is the derivation of a money market equilibrium curve. Following this, both markets and their respective curves are brought together to analyse the effects of fiscal and monetary policy changes on both interest rates and income levels. Finally, the differences in policy between Keynesians and monetarists are briefly discussed.

14.1   THE GOODS MARKET AND THE IS CURVE

The IS (Investment/Savings) curve is the goods market equilibrium curve. The IS curve depicts the negative relationship between interest rates and income that exists in the goods market.[5] It can be derived from the Keynesian income determination model. However, we must first examine investment and its determinants in greater detail before we can derive the IS curve. In Chapter 12 we assumed that investment was independent of the explanatory variable, income. Investment was exogenous: it was determined by variables outside the model. We now adjust this in order to incorporate interest rates as an explanatory variable. With this adjustment to the model, investment is now a function of the interest rate. Figure 14.1 shows the relationship between interest rates and the level of investment when all other factors including expectations are held constant.

Figure 14.1: The investment function

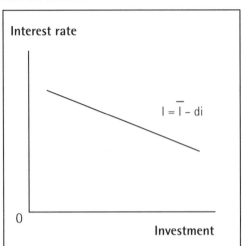

The level of investment expenditure is related to the cost of borrowing investment funds. The investment function is downward sloping, depicting a negative relationship between interest rates and investment. Lower interest rates induce higher investment expenditure. Likewise, high interest rates induce businesses to defer or postpone investment decisions. A change in expectations for future corporate earnings causes the entire curve to shift.

Another possibility is for a firm to use its own funds to finance capital projects. However, if the market rate of return on these funds is high, there is an opportunity cost involved. The firm can place the funds into an interest-bearing account rather than undertake the investment project. The higher the rate of return, the less likely the investment project is to be financed from these funds. The negative relationship still holds.

The equation for the investment function is as follows:

$$\mathbf{I = \bar{I} - di}$$ **[14.1]**

where: I = total investment expenditure; $\bar{I}$ = autonomous investment expenditure; d = the investment sensitivity to interest rates; i = interest rates.

The position of the investment function is determined by the level of autonomous investment whereas the slope is given by the sensitivity of investment to interest rate changes, measured by d. This sensitivity measure plays an important role in the slope of the IS curve and the subsequent effectiveness of both fiscal and monetary policy.

Investment decisions must include interest rates as an explanatory variable in order to derive the IS curve. We begin with the Keynesian income determination model. Changes in interest rates will cause investment and ultimately income to change.

The IS curve: derivation, position and slope

The IS curve is derived from the Keynesian cross diagram as shown in Figure 14.2.

Figure 14.2: Derivation of the IS curve

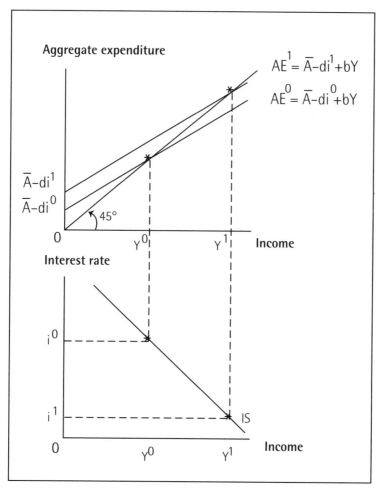

In the top diagram the AE curve, AE^0 is drawn for a particular level of interest rate, i^{0}.[6] This corresponds to an equilibrium level of income, Y^0. In equilibrium, expenditure is equal to income, AE = Y. This, in turn, gives us our first point in (i,Y) space.

Let us suppose interest rates decline, from i^0 to i^1. Lower interest rates increase the level of investment expenditure and, subsequently, aggregate expenditure. The higher AE function results in a new and higher equilibrium level of income, Y^1. This lower interest rate and higher income level gives us the second point in (i,Y) space. We could continue to change the interest rate and find corresponding levels of income. The locus of points results in a downward sloping curve, illustrating the inverse relationship between interest rates and income.

We know that when the aggregate expenditure curve crosses the 45° line, the goods market is in equilibrium. Therefore, since every point on the IS curve is derived from these equilibrium points, the goods market is in equilibrium at every point along the IS curve. In other words, this locus of points reflects equilibrium in the goods market.

Definition
The IS curve depicts the combination of interest rates and income levels that is consistent with equilibrium in the goods market.

The equation for the IS curve is derived algebraically in Appendix 14.1.

The position of any given IS curve is determined by the level of autonomous spending. $\bar{A}$, consisting of autonomous consumer, investment and government expenditure, remained constant throughout the derivation of the IS curve. Any discretionary change in $\bar{A}$ will result in a shift of the IS curve. An increase in $\bar{A}$ results in a rightward shift whereas a decrease in $\bar{A}$ results in a leftward shift. In terms of broad macroeconomic policies any change in fiscal policy, either expansionary or contractionary, results in a change in the position of the IS curve. This, in turn, helps us to analyse the effect of fiscal policy changes on the equilibrium level of interest rates and income. This is discussed in Section 14.4 below.

The two factors which largely determine the slope of the IS curve are the interest rate sensitivity of investment and the expenditure multiplier. For example, the IS curve is relatively steep when investment is insensitive to changes in interest rates and the multiplier is relatively small. The opposite is true for a relatively flat IS curve. The slope of the IS curve has important implications for the effectiveness of fiscal and monetary policy.

As an exercise, draw the relevant IS curves when the multiplier is low/high and for low/high interest rate-investment sensitivity measures.

We will now turn to the money market to derive the LM curve.

14.2 THE MONEY MARKET AND THE LM CURVE

The LM curve is the money market equilibrium curve. It depicts the positive relationship between interest rates and income that exists in the money market.

The LM curve: derivation, position and slope

The LM (Liquidity/Money supply) curve is derived from equilibrium points in the money market as shown in Figure 14.3. Keynes suggested that the demand for money is inversely related to the interest rate. Therefore, the demand curve is downward sloping: as interest rates rise, the demand for money falls. The money supply is determined by the monetary authorities and is therefore independent of the rate of interest. Hence, the supply curve for money ($\frac{\bar{M}}{P}$) is vertical (denoted by M_s in Chapter 13).[7] At the intersection between the demand curve and the supply curve, the money market is in equilibrium. At this particular rate of interest, the demand for real balances equals the supply of real balances. This is shown in the right-hand panel of Figure 14.3 (see the money market as illustrated in Figure 13.10).

Figure 14.3: *Derivation of the LM curve*

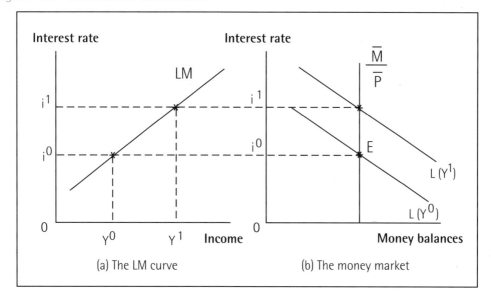

(a) The LM curve   (b) The money market

The interest rate and the level of income at point E in the money market gives us our first point in (i,Y) space, (i^0,Y^0). The demand for money curve is drawn for a particular level of income.

Suppose that the level of income increases to Y^1. As a result, the demand for money increases. This is shown by a rightward shift of the money demand curve. If the supply of money is held constant, the subsequent excess demand of money pushes up equilibrium interest rates. Thus, as income increases, interest rates increase.

If we plot interest rates against income, we get the second point in (i,Y) space, (i^1,Y^1). We could continue to change the income level and find corresponding rates of interest. The locus of points results in an upward sloping curve illustrating a positive relationship between income and interest rates in the money market. This is the LM curve.

Definition
The LM curve depicts the combination of interest rates and income levels that is consistent with equilibrium in the money market.

The equation for the LM curve is derived algebraically in Appendix 14.1.

The position of the LM curve is determined by the real money supply. When we derived the LM curve, the real money supply was held constant. Any discretionary change in the real money supply, $\frac{\overline{M}}{\overline{P}}$ will result in a shift of the LM curve. For example, an increase in $\frac{\overline{M}}{\overline{P}}$ results in a rightward shift of the LM curve. Similarly, a decrease in $\frac{\overline{M}}{\overline{P}}$ results in a leftward shift of the LM curve. Monetary policy aimed at changing the real money supply will cause the position of the LM curve to change. This, in turn, affects the equilibrium level of interest rates and income. Section 14.4 below deals with these matters in greater detail.

The slope of the LM curve is largely determined by the income and the interest rate elasticities of money demand. A large income elasticity of money demand combined with a small interest rate elasticity of money demand results in a relatively steep LM curve. A relatively flat LM curve results from a combination of a small income sensitivity and a large interest rate sensitivity of money demand. The slope of the LM curve has important implications for the effectiveness of fiscal and monetary policy.

As an exercise draw the relevant LM curves for different combinations of income elasticities of money demand and interest rate elasticities of money demand.

14.3 EQUILIBRIUM IN THE IS/LM MODEL

The IS curve depicts the negative relationship that exists in the goods market between interest rates and income. At all points along the IS curve, the goods market is in equilibrium. The LM curve shows the combinations of interest rates and income at which the money market is in equilibrium. All points on the LM curve are points where money demand equals the stock of money. The IS and LM curves together determine the equilibrium interest rate and the equilibrium income level. We know from Chapter 12 that the equilibrium income level may not coincide with the full-employment output level: it is independent of the labour market. The market clearing position is illustrated in Figure 14.4.

Figure 14.4: Equilibrium in the IS/LM model

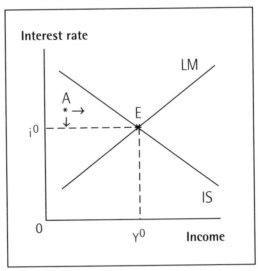

In this diagram the IS and LM curves intersect at (i^0, Y^0). This point E represents the equilibrium interest rate, i^0, and equilibrium income level, Y^0. At this point, the goods market and the money market are in equilibrium simultaneously. The forces of excess demand and excess supply act together to move the economy towards this equilibrium position. Let us take an example.

Consider point A in Figure 14.4. Point A is to the left of the IS curve. It is a point of excess demand in the goods market.[8] This excess demand will result in unplanned inventory depletions, and eventually to an increase in output. There is a subsequent move to the right, towards the IS curve.

In addition, point A is above the LM curve. It is a point of excess supply in the money market.[9] This excess supply of money will result in a downward movement of interest rates. There is a move towards the LM curve. Taken together, the economy moves from a point of disequilibrium to the one point where the goods market and the money market are in equilibrium simultaneously.

The separate analysis of the goods market (Section 14.1) and the money market (Section 14.2) is a deliberate exercise in understanding the framework to this model. In the real world, however, the goods market and the money market are dependent on each other. The interdependency between these two markets is explained in two examples below.

Example 1

The demand for money (a money market concept) is influenced by the level of income which is determined in the goods market.

Example 2

The level of investment expenditure (a goods market concept) is influenced by the rate of interest which is determined in the money market.

This interdependency has important consequences for government policy. For example, a policy which is targeted exclusively at the goods market may have implications for the money market. The inverse is also true.

Finally, any change in fiscal and/or monetary policy will change the position of the respective IS or LM curves and, in turn, affect the equilibrium interest rate and income level. A more detailed analysis follows.

14.4 FISCAL AND MONETARY POLICY

Fiscal policy is concerned with government expenditure and taxation and how they affect national output. Monetary policy refers to the use of money supply, credit and interest rates to influence national output. Changes in these policies and in particular their effect on interest rates and national income can be explained by using the IS/LM framework. Let us begin with a fiscal policy change.

Fiscal policy

Suppose the government decides to increase expenditure. We know from the Keynesian income determination model that an increase in expenditure will increase national income and do so by a multiple of itself. The increase in income may be quite large, depending on the size of the multiplier. However, this is a very simple model where interest rates are assumed to be fixed. The analysis is a little more complicated when interest rates are allowed to vary.

Figure 14.5 illustrates the effect of a change in government expenditure. The original equilibrium point reflects the old level of government expenditure. We know from our analysis of the IS curve that an increase in expenditure shifts the IS curve out and to the right. Interest rates rise, from i^0 to i^1. There is also an increase in the level of equilibrium income. A more detailed explanation is required.

Figure 14.5: Expansionary fiscal policy – an increase in $\bar{G}$

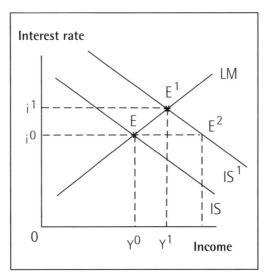

The Keynesian model predicts an increase in income arising out of an increase in government expenditure. Higher income levels increase money demand. The subsequent excess demand for money forces up interest rates. Higher interest rates have a negative effect on investment expenditure. The decline in investment expenditure causes a reduction in national income. As a result the overall increase in national income is not as large as originally predicted. This knock-on effect is known as crowding out. The extent of the crowding out can be measured by the move from E^2 to E^1, in Figure 14.5. In summary, higher public expenditure and its subsequent effect on national income is crowded out by higher interest rates and lower private spending.[10]

Expansionary fiscal policy and its effect on economic variables is shown below.[11]

Increase in $\bar{G}$ → increases Y → increases L → increases
i → reduces I → reduces Y

In this example, the initial increase in government spending does increase national income, but by less than it would if the interest rate was fixed (as in the Keynesian model of income determination).

Belief in the effectiveness of fiscal policy has changed over the years. Fiscal policy was in the ascendancy after World War II and in particular (as we saw in Chapter 12) during the 1960s. Changes in public expenditure or taxes were believed to have a large influence on the level of aggregate expenditure and, in turn, on national output. The belief in the active use of fiscal policy was particularly strong in the US and in the UK.

In the 1970s most governments, with few exceptions (Ireland being one), abandoned fiscal policy as a method of increasing national output and employment. In the 1990s, the use of fiscal policy re-emerged as an alternative policy to the supply-side measures advocated by the followers of Reaganomics and Thatcherism. One of its strongest contemporary supporters is J. K. Galbraith (b. 1908) who has strongly advocated the use of fiscal policy. As recently as 1993, Galbraith suggested counter-cyclical fiscal policy was appropriate for Ireland.

Monetary policy

A change in monetary policy is now considered. Suppose the monetary authorities decide to increase the supply of money in the economy. The effect of a change in the stock of money is shown in Figure 14.6. The original equilibrium point, E reflects the old level of money stock. We know from our discussion in a previous section that an increase in the real money supply shifts the LM curve to the right. Interest rates fall, from i^0 to i^1. A higher level of equilibrium income (Y^1) also results. A more comprehensive explanation follows.

Figure 14.6: Expansionary monetary policy – an increase in $\frac{\bar{M}}{\bar{P}}$

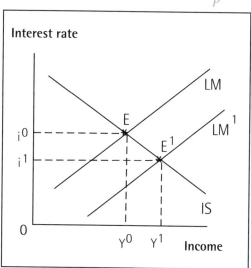

Lower interest rates induce higher investment expenditure. The increase in expenditure will contribute to an increase in national income. Higher income levels increase the demand for money which puts upward pressure on interest rates. As a result the initial easing of interest rates may be partly offset by this subsequent increase.

Definition

The process where a change in monetary policy affects aggregate expenditure and national output is called the monetary transmission mechanism.

Expansionary monetary policy and its effect on economic variables is shown below.

$$\text{Increase in } \frac{\overline{M}}{P} \rightarrow \text{reduces i} \rightarrow \text{increases I} \rightarrow \text{increases Y}$$

Monetary policy as a tool to control inflation became popular once again in the early 1970s with the advent of monetarism and the downfall of Keynesian economics. In more recent times, however, monetary policy has been used to help countries out of recession. For example, in both Japan and the EU, monetary policy has been used as an instrument to boost spending and ultimately national income.

A policy mix

A policy mix is the simultaneous use of fiscal and monetary policy. One example which is quite common among policy-makers is a monetary accommodation of a fiscal expansion. This is where the adverse effects of fiscal expansion, namely higher interest rates, are lessened by deliberate increases in the money supply.[12] National output increases but there is no corresponding rise in interest rates. This is illustrated in Figure 14.7.

Figure 14.7: A policy mix – a monetary accommodation of a fiscal expansion

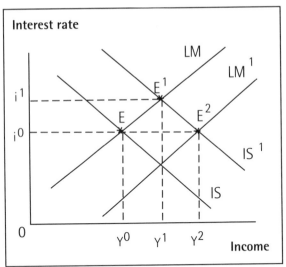

Expansionary fiscal policy shifts the IS curve rightwards, from IS to IS^1. As a result, income and interest rates rise, from Y^0 to Y^1 and from i^0 to i^1 respectively. To counteract the rise in interest rates, the Central Bank increases the money stock. This shifts the LM curve to the right, from LM to LM^1. This expansion of the money supply causes a further increase in income from Y^1 to Y^2 and a fall in interest rates from i^1 to i^0. The net effect of this particular policy mix is a relatively large increase in income from Y^0 to Y^2 combined with no change in the interest rate level. The monetary accommodation of the fiscal expansion keeps interest rates at the original level, i^0.

Monetary accommodation of fiscal expansion was used by the US authorities during the recessionary period 1974–75 and again in 1981–82.

CASE STUDY

Extract from *The Economist*
Up and down

Although Japan's economy is officially in recession again, it is stronger than it looks.

The Japanese economy is following in the footsteps of the Grand Old Duke of York. Having marched up the hill, earlier last year, it now appears to be marching swiftly down again. After the massive fiscal stimuli injected into the economy in recent years, along with near-zero short-term interest rates, Japan's latest slump suggests that the economy is even sicker than originally thought. Below the surface, however, there are reasons to believe that it is slowly on the mend.

In the first half of 1999, Japan's GDP grew at an annual rate of 5.1%. But it then shrank in the third quarter, and the head of the country's Economic Planning Agency has warned that GDP probably fell again in the fourth quarter of last year (official figures are not due until next month). Two consecutive quarters of contraction technically put Japan back into recession. However, Japan's GDP figures are notoriously unreliable, swinging wildly from quarter to quarter and subject to large revisions. The official figures probably overstated growth during the first half of the year, and then overstated the slowdown in the second half. Some economists reckon that a better gauge is industrial production, which continued to expand throughout the second half of last year.

For 1999 as a whole, Japan's economy grew by an estimated 0.6%. Disappointing, yes, but better than the 1.1% decline expected by *The Economist*'s poll of forecasters in the middle of last year. This shows that fiscal policy does work. Indeed, one reason why growth stumbled in late 1999 is that by then the fiscal stimulus had been exhausted. The latest budget package will spur the economy again this spring. The snag is that with a budget deficit already at 8% of GDP, the path of Japan's public-sector debt now looks scary. Government borrowing cannot permanently prop up the economy; private-sector spending needs to revive.

Household spending has been depressed by continuing deflationary pressures: prices, wages and bank lending are all falling. Despite this, some on the Bank of Japan's policy board are talking about raising interest rates. Instead, the bank should be pursuing more aggressive monetary expansion, either through unsterilised foreign-exchange intervention or by buying government bonds. Not only would this help to take some of the strain off fiscal policy, but by adjusting the monetary and fiscal mix, it would also help to hold down the yen. The currency has in fact weakened over the past few weeks, but any renewed strength would risk choking exports.

. . .

Source: *The Economist*, 12 February 2000, p. 15.

Questions

1. Using the IS/LM model, outline the predicted effects of a fiscal stimulus and a monetary expansion. How has the Japanese economy actually performed?

2. Why does the author favour expansionary monetary policy instead of an interest rate increase? Explain using the IS/LM model.
3. Aside from foreign trade and the exchange rate issue, why is the IS/LM model more appropriate in analysing the Japanese economy rather than, say, the Irish economy, at the start of the new millennium?

Answers on website

14.5 THE KEYNESIAN-MONETARIST DEBATE

How effective fiscal and monetary policies are can be explained by the slopes of the IS and LM curves. The slopes in turn are determined largely by a range of sensitivity measures which were outlined in Sections 14.1 and 14.2 above.

Fiscal policy is more effective when the LM curve is flat and the IS curve is steep. We know from our discussion of the IS curve that a steep IS curve results from investment expenditure which is insensitive to interest rate changes. Likewise, it is the particular combination of a demand for money which is insensitive to income and highly sensitive to interest rates which results in a flat LM curve. The inverse is true for the case of ineffective fiscal policy.

Monetary policy, in contrast, is relatively effective when there is a flat IS curve and a steep LM curve. When the sensitivity of investment to changes in interest rates is high, the subsequent IS curve is relatively flat. A steep LM curve results from a demand for money which is sensitive to income and insensitive to interest rates. The opposite is true for ineffective monetary policy.

This rather technical discussion prepares us for the debate between the Keynesian view and the monetarist view of either policy.

Keynesians argue that the IS curve is relatively steep, and is so because investment is insensitive to changes in interest rates. A steep IS curve results from investment pessimism. A change in interest rates does not entice investors to undertake new projects which would lead to an increase in economic activity. Of greater importance is their belief in a relatively flat or, in the extreme case, a horizontal LM curve.

This hypothetical situation is known as the liquidity trap which, in theory, could exist at very low interest rates where the demand for money may be infinitely large. In effect, people are willing to hold any amount of money at this given interest rate. However, even Keynes himself doubted the very existence of such a case. Nonetheless, since it was felt that the IS curve was relatively steep and the LM curve relatively flat, fiscal policy was preferred to monetary policy.

In contrast, monetarists argued that the IS curve is relatively flat, reflecting investment expenditure which is highly responsive to changes in interest rates. Their belief in a relatively steep LM curve, and vertical in the extreme, is a return to the classical doctrine. The vertical LM curve arises from an absence of any speculative demand for money. The demand for money does not change in response to changes in interest rates. Any increase in output which results directly from a rise in public expenditure is offset by subsequent increases in interest rates which have an adverse effect on private spending. This possibility is known as crowding out. In these circumstances, fiscal policy is largely ineffective.

The Keynesian/monetarist controversy is illustrated in Figure 14.8. In Figure 14.8(a) the IS curve is relatively steep, reflecting the Keynesian position. The monetarist position of a vertical LM curve is depicted in Figure 14.8(b).

Figure 14.8: The Keynesian and monetarist debate

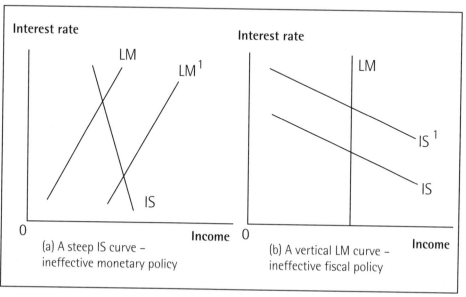

(a) A steep IS curve – ineffective monetary policy

(b) A vertical LM curve – ineffective fiscal policy

Both the liquidity trap and crowding out are extreme cases and are unlikely to exist in reality. Notwithstanding this fact, the above analysis is worthwhile in that it provides us with a brief account of some of the differences between two of the main schools of economic thought. It is also important to acknowledge that both these alternatives, as represented above, ignore supply-side considerations and changes in the price level. These must be included in a more comprehensive discussion of the Keynesian/monetarist controversy.

SUMMARY

1. The IS/LM model is a static, short-run model which integrates the goods market with the money market. It is similar to the Keynesian model of income determination in that prices are fixed and demand determines output and employment. It is a model for a closed economy. It differs to the extent that interest rates are endogenous and the money market matters.
2. The IS curve illustrates the combinations of interest rates and income levels for which the goods market is in equilibrium. It is negatively sloped. Lower interest rates increase the level of investment which, in turn, increases national income. Its position is determined by the level of autonomous spending. The interest rate elasticity of investment and the multiplier determine its slope.
3. The LM curve shows the combinations of interest rates and income levels where the demand for and supply of money are equal. It is positively sloped. Higher income

levels increase the demand for money which, in turn, increases interest rates. The stock of money determines the position of the LM curve. Its slope is determined by the interest rate and income elasticities of money demand.

4. The goods market and the money market do not operate independently. The intersection of the IS curve and the LM curve is the equilibrium point. Both markets are in equilibrium simultaneously at this point. A change in fiscal policy shifts the IS curve whereas a change in monetary policy shifts the LM curve. Changes in equilibrium interest rates and income levels will result.

5. Expansionary fiscal policy results in higher interest rates and higher income levels. Crowding out limits the increase in national income. Expansionary monetary policy results in lower interest rates and higher income levels. An example of a policy mix is a monetary accommodation of a fiscal expansion.

6. The IS/LM framework is very useful in explaining the divergent views of Keynesians and monetarists. The liquidity trap is the extreme Keynesian case. The classical case of full crowding out is supported by the monetarists.

KEY TERMS

IS curve
Marginal efficiency of capital
Interest rate elasticity of investment
LM curve
Income elasticity of money demand
Interest rate elasticity of money demand
Fiscal policy
Monetary policy
Transmission mechanism
Monetarists
Policy mix
Liquidity trap
Crowding out

REVIEW QUESTIONS

1. What are the differences between the Keynesian model of income determination and the IS/LM model? What are the limitations to the IS/LM model?

2. Explain why the IS curve slopes down from left to right. What factors determine the position and the slope of the IS curve?

3. Why is the money market equilibrium curve upward sloping? What factors determine its slope?

4. Explain what effect a contractionary monetary policy would have on the equilibrium level of interest rates and national income.

5. What effect would a contractionary fiscal policy have on (a) the IS curve; (b) equilibrium income and, finally (c) equilibrium interest rates.

6. Explain 'crowding out'. What action can the Central Bank take to avoid the rise in interest rates which is usually associated with crowding out?

WORKING PROBLEMS

1. The following equations describe an economy:

$$C = .85Y$$
$$I = 700 - 25i$$
$$\bar{G} = 540$$
$$L = .5Y - 70i$$
$$\frac{\bar{M}}{P} = 400$$

   (a) Derive the IS equation.
   (b) Derive the LM equation.
   (c) Calculate the equilibrium levels of interest rates and income.
   (d) Sketch the equilibrium position.

[Calculations to two decimal places]

2. If investment is insensitive to changes in the interest rate, is monetary or fiscal policy more effective? Explain your answer.

MULTI-CHOICE QUESTIONS

1. The IS/LM model is an extension of the Keynesian income determination model with an adjustment for:
   (a) wages;
   (b) income levels;
   (c) exchange rates;
   (d) interest rates;
   (e) none of the above.

2. The IS curve:
   (a) is derived from the goods market;
   (b) shows combinations of interest rates and income such that expenditure equals income;
   (c) is the goods market equilibrium curve;
   (d) is drawn for a given level of autonomous spending;
   (e) all of the above.

3. The slope of the LM curve:
   (a) is determined by the interest rate elasticity of investment;
   (b) is relatively flat given a small income elasticity of money demand;
   (c) is relatively steep given a high interest rate elasticity of money demand;
   (d) both (a) and (b) above;
   (e) both (a) and (c) above.

4. Suppose investment becomes less responsive to changes in interest rates. As a result the:
   (a) IS curve will shift to the left;
   (b) IS curve will shift to the right;
   (c) IS curve will become flatter;
   (d) IS curve will become steeper;
   (e) none of the above.

5. Suppose the government decreases public expenditure. All other things equal, the likely result will be:
   (a) an increase in interest rates;
   (b) a decrease in national income;
   (c) a decrease in interest rates;
   (d) both (a) and (b) above;
   (e) both (b) and (c) above.

6. The extreme case of crowding out:
   (a) occurs when the LM curve is horizontal;
   (b) is caused by a large interest rate elasticity of money demand;
   (c) leads to ineffective fiscal policy;
   (d) is supported by Keynesians;
   (e) none of the above.

TRUE OR FALSE (SUPPORT YOUR ANSWER)

1. The IS/LM model is a demand-side model.

2. Equilibrium prices and income can be determined by the IS/LM model.

3. The position of the IS curve is determined by the size of the multiplier and the interest rate sensitivity of investment.

4. The real money supply is constant along any given money market equilibrium curve.

5. A cut in taxes is an example of contractionary fiscal policy and is likely to result in lower income and interest rate levels.

6. In the case of full crowding out, fiscal policy is ineffective.

CASE STUDY

Extract from *The Economist*
Phew

Until recently, it seemed that the most embarrassing section in the government's report would be on the economy. Surveys of business opinion and consumer confidence indicated that recession was on the way. Now, the economy is the government's chief source of self-satisfaction. For once, slowdown has not given way to recession: the fourth quarter of last year, when GDP was flat, was probably the low point.

. . .

All this is largely the result of luck: the world economy did not fall to bits after all. Most of the credit for good judgement belongs to the Bank, whose string of interest-rate cuts, beginning last October, helped stave off recession. This has not, of course, stopped the government from claiming some glory. Fair enough. It was Mr Brown who gave the Bank control of interest rates in May 1997. And he would surely not have escaped blame had there been a recession.

In budgetary policy, Mr Brown stuck to tight Tory spending plans for his first two years. Now the government is emphasising how much it is spending rather than how little. In 1999–2000 and the next two years, ministers expect expenditure to grow by $2^3/4\%$ a year in real terms – in all likelihood, faster than GDP. To finance this, taxes will also rise. As a result, the chancellor still expects to keep to the two rules he has set himself: that he will maintain a 'current surplus' over the economic cycle; and that net public-sector debt should average no more than 40% again over the cycle.

Yet Mr Brown sees macroeconomic stability as only the first stage of his ambitions for the British economy. He also wants to raise the country's long-run rate of economic growth, and to that end ministers are dreaming up a host of microeconomic ideas.

. . .

Source: *The Economist*, 31 July 1999, p. 35.

Questions

1. Explain, in words, how a 'string of interest-rate cuts' could help to 'stave off recession'.
2. Using the IS/LM framework, explain the effects on the economy of higher public spending. Why would the Chancellor have kept spending plans tight in the first two years of the administration only to loosen them later on?
3. How does an increase in taxes affect (i) the IS curve; (ii) the government budget surplus; (iii) output? Do this exercise for both cases, that is, with and without the increase in government spending (mentioned in Question 2 above).

APPENDIX 14.1: ALGEBRAIC DERIVATION OF THE IS AND LM CURVES

To derive the equation for the IS curve we begin with the aggregate expenditure function:

$$AE \equiv C + I + G \qquad \text{[14.2]}$$

In the Keynesian aggregate expenditure model, investment was autonomous. In the IS/LM model, it depends on the interest rate. Therefore, we will define the components of aggregate expenditure in the following way:

$$C = \overline{C} + bY \qquad \text{[14.3]}$$

$$I = \overline{I} - di \qquad \text{[14.1]}$$

$$G = \overline{G} \qquad \text{[12.14]}$$

Substitute these equations into Equation 14.2:

$$AE = \overline{C} + bY + \overline{I} - di + \overline{G} \qquad \text{[14.4]}$$

Let $\overline{A} = \overline{C} + \overline{I} + \overline{G}$ the autonomous components of aggregate expenditure.

Substitute $\overline{A}$ into Equation 14.4:

$$AE = \overline{A} - di + bY \qquad \text{[14.5]}$$

Equilibrium in the goods market is where:

$$Y = AE \qquad \text{[12.9]}$$

Substitute Y for AE in Equation 14.5 and solve for Y:

$$Y = \frac{1}{1-b}(\overline{A} - di) \qquad \text{[14.6]}$$

Let $k = \dfrac{1}{1-b}$ as in Chapter 12. Substituting this expression into Equation 14.6 yields:

$$Y = k(\overline{A} - di) \qquad \text{[14.7]}$$

Equation 14.7 shows that the relationship between the interest rate and income in the goods market is negative. Therefore, the IS curve is downward sloping. The strength of the relationship will be reflected in the slope of the line. This is determined by the expenditure multiplier, k and the interest rate elasticity of investment, d.

To derive the equation for the LM curve, we begin with the money market. The demand for money equation is:

$$L = jY - hi \qquad [14.8]$$

where j is the sensitivity of money demand to changes in income and h is the sensitivity of money demand to changes in the interest rate.

In equilibrium in the money market, money demand equals real money supply $(\frac{\overline{M}}{\overline{P}})$. Hence,

$$jY - hi = \frac{\overline{M}}{P} \qquad [14.9]$$

Solve for Y:

$$Y = \frac{1}{j} \left(hi + \frac{\overline{M}}{P} \right) \qquad [14.10]$$

In terms of i:

$$i = \frac{1}{h} \left(jY - \frac{\overline{M}}{P} \right) \qquad [14.11]$$

We can see that the relationship between the interest rate and income in the money market is positive. The LM curve is upward sloping. The strength of the relationship is reflected in the slope of the line. The variables which affect the slope of the LM curve are the two elasticity measures, j and h.

CHAPTER 15

OPEN ECONOMY MACROECONOMICS

'There is no way in which one can buck the market.'[1]

Margaret Thatcher

'In short, there is *no* meaningful economic argument for a single currency in Europe – now or ever.'[2]

Bernard Connolly

CHAPTER OBJECTIVES

Upon completing this chapter, the student should understand:

- the balance of payments;
- exchange rate determination;
- devaluation and the currency crisis;
- Ireland's record within the ERM;
- Economic and Monetary Union and the single currency.

OUTLINE

15.1 Balance of payments
15.2 Exchange rate determination
15.3 Exchange rate regimes and the balance of payments
15.4 The European Monetary System (EMS)
15.5 Economic and Monetary Union
15.6 The Irish experience

INTRODUCTION

In Chapter 10 we examined the circular flow of economic activity. We began by studying the exchange between households and firms. We then adjusted this model to include the government and the foreign sector. A similar method of analysis was used for the income determination model. Variables such as prices, wages and interest rates were assumed to be fixed. Moreover, the government and the foreign sector were initially excluded before they were eventually incorporated into the model.

Even with these adjustments for the foreign sector, our examination of macro-economics until now has largely ignored the value of the domestic currency *vis-à-vis*

oreign currencies and its role in the economy. Foreign interest rates, exchange rate
volatility, foreign markets and external trade were only briefly mentioned. In reality,
these variables are very important and play a vital role in any modern economy. We
now examine these variables in detail.

15.1 BALANCE OF PAYMENTS

We begin our investigation of the foreign sector by discussing the balance of payments.

Definition

The balance of payments is a set of accounts showing all economic transactions between
residents of the home country and the rest of the world in any one year.

It is a 'flow' concept rather than a 'stock' concept. We are not measuring the assets and
liabilities at a point in time. Rather, we are looking at outflows and inflows over a
period of time, usually a year.

Receipts of foreign exchange from the rest of the world (e.g. arising from exports,
sale of government bonds or 'gilts' etc.) are treated as a credit item and are denoted
by a positive (+) sign in the balance of payments. Payments of foreign exchange to
the rest of the world (e.g. arising from imports, purchase of French works of art etc.)
are treated as a debit item and are denoted by a negative (–) sign.

At the end of the calendar year this statement must balance, i.e. receipts or inflows
equals payments or outflows. It does so by following the principles of double-entry
book-keeping.

The balance of payments consists of two subsections: the current account and the
capital and financial account. These are explained below.

Current account balance

Definition

The current account in the balance of payments records all visible and invisible trade.

Merchandise trade is an example of visible trade. Invisible trade includes services such
as tourism and travel.

This section of the Irish balance of payments is subdivided into four categories,
including:

- merchandise trade, as explained below;
- services such as tourism and travel, communications and financial services;
- net income. This includes investment income arising from Irish investors' investment
  abroad and foreign investors' investments in Ireland;
- current transfers such as Irish aid to developing countries and monies from EU funds.

The addition of all these plus a number of miscellaneous items is defined as the current
account balance. If the value of receipts is greater than the value of payments, a surplus

is recorded. If the value of receipts is less than the value of payments, a deficit is recorded. In 1999 there was a current account surplus of £446m (€567m).

Merchandise trade balance

The merchandise trade balance is the most publicly discussed component of the current account.[3]

Definition

The merchandise trade balance, or the balance of trade as it is sometimes called, is a record of transactions of merchandise exports (X) and imports (M) during a year.

If the value of exports exceeds the value of imports (X > M) a trade surplus results. A trade deficit results when the value of imports exceeds the value of exports (M > X). If the value of exports and imports is equal (X = M) we have a trade balance.

Figure 15.1 shows the record of the Irish trade balance between 1975 and 1999.

Figure 15.1   Trade balance in Ireland, 1975–99

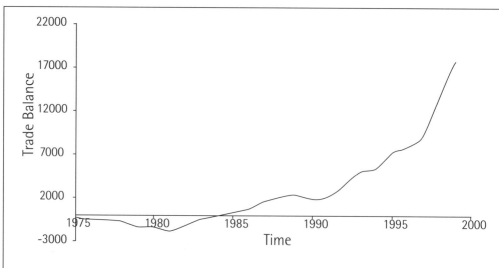

It is evident from the figure above that Ireland's first trade surplus in modern economic times was recorded in 1985. This 'favourable' trend has been repeated in each year, with a record surplus of £17,903m (€22,732m) in 1999. It is widely believed that this improvement in the trade surplus is due, in no small part, to the activities of multinationals operating in Ireland.

The composition of trade by commodity and geographical location is shown in Tables 15.1 and 15.2 respectively.

Table 15.1: *Trade by commodity, 1999*

Category	Exports (%)	Imports (%)
Food and live animals	8.2	5.8
Beverages and tobacco	1.2	1.2
Crude materials (except fuels)	1.2	1.5
Mineral fuels, lubricants and related materials	0.3	2.8
Chemicals and related products	31.8	11.4
Manufactured goods	2.7	8.7
Machinery and transport equipment	39.2	50.9
Miscellaneous manufactured	11.0	11.1
Others	4.4	6.6

Source: CSO, *Statistical Bulletin*, December 1999.

Table 15.2: *Trade by geographical area, 1999*

Destination	Exports (%)	Imports (%)
UK	21.7	32.6
Rest of EU	42.9	22.2
Other European countries	5.0	2.9
USA, Canada and Mexico	16.2	17.7
Others	12.3	21.1
Unclassified	1.9	3.5

Source: CSO, *Trade Statistics*, December 1999.

This chapter deals with the monetary aspects of international trade. The gains from trade are discussed in detail in Section 17.3.

Capital and financial account balance

Definition
The capital and financial account in the balance of payments is a record of a country's inflows and outflows of capital or assets.

More specifically, the capital account records all transfers intended for capital purposes whereas the financial account reports foreign financial assets and liabilities, that is, claims on and obligations to non-residents. In the financial account, there are four categories of investment, namely direct investment, portfolio investment, other investment and reserve assets. A full description of each category can be found in the CSO *Statistical Bulletin*.

Purchases of Irish financial stocks and loans to Irish residents by foreigners are capital inflows. Capital outflows include purchase of foreign financial securities and loans to foreigners by Irish residents. In 1999, the balance on the capital account was £441m (€560m). The balance on financial account was £121m (€153m).

The Irish balance of payments for the year 1999 is reprinted in Table 15.3.

Table 15.3: The Irish Balance of International Payments 1999[1, 2]

Current Account	£m	€m
Merchandise	17,903	22,732
Services	−8,424	−10,697
Net income	−9,984	−12,677
Current transfers	951	1,208
Balance on current account	**446**	**567**
Balance on capital account	**441**	**560**
Financial Account		
Direct investment	10,008	12,707
Portfolio investment	−11,059	−14,042
Other investment	−203	−258
Reserve Assets	1,375	1,746
Balance on financial account	**121**	**153**
Net errors and omissions	*−1,008*	*−1,280*

Source: *Central Bank of Ireland Bulletin,* Autumn 2000.
1. A new presentation for Balance of Payments data was introduced by the CSO in May 2000.
2. The new series of Balance of Payments estimates incorporates the activities of the International Financial Services Centre (IFSC).

In principle, the sum of the debit entries should equal the sum of the credit entries in the balance of payments. Differences in coverage, timing and valuation in the three accounts mean that, in practice, this does not occur. The entry called 'net errors and omissions' as shown above in the balance of payments is a balancing item. This entry ensures that there is an overall balance in the account. In 1999, net errors and omissions was − £1,008m (− €1,280m).

15.2 EXCHANGE RATE DETERMINATION

We will continue our discussion of the foreign sector by considering exchange rates.

Definition
The exchange rate between two currencies is the price of one currency in terms of another.

Similar to interest rate determination, the equilibrium price can be explained in terms of demand and supply analysis. It is the equilibrium price that we call the exchange rate. The market in this case is the foreign exchange market.

There are many similarities between a market for a product and the foreign exchange market. However, there are a few important differences. We consider the market of a single good, like tea. When we discuss the foreign exchange market, we are considering two currencies, e.g. the US dollar (US$) and the euro. For example, in the market for €/US$, a demand for euros implies a supply of US$ and a supply of euros implies a demand for US$. This is evident in our analysis of the €/US$ market below.

Another important difference which we will explain shortly is that the demand for and the supply of foreign exchange is derived. In spite of these differences, we will see that the foreign exchange market looks, and in many ways behaves, like a product market.

The state often intervenes in the foreign exchange market and we will discuss that in the next section. However, we will begin our discussion of exchange rate determination by considering a foreign exchange market where the state does not intervene. We will see that the exchange rate is determined by the forces of demand and supply.

We will explain how the exchange rate is determined using a simplified example.

Assume there are only two countries, Europe and the US, with respective currencies, the euro and the American dollar, US$. In this case the price will be expressed as the number of dollars per one euro.[4] We must examine both the demand for and the supply of euros in order to derive the market exchange rate.

The demand for euros

The demand for euros on the foreign exchange market is a derived demand. Holders of American dollars purchase euros in order to pay for:

- European goods and services;
- European assets including shares, government gilts and property.

When Americans buy European goods and assets, they supply dollars in exchange for euros. For example, if the rate of exchange is €1 = $1, €1m of European goods costs an American importer $1m.

Suppose the value of the euro increases or appreciates relative to the dollar. The new rate of exchange is €1 = $2. The same €1m of European goods now costs the American importer $2m. In other words, European goods are more expensive in the American market after the euro appreciates. At this exchange rate, the demand for goods, and therefore the demand for euros will be less than at the previous rate.

Alternatively, the euro could decrease in value or depreciate relative to the dollar. Suppose the new exchange rate is €1 = $0.5. The delighted importer can now purchase €1m of European goods for only $500,000. At this exchange rate, the demand for European goods will be higher and so will the demand for the euro.

In summary, the higher the exchange rate of dollars for euros, the lower the demand for euros. As the euro depreciates, the demand for the euro increases. Therefore, the demand curve for the euro is downward sloping as drawn in Figure 15.2.

Figure 15.2: The demand curve for euros

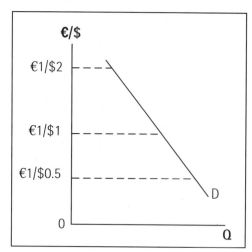

The supply of euros

The supply of euros on the foreign exchange market is also derived. Holders of euros wish to purchase dollars to pay for:

- American goods and services;
- American assets including shares, US government bonds and real estate.

When European residents buy American goods and assets, they supply euros in exchange for dollars. For example, if the rate of exchange is €1 = $1, $1m of imports from the United States costs a European importer €1m.

Suppose the value of the euro appreciates. At the new rate of €1 = $2, the same $1m of merchandise will cost the European importer only €500,000. In other words, US goods are cheaper at this exchange rate. European importers may now be willing to supply more euros in exchange for US dollars.

Alternatively, the euro could depreciate relative to the dollar. Consider another exchange rate of €1 = $0.5. The European importer will have to exchange €2m in order to purchase the goods valued at $1m. At this exchange rate, US goods are more expensive in the European market. The demand for US goods will be less and so will the quantity of euros supplied on the foreign exchange market.

In summary, the higher the exchange rate of dollars for euros, the higher the supply of euros. As the euro depreciates, the supply of the euro decreases. Therefore, the supply curve is upward sloping as drawn in Figure 15.3.[5]

Figure 15.3: The supply curve for euros

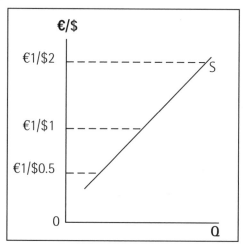

Equilibrium in the foreign exchange market

The demand for euros, represented by D, and the supply of euros, represented by S, determine the equilibrium rate of exchange in the €/US$ market. This is illustrated in Figure 15.4.

Figure 15.4: The equilibrium exchange rate

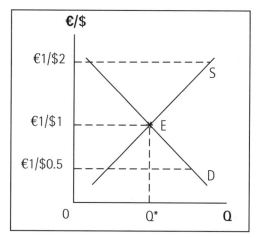

The demand curve for euros and the supply curve for euros intersect at point E, the equilibrium exchange rate. As in all markets there is an automatic process which moves the market towards equilibrium.

If the exchange rate is above equilibrium, the supply of euros exceeds the demand. At the exchange rate indicated by €1/$2 in Figure 15.4, American imports to the European market are relatively cheap and European importers are willing to trade euros for dollars in order to buy them. However, European exports to the American market are relatively expensive. At this exchange rate, the American importer of European goods does not demand as many goods and therefore does not need euros to pay for them. In a market without restrictions, the exchange rate will fall. Equilibrium is restored when quantity demanded equals quantity supplied.

Similarly, if the exchange rate is below the equilibrium, at the rate indicated by €1/$0.5 in Figure 15.4, demand for euros exceeds the supply. American imports are relatively expensive and European importers are not willing to trade euros for dollars in order to purchase them for the European market. However, European exports to the American market are relatively cheap and the American importers are willing to purchase euros in order to buy them for the American market. The shortage of euros will lead to an appreciation of the exchange rate. Equilibrium is restored when quantity demanded equals quantity supplied.

Factors which shift the demand curve or the supply curve

The foreign exchange market considers the relationship between the exchange rate and the quantity of euros demanded and supplied, *ceteris paribus*. Other variables which influence the exchange rate between the two currencies are held constant. These include interest rate differentials, inflation differentials, income differentials and speculation. A change in any of these factors will cause the demand curve and/or the supply curve to shift. We will examine each of these factors briefly.

1. *Interest rate differentials* Suppose European interest rates rise above US interest rates. American investors, seeking the highest rate of return, respond to this interest rate differential by investing in European assets. The change in demand for capital assets, caused by the interest rate differential, leads to a change in demand for the euro. The demand curve for the euro shifts out and to the right, as shown in Figure 15.5.

Figure 15.5: A shift of the demand curve and the supply curve caused by an interest rate differential

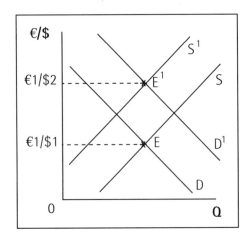

We can see that at every exchange rate, the demand for euros has increased.

In this situation, the supply curve may also shift. European investors are unwilling to purchase American assets since the return on European assets is higher. Fewer euros are supplied to the market. This change in the underlying variable causes the supply curve to shift to the left as shown in Figure 15.5. At each exchange rate, the supply of euros has decreased.

We can now compare the old equilibrium E with the new equilibrium E^1. The combination of increased demand and decreased supply results in an increase in the €/US$ exchange rate. Hence, the higher interest rate in Europe *vis-à-vis* the United States causes an increase in the value of the euro against the dollar. Alternatively, lower interest rates in Europe will cause a decrease in the exchange rate, all other things being equal.

2. *Inflation differentials* Suppose the European inflation rate increases, resulting in an inflation differential with the United States. European goods are now relatively more expensive. This may lead to a decrease in demand for euros in the US, depending on the elasticity of demand for European exports. This change in an underlying variable means that the demand curve for euros shifts to the left.

The supply curve for euros also changes because the relatively low inflation rate in the US causes the demand for US goods, which are relatively cheaper, to increase. These goods must be paid for by exchanging euros for US dollars. As the demand for US dollars increases, the supply of euros increases. The supply curve for euros shifts to the right.

As a result, the higher inflation rate in Europe *vis-à-vis* the United States leads to a decline in the value of the euro against the dollar. The relationship between exchange rates and inflation rates is expressed in terms of Purchasing Power Parity. For more on this subject, see Appendix 15.1 and Section 15.6 on the Irish experience.

3. *Income differentials* Suppose European GDP increases at a rate that is higher than her trading partners. As national income increases, domestic consumption increases. Part of this increase in consumption is met by purchasing more imports. As demand for imports (and, with that, US dollars) increases, the supply of euros increases. As a result, the exchange rate falls. Hence, the higher income level in Europe causes a decline in the value of the euro against the US dollar, all other things being equal.

4. *Speculation* This is a curious but powerful factor in the determination of the exchange rate. Suppose the demand for the euro is expected to be weak. Expectations are for a fall in the value of the euro. Market participants, in anticipation of making a capital gain, sell their euro holdings.[6] As a result, the supply of euros in the foreign exchange market increases. This is represented by a rightward shift of the supply curve. If enough market participants act on this expectation, the value of the euro will fall. The actions of speculators, as described in this example, caused the fall in the value of the euro. Although it is difficult to assess the level of speculation on the foreign exchange markets, it is estimated that less than one-fifth of daily foreign exchange transactions in London is trade/investment related, with speculation accounting for the remainder.

We now examine the relationship between the balance of payments and the exchange rate. Also, the different exchange rate regimes are explained.

15.3 EXCHANGE RATE REGIMES AND THE BALANCE OF PAYMENTS

The composition of the balance of payments and how it actually balances depends on the ability of the domestic currency to adjust in value to other currencies. There are different types of exchange rate systems. The flexible and fixed exchange rate systems are polar opposites and do not reflect the exchange rate systems which operate in practice. However, we will begin by discussing the extremes (and the arguments in favour of each) and then explain the semi-fixed and managed exchange rate systems which we often observe. Figure 15.6 illustrates the range of exchange rate regimes.

Figure 15.6: Exchange rate systems

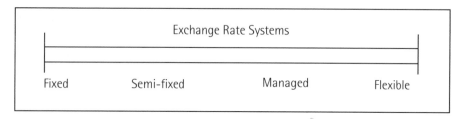

Flexible exchange rate systems

Under this regime, the value of the domestic currency is allowed to change, *vis-à-vis* other currencies.

Definition
A flexible exchange rate system operates on the basis of market forces whereby the exchange rate between two currencies is determined by demand and supply.

The Central Banks are not required to intervene on the foreign exchange market.

Under a flexible exchange rate regime there is an automatic adjustment process in operation. For example, a current account deficit is financed by an equal capital account surplus. How does this work?

If a country records a current account deficit, it means that it is importing more goods and services than it is exporting. The foreign exchange needed to pay for these imports must come from some source. It comes from either borrowing from foreigners or from the sale of domestic assets. When a country sells more assets than it buys, it runs a capital account surplus. This net inflow of foreign exchange is the source used to finance the deficit in the current account.[7] Likewise, a current account surplus is matched by an increase in the ownership of foreign assets.

A current account deficit may result in a change of the exchange rate. All other things being equal, a current account deficit causes the home country's currency to depreciate. This is because at the old exchange rate, there exists an excess supply of the home country's currency. With flexible exchange rates, the excess supply leads to a depreciation. As a result, exports become cheaper whereas imports become more expensive. Likewise, a current account surplus is eliminated by an appreciation of the exchange rate.

In theory, flexible exchange rates will eliminate a current account surplus or deficit. Like any market system, it is the price mechanism that will eliminate any disequilibrium. If the foreign exchange market is at equilibrium, the balance of payments should balance. In practice there may be a discrepancy caused by book-keeping errors and omissions.

The arguments in favour of a flexible exchange rate system are listed below.

1. Adherence to a flexible exchange rate system does not involve any costly interventions by the monetary authorities. Imbalances will be corrected automatically if there are any shocks to the economy. The costs which are normally associated with the depletion of a country's external reserves are eliminated.
2. There is no loss of autonomy with a flexible exchange rate system. There is no balance of payments constraint on domestic policy. Hence, the government is free to pursue whatever policy suits domestic conditions.
3. In times of severe recession the government may allow the currency to depreciate. This would increase the volume of exports and in doing so boost demand. Also, during inflationary times the government may allow the currency to appreciate. In doing so, it may stem the inflationary pressures from abroad. Also, flexible exchange rates can insulate the domestic economy from external shocks.
4. The exchange rate at any given time is the 'true' exchange rate; true in the sense that it is determined by the forces of demand and supply. There is no Central Bank intervention. Currencies are not under- or over-valued or misaligned.
5. Under a flexible exchange rate system, monetary policy is effective.

Fixed exchange rate systems

Alternatively, governments often attempt to maintain the value of their currency *vis-à-vis* other currencies.

Definition
Currencies that belong to a fixed exchange rate system are pegged to each other at rates which are usually agreed by their respective Central Banks.

In order to maintain the currencies at the fixed rates, intervention by the Central Banks is required.[8]

Under a fixed exchange rate regime, the balance of payments will balance with the external reserves playing a central role.

Definition
The external reserves are the stock of foreign currency held by the Central Bank for the purpose of intervention in the foreign exchange market.

To illustrate the operation of external reserves, we will consider the balance of payments for a fictitious state for the year 2000, as outlined in Table 15.4.

Table 15.4: Balance of payments, 2000

Current account	2,500	Change in external reserves	800
Capital account	−1,700		
	800		800

In Table 15.4, we observe a current account surplus of 2,500 units which is partially offset by a capital deficit of 1,700 units. Under these circumstances, there is excess demand for the domestic currency which should lead to a rise in its value. However, under a fixed exchange rate system, the Central Bank is obliged to intervene to maintain the value of the domestic currency *vis-à-vis* other currencies. To eliminate the shortage, the Central Bank purchases external reserves. In other words, foreign currencies are exchanged for the domestic currency. The stock of external reserves increases and with it, the foreign currency reserves of the Central Bank. In this example, the external reserves increase by 800 units.

On the other hand, a negative balance in the current and capital accounts means that there is an excess supply of the domestic currency. In this situation, the Central Bank sells external reserves and purchases the domestic currency to eliminate the surplus. The balance of payments statement at the end of the year would show a decrease in the external reserves.

The arguments in favour of a fixed exchange rate are as follows:

1. It creates a more stable trading environment. It facilitates international trade with importers and exporters assured of fixed payments in terms of their domestic currency. Governments need not fear the damage caused by market uncertainty or volatile exchange rate movements. International institutions operate more effectively under a fixed exchange rate system.
2. Adherence to a fixed exchange rate system can result in favourable economic conditions at home. For example, low inflation, stable interest rates and a favourable trade balance can all result from a fixed exchange rate policy.
3. The transition to a single currency is easier from a fixed exchange rate system than it is from a flexible exchange rate system. Fewer adjustments and fewer sacrifices are necessary.
4. Fiscal policy is effective under a fixed exchange rate system.
5. By imposing increased discipline on internal economic policy, it can sometimes prevent national governments from adopting irresponsible economic policies for short-term political gain.

It was within the context of fixed exchange rates that the concept of Optimum Currency Areas (OCA) was developed. This is discussed in Appendix 15.2.

Managed floating exchange rate systems

The managed floating exchange rate system closely resembles the flexible exchange rate system.

Definition

The managed floating exchange rate system is characterised by an exchange rate which changes with the market forces of demand and supply. However, the Central Bank intervenes periodically, particularly when the currency is very weak or very strong.

The danger of a weak currency is that inflationary pressures may arise. A strong currency may have a negative effect on the volume of exports. To avoid both of these threats to the domestic economy, the Central Bank may intervene.[9]

Semi-fixed exchange rate systems

The semi-fixed exchange rate system closely resembles the fixed exchange rate system but it is more 'flexible'.

Definition

Member states of a semi-fixed exchange rate system set the value of their currencies in relation to other participating currencies. However, currencies are permitted to fluctuate above and below these rates.

The 'fluctuation bands' are normally one or two percentage points above and below the established rate. If the domestic currency fluctuates within the band, the Central Bank does not normally intervene. If the domestic currency approaches the limit of the band, the Central Bank intervenes in the market to stabilise the exchange rate within the band.

Countries that participate in a semi-fixed exchange rate system must offset their interventions using external reserves.

One example of a semi-fixed exchange rate system was the European Monetary System, or the EMS. Since Ireland was a member of this system, we will discuss it here.

15.4   THE EUROPEAN MONETARY SYSTEM (EMS)

The EMS came into operation on 13 March 1979. Its aim was the 'creation of closer monetary co-operation leading to a zone of monetary stability in Europe'.[10] How did the EMS operate?

There were three separate components to the EMS. The first was the ECU, the European Currency Unit. It was a weighted basket of EU currencies, with the weightings changed every five years or when a new currency joined the system. The weights were based on a country's GNP and level of intra-EU trade.

The second component was the EMCF, the European Monetary Co-operation Fund. On joining the system member states were obliged to submit 20% of their holdings of gold and foreign exchange reserves in return for ECUs. These funds were used for settling accounts after foreign exchange intervention.

The third and most important part of the EMS was the Exchange Rate Mechanism (ERM). This was a semi-fixed system where members' currencies were allowed to fluctuate against each other's currencies within an agreed band.[11]

All currencies of the ERM were assigned a central rate against the ECU. Each member's currency was also committed to a central rate against other currencies, with bands of fluctuation.

When the ERM was first established, it was decided to operate two bands of fluctuation: a narrow band of 2.25% and a wide band of 6%. The wider band was perceived to be a temporary measure and was assigned to member states with volatile currencies. It was hoped that as their economies converged towards the European average their currencies would become more stable and they would eventually enter the narrow band.

We will explain how the ERM operated by discussing an example. Consider the relationship between the Irish pound and the German mark.[12] Before January 1993, the central rate for the IR£/DM was IR£1 = 2.6789DM. This means that one Irish pound was worth approximately 2.68 German marks. At that time, both the Irish pound and the German mark operated within the narrow band. The upper and lower limits are shown in Figure 15.7.

Figure 15.7: IR£/DM trading range

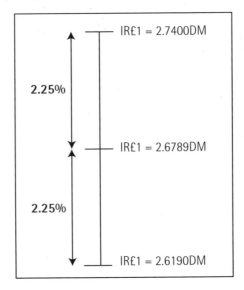

The Irish pound could move between the lower band of 2.6190DM and the upper band of 2.7400DM. These figures are 2.25% below and 2.25% above the central rate. In other words, if the value of the Irish pound fell below 2.6190DM or rose above 2.74DM, the Central Bank was obliged to intervene.

In a 'normal' day's trading, the IR£/DM would trade within these limits. The Central Bank used a number of instruments to ensure that its currency stayed within these limits.

There were three options available to any central bank involved in maintaining the value of its currency within the ERM fluctuation bands. A short-term measure was foreign exchange intervention which altered the external reserves. Central banks could intervene on a daily basis. Domestic currency was bought and sold in exchange for foreign currency. According to the rules of the ERM, intervention was a joint responsibility, i.e. it involved the respective central banks of the strongest and weakest currencies. For example, if the IR£/DM rate was close to its intervention limits both the Central Bank of Ireland and the Bundesbank were required to act. Of course, there is a finite stock of external reserves. Hence, this was only used as a short-term measure.

A medium-term measure was an interest rate change. If a currency was continually weak and central bank intervention was unsuccessful, the monetary authorities could decide to increase domestic interest rates. We have already seen from Section 15.2 that there is a positive relationship between interest rates and the exchange rate. Frequent changes in interest rates have a destabilising effect on the economy. In theory, this was not a long-term option. However, it became a long-term practice for many countries.

The long-term measure was a realignment of a currency within the ERM. Both devaluation and revaluation involved a change in the central rate between two currencies.

Definition

Devaluation is a reduction in the value of a currency *vis-à-vis* other currencies. In terms of the ERM, the central rate is lowered by a certain percentage.

In a market without restrictions, the currency may depreciate due to the forces of demand and supply. Within the ERM the devaluation of a currency had to be negotiated with other participating members. However, the reason for the devaluation was generally a disequilibrium in the market for the currency.

For example, suppose that the demand for the Irish pound was continually weak, indicating that Irish goods were not competitive on the international market. Foreign exchange intervention and interest rate changes failed to strengthen the pound. The only option left for the Central Bank was to negotiate a devaluation of the Irish pound. Alternatively, increased demand for Irish goods and for the Irish pound could lead to a revaluation.

Definition

Revaluation is an increase in the value of one currency *vis-à-vis* other currencies. In terms of the ERM, the central rate is raised by a certain percentage.

We now examine devaluation as a possible policy option within a semi-fixed exchange rate system.

Devaluation as a policy option

The end of the currency crisis in 1993 was the last major realignment of the European currencies. In order to understand the issues surrounding devaluation, we will explore the currency crisis in some detail. Information Box 15.1 explains the issues surrounding the crisis.

INFORMATION BOX 15.1

The currency crisis, the devaluation of the Irish pound and the demise of the ERM

For most people, the currency crisis began in the autumn of 1992 with the decline in the value of sterling and finished in the spring of 1993 with the devaluation of the Irish pound. In reality, events leading to the currency crisis date as far back as 1989 and only came to a conclusion in the autumn of 1993.

The reasons behind the currency crisis are many and varied. Possible contributing factors are categorised into long-term factors (dating back years) and medium-term factors (dating back months).

Long-term factors

1. *Sterling's entry into the ERM*   Sterling entered the ERM in October 1990. Many commentators viewed sterling's entry as a decision taken on the basis of political expediency rather than on economic fundamentals. In particular, one of the conditions that Mrs Thatcher stipulated prior to ERM entry was for the UK inflation rate to be close to the European average. However, it was then decided that entry into the ERM would aid the British effort to control inflation. When the UK entered the ERM, the inflation rate differential between the UK and core EU member states was substantial. This differential was likely to cause tension within the system. Also, some felt that the central rate of UK£1 = 2.95DM was too high and therefore unsustainable. However, British authorities believed that they could maintain this rate within the wider 6% band.

2. *German re-unification*   The re-unification of West and East Germany had some destabilising effects. First, prior to unification the old East German mark, the oestmark, was abolished. East Germans were allowed to convert a part of their savings into deutschmarks at the very favourable one-for-one exchange rate. This increased the purchasing power in the newly unified state and ultimately led to an increase in the inflation rate. Second, rejuvenating the East German economy led to substantial expenditure increases and ultimately to a large budget deficit. The Bonn administration was reluctant to completely finance this extra spending from higher taxes. Most of the expenditure was financed by borrowing which led to higher interest rates in Germany. This occurred at a time when the Bundesbank was trying to stem inflationary fears by operating a tight monetary policy. This caused the already high interest rates to increase even further. These high interest rates in Germany were the predominant factor behind the high interest rate regime prevalent throughout most of western Europe in the early 1990s.

Medium-term factors

3. *US-German interest rate differentials*   The low interest rates adopted by the US authorities (in order to thwart the American recession of the 1990s) combined with

→

the high interest rate policy in Germany (in order to stem inflation) resulted in a significant interest rate differential between the two countries. This, alongside other factors, led to a large capital inflow to Europe, and particularly Germany. This increased demand for the mark caused it to increase in value and created tension and uncertainty within the ERM. The combination of the weak dollar and strong mark added to the exchange rate pressure between sterling and the mark during the summer of 1992.

4. *The Scandinavian connection* Prior to the currency crisis all three Scandinavian currencies were shadowing the ECU. Shadowing is an informal arrangement. Currencies outside the ERM, particularly those with strong trading links to EU member states, attempted to maintain the value of their currency within the narrow or the wide band. Adherence to this policy in the Scandinavian countries became unpopular during the summer of 1992. Many felt that sustaining the value of the domestic currency against the currencies within the ERM was responsible for the depleted external reserves, high interest rates and high unemployment which were evident at the time.

5. *The Treaty on European Union* The failure by the Danes to ratify the Maastricht treaty in June 1992 and the decision by the French to hold a referendum created further tension within the markets and the ERM. The European Monetary System without the Maastricht treaty was suddenly becoming a possibility that no one (with the exception of the Euro-sceptics) had imagined. The future existence of the EMS was now in doubt.

Other events, including the removal of exchange controls and the perceived overvaluation of the French franc, were contributing factors.

Each of these factors individually placed the ERM under pressure. The combination of the factors made the entire system unstable. The instability quickly spread to the financial markets. On 16 September, sterling collapsed on the foreign exchanges. The UK Chancellor raised interest rates by five percentage points but to no avail. Sterling's (and the lira's) membership of the ERM was suspended. Attention then turned to other currencies, including the Spanish peseta, the Portuguese escudo and the Irish pound. On 30 November, the Irish Central Bank raised its overnight lending rate from 30% to 100% in an attempt to limit capital outflows and to deter further speculative pressures on the Irish pound. Once again, intervention by the authorities proved futile. On 30 January, the EU Monetary Committee devalued the Irish pound by 10%. The new IR£/DM central rate was IR£1 = 2.41105DM with an upper limit of IR£1 = 2.4660DM and a lower limit of IR£1 = 2.3570DM.

The uncertainty which was prevalent in the foreign exchange market for the previous six months subsided because of the devaluation of the Irish pound, further Central Bank intervention and the cut in German interest rates.

The lull in the storm lasted until the summer of 1993 when speculators began to focus on the French franc and the Danish krone. Events came to a head in late July. Financial markets, certain that the ERM was about to collapse, were already discounting that event. However, their post-mortem was premature. The ERM was saved by the decision taken on the first weekend of August to extend the fluctuation bands to 15%.

The process involved in a devaluation of the Irish pound is described above. The controversy regarding devaluation relates to the possible benefits and drawbacks which may result from the decision. We will illustrate both the advantages and disadvantages involved by example.

On 30 January 1993 the Irish pound was devalued by 10%. For several months prior to this, the Irish pound weakened against the core currencies of the ERM (German mark, Dutch guilder and Belgian franc). This problem was aggravated by a weak US dollar and an even weaker pound sterling.

The Irish and the British currencies were linked in the foreign exchange markets. This is because of the strong trade links that persist between the two countries. Therefore, if the Irish pound gained in strength relative to the pound sterling, Irish exports became dearer in their main market. Under those conditions, the foreign exchange markets often anticipated a devaluation of the Irish pound.

Between the months of July and September 1992, the IR£/UK£ exchange rate increased from IR£1 = UK£.93 to parity and then to IR£1 = UK£1.09. Irish firms exporting to the UK faced severe difficulties. Margins were squeezed. In addition, interbank interest rates were extremely high, with the one month lending rate close to 50%. As speculators continued their domination of the foreign exchanges, the situation became unsustainable.

Arguments favouring devaluation

A devaluation improves a country's competitiveness by increasing the domestic price of imports and reducing the foreign price of the country's exports. In the Irish context such a devaluation would probably return the IR£/UK£ exchange rate to its former trading rate. Prior to the currency crisis the IR£/UK£ exchange rate had traded at approximately IR£1 = UK£.93 for a period of over two years.

A weaker Irish exchange rate was particularly important for indigenous firms who rely, often exclusively, on the British market. Because the firms are often small, they cannot afford to 'hedge' against exchange risk.[13] This contrasts sharply with their Irish-based multinational competitors who either hedge or simply invoice their Irish exports in US dollars. Either way, their exchange risk is lessened. Also, indigenous companies do not have the resources to maintain operations until the exchange rate becomes more favourable. Because the Irish firms are more labour intensive than foreign multinationals, the likely closure of indigenous firms added to an already serious unemployment problem.

Also, a devaluation would allow the Central Bank to lower interest rates as it would no longer have to defend the currency. High and rising interest rates were particularly devastating to mortgage holders, whose monthly payments increased. They had less income to spend which negatively affected consumer spending. Firms were unable to borrow money at the penalising rates of interest. The consequences of this lack of investment were felt in the medium term and the long term.

Arguments opposing devaluation

A devaluation is inflationary, particularly for a country that imports as much as Ireland. A devaluation has the effect of increasing the price of imports. If there are domestic substitutes, they become more competitive and so a devaluation can have a positive impact on indigenous industry. However, because the Irish economy is small, many goods are not produced here and many raw materials are not found here. Therefore, consumers and firms are forced to pay for higher priced imports which leads to inflation.

Devaluations can also lead to a vicious circle of inflation and devaluation which, once established, is difficult to break. For example, suppose a number of Irish firms lobby the government for a devaluation of the Irish pound. The government subsequently devalues the Irish pound. Irish firms gain a short-term competitive advantage over their trading partners. However, as import prices begin to rise, the Irish inflation rate increases. Consequently, the inflation rate differential with the UK worsens. Irish firms become even less competitive. As a short-term solution to the problem, Irish industry requests another devaluation. The government, facing a general election in the near future, devalues again. The inflation rate in Ireland increases, again. Another cycle begins. This is the devaluation-price inflation spiral which is sometimes used as an argument against devaluation.

Also, as we mentioned in Chapter 10, part of the national debt is denominated in foreign currency. If the Irish currency is devalued relative to these foreign currencies, the size of the foreign debt increases along with the debt service repayments. Therefore, the decision to devalue undermines the government's commitment to contain the national debt.

Short-term interest rates usually decline following a devaluation. However, the devaluation itself could lead investors to believe that the Irish pound is volatile and that investments denominated in Irish pounds are risky. Investors would demand a premium on Irish interest rates relative to, for example, German interest rates to compensate for the risk. Therefore, the benefit of lower interest rates might only last for a short time. Long-term interest rates may be higher as a result of the decision to devalue.

To summarise, those who oppose devaluation argue that the decision to devalue places too much emphasis on the short-term goal of preserving employment. The long-term goals of the economy include maintaining low inflation rates, low interest rates and a stable exchange rate regime. Attaining these goals would encourage long-term growth and promote increased employment. The devaluation is a political expedient at the expense of the long-term national interest, it is argued.

In conclusion, it can be seen from the above analysis that the decision to devalue is a difficult one to make. There are many who favour devaluation as a credible policy option; others are not so supportive. For one, Harold Wilson, the former UK Prime Minister who, in 1963, said 'Devaluation, whether of sterling, or the dollar, or both, would be a lunatic, self-destroying operation.' Incidentally, four years later he had this to say: 'From now on the pound abroad is worth 14% or so less in terms of other currencies. It does not mean, of course, that the pound here in Britain in your pocket or purse, or in your bank has been devalued.' Not surprisingly, this statement followed the decision to devalue sterling, in 1967. It is left to the readers to decide for themselves the reason behind the change of opinion!

Membership of the ERM was a precondition for participation in Economic and Monetary Union. This is the subject of the next section.

15.5   ECONOMIC AND MONETARY UNION

The origins of Economic and Monetary Union, or EMU, date back to 1957, the year that the European Economic Community (EEC) was established.

The main features of an economic union are:

- the free mobility of capital, labour, goods and services;
- a community-wide competition policy;
- co-ordination of macroeconomic policy;
- economic and social cohesion and regional development.[14]

The main features of a monetary union are as follows:

- the abolition of all exchange controls culminating in the complete liberalisation of all capital transactions;
- the irrevocable fixing of exchange rates culminating in a single currency;
- a European Central Bank and a common monetary policy.

The Delors Report, published in 1989, established a three-stage process and a timetable to achieve these goals. These were slightly modified at the Intergovernmental Conference in 1991. They were published in the Treaty on European Union, more commonly known as the Maastricht treaty, in December 1991. Because of problems in achieving the objectives set out in the Delors Report, the timetable was amended by the European Council at a meeting in Madrid during December 1995. The three stages for achieving EMU and the amended timetable are outlined below.

Stage 1: Laying the foundation

This stage began in July 1990 and ended in December 1993. One of the goals of the stage was to complete the Internal Market, made possible by the passage of the Single European Act in 1987. Theoretically, within the Single European Market there is free movement of people, goods, services and capital. All barriers to entry between European Union member states were to be eliminated. In other words, it was to be a Europe without national frontiers. Although much has been achieved, work continues to harmonise tax systems, to standardise technical specifications across member states and to reduce national incentives to industries.

Another goal of this phase was to co-ordinate macroeconomic policies between member states. It was hoped that the exchange rates of member states could be maintained within their 'narrow bands'. Exchange rate stability and the discipline that it imposes on national governments was to pave the way to the single currency.

In order to reduce disparities in the living conditions between member states, structural funds were awarded, particularly to countries whose GDP per capita was significantly below the EU average.

Stage 2: Moving towards union

Stage 2 was designed as a transitional phase. The European Monetary Institute (EMI) was established in Frankfurt to begin the transition from independent national monetary policies to a common European monetary policy. The EMI itself was a 'transitional' institution and it was to be replaced by a European Central Bank. This happened in June 1998.

Under the terms of the Maastricht treaty, the EMI and the Commission were to report to the EU Council at the end of 1996 on the progress made by member states in fulfilling the convergence criteria. At the summit in Madrid, the Council extended this deadline. In May 1998 eleven countries were deemed eligible to participate in EMU. Of the remaining four, Greece was the only country deemed ineligible. The UK, Sweden and Denmark decided not to participate. The irrevocable conversion rates for the euro, based on the ERM bilateral central rates were announced. These rates are shown in Table 15.5.

Table 15.5: Euro conversion rates

BEF	40.3399
DEM	1.95583
ESP	166.386
FRF	6.55957
IEP	0.787564
ITL	1936.27
LUF	40.3399
NLG	2.20371
ATS	13.7603
PTE	200.482
FIM	5.94573

Stage 3: Completing the union

Under the terms of the Maastricht treaty, Stage 3 was to begin between 1997 and 1999, at the latest. The Council in Madrid confirmed the starting date for the irrevocable fixing of the exchange rates for 1 January 1999. With the launch of the single currency in January 1999, the euro became a currency in its own right, with the national currencies (including the Irish pound) becoming, in effect, units of the euro. The changeover to the single currency, called the euro, begins no later than 1 January 2002 and can last for a period of up to six months.[15] The new European Central Bank and the national central banks of the EU countries constitute the European System of Central Banks (ESCB). These institutions will be responsible for the formulation and implementation of a common, EU monetary policy.

The road to EMU is highlighted in Figure 15.8.

Figure 15.8:   The road to EMU

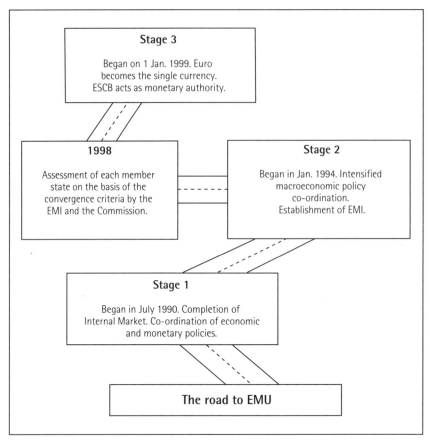

Convergence criteria to join the single currency

To prepare for the transition to a single currency, the Maastricht treaty established a set of targets called the convergence criteria. The treaty did not specify policies. It was up to the national governments of each member state to determine how to achieve each criterion. The convergence criteria are listed below (with the direct quote from the treaty in quotation marks).[16]

- Inflation rates: 'an average rate of inflation . . . that does not exceed by more than 1.5 percentage points that of, at most, the three best performing Member States in terms of price stability';
- Interest rates: 'a Member State has had an average nominal long-term interest rate that does not exceed by more than two percentage points that of, at most, the three best performing Member States in terms of price stability';
- Exchange rates: 'the observance of the normal fluctuation margins provided for by the exchange-rate mechanism of the European Monetary System, for at least two years, without devaluing against the currency of any other Member State';

- 'the sustainability of the government financial position', as judged by the following two measures:

Government deficit: 'the ratio of the planned or actual government deficit to gross domestic product at market prices' should not exceed '3%'.
Government debt: 'the ratio of government debt to gross domestic product at market prices' should not exceed '60%'.

If the deficit is above the reference value, it would still be deemed suitable if either the ratio has declined substantially or, alternatively, the excess is only exceptional and temporary. If the debt is above the reference value, it would be deemed suitable if the ratio is sufficiently diminishing and approaching the reference value at a satisfactory pace.

These conditions (known as the Excessive Deficit Procedure) were written in the knowledge that it would be at least six years before any assessment would take place. Hence, the wording had to allow for a certain amount of leeway. Given the difficult economic conditions that prevailed after the Maastricht treaty was adopted, a loose interpretation of the convergence criteria was indeed required.

As stated earlier, the decision on eligibility was taken in May 1998. It was based on data for the fiscal year 1997. Table 15.6 reports the outcome of the fiscal criteria for all member states of the EU, as these proved the more difficult to satisfy. It would appear that all three non-participating countries (UK, Sweden, Denmark) were 'suitable' whereas both Belgium and Italy were 'ineligible'. For obvious political reasons, Belgium and Italy were deemed suitable.

Table 15.6: Fiscal convergence, 1997

Country	Deficit/GDP[1]	Debt/GDP[2]
Austria	−1.9	64.3
Belgium	−1.9	123.4
Denmark	+0.4	63.6
Finland	−1.2	54.9
France	−3.0	58.1
Germany	−2.7	61.5
Greece	−3.9	109.4
Ireland	+1.1	61.3
Italy	−2.7	122.4
Luxembourg	+2.9	6.4
Netherlands	−0.9	71.2
Portugal	−2.5	61.7
Spain	−2.6	67.5
Sweden	−0.7	76.7
UK	−1.9	52.1

Source: ECB *Annual Report 1998*, 1999.
Notes: 1. General Government Deficit (−)/Surplus (+).
      2. General government, consistent with the Maastricht treaty definition.

In order to reassure Germany (and the financial markets) a Stability and Growth Pact was agreed at the Dublin summit in December 1996. Driven by a fear of unsustainable deficits, the aim of the Stability Pact was to achieve sustained financial stability by penalising national governments for overspending. Member states of the single currency are required to keep their fiscal deficits below 3% of GDP. Any deficit in excess of this limit would result in a fine imposed by Brussels. These limits could only be breached under 'exceptional circumstances', i.e. if the economy recorded a negative growth rate of 2% or more per annum. A decline in output of between 0.75% and 2% would result in a reduced fine.

There was a genuine concern expressed about the effect that this Pact might have on a country whose economic growth was 'negative'. Adherence to the Stability Pact precludes governments from adopting counter-cyclical policies to offset fluctuations in economic activity. Some feared that the Pact would only succeed in exacerbating cyclical fluctuations in the economy. In contrast, its supporters argued that fiscal policy within the single currency should be subject to rules that preclude a member state from opting for unsustainable budget deficits and, in the process, imposing negative externalities on all others.

Economic policy in EMU

'In short, most domestic macroeconomic policy instruments will, for good or ill, be removed.'[17] (Honohan, 1999). For national authorities, the loss of policy autonomy is one of the most significant implications of EMU membership. As participants in the euro area, no independent exchange rate instrument is available. The objective of exchange rate policy is to maintain price stability. According to the Maastricht treaty (Article 109), responsibility for the formulation of exchange rate policy is shared between the Council of Ministers and the ECB. Ireland's reliance in the past on exchange rate realignments is no longer a policy option.

The same applies to monetary policy. Interest rate adjustments, either to dampen down inflation or to boost spending, are no longer available to the national authorities. A single monetary policy, aimed at achieving price stability in the euro area, is unlikely to reflect economic conditions in the Irish economy, or for that matter, in other small countries in the euro area. Economic conditions in the large European economies are more likely to influence the monetary decision-making authority, namely the European Central Bank.

With independent exchange rate and monetary policy constrained, the national authorities will be more reliant than ever before on fiscal policy. However, we know from the previous section that fiscal policy is, in theory at least, constrained by the Stability and Growth Pact. Without fiscal federalism in the EU, adherence to the Pact may impose a deflationary bias on EMU member states i.e. in a downturn, countries may have to adopt contractionary (pro-cyclical) as opposed to expansionary (counter-cyclical) policies to avoid the imposition of fines. Recall from Chapter 12 that the General Government Deficit (GGD) is calculated by subtracting tax and non-tax revenue from government expenditure. During a recession, expenditure automatically increases as more people collect the dole and income-related benefits. Tax revenue automatically falls because fewer people are working and corporations are less profitable. To maintain a deficit of less than 3% of GDP (and to avoid large fines) national governments may have to cut back on regular services. As a result, government expenditure may decrease during a recession to comply with the terms of the Stability and Growth Pact. Adherence to the Stability Pact may mean that recessions in the EU will be intensified.

The implication for economic policy arising from this loss of economic independence is that the national authorities will have to rely on, to a much greater extent than in the past, wage bargaining and price flexibility to ensure competitiveness in the face of economic shocks. This will apply to all EMU member states, including Ireland.

15.6   THE IRISH EXPERIENCE

In this section, we will examine Ireland's participation in the fixed or semi-fixed exchange rate systems in the context of exchange rate policy. Price stability, characterised by a low and stable inflation rate, has been the primary objective of Irish exchange rate policy. We begin with Ireland's decision to join the EMS.

Ireland and the EMS

Ireland joined the EMS in 1979. It was a difficult decision to make for the Irish authorities. We will begin by discussing the arguments advanced by those who favoured membership in the EMS and then consider the arguments of the opponents.

Arguments favouring entry to the EMS

The main argument in favour of membership was the prospect of lower inflation. Until 1979, the pound was linked with sterling and its inflation rate mirrored the British rate. At the end of the 1960s and throughout the 1970s, both countries experienced persistently high inflation rates, peaking at almost 25% in the mid-1970s. The Irish monetary authorities believed that a link with a 'hard currency' which appreciates over time, like the German mark, was preferable to the British link with its inflationary tendency. They hoped that the link with the mark would result in a convergence of the Irish inflation rate to the German inflation rate which fluctuated between 3% and 4% per annum.

Also, the policy-makers believed that membership of the EMS would facilitate stronger trading links with other member states. This would diminish the reliance of indigenous industries on Britain as a destination for their products.

Finally, Irish authorities expected financial aid from the European Economic Community to assist Ireland to adjust to the new system.

Arguments opposing entry to the EMS

The main argument advanced by those who opposed EMS membership was that the UK decided not to enter. British authorities, under a Labour administration, were opposed to membership on the basis that it would result in a loss of autonomy, particularly in the area of monetary policy. They believed that Britain, as an exporter of oil, was subject to different, oil-related shocks than the other European countries. They wanted to maintain control over their monetary policy to respond to these shocks. See Information Box 15.2 for a discussion of Britain's ambivalent relationship with Europe and the single currency.

INFORMATION BOX 15.2

The UK, the ERM and the single currency

Sterling's participation in the ERM and later its opt-out of the single currency in Europe have been hotly debated in the UK. When the EMS was set up in 1979, the UK government decided to keep sterling out of its exchange rate mechanism. The UK authorities were insistent on allowing sterling to float freely on the foreign exchanges and on maintaining control over UK interest rates. There was little or no change in this policy until the mid-1980s when the UK Chancellor of the Exchequer, on recognising the benefits of the ERM, allowed sterling to shadow the German mark.

In October 1990, after much debate, sterling joined the wide band of the ERM at the central rate of UK£1 = 2.95DM. Although the decision to join was not surprising, some of the details took the market by surprise. In particular, many commentators believed that the central rate of UK£1 = 2.95DM was too high. The argument in favour of a high rate was its anti-inflationary bias. The argument against a high rate was its likely effect on UK industry and UK exports.

In Ireland, the authorities, not to mention the business community, were delighted with the decision. The IR£/UK£ exchange rate was now limited to a particular and favourable range. The central rate was IR£1 = UK£.908116 with an upper limit of IR£1 = UK£.96424 and a lower limit of IR£1 = UK£.85526. Unfortunately, this new trading environment did not last.

The critics were proven correct. During the currency crisis, Britain could not maintain its exchange rate with the mark within the 6% band. The British monetary authorities increased their interest rates and attempted to fight the speculators. Ultimately they decided that the damage to the domestic economy was too great. In September 1992, less than two years after joining, sterling's membership of the ERM was suspended. The IR£/UK£ exchange rate went above parity and traded close to IR£1 = UK£1.10. With sterling no longer tied to the mark, the IR£/UK£ exchange rate was once again exposed to conflicting forces.

As sterling remained outside the ERM and with the IR£/UK£ trading close to parity, Irish firms exporting to the UK remained vulnerable to any sterling weakness. Even with the changes that have taken place over the past twenty years, the UK remains Ireland's largest trading partner. In 1999 we delivered 21.8% of all exports to the UK and 32.8% of all imports came from the UK. Sterling's strength in 1999 provided the Irish authorities with a different problem, namely, inflation.

On the broader issue of a single currency, the UK authorities negotiated an opt-out clause in the Maastricht treaty. For the moment, the UK sits on the fence while

$\longrightarrow$

assessing the performance of the euro. It is likely that a referendum will decide the fate of sterling. Given the importance of the UK market to Irish industry, Britain's opposition to a single currency causes Irish industry continuing pain and anguish.

Hence, the attraction to joining a fixed exchange rate system was dampened by the absence of Ireland's largest trading partner, the UK. Although Irish exporters were promised a more favourable trading environment as members of the ERM, the prospect of a flexible, not to mention a volatile IR£/UK£ exchange rate, was chilling. In the end, the Irish authorities were attracted more by the fixed exchange rate with the mark than by the old link with sterling. So, after much deliberation, Ireland decided in favour of the ERM. In 1979, the 153-year, one for one, no margins link with sterling was broken.

Next, we will attempt to evaluate Ireland's performance within the ERM.

Ireland's experience within the ERM

An assessment of Ireland's experience within the ERM is normally divided into two distinct periods, 1979–86 and 1987–92.[18] The first period was, in general, disappointing. Ireland's inflation rate remained high, as did Irish interest rates. Trade with member states of the ERM increased but not by a significant amount.

There are a number of reasons for the poor performance during these early years of membership. Possibly the most significant reason was the 'sterling' problem. Sterling was not a member of the ERM and subsequently the IR£/UK£ exchange rate was not subject to any fluctuation bands. Nonetheless, Irish authorities shadowed sterling and at the same time attempted to maintain the formal links with the member states of the ERM. The authorities were literally caught between a rock and a hard place because sterling and the mark often moved in opposite directions.

The financial markets, both at home and abroad, were aware of this dual policy. It caused the markets to question Ireland's commitment to the ERM. The market scepticism led to speculation whenever the Irish pound appreciated relative to sterling. The tendency for the Irish authorities to devalue in the face of uncertainty reinforced the market view of Ireland's relaxed attitude towards ERM membership.

The belief that Ireland's inflation rate would fall towards the German level on membership of the ERM was based on the theory of purchasing power parity (PPP). PPP is a theory of exchange rate determination. It states that changes in the exchange rate are accounted for by inflation differentials. In the context of Ireland's membership of the ERM, PPP implies that Ireland's inflation rate will be equal to the core member's (Germany) inflation rate, if the exchange rate between the Irish pound and the German mark is fixed. In this context, PPP is a theory of inflation. See Appendix 15.1 for more on the theory of PPP.

For PPP to hold, a sizeable amount of trade must exist between the two countries. A country cannot benefit from having a fixed exchange rate with another unless a sufficient amount of foreign trade is evident between the two states. Unfortunately, trade between Ireland and other ERM member states did not increase sufficiently during the early years of membership.

Finally, a precondition of entry to a semi-fixed exchange rate system is the agreement to sacrifice national autonomy over certain macroeconomic policies and to co-ordinate policies with other member states. A single member state cannot expect the benefits of a fixed exchange rate system unless its mix of demand-management policies is broadly in line with other member states. This did not happen in the early years of the ERM. Some member states, including Ireland, adopted short-term demand policies which sharply contrasted with the policies adopted by the core member states of the ERM. This is another reason for Ireland's poor performance from 1979 to 1986 (see Appendix 15.3 for a discussion on fiscal and monetary policy in the context of alternate exchange rate regimes).

The performance generally improved during the second period between 1987 and 1992. Unexpectedly, the Irish inflation rate fell below the EU average and the German rate. Interest rates also declined. The differential between Irish and German interest rates narrowed from 9% in 1986 to 3% in 1988. The trade account recorded a surplus, as did the current account. The IR£/DM exchange rate stabilised with the Irish pound reaching the top of the ERM band on a number of occasions.

The improvement in performance came from two sources, domestic and international. The domestic source was the fiscal restraint exercised by the government beginning in 1987. The improvement in industrial relations and the moderate wage increases arising from the Programme for National Recovery also contributed to an Irish environment characterised by low inflation. The international economy, so important to the Irish domestic economy, was buoyant, contributing to the combination of low inflation rates and strong demand for Irish products. The combination of internal discipline and external demand helped Irish policy-makers to maintain the value of the pound within the ERM while experiencing strong rates of economic growth.

Exchange rate policy 1993–98

After the currency crisis the Irish authorities operated exchange rate policy under wide bands within an ERM that was no longer a semi-fixed exchange rate system. With the British pound and the German mark going in opposite directions, the Irish authorities tried to straddle the Irish pound between the two currencies. Although no explicit policy announcement was made, the effective or exchange rate index for the Irish pound remained remarkably stable in this period.

Definition

The effective or trade-weighted exchange rate index for a currency is the weighted average of the value of the currency against its largest trading partners.

By assigning trade weights for each country which reflect the importance of various foreign currencies in Ireland's international trade, we can calculate an index of the average value of the Irish pound *vis-à-vis* currencies of our largest trading partners. For example, the largest weight is assigned to the UK as it is Ireland's largest trading partner. Using bilateral exchange rates, the trade-weighted exchange rate index is calculated by multiplying each bilateral exchange rate, expressed as an index, by the respective trade weights. Summing for all of Ireland's major trading partners, we find the effective exchange rate index.

The effective exchange rate index for the Irish pound for the period 1994–97 is shown in Figure 15.9.

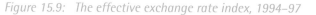

Figure 15.9: The effective exchange rate index, 1994–97

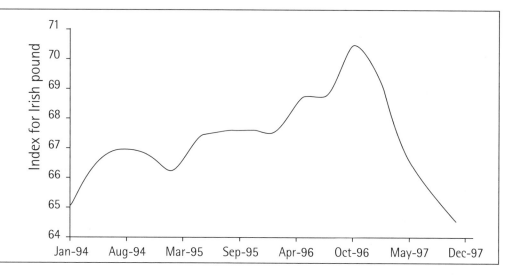

In view of the fall in the value of the Irish pound against the German mark in late 1997 and the subsequent fear of inflation ahead of the 1999 launch of the single currency, a decision to revalue the Irish pound was taken. In March 1998, the authorities announced a 3% revaluation of the Irish pound, resulting in a new central rate of DM2.4833. This was the last realignment before the changeover to the single currency in January 1999.

At the same time that this was happening, it was recognised that Irish interest rates would have to fall in order to converge with German levels. Given the level of domestic demand, the Irish authorities delayed the interest rate reductions for as long as possible. In late 1998, the Central Bank of Ireland reduced interest rates on three separate occasions, by over 3% in total. By December 1998, Irish interest rates were in line with interest rates in other EMU countries.

Ireland and the single currency

From an Irish perspective there are arguments in favour of and against the adoption of a single currency.[19] We begin by examining the arguments favouring a single currency.

Arguments supporting Irish participation in the single currency

A transformation to a single currency should result in lower transaction costs. One important transaction cost which will be eliminated is the cost of converting the domestic currency to foreign currencies when goods are imported and exported. Since most of Irish trade is conducted with other EU countries, this saving should be significant. At present, it is estimated that the elimination of transaction costs alone should increase Ireland's GDP by an additional 1%.

Also, exchange rate risk will be eliminated. Exchange rate risk occurs because exchange rates may change between the time when a sale is negotiated and when the goods and services are actually delivered. Large firms can eliminate this risk by purchasing foreign currencies in the forward exchange market to ensure that they pay in the future the price that they agree today. However, this is costly and requires a level of expertise, often lacking in small exporting/importing firms.

Many believe that a single currency will lead to increased competition and trade within the single currency area. Price discrepancies will be more obvious to firms. A higher price, charged in a market of a member state, should signal firms from other countries that opportunities exist in that market. Increased competition should lead to lower prices for consumers. Additionally, heightened competition should strengthen European firms and prepare them to compete in other markets like North America and the Far East.

Another argument in favour of the move to a single currency area is the positive effects which have resulted from the convergence criteria. These requirements have acted as a constraint on the Irish authorities when dealing with the public finances. Given the events of the late 1970s and the early 1980s when public expenditure was out of control, restrictions on the public finances are a welcome feature of Irish budgetary policy. In terms of its financial position, Ireland's ranking within the EU has improved enormously.

Finally, a European Central bank is independent from national governments and political favouritism. This is likely to enhance the credibility of the new monetary institution, it is argued. A country such as Ireland which relies heavily on foreign trade is likely to benefit from such an institutional change.

All of these changes are likely to impact favourably on Irish economic growth, as measured by GDP.

Arguments opposing Irish participation in the single currency

By far the most important economic argument against participation is the future consequences for the Irish economy if Britain continues to 'opt out'. Although the level of trade with Britain has fallen in the past thirty years, it is still Ireland's most important trading partner and the outlet for most indigenous exports. Opponents of EMU are particularly concerned that the exchange rate links between EU countries inside the single currency area and those outside will not be strong enough. A weak sterling hurts Irish exporters. A strong sterling causes inflationary worries in Ireland. Either way, Britain's refusal to participate makes EMU an unattractive proposition for Ireland.

Another significant issue is the problem of peripherality and whether EMU can lead to economic convergence. A brief look at history would indicate that economic activity tends towards the centre, where the benefits of economies of scale are most evident. Although labour costs tend to be much lower in the peripheral regions compared to the more central regions, further economic integration may result only in a widening of the wealth gap between the core nations and the weaker nations of the EU.[20]

Another drawback is the absence of a fiscal union, which exists in other monetary unions like Australia and the United States. Member states of the EU do not share common tax and welfare systems. If there is a localised demand or supply shock in the US, the tax burden is reduced and social welfare payments increase, acting as 'automatic stabilisers' for the local economy. An adverse shock to an EU state is not followed by an automatic transfer of funds from the EU or a reduction of tax payments to the EU. Because of the stability pact, the national government is limited in its response to negative shocks. Given the UK's fierce resistance to a fiscal union, it is unlikely that it will be adopted by the EU in the near future.

Finally, devaluation as a policy option will no longer be available in a single currency market. In the past, public authorities have tackled unemployment by devaluing the domestic currency in order to boost foreign demand for Irish products. This will no longer be possible. Related to this is the issue of policy sovereignty. Membership in the EMU is likely to result in a loss of autonomy, and in particular control over monetary policy. This is an important issue in the UK where an independent monetary policy is a central part of their overall economic strategy. In Ireland, it was not such an important issue because monetary policy was largely outside the control of the Irish authorities.

The single currency since its launch in January 1999

The euro was launched in January 1999. The prediction was for a strong currency, with early gains against the US dollar and sterling expected. The outcome was very different, as Figure 15.10 shows.

Figure 15.10:   Euro exchange rates, January 1999–October 2000

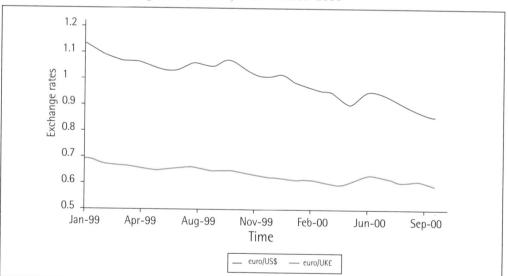

In the first month of its launch, the average exchange rate was 1.161 US dollars to one euro. The average €/UK£ exchange rate for the same month was 0.703 (UK£ per one €). Eleven months later, the €/US$ had fallen in value to 1.011, a decline of almost 13%.

Likewise, the euro fell in value against the UK£, to 0.627 in December 1999. The euro continued to fall in value for most of the following year. Eventually, the ECB intervened to support the currency. At first, it increased interest rates. Numerous ECB interest rate hikes followed. Later in the year and with the support of other central banks, it intervened in the foreign exchange market. Despite this support, the euro's perception as a weak currency persisted. Let us consider some possible explanations for this fall in the value of the euro.

On economic grounds, the fall in the value of the euro can be explained partly by the growth differential between the US economy and the euro area economies. Whereas the US economy was booming throughout 1999, economic growth in the big euro area countries such as Germany and Italy was sluggish. In addition, better returns on assets in the form of higher interest rates attracted capital flows to the US and UK in preference to Euroland.

Aside from these economic reasons, there are institutional and political reasons for the weak currency. The new ECB is the sole monetary institution responsible for exchange rate policy within the euro area. Although the Maastricht treaty conferred unprecedented powers of independence on the ECB, the euro was subject to political pressure within weeks of its launch. It would take some time before the ECB could gain the same anti-inflation reputation that the Bundesbank had earned. Aside from political interference, the credibility of the ECB was not helped by a number of events in its first two years. A perceived lack of accountability and openness, unhelpful comments by ECB personnel (including its President) and indecisive action by its Governing Council contributed to the euro's weakness on foreign exchange markets. By October 2000, twenty-two months after its launch, the single currency had lost over 26% of its value against the US dollar. In the same period, it lost almost 30% of its value against the Japanese yen and 16.2% against the UK pound.

The fall in the value of the euro had serious implications for EMU member states. This was particularly true for Ireland where external trade is sizeable and exchange rate movements are a significant determinant of inflation. Consider the case study below.

CASE STUDY

Extract from *The Sunday Independent*
Light a penny candle for our economy
by Colm McCarthy

The record of Irish economic expansion in recent years is well known. This is the seventh straight year of growth at eight per cent and above. Unemployment has fallen to one-third its peak levels. Employers and State agencies are actively seeking immigrant workers. On any reckoning, the economy has been operating at a high rate of capacity utilisation for some years past. The danger of overheating has been flagged repeatedly. But the expressions of concern have become more vociferous in the last few weeks. Wim Duisenberg, the European Central Bank President, and the authors of the recent ESRI report on the Irish economy, have drawn attention to the evidence of inflationary

⟶

pressure, and both have called for fiscal restraint, which means the deferral of whatever tax cuts were in the pipeline. But neither has produced a complete explanation of the rise in economic temperature, nor have they convinced the Government that fiscal tightening is the way to go. But in all the discussion of the recent rise in inflationary pressure in Ireland, there is a Dog that Did Not Bark. It is the exchange rate of the Irish currency, since January 1998 [sic], the euro. This currency has been a lead balloon over the last 15 months, showing spectacular weakness against sterling and the dollar in particular.

In order to get a measure of the extent of a currency's movements it is necessary to apply weights which reflect the importance of the various foreign currencies in external trade. The trade-weighted index for the Irish pound is computed daily by the Bank of England, and it shows that the Irish currency has effectively been devalued by around 9 to 10 per cent from the levels prevailing at the end of 1998. In addition, interest rates are down, notwithstanding the recent rebound, by about 2.5 per cent compared to the levels of 1998. Either of these developments would have imparted a huge expansionary stimulus to the Irish economy, already running up against resource constraints prior to our entry to the euro in January 1999. Taken in combination, they have created a situation that is virtually unmanageable.

Something like this was always on the cards. Ireland does more trade in dollars and in sterling than it does in euros. This is not true of any other euro member. So the weak euro has had a bigger impact in Ireland than it has had in other euro members, who in any event, needed some stimulus last year.

The European Central Bank, and the ESRI, are thus quite correct to argue that the Irish economy is overheating. They are, however, quite wrong if they believe that excessive tax giveaways have caused the overheating. A tax increase, the preferred policy of both the European Central Bank and the ESRI, would have limited power to slow the economy, even if tax reductions had caused the problem, which they have not. Irish imports plus exports total 157 per cent of GDP, and this renders domestic fiscal policy ineffective. It is the exchange rate that works in this type of economy. The huge stimulus of the post-euro period has come from the combined impact of the exchange rate fall and the cut in interest rates. Since we can no longer alter either our exchange rate or our interest rate, the task of macroeconomic stabilisation is akin to playing tennis without a racket.

. . .

If, in future years, the Irish economy experiences big swings in the effective exchange rate – and there is every likelihood that this will happen if Britain stays out – we can pursue no available practical course of action to neutralise the impact, aside from prayer. We can light penny candles at two locations. The first is at the UK Treasury, seeking the favour of an early decision from Her Majesty's Government to join the euro and thus resolve our dilemma. The second is at the European Central Bank HQ in Frankfurt, where we would implore Mr Duisenberg and his colleagues to so orient European monetary policy as to stabilise the economy of the Republic of Ireland. I could not recommend that we commission a fresh report from the ESRI, or from any other source, on the options for macroeconomic management. Prayer is the course we have chosen.

Source: *The Sunday Independent*, 23 April 2000.

Questions

1. According to this article, what are the policy implications arising from Ireland's membership of EMU? How different is Ireland's position compared with the position of other euro members?
2. What was the main reason for the fall in Irish interest rates in the run-up to the euro launch? What factors were behind the more 'recent rebound' in euro interest rates?
3. What constraints are there on the Irish government's use of fiscal policy within the context of EMU membership? Outline the arguments in favour of the Irish government's tax reduction policies and of the alternate fiscal restraint proposals favoured by the ECB and the ESRI.

Answers on website

SUMMARY

1. The balance of payments is an accounting record of all transactions between economic agents of one country and the rest of the world. It comprises a current and a capital account. The current account records the movement of all goods and services whereas the capital account is a statement of all capital transactions into and out of a country. The way in which the balance of payments actually balances depends largely on the exchange rate regime.
2. An exchange rate is the price of one currency in terms of another. Factors which influence the exchange rate include the level of foreign trade, interest rate differentials, inflation differentials, speculation and income differentials. There are a number of different exchange rate regimes. Under a fixed exchange rate system the Central Banks are obliged to maintain currencies at predetermined rates in terms of gold or of a 'hard' currency. Under a flexible exchange rate system, the exchange rate is determined by the forces of demand and supply. Semi-fixed exchange rate systems and managed floating systems are other examples of exchange rate regimes.
3. The European Monetary System is an example of a semi-fixed exchange rate system. Its aim was to create a zone of monetary stability. Central to the EMS is its exchange rate mechanism wherein member states are committed to a central rate and a band of fluctuation. Central Banks, in attempting to support the value of a currency, can intervene using external reserves or by changing interest rates or realigning the currency within the ERM.
4. A devaluation (revaluation) is a reduction (increase) in the value of a currency *vis-à-vis* other currencies. With a devaluation the level of exports is likely to increase, jobs in the exposed sector may be saved and the pressure on interest rates may be reduced. The drawbacks include higher import prices, the possibility of higher interest rates in the long term, an increase in the size of the foreign debt and larger debt service repayments. Devaluation is no longer a policy option for the euro area countries.
5. Economic and Monetary Union has been an aim of the EU since its foundation. Central to the economic union is the creation of a single market where the flow of

goods, services, labour and capital is unrestricted. Monetary union involves the creation of a single currency and one Central Bank. Co-ordination of economic policies is another feature of EMU. The three stages towards EMU were laid out in the Maastricht treaty. The convergence criteria related to inflation rates, interest rates, exchange rates and a country's fiscal position.

6. The aim of Irish exchange rate policy is price stability. Within the ERM, this was best achieved, according to the monetary authorities, by fixing the Irish pound to other member states' currencies. Ireland's experience within the ERM was mixed. Sterling's absence from the exchange rate mechanism of the EMS caused policy problems for the Irish authorities, and trading problems for Irish businesses. Sterling's absence from the single currency causes similar problems for Ireland, despite the lower transaction costs that accrue from EMU participation.

KEY TERMS

Balance of payments	Realignment
Current account	Devaluation
Merchandise trade balance	Revaluation
Capital account	Economic and monetary union
Exchange rate	The Maastricht treaty
Flexible exchange rate system	Internal market
Fixed exchange rate system	European Monetary Institute
External reserves	Euro
Optimum currency areas	Convergence criteria
Managed floating	Excessive Deficit Procedure
Semi-fixed exchange rate system	Stability and Growth Pact
European Monetary System	Purchasing power parity
European currency unit	Effective exchange rate index
Exchange rate mechanism	Economic and social cohesion
Fluctuation bands	Peripherality
Foreign exchange intervention	Fiscal union

REVIEW QUESTIONS

1. Explain the term 'balance of payments'. Distinguish between the trade balance, the current account balance and the capital account balance.
2. Imagine that the only two currencies traded on the foreign exchange market are the UK pound sterling and the Japanese yen. Explain how the UK£/yen exchange rate is determined. What factors influence this exchange rate? Explain.
3. Explain the link between the balance of payments and the different exchange rate systems.
4. Explain how the ERM operated. Briefly outline the background to and the details of the 1992–93 currency crisis.
5. What is the objective of exchange rate policy? In the Irish context, explain how it was to be achieved (i) pre-1979; (ii) in the ERM; (iii) in EMU.

6. (a) Outline the three stages to EMU as laid down in the Maastricht treaty.
    (b) What are the benefits and drawbacks to EMU as they relate specifically to Ireland?

WORKING PROBLEMS

1. Items normally found in a balance of payments statement are randomly listed in Table 15.7. You are a Central Bank employee and it is your job to set up the balance of payments statement in its new format. You are also required to insert headings where appropriate.

Table 15.7: The balance of payments, m

Reserve Assets	-2,280	Other investment	7,459
Balance on current account	706	Merchandise	17,771
Direct investment	4,422	Balance on capital account	840
Net income	-9,382	Portfolio investment	-8,466
Balance on financial account	1,135	Net errors and omissions	-2,681
Services	-9,002	Current transfers	1,319

2. Using monthly data, tabulate the value of the euro against both the UK pound and the US dollar in the twelve-month period January 1999 to December 1999.

[Note: The European Central Bank *Annual Report* or *Monthly Bulletin* is a good source. The ECB's website is www.ecb.int.]

MULTI-CHOICE QUESTIONS

1. In the case of the UK£/US$ exchange rate, an increase in UK imports will:
   (a) push the supply curve of UK pounds to the left, leading to an increase in the UK£/US$ exchange rate;
   (b) push the demand curve for UK pounds to the right, leading to an increase in the UK£/US$ exchange rate;
   (c) push the demand curve for UK pounds to the left, leading to a reduction in the UK£/US$ exchange rate;
   (d) push the supply curve of UK pounds to the right, leading to a reduction in the UK£/US$ exchange rate;
   (e) none of the above.

2. Suppose US national income increases. All other things being equal, the euro/US$ exchange rate:
   (a) increases on account of a rise in US imports;
   (b) decreases on account of a rise in US imports;
   (c) increases on account of a rise in US exports;
   (d) decreases on account of a rise in US exports;
   (e) none of the above.

3. There is a surplus in the current account of the balance of payments. Under a fixed exchange rate system this is reflected in:
   (a) a rise in external reserves;
   (b) a fall in the exchange rate;
   (c) a fall in external reserves;
   (d) both (a) and (b) above;
   (e) both (b) and (c) above.

4. The central rate of the DM/Frf before August 1993 was DM1 = 3.3539Frf, with a 2.25% band of fluctuation. The upper limit (rounded off to two decimal points) was:
   (a) 3.56;
   (b) 3.41;
   (c) 3.28;
   (d) 3.43;
   (e) none of the above.

5. The Treaty on European Union:
   (a) is an amendment to the Treaty of Rome;
   (b) arose out of the Intergovernmental Conference of 1991;
   (c) sets out the path to EMU;
   (d) is commonly known as the Maastricht treaty;
   (e) all of the above.

6. The Stability and Growth Pact restricts the use of:
   (a) exchange rate policy;
   (b) competition policy;
   (c) fiscal policy;
   (d) monetary policy;
   (e) none of the above.

TRUE OR FALSE (SUPPORT YOUR ANSWER)

1. The balance of payments statement always balances.

2. If the euro is the base currency and the US dollar is the counter currency, then the exchange rate is expressed as the number of US dollars per one euro.

3. Ireland and Britain joined the EMS on its inception in 1979.

4. Devaluation is simply another term for depreciation.

5. The ultimate aim of Irish exchange rate policy is parity with sterling.

6. EMU involves a monetary and fiscal union.

CASE STUDY

Extract from *The Sunday Tribune*
Poor prognosis for euro: Sick currency is showing no signs of speedy recovery
by Matt Cooper

Ireland, one of the best performing economies in the world, is irrevocably tied to a seriously ailing currency. Membership of the euro threatens to ruin the wonderful advances of recent years: exporters to Britain and America have been coining it because of the currency advantages provided by the value of the euro against sterling and the dollar, but inflation is now at its highest level in ten years. Inflation threatens to wipe out many of the benefits of economic growth.

Our government's policy seems to be one of waiting for the euro to recover. If it does, that should help to drive inflation down. The problem is that confidence in the euro is now so diminished that the chances of a quick recovery in its value on international currency markets are poor. Even higher interest rates are unlikely to restore investor confidence in the currency. The euro is so unpopular that it will go lower still. The 0.25% rise last Thursday will have minimal effect and it is expected that rates will have to rise by at least 1% more between now and year-end in an effort to provide support for the currency. Such an increase would be good news for Ireland but unfortunately it is likely to be too little, too late. There is likely to be a lengthy period of sustained currency weakness, which is bad news for Ireland.

Nobody is willing to take the chance on buying the euro, because nobody is confident about when it is likely to recover. Money is leaving the euro-zone because investors see better opportunities elsewhere. The outward flow is larger than the inward flow from the region's current account surplus. At some stage, the currency will recover. It may reach such a low that suddenly investors will reckon they can profit from buying it and there will be a surge in interest. But the recovery may be limited as a percentage of the previous fall.

The European Central Bank must shoulder a considerable portion of the blame. It has been guilty of bad presentation and now nobody believes what is says. Since the ECB embarked on its programme of interest rate rises to boost the currency it has fallen by more than 10% in value against the dollar. There is no doubt that the euro is now cheap but that doesn't mean that anyone wants to buy damaged goods. The EU's overall growth is likely to be 3.5% this year. Inflation is just over 2%. Those figures in themselves should boost interest in the euro. But Britain is likely to grow by at least as much and the US by twice as much, despite their overvalued currencies. Why should investors abandon economies that have shown consistently high returns in recent years and seem

→

better able to adapt to changing economic circumstances?

. . .

Euroland exporters have enjoyed the benefits of the weak currency. Both the US and euroland export only 10% of output. Policy is set to suit the remaining 90%. It is hard to argue with this, even if it is totally unsuited to Ireland's position. Our

currency has undergone a massive and inadvertent devaluation of 28% against the dollar and 22% against sterling. The people who say that the euro must recover are among those who always insisted that sterling would later join the euro if we did first. There is little chance of that now. So should anyone believe them when they say that the euro 'must' recover?

Source: *The Sunday Tribune*, 30 April 2000.

Questions

1. What are the economic benefits of a weak currency? Why, in present circumstances, is a weak euro 'bad news for Ireland'?
2. What short-term options does the ECB have to support the 'sick currency'?
3. In the context of the adoption of a single currency, what are the main differences between the US and Euroland? [Note: See Appendix 15.2 on Optimum Currency Areas]

APPENDIX 15.1: PURCHASING POWER PARITY

Purchasing power parity (PPP) or the law of one price explains changes in exchange rates in terms of inflation differentials. PPP can be expressed in many different ways.

In its simplest form, the law of one price states that the price of a commodity in different countries, but expressed in a common currency, should be equal. It can be written as follows:

$$P_{UK} \times E = P_{US}$$ [1]

where P_{UK} is the price of the good in the UK, E is the exchange rate (expressed as the number of dollars per one UK pound) and P_{US} is the price of the same good, sold in the US and expressed in US dollars. This is called the strong version of PPP.[21]

For example, we can compare the price of a McDonald's Big Mac in London with a Big Mac in New York by adjusting for the exchange rate.[22] In April 2000, a Big Mac cost UK£1.90 in London and US$2.51 in New York. The actual UK£/US$ exchange rate in April 2000 was UK£1 = US$1.58. We can compare the two prices by converting into a common currency. Consider converting sterling into dollars, as follows,

UK£1.90 × 1.58 = US$3.00

By converting into a common currency, in this case US$, we can compare the price of a Big Mac in New York with the price in London. If these prices are equal we can say that the law of one price holds. In this case they are not equal. In New York, a Big Mac costs US$2.51 whereas according to the law of one price a Big Mac in New York should cost US$3.00. This begs the question – why, in theory at least, should they be equal and why, it seems in practice, are they not equal? In theory, prices should equate across frontiers because of price competition and arbitrage where arbitrage is the buying and selling of goods in different markets in order to exploit price differentials and to make a riskless profit. Suppose, for example, that a personal computer is relatively cheap in the US compared to the UK. By buying them in the US and selling them in the UK, a profit can be made. As a result, US exports will increase. Holding all other things equal, this will give rise to a balance of payments surplus in the US.

Two possible results may emerge. First, the balance of payments surplus will cause an increase in the exchange rate (explained in Section 15.3). Second, the increase in demand for computers will push up the domestic price level. Either way, the differential between the domestic price level and the foreign price level diminishes. Over time, the price differential between the personal computer sold in the US and that sold in the UK disappears.

In the real world, however, factors exist which allow price differentials to persist. These factors include transport costs, tariffs, quotas and indirect taxes. These drive a wedge between prices.

APPENDIX 15.2: EMU AND OPTIMUM CURRENCY AREAS

The Palgrave *Dictionary of Economics* defines an OCA as 'the "optimum" geographical domain having as a general means of payment either a single common currency or several currencies whose exchange rates are immutably pegged to one another with unlimited convertibility for both current and capital transactions, but whose exchange rates fluctuate in unison against the rest of the world.'[23] By the end of the 1990s, Optimum Currency Areas (OCA) had re-emerged to become one of the most recognised theories in the economics profession. This coincided with the launch of the single currency in 1999 and, in the same year, the awarding of the Nobel prize in Economics to Robert Mundell, the person most responsible for the advancement of OCA theory. It is within the context of the viability of European Economic and Monetary Union and the suitability of its participating member states that we briefly review the theory of Optimum Currency Areas.

The benefits of monetary union, namely lower transaction costs, policy credibility and elimination of exchange rate variability need to be assessed against the costs of monetary union, namely loss of monetary policy autonomy associated with the exchange rate instrument. For a monetary union to work, participating regions or countries should be closely integrated. Integration of factor and product markets is considered necessary. More specifically, the theory outlines a number of criteria for assessing the degree of economic integration. The criteria are as follows:

- factor mobility;
- wage and price flexibility;
- similarity of economic structures;
- diversity of production.

Regions with a high degree of labour and capital mobility and where wages and prices are flexible are considered suitable for a currency area. In addition, regions that have similar economic structures and high industrial diversification tend to be suited to a single currency area. It is argued that highly diversified countries are better candidates as the diversification provides some insulation against shocks.

Essentially, the theory of OCA depends on the type and size of disturbances and the speed with which the economy or region can adjust to these disturbances. In the case of a currency area, it is asymmetric or country-specific shocks (i.e. shocks that affect different countries differently) that matter. As for the speed of adjustment, this depends on the adjustment mechanisms that are available. In the absence of exchange rate autonomy, the remaining adjustment mechanisms are factor mobility, flexibility of prices and fiscal stabilisers. If, for whatever reason, these are absent, output and employment levels will adjust, resulting in higher emigration and unemployment.

These adjustment mechanisms weaken the case for a European monetary union, it is argued. Within the EU, labour mobility is low, more due to cultural and linguistic differences and rigidities in housing markets than to border controls. There is evidence of wage rigidities across the EU member states. As for fiscal federalism, the absence of a centralised budget and any meaningful fiscal redistribution in the EU means that a region adversely affected by an asymmetric shock will not be compensated with lower taxes and higher transfers. The EU budget is small and lacks any automatic mechanism that would transfer funds to adversely-affected regions. Taking these into account, it would appear to be the case that the European Union is less of an optimum currency area than, say, the United States. There is considerable evidence to support this claim. However, supporters of European EMU point to the endogeneity of OCA, that is, the suitability of regions or countries participating in a currency area may increase as membership of the currency area becomes more likely. In the context of EMU, the euro itself may encourage closer economic integration. For example, the European Commission has argued that greater economic integration in the EU will reduce the probability that countries will be hit by asymmetric shocks. This claim is subject to debate.

APPENDIX 15.3: THE MUNDELL-FLEMING MODEL

We use the Mundell-Fleming model, which was first developed in the early 1960s, to assess the effectiveness of fiscal and monetary policy within an open economy framework. We examine both policies under fixed and flexible exchange rate systems with the assumption that capital flows are perfectly mobile.

Monetary policy under a fixed exchange rate regime

Consider an increase in the money supply by the Central Bank. As the money supply increases, interest rates fall and national income increases. Because domestic interest rates are lower than world interest rates, an outflow of capital results. A deficit in the current account also emerges as a result of the higher income levels and the subsequent higher import levels. We know from our analysis of the exchange rate market that an overall balance of payments deficit causes a depreciation of the domestic currency against other currencies. Because of its membership in the exchange rate system, the Central Bank is obliged to maintain the value of its currency between certain limits. Hence, the Central Bank intervenes by selling the stock of foreign currency in exchange for domestic currency. By taking this domestic currency out of circulation the domestic money supply decreases. In doing so, the economy reverts to its original level of national income. Hence, an independent monetary policy is ineffective.

Fiscal policy under a fixed exchange rate regime

Consider an increase in spending by the government. As government expenditure increases, interest rates and national income levels rise. Because domestic interest rates are now higher than world interest rates, an inflow of capital results, leading to a capital account surplus. This surplus is only partly offset by a deficit in the current account which arises because the higher income level means that more goods are imported. The overall surplus results in an increase in the exchange rate. The Central Bank intervenes in order to maintain the value of the domestic currency between certain limits. It buys foreign currency and sells domestic currency. By injecting more pounds into circulation, the Central Bank increases the domestic money supply. In doing so, it increases income levels further. Hence, fiscal policy is effective.

Monetary policy under a flexible exchange rate regime

Consider an increase in the money supply by the Central Bank. As the money supply increases, interest rates fall. With domestic interest rates now lower than world interest rates, an outflow of capital results. A capital outflow results in a lowering of the domestic currency against other currencies. As the domestic currency depreciates, imports become more expensive and exports become cheaper. We know from the Keynesian income determination model that an increase in exports will increase the level of national income. Under this flexible exchange rate system national income increases, initially out of the increase in the money supply and subsequently from an increase in exports. Hence, monetary policy is effective.

Fiscal policy under a flexible exchange rate regime

Consider an increase in spending by the government. As government expenditure increases, interest rates and income levels rise. The increase in interest rates leads to an inflow of capital, resulting in a capital account surplus. This surplus is partly offset by a deficit in the current account which arises from the higher income levels and the higher import levels. This overall balance of payments surplus results in an increase in the exchange rate. As the exchange rate appreciates, exports become more expensive whereas imports become cheaper. The subsequent decline in exports reduces the income level which in turn reverts to its original position. Hence, fiscal policy is ineffective.

In summary, under a fixed exchange rate system fiscal policy is more effective than monetary policy whereas under a flexible exchange rate system monetary policy is more effective than fiscal policy.

CHAPTER 16

EXPLAINING THE MACROECONOMY – THE AD/AS MODEL

'Although economists can tell the government much about how to influence aggregate demand, they can tell it precious little about how to influence aggregate supply.'[1]

Alan S. Blinder

'To many economists this [supply-side economics] has the potential to be the greatest single breakthrough in economic thinking since the Keynesian revolution.'[2]

Mark Brownrigg

CHAPTER OBJECTIVES

Upon completing this chapter, the student should understand:

- aggregate demand;
- aggregate supply and potential output;
- short-run and long-run aggregate supply;
- macroeconomic equilibrium;
- demand-management policies;
- supply-side policies.

OUTLINE

16.1 Aggregate demand
16.2 Aggregate supply
16.3 The policy debate
16.4 The Irish experience

INTRODUCTION

Until now our analysis of macroeconomics has been limited. Our model of the economy is incomplete. For one, the focus has been exclusively on the demand side of the economy. We considered planned expenditure or spending. We assumed that the supply side of the economy was passive, reacting largely to changes in aggregate demand. Policy considerations were limited to demand-side policies, i.e. fiscal or monetary policy. In addition, prices were fixed throughout the model. Therefore, we could not explore inflation, a possible side-effect of government demand-side policies.

A complete model of the economy is inherently complex with many different variables. In this chapter, we discuss a model called the aggregate demand/aggregate supply (AD/AS) model. Both the demand and the supply sides of the economy are considered. Price is a variable. The purpose of the AD/AS model is to provide the student with a complete framework which can be used to analyse macroeconomic principles and policy options.

16.1 AGGREGATE DEMAND

In the Keynesian model of income determination we defined aggregate expenditure as the total spending in the economy by all economic agents. It is comprised of consumer expenditure, investment expenditure, government expenditure and net exports. With the help of the income determination model, we examined the level of expenditure at each level of income. We now examine the level of expenditure at each price level.

Definition
Aggregate demand is the total output which is demanded at each price level holding all other variables constant.

The curve which shows the relationship between the level of demand and the aggregate price level is called the aggregate demand curve, or simply the AD curve.

The AD curve is normally downward sloping, showing that the lower the price level, the greater will be the aggregate quantity of goods and services demanded in the economy. The demand for national output is inversely related to the price level.

This negative relationship between price and the aggregate quantity of goods and services demanded exists for a number of reasons. First, as the price level falls, the purchasing power of money balances increases. This results in an increase in people's wealth. This so-called real balance or wealth effect leads to a rise in consumption.[3] As consumption increases, aggregate demand increases. This effect may be small on account of the weak link between prices, wealth and consumption.

Second, the increase in purchasing power arising out of lower prices may induce a separate effect. Less money is required to carry out a fixed level of transactions. As the excess money is saved, there is an increase in the supply of money. This, in turn, forces interest rates downwards. The lower cost of borrowing induces greater investment expenditure by firms and possibly greater spending by households. As investment increases, aggregate demand increases. This is called the interest rate effect and it may also be weak.

A third reason why the AD curve slopes downwards is called the international trade effect. As the price level falls (or, to be more accurate, as the domestic price level falls relative to the foreign price level) domestic firms become more competitive. Accordingly, the level of domestically produced goods sold in foreign markets increases, i.e. exports increase. As exports increase, aggregate demand increases.

Derivation of the AD curve

In order to derive the AD curve we return to the income determination model. The top panel of Figure 16.1 is similar to Figure 14.2. Aggregate expenditure is measured on the vertical axis and income is measured on the horizontal axis. The AE curve shows total spending for each level of income at a particular price level.

Figure 16.1: Deriving the AD curve

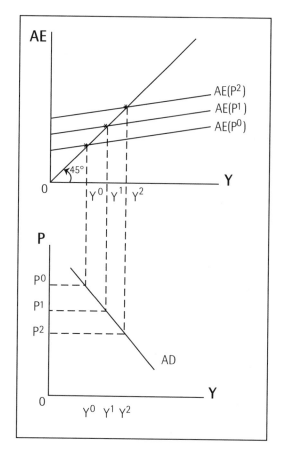

We now examine the relationship between aggregate expenditure and price. The AE curve is drawn for a price level, P^0. The equilibrium level of income is Y^0. Suppose prices fall. We know from our previous discussion that as prices fall aggregate expenditure rises. This is reflected in the higher AE curve, AE (P^1). The higher AE level results in a higher level of equilibrium income, in this case, Y^1. As price continues to fall, to P^2, AE rises further leading to, yet again, a higher level of income, Y^2. The result in (P,Y) space is a locus of points which form a downward sloping AD curve.

Definition

The aggregate demand (AD) curve shows the level of national output demanded at different price levels.

As the aggregate price level rises, the quantity of output demanded falls. An alternative way of deriving the AD curve is depicted in Appendix 16.1.

We have already stated that the real balance and interest rate effects may be quite small. Hence, the increase in aggregate expenditure arising out of the fall in prices is small. In graphic terms, the upward shift of the AE curve is quite modest. As a result, the subsequent AD curve is likely to be relatively inelastic or steep.

The AD curve depicts the relationship between price and total output demanded, *ceteris paribus*. The variables which we are holding constant include government spending, taxes and the money supply. A change in any of these factors will cause a shift of the aggregate demand curve. We will examine changes in the underlying variables in greater detail in Section 16.3.

16.2 AGGREGATE SUPPLY

The term 'aggregate supply' is a macroeconomic concept.

Definition
Aggregate supply describes the total quantity of national output supplied by all producers at each level of price.

It is closely associated with the capacity of the economy to produce. This is often referred to as potential output.

Definition
Potential output represents the maximum level of output that can be produced given a country's productive capacity.

It is determined by the amount of natural, capital and human resources available and the efficiency with which these resources can be put to use.

The aggregate supply curve or simply the AS curve is to macroeconomics what the supply curve (of Chapter 2) is to microeconomics. It is, however, much more complex than the individual or market supply curve.

Definition
The aggregate supply (AS) curve shows the output of GDP produced at different price levels.

There is a distinction between the short-run AS curve and the long-run AS curve. This distinction is largely based on the speed at which factor inputs, particularly labour, react to a change in economic conditions.

In the short run, the costs of factors of production are assumed to be constant or at least to respond slowly to changes in the demand for the factor input. For example, wage rates may be constant in the short run because of contracts between employers and employees.

The positive relationship between output and prices in the short run is depicted in an upward sloping AS curve. It is drawn in Figure 16.2.

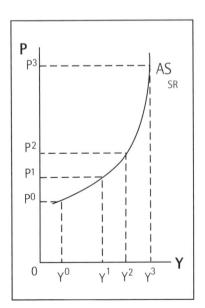

Figure 16.2: The conventional short-run AS curve

The AS curve, as drawn in Figure 16.2, becomes steeper as the level of national income increases. Why?

Initially, the AS curve is elastic. At low levels of output, there is excess capacity in the economy. Thus, a small increase in the price level, from P^0 to P^1, elicits a large increase in output, from Y^0 to Y^1.

The next portion of the AS curve is steeper. From our discussion in Chapter 5, we know that in the short run, some inputs are fixed and others are variable. As production levels increase, some firms reach full capacity. Further, as all firms demand more labour and other variable inputs, the cost of those inputs may increase. If prices continue to rise, output increases, but only by small increments. An increase in the price level from P^1 to P^2, similar in magnitude to the last price increase, leads to a much smaller increase in output, from Y^1 to Y^2.

The final section of the short-run AS curve is inelastic. We can think of Y^3 as the limit of what this economy can produce if all of its factors of production are fully employed. Even if the price level increases above P^3, the level of national output will not expand.

The AS curve is drawn to show the relationship between national output and price, *ceteris paribus*. The variables which are held constant include technology, the capital stock and the skills of the labour force. Any change in these determinants will alter the position of the AS curve. We will examine changes that shift the AS curve in greater detail in the next section.

This version of the AS curve combines the extreme classical and Keynesian views which are based on different assumptions about the labour market (see Section 11.3 for a more complete discussion on the differences between the classical and Keynesian interpretations of the labour market). We will look briefly at the two perspectives.

The classical view

According to classical economists, the output of the economy is based on the labour market. As long as wages and prices are flexible, the labour market returns to full-employment equilibrium. Labour is combined with the economy's other inputs to produce goods and services. Therefore, in the classical view, the real output of the economy is the same as the potential output because all factors of production are fully employed. The short-run AS curve is vertical at the full-employment output level, as shown in panel (a) of Figure 16.3.

Figure 16.3: The extreme classical and Keynesian short-run AS curves

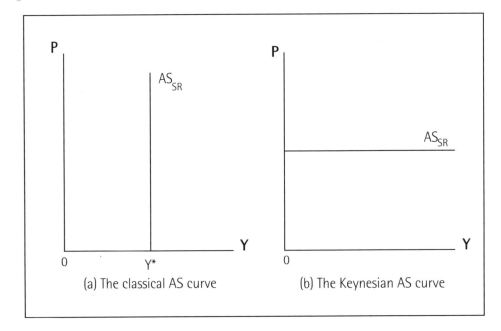

(a) The classical AS curve   (b) The Keynesian AS curve

The inelastic AS curve means that output is unresponsive to changes in the price level. Any change in output occurs because of a shift of the aggregate supply curve.

The Keynesian view

Recall from our discussion in Chapter 11, that from the Keynesian perspective, demand for labour depends on the demand for output. In other words, causation is reversed. In the classical model, national output is determined by the number of people employed when the labour market is at equilibrium. From the Keynesian perspective, the number of people employed is derived from the demand for goods.

Also, recall that Keynes believed that there are institutional factors which cause wages to be rigid in the short run. In other words, firms can hire additional workers at the same wage that they are paying their current labour force. If firms are producing at less than full capacity, they can increase their variable inputs and increase production at a constant cost per unit.

This means that as demand increases, the level of output will increase, even though the price level has not changed. In other words, the short-run AS curve is perfectly elastic as shown in panel (b) of Figure 16.3.

As stated previously, the upward sloping AS curve is a compromise between the extreme views of the classicals and the Keynesians.

The elastic portion of the AS curve as shown in Figure 16.2 is Keynesian. At low levels of output, where there is excess capacity, changes in output can occur without increasing the price level. This means that over a range of production, the cost of variable inputs, particularly labour, is not changing. The upward sloping portion of the

AS curve means that, as the price level rises, the level of production increases. The vertical section of the AS curve reflects the classical view that the maximum output of an economy is constrained at the level where all factors of production are fully employed.

In the long run, changes to factor prices and, in particular, wages are incorporated into the model. Input prices adjust fully to changes in the price level in the long run. There is no dispute between Keynesians and classical economists concerning the aggregate supply curve in the long run. The vertical long-run AS curve is drawn in Figure 16.4, at the potential level of national output, Y*. It shows the maximum output that the economy is able to produce at different price levels, assuming that input prices fully adjust to changing economic conditions.

Figure 16.4: The long-run AS curve

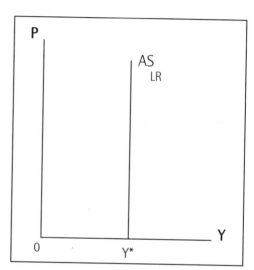

16.3 THE POLICY DEBATE

The AD/AS model is the centrepiece of modern macroeconomics. Both the demand and supply aspects of the economy are considered. Price changes are also incorporated in the analysis. Short-run equilibrium in the AD/AS model is shown in Figure 16.5.

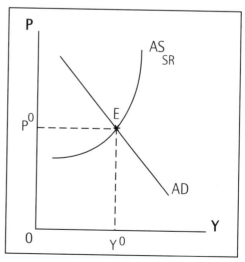

Figure 16.5: Equilibrium in (P,Y) space

The downward sloping AD curve depicts the relationship between total spending and different price levels. The upward sloping, short-run AS curve shows the level of output which the economy produces at different price levels. Macroeconomic equilibrium occurs at (P^0, Y^0), the intersection of the AD and the AS curves. At this point the output which households and firms demand is equal to the output which firms are willing to supply. Hence, equilibrium price and output are simultaneously determined by the interaction of aggregate demand and supply.

If the price level is above equilibrium, aggregate supply exceeds aggregate demand resulting in a rise of unplanned stocks. For equilibrium to be restored, price must adjust downwards. Similarly, if the price level is below equilibrium, aggregate demand exceeds aggregate supply resulting in an excess demand of goods and services. In order for equilibrium to be restored, price adjusts upwards. At P^0, aggregate demand equals aggregate supply.

With a more complete model of the economy than before, we can analyse the full effects of both demand-management policies and supply-side policies. The analysis is divided into short-run and long-run effects.

We begin, however, with a brief explanation of both types of policies. We previously defined demand-management policies as the collective term used to explain various government policies which target the level of aggregate demand in the economy. Examples of demand-management policies include changes in government spending, the tax rate, the money supply or the interest rate. Any of these policies will shift the AD curve.

Definition
Supply-side policies are targeted at increasing the productive capacity of the economy.

Measures include improving the infrastructure, adopting training programmes to reduce the costs of production and developing new technologies.

Any of these policies will shift the AS curve.

Short-run analysis

Demand-management policies

We will use the AD/AS model to assess the effect of discretionary fiscal policy on the aggregate price level and national income.

Definition
Discretionary fiscal policy refers to deliberate, as opposed to automatic, changes in government expenditure or tax rates in order to influence national income.

Expansionary fiscal policy involves increasing government spending or cutting the tax rate in an effort to increase national income. Contractionary fiscal policy is initiated by decreasing government spending or raising the tax rate.

The AD curve is initially drawn for one set of fiscal policy variables, i.e. a particular level of government spending and a particular tax rate. Any change in a fiscal policy variable causes the AD curve to shift. Figure 16.6 illustrates the effect that an increase in government spending has on the aggregate demand curve.

Figure 16.6: An increase in government expenditure and the AD curve

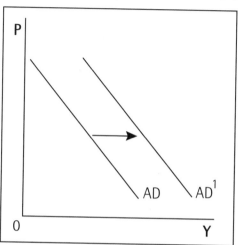

In effect, the increase in government expenditure shifts the original AD curve to the right. Along AD^1, there is a higher level of output demanded for each given price level. Alternatively, contractionary fiscal policy, initiated by a decrease in government spending, shifts the AD curve to the left.

The analysis is incomplete without the supply side of the economy. The overall effect in the short run is illustrated in Figure 16.7 (assuming factor prices are not completely flexible).

Figure 16.7: Expansionary fiscal policy in the short run

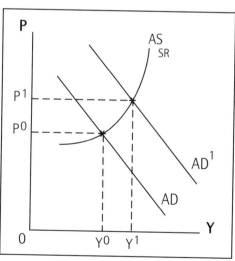

The conventional short-run AS curve is depicted in Figure 16.7. The economy is initially in equilibrium at the intersection of the AD curve and the AS curve: at the point (P^0, Y^0). We know from our previous analysis that an increase in government expenditure shifts the AD curve to the right, from AD to AD^1. At the original price level, P^0, there is excess demand caused by the increase in government expenditure. In order to re-establish equilibrium, the price level must rise. At the new equilibrium (P^1, Y^1), both price and output have increased. The extent of the output increase and the price rise will depend on the potential output of the economy and in particular the sensitivity of output changes to price changes. This is reflected in the slope of the AS curve.

In this model, the increase in aggregate demand causes the price level to rise, which partly offsets any subsequent change in output. The final result is a combination of higher prices and higher output but with a smaller change in output than in the Keynesian model of income determination (see below).

We have illustrated demand management using the example of an increase in government spending. However, a tax cut or an increase in the money supply would result in a similar rightward shift of the AD curve. Contractionary monetary or fiscal policy results in a leftward shift of the AD curve.

Keynes and the classicals

The increase in output from Y^0 to Y^1 in Figure 16.7 is less than the increase which arose out of the simple Keynesian model. The difference is accounted for by the price change. In the Keynesian income model, prices are fixed. We assume that firms expand their output without increasing the price. In terms of the economy production can expand without increasing the price level. Hence, any change in autonomous spending results, via the multiplier process, in a change in equilibrium output.

The Keynesian AS curve is depicted in panel (a) of Figure 16.8. We can see that a change in demand, caused by an increase in government spending, has a different result than what emerged from the conventional short-run AS curve.

Because the aggregate supply curve is perfectly elastic, an increase in government expenditure leads to a change in national income without changing the price level. For Keynes, excess capacity meant that idle factors of production could be put to work without fuelling inflationary pressures. If the AS curve is horizontal, the expansionary fiscal policies which Keynes advocated are rational and advisable.

Figure 16.8: Expansionary fiscal policy: the Keynesian and classical cases

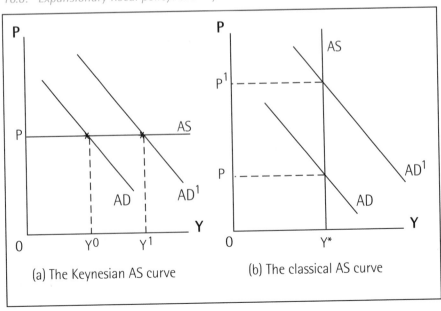

(a) The Keynesian AS curve

(b) The classical AS curve

The classical aggregate supply curve is depicted in panel (b) of Figure 16.8. From the classical perspective, expansionary fiscal policy is indefensible. With a vertical AS curve, an increase in government expenditure results only in higher prices. There is no change in the level of national output. Again, this reflects the classical assumption that output is determined by real factors such as technology and the training of human capital. From the classical perspective, demand-management measures can only lead to changes in price.

Supply-side policies

Aggregate supply is determined by a number of factors, including technology, population size and expectations. Supply-side policies generally promote private enterprise within the market system by cutting costs or increasing incentives in order to stimulate output.[4] These policies found favour with both the US President Ronald Reagan and the UK Prime Minister Margaret Thatcher during their time in office (see Information Box 16.1). Examples of supply-side policies are included below.

The functioning of the market is enhanced by:

* reducing government controls;
* promoting competition;
* privatisation and deregulation;
* legislating against monopolies.

Costs are reduced by:

* cutting tax on labour (reductions in marginal tax rates and PRSI rates);
* cutting benefits and reforming the welfare state.

The incentive system is improved by:

* lowering capital gains tax and corporation tax;
* encouraging profit-related pay and wider share ownership.

Many commentators regard the disinflationary aspect of tax cuts as the central plank of supply-side economics. Whereas Keynesians emphasise the demand-side effects of a tax cut, supply siders focus in on the supply-side effect. They argue that lower taxes increase incentives and, in turn, stimulate work, savings, risk-taking and investment. For Keynesians, a tax cut shifts the aggregate demand curve to the right, while for supply siders, a tax cut shifts the aggregate supply curve to the right. Although this seems to be a relatively minor point, the implications are not. For the Keynesians, government action is leading to an increase in output. For the supply siders, the reduction of government involvement is improving the incentive system which promotes expansion in the private sector. The key to long-term growth for supply siders is to unleash the productive capacity of the private sector.

The short-run AS curve describes the relationship between price and national output, *ceteris paribus*. Among the variables which are held constant are the level of technology, the skills of the labour force and the availability of natural resources. Any change in these factors causes a shift of the AS curve. An example is illustrated in Figure 16.9.

Figure 16.9: A rightward shift of the AS curve

Equilibrium is initially at the point (P⁰, Y⁰). Let us suppose that the discovery of a new national source of oil allows for an expansion of the productive base of the economy in the short run. As production costs are lowered, the AS curve shifts rightwards; firms are willing to produce more output at any given price level. The lower costs increase the likelihood of profits which, in turn, induces greater production. A new equilibrium is reached at a higher output level and a lower price level. This new equilibrium is at point (P¹, Y¹). The extent of these changes will depend on the shape of the AD curve.

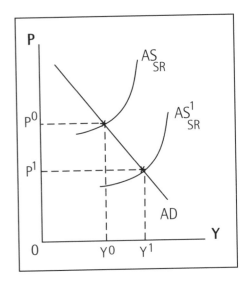

INFORMATION BOX 16.1

The supply-side policies of the 1980s

The disillusionment with Keynesian economics set in well before Reagan became the President of the United States in January 1981. The emergence of stagflation in the early 1970s left the economics profession asking many questions about the usefulness of Keynesian policies. A decade earlier, Milton Friedman criticised the active demand-management policies of previous administrations and advocated non-interventionist policies. With the 1980 election of Ronald Reagan, this economic philosophy found a political advocate. The emergence of supply-side economics is associated with the Reagan administration between 1981 and 1982.

The background to 'Reaganomics' reportedly dates back to a December evening in 1974. In the Two Continents restaurant in Washington DC, three individuals were discussing the state of the US economy: Arthur Laffer, a young economist; Richard Cheney, a White House aide under President Ford; and Jude Wanniski, an editorial writer for the *Wall Street Journal*. Laffer convinced his colleagues that the fundamental problem with the economy was the high marginal tax rates. This is the rate paid on each additional dollar earned. Laffer was discussing the relationship between the tax rate and the total tax revenue collected by the government. At low tax rates, he claimed, when tax rates rise, tax revenue increases. There was nothing sensational about this assertion.

It was his additional proposition that beyond a certain point, a cut in taxes may also increase tax revenue, which surprised his colleagues. In support of his proposition, he argued that high taxes act as a disincentive. Work, savings and investment are discouraged. By cutting taxes, the supply side of the economy is stimulated. Lower taxes increase the attractiveness of work relative to leisure. Tax avoidance declines. In addition, investment and production increase. Encouraged by lower tax rates, new workers and firms broaden the tax base. Theoretically, these new sources of tax revenue meant that the total tax revenue collected by the state would increase.

The relationship, which is known as the Laffer curve, is illustrated in Figure 16.10.

Figure 16.10: The Laffer curve

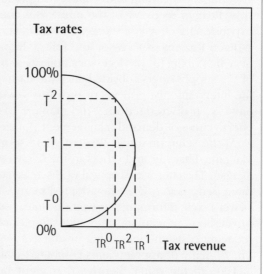

The tax rate is measured on the vertical axis and tax revenue is measured on the horizontal axis. If taxes are zero, total revenue amounts to zero. As tax rates increase, first from 0 to T^0 and then from T^0 to T^1, tax revenue increases from 0 to TR^0 and then to TR^1. Tax revenue is maximised when the tax rate is T^1. Any subsequent increase in the tax rate, from T^1 to T^2 for example, will only reduce tax revenue, in this instance from TR^1 to TR^2. Finally, if taxes are raised to 100%, nobody will work, resulting in zero tax revenue.

This diagram illustrates the essence of Laffer's argument. According to Laffer, marginal tax rates in the US had risen during the 1970s to levels beyond T^1. A tax cut would increase the incentive to work and to invest and possibly lead to an increase in tax revenue. On that basis, cuts in personal and business taxes were justified, even though there was a national debt which the state was trying to reduce.

While many people were sceptical of these proposals, they had the support of Ronald Reagan, the Republican candidate in the 1980 presidential election. Reagan was influenced heavily by Jack Kemp, the New York Congressman who three years earlier, together with Senator William Roth of Delaware, had introduced a bill to Congress proposing a 30% cut in personal income tax over a three-year period.

On taking office, Reagan appointed Murray Weidenbaum as his first chairman of the Council of Economic Advisers. Their economic plan centred around 'the four pillars of wisdom' which were:

- steady growth of the money supply;
- regulatory reform;
- cutting personal and business taxes;
- reducing federal spending.

The Kemp-Roth tax cuts (1981–83), enacted by the Economic Recovery Tax Act of 1981, were the centrepiece of Reaganomics – cited by President Reagan as a 'second American Revolution'. The proposal was designed to cut marginal tax rates by 10% per year over a three-year period.

Supply-side economists were criticised by their peers within the neoclassical school and by Keynesian economists. Their critics included J. K. Galbraith, Walter Heller (President Kennedy's chief economist) and Herbert Stein (President Nixon's chief economic adviser). All of these economists questioned the wisdom of the supply-side policies of the Reagan administration. In the words of Heller 'Only an ostrich could have missed the contradictions in Reaganomics.' In criticising supply siders, they highlight the record of supply-side policies – a large and rising federal debt, a failure to curtail government spending and sluggish output. They also assert that the so-called 'supply-side' Reagan recovery of the mid-1980s was largely attributable to the demand-side expansionary effects of the Reagan tax cuts rather than the supply-side effects.

Even Reagan's successor and fellow Republican George Bush was not convinced, once describing his predecessor's policies as 'voodoo economics'. Although the influence of the supply siders subsided after the early 1980s, there was a reluctance to return to the interventionist policies of previous governments. While supply-side policies may have been discredited they did manage to raise some 'justifiable' doubts about the effectiveness of demand-management policies. That is their legacy.

At the same time that Reagan was espousing the virtues of supply-side policies, Margaret Thatcher and others in the UK were embracing free-market economics. Like Reagan, Thatcher was sceptical of discretionary monetary and fiscal policies. During her three periods in office, she adopted many of the policies advocated by supply siders. Lower taxes, reforming the welfare state, reducing the power of trade unions and the privatisation programme were all examples of policies aimed at increasing competition, reducing costs and increasing productivity. Similar to the US experience, the record is one of many disappointments combined with limited successes.

Like all the other theories that went before it, supply-side policies have their shortcomings. For one, supply siders failed to produce a coherent and rigorous model of the economy. Also, the assertion that a tax cut could possibly increase tax revenue was proven incorrect by the significant increase in the US budget deficit in the early 1980s. More critically, the evidence asserting a link between tax cuts and work incentive is conflicting. Moreover, a cut in the rate of personal taxation may have demand-side as well as supply-side implications. In the long run, the output of the economy might increase. However, in the short run, if income increases in excess of output, excess demand can lead to inflationary pressures.

On a broader level, welfare 'reform', even if it is combined with lower taxes, can often lead to greater hardship for the poor in society. The removal of statutory restrictions can often lead to a return of the abuses, to the environment for example, which were responsible for the imposition of the regulations in the first place. Many of these side-effects are the 'unacceptable face of capitalism', as described by former UK Prime Minister Ted Heath.

We leave the last few words on supply-side economics to Martin Feldstein. 'Experience has shown that the notion "supply-side economics" is a malleable one, easily misused by its supporters, maligned by its opponents, and misinterpreted by the public at large.'[1]

1 M. Feldstein, 'Supply Side Economics: Old Truths and New Chains'. *American Economic Review*, 76, May 1986.

A supply-side shock

Definition

A supply-side shock or a supply disturbance refers to sudden changes in the conditions of productivity or costs which in turn impacts on aggregate supply.

Supply-side shocks were uncommon prior to the 1970s. In 1973, however, the world economy suffered a sudden supply-side shock in the form of higher oil prices. For more on the oil crisis see Section 6.4.

The effects of such a supply-side shock in the short run are illustrated in Figure 16.11.

Figure 16.11: A supply-side shock

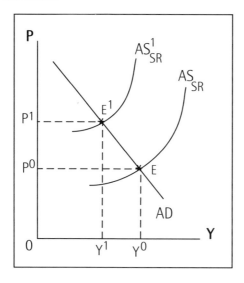

The economy is initially in equilibrium at $(P^0, Y^0$, the intersection of the AD curve and the AS curve. The increase in costs arising out of the rise in the price of oil causes a leftward shift of the AS curve. In the short run, the excess demand gives rise to an increase in the price level. Equilibrium in the short run is restored at the intersection of AD and the new AS curve, AS^1 at the point (P^1, Y^1). This rather unusual combination of higher prices and sluggish output became known as stagflation. Another period of stagflation occurred at the end of the 1970s.

Long-run analysis

In the long run, factor costs adjust to changing economic conditions. In particular, wages will respond to changes in prices.

We know from our discussion in Section 16.2 that the long-run AS curve is vertical at the full-employment level of output. We now examine the effectiveness of demand-management policies and supply-side policies in the context of a vertical AS curve.

Demand-management policies

Consider an increase in government expenditure. We have already discovered that an increase in government expenditure shifts the AD curve to the right. In the short run output and prices adjust upwards. In the long run, the only effect is an increase in prices: there is no change in output. This is illustrated in Figure 16.12.

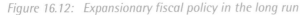

Figure 16.12: Expansionary fiscal policy in the long run

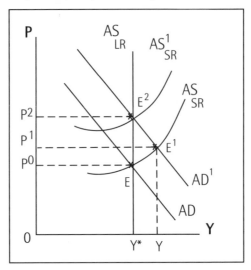

We begin at the full-employment equilibrium in the short run with the AD curve intersecting the short-run AS curve, AS_{SR} at point E. Y*, the actual output of the economy, equals the potential output. The increase in government expenditure shifts the AD curve out to the right, from AD to AD^1. The new point of intersection occurs at E^1, with prices at P^1 and output temporarily raised beyond the potential level, to Y. As a result many firms begin to experience supply bottlenecks; they want to increase production but limited resources do not permit such an increase.

The higher price level induces wage increases. The rising costs of production shift the short-run AS curve leftwards, to AS^1. The long-run equilibrium is shown by the intersection of AD^1 and AS_{LR} which is point E^2 and combination (Y*, P^2). We can see that demand-management policies led to an increase in price from P^0 to P^2, but that output does not increase beyond the full-employment level in the long run.

To summarise, in the long run, this model predicts that a change in aggregate demand cannot affect output. The only change is a change in the level of prices.

Supply-side policies

Consider a supply-side policy directed at increasing potential output in the long run. It is illustrated in Figure 16.13.

Figure 16.13: Supply-side policies in the long run

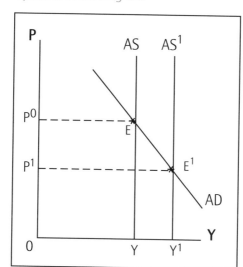

The long-run AS curve is vertical. A supply-side policy intended to increase potential output results in a rightward shift of the AS curve, from AS to AS^1. The net effect is an increase in output combined with a lower price level. This occurs because the quantity of the factor inputs increases or because existing resources are employed more efficiently. An example that will shift the supply curve is an improvement in the education or training of the labour force.

Keynes and the classicals

Keynesians and classical economists disagree about the effectiveness of supply-side policies. Essentially, the classical case is depicted above. The economy is always moving towards full-employment equilibrium. Technology and the magnitude and quality of capital and labour constrain the level of output in the economy. An economy may be able to move beyond the full-employment level of output in the short run by working overtime, but ultimately, technology or the factors of production must change to expand national output in the long run. Therefore, if the state wishes to facilitate an increase in output, policies which shift the AS curve are the only ones which will achieve this goal.

Keynes did not agree that the economy moved toward full-employment equilibrium in the short run. If people are unemployed, labour is available for employment at the market wage. It is only if the short-run equilibrium of the AD curve and AS curve is at full employment, that demand-side polices put pressure on wages and ultimately on prices. Otherwise, demand management can be used to move the economy to full employment.

Supply-side policies, on the other hand, are completely ineffective. When Keynes wrote during the Great Depression, there was excess capacity and labour was idle. Supply-side policies have the effect of increasing capacity. This scenario is illustrated in Figure 16.14.

Figure 16.14: The Keynesian view of supply-side policies

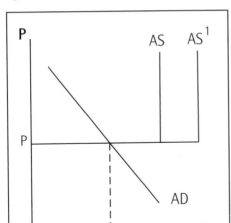

Figure 16.14: The Keynesian view of supply-side policies

In Figure 16.14 the AS curve is drawn with a 'kink' at a point where the factors of production are fully utilised. An increase in the aggregate supply, in this case from AS to AS[1] will have no effect on the actual output level, according to Keynesians. Output can only be increased by boosting aggregate demand.

In terms of the long run, it is not clear what Keynes thought. In effect, he saw the economy moving from short run to short run. So the question of whether an economy ever reached its long-run capacity was not an issue.

A summary of policy effectiveness

At this stage, there is a need to sum up the policy conclusions. In the short run where there are unemployed resources, there appears to be a role for demand management. Wage and price rigidities allow output to respond to changes in aggregate demand over a short period of time. In the long run, however, fiscal and monetary policies have no effect on output. Output can only be expanded in the long run by supply-side policies.

Finally, one way of explaining the differences between demand-management policies and supply-side policies is by focusing on the business cycle. Figure 16.15 illustrates the business cycle.

Figure 16.15: The business cycle

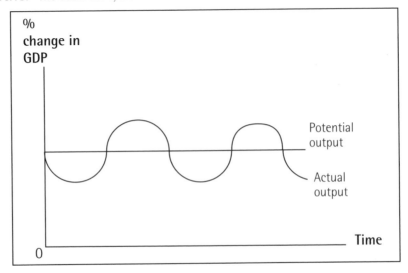

The actual output line depicts the annual increase in national output, as measured by changes in GDP. The potential output line depicts the rate at which the economy would grow if all resources were fully utilised. The purpose of demand-side policies is to stabilise actual output close to its potential. In terms of Figure 16.15 this involves the convergence of the actual output and the potential output lines. This entails short-term fine-tuning of the economy through frequent changes in tax rates, money supply, interest rates and expenditure levels.

In contrast, the purpose of supply-side policies is to increase potential output beyond its present levels. In terms of Figure 16.15 an upward shift of the potential output line is sought. This involves a long-term strategy, enhancing the efficiencies of the market system and lowering production costs wherever possible.

We will end this section with a note by A. Protopapadakis which summarises the value of both demand-management and supply-side policies:

'supply-side policies should not be looked at to replace counter-cyclical demand-management policies. Demand management may be the appropriate policy response to recessions that periodically are brought about by special sequences of economic events. But these policies are ill-suited to improving long-term growth in productivity and output, because they don't necessarily increase incentives to produce, save and invest. Supply-side policies do precisely that, but they are likely to work slowly and therefore can't be used to combat recessions'.[6]

16.4 THE IRISH EXPERIENCE

Ireland's experience of demand-management policies has been well documented. Extensive use of fiscal policy was the norm during the 1970s and 1980s. At different times, this was combined with a mix of monetary, exchange rate and incomes policies.

Supply-side policies were not as prevalent in Ireland in the 1980s as they were in the UK or the US. This was due to a number of factors.

First, in other countries there was a deeper divide between the left and right political parties. This focused the economic debate between those who favoured state intervention and those who preferred a limited role for the state. The 'right', who initiated the supply-side policies, were represented by the Republicans in the US and by the Tories in the UK. Until the formation of the Progressive Democrats in 1985, the economic policies of the 'right' were not coherently presented by any political party in Ireland. This partly explains why Irish policy-makers were slow to adopt supply-side policies.

Second, given the state of the public finances in the early 1980s, the Irish authorities were concerned less with ideology and more with restoring order and confidence to the financial markets at home and abroad.

By the late 1980s there was some evidence of a change in policy. Two semi-state companies, Irish Life and Irish Sugar (Greencore), were privatised. Other state bodies such as B&I and Irish Steel were sold to foreign companies. A plan to restructure Aer Lingus was agreed and implemented. The remaining semi-state companies were encouraged to cut costs with a view to competitiveness, commercialisation and future competition from foreign companies.

Taxes on labour were cut in order to increase the incentives for both employers and employees. Controls on public expenditure were also implemented. Pump-priming the economy was frowned upon. The business sector was also targeted via a lowering of corporate taxes, an expansion of the Business Expansion Scheme (BES), an increase in profit-sharing schemes and tax reliefs relating to capital acquisition.

During the 1990s, the Culliton report became the blueprint for job creation in Ireland.[7] Among its many recommendations were a fundamental reform of the tax system, greater competition in air services, telecommunications and energy supply and an improvement in training in Ireland. These and many of the other sixty-plus recommendations are 'essentially supply-side in tone'.[8]

By the late 1990s, government policy was certainly supply-side in tone. Greater competition, deregulation, privatisation and tax cuts were introduced by successive governments to increase the productive capacity of an already booming economy. Paul Tansey (1998) goes further and claims that Ireland has witnessed a supply-side revolution, albeit by stealth.[9] The combination of foreign direct investment, low taxes, EU funding and an improvement in human capital has raised Ireland's productive capacity. Yet, this supply-side revolution was different from the UK and US experience. It relied much more on social partnership, government spending and public consensus than the ideological, class-based, private sector revolution associated with Reagan and Thatcher.

In conclusion, in contrast to the late 1970s and the early 1980s, Irish policy-makers appear to be concentrating on the supply side of the economy. Economic policies are aimed at the private sector. This is obvious in the privatisation of semi-state companies. A sustained effort to improve the incentive system through tax and welfare reform has broad support across the political spectrum and has featured prominently in the recent budgets. Irish industrial policy encourages technological change and constant upgrading of the factors of production. All of these policies are aimed at increasing the potential national output. In short, they are designed to shift the aggregate supply curve.

CASE STUDY

Extract from *The Financial Times*
Growth raises real spectre of over-heating IRELAND
by John Murray-Brown

Ireland's economy continues to grow at record levels, outpacing the rest of Europe. With the republic now part of the euro-zone, interest rates are close to historic lows. Consumer demand looks set to continue to grow, with the government promising tax cuts to sweeten the unions. At first glance, it would seem a recipe for over-heating. Add to that a housing market which is booming for the fifth straight year, and it is little wonder international commentators such as the Organisation for Economic Co-operation and Development are starting to get the jitters about sustainability of the Irish miracle.

The OECD, in its twice-yearly *Economic Outlook*, says the risks of over-heating are rising, pointing out that unemployment is set to fall, wages are picking up steadily and house prices continuing to

$\longrightarrow$

soar. Ireland, it says, has 'no choice' but to limit domestic demand through a contractionary budget policy. It also warns the government should not accede to wages demands from the unions in the latest negotiations on a new pay agreement which would put Irish industry at a competitive disadvantage to its continental partners.

. . .

Part of the problem is the government is tied into a bargaining process on pay in which moderate wages are bought in exchange for tax cuts and a say in economic policy. The unions believe, with some justification, the last three-year deal did not adequately reflect the strong performance of the economy. Corporate profits are currently rising in excess of 20 per cent, while the unions are restricted by the agreement to annual wage increases of just over 2 per cent, with some local bargaining flexibility. Pressure on wages is being fuelled by considerable labour supply problems in construction and the increasingly important information technology sectors. Eunan King, senior economist with NCB stockbrokers, says labour shortages will increase unless immigration rises as employment opportunities are rising faster than current growth in the labour supply. According to official figures, employment rose by 97,000 in the year to May while the numbers in the labour market only grew by 67,000. As a result unemployment has fallen. Mr King says the government needs to consider policy changes to stimulate more immigration flows, whether through a liberalisation of non-EU immigration or a policy which targets UK labour by lowering taxes, which

still act as a disincentive to workers coming to Ireland from the UK.

The other pressure on prices comes from the threat posed by increased competition and privatisation. The recent arrival of Bank of Scotland in the mortgage market and Northern Rock undercutting local banks in the deposit market has underlined that banking in Ireland is due for a further shake out. Telecom and other utility prices have further to fall if Irish services are going to come down in line with the UK and other continental European economies – all of which will put downward pressure on inflation. A more long-term challenge for the authorities is the strain Ireland's recent growth rate is putting on the country's infrastructure, with bottlenecks appearing. The strains on the system were underlined on one Friday last month, when telephone and mobile systems in the whole of the south Dublin area went down for more than two hours after an overload at one of the main telephone companies.

The government's response to this crisis is pure Keynes, increasing the capacity of the economy through a major programme of public works. In mid-November, Charlie McCreevy, the finance minister, announced a £40bn national development plan aimed at boosting the infrastructural capacity of the economy, with major spending in transport, education and energy. Bernard Feeney, director with Goodbody stockbrokers, says that while the ambitious spending programme is welcome, 'its success depends on the government's commitment to speed up the planning and procurement processes and take action to address the labour supply shortages'.

Source: The Financial Times, 3 December 1999.

Questions

1. Show, using the AD/AS model, how each of the following demand policies affect prices and output:
   (i) a Keynesian-style public works programme;
   (ii) a contractionary budget policy.
2. Comment on the statement that the 'government's response to this crisis is pure Keynes, increasing the capacity of the economy through a major programme of public works.'
3. What supply-side measures are referred to in the article?

Answers on website

SUMMARY

1. Aggregate demand refers to the total quantity of output demanded at different price levels. There is a negative relationship between aggregate demand and price and this is represented by a downward sloping AD curve. The wealth effect, the interest rate effect and the international trade effect are the reasons for the negative relationship. The AD curve is drawn for given levels of autonomous spending. Any change in autonomous spending or monetary variables results in a shift of the AD curve.
2. Aggregate supply is the total output supplied at different price levels. Potential output refers to the maximum output that a country can produce given the resources available and the efficiency with which they are put to use. The AS curve relates output levels to price levels. Factors such as technology, the level of human capital and expectations determine the position of the AS curve.
3. There is a distinction between the AS curve in the short run and the long-run AS curve. The assumption underlying the short-run AS curve is that factor costs are constant. Hence, higher prices are associated with higher output levels and result in an upward sloping AS curve. In the long run factor costs can vary; they adjust fully to price changes. With complete adjustments in the long run possible, the AS curve is vertical at the full-employment level of output. It is unresponsive to changes in the price level.
4. Demand-side policies include both fiscal and monetary policy. They are designed to influence the level of expenditure in the economy and, in turn, the level of output. In the short run, expansionary demand-side policies result in higher output levels and higher prices. Contractionary demand-side policies reduce both output levels and prices. In the long run a change in aggregate demand cannot affect output. The only change is in the level of prices.
5. Supply-side economics is concerned with changing the aggregate supply. Supply-side policies seek to influence production directly, by lowering production costs or by increasing incentives. A supply-side shock refers to changes in the conditions of productivity or costs which in turn affect aggregate supply. The adverse effects of a negative supply-side shock are twofold: higher prices and lower output.

6. The Irish authorities were slow to adopt demand-management policies. Active use of short-term fiscal policy only became the norm in the mid-1970s. Once tried, demand-side policies were extensively used thereafter. Supply-side policies were largely absent until the late 1980s. Possible reasons include the absence of a right-left political divide and the unsatisfactory state of the public finances. There was some evidence of supply-side influences in economic policy by the 1990s.

KEY TERMS

Aggregate demand
Real balance effect
AD curve
Aggregate supply
Potential output
Short-run AS curve
Long-run AS curve
Full-employment output level
Macroeconomic equilibrium
Demand-management policies
Supply-side policies
Discretionary fiscal policy
Reaganomics
Laffer curve
Supply-side shock
Business cycle

REVIEW QUESTIONS

1. Outline the reasons why the AD curve is downward sloping. What causes a shift of the AD curve?
2. Explain why the short-run AS curve slopes upwards. What accounts for the difference between the short-run and the long-run AS curves?
3. Using a short-run AD/AS model, explain what effect a contractionary fiscal policy would have on the equilibrium price and output.
4. What is a supply-side shock? Use the AD/AS model to illustrate the effect of an adverse supply-side shock on the equilibrium price and output.
5. Assess the use of supply-side policies both in the US and the UK since the early 1980s.
6. Comment on Ireland's use of both demand-management and supply-side policies.

WORKING PROBLEMS

1. Data (expressed in billions of euros) for aggregate demand and aggregate supply curves are presented in Table 16.1. The price level is presented as an index number.

Table 16.1

Price level	100	110	120	130	140	150	160	170	180
Aggregate demand	7.0	6.7	6.4	6.1	5.8	5.5	5.2	4.9	4.6
Aggregate supply	1.4	2.4	3.4	4.3	5.0	5.5	5.8	5.8	5.8

(a) Plot the aggregate demand and aggregate supply curves.
(b) What do the portions of the AS curve reflect?

2. Sketch appropriate AD/AS diagrams (as they relate to Ireland) for the following:
(a) the expansionary phase of fiscal policy during the 1970s;
(b) the fall in oil prices in the early 1980s.

MULTI-CHOICE QUESTIONS

1. The AD curve slopes down from left to right because of:
(a) the international trade effect, the income effect and the substitution effect;
(b) the price effect, the real balance effect and the substitution effect;
(c) the income effect, the price effect and the interest rate effect;
(d) the interest rate effect, the real balance effect and the international trade effect;
(e) none of the above.

2. If the AD curve is relatively steep, which of the following is a likely source?
(a) This is because the changes in AE arising out of price changes are relatively small.
(b) A weak international trade effect.
(c) The real balance effect is weak.
(d) A weak interest rate effect.
(e) All of the above.

3. Assuming spare capacity, constant inputs costs and a demand-constrained economy, the AS curve is:
(a) vertical;
(b) horizontal;
(c) perfectly inelastic;
(d) upward sloping;
(e) both (b) and (c) above.

4. Under short-run conditions, contractionary demand-side policies are likely to:
(a) reduce output and prices;
(b) increase output, reduce prices;
(c) increase prices, reduce output;
(d) increase output and prices;
(e) none of the above.

5. According to supply siders:
    (a) more government intervention is necessary;
    (b) high taxes are necessary to finance the welfare system;
    (c) higher government spending is always desirable;
    (d) tax rate cuts can cause total tax revenue to increase;
    (e) both (c) and (d) above.

6. In the long run, a change in which of the following is likely to cause a shift of the AS curve?
    (a) welfare expenditure;
    (b) money supply;
    (c) interest rates;
    (d) technology;
    (e) none of the above.

TRUE OR FALSE (SUPPORT YOUR ANSWER)

1. The AD curve shows total spending for each level of income at a fixed price level.

2. Underlying the upward sloping short-run AS curve is the assumption that all prices are constant.

3. The classical AS curve reflects supply constraints.

4. Both Keynesians and classical economists agree that the AD curve is downward sloping.

5. Supply siders perceive tax cuts as, among other things, disinflationary.

6. An adverse supply-side shock can lead to higher prices and lower output.

CASE STUDY

Extract from *OECD Economic Surveys: Ireland*
Effectiveness of policy mix of fiscal and incomes policies

Since the start of EMU in January 1999, fiscal and incomes policies have become the only demand management tools available. One of the objectives of the Stability and Growth Pact is to make budgetary room for manoeuvre. But the effectiveness of fiscal policy is perceived to be quite limited in the first place because of the openness of the Irish economy. Although joining EMU may in theory strengthen the effectiveness of fiscal policy in the short run because of the disappearance of crowding-out effects as domestic interest and exchange rates become virtually exogenous, in practice the effectiveness of fiscal policy is likely to be rather small and will be eroded further by greater regional integration in the long run. Thus, the effect of fiscal policy on output seems limited; indeed, how sensible it is for a 'regional' government to adopt active demand management is unclear.

. . .

It is not easy to assess the impact of a discretionary fiscal action on the economy when its supply-side effect is significant. Suppose, for example, that the announced future cuts in income tax rates by 4 percentage points were to be postponed as a way of restraining aggregate demand. If the postponement is perceived to be temporary, thereby leaving aggregate demand almost unchanged, inflation might even pick up as labour supply decreases (compared with the baseline of no postponement) in response to this announcement. The elasticity of labour supply in Ireland is likely to remain higher than those of other countries because another source of labour supply, migration, is available in addition to intertemporal substitution. Hence, only if the postponement is perceived to be permanent will the effect on demand be important. However, because people understand that the partnership approach ensures low nominal pre-tax wage growth and competitiveness in exchange for tax cuts, the permanence of any postponement might not be credible. Thus, taking account of the effects on the supply side, the effectiveness of discretionary fiscal policy seems even more limited.

The authorities' inclination to use the budget as a policy instrument to improve the supply side, rather than to manage aggregate demand, makes sense. Given the current low tax rate compared to other countries, however, tax tools should be used selectively. In this sense, tax measures to reinforce work incentives incorporated in the 1999 Budget can be considered as a step in the right direction.

. . .

Source: *OECD Economic Surveys: Ireland,* 1999, pp. 92–95.

Questions

1. Using the AD/AS model, show how active demand-management policies can affect prices and output.
2. Outline, using the AD/AS framework, the favourable supply-side effects arising from the type of discretionary fiscal policy outlined in the extract.

3. Outline the reasons why, in the current economic climate, demand management is not the preferred option of the Irish authorities.

APPENDIX 16.1:   USING THE IS/LM MODEL TO DERIVE THE AD CURVE

An alternative way to derive the AD curve is by using the IS/LM model. The IS curve is drawn for a given level of autonomous spending. The LM curve is drawn for a given real money supply. At a given price level P^0 the IS and LM curves intersect, giving us our first equilibrium level of national income, Y^0. In turn, we have our first point in (P,Y) space.

Figure 16.16: Deriving the AD curve

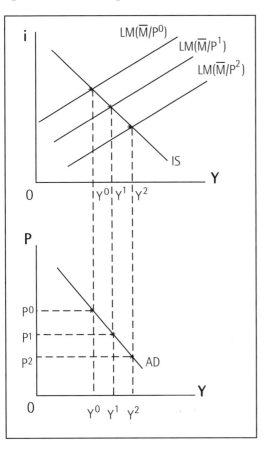

Suppose the price level falls. As price falls from P^0 to P^1, the real money supply increases from $\underline{\overline{M}}{P^0}$ to $\underline{\overline{M}}{P^1}$. The LM curve shifts rightwards, from LM $\underline{\overline{M}}{P^0}$ to LM $\underline{\overline{M}}{P^1}$. This results in a new and higher level of equilibrium income, Y^1 and our second point in (P, Y) space.

Assume the price level falls further. The fall in price from P^1 to P^2 results in a further increase in the real money supply, causing another rightward shift of the LM curve. This new equilibrium point results in another and yet again higher equilibrium level of income, Y^2. This is our third point in (P,Y) space.

A similar exercise can be carried out for all possible price levels. The subsequent income levels provide us with a relationship between the aggregate price level and national income. The relationship is depicted by a downward sloping AD curve. The goods market and the money market are both in equilibrium at every point on the AD curve.

CHAPTER 17

MACROECONOMIC ISSUES

'Inflation occurs when too much money is chasing too few goods.'

Anonymous

'We believe that if men have the talent to invent new machines that put men out of work, they have the talent to put those men back to work.'[1]

John F. Kennedy

'No nation was ever ruined by trade.'[2]

Benjamin Franklin

CHAPTER OBJECTIVES

Upon completing this chapter, the student should understand:

- the meaning of inflation;
- the causes, consequences and remedies;
- problems of defining and measuring unemployment;
- the costs and theories of unemployment;
- traditional trade theory, comparative advantage and trade barriers;
- new trade theory and economies of scale.

OUTLINE

17.1 Inflation
17.2 Unemployment
17.3 International trade

INTRODUCTION

There are many important and controversial issues in macroeconomics. Throughout the centuries, economists, sociologists and philosophers together with lorry drivers, domestic workers and shopkeepers have argued over the costs of inflation, the evils of unemployment and the merits of free trade. The debate remains lively because problems relating to these issues remain unresolved.

In this chapter, we will begin by discussing the issue of inflation and then continue with the topics of unemployment and international trade.

17.1 INFLATION

17.1.1 *Defining and measuring inflation*

We will begin by defining the relevant terms.

Definition

Inflation refers to a rise in the general or aggregate price level.

Alternatively, inflation can be defined as a fall in the value of money because it erodes the purchasing power of money. In any discussion on inflation, we generally refer to changes in the inflation rate.

Definition

The inflation rate is the percentage change in the price level from one period to the next period.

Since inflation refers to an increase in the price level, the percentage change is positive.

Definition

Deflation is a fall in the general level of prices.

In this situation, the percentage change in the price level is negative; the price level is falling from one period to the next. This phenomenon has not been observed on a yearly basis in Ireland since the mid-1940s. Often, this term is used loosely, to refer to policies or events which will lead to a slowdown in economic activity. Contractionary monetary and fiscal policies are sometimes labelled as 'deflationary'. A more accurate description is 'disinflationary'

Definition

Disinflation is defined as a reduction in the rate of inflation.

In this case, the rate of inflation is positive but decreasing from one period to the next. Contractionary policies normally reduce, rather than reverse inflation.

There are different categories of inflation including creeping inflation, hyper-inflation and stagflation. Creeping inflation exists when the rise in the price level is both relatively modest and stable. Hyper-inflation refers to a situation where inflation is escalating and the value of money diminishes so quickly that it ceases to perform its main functions. Table 17.1 shows the unfortunate state of the Hungarian currency between 1938 and 1946. Finally, stagflation refers to the simultaneous existence of both high rates of inflation and stagnant or negative economic growth. Unemployment is often a problem during periods of hyper-inflation or stagflation.

Table 17.1:   The Hungarian hyper-inflation 1945–46

	Mid-1938 = 100	% increase at an annual rate
Mid-1939	100	–
Mid-1941	139	18
Mid-1943	217	25
15 July 1945	9,200	527
31 Aug.	17,300	15,000
30 Sept.	38,900	1,700,000
31 Oct.	250,300	5.0×10^{11}
30 Nov.	1,545,700	3.1×10^{11}
31 Dec.	3,778,000	4.5×10^{6}
31 Jan. 1946	7,089,000	1.9×10^{5}
28 Feb.	45,845,300	5.4×10^{11}
31 Mar.	205,060,000	6.4×10^{9}
30 Apr.	3,575,600,000	7.9×10^{16}
31 May	1,076,400,000,000	5.5×10^{31}
30 June	470,300,000,000,000	4.8×10^{33}
31 July	12,572,000,000,000,000,000	1.3×10^{55}

Source: Falush, P. 'The Hungarian Hyper-Inflation of 1945–46' *NatWest Quarterly Review*, August 1976.

Inflation is measured using a price index.

Definition

A price index measures the level of prices in one period as a percentage of the level in another period called the base period.

The price index most frequently discussed by the media in Ireland is the Consumer Price Index.

Definition

The Consumer Price Index (CPI) is designed to measure the average change in the level of the prices paid (inclusive of all indirect taxes) for consumer goods and services by all private households in the country.

A price index is composed of a number of goods and services, each with its own weighting. For the CPI, these weights express the proportion of the household's budget which is spent on each category of good and service. The weights are updated every seven years following the publication of the *Household Budget Survey*.[3] The 'basket of goods' used for the Irish CPI and the respective weightings of each category are shown in Table 17.2.

Table 17.2: Weights used for the CPI in 1996

Food	22.8497
Services and related expenditure	16.7232
Transport	13.9402
Alcoholic drink	12.6298
Housing	8.0385
Clothing and footwear	6.1311
Fuel and light	4.9038
Other goods	6.3810
Household durables	3.5786
Tobacco	4.8242
	100.0000

Source: Central Statistics Office.

We will calculate the Irish rate of inflation for the year 1999 using the CPI. The base year is 1990. The CPI was 119.6 in 1998 and 121.5 in 1999. To find the annual inflation rate for 1999 we use the following formula:

$$\textbf{1999 Inflation rate} = \frac{\textbf{CPI 1999} - \textbf{CPI 1998}}{\textbf{CPI 1998}} \times \textbf{100}$$

[17.1]

Insert values for CPI 1998 and for CPI 1999 to get:

$$\frac{121.5 - 119.6}{119.6} \times 100 = \frac{1.9}{119.6} \times 100 = 1.6\%$$

Using the CPI as an index, the inflation rate for 1999 was approximately 1.6%. In other words, the general price level in Ireland rose by 1.6% in 1999.

In Ireland the inflation rate is measured by the Central Statistics Office (CSO) on a monthly and yearly basis.

Although used in both the US and Ireland, the CPI has a number of weaknesses. Its shortcomings include the use of a constant market basket despite frequent changes in consumption patterns, the difficulty in capturing changes in quality and the inclusion of mortgage costs which may explain why inflation is sometimes overstated. This measurement bias has meant that the CPI has probably overstated the 'true' rate of inflation. In the US, the CPI commission concluded that changes in the CPI overstated the change in the cost of living by about 1.1 percentage points per annum. Despite this, the CPI is considered to be the best measure of Irish inflation.

However, the Harmonised Index of Consumer Prices (HICP) is also an important measure. The HICP was introduced in 1997 as an international measure of comparison for EU member states. It was used to determine if countries met the convergence criterion on inflation for participation in the single currency. The HICP includes about

87% of the basket of goods and services used for the CPI. One notable item that is missing from the HICP is mortgage interest repayments.

Finally, the GDP deflator is a price index which measures changes in the entire range of goods and services produced in the economy. It is the most comprehensive measure of inflation. We can calculate the GDP deflator by using the following formula:

$$\text{GDP deflator} = \frac{\text{Nominal GDP}}{\text{Real GDP}} \times 100 \qquad [17.2]$$

In 1999, nominal GDP (GDP at current prices) was £69,052m. Real GDP or GDP at constant prices was £58,876m. With a base year of 1995, the GDP price index or deflator is 1.17 approximately. This indicates that prices increased by about 17% between 1995 and 1999.

17.1.2 Consequences of inflation

The consequences of inflation are many and varied. Before we discuss them, we will define some relevant terms.

Definition
The nominal rate of interest is the actual rate of interest which is charged when money is borrowed.

Definition
The real rate of interest is the nominal rate of interest adjusted for the inflation rate.

It is calculated by subtracting the inflation rate from the nominal rate of interest. For example, if the nominal interest rate is 12% and the inflation rate is 5%, the real rate of interest is 7%.

Definition
People are on fixed incomes if their income is set at a particular nominal amount which is not adjusted for inflation.

Definition
Menu costs refer to the costs which result when prices are adjusted.

For example, wholesalers must publish and mail new catalogues if prices increase. At the retail level, vending machines must be reprogrammed and merchandise must be physically reticketed when prices change. These costs are explicit and are fairly easy to monitor. What is more difficult to calculate is the loss of goodwill which firms encounter if they constantly increase their prices. Also, retailing firms may be slower to reorder if all of their current stock must be repriced.

The following is a comprehensive, although not exhaustive list of the possible effects of inflation.

- Depending on the level of real interest rates, inflation can involve a redistribution of income from lenders to borrowers. For example, suppose Helen borrows €2,000 from her local bank manager at a fixed rate of interest of 6% for one year. Unexpectedly, the annual inflation rate increases to 10%. The real rate of interest paid by Helen is negative, at minus 4%. When repaying the loan, Helen will return euros to the bank which are worth less in purchasing power terms than the euros lent to her by the bank. As a result of inflation, the borrower gains at the expense of the lender. In general, borrowers welcome unanticipated inflation. Interestingly, the biggest borrower of all can often be the government.
- Savings are adversely affected by inflation. Since inflation reduces the value of money, any stock of savings over time will lose its purchasing power. The inflation-adjusted interest rate, i.e. the real rate of interest, may be low or even negative. Hence, during inflationary times savings are discouraged and consumption is encouraged.
- Those sections of society that are on fixed incomes lose. Moreover, it is usually the more vulnerable sections of society, pensioners for example, who are on fixed incomes. In this instance inflation is a form of 'tax' on money holdings. The adjustment of incomes in line with price changes, called indexation, allows for some protection against inflation.
- Inflation often changes the pattern of investment. Capital moves out of assets like government bonds or gilts because the real rate of interest is low or negative. Investment in 'real' assets like property, fine art or gold increases because, in general, they appreciate over time. These assets are safe but unproductive. In a period characterised by growing inflation, productive investments, which lead to national economic growth, may be avoided because firms are unable to evaluate the potential for profit. Inflation breeds uncertainty which is generally unfavourable to investment decisions.
- Inflation can also affect the level of government expenditure and revenue. For example, if there is no indexation built into the tax system, tax revenues automatically increase as inflation forces more taxpayers into higher tax brackets. This is commonly known as fiscal drag. In effect, it is a transfer of resources from the taxpayer to the government.
- Inflation has serious implications for international competitiveness. For example, if Ireland's inflation rate is low relative to her trading partners' inflation rate within a fixed exchange rate system, a competitive advantage is gained. Exports increase and contribute to an increase in Irish GDP. In the absence of a fixed exchange rate system, inflation differentials can cause movements in exchange rates.
- Inflation can lead to money illusion. Money illusion exists when economic agents confuse changes in money variables with changes in real variables. In times of inflation, workers who receive higher wages might be fooled into thinking that they are better off. In reality, however, the wage increase is offset by the higher prices. These workers are said to be suffering from money illusion.
- Inflation prevents money from fulfilling its functions effectively. The primary function of money is as a medium of exchange. During periods of hyper-inflation, the domestic currency is shunned because of its rapid loss of value. If possible, exchanges are transacted in a reliable, foreign currency. Bartering, which is both time-consuming and inefficient, is often a feature of an economy experiencing hyper-inflation.

Finally, the effects of inflation are often different depending on whether inflation is anticipated or unanticipated. In general, anticipated inflation imposes fewer costs on society than unanticipated inflation. The normal costs to anticipated inflation are changes in menu costs and the extra time spent managing the finances. In turn, this may involve more frequent visits to the bank. The cost of these extra trips is called the 'shoe leather' effect.

Unanticipated inflation is not built into wage contracts or tax brackets/bands. The additional costs associated with unexpected inflation include misallocation of resources, income redistribution, tax distortions and the adverse impact on the incentive to save.

17.1.3 *Explanations of inflation*

Many explanations of inflation have been advanced over the years. In this section, we will look at four: demand pull, the Quantity Theory of Money, cost push and imported inflation. We will also briefly discuss the role of expectations. Although we will discuss each case separately, in reality they may occur simultaneously.

Demand pull inflation

We will begin by defining the concept of demand pull inflation and then we will explain it within the context of the model of income determination.

Definition

Demand pull inflation occurs when the total demand for goods and services is greater than the total supply of goods and services.

There is unsatisfied demand at the existing price level. The excess demand 'pulls up' the price level.

Demand pull inflation is generally but not exclusively associated with the Keynesian school. Although Keynes was primarily concerned with the issue of unemployment, he did consider the implications of inflation in an essay that was published in 1940 entitled *How to Pay for the War*. In this essay, Keynes looked at the problem of an increase in government spending caused by a war, particularly if the economy is at full-employment equilibrium at the outbreak.

We can illustrate this idea by returning to the model of income determination described in Section 12.1. Although the equilibrium can exist at any point along the 45° line, we are specifying that initially equilibrium is at full employment. This is shown as point E in Figure 17.1 where the aggregate expenditure curve AE cuts the 45° line.

Figure 17.1: The inflationary gap caused by demand pull inflation

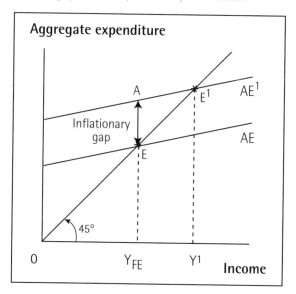

Recall that any increase in autonomous expenditure, of which government spending is one component, causes the AE curve to shift upward. In this case, government spending increases to purchase the arms and supplies needed to fight the war. The AE curve shifts upwards from AE to AE^1. Output at the new equilibrium, E^1, is above full employment. Keynes agreed that in this situation, inflation would logically result (see Appendix 17.1 on the Phillips curve).

Price is not a variable in this model. However, we have labelled the 'inflationary' gap in the diagram.

Definition

An inflationary gap exists when the equilibrium of the economy is greater than the full-employment level of output.

In Figure 17.1 the inflationary gap is measured by $|AE|$.

This model demonstrates the essential features of demand pull inflation. Inflation is caused by excess demand which causes the price level to increase. In the first instance, the excess demand may be caused by greater spending or tax cuts or some combination of these factors.

The Quantity Theory of Money

The Quantity Theory of Money (QTM) is the oldest theory of inflation. It is attributed to the classical economists, but it was popularised by Irving Fisher at the beginning of this century (see Information Box 17.1). In the years following World War II, inflation was not a pressing issue and the QTM was considered to be an appropriate topic for a course on the history of economic thought. However, the monetarist Milton Friedman revived the QTM in 1956 with the essay 'The Quantity Theory of Money – A

Restatement'.[4] The powerful policy conclusions of this model concerning the ineffectiveness of monetary policy continue to influence the thinking of monetarists in particular and neoclassical economists in general.

The classical view

In its simplest form the QTM states that there is a relationship between the money supply and the price level. It predicts that the price level will change with changes in the money supply. The more rapid the rate of increase in the money supply, the higher the inflation rate.

The following equation describes the income version of the QTM.

$$M \bar{V} = P \bar{Y}$$ [17.3]

where: M = money supply; V = velocity of money; P = the price level; Y = real income or output or GDP.

Notice that there is a bar over V and Y. This means that these variables are held constant. This is not an arbitrary decision, but reflects the assumptions of the classical economists. We can think of the velocity of money as the number of times a sum of money changes hands in a year. Advocates of this model believe that velocity is determined by institutional factors which change slowly over time. Holding real output as constant reflects the classical belief that the economy is always close to its full-employment output level.

If we hold velocity and output constant, any change in the money supply is reflected by a proportional change in the price level. Continuous increases in the money supply cause inflation. This model implies that monetary policy is ineffective. It causes deflation or inflation, but does not lead to changes in 'real' variables like output or employment.

INFORMATION BOX 17.1

The Quantity Theory of Money

Irving Fisher, the great American economist of the early twentieth century, is credited with popularising the Quantity Theory of Money.[1] In his book *The Purchasing Power of Money* (1911) he began with the simple equation of exchange MV = PT where M is the quantity of money, V is the rate of turnover of money or the velocity of money, P is the price level and T is the number of transactions. Since T is difficult to measure it can be replaced by output, Y.

As it stands, this equation is simply an identity or truism – something which is true by definition. It states that for the aggregate economy, the value of transactions, PT, is equal to the value of receipts, MV. A number of assumptions have to be made about the level of transactions and the velocity of money in order for this identity to be converted into a theory of inflation.

⟶

Fisher assumed that the level of transactions was fixed because it bore a close relationship with income which in the classical model was fixed at a level consistent with full employment. In addition Fisher argued that the velocity of money was determined by institutional factors which had a stabilising effect in the short term. If velocity and transactions are fixed, these assumptions transform the equation of exchange into a theory of inflation where changes in the money supply determine the price level.

Although the Cambridge version of the Quantity theory is similar, there are some important differences. Whereas Fisher focused solely on the transactions demand for money, the approach developed by Marshall and Pigou extended the functions of money to include the store of value function. This cash-balance approach also allowed for some flexibility in terms of how much money was held, with individual choice playing an important role. In the Fisher model, institutional constraints prevented any freedom in terms of the amount of money held. Finally, interest rates were not ruled out of the Cambridge version as a possible factor explaining changes in money demand. It was left to others, however, including Keynes to investigate the possible relationship between interest rates and money demand.

1 Fisher was not the first to develop the theory. It is believed that the first attempts at formulating the Quantity Theory of Money were independently made by David Hume in 1752 and Simon Newcomb in 1885.

The monetarist view

The monetarist view can be easily understood if we return to the AD/AS model developed in Chapter 16. Recall the downward sloping AD curve which depicts the relationship between the price level and national output, *ceteris paribus*. One variable which was held constant was the money supply.

The AS curve also depicts the relationship between the price level and national output, holding the characteristics of the labour force, technology and expectations constant. The aggregate supply curve is depicted as upward sloping in the short run as shown in Figure 17.2.[5]

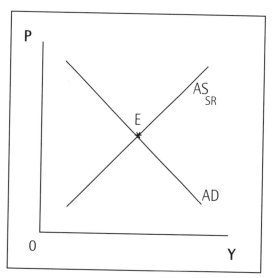

Figure 17.2: The AD/AS model

The AS curve is upward sloping, which reflects the assumption that as price rises, the output level also rises. The monetarists agree with the classical economists that the economy returns to full-employment equilibrium, represented by point E in Figure 17.2.

During the period when interest in the QTM resurged, monetarists believed in adaptive expectations (see Appendix 17.2 on expectations). Briefly, adaptive expectations refers to a phenomenon where neither management nor labour accurately interpret the meaning of a change in the price level. In the short run, they may be temporarily fooled into producing at a level of output which is higher than full employment. In the long run, the economy will return to full employment, at a higher price level.

We will demonstrate the model by illustrating an increase in the money supply which shifts the AD curve to AD^1, shown in Figure 17.3.

Figure 17.3: AD/AS model featuring adaptive expectations

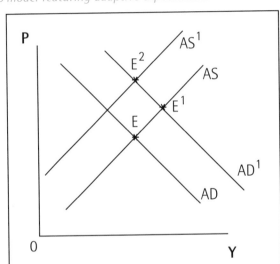

The change in the money supply has caused the price level to increase.

Firms interpret upward pressure on price as a signal to increase production. To do this, they hire more labour. Since the labour supply curve is upward sloping, they must pay a higher nominal wage. A new equilibrium is reached in (P,Y) space at E^1.

Recall that we began at full employment. The wage has increased, but so has the price level. Labour has not correctly understood that the change in the price level is eroding their purchasing power. In other words, although their nominal wage is increasing, their real wage has not increased.[6] When labour 'cops on', they will cut back the amount of labour that they are willing to supply at the new price level. This causes the AS curve to shift to AS^1 as shown in Figure 17.3. At the new equilibrium, E^2, the price level is higher, but the level of output returns to the full-employment level.

This led the monetarists to conclude that changes in the money supply have short-term effects on output, but in the long run, they are inflationary. According to Friedman, 'Inflation is always and everywhere a monetary phenomenon in the sense that it is and can be produced only by a more rapid increase in the quantity of money than in output.'[7] Essentially, he revived the QTM. For more information on Milton Friedman and monetarism, see Information Box 17.2.

INFORMATION BOX 17.2

Monetarism

Monetarism is the economic school of thought which lays special emphasis on the role of money in the economy. It does not, however, confine itself to the topic of money. Monetarists have a view on the role of government, the role of the market, fiscal policy, unemployment, inflation and many other issues.

Just as the classical economists succeeded the Physiocrats, the monetarists are the modern bearers of the classical tradition. Like the classicals, monetarists believe in the efficacy and the efficiency of the market. They are suspicious of government intervention in the economy. Gaining insights from extended periods of demand management, they cast a jaundiced eye on the efforts of government to change the level of output and employment by altering government expenditure.

It is their view of money, however, which distinguishes monetarism from other economic doctrines. According to monetarists, the rate of money growth is paramount in the determination of short-run output and long-run inflation. In order to combat inflation, money growth must not exceed output growth. A steady rate of money growth ensures low levels of inflation and facilitates long-term economic prosperity.

The emergence of monetarism in the 1970s in the US was largely due to the Nobel Laureate Milton Friedman. His most famous works include *A Monetary History of the United States* and the best-seller *Free to Choose* in which he makes a strong defence of free enterprise and the market. Although he has written widely on many different issues in economics he will be remembered for restoring many of the tenets of the classical doctrine of economics.

The most famous proponent of monetarism was the British Prime Minister, Mrs Thatcher. With the support of Keith Joseph and Professor Alan Walters, Mrs Thatcher strongly advocated the principles of monetarism. Combating inflation became the ultimate priority for the Tory government. The economic instrument used to achieve this objective was the money supply. Monitoring the money supply growth rate was central to the Medium Term Financial Strategy (MTFS). Fiscal spending was no longer used to increase aggregate demand. Mrs Thatcher was more concerned with how spending was to be financed.

By the late 1980s, the star of monetarism began to fall. Fiscal rectitude and scrupulous adherence to monetary targets did not ensure employment creation. While these goals have not been abandoned, some governments believe that some intervention is necessary to combat the high rates of unemployment that persist across western Europe. This does not signal a return to Keynesian demand management, but it does suggest a more prominent role for government in the economy than advocated by either the classicals or the monetarists.

Cost push inflation

During the post-war years inflation continued even in times when there was little or
no evidence of excess demand in the economy. This prompted economists to examine
other explanations and, in particular, possible causes arising from the supply side of
the economy.

We begin by defining cost push inflation and then we will explain its application
using the AD/AS model.

Definition
Cost push inflation occurs when the source of upward pressure on prices is the rising costs
of the factors of production in the absence of any corresponding increase in productivity.

The most important factor cost is labour. Consider a situation where an important labour
union signs an agreement for a significant wage increase which sets off a round of
wage increases throughout the economy. This causes the AS curve to shift to the left
as shown in Figure 17.4.

Figure 17.4: Cost push inflation

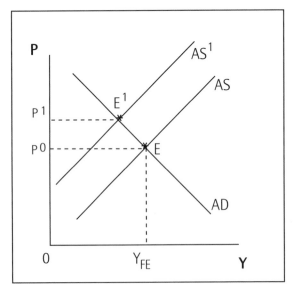

The original equilibrium, E, represents a level of output where all factors of production
are fully employed. At the associated price level P^0, aggregate supply is now less than
aggregate demand. In response to the wage increase, firms are unwilling to supply the
original level of output to the market at that price. Eventually, the economy reaches a
new equilibrium at E^1, at a higher price level and a lower level of output. Higher taxes
or the imposition of more extensive legislation would result in a similar outcome.

This particular pattern of inflation can lead to a wage-price spiral. Labour unions
force a wage increase. To return the economy to full employment the state responds
by adopting expansionary monetary and/or fiscal policies. This shifts the AD curve to

the right resulting in another increase in the price level. Labour unions look for another wage increase to compensate for higher inflation. The AS curve shifts leftwards. Once started, the spiral is difficult to end.

Imported inflation

This type of inflation is another form of cost push inflation which is particularly relevant to countries, like Ireland, with open economies. Suppose the domestic currency falls in value. Many raw materials and inputs for industry are imported. As a result of the fall in the value of the domestic currency, Irish-based firms are faced with higher import costs which, in turn, are reflected in higher prices for their finished good. This leads to inflation in the domestic market, which again leads to problems with competitiveness in foreign markets.

Expectations

In an economy where people become accustomed to high rates of inflation, they expect it to persist into the future. Workers incorporate the inflation rate into their contract demands. To compensate for the higher prices, higher wages are sought. This, in turn, causes the price level to increase further. We can see from this that the expectation of inflation is validated by actual increases in the inflation rate. Even after the initial causes of inflation have been removed, people's expectations may cause the inflationary process to continue.

The importance of expectations in explaining the actual rate of inflation (and other related topics) has become increasingly recognised by economists in recent years. As you might expect, there is considerable disagreement, and it is one of the most controversial topics in economics today.

17.1.4 Counter-inflationary policies

Policies aimed at combating inflation are usually categorised as either demand-side policies or supply-side policies. Although the solutions to inflation should redress the specific source of the rise in the price level, it may be difficult in reality to correctly assess the actual cause. If there is more than one source, a package of measures may be required. It may also be difficult to completely eradicate inflation. In fact it has been argued that a little inflation is not necessarily a bad thing as it may be conducive to economic growth.

Demand-side policies

In the last section, we discussed inflationary pressures placed on an economy due to a country's entry into a war. Theoretically, that increase in autonomous expenditure could be offset by either contractionary monetary or fiscal policy. Contractionary monetary policy causes an increase in the interest rate and leads to a fall in the level of private investment. Contractionary fiscal policy can take the form of a tax increase which would cut disposable income and therefore income-induced consumption. Either alternative will cause the aggregate expenditure curve to shift down towards the full-employment level of output in Figure 17.1 and in doing so eliminate the inflationary gap.

Supply-side policies

There are two objectives of supply-side policies. One is to moderate inflation by increasing the rate of growth of output. The other objective is to reduce the rate of increase of the costs of production. Achieving either of these objectives shifts the AS curve to the right and is therefore deflationary as we can see from Figure 17.5.

Figure 17.5: Deflationary supply-side policies

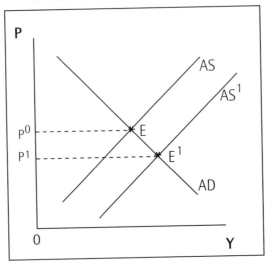

Supply-side policies generally focus on promoting competition, containing labour costs and increasing work incentives. Examples of policies which promote competition include restricting the number of mergers and takeovers. Monopoly powers are curbed to limit the control over price and profits.

Supply-side economists recommend lowering the corporate and personal tax rates which they believe will have beneficial effects on the competitiveness of firms (see Section 16.3). Although Keynes argued that the tax changes work by altering the demand side of the economy, this group of economists believe that this particular type of fiscal policy affects the supply side. The primary focus of these policies is to increase national output.

Containing labour costs can take two forms. Traditionally, supply-side economists advocate restricting the power of labour unions and avoiding legislation which guarantees a minimum wage. In neoclassical models, the economy moves towards full employment if – and only if – wages are flexible. Unionised labour, it is believed, can negotiate a wage rate above the equilibrium wage rate, causing unemployment. They argue that minimum wage legislation has the same effect. Many feel that if labour is unorganised and if contract arrangements are decentralised, wage demands will be lower and more flexible.

A different model has been used in Ireland since 1987 (see Section 7.5). The social partners negotiated successive national wage agreements beginning with the Programme for National Recovery (1987). This was replaced by the Programme for Economic and Social Progress (1991), the Programme for Competitiveness and Work (1994) and Partnership 2000 for Inclusion, Employment and Competitiveness. The current agreement is the Programme for Prosperity and Fairness. This process allows the economic interests of different sections of society to be considered in an organised way. The wage increases negotiated under these programmes have been modest, influenced by the high rates of unemployment in the early 1990s. While many have argued that these agreements promote price stability, some commentators have argued that returning to decentralised agreements would increase labour market flexibility and lower the wage bill.

Finally, a strong currency is anti-inflationary because it ensures stable import prices from the country's main trading partners. In the context of EMU, Irish authorities have lost control over exchange rate policy. The policy of a 'strong' euro must be implemented by the European Central Bank.

The success of all anti-inflationary policies depends on the credibility of government. Trade unions, firms and consumers form their expectations based on government actions, rather than government statements. Policies must be both reasonable and consistently applied.

17.1.5 *The Irish experience*

Ireland is a small open economy (SOE). On account of its size, it has little or no control over the international price of goods and services. In other words, it is a price taker in an international environment.

In 1999, exports were valued at £60.5 billion which is approximately 88% of Irish GDP. Imports were valued at over £51 billion which represents approximately 74% of GDP. Both of these figures attest to the extreme openness of the Irish economy.

As Ireland is a SOE, Irish policy-makers must take the issue of inflation seriously. A high domestic inflation rate erodes the competitiveness of Irish goods on foreign markets. High foreign inflation rates, particularly from Ireland's main trading partners, can be quickly imported to the Irish economy. It is widely accepted that inflation in Ireland is largely determined by exchange rate movements and inflation in its major trading partners.

Until 1979 when the fixed exchange rate between Ireland and Britain was finally broken, the Irish inflation rate was largely determined by the UK inflation rate, and the Irish authorities had little control over Irish inflation. The level of trade with the UK, UK interest rates, UK monetary policy and sterling's value on the foreign exchange markets were the primary factors in determining the Irish inflation rate.

Ireland joined the exchange rate mechanism of the EMS in 1979. Although the 'sterling factor' did not disappear, the IR£/DM exchange rate and the inflation rates of EU countries participating in the ERM became determining factors of Irish inflation.

The Irish inflation rate for the period 1970–99 is illustrated in Figure 17.6.

Figure 17.6: Irish inflation rate 1970–99

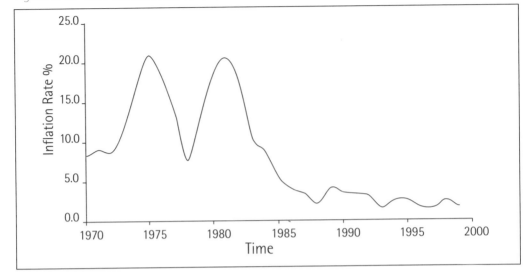

It is evident from Figure 17.6 that inflation in Ireland was high from 1973 to 1982. From the early 1980s the inflation rate began to decline. By the early 1990s the Irish inflation rate was close to, and often below, the EU average. Ireland had become a low inflation economy. However, by late 1999, there was evidence of a pick-up in Irish inflation.

The inflationary period 1973 to 1980 coincided with an increase in inflationary pressures throughout western Europe. The main sources of Irish inflation were the volatility of sterling and the supply-side shocks of 1973 and 1979 arising from the increase in the price of oil. As a small open economy, Ireland is likely to record similar rates of inflation to its main trading partners. Expansionary fiscal policy practised by Irish governments after 1973 also contributed to the high inflation rates.

Likewise, the decline in the inflation rate experienced by most EU countries in the mid- to late 1980s was also evident in Ireland. Although the international experience of low and stable inflation was a contributory factor in reducing the Irish inflation rate, it was not the only factor. Domestic policy was largely deflationary in the late 1980s. The combination of tight fiscal policy and moderate pay increases reinforced the international anti-inflationary experience of the time.

The firm exchange rate policy followed by the Irish authorities may also have contributed to the reduction of Irish inflation. Price stability had become the sole objective of domestic exchange rate and monetary policy. Interest rate levels were set in order to attain low and stable inflation. By the mid-1990s, the Irish inflation rate was one of the lowest in the EU. In addition, by achieving a low inflation rate, Ireland met the inflation criterion as set down in the Maastricht treaty. Given the Irish authorities' determination to participate in the single currency, Ireland's commitment to achieving a low and stable inflation rate was both desirable and necessary.

A number of factors may account for the high inflation rate in late 1999 and throughout 2000. External factors, proven in the past to be the main determinant of Irish inflation, include, in this period, the fall in the value of the euro and the rise in the price of oil. Although external factors are more prevalent in explaining the inflation rate of a small and open economy, domestic factors may also have played a role during this period. Discretionary tax changes and the fall in Irish interest rates arising from the convergence of interest rates across EMU-participating states gave a boost to an already booming economy. Claims of extensive labour shortages and evidence of rising wage inflation in certain sectors of the economy fuelled, if not reinforced, inflationary expectations. In addition, rising equity and house prices gave rise to rapid asset price inflation and the fear of a collapse of an asset price bubble.

This pessimistic view is disputed by many in the economics profession and elsewhere. It is argued that the rise in house prices in Ireland has not been driven by an inflow of speculative capital, as has happened in many of the real estate booms elsewhere, but has been due to changes in economic fundamentals, namely, demographics factors, the economic boom, fall in mortgage rates, shortages of supply and so on. Likewise, Ireland's membership of the single currency changes the future dynamics of inflation. In the context of EMU, higher wage inflation in one fast-growing region (Ireland, for example) will translate into a deterioration of this region's competitiveness *vis-à-vis* other regions in the monetary union. This will result in output and employment losses, associated with a slowdown in the region's economic activity. This may be what lies ahead for Ireland as a member of a currency area.

As a member of the euro area, the Irish economy could be viewed as a region within a low-inflation trading area. Despite a single monetary policy, price differentials may still exist. With the fastest growing economy or region within the euro area, Irish inflation may, at times, be higher than the average inflation rate across participating states. This was the case in the first year of the new millennium when the Irish inflation rate was the highest in the euro area (see Case Study).

CASE STUDY

Extract from *Central Bank of Ireland Bulletin*
Consumer Prices

Inflation, as measured by the CPI, averaged 1.6 per cent in 1999, compared with an average rate of 2.4 per cent in the previous year. This lower rate of inflation reflected the effect of a series of mortgage interest rate reductions during the year, which offset significant increases in other components of the index. The HICP which does not include mortgage interest rates increased at an average rate of 2.5 per cent last year, an acceleration from the 2.1 per cent rate recorded in 1998.

The combined effect of higher energy prices, a pick-up in service sector inflation and a decline in the value of the exchange rate has resulted in a marked acceleration in HICP inflation since the Summer of 1999. Mortgage interest rate reductions delayed the acceleration in CPI inflation until November, but since then this measure of inflation has also increased sharply. The increase in tobacco excise duties in Budget 2000 was one element in this, adding 0.8 per cent to the CPI and (reflecting a higher weight in the index) 0.9 per cent to the HICP. In the three months to January 2000, HICP inflation averaged 3.8 per cent, year-on-year, up from 2.6 per cent in the previous three months and 2.1 per cent in the same period last year. The CPI, which is still being restrained by the effect of lower mortgage interest rates, averaged 3.2 per cent in the three months to January 2000, compared with 1.5 per cent in the previous three months and 1.6 per cent in the same period last year. The factors which have led to the increase in consumer price inflation in recent months will continue to exert upward pressure on inflation during the first half of this year at least.

. . .

The effect of the increase in excise duties on tobacco will remain in the index until December. In addition, the stimulus to domestic demand engendered by the other tax and spending measures announced in Budget 2000 (and subsequently) will put additional upward pressure on service sector inflation in particular.

. . .

Source: *Central Bank of Ireland Bulletin*, Spring 2000, pp. 36–37.

Questions

1. Explain what is meant by the CPI? How is the inflation rate derived from the CPI? What is the difference between the CPI and the HICP?
2. What effect did the discretionary changes in excise duties in Budget 2000 have on the CPI?
3. Although mortgage interest rates are included in the calculation of CPI inflation, house prices are not included. Explain why house prices are not included in the index.

[NB: The Central Statistics Office website www.cso.ie is a useful source.]

Answers on website

17.2 UNEMPLOYMENT

Undoubtedly, the most serious economic problem facing society is unemployment. A section discussing this topic is an exercise in humility for any economist. We have trouble defining it. The number of unemployed depends on the statistic that we use. We cannot come close to measuring the opportunity cost of unemployment. Many of the theories that we cling to may have never been appropriate. The persistently high rates of unemployment observed in western Europe offer no consolation that our policies are effective. Incidentally, this applies to the reverse case, that is, a fall in unemployment (as evident in Ireland in recent times) is no guarantee that our policies will work in the future.

Unfortunately, we cannot offer a solution to the unemployment problem in this section. Hopefully we can explain the issues in such a way that the policy discussions which you hear and read about will make more sense. You are already familiar with many of the definitions and the models.

17.2.1 *Defining unemployment*

Unemployment is surprisingly difficult to define and to measure. We will begin by looking at the Quarterly National Household Survey (QNHS) and the Live Register (LR), two measures of Irish unemployment. The two measures have one thing in common. In both, unemployment is a stock concept; they look at the number of unemployed at a point in time.[8] However, each measure defines unemployment differently and, as a result, the number of people which they count as unemployed differs widely.

Quarterly National Household Survey

The QNHS replaced the annual Labour Force Survey (LFS) in 1997. The survey was changed in order to harmonise the collection of labour market statistics throughout the EU. About 39,000 households are surveyed four times per year. For QNHS results, the primary classification used is the International Labour Organisation (ILO) labour force classification. According to the classification, the population includes everyone who is 15 years or older. It is divided between those who are in the labour force and those who are not in the labour force. Those who are not in the labour force are classified as students, on home duties, retired or 'other'.

Definition

The labour force includes those who are employed and those who are unemployed.

Definition

The unemployed include those who are not working and who are available for, and are actively seeking work. People are unemployed because they lost or gave up their previous job. Also included are school-leavers and people who are looking for their first regular job.

Definition

The unemployment rate is the number of people unemployed divided by the labour force.

The QNHS allows people to classify their own employment status.

Live Register

The LR figures are released on the last Friday of each month and published by the CSO in the *Statistical Bulletin*. The LR defines unemployment in the following way.

Definition

The Live Register counts as unemployed the people who are registered at local offices of the Department of Social, Community and Family Affairs for either unemployment benefits or unemployment assistance.

As the LR is a count of claimants eligible for unemployment benefit (UB) or assistance (UA), it is not really designed to measure unemployment. For example, the LR includes part-time workers (those who work up to three days a week) and seasonal and casual workers entitled to UB or UA.

The LR excludes the following categories of people who receive unemployment benefit or assistance: smallholders/farm assists, persons on systematic short-time and self-employed individuals. Individuals who are involved in industrial disputes are also excluded.

The difference between the two measures

The difference between the two measures is a matter of some interest in the media. There is a large gap between the two measures which is shown in Table 17.3.

Table 17.3: Difference between those classified as unemployed on the LFS/QNHS and those receiving social welfare benefits

Year	LR (April) (thousands)	LFS[1]/QNHS[2] (thousands)
1992	280.9	206.6
1993	294.6	220.1
1994	284.5	211.0
1995	276.0	177.4
1996	281.3	179.0
1997	255.5	159.0
1998	231.3	126.6
1999	196.5	96.9
2000	161.8	74.9

Source: Central Statistics Office.
1. April
2. March–May

What accounts for the gap? Recall that for the LFS/QNHS, people classify themselves. Women particularly classify themselves as 'on home duties' if they are not employed. In the LFS/QNHS, this classifies them as 'not in the labour force'. However, since the equality legislation of the mid-1980s, they may also be entitled to social welfare payments and therefore appear on the Live Register. Therefore, on the LR, they are classified as both in the labour force and unemployed. Each measure is defining 'unemployment' differently.

Social welfare fraud appears to be another reason why the two statistics differ. A survey commissioned by the government to compare the LR with the LFS found that for a sample of 2600 cases, 16% of the people claiming unemployment benefits were working and not entitled to those benefits. Promises made by the government to prosecute cases of social welfare fraud led to an immediate drop in the Live Register. In October 1996, for example, over 11,000 'signed off' the dole. Other possible reasons for the difference include arrangements for splitting entitlements between spouses and the introduction of signing on as an eligibility requirement for subsequent participation in training and/or employment schemes.

Unravelling the differences between the two statistics is difficult. Parties in power tend to focus on the lower unemployment rates derived from the LFS/QNHS. These are also the figures which are used for international comparisons. Opposition parties concentrate on the higher LR figures.

The 'best measure' probably depends on the policy issue. One thing is certain. Each measure should be fully understood prior to the policy discussion.

Unemployment can be classified into a number of different types. These include frictional, seasonal, structural, demand deficient and classical. These classifications correspond broadly with the causes of unemployment.

Frictional   This arises when workers who are 'between jobs' find themselves unemployed for a short period of time although work is available. A job vacancy may remain unfilled for a period of time because of imperfect information in the labour market or because of an immobile work force. This is also called search unemployment. Economists and policy-makers are not overly concerned with frictional unemployment which they see as inevitable in any dynamic economy. Measures that will shorten the job search time are likely to reduce frictional unemployment.

Seasonal   Employment in certain industries is seasonal in nature, requiring a work force for only a particular time of year. Employees are then laid off when the season ends. This is also called 'casual' unemployment. Industries which hire seasonally include tourism, construction and farming.

Structural   Economies sometimes face fundamental or structural changes which lead to unemployment. Technological change and the invention of new products may make old products and even whole industries obsolete. If that industry is important to a region or to a national economy, unemployment may persist until new firms and new industries are developed or until labour can be retrained to work in different industries. Examples include the mining industry in the UK and the linen industry in Northern Ireland.

Demand deficient   This type of unemployment arises from a deficiency in aggregate demand in the economy. It occurs during the downturn of the business cycle. It is caused by too much savings and an insufficient amount of spending.

Classical   This is the explanation of unemployment associated with the classical school. It arises from a combination of uncompetitive forces at work in the labour market. Powerful trade unions, costly labour legislation and monopoly influences are all sources of wage inflexibility which are thought to cause unemployment. This is also called 'real wage' unemployment.

17.2.2   *The costs*

So far, we have stated that unemployment is difficult to define and to measure. We will begin this section by admitting that the costs of unemployment are impossible to calculate. Some of the costs, like the total of social welfare payments, can be determined. Many costs, including the loss of production, of tax revenue and of self-

esteem are difficult to quantify. They are felt by all sections of society, but disproportionately by the unemployed and their dependants.

The unemployed do not earn an income. This is only partially offset by the state in
the form of unemployment allowances, rental allowances and medical cards. Although
a person on the dole may not be literally dying of hunger, their relative standard of
living is below that of people who are working. In a world where success is measured
by our accumulation of material goods, there is a stigma attached to those who cannot
participate in that accumulation. Higher security costs, both public and private, are
incurred by societies as the size of the gap between the social classes widens. Length
of life can be affected along with the quality of life. The poverty associated with
unemployment leads to increased physical and mental breakdowns.

The unemployed tend to be 'ghettoised'. They live in areas where the rates of
unemployment are substantially higher than the national average. These neigh-
bourhoods face high levels of crime and substance abuse. Few students finish with
second-level qualifications. Fewer still participate at third level. Not only are their
surroundings bleak, their exits are blocked by a lack of access to education.

Society loses if people are unemployed. The unemployed are a resource which is
not being utilised. If all of the unemployed were working, an economy would produce
more and the national income would increase. If everyone was working, the tax base
would be broader; there would be more sources of tax revenue. More public goods
could be provided.

The money transferred to the unemployed is taken from the taxpayer. This constitutes
a redistribution of resources from one section of society to another. This is not
considered to be a cost to society in an economic sense. However, if the unemployment
rate is high, the tax base is relatively narrow and individuals who are working must
pay high rates of taxes to finance government spending. Some economists suggest that
high tax rates act as a disincentive to employment, so the productive capacity of the
economy may again be affected.

This brief discussion shows the difficulty of 'counting the costs'. The costs that we
can count are huge. The magnitude of the opportunity cost of unemployment is painful
to contemplate. We will now discuss some of the theories developed to explain
unemployment.

17.2.3 The theories and policies

There are a number of different theories of unemployment. Some of them are
conventional, others are radical; some are modern whereas others are centuries old;
some blame government and the state while others apportion blame to the market.
The one feature common to the different theories is the recognition of the social and
economic costs associated with unemployment. We begin with the classical explanation.

The classical theory

The classical model of the labour market was explained in detail in Section 7.1. The
downward sloping demand curve for labour is based on the diminishing margina

productivity of labour. In order for firms to hire more labour, the real wage must fall. The upward sloping supply curve of labour is based on the idea that workers trade off the disutility associated with work with the utility associated with consuming goods and services. In order for labour to work additional hours or for more people to enter the labour market, the real wage rate must increase.

Figure 17.7 shows the classical labour market.

Figure 17.7: The classical labour market

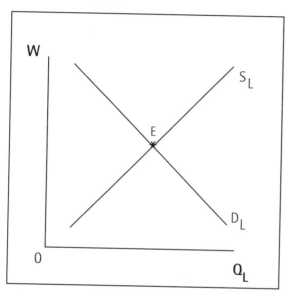

Full employment is shown at point E. The level of output of goods and services is determined by the number of people working. The classicals believed that the labour market moves automatically toward full employment, if wages are flexible. At point E, there is no involuntary unemployment. The supply curve above point E represents people who are voluntarily unemployed. Their utility-maximising decision is to withhold their services, preferring leisure to labour.

If unemployment persisted in the economy, the classicals believed that the source of the unemployment must be in the labour market itself. Since full employment depended on wage flexibility, unemployment meant that wages were not flexible. Rigidities were caused by labour unions, minimum wage legislation or other anti-competitive practices.

The solution to classical unemployment follows directly from their model; the sources of wage rigidity must be eliminated. The labour market will then return to full employment.

The Keynesian theory

The Keynesian theory of unemployment can be explained within the context of the model of income determination. Keynes did not think that the source of unemployment was to be found in the labour market. Instead, he believed that the source of unemployment was in the goods market. Labour demand was derived from the demand for goods. There was nothing automatic about full employment. Deficient demand led to persistent unemployment.

Suppose we begin at a point where the level of output corresponds coincidentally with full employment in the labour market. Panel (a) of Figure 17.8 shows the model of income determination. The equilibrium level of output is determined by adding together the different sources of aggregate expenditure including personal consumption, investment, government spending and net exports. The economy is at equilibrium indicated by point E, which corresponds to full employment in the labour market shown in panel (b).

Figure 17.8: Involuntary unemployment explained using the Keynesian model

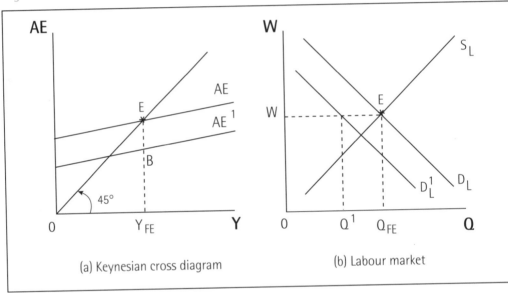

(a) Keynesian cross diagram   (b) Labour market

Now, suppose that war breaks out between the states of the former Yugoslavia, and the markets are concerned about future economic stability in the Balkan regions. Firms, facing uncertainty, decide to postpone their expansion plans. Investment falls, causing the AE curve to shift downwards to AE^1.

Because labour demand is determined by the demand in the goods market, the decrease in investment means that the demand for labour falls. This is shown by a shift of the demand curve for labour to D_L^1. An additional feature to the Keynesian model is the assumption that wages are rigid for institutional reasons such as the existence of labour contracts. Therefore, the wage rate does not fall, but remains at W. The gap between Q^1 and Q_{FE} represents involuntary unemployment. In the goods market, the distance $|EB|$ measures the deflationary gap.

Keynes did not argue in favour of flexible wages. He believed that the source of unemployment was demand-determined. A fall in wages would lead to a fall in consumption, another component of aggregate expenditure. Government intervention in the form of expansionary monetary or fiscal policy is the preferred solution. Only government controls a sufficient level of resources to overcome the deficiency in demand.

The monetarist theory

The monetarist theory essentially agrees with the classical conception of the economy and of the appropriate role of government. Additions to the theory resulted from their observation of what they considered to be inappropriate demand-management policies enacted by the Keynesian economists who influenced policy-makers in the 1960s and the 1970s.

The monetarists believe that the existence of unemployment in the labour market is due to imperfections in the market system and misguided demand-management policies. A flexible labour market without excessive government interference should return to the 'natural rate' of unemployment.[9] Examples of market imperfections include the existence of monopolies, strong labour unions and minimum wage legislation.

The source of employment creation, according to monetarists, is in the private sector. Demand-management policies are not only ineffective in increasing the level of employment, but are also inflationary. Inflation interferes with the price mechanism, the most important source of information between households and firms. Inflationary policies short-circuit the price mechanism and counteract the ability of the private sector to create jobs.

The supply-side theory

Supply-side economists also begin with the classical conception of the economy. Total output depends on factors such as the level of technology, the training of the labour force and the accumulation of capital. One source of unemployment in the economy is 'supply-side' shocks. The most memorable example of a supply-side shock is the oil crisis. Figure 17.9 shows how a negative supply-side shock moves an economy to a level of output which is less than full employment.

Figure 17.9: A supply-side shock

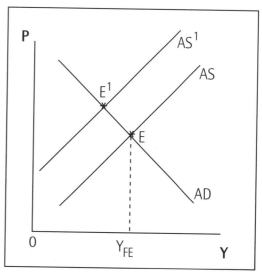

The supply siders also agree with the monetarists that government policy impedes the natural progress of the economy to full employment. Some of the supply-side economists believe in the validity of the Laffer curve relationship (see Information Box 16.1). Briefly, this economist suggested that tax rates act as a disincentive to work. The more heavily that work is taxed, the greater the disincentive. Onerous tax rates limit the productive output of the economy. For this reason, supply siders advocate a revision of the tax system to limit this disincentive.

The supply-side economists differ from the Keynesians because they believe that tax reform will affect the supply side, rather than the demand side of the economy. Tax reform pushes the aggregate supply curve out and to the right, increasing the economy's output. Supply siders differ from the monetarists because they focus primarily on fiscal policy rather than monetary policy.

The Marxian theory

Marxian unemployment theory is based on the conflicting relationship between labour and the capitalist. Marx believed that labour is productive and the source of all surplus. This surplus is divided between labour and the capitalist, depending on who is the most powerful. If labour is more powerful, wages rise above the subsistence level. If the capitalist is more powerful a larger share of the surplus goes to the capitalist in the form of profit.

Marx agreed with Keynes that the capitalist system is prone to periodic expansions and contractions.[10] Involuntary unemployment of labour is a feature of both models in recessions and depressions. In the Keynesian model, involuntary unemployment is caused by the failure of private investment which occurs because of the 'animal spirits' of investors. In the Keynesian model, the failure of investment is a consequence of instability; in the Marxian model, it is a tactic designed to create instability.

In the Marxian model, high levels of unemployment serve a regulatory purpose. During periods when workers are powerful, profits decline. If profits are falling, capitalists reduce investment. This leads to a recession, which reduces labour power. When unemployment is high, workers are in a weaker bargaining position. The capitalist can force workers to increase productivity and to work for less. Workers realise that there is a 'reserve army of unemployed' waiting to take their place.

We have already observed that differences in modelling the unemployment problem lead to different policy prescriptions. The Marxian model is no exception. Marx believed that government, in protecting the private property rights of the capitalist, was an active participant in the problem of unemployment. Profits, extracted from the workers who produced the surplus, were protected by the police and the legal system. The source of unemployment in the Marxian model is the link between profits and investment. The solution is to break that link. It was in this sense that Marx advocated the abolition of private property. To end the exploitation of labour and to eradicate unemployment, the capitalist system had to be destroyed. For more on the life of Marx, see Information Box 17.3.

INFORMATION BOX 17.3

Karl Marx (1818–83)

Karl Marx was born in Germany and educated at the University of Bonn where he studied law. He furthered his education at the University of Berlin where he began to take a keen interest in philosophy. His teacher was the radical philosopher Georg Hegel. Marx was influenced by Hegel and began work on a thesis with a view to getting a university lectureship. He received his doctorate in 1841.

Marx's radical views, however, were a major obstacle in his search for an academic position. Instead he worked as a freelance journalist. After marrying his childhood sweetheart, Marx moved to Paris, the centre of radical reformers, where he met Friedrich Engels, the revolutionary socialist. They became lifetime friends and collaborators.

Marx and his family were expelled from France in 1845, and subsequently moved to Brussels where he organised a Communist Correspondence Committee. Three years later, the outline to Marx's theory *The Communist Manifesto* was complete. According to Engels it was 'to do for history what Darwin's theory has done for biology'. It concluded with the famous lines 'The workers have nothing to lose in this but their chains. They have the world to gain. Workers of the world, unite!'

After being expelled from a number of European cities, Marx moved to London where he lived for the rest of his life. Although he contributed regularly to the *New York Tribune*, he and his family spent many years in poverty. It was during this time that he wrote his most famous work *Capital* wherein he prophesied that capitalism would collapse and would be replaced by an alternative economic system – socialism. Socialism in turn would be replaced by the utopian state of communism.

While his personal finances improved considerably in the later years of his life, due to inheritances, his personal life was shattered by the early deaths of his children and his grandchildren. This was followed by the death of his wife in 1881 and his eldest daughter in 1883. He died of bronchitis at the age of 65 in March 1883.

In recent times, explanations of unemployment focus on specific features of the economic system in general and the labour market in particular. These include the time and effort involved in searching for employment, the insider-outsider composition of the labour market and the effects of long-term wage contracts.[11]

17.2.4 *The Irish experience*

One of the most unforgettable comments by a senior political figure in Ireland was made in 1978. The Taoiseach and leader of Fianna Fáil, Jack Lynch, was interviewed by RTE's 'This Week' programme. In response to a question on unemployment and whether the electorate should put the government out of office if the figures rose to 100,000, Mr Lynch replied, '. . . if we don't deliver then the electorate are entitled to put us out of office.'[12]

Since then governments from different political parties have come and gone. Yet the unemployment figure increased steadily until it was over 300,000 by January 1993. It had become the second highest rate within the EU (second to Spain) and the third highest within the OECD (behind Spain and Finland). One in five of the labour force was unemployed.

High unemployment is not a recent phenomenon in Ireland. In the past there have been periods of high and rising unemployment. Our analysis of unemployment is limited to the period since the early 1970s.

The unemployment rate in Ireland during the period 1970–2000 is shown in Figure 17.10.

Figure 17.10: Unemployment rate in Ireland 1970–2000

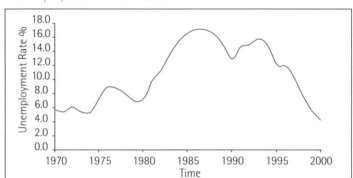

We will separate the discussion of unemployment during this thirty-year period into two sections. We will begin with the 1970s and 1980s. During this period, the numbers unemployed increased and then remained persistently high. We will then look at the 1990s, a period of falling unemployment.

The rise and persistence of Irish unemployment

The causes of the high Irish unemployment rate of the 1980s were many and diverse. Factors such as the lack of natural resources, peripherality and the absence of entrepreneurial spirit are some of the causes which often get a mention. In reality, their contribution to the high unemployment rate is questionable.

The unemployment problem is complex. In order to gain some understanding of the nature of the problem, we will begin by attempting to group possible causes into four classifications: demographic factors, external factors (incorporating UK unemployment), inappropriate demand-management policies and other domestic factors.

The demographic factor

There is considerable disagreement over the relationship between population changes, changes in the labour force and changes in unemployment in Ireland. As a result of the increase in birth rates and the reversal of the emigration pattern from the 1960s onwards, the Irish labour force began to record significant increases in new entrants. Although many new jobs were created during this period, unemployment numbers also rose. Many experts, however, do not view these demographic changes as a significant factor contributing to the increase in Irish unemployment. In support of their argument, they highlight the following points: Irish birth rates peaked in the early 1980s

(21.9 per 1,000), falling close to EU levels thereafter; and other countries, including the US and Japan, recorded similar increases in population without any matching increase in unemployment levels.

External

A number of shocks external to the economy contributed to the poor performance of the Irish labour market. These include the two oil crises, the break-up of the Bretton Woods system, the liberalisation of financial markets and high real interest rates, the world recessions of 1980–82 and 1990–91 and the poor performance of the UK economy. The supply-side shocks of the 1970s were price inflationary and demand deflationary. This caused problems for policy-makers throughout the western world, including Ireland. Higher oil prices added to the production costs of many Irish and Irish-based firms. The break-up of the fixed exchange rate system created uncertainty in financial markets both at home and abroad. Exchange rate volatility and greater interest rate fluctuations caused problems for both exporters and importers. World recession, and in particular the sluggish growth recorded in the UK, contributed to the already weak domestic demand. In fact, the trend in Irish unemployment during this period was similar to the trend in UK unemployment; this suggests, unsurprisingly, the existence of a strong link between the Irish and UK labour markets. Conditions in the UK labour market impact on Irish unemployment, via inward and outward migration. The combination of all these events had an adverse effect on Irish economic growth and, likewise, Irish unemployment.

Inappropriate demand-management policies

The fiscal, monetary, incomes and exchange rate policies adopted by different governments may have contributed in different ways to the high unemployment rates of the 1970s and 1980s. In terms of fiscal policy, a number of mistakes were made. First, the authorities responded to the supply-side shocks of the 1970s with orthodox demand-management policies.[13] Second, the borrowing which subsequent governments undertook was partly to finance day-to-day spending.[14] Third, fiscal policy from the mid-1970s until the mid-1980s was largely pro-cyclical.[15] Fourth, although the Fine Gael/Labour Coalition government of the 1980s was forced by the burgeoning debt to enact contractionary fiscal policy, their policy mix was flawed.[16] Hence, we arrive at the assessment of some commentators that the legacy of Irish fiscal policy of the 1970s and early 1980s was one of high unemployment and massive debt.

Fiscal policy was not the only culprit during this period. Job creation was hindered by the combination, at different times, of high interest rates arising from tight monetary policy, a real exchange rate appreciation arising from Ireland's participation in the EMS exchange rate mechanism and excessive increases in wage levels arising from pay agreements between the government and the social partners.[17]

Other domestic factors

There are a large number of other domestic factors which have contributed to high unemployment in Ireland; most of these have affected the supply side. Production was adversely affected because of factors which contributed to high costs. We deal with two: taxation and labour market rigidities.

Taxation

There were many aspects of the tax system which hindered job creation and contributed to the high unemployment rates. A number of these are considered below:

- The Irish tax system treats labour and capital differently. Since the early 1960s the cost of capital has been subsidised by the state in order to attract foreign investment. Allowances against corporate tax for capital expenditure in addition to flexible depreciation allowances were offered to multinationals as part of the incentive package. Tax on labour, on the other hand, was considered, by many, as excessive. Labour was the main source of tax revenue, with the PAYE sector carrying the burden. In particular, marginal tax rates on labour were high and were applicable at low income levels. With a large excess supply of labour, it was surprising to see labour treated in this fashion.
- The lack of integration between the tax and welfare systems in Ireland was highlighted as a possible contributing factor to the unemployment crisis in Ireland. The non-integration of the tax and welfare systems resulted in many anomalies. One such anomaly is referred to as the unemployment trap. This occurs when an unemployed person finds that he is financially worse off if he accepts a job offer. One measure of the unemployment trap is the replacement ratio (RR), described in [17.4] below.

$$\text{Replacement ratio} = \frac{\text{unemployment benefits}}{\text{after-tax income}} \times 100 \qquad [17.4]$$

This is the proportion of a worker's after-tax income that is replaced by unemployment benefits. As the replacement ratio approaches 100, the gap narrows between working and remaining unemployed. The higher the ratio, the less financial incentive there is to work.

High replacement ratios were not uncommon in the 1980s and early 1990s in Ireland. For example, for a single person earning £6,000 or less a year, the welfare system might have replaced over 75% of take-home pay. The disincentive to work was more striking for larger families. Welfare payments could have been up to 1.5 times higher than the after-tax income of a married couple with two children. For families earning close to the average industrial wage, the replacement ratio could have been close to 70%.

Replacement ratios increased in Ireland during the period 1977–94. There is both international and domestic evidence to indicate a correlation between rising replacement ratios and the persistence and duration of unemployment.[18]

- Another anomaly within the tax system is the occurrence of a poverty trap. A poverty trap exists when there is no financial incentive for an employed person to take up a better job offer. Given the nature of the tax and welfare systems in Ireland, a poverty trap existed for low-paid workers who were supporting large families. Before the tax reductions that were initiated in the mid- to late 1990s, many low-paid workers had little or no financial incentive to accept higher (gross) paid jobs. This is because the increase in their income resulted in a decrease in their social welfare benefits and a larger tax liability to the state. The worker in this position was caught in a poverty trap. An increase in gross pay led to a decrease in net income.

- For there to be low unemployment, employees must have an incentive to accept employment in addition to the employers having an incentive to hire additional workers. Central to this issue is the level of labour costs and the tax applied to wages. The tax wedge, as it is commonly referred to, is the difference between the after-tax earnings of the employee and the gross cost incurred by the employer. A significant tax wedge acts as a dual disincentive. Considering the supply curve for labour, a low take-home pay does not overcome the disutility of labour. The tax-inflated marginal cost of hiring another worker is a disincentive on the demand side of the labour market.

  In 1980/81 the tax wedge for a single person earning the average industrial wage amounted to £1,835.93. Ten years later, the tax wedge was £5,004.57. This 173% increase far exceeds the rise in prices over the same period.[19] Arthur Andersen & Co. (1991) estimated that the marginal tax wedge for a single person in Ireland was 61%, the second highest of the countries surveyed.[20] An OECD study in 1991 calculated that the economy-wide tax wedge in Ireland was the fourth highest in the OECD, behind the wealthier nations of Denmark, Holland and Sweden.[21]

Labour market rigidities

Neoclassical labour market models predict that in a market without rigidities, the wage rate should fall, eliminating involuntary unemployment. Similar to other national labour markets, the Irish labour market is characterised by a number of rigidities.

Obviously, we cannot talk about the elimination of rigidities without acknowledging that this will lead to an erosion of the institutional arrangements, developed over the years to protect labour. It is not easy to strike a balance. In this section, we will describe some of the economic problems which arise because of the rigidities. However, we acknowledge that the resolution of these issues must take place within the context of a wider social debate.

- The wage bargaining process in Ireland has been characterised as an example of the insider-outsider model. Those employed are 'insiders' who negotiate for their own income and job security to the detriment of the 'outsiders' who are the unemployed. The insiders' demands impose a floor on wages which is above the market clearing wage.

  Since 1987, centralised wage agreements have been the norm. Until 1996 the negotiations between the government and the social partners excluded the unemployed. Between 1987 and 1993 real earnings in Ireland, as measured by the average hourly earnings index, rose by over 30%. Over the same period unemployment increased by 47,000. In the words of Dermot McAleese 'The insiders did what came naturally – put themselves first, while protesting concern for the unemployed – and the outsiders stayed outside.'[22] Not everyone accepts the validity of Professor McAleese's claim. For a contrasting view, see Information Box 17.4.

INFORMATION BOX 17.4

Do high wages cost jobs?

Two contrasting views

The debate over the relationship between wage rates and unemployment levels dates back to the classical school of economics. Followers of the classical school argued that high unemployment was caused by uncompetitive forces in the labour market. If wages were high, an excess supply of labour can result. The solution to high unemployment levels was a reduction in wages levels. Keynes took a very different view of the labour market. Deficiencies in demand were largely responsible for rising unemployment. Any attempt to pursue the classical policy response of a cut in wages may only make the situation worse; by cutting wage levels, workers' ability to boost demand is reduced. The solution lies with government and active fiscal policy.

Professor Dermot McAleese of TCD says Yes, high wages can cost jobs. He supports this view by examining the increases in the public services pay bill since 1987. If a 2.5% increase had been granted (sufficient to compensate for inflation) rather than the recorded 6% increase, the remaining £600m 'could have been used to generate extra employment'. Such a saving could have financed tax cuts or increased public sector employment, he argues. In relation to public sector pay he concludes by saying 'Many thousands of jobs have been priced out of existence because of public sector unions' success in obtaining high increases in remuneration'. His criticisms are not solely directed at the public sector. He estimates that at least 10,000 extra jobs could have been provided in the private sector if the same pay criteria which he applied to the public sector was applied to the private sector.

Peter Cassells, General Secretary of the ICTU says No, high wages do not cost jobs. He defends his position by outlining the positive aspects of high earnings and by examining Ireland's record against international standards. A summary of his main points is listed below.

1. Lower wages reduce purchasing power which in turn reduces the demand for goods and services. The demand for labour to provide these same goods and services is subsequently lowered.
2. Lower wages result in less tax revenue for the government. Less revenue translates into less expenditure and fewer social services. Consequently, fewer people are required to provide these services.
3. High wages do not necessarily translate into uncompetitiveness. Wage increases are justified if they are in line with productivity gains.
4. Ireland's wage levels or increases in wage levels are not out of line with other EU countries. The evidence that he provides indicates relatively low wage levels and moderate increases in the period 1987–91.

The views expressed above reflect a much wider debate concerning the different approaches to tackling unemployment.[1] Is the low-wage, low-skilled, hire-and-fire approach followed in the US preferable to the high-wage, high-skilled, heavily protected approach adopted by the EU? The passage of time has not lessened the intensity of this debate.

1 *The Irish Times*, 18 September 1992.

- In terms of trade union membership, Ireland is quite similar to many continental European countries. The trade union density, which refers to the percentage of all wage and salary earners who are trade union members in Ireland, was 31% in 1999. This translates to approximately 514,000 workers affiliated to a trade union. This union density, although declining, is much higher than the union densities for either the UK or the US, the two countries whose labour markets are most relevant to Ireland. The US has traditionally been a low-union membership country whereas in the UK the trade union movement was badly damaged by Thatcherite policies. Trade unions seek to improve the working conditions of their members. In addition, they negotiate wage increases for workers.
- In the past thirty years Irish workers have benefited from protective labour legislation. Notwithstanding the importance of protecting workers' rights, the drawback of such extensive legislation is the added cost to the employer. The net effect for many indigenous firms is higher costs, a loss of business and subsequent job losses. When confronted with extensive labour legislation in Ireland, multinationals may be enticed abroad to countries where labour costs are lower (Greece) or to countries where legislation is not as extensive (UK). A study by Emerson in 1988 concluded that workers in Ireland were no worse off in terms of protection than their counterparts in other EU countries.[23]

We now turn our attention to the fall in unemployment that took place in Ireland in the mid- to late 1990s.

The fall in Irish unemployment

It appears that the significant fall in unemployment that took place in the mid- to late 1990s was due largely to the rapid growth in the Irish economy. In the six years from 1993 onwards, the economy grew, as measured by changes in GNP, by 57% in real terms. In the same period, the unemployment rate fell by 10 percentage points, from 15.7% of the labour force in 1993 to 5.7% of the labour force in 1999. This can be explained by Okun's Law.

Definition

Okun's Law depicts the inverse relationship between output growth and unemployment.

It is named after the American economist, Arthur Okun, who studied the relationship between changes in real GDP and fluctuations in unemployment in the US. In his study, for every one percentage point decrease in the unemployment rate, output increased by about three percentage points.

It is recognised that the relationship between changes in the unemployment rate and output growth may not be as strong in Ireland as it is in the US. On account of the close link between the Irish and the UK labour market, the trend in the Irish unemployment rate has been remarkably similar to the UK trend in unemployment. This similarity in the historical behaviour of Irish and British unemployment rates is well documented in the unemployment literature. With migration flows sensitive to labour market conditions in both countries, the *a priori* relationship between unemployment and output in Ireland might prove weak. Despite this, the association between changes in unemployment rates and output growth in Ireland appears quite strong. In Figure 17.11 we plot the change in the unemployment rate (as measured by labour force data) on the horizontal axis and the percentage change in real GNP on the vertical axis. We use GNP rather than GDP for the reasons outlined in Chapter 10. We can see from the scatterplot that there is a negative relationship between the two variables. Although we show the relationship for the twenty-five-year period 1975–99, we are particularly interested in the six-year period beginning in 1994. These points, marked 1994 to 1999, are all clustered in the top left-hand corner of the graph. The rapid fall in unemployment appears closely associated with the remarkable growth in the Irish economy over the past six years. According to one expert, GNP growth in Ireland in excess of 3.5% per annum leads to falling unemployment.[24] Although simplified, this provides a reasonable explanation for the fall in Irish unemployment.

Figure 17.11: Unemployment and economic growth, 1975–99

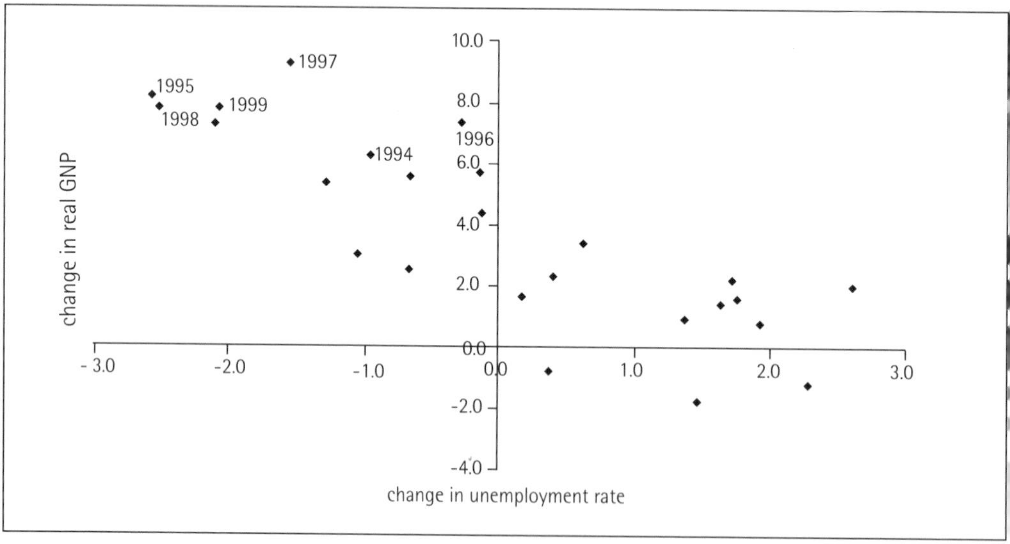

This raises another question, that is, an explanation for Ireland's remarkable growth rates throughout most of the 1990s and into the early part of the new millennium. Ireland's long-term growth performance is explained in the next chapter. A brief outline follows.

In simple terms, we can account for economic growth by increases in the quantity of factor inputs, that is capital and labour, and by increases in productivity, that is output per unit of input. As ever, it is difficult to assess the contribution of capital due to the paucity of data on physical capital stock. What we can say is that the capital stock has been upgraded and modernised by the inflow of foreign direct investment. Nonetheless, there is no doubt that the most significant input contribution comes from labour. In the Irish case, an elastic supply of labour, arising from a combination of factors including rising female labour force participation, favourable demographics and a drawdown of a large stock of unemployed, has resulted in a rapid rate of growth in employment in the 1990s. The remarkable increase in employment numbers for the period 1994–2000 is shown in Table 17.4.

Table 17.4: Employment Numbers 1994–2000

	1994	1995	1996	1997	1998	1999	2000
Employment ('000s)[1]	1220.6	1281.7	1328.5	1379.9	1494.5	1591.1	1670.7
Annual change (%)	3.2	5.0	3.7	3.9	8.3	6.5	5.0

Source: Central Statistics Office.
Note: 1. For the QNHS, we report the results from the 2nd quarter (March–May) surveys.

These employment growth rates are unusual for a developed country. They are more associated with high-growth developing countries whose agricultural sector supplies a large stock of labour. Interestingly, given its history of immigration, another developed country that has recorded, in its recent past, rapid increases in employment contributing to economic growth is the United States.

In addition to the increased labour supply, real productivity gains have contributed to the growth performance. Advances in technology allow for a more efficient use of available inputs.

Definition
Total factor productivity (TFP) growth is the change in output that arises from technological progress.

Several different studies indicate that total factor productivity growth increased by between 4% and 4.5% per annum in Ireland in the period 1987–97.[25] This compares favourably to productivity growth in Ireland in the late 1970s and 1980s and also, surprisingly, to the productivity growth achieved by the East Asian countries during their period of rapid economic growth. It is somewhat similar to the total factor productivity growth attained by the big western European economies during the post-war Golden Age era. The conclusion of the OECD report into Ireland's economic boom is that '. . . it is clear that while factor input increases have played an important part in fuelling the growth process, total factor productivity gains have played at least as large a role . . .' (OECD, 1999).

As for these productivity gains, it is yet again a combination of factors that has been responsible. Among others, they include investment in human capital, an industrial policy that opened up trade and allowed for an inflow of foreign direct investment (FDI), a shift from traditional, low-productivity sectors to high-technology sectors, corporatism or centralised wage agreements and improvements in demand management that involved tax reform and fiscal prudence. Of course, many of these factors were in place before 1994 and, in some cases, were initiated before the 1987 regime change. This suggests that the remarkable achievement that has happened, namely the transformation of one of western Europe's poorest countries (the 'poorest of the rich' as *The Economist* described it in 1988) to one of its richest ('Europe's shining light' as *The Economist* described it ten years later), required the right mix of mutually-reinforcing factors and policies.[26] Despite this, problems still remain. Of the current numbers who are unemployed, about one-third are long-term unemployed. Given the level of FDI in certain key sectors, the Irish economy remains vulnerable to economic shocks. Infrastructural bottlenecks continue to act as a constraint. In this last section, we outline the policies that can help to keep Irish unemployment at low levels.

Favourable economic climate

It is generally agreed that the Irish and EU authorities should maintain an economic climate at home conducive to economic growth and job creation. This environment is characterised by low inflation rates, low interest rates and low public sector borrowing. This is achieved by implementing consistent and credible macroeconomic policies.

Because of Ireland's participation in the single currency, Irish authorities have little control over these macroeconomic policies. Monetary and exchange policies are determined at 'euro' level. The use of fiscal policy is constrained by the Stability and Growth Pact.

Even with a favourable economic climate at home and abroad, maintenance of low unemployment requires continued structural changes in the Irish economy, particularly in the area of competition, tax and welfare reform, pension reform and other areas of public policy. The most urgent are listed below.

- *A reform of the tax and welfare systems* Greater integration of the tax and welfare systems is required. A widening of the tax base is considered important as is an elimination of the anomalies that exist in the tax system. Other forms of tax such as property, wealth and energy should be considered in order to widen the tax base. The level of bureaucracy and red tape should be minimised. More investment in training and education is required by the state in order to avoid the move from short-term unemployment to long-term unemployment.
- *Increasing the competitiveness of commercial state bodies* The commercial state bodies face challenging times ahead. They must be prepared for greater competition. This requires a radical restructuring in many of the semi-state bodies. Restrictive practices, excessive overheads and state subsidisation require examination. Only those companies that are cost competitive will survive in the single European market. This challenge applies equally well to private sector companies.
- *Adjustments in the wage bargaining process* There is a recognition that the wage bargaining process has worked well up to now. However, given the change in the economic environment, there is a need to question whether local wage bargaining should replace the centralised wage agreements which have dominated incomes policy since 1987. Opinions are mixed. Some argue that localised bargaining will lead to lower wage agreements. Others believe that the national agreements have led to modest wage increases and have imposed order on an otherwise chaotic process. What is indisputable is the need to maintain our competitiveness. This objective can be achieved by controlling costs. Wages increases must be based on

productivity gains and they must also reflect employment conditions in the labour market.

- *Changes in education and training* Notwithstanding the past achievements of the Irish educational system, there is a need for change in education policy. Features of other European educational systems may be useful. These include the focus on vocational and technical training in Germany and Switzerland, the emphasis on languages and oral communications found in central and eastern Europe and, finally, the focus on non-academic skills such as music and art as established in the former Soviet Union. The educational system must help students to develop entrepreneurial skills. Active manpower policies, the upgrading of existing skills and the search for new skills is an area which requires improvement in Ireland. All members of the labour force, those at work and those out of work, require further training to adapt to our knowledge-based society.

- *A reappraisal of industrial policy* This process began in the early 1980s. Although many reports and countless recommendations have followed, more action is required. While acknowledging the success of the multinational sector in Ireland, the performance of the indigenous sector has been less successful. More attention needs to be paid to small Irish-owned firms. Within this sector, there needs to be a greater awareness of the importance of ancillary activities such as R&D, marketing, management, product design and development. The amount of time spent on paperwork to comply with various government regulations needs to be reduced.

- *Infrastructural spending* It is widely recognised that if Ireland is to continue to grow, it must alleviate the supply-side constraints evident in the economy. This requires a significant upgrading of the economy's infrastructure, as indicated by the National Development Plan. Housing, the environment and transport are the areas that need urgent attention. All these areas of public policy will require significant increases in capital spending in the coming years.

- *Labour supply* Another constraint on growth is the labour supply. Policy initiatives in the areas of taxation, housing and immigration can help to alleviate the labour shortages. By encouraging female participation, and by facilitating immigration by Irish emigrants and non-nationals, the authorities can help to ensure an adequate supply of labour.

CASE STUDY

Extract from *The Irish Times*
Unemployment figures at lowest levels since 1980
by Padraig Yeates

The number of people unemployed in the Republic has fallen below 100,000 for the first time in 19 years, according to the latest figures from the Central Statistics Office. These are based on the quarterly national household survey, which is generally accepted as the most accurate measure of unemployment in the State. The survey was introduced in 1997 and strict comparisons with earlier figures are

→

not possible. Nevertheless, the figures show a drop of 43,500 in the number of unemployed in the year ending February 1998 [sic] and an increase in the number at work of 71,900. The last time the number of unemployed fell below 100,000 was 1980. The following year it rose to 126,000.

The Tánaiste, Ms Harney, welcomed the figures released yesterday and said they showed 'the tiger economy is benefiting all sectors of society'. She said unemployment now stood at 5.8 per cent and long-term unemployment at 2.6 per cent of the labour force. Seamus Brennan, said that, 'We are now tantalisingly close to full employment.' The Labour Party spokesman on Finance, Mr Derek McDowell, gave it a more qualified welcome. He focused on the rise in the number of 'marginally attached' people in the workforce – those who had not actively sought work in the previous month. He said there was a danger that this group of predominantely long-term unemployed people with low skill levels,

would be left behind. The figure for marginally attached unemployed rose from 17,100 in the quarter ending November 1998 to 19,300 in the quarter ending February 1999. However, this [sic] still well below the recent peak of 20,800 in the quarter ending August 1998.

. . .

The Workers Party described the figures as a 'fabrication' and pointed out that there were 197,395 people signing on the live register last month.

The dramatic fall in the number of long-term unemployed, especially the 8,000 drop in the fourth quarter of 1998, coincides with the introduction of the Government's National Manpower Plan, requiring under-25s signing on for over a year to attend for interview at their local FÁS office. Another striking feature of the figures is the drop of 38,000 in the size of the workforce between August and September 1998. This is largely accounted for by students returning to full-time study.

Source: *The Irish Times*, 22 July 1999.

Questions

1. Two measures of Irish unemployment are referred to in the article. What are they and how do they differ?
2. How are the long-term unemployed defined? Using the Quarterly National Household Survey, report the quarterly long-term unemployment rate for the period September 1997–August 2000. In the same table, report the total unemployment rate for the same period.
3. What is meant by the 'marginally attached'? How does this relate to other classifications used in the QNHS? Report figures for the classifications for the three-month period June–August 2000.

[NB: The Central Statistics Office website www.cso.ie is a useful source.]

Answers on website

17.3 INTERNATIONAL TRADE
by Eithne Murphy

17.3.1 Traditional trade theory

Mercantilism

Mercantilism was the principal economic doctrine of the seventeenth and eighteenth centuries. As a doctrine it probably reflected as well as influenced the prevailing commercial practices of the period. According to mercantilists, countries get wealthy through the accumulation of precious metals; in that instance, gold and silver. Since gold and silver were the means of payment for goods and services, a country could accumulate such wealth if it ran continuous balance of payments surpluses; that is to say, if it exported more than it imported. Hence policies designed to achieve this end were those that limited imports (especially imports of high value-added products) and encouraged exports.

This philosophy, although subsequently discredited intellectually, has continued to influence international trade practice. The few exceptions were the UK in the nineteenth century and contemporary Hong Kong. Most policy-makers consider a balance of payments surplus to be a positive economic sign. Most policy-makers consider the removal of trade barriers in their national markets to be a concession on their part and one that has to be paid for by reciprocal trade barrier dismantlement on the part of other countries. This is simply mercantilist philosophy in modern guise.

Absolute advantage

Adam Smith is generally considered to be the founding father of economics.[27] For the purposes of the history of international trade theory, two aspects of his philosophy will be highlighted. Firstly, he considered that the objective of all economic activities was consumption. Here we have the first blow against mercantilism. Gold and silver do not contribute directly to our individual welfare, the consumption of goods and services do. Metals are only useful to the extent that they aid consumption. A country that runs a continuous balance of payments surplus is akin to the miser who will not spend his money.

Secondly, individual self-sufficiency is never efficient, in the sense of representing an optimum use of an individual's energies and talents. Most individuals specialise in their choice of work which still allows them to consume a wide variety of goods and services if they trade with one another.

Laissez-faire, which is a policy of non-interference in the economic affairs of individuals, will ensure that the goods produced in the economy will be those that consumers want, while competition will ensure that the consumer gets these goods at the cheapest possible price. What holds for the individual also holds for the nation state. If self-sufficiency is inefficient for an individual, it must also be inefficient for a country. A country should specialise in production, producing what it does best, and import other products; this will ensure global efficiency, and it will also allow a country to enjoy a higher overall level of consumption.

	Ireland	Britain
Beef	20 kg	5 kg
Grain	2 kg	10 kg

If one person fewer engages in grain production in Ireland and instead devotes his energies to beef production, then grain output will fall by 2 kilos per day and beef output will increase by 20 kilos per day. Do the opposite in Britain and beef output will fall by 5 kilos while grain production will rise by 10 kilos. The net effect is that overall beef production rises by 15 kilos per day and overall grain production rises by 8 kilos per day. If both countries trade with each other then both can enjoy the benefits of higher overall production.

Comparative advantage

The problem with the theory of absolute advantage is that it assumes that countries and the world can gain from specialisation and trade if they are absolutely more efficient than other countries in some line of production. David Ricardo however showed that a country and the world can gain from specialisation and trade even if one country is better at producing all goods. He called this the theory of comparative advantage.[28]

Table 17.6: Production per person per working day

	Ireland	Britain
Beef	6 kg	10 kg
Grain	2 kg	10 kg

Workers in Britain are more productive in both beef and grain production. How then can Ireland and Britain gainfully trade? According to David Ricardo, if each country specialises in what it does 'relatively' best, both can gain from trade. We can see that in grain production, Britain is five times more productive than Ireland, whereas in beef production it is less than twice as productive. Accordingly, Ireland should specialise where its absolute disadvantage is least, i.e. in beef production, and Britain should specialise where its absolute advantage is greatest, i.e. in grain production.

In Ireland the true cost of a kilo of grain is 3 kilos of beef. Taking a person away from beef production and employing them in the grain sector means sacrificing 3 kilos of beef daily in order to have 1 kilo of grain. In Britain the cost of a kilo of grain is 1 kilo of beef. True cost is opportunity cost. Alternatively the cost of 1 kilo of beef in Britain is 1 kilo of grain. If Britain can import beef and pay less than 1 kilo of grain for it then Britain is better off than it was before. If Ireland can import grain and pay less than 3 kilos of beef for 1 kilo of grain then Ireland is better off than it was before.

So an exchange of beef for grain at a price somewhere between 1:1 and 1:3 will benefit both countries. In other words, if international terms of trade (the cost of a unit of imported goods in terms of the amount of exports required to purchase them) are different to a country's opportunity cost of production, then the country can gain from specialising and trading. If, for example, the international terms of trade were 2 kilos of beef for 1 kilo of grain, then the gains to Ireland and Britain from specialising in beef and grain respectively would be the following:

Ireland

Take a person away from grain production and put them working in the beef sector. Output of beef would rise by 6 kilos a day while output of grain would fall by 2 kilos a day. But 6 kilos of beef buys 3 kilos of grain on the international market. So Ireland can actually enjoy a higher level of grain consumption than before.

Britain

As an exercise, see how Britain can also gain and enjoy a higher level of beef consumption than it did before, by specialising out of beef and into grain.

We can represent graphically the production and consumption possibilities of both countries both before and after trade. The only additional information that we need are the number of workers in an economy. For simplicity let us assume that both countries have 1 million workers.

Figure 17.12: Production possibilities for Ireland and Britain

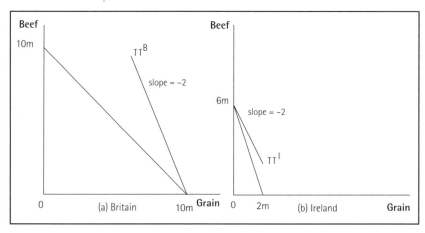

Figure 17.12 shows both countries' production possibilities for a day. If all workers are fully employed in Britain in the beef sector only, it can produce 10 million kilos of beef daily. Alternatively, if all workers are employed in the grain sector, it can produce 10 million kilos of grain daily. Or if some workers are employed in the beef sector and others in the grain sector it can produce less than 10 million kilos of both goods daily. For example, if 70% of the labour force were employed in the beef sector and 30% in

the grain sector, it could produce 7 million kilos of beef and 3 million kilos of grain daily. The production possibility frontier (PPF) shows all the different combinations of beef and grain that are feasible, given the resource base and given the productivity of the resource base in both sectors (see Chapter 1). The slope of the PPF shows the cost of a kilo of grain in terms of beef which is –1. Before trade, Britain is forced to consume exactly what it produces.

Similarly Ireland can produce either 6 million kilos of beef daily or 2 million kilos of grain daily or some combination thereof. The slope of the PPF is –3 indicating the cost of a kilo of grain. Again before trade Ireland can only consume what it produces.

With trade Ireland produces only beef and Britain only grain. The international terms of trade are 2 kilos of beef for 1 kilo of grain. Both countries are now no longer obliged to consume exactly what they produce: they are merely obliged to ensure that the value of domestic production equals the value of domestic consumption, where prices are determined internationally. The line TT^I for Ireland shows us Ireland's potential consumption. We can see that potential consumption with trade is greater than it was without trade. Similarly for Britain, the line TT^B shows us Britain's potential consumption post-trade and we can see that it dominates pre-trade consumption possibilities. The rate at which goods exchange internationally is determined by international demand and supply.

What we can conclude from David Ricardo's analysis of trade is that all countries, even the most inefficient, can gain from trade, provided that they specialise in what they do relatively best and provided that the international terms of trade differ from the domestic opportunity cost of production.

Revealed comparative advantage and competitiveness

How do we know where a country's comparative advantage lies? One way is to look at the unit cost of producing different goods; another is to look at the prices of these goods before trade, assuming, of course, that prices equal unit costs. If the only factor of production is labour and all labour gets paid the same wage, then the price of grain in Ireland will be three times the price of beef since workers in the grain sector are only one-third as productive as workers in the beef sector. In Britain the price of a kilo of grain will be the same as the price of a kilo of beef since workers are equally productive in both sectors and get paid the same amount.

	Ireland	Britain
$\dfrac{P\ \textbf{beef}}{P\ \textbf{grain}}$	$\dfrac{1}{3}$	$\dfrac{1}{1}$

Since one-third is less than 1, indicating that Ireland's relative price of beef is less than that of Britain, it follows that Ireland has a comparative advantage in beef production.

	Ireland	Britain
$\dfrac{P\ \textbf{beef}}{P\ \textbf{grain}}$	$\dfrac{3}{1}$	$\dfrac{1}{1}$

Since 1 is less than 3, indicating that Britain's relative price of grain is less than that of Ireland, it follows that Britain has a comparative advantage in grain production. It is interesting and important to note that in our stylised two-good, two-country world, as long as the domestic opportunity cost of production is different in both countries, then it is impossible for one country to have a comparative advantage in the production of both goods.

Many individuals still find the theory of comparative advantage counter-intuitive. It is all very well to say that what matters for trade purposes is domestic opportunity, cost of production or domestic relative prices, but in the real world what matters are absolute prices. How then in the real world can an Ireland of the above example compete with Britain if it is less productive in all lines of production?

The answer to this puzzle is to realise that prices are determined by two elements, the productivity of factors of production and the cost of employing factors of production. Since workers in Ireland are less productive than workers in Britain, they will earn less, even after trade. For example, if Irish workers were paid €10 a day and British workers UK£6 a day and the euro–sterling exchange rate was €1 = £0.6, then we can see the Irish and British workers get the same return. In this situation Ireland would not be able to export anything to Britain; it would be uncompetitive as its prices would be too high.

If on the other hand, Irish wages were €4 a day to Britain's UK£6 and the exchange rate was still €1 = £0.6, then Ireland would be able to successfully export beef at a lower price than the British. This is because although the Irish worker in the beef sector has a productivity of only 60% of his British counterpart, his wages are only 40% of British wages. They would still, however, not be able to export grain as the price of grain in Ireland would still be higher than in Britain. This is because an Irish worker has a productivity in the grain sector which is only 20% of that of a British worker in grain production but his wages are 40% of British wages.

So lower wages in the less productive country allow it to compete successfully against the more productive country. This does not mean that the less productive country does not gain from trade. If the imported good costs less than it did before trade, then the country has gained.

Another means by which a less productive country pays its workers less than the more productive country is through a depreciation of its currency. Let us return to the example where Irish workers were paid €10 a day to Britain's UK£6. At the €1 = £0.6 exchange rate, Ireland would want to import both grain and beef from Britain, and Britain would not want to import anything from Ireland. The excess demand for sterling and the excess supply of euros would cause a depreciation of the euro against sterling. This depreciation would continue until such time as the excess demand for sterling and the corresponding excess supply of euros had been eliminated. If the exchange rates were for example €1 to £0.3 then Ireland would be able to successfully export beef at that exchange rate.

It should be noted that an exchange rate depreciation is analogous to a reduction in the return to domestic factors of production. In this example, the exchange rate depreciation is the same as a cut in the domestic wage rate.

The sources of comparative advantage

In the previous section we have seen that all countries can engage in mutually beneficial trade, provided that the relative prices of their goods prior to trade differ. This naturally begs the question, what determines pre-trade relative prices? The answer is straightforward. Prices of goods in a country are determined by the interaction of supply and demand. If pre-trade relative prices differ among countries, this is indicative of inter-country differences in domestic conditions of supply and demand. All other things being equal (*ceteris paribus*), the greater the supply of a good, the lower its price; and the greater the demand for a good, the higher its price. There are two principal theories as to why supply conditions differ among countries. These are, firstly, technological and climatic differences and secondly, resource differences.

David Ricardo's explanation of international trade, which was based on differences in the levels of productivity per person per day in various industries, could be an example of technological or climatic differences among countries. In the example of Britain and Ireland, the British worker has a higher productivity in all sectors compared to the Irish worker. This could be due to a climate that is more conducive to higher yields or alternatively, it could be due to superior British technology.

Ricardo's model is essentially based on a labour theory of value, since labour is the only factor of production that he considers and it is the productivity of labour that determines the domestic opportunity cost of production. There are no distribution effects in Ricardo's model because labour is considered to be the only factor of production. Hence, if free trade benefits a country, then it must be benefiting all of its workers, since all income earned accrues to workers.

At the beginning of this century two Swedish economists, Eli Heckscher and Bertil Ohlin offered a new explanation as to why supply conditions and hence relative prices differ among countries; countries differ in terms of natural endowments.[29] These endowments (for example land, labour and capital) are inputs that are used in the production of goods and services. So differences in endowments get reflected in differences in the cost of producing various goods. For example, one would expect that a country with an abundance of good farmland would be an efficient producer of agricultural products. The reasoning is simple: an abundance of good farmland means low rental values for land and hence low prices for agricultural products, since agricultural products are intensive users of land.

The Heckscher-Ohlin model of trade (as it is popularly known) differs from the Ricardian model in another respect: the distribution consequences of free trade. In this model, notwithstanding the fact that the country as a whole gains from trade, there are income redistribution effects within a country. Putting it more starkly, there are winners and losers when a country opens its borders and engages in free trade. This is a consequence of the fact that there is more than one factor of production. Free trade will not only change the production structure of a country (more specialisation) it will also change the demand for factors of production.

Take the example of a country that, as a result of free trade, now specialises in the production of land-intensive agricultural products, whereas before free trade, it was also producing capital-intensive industrial products. The change in the country's production structure would have increased the demand for land and reduced the demand for capital. This would have resulted in increased returns for landowners and decreased returns for the owners of capital. Landowners gain and capitalists lose as a result of free trade.

These two principal theories of comparative advantage are similar, to the extent that they conclude that a country will have a comparative advantage in products which they produce in relative abundance, regardless of whether that abundance is determined by climate, technology or resource availability.

Demand conditions can also help determine a country's comparative advantage. If, for example, two countries had identical supply conditions but different tastes, pre-trade relative prices would differ. If the Irish consumer displayed a relatively stronger preference for grain than her British counterpart, this would lead to higher pre-trade prices for grain in Ireland compared to Britain (assuming identical supply conditions) thus indicating comparative disadvantage in Ireland in grain production. So in trade between Ireland and Britain, we would expect Ireland to be an importer of grain.

Although demand differences across countries can help explain comparative advantage, it is little more than a theoretical curiosity since it is unlikely that it is the principal determinant of comparative advantage.

Policy implications of traditional trade theory

The common feature of traditional trade theories (be they of the Ricardian or Heckscher-Ohlin variety) is that economic agents are assumed to be operating in perfectly competitive markets. In other words increasing returns to scale or spillover effects do not exist and no individual or firm can influence prices. Countries trade because they are different and the greater the differences between countries the greater the gains from trade. We also expect trade between countries to be of an 'inter-industry' variety. In other words countries will not have two-way trade in the same product: they will either be an exporter or importer of that product.

In an earlier section we saw how a country can enjoy a higher level of consumption in the aggregate if it removes its trade barriers. If all countries remove barriers to trade, all countries will enjoy a higher level of aggregate consumption and income. But even if some countries continue to pursue protectionist policies, the countries that unilaterally remove their trade barriers increase their level of national income. This is an incredibly strong result: it implies that all policy-makers can increase real national income simply by removing trade barriers. Moreover, it also means that policy-makers can increase national welfare through trade barrier dismantlement and a proper redistribution of the gains from trade.

Of course in practice, liberalisation will hurt some sections of society, but if the national cake has grown, a taxation and transfer policy that taxes the beneficiaries of trade liberalisation and transfers the proceeds of this tax to those whom trade liberalisation has made worse off, could ensure that everybody gains. This does of course presuppose that there are no inefficiencies associated with a tax and transfer policy. If we ignore the possibility of a tax and transfer system, then we can assert that the principal beneficiary of free trade is the consumer, who is now able to enjoy cheaper imported goods than was previously the case.

If trade liberalisation is so beneficial we must ask why the world is not characterised by free trade? What causes governments to interfere with trade? A whole literature has developed to answer this question and we will address it in a later section. For the moment the most important thing to remember is that the gains from trade outlined so far all depend on the assumption that markets are perfectly competitive. Remove this assumption (as we will do later) and the whole edifice of unilaterally realisable gains from trade becomes much more fragile.

Trade barriers

Governments interfere with the international movement of goods and services for a variety of economic, political and fiscal reasons. In this section we will identify the principal instruments that governments use which impede free trade. A good overview of the effects of trade policy is provided by Corden (1971).[30]

Tariffs

A tariff is a tax on imports and is usually *ad valorem*; a percentage of the price of the imported goods. It is inherently discriminatory, since it does not apply to domestic goods that compete with imports. It results in a redistribution of income away from consumers in favour of domestic producers and the government. Governments have a new source of revenue while domestic producers can now charge a higher price thanks to the protective effect of the tariff. The real income of consumers is reduced as they must now pay more for those goods that are subject to tariffs.

Quotas

Tariffs operate by taxing imports and allowing demand and supply to adjust to the new domestic price. Quotas operate by restricting the volume of imports and allowing the domestic price to adjust in such a way that the domestic market clears, i.e. domestic demand equals domestic and foreign supply. If a quota is to be effective in restricting imports it will inevitably result in higher domestic prices for the product subject to such a restriction. This is because the restriction of foreign supply will result in excess demand for the product which will increase its price.

Again, as with the tariff, the consumer will suffer a loss in real income due to higher domestic prices for the good subject to quantitative import restrictions. Domestic producers of competing products will gain due to higher prices for their output but there will be no fiscal gain for the government. Those fortunate enough to hold import licences (or quotas) will gain as they now hold a valuable asset: the right to import good(s) at world prices and sell them at inflated domestic prices.

Voluntary restraint on exports

This is very similar to a quota except in this instance it is the exporting country that agrees to limit the quantity of its exports to the importing country, thus increasing the price of such goods in the countries that import them. The only difference in the income redistribution effect of this measure compared to quotas is that it is the foreign exporter as opposed to the holder of import quotas, who enjoys the rent (the difference between the domestic price of the good in the importing countries and its world price) associated with this form of trade restriction. It is also a very popular means of restricting trade, as it is not very visible and it allows countries to contravene international trade laws in a way that would be impossible with tariffs or import quotas.

Administrative barriers

The governments of many countries make it difficult for foreign exporters to penetrate their domestic markets by putting in place a whole series of rules and regulations with which the foreign exporter must comply, at some cost. These rules often come in the guise of health and safety standards or measures designed to give consumers protection.

Frontier delays and the paperwork associated with crossing national borders add to the cost of trying to penetrate certain markets and hence is akin to a tax on imports.

Governments are important players in an economy, not just as the overseer who determines the rules of the game, but also as a player in the market. In a free international market, governments would purchase goods from the supplier who offers the product(s) that they desire at the best price, regardless of the nationality of the supplier. In reality, public procurement tends to have a decidedly nationalistic bent; in other words public contracts invariably go to domestic firms.

Export subsidies and export taxes

Giving domestic producers a subsidy when they export encourages them to produce more for foreign markets at the expense of the domestic market. The cost of this policy is borne by the taxpayer and the domestic consumer, since the diversion of supply away from the domestic market raises domestic prices. Export taxes have the opposite effect of penalising producers who serve foreign markets, with positive fiscal consequences for the government and lower prices for the domestic consumer.

All the above measures, be they designed to protect producers who serve the domestic market or aid producers who serve foreign markets, are an interference with free trade. In a perfectly competitive world, such measures reduce national and global income through their interference with the market mechanism. They distort the allocation of resources between different sectors of the economy, promoting some sectors at the expense of others.

Justifying trade restrictions

Non-economic reasons

The government of a country may restrict the importation of certain goods in order to be self-sufficient in those products. Self-sufficiency, although it entails an economic cost, may be desired to achieve some political goal. This goal could be national security, it could form part of a country's international strategic objectives or merely be designed to protect a country from foreign influences that are considered dangerous and pernicious. For example, self-sufficiency in agriculture and armaments could be justified as a precautionary measure in case imports of these products are cut off in times of war. One means of settling scores, when countries' governments disagree politically with one another, is to impose a trade embargo. The importation of animals into rabies-free countries is restricted for obvious national health reasons; the same goes for drugs. All these restrictions are costly, but that is not to say that the realisation of such objectives does not merit such a cost.

Economic reasons

A good survey of economic arguments for and against protectionism is provided by Corden (1974).[31]

The principal economic reasons given for interfering with free trade are the protection of infant industries and the maintenance of employment. The infant industry argument is associated with the German economist Friedrich List (1789–1846), who advocated the protection of industries from foreign competition in order to allow them to develop. Without such protectionism, such industries would not be able to withstand foreign competition. Once these industries had developed sufficiently so as to be in a position to compete with foreign producers, such protection could be removed.

There are two principal criticisms of this theory: the first criticism questions the *a priori* assumption that there are market factors which prevent the spontaneous emergence of these industries in an unrestricted market, and the second criticism asserts that overprotected infants never mature.

Recall that traditional trade theory operates within the neoclassical framework of perfect competition. Perfect competition implies, *inter alia*, perfect knowledge, no barriers to entry and no spillover effects or externalities. In such a world, if there are potentially profitable industries that are as yet undeveloped, then entrepreneurs, driven by a desire to make profit, will enter these industries. If those industries are potentially profitable, even if that profit is not immediately realisable, then there is no need for government-inspired protection to help them develop. The second criticism makes the point that protectionism, instead of aiding the development of industries, can often inhibit their development by shielding them from the forces of international competition.

Protectionism allows workers in protected industries to retain jobs that would otherwise have been lost. However, in a perfectly competitive world, removing trade restrictions would cause the import competing sector to shrink but the export sector would expand, so workers and resources would move from the import competing sector to the export sector. Unemployment should only be a temporary phenomenon, lasting as long as it takes displaced workers to find new jobs. If it persists, then according to economists there must be some reason (other than the removal of trade barriers) that is causing its persistence, such as inflexible labour markets and minimum wages. Removal of these institutionally imposed rigidities will solve the problem of unemployment. Protectionism is a more costly way of achieving the same objective.

Distributional reasons

As mentioned earlier, the removal of trade barriers, like any other form of structural adjustment, involves winners and losers. Losers are those who witness a reduction in their real income as a result of trade liberalisation. Governments are very susceptible to political pressure and those sections of society that are threatened with a reduction in income, as a result of trade liberalisation, have every incentive to organise in order to lobby the government against such measures.

Many political economists argue that the protectionist bias of most governments reflects the political power of interest groups associated with protected industries. But just as some sections of society are adversely affected by free trade, others are adversely affected by protectionism; namely consumers. If commercial policy has a protectionist bias, it must mean that the political power of pro-protectionist groups is greater than the political power of free trade groups.

How can this be? Olson (1965) discusses the logic of collective action and the impact of interest groups on the political process.[32] Consumers, who are the main beneficiaries of free trade policies, are a large dispersed group. So the benefits of free trade are spread over a large body of people. Hence, even though in the aggregate the gains to consumers outweigh the losses to those associated with protected sectors, their *per capita* gains must be much less than the *per capita* losses of the losers.

Moreover, these gains, since they come in the form of lower prices, are not very visible whereas the losses (which usually take the form of a fall in earnings) are highly visible. Thus there exists an asymmetry in the incentive to organise and lobby among consumers and protectionist interests; the latter having a much greater incentive than the former to defend their position. It is also much easier to organise a lobby group when the number is smaller and geographically and sectorally concentrated, which is usually the case with protected industries.

Concluding remarks on traditional trade theory

All of the preceding analysis takes as its starting point the assumption of perfectly competitive markets. As a consequence, we see that protectionism unambiguously reduces national income and that there is no economic or even distributional justification for its existence. In the next section we will look at new theories of trade and specialisation that assume that markets are imperfect. We will see that in the context of imperfect markets, trade restrictions may not necessarily be welfare reducing. However, we will also see that trade restrictions are a second-best means of achieving certain economic and distributional objectives. In other words, free trade combined with other policies can realise the same objectives at a lower social cost.

17.3.2 New trade theory

Traditional trade theory dominated intellectual thinking for more than a hundred years. However, increasingly, academics, students and general observers began to notice the disparity between theory and reality. Most world trade in the post-war period was not trade between very different nations but trade between developed countries with similar resource bases, similar technology and similar tastes. Moreover, most trade between these nations was not of an inter-industry variety but rather of an intra-industry type; that is the simultaneous import and export of similar products.

In the 1980s, economists put forward new theories to explain this phenomenon. Foremost among them has been Paul Krugman; in fact his name has become almost synonymous with new trade theory.[33] Firstly, they claimed that consumers desire diversity. Some Germans drive BMWs and some drive Peugeots: likewise in France. If diverse consumer tastes cannot be satisfied by domestic supply, we will witness a two-way flow of trade in similar products, in this instance a two-way flow in car trade.

What makes intra-industry trade in identifiable branded products more probable and profitable is the existence of economies of scale. When technology exhibits economies of scale, it tends to result in high levels of output, since the more a firm produces the lower the unit cost of production. So it does not make sense for French or German manufacturers of cars to try and produce all varieties themselves, since this would lead to much shorter production runs, and much higher costs and prices as a result. Therefore, the combination of diverse consumer tastes and economies of scale are sufficient to ensure trade of an intra-industry variety.

It should also be noted that the market structure in which such trade takes place is necessarily imperfect, since goods are distinguishable by brand (which is never the case under perfect competition) and economies of scale tend to promote large firms who dominate an industry. The industrial structure may be monopolistic or oligopolistic, depending on the degree of competition that exists in an industry.

According to traditional trade theory, if two countries had identical demand and supply conditions and hence identical pre-trade prices, there would be no basis for mutually beneficial trade. When, however, economies of scale exist, two identical countries can engage in mutually beneficial trade by specialising and realising the lower unit cost that specialisation brings. Unlike trade based on comparative advantage, trade based on increasing returns to scale is hard to predict in advance of its occurrence. We cannot with confidence predict what country is likely to produce what product. All we know is that the country with the largest domestic market is probably more likely to be competitive in industries exhibiting increasing returns to scale.

Other forms of market imperfections that have important implications for trade policy are externalities or spillover effects. In many instances the private and social cost of an action differs. An individual entrepreneur thinking about setting up a plant in a certain region will weigh up the private costs and benefits of such a decision. He will reject the option if, *ex ante*, it appears to be unprofitable. Yet if many firms take this decision, what appeared initially as a non-viable option could become viable due to positive spillover effects. Without being exhaustive, these spillover effects (or externalities) could be: the availability of cheaper and more varied services (which are greater, the greater the concentration of industry); greater access to skilled labour (which tends to be attracted to regions with a high firm density); and easier access to vital information, which is so crucial to the success of business in a competitive environment.

The policy implications of new trade theory or the policy implications of imperfect markets

When markets exhibit imperfections there is always a justification for government intervention to correct the market imperfection; this does not mean that intervention always improves upon the market outcome. Efficiency-improving intervention requires appropriate information in order to know where market imperfections exist and their extent. It also requires the choice of the correct instrument of intervention.

All the aforementioned is relevant to new trade theory, since the latter is firmly rooted within an imperfect market context. For example, in a world characterised by diverse industries, some of which exhibit increasing returns to scale, while others exhibit decreasing or constant returns to scale, the effect of trade liberalisation is much less clear. The beauty of traditional trade theory was that it showed that trade liberalisation benefited all countries, even the most technologically backward. New trade theory, on the other hand, can make a case for free trade based on global efficiency or even the need for good international relations between countries, but it cannot unambiguously claim to benefit all countries.

Free trade brings about a restructuring of an economy. If a country witnesses a decline in its increasing returns industries and growth in its decreasing or constant returns industries, due to trade liberalisation, then the average productivity of resources will have declined. This does not mean that the country is necessarily worse off as a result, since this loss in terms of the productivity of its resources has to be weighed against the gain to consumers from cheaper imports.

The situation is no longer clear-cut. Such a result is not as startling as it may first appear, since we are all familiar with the phenomena of declining or economically backward regions within what is often a prosperous country. Since free trade exists between regions within a country, it is not obvious all have benefited from free inter-regional trade.[34]

The policy implication of new trade theory is that it creates a 'case' (that is to say a necessary but not sufficient condition) for intervention. Intervention could take the form of import barriers or export subsidies or even production subsidies in those industries where economies of scale exist. The objective is clear: to try and ensure that a country has a high percentage of increasing returns or high value-added industries. The decline of the traditionally high wage manufacturing sector in the UK and its replacement by low wage services should not be a matter of policy indifference. Of course the negative side of the intervention argument is that it is a zero sum game. Not all countries can have a monopoly on increasing returns industries. If all try, then all will suffer as a consequence. Also, certain kinds of intervention such as export subsidies only serve to antagonise international competitors and can easily degenerate into a trade war from which no one emerges as victor.

Externalities are in essence the core of the infant industry argument. Social and private benefits and costs differ, so governments protect certain industries, where they consider that the social benefits of that industry's existence outweigh the private benefits to the industry's proprietors. Often, however, there are more effective and direct means of tackling market imperfections. If, for example, private entrepreneurs are unable to exploit a sector where a country may have a potential comparative or competitive advantage, due to lack of availability of finance, the correct response by policy-makers is to improve the nature of financial institutions, to overcome this imperfection. Barring this strategy, capital or loan subsidies may be appropriate. Protectionism, according to economists, is down this list of appropriate policy measures to combat market imperfections.

Even though theoretically there is a strong case to be made against unlimited free trade, very few of the new trade theorists actually advocate protectionism or other forms of interference with the market mechanism. Their failure to breach the gap between theory and policy could be due to an innate conservatism or to their fear of what can be broadly termed political failures. The market is not the only social system riddled with imperfections. The informational requirements necessary to intervene correctly are enormous and, at a more serious level, there is always the fear that governments will become hostages to vested interests if they make it standard politics to intervene in trade policy.

For these reasons, notwithstanding the less rosy picture presented by new trade theory (especially for poorer and smaller countries), new trade theorists still advocate free trade as the best option in an imperfect world.

17.3.3 *The Irish experience*

Irish trade policy

It is difficult to find real-world examples of the polar extremes of trade policy as defined in theory; that is to say self-sufficiency and complete free trade. The reality is that nearly all countries engage to some extent in the international exchange of goods and services and nearly all countries have rules and regulations in place, that interfere to some extent with the volume and direction of international trade. However, along the spectrum from self-sufficiency to free trade, we can judge the bias of a country's trade policy over time and also make comparisons between countries.

It is in this context that we can say that Ireland's trade policy was relatively liberal (free-trade oriented) in the 1920s, highly protectionist from the 1930s to the end of the 1950s, and progressively liberal ever since. The global environment during the period of protectionism varied considerably. The 1930s witnessed a worldwide global depression, followed by a world war, followed by a period of reconstruction and very rapid growth in the post-war period.

Despite the varying fortunes of the world economy in this period, the contemporaneous Irish economic experience singularly failed to live up to expectations. The disillusionment with protectionism as a strategy for economic development led to a reversal in the direction of commercial policy. This shift in policy direction was reflected in a unilateral cut in tariffs in 1963 and 1964, followed by the Anglo-Irish Free Trade Agreement in 1965 and culminating in our admission to what was then the European Economic Community in 1973.

The principal aim of the European Economic Community (EEC), which was set up by the Treaty of Rome in 1957, was to foster free trade among its member states and to pursue a common trade policy with regard to non-member states. Hence since 1973 Ireland has essentially waived its right to an autonomous trade policy, by agreeing to abide by the rules and regulations of the EEC. The European Economic Community has itself evolved since its original inception. It now has many more member states (and potential applicants knocking on the door) and has renewed itself and its commitment to freer internal trade through the Single European Act, which came into force in July 1987, the Treaty on European Union (which was finalised at Maastricht in December 1991), the Amsterdam Treaty 1997 and the Nice Treaty 2000 which still has to be ratified by the member states.

The European Union (as it is now known) has also participated in international agreements and signed treaties designed to foster freer trade at a more global level. Some of these arrangements are bilateral, such as its free trade agreement with EFTA (European Free Trade Association), while others are more global and non-discriminatory such as its participation in the GATT (General Agreement on Tariffs and Trade), which was itself replaced by the WTO (World Trade Organisation) in 1995.

GATT has been the most important organisation governing world trade in the post-war period. It has been committed to global free trade as enshrined in its principles of National Treatment and Non-Discrimination. 'National Treatment' is a commitment to give equal treatment to national and international transactions, while 'Non-Discrimination' is a commitment to not distinguish between countries on the grounds of origin. It has also overseen successive rounds of multilateral trade barrier reductions, whereby all member countries agreed to reduce trade barriers by some agreed amount. The last round of multilateral trade negotiations was held in Seattle in 1999 but had to be abandoned due to popular protests. Notwithstanding the suspension of talks, the WTO is still making progress on further liberalisation, particularly in the areas of services and agriculture.

What should be clear is that Ireland's trade policy has to be looked at within the international institutional framework, firstly as a member of the EU and secondly within the context of the EU's membership of the WTO. The fact that Ireland and all the other member countries of the EU and WTO have agreed to bind themselves to rules that increasingly curtail these countries' rights to interfere with international trade, is testament to the general faith that global prosperity requires the unfettered movement of goods and services between countries.

SUMMARY

1. Inflation is a rise in the general price level. There are many different causes of inflation. The Quantity Theory of Money is the earliest model of inflation. It suggests that the price level increases with the money supply and that monetary policy is ineffective in changing an economy's level of output. Demand pull inflation is caused by increases in aggregate demand. Cost push inflation results from a rise in costs in general, and of wages in particular. A depreciating currency, unless checked, results in imported inflation. Expectations also play an important role. During inflationary periods, debtors gain at the expense of creditors, individuals on fixed incomes lose, consumption is encouraged, and fixed-income assets become less attractive.

2. Policies to combat inflation concentrate on either the demand side or the supply side of the economy. Tighter control over the money supply, increases in tax rates and reductions in public expenditure are all examples of demand-side measures. Increasing competition and cutting labour costs are examples of supply-side measures.

3. Unemployment is a stock concept: it measures the number of people who are out of work at a particular point in time. There are different types of unemployment. They include frictional, seasonal, structural, demand deficient and classical. The costs of unemployment are both private and social. They accrue to the unemployed, to

the taxpayer and to society at large. Whereas it is possible to measure the economic costs arising from unemployment, it is very difficult to estimate the social costs.

4. There are many different explanations of unemployment. With the assumption of freely flexible wages, unemployment in the classical world is temporary and voluntary. For Keynes, unemployment could be long-term and involuntary. It is caused by insufficient aggregate demand and requires government action. Fiscal policy is the preferred option. The monetarist and the supply-side theories of unemployment are similar to the classical explanation. Government intervention is seen as part of the problem rather than the solution. A large number of unemployed is a cyclical characteristic of the capitalist system, according to Marx: unemployment is the result of the inevitable class struggle between capitalists and workers.

5. Trade theories attempt to explain the causes and consequences of the international exchange of goods and services. The multiplicity of theories can be broadly categorised into two schools of thought: traditional trade theory and new trade theory. The essential difference between the two approaches is that traditional trade theory assumes that markets are perfectly competitive, while new trade theory assumes that markets are imperfectly competitive to a greater or lesser extent.

6. The key concept in traditional trade theory is 'comparative advantage'. It says that all countries can engage in mutually beneficial trade by specialising in what they do 'relatively' best. Countries trade because they are different and this difference reflects itself in their domestic relative costs. The greater the differences between countries, the greater the gains from trade. Such trade will be inter-industry in type. The optimal trade strategy in a perfectly competitive environment is unilateral trade barrier dismantlement. The bases for new trade theory are economies of scale and consumer demand for product diversity. Such trade tends to be intra-industry in type and to take place between relatively similar countries. It results in global production efficiency but all countries may not necessarily gain from such trade. The optimal trade strategy in this context may be interventionist in order to maximise a country's share of the gains from trade.

KEY TERMS

Inflation	*Unemployment*	*International trade*
Inflation	Quarterly National	Mercantilism
Inflation rate	Household Survey	Absolute advantage
Deflation	Live register	Comparative advantage
Disinflation	Labour force	International terms of trade
Creeping inflation	Unemployment rate	Opportunity cost of
Hyper-inflation	Frictional unemployment	production
Stagflation	Seasonal unemployment	Production possibility frontier
Price index	Structural unemployment	Pre-trade relative prices
Consumer Price	Demand-deficient	Revealed comparative
Index	unemployment	advantage

Inflation (cont.)	Unemployment (cont.)	International trade (cont.)
Harmonised Index of Consumer Prices	Classical unemployment	Factor endowments
	Voluntary unemployment	Inter-industry trade
GDP deflator	Involuntary unemployment	Tariffs
Nominal interest rate	Deflationary gap	Quotas
Real interest rate	Natural Rate of	Voluntary export
Menu costs	Unemployment	restraints
Indexation	Reserve army of	Export subsidies/taxes
Fiscal drag	unemployed	Infant industries
Money Illusion	Unemployment trap	Imperfect markets
Shoe leather effect	Replacement ratio	Economies of scale
Unanticipated inflation	Poverty trap	Externalities
Anticipated inflation	Tax wedge	Intra-industry trade
Demand pull inflation	Labour market rigidities	
Inflationary gap	Wage bargaining process	
Quantity Theory of Money	Insider-outsider model	
Money Velocity	Labour legislation	
Monetarism	Okun's Law	
Adaptive expectations	Total factor productivity growth	
Cost push inflation		
Imported inflation		
Rational expectations		

REVIEW QUESTIONS

1. Explain the term 'inflation'. Why is inflation undesirable? Who benefits from inflation?
2. Explain the causes of inflation. Suggest how each cause can be tackled.
3. What are the costs of unemployment?
4. Explain the theories of unemployment. How do they relate to the Irish experience of unemployment?
5. Explain the theory of comparative advantage. How does it differ from absolute advantage? According to the theory of comparative advantage, what countries are most likely to engage in mutually beneficial trade?
6. By what mechanism is comparative advantage translated into absolute competitiveness?

WORKING PROBLEMS

1. The figures in Table 17.7 were taken from the annual report entitled *National Income and Expenditure*, published by the CSO. It shows GDP at current market prices and GDP at constant market prices.

Table 17.7: GDP at constant and current market prices (1990–98)

Year	Current GDP (£ million)	Constant GDP (£ million)
1990	28,598	32,986
1991	29,675	33,622
1992	31,529	34,746
1993	34,054	35,682
1994	36,624	37,736
1995	41,409	41,409
1996	45,634	44,594
1997	52,760	49,382
1998	60,582	53,609

(a) What is the base year? Explain your answer.
(b) Calculate the GDP deflator for each year. What is the general trend?
(c) Calculate the inflation rate for 1998.

2. The working population of the home country is two million. The working population of the foreign country is ten million. Both countries can only produce two goods: beer and grain. The average productivity of labour in the production of both goods is shown in Table 17.8.

Table 17.8

	Home	Foreign
Beer (litre per person per day)	4	16
Grain (kg per person per day)	8	8

Describe and explain the pattern of trade between the home country and the foreign country.

MULTI-CHOICE QUESTIONS

1. The inflation rate for 1999 was 1.6%. The CPI for 1998 was 119.6. What was the CPI for 1999?
   (a) 115.1;
   (b) 124.6;
   (c) 121.5;
   (d) 118.2;
   (e) none of the above.

2. Anticipated inflation:
   (a) imposes no costs on society;
   (b) can result in menu costs and the shoe leather effect;
   (c) imposes more costs on society than unanticipated inflation;
   (d) both (b) and (c) above;
   (e) none of the above.

3. For monetarists, unemployment:
   (a) is largely involuntary;
   (b) is caused by a deficiency in demand;
   (c) often results from inappropriate demand-management policies;
   (d) can be cured by active demand-management policies;
   (e) both (b) and (d) above.

4. Involuntary unemployment:
   (a) is caused by a deficient demand for goods;
   (b) is closely associated with Keynesian unemployment;
   (c) is difficult to measure accurately;
   (d) is a measure of those who are willing to work but who cannot find a job at the market wage rate;
   (e) all of the above.

5. In working problem 2, what is the domestic opportunity cost of grain production in the home country?
   (a) 2 litres of beer per 1 kg of grain;
   (b) 1 litre of beer per 1 kg of grain;
   (c) 5 litres of beer per 1 kg of grain;
   (d) $\frac{1}{2}$ litre of beer per 1 kg of grain;
   (e) there is no opportunity cost.

6. Refer again to working problem 2. If wages are identical in both countries then the 'competitive' position of home and foreign will be as follows:
   (a) Home is competitive in grain only and foreign in beer only.
   (b) Home is competitive in beer only and foreign in grain only.
   (c) Home is competitive in grain and foreign is competitive in both grain and beer.
   (d) Home is not competitive in either grain or beer and foreign is competitive in both grain and beer.
   (e) None of the above.

TRUE OR FALSE (SUPPORT YOUR ANSWER)

1. Disinflation is defined as a continuous decline in the price level.

2. In combating inflation, monetarists advocate a steady rate of growth of the money supply.

3. The total cost of unemployment can be measured by summing the amount of money spent on social welfare benefits.

4. The poverty trap is the estimated number of citizens below the poverty line.

5. A country can have a 'comparative advantage' in the production of 'all goods' if it is more efficient at producing all goods than its competitors.

6. The infant industry argument for protection is only valid if some market imperfection has prevented thus far the emergence of that industry.

CASE STUDY A: INFLATION

Extract from *The Irish Independent*
Upward trend in inflation shows no signs of abating
by Austin Hughes

Irish consumer price data for March indicate that the worsening trend in inflation evident since the middle of last year remains in place. In contrast to many other forecasters, we do not expect to see a material improvement later this year and would suggest that upside risks persist even from current levels. We reckon that this trend is both symptom and harbinger of increasing strains on the Irish economy's capacity to sustain the exceptional performance of recent years. The full extent of these strains will only become clear in the next 12 to 24 months. Comparable inflation data for the euro area suggest that price pressures within the single currency area as a whole remain muted.

. . .

Irish Inflation rose to 4.6pc in March from 4.3pc in the previous month, the highest rate since November 1989. Ireland's harmonised rate, used for EU comparisons (and as a reference rate by the European Central Bank), rose sharply to 5.0pc last month from 4.6pc in February. March figures for the euro area as a whole saw an altogether more modest increase, with an annual rate edging up to 2.1pc. Looking at underlying or 'core' inflation – Irish prices are rising at a 3.2pc annual rate against a comparable figure for the whole Euro area of 1.2pc. In July 1999, the corresponding 'core' figures were 1.9pc for Ireland and 1.1pc for the euro area. It seems clear that there has been a sharp deterioration in Ireland's underlying inflation performance in recent months in absolute and relative terms.

. . .

⟶

A number of factors contributed to the pick-up in Irish inflation in March. An increase in oil prices in the early part of March pushed up transport costs by 15.2pc year on year. The effects of a subsequent easing in world oil prices may be more than offset by continuing upward pressure on prices in a range of areas. Housing costs increased last month but are still 1.6pc below earlier year levels. This element is likely to become a source of pronounced upward pressure on the headline inflation rate later this year as a sequence of ECB rate hikes feeds into the index and the sharp drop in mortgage rates that occurred during the year falls out. Services prices remain strong, with an annual rate of inflation stuck at 5.8pc. Irish March data shows a modest monthly increase in clothing and footwear prices, keeping the annual rate at 6pc lower than a year ago. A rise in the goods prices (newspapers, magazines, detergents and cosmetics) last month suggests the weak euro and higher domestic costs are beginning to feed through to higher inflation. We also see scope for further rises in prices of food and drink as a result of the combination of a weak euro and strong demand in the months ahead. The rise in drink prices also reflects the combination of strong domestic demand and rising wage costs.

. . .

We see higher inflation posing threats in a number of areas. The most obvious of these is a likely impetus to higher wages. The higher the recorded inflation rate goes, the larger the indexation element in pay demands. Other potentially negative implications are reduced borrowing costs. In the past year the 'real' mortgage rate has fallen by about 4pc points to around zero and this is imparting a powerful stimulus to borrowing that could lead to debt burdens overshooting their sustainable level. Ireland may be unable to rely on external or domestic developments to deliver a gentle slowing of Irish inflation.

. . .

Source: *The Irish Independent,* 25 April 2000

Questions

1. What is meant by the underlying or 'core' inflation rate? Explain its rationale.
2. Explain how a weak euro can cause higher inflation in Ireland.
3. Report the monthly trend in the consumer price index in Ireland, for the year 1999. How does Ireland compare to the average for the euro area? Use the EU HICP in both cases.

[NB: The Central Statistics Office website www.cso.ie is a useful source.]

CASE STUDY B: UNEMPLOYMENT

Extract from *Business and Finance*
Ireland Cut Off by Fog
by Chris Johns

From an economic perspective at least, immigration is unambiguously a good thing.

. . .

There are many aspects to the discussion, many 'economic' reasons why people object to immigration, first and foremost among which is the idea that importing workers will somehow 'steal' jobs from the indigenous population. Economists call this the 'lump of labour' fallacy: the idea that there is a fixed number of jobs is simply nonsense. An increase in the supply of labour, in a properly functioning market economy, can easily be handled. In a fully employed, resource constrained economy, like Ireland, the labour market benefits that will flow from importing people are simply enormous.

Bringing in extra workers at a time where every employer seems to be bemoaning a lack of both skilled and unskilled labour would seem to be a reasonable, if not un-controversial, idea. And yet it has become one of the hottest of political potatoes. There seems to be two main reasons why this has happened, one of which is rooted in good old-fashioned xenophobia. The other is couched in terms of another resource constraint. We might need the extra labour and could put it to very good use but, goes the objection, we have no-where to house these people, no transport system to get them to work, no space in our schools for their children, no spare hospital beds should they get sick. And this is where the debate usually ends, instead of begin-ning: we certainly do lack the infrastructure to support the existing population, let alone a significantly enlarged one. But this should merely serve to sharpen the focus on the question, not to stifle debate. We need the extra people and the infrastructure. Instead, poverty of imagination – not lack of cash – will ensure we get neither.

. . .

It is often said that one of the basic reasons for allowing immigration is that immigrants are typically self-selecting elite. In the US, even today, there is a very high probability that your doctor, chemist, or children's schoolteacher will be a first generation immigrant. And an even higher probability than the Silicon-Valley high tech company whose shares have just made you a millionaire was founded by an immigrant. Also true is the image of the immigrant farm labourer and tax-driver. But all of these occupations are important: if we can't get people to fill the vacancies, wherever they occur, the whole economy suffers. Surely if there is one economy in the world that recognises these basic truths it is the US though sadly, there is another long history of attempting to stifle immigration.

A good reason for any country to allow more people to enter is demographic. Ireland is less troubled than Germany, France or Italy in this regard but Europe generally is getting older. This simple fact is creating a so-called demographic time-bomb whereby the pension requirements of a rapidly ageing population cannot be met. Importing people is actually a very neat solution to this problem.

. . .

Source: Business and Finance, 4 May 2000, p. 16.

Questions

1. What pull factors drawing immigrants to Ireland are inferred in the article? How does this compare to the situation in the mid-1980s?
2. Using CSO data, report the net migration flow for the period 1989–98. How does this compare to the natural increase for the same period?
3. (i) Explain the employment dependency ratio? Comment on the trend in the dependency ratio in Ireland.
   (ii) Explain the participation rate? Using real data, estimate the participation ratio in Ireland for any quarter of 2000.

[NB: The Central Statistics Office website www.cso.ie is a useful source.]

CASE STUDY C: INTERNATIONAL TRADE

Extract from the *Guardian Weekly*
Putting Trade in its Proper Place
by Larry Elliott

Fauchon's, in the Place de la Madelaine in Paris, is a gastronomic paradise. In the section devoted to fruit and veg. there are dainties to whet the appetite of Parisian foodies – mangoes from Mali, maracujas from Colombia and kiwanos from Portugal. This is the way supporters of global liberalisation would have us believe it could be everywhere from Kuala Lumpur to Knightsbridge. It is taking as read that the meshing of free trade and unfettered capital flows lead to rising world prosperity and a way out of poverty for the developing world.

Last week the Organisation for Economic Co-operation and Development summed up current thinking when it said globalisation 'gives all countries the possibility of participating in world development and all consumers the assurance of benefit from increasingly vigorous competition between producers'.

The theory is that liberalisation and deregulated capital flows allow countries to specialise in what they are good (or least bad) at, and this international division of labour raises global income.

. . . the developing countries that do best are those with the least state intervention and the freest trade and those new 'tiger economies' pose a massive competitive threat to living standards in the developed world.

Source: Guardian Weekly, 2 June 1996.

Questions

1. Why does the OECD think that freer trade can be beneficial to all countries?
2. If workers in developing countries are not as productive as workers in developed countries (due to the superior technology that is to be found in developed countries), how will such countries be able to compete in an era of globalisation?
3. Who gains and who could possibly lose in the so-called developed countries from freer world trade?

APPENDIX 17.1: THE PHILLIPS CURVE

The Phillips curve was named after A. W. Phillips, a professor at the London School of Economics. In 1958, he published a paper based on an empirical study. He stated that in the UK, during the period between 1861 and 1957, there was a stable, inverse relationship between the rate of change in money wages and the unemployment rate.[35] In other words, a high rate of money wage inflation was associated with a low rate of unemployment.

In 1960, Samuelson and Solow redefined the variables to look at the relationship between the inflation rate and the unemployment rate. This adaptation, shown in Figure 17.13 is called the Phillips curve.

Figure 17.13: The Phillips curve

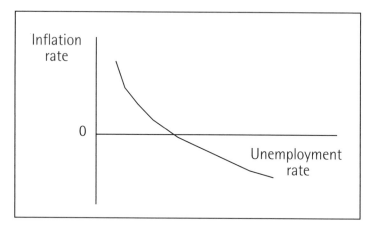

Keynesian economists accepted the Phillips curve relationship into their theoretical framework. The omission of a price variable was one of the main weaknesses of the Keynesian model.

The Phillips curve appeared to offer a 'menu of choice'. Economists could choose between different rates of inflation and unemployment. Unfortunately, when the relationship was exploited, it broke down. To combat the high rate of unemployment in the 1970s, many western governments followed policies which were inflationary. Unfortunately, the unemployment rates did not fall.

Friedman (1968) and Phelps (1967) tried to explain the breakdown of the Phillips curve relationship in terms of price expectations. Friedman argued that there is a natural rate of unemployment associated with variables like the skills of the labour force, the size of the capital stock and the level of technology. Figure 17.14 depicts the natural rate of unemployment (U*), at 5%.

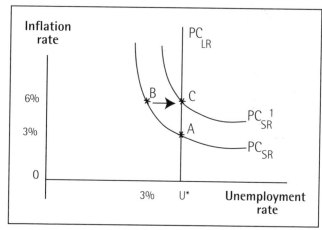

Figure 17.14: The Phillips curve

Initially, the economy is at equilibrium at point A. The inflation rate is stable at 3% and unemployment is at the natural rate. Suppose the government decides to reduce the unemployment rate by adopting expansionary policies. On the initial short-term Phillips curve PC_{SR}, the economy moves from point A to point B. The inflation rate rises from 3% to 6% and the unemployment rate falls below the natural rate, U^*, to 3%.

According to Friedman, workers do not realise that increasing inflation means that the real wage is falling. However, they are not fooled for long. A change in expectations shifts the Phillips curve upwards, from PC_{SR} to PC_{SR}^1. The economy returns to equilibrium at point C. Unemployment is again at the natural rate, but the inflation rate is higher.

The inverse relationship between inflation and unemployment is temporary, according to Friedman. Unemployment returns to the natural rate as soon as expectations adjust. A continuation of expansionary policies leads inevitably to accelerating inflation.

In the long run, Friedman argued that the Phillips curve is vertical, at the natural rate of unemployment, U^*. For Friedman, inflation has no long-run effect on the unemployment rate. The long-run expectations-augmented Phillips curve is labelled PC_{LR} in Figure 17.14.

The policy implications differ from the simple case. In attempting to reduce unemployment below its natural rate, the government only succeeds in accelerating domestic inflation. In the long term the natural rate of unemployment can only be reduced by supply-side measures. These changes result in a shift of the aggregate supply curve.

Incidentally, the Phillips curve is simply another way of depicting the AS curve. Consider the different types of AS curves. The conventional AS curve depicts a positive relationship between prices and output levels. Unemployment fluctuates inversely with output. Hence, the rate of change in the price level and unemployment are inversely related. This is depicted in the downward sloping Phillips curve.

The classical AS curve is vertical. Output is independent of the price level; a price rise has no effect on the level of output. Unemployment remains constant. This is depicted by the vertical Phillips curve where the inflation rate and the unemployment rate are unrelated.

From this brief analysis we can see that the Phillips curve is another way of expressing and explaining aggregate supply.

APPENDIX 17.2 EXPECTATIONS

Because of Keynes, expectations are an important feature of all modern macroeconomic models. Recall that Keynes believed that investors' expectations about the future were the main cause of instability in the national economy. He discussed the 'animal spirits' of investors, which is very different from the careful, cost-benefit analysis which many believe underlie any profit-maximising investment decision.

The volatility of expectations, so colourfully described by Keynes, was very difficult to model and too unpredictable to be accepted by the neoclassical economists. Until the 1970s, the neoclassicals believed that adaptive expectations could be used to explain the behaviour of economic agents. According to this theory, expectations for the current period are based on what actually happened in the past. If we use this concept in a model, the success of that model depends on how accurately the past explains the present and can be extrapolated into the future.

For example, we can develop a model incorporating adaptive expectations to predict the inflation rate. The most basic model is described by Equation [1]

$$\Pi^*_t = \Pi_{t-1}$$ [1]

which states that the predicted inflation rate (Π^*t) for period t is the same as the actual inflation rate for the previous period (Π_{t-1}).

We can expand this model to take account of errors which we made in our previous prediction. In other words, we are adapting our predictions based on our previous mistakes. One such model is described by Equation [2]

[2]

$$\Pi^*_t = \Pi^*_{t-1} + \emptyset \,(\Pi_{t-1} - \Pi^*_{t-1}) \quad 0 < \emptyset < 1$$

where:

Π^*_t = inflation forecast for the present period.
Π^*_{t-1} = inflation forecast for the previous period.
$\emptyset$ = weight attached to last period's forecasting error.
Π_{t-1} = actual inflation rate for the previous period.

The expression inside the parenthesis represents the forecasting error. It shows the discrepancy between the actual inflation rate in period t – 1 and the predicted inflation rate. $\emptyset$ represents the importance which we attach to that discrepancy. If we think that the discrepancy will persist into the future, $\emptyset$ will have a value close to one. Then our new inflation rate will equal our old inflation rate plus last period's mistake. If we think that the discrepancy will not persist, we will assign to $\emptyset$ a number which is close to zero. This means that we expect the inflation rate in period t to equal the predicted inflation rate in the previous period.

The importance of this model is that it allows us to incorporate our previous errors into our predictions. Our predictions for the future are based on the mistakes that we made in the past. Unfortunately, if we made consistent errors in the past, they will persist into the future. The adaptive expectations models were criticised for this and also because they limit the information which economic agents utilise.

The concept of adaptive expectations was replaced by rational expectations. Rational expectations assumes that economic agents will use all relevant past and current information when making decisions. In the inflation example, agents consider the past inflation rate but also changes in government monetary and fiscal policy, pressures in the labour market and international problems. Models based on rational expectations assume that all agents have 'perfect information'. They are fully informed of all relevant information which they need to make their forecast.

This simple concept has surprising implications for the effectiveness of economic policy and, in the broader sense, of government intervention in the economy. An important assumption of this model is that wages are fully flexible and that labour, as rational economic agents, will increase their wage demands in line with any inflationary pressures. Under these circumstances, the aggregate supply curve is vertical in the short run.

Under the rational expectations hypothesis, governments cannot 'fool' the people. People will anticipate the government's behaviour and act accordingly. Hence, any demand-management policies of the state will lead only to a change in the price level. Fiscal and monetary policies are ineffective in the short run and in the long run. Proponents of the rational expectations hypothesis were also concerned with policy issues of credibility and sustainability.

The leading proponents of rational expectations were Robert Lucas of Chicago, Thomas Sargent of Stanford and Robert Barro of Harvard.[36]

The New Keynesians responded to this with another modification to the expectations story. While acknowledging the possibility of rational expectations in the long run, new Keynesians were primarily concerned with the short run; a period of time when full adjustments in the labour market were unlikely. This allowed for the existence of high unemployment and as a policy response, active demand-management policies. As for the long run, '. . . we are all dead'.[37]

Regardless of which doctrine you support, expectations are considered to be a crucial feature of modern macroeconomics.

CHAPTER 18

ECONOMIC GROWTH AND THE IRISH ECONOMY

by Matthew Coffey

'People are the common denominator of progress. So . . . no improvement is possible with unimproved people, and advance is certain when people are liberated and educated. It would be wrong to dismiss the importance of roads, railroads, power plants, mills, and the other familiar furniture of economic development. . . . But we are coming to realise . . . that there is a certain sterility in economic monuments that stand alone in a sea of illiteracy. Conquest of illiteracy comes first.'[1]

John Kenneth Galbraith

'I had one fundamental question about economics: Why do some places prosper and thrive while others just suck?'[2]

P. J. O'Rourke

CHAPTER OBJECTIVES

Upon completing this chapter, the student should understand:

- the basic theory of economic growth and the Solow growth model;
- the influence of population and capital stock on economic growth;
- the factors which have led to economic growth in different countries around the world;
- the factors which have led to economic growth in Ireland.

OUTLINE

18.1 Economic growth: the basic theory
18.2 Economic growth around the world
18.3 Lessons from the Irish experience

INTRODUCTION

This chapter explains how a nation can increase the size of its macroeconomy. In Chapter 10 we discussed the measurement of economic activity, but how does a country increase that activity? This chapter focuses on long-run changes in economic activity and the living standards of a nation. The first step is to provide a simple model to explain this growth, namely, the Solow growth model. However this model, while instructive, omits many factors which are important for an economy's growth.

These factors are best illustrated and explained by telling the stories of economic growth from around the world. These stories give us a wide range of examples with which to illustrate the importance of factors such as government and education. The chapter ends by presenting the story of economic growth of the Irish economy and provides a number of possible explanations for the 'Celtic Tiger'.

18.1 ECONOMIC GROWTH: THE BASIC THEORY

The wealth of a nation and the living standards of its citizens are typically measured using Gross National Product (GNP) and Gross National Product per person. But once wealth and living standards are measured, the next basic questions facing students of economics are the following: how can that wealth be increased over time? What can a nation's government and citizens do to increase their own living standards? These are the questions and problems of economic growth.

GNP measures the amount that is produced by a nation within a given year. As such it is a measurement of the nation's income in that year because everything produced is sold and becomes income for someone. GNP also gives us a measure of a nation's wealth; not one based on gold, silver and money, but one determined by the production potential of a country. That is, the ability of a nation to produce food, health care, cars and other goods is the real measure of its wealth and living standards. Increasing this production potential so that the wealth and living standards of a nation increase can be studied in two different ways.

One approach focuses on the short-run effects on national income. This approach notes that **GNP = Consumption + Investment + Government Spending + Net Exports**. It focuses on the short run and the actions taken by consumers, businesses and the government to change GNP over a few months or years. The main focus of this approach to measuring national income is on its components. GNP is divided into its components of consumption, investment, net exports and government spending. Each of these components is studied individually with a view to how they change. National wealth and living standards are constructed from their basic components.

Alternatively, the second approach takes a larger, long-run view of a nation's wealth. Over longer periods of time, trends in population, capital, geography, technology and other factors will lead to changes in GNP and living standards. These changes occur over the course of years and even decades. It is this long-run view that is discussed in this chapter. This chapter presents the story of economic growth over a long period of time, both in Ireland and in the rest of the world.

There are of course a number of different ways to tell the story of economic growth.[3] We could start with the most common model of economic growth and work with that model to derive predictions and descriptions of how economies grow. Or we could examine a wide range of countries and look at which countries have done well and which have not. Then we could derive the lessons of growth from those countries that have thrived. Or we could look at one particular country, examine its history and evaluate its actions and policies. Each of these three approaches will give us a different part of the growth story and all three will be presented here.

First, however, let me add a word of caution. When studying the economic growth of nations, it is tempting to develop an economic model, present some economic statistics, or tell the story of one nation's growth and then proclaim that the problem of economic growth has been solved. To be sure, every economic growth model or story of national economic growth from around the world offers lessons to be learned for students and for other nations. However, the question of how to increase living standards and national wealth remains too complex to have any single answer.

Therefore, this chapter will not present a single answer to the question of how to increase living standards and economic growth. Rather it will provide some theory from a model of economic growth, some evidence of economic growth from economies throughout the world, and some of the recent economic history of Ireland in an attempt to provide an understanding of some of the factors that may help or hinder growth.

To begin with, let us look at the growth in the Irish economy over a forty-year period beginning in 1950. Table 18.1 shows GDP per capita, population and capital stock per worker from 1950 to 1990. GDP per capita is simply national income divided by the population, which is also listed in the table. Capital stock per worker is a measurement of the total value of factories and machines in an economy divided by the number of workers.[4]

Table 18.1: The Irish economy, 1950–90

Year	GDP/capita Value (1985 US$)	5 year % change	Population (thousands)	Capital stock per worker
1950	2,716	..	2,969	..
1955	3,081	13.4	2,921	..
1960	3,299	7.1	2,832	..
1965	3,991	21.0	2,876	6,925
1970	5,012	25.6	2,950	10,266
1975	5,809	15.9	3,177	13,941
1980	6,828	17.5	3,401	17,585
1985	7,275	6.5	3,540	20,700
1990	9,261	27.3	3,503	21,660

Source: Penn-World tables version 5.6 and author's calculations.[5]

Looking at Table 18.1, we can make a number of observations. First, despite all the recent stories about the 'Celtic Tiger', Ireland's economy has actually grown significantly since the 1950s. The average annual growth over this period was 3.1% but there have been periods when it has been much higher. The exceptions are the periods 1955–60 and 1980–85, both exhibiting quite low growth; in some of the intervening years the economy actually shrank. However, the most notable change has been that the GDP per person grew more than threefold between 1950 and 1990. Although this table stops at 1990, we know that growth has continued strongly, as we will discuss in Section 18.3.

The second notable fact is the following: along with a steady increase in the Gross Domestic Product per person, there have also been increases in the population and the amount of capital stock per worker. The population increased only slightly. For much of this period emigration was still the norm in the Irish economy. During the 1950s and the late 1980s the population decreased as a result of a net outflow of migrants. However, coupled with the threefold increase in GDP per capita, there has been a tripling in capital stock per worker. In the simplest terms, over this time period there has been a dramatic increase in the number of factories and machines at the disposal of workers. This increase is largely the result of a change in Irish economic policy away from protectionism and toward an outward-oriented economic growth strategy. This included an active pursuit of foreign investment, encouragement of exports and an era of more openness toward international trade, including joining the European Union.[6]

Solow growth model

Table 18.1 focuses on three factors: national income per person, population and the capital stock per worker. These factors are the main ingredients of one basic explanation for economic growth known as the Solow growth model[7] which was developed by Robert Solow, a Nobel prize winning economist from the Massachusetts Institute of Technology.[8] This model provides a picture of the economy and how it produces goods and services for its residents to consume. Its use of the relationship between labour and capital is similar to a firm's production function. National income, which we denote as Y, is the amount of goods and services produced in a nation's economy. To produce a certain level of output, labour, factories and machinery are required. We summarise this relationship by writing:

$$Y = F(K,L)$$ [18.1]

In this equation, Y is national income or GDP, K is the capital stock, that is, the amount of machines and factories that can be used to produce goods, and L is the labour supply, or more simply, the population. The function F(K,L) tells us that capital stock is combined with the population in (ideally) an efficient way to produce goods. While it is simple enough to write this function, specifying the actual relationship between K and L is quite difficult, as we will see shortly.

In microeconomics, we studied a firm and saw that its output depended on the capital and labour that it used. It also depended on the particular production function. The Solow growth model uses the same idea, but for the whole economy. So the amount that can be produced by a country at any given time depends on its available population and its capital stock. Table 18.1 shows an increase in GDP per person as well as an increase in population and capital stock. So one simple theory of economic growth which we can state immediately is that just increasing a country's population L or amount of capital K will increase its income.

Let's look first at population growth, which introduces a number of interesting issues. Population can be increased by allowing increased immigration or through more traditional methods. But despite the theoretical prospect that the economy grows when the population grows, most countries take actions to limit their own population growth. These limitations range from quotas on immigrants in the United States to China's one child policy.

Another contradiction is that some of the best economic growth in the world has taken place in countries with little or no population growth. Consider Ireland, and compare the population and growth rate in Table 18.1 between 1950 and 1970. Over the twenty-year period, the population fell while the income per capita increased by 85%. At the same time, some of the countries with the lowest economic growth have had very high increases in population. For example, China and India are the two most populous nations and yet they are ranked 149th and 165th in the world in terms of GNP per capita.[9] However it is too simple to blame only a low or high population growth rate for the state of a country's economy. Remember it is the combination of labour and capital that is important. Population increase alone may not yield very high growth, because the interaction between labour and capital is an important factor. So in addition to population, we must study capital stock. But where do these machines and factories come from?

A closed economy, one that is isolated from the rest of the world, must produce any capital stock independently. That is, the amount of capital stock, K used to produce output, Y in any one year must have been produced in the previous years. If your country needs a factory to produce goods in the year 2005, you must build that factory sometime in the years before then. So part of today's output is used in future years. The only other possible use of this output is to consume it.

So, a major determinant of future K is today's consumption, or more specifically, the amount of today's output that is not consumed and is saved for use as tomorrow's capital stock. An equivalent way of thinking about the accumulation of capital is to consider investment. The only use for output is savings or consumption and the only use of savings is for it to be invested in the economy. For example, you place your money in a savings account and the bank loans the money to businesses to build machines and factories. If your economy is isolated from the rest of the world, the only source of investment is domestic savings and the only use of savings is investment. The amount of savings equals the amount of investment. Isolated economies therefore limit themselves to using only capital stock produced domestically. (Removing this limitation has benefited many countries, as we will see in Sections 18.2 and 18.3).

We can now outline a process by which national output and national income grow. If more is saved and invested, more capital stock is available for future production of output. A country that saves more of its output to invest will accumulate capital stock and increase its production of Y. However, this process of capital accumulation has a limit. When a country has more machines and factories, it must invest more money in their repair and upkeep. If a country has a certain level of savings, its capital stock K and output will grow until its entire savings is being used to repair and replace the old machines and factories. If savings increases, the amount of capital will increase at first, but then the additional machines will need to be repaired also. Just because a country is saving and investing more does not imply that its capital stock is increasing without limit.

The process by which machines and factories break down, become obsolete, and must be replaced is called depreciation. A country can grow only if its savings and investment outweigh the amount of depreciation. When the level of savings equals the amount of depreciation, the capital stock K and output Y remain the same. This final stable point is known as the steady state level of capital.

Definition

The steady state consists of a level of capital and a savings rate such that the level of savings and investment equal the capital that is lost due to depreciation.

At first glance then, countries with higher savings rates will grow faster since they accumulate capital more quickly. But it is possible to go a bit further and say that poor countries with low levels of capital tend to grow more quickly than wealthier countries that have abundant capital. The extra savings and investment in a country with very few machines and factories has a larger impact whereas wealthier countries already have a lot of capital and find it harder to increase their level of K by as much. This point can be illustrated numerically.

Suppose, in the imaginary country of Aslan, K=100. Savings and investment add 10 units of capital. Therefore, its growth in capital is 10%. In the poorer imaginary country of Beowulf, K=50. The same addition of 10 units of capital represents a much higher increase of 20%. Assuming each country's population remains the same, the output of Beowulf will grow faster than Aslan's. Therefore savings, along with the existing level of capital stock, affects the growth rate of output. A major question and problem for a nation's government is the following: what level of capital and savings is best for an economy?

This question is not as straightforward as it might seem. One might be tempted to conclude that a country should save and invest as much as possible because higher levels of K are better. And while a country that saves more will boost its capital, it may not need that extra capital. It may also fail to recognise the opportunity cost of that savings. Remember that in order to save, people have to consume less. If we consider that it is consumption that makes people happy, then the best level of savings and capital will maximise the amount of people's consumption.

For example, a country saving 0% of its output will not have any capital stock in the future. Eventually all its K will depreciate away and it will not be able to produce anything. On the other hand, a country saving 100% of its output will have nothing available for its people to consume. The workforce starves and nothing is produced. Between these two extremes lies an optimal savings rate. This optimal savings rate allows for investment to accumulate and maintain the optimal level of K. This optimal level of capital allows a country's citizens to have the highest possible consumption from year to year. The goal for a government is to find the Golden Rule level of capital.[10]

Definition

The Golden Rule level of capital is the steady state with the highest level of consumption.

Consumption is maximised not just today but for all future generations, hence treating future generations as you wish past generations had treated you. If the economy currently has too little capital, savings should be increased and capital accumulated. If the economy has too much capital, savings and investment should be decreased until the capital stock falls to the Golden Rule level.

In conclusion, a higher level of savings will in turn lead to more capital stock with which to produce a larger output. Further, there is a level of K which leads to the maximum consumption per capita. However, once the savings rate equals the rate of depreciation, there will be no further changes in K. With no changes in capital there will be no further changes in output. Growth stops. The simplified Solow model describes economies growing to a certain level depending on their savings rates and then staying at that level of national income forever after that. This leads to the following predictions.

1. Countries that save more of their national output will grow faster. These countries will invest more and will accumulate a larger amount of capital. The higher level of capital will allow them to produce more in future years. But, there is a limit to the amount of savings and investment that can occur. Any time the capital stock is increased, depreciation, the cost of maintaining that capital, increases as well. Eventually savings will just cover the replacement value of depreciated capital. There are a few notable exceptions to this prediction. For example, the United States has had strong growth in its history despite having a lower savings rate than many other countries.

2. Poor countries tend to grow more quickly than rich countries. There is convergence between economies around the world. This does not mean that the poorest countries in the world are quickly approaching the richest; the opposite is actually occurring. It means that among countries with similar characteristics, savings rates and technology, the poorer countries within a given group are approaching the richer ones within the same group. For example, Japan started out as a poor industrialised country and grew very quickly to become one of the richest. Ireland's living standards have surpassed the UK's level as measured by GDP per capita. This is due to the faster growth evident in the Irish economy in the last forty years. However, the gap between countries such as the United States and Ethiopia is actually increasing. Convergence tends to occur within similar groups, not between them.

3. Capital and labour are paid their marginal products. This is not really a prediction, but rather the result of using a production function. When studying the firm in microeconomics, we found that the theory of the firm predicts that labour is paid a wage equal to its marginal product. Also, capital receives a wage or rent equal to its marginal product. The same is true if we consider a national economy with its production function. Now, the returns to capital and labour must be paid from total output, so capital and labour receive shares of GNP. Depending on the production function that we apply to a country's economy, the theory predicts a percentage of GNP paid to capital and a percentage paid to labour in a country. These can be compared to the actual economic statistics.

The Solow growth model, while simple, yields all of these predictions and results. In this regard, the model does a fairly good job of explaining some facts of economic growth. However like many economic models, there are limitations. The equation offered for an economy Y=F(K, L) contains a relationship between output, labour and the capital stock. This relationship can be examined using the statistics of a country; it is possible to add up the L and K and see how much output was produced. But the main limitation of the Solow growth model is that it offers no explanation of how labour and capital interact to produce Y. With the Solow growth model, we have a form of growth accounting and the measurement of some key factors, but the model only explains so much.

In fact, the Solow growth model is interesting partly because of what it cannot explain and the factors for economic growth that it does not include. When the equation is given for a country, no matter what the savings rate is, the Solow growth model predicts that growth will eventually stop unless other factors are 'added in'. For example, technology can be added to the Solow growth model, but only in a way that leaves the exact role of technology unexplained. Technology is this special extra 'something' which creates growth. Because growth stops unless we add technology and other factors to the model, the Solow growth model points to the importance of such factors.

The bottom line: There is more to the story of economic growth than is contained in this one model, and we only have to look at economic growth in different countries to see this.

18.2 ECONOMIC GROWTH AROUND THE WORLD

The main limitation of the Solow growth model is its simplicity. While on the one hand this gives us some nice explanations about economic growth, it neglects some key factors that we would expect to be important to a country's economy. While these factors may not be included easily into our growth model from the previous section, it does not mean that they cannot be discussed. The principal aim of this section is to categorise and explain other factors that influence a country's prospects for growth. To do so, we will make some broad comparisons between different economies.

Cross-country comparisons are quite common in the study of economic growth. Typically these take the form of 'horse races' where most of the attention is paid to the winners. The best current example of this is the 'Celtic Tiger' economy of Ireland, and past examples include the Asian tigers in the early 1990s and the German and Japanese economies of the 1970s and 1980s. Usually when these winners are identified, economists and politicians comment on the lessons that these winners have to teach the rest of the world.

Let us take Table 18.2, listing fifteen countries, their GNP per capita and their growth rates since 1950. What lessons can be learned from the experiences of these countries? Why have some of them languished while others have thrived? And finally, what lessons do the 'winners' provide for the Irish economy and other economies overall?

Table 18.2: Economic growth around the world[11]

Country	GNP/capita 1998 (US$)	Annual Growth 1997–98	Average Annual Growth 1950–92
China	750	6.5%	3.3%
Denmark	33,260	2.6%	2.4%
Egypt	1,290	3.3%	2.3%
Ethiopia	100	-3.2%	1.0%
France	24,940	2.9%	3.0%
Germany	25,850	-0.4%	3.5%
India	430	4.2%	2.0%
Ireland	18,340	8.5%	3.1%
Italy	20,250	2.2%	3.7%
Japan	32,380	-2.8%	5.8%
Poland	3,900	5.4%	1.4%
South Korea	7,970	-7.1%	6.1%
United Kingdom	21,400	1.9%	2.1%
United States	29,340	2.8%	1.8%
Venezuela	3,500	-2.4%	1.1%

Source: Penn-World tables version 5.6, *World Development Report 1999/2000*, The World Bank, and author's calculations.

From this table, looking at the average annual growth in the economy from 1950–92, we can see that the 'winners' in this economic growth race are Japan and South Korea followed by Italy, Germany, China, Ireland and France. The growth of Japan, Germany and to a certain extent Italy and France can be attributed to the massive reconstruction that occurred after World War II. In these countries, massive investments in capital stock occurred after the war. There was also a large degree of catching up. These countries had their economies devastated by the war and consequently they grew very quickly as they caught up to the United States. South Korea and China are examples of countries with low levels of capital which grew quickly because they were starting from a relatively low base. Any increase in the economy will seem like a larger percentage simply because the starting level of output is lower. We will leave the case of Ireland until Section 18.3.

The rest of the countries all have an average growth rate of less than 3% with the lowest growth occurring in Ethiopia and Venezuela. These two countries have grown, but compared to most of the rest of the world, they have become relatively poorer. Our theory of economic growth must not only account for high growth, but must also be able to explain these low growth cases. Poland with its relatively low growth is an exception because that country was operating under a communist system for most of the time studied. It has recently been growing much faster as it makes the transition to a market economy and it provides an illustration of the impact that the political system can have on an economy.

This leaves the countries where economic growth has not been exceptional nor can it be described as a failure. Denmark, Egypt, India, the United Kingdom and the United States have all had growth rates around 2%. While this is low compared to Japan and South Korea, it still leads to a substantial change in living standards over time. In fact, even with a growth rate of 'only' 2%, the living standards of a country as measured by GNP per capita will double in about thirty-five years. It is hard to consider these countries as failures at all. The implication is that over thirty-five years, the average citizen realises such large gains in material living standards that they are twice as wealthy. So, even a low growth rate will, over time, imply more national wealth. Of course, GNP per capita will double much more quickly in Japan and South Korea, around every ten to twelve years. However, the most recent evidence points to slower growth in these countries as they approach the levels of the US and Europe. For the low growth countries, the economy can take up to seventy years to double in size, so they fall further behind in terms of poverty relative to the rest of the world.[12]

As Table 18.2 shows, there is a wide disparity in living standards among different countries, and a wide disparity in growth rates. What are the reasons for these differences in growth rates? Why have some countries done remarkably well, while others have stagnated or even fallen behind? While economists do not have the answers for every country, it is possible to identify some key characteristics and properties that provide a good environment for economic growth. Although not an exhaustive and complete list, the growth of a nation is influenced by:

1. the political system and government,
2. openness to the world economy,
3. human capital and education and
4. technology.

We begin with the political system and the quality of governance.

Political system and government

A quick comparison of economies may lead one to conclude that democracy and capitalism are best for economic growth. In Table 18.2, the richest eight countries, namely, Denmark, France, Germany, Ireland, Italy, Japan, the UK and the US are all advanced democracies whose markets have a large degree of freedom. Now some economists may argue that they are stable, free market democracies because they are rich, while others would argue that they are rich because they are stable, free market democracies. In any case, all of these countries have a number of helpful characteristics with regards to the political and economic systems. These include a stable, independent judicial system which can enforce contracts and settle disputes, clearly defined property rights which allow entrepreneurs to profit from industry, and a government which does not intervene unnecessarily in the daily actions of the economy.

It does not mean that all economies must have these factors in order to grow, but the government of a country can hinder the growth of its economy through actions that make the business environment unstable and uncertain. It is also quite probable that heavy government interference in the market can divert resources away from their most productive use.

For example, for decades industries in the economies of central and eastern Europe relied on a captive market dictated by the Soviet Union. This allowed businesses to remain in existence even though they were not competitive, because they were guaranteed a closed market in which to sell their goods. Once the Soviet Union dissolved and these markets were no longer guaranteed, many firms in Central and Eastern Europe found themselves uncompetitive when compared to firms from the western industrialised countries. The heavy government interference of the communist system allowed inefficient firms to stay in business and reduced the incentives to innovate and grow. Hence the poor growth exhibited in Poland over the years 1970–92.

Openness to the world economy

This concept could also be called a country's degree of globalisation. A country opening its economy to the world economy faces some benefits and drawbacks. The benefits of openness include the ability to buy cheaper imports, to export and sell goods to the world market and the ability to attract foreign businesses to invest in your country. If a country is open to the world economy, it has the possibility of importing the latest technology. The drawbacks include competition from cheap imports harming domestic firms and the exposure to foreign capital flight. That is, foreigners that invest money into your country can just as quickly pull their money out, often with dire effects.[13]

As for the effect of openness on growth, it is almost universally agreed that countries with a larger degree of openness will grow faster than those countries that try to shut themselves off from the rest of the world. Again, there is a debate among economists over causation: are they open economies because they have grown or vice versa, but there is agreement that the two main facets of globalisation that benefit growth are export-led growth and the attraction of foreign direct investment.

One strategy available to an economy is to try to increase its level of exports. If successful, this country engages in export-led growth. An economy would specialise in a number of goods for exports. Examples include textiles or electronic goods. Exports provide more money for a nation to use for its development. Some countries may attempt to climb an export ladder. They start by exporting cheap low technology goods such as clothing and simple manufactures. After gaining success there, they invest their profits in technology and more capital to begin exporting more expensive high technology goods such as cars and electronics. Japan grew in this fashion. It started producing cheap goods like toys and simple consumer goods before moving on to advanced technology products such as computer chips and televisions.

An alternative strategy for an economy opening to the world economy is to actively attract foreign direct investment. This investment usually takes the form of a foreign multinational building a factory locally and producing goods for export. To attract this investment, a country may offer low tax rates or subsidies to foreign firms. The benefit of this type of investment is that it provides capital and technology to a home country when they may not have been able to afford the investment. The foreign multinational provides the capital and the technology, while the host nation usually provides tax incentives and relatively cheap labour.

Education and human capital

While capital stock K consists of factories, machines and technology, human capital refers to human knowledge and know-how. It can be accumulated like regular capital, and countries can invest and increase their level of human capital by spending on training and education. One of the stories told about the Irish economic growth experience is that it results from the exceptional educational system, though there is some debate about this (see Case Study). If, however, we look at Table 18.3, we can see some statistics on human capital and education for our fifteen countries.

Table 18.3: Measures of education

Country	Public expenditure on education % of GNP 1996	Expected years of schooling 1995	
		Males	Females
China	2.3%	..	..
Denmark	8.2%	15	15
Egypt	4.8%	11	9
Ethiopia	4.0%	..	..
France	6.1%	15	16
Germany	4.8%	15	15
India	3.4%	..	..
Ireland	5.8%	14	14
Italy	4.7%	..	..
Japan	3.6%	14	14
Poland	5.2%	13	13
South Korea	3.7%	15	14
United Kingdom	5.4%	16	17
United States	5.4%	15	16
Venezuela	5.2%	10	11

Source: World Bank, *World Development Report 1999/2000*.

Although data are missing for some countries, we can see the large expenditure on education made by many countries. Like investment in machines and factories, we can consider the money spent on education to be an investment in the human capital of a nation. We would expect that the larger amount of human capital accumulated would translate into higher growth. Also, all the countries that can be considered middle to high income have high figures for expected number of years of schooling obtained by their citizens.

While all economists and the available economic data would agree that education and investment in human capital are important factors in a nation's growth, it is useful to clarify what kind of education. The type of education required to promote growth in an economy depends in part on the stage of a country's development. A nation that is just transforming itself from an agricultural economy to a manufacturing economy does not necessarily need to teach all of its citizens philosophy, physics, or even economics. Rather, if a country is newly industrialising, a basic level of literacy and technical training is necessary. On the other hand, if a country is an advanced industrial economy, it needs people trained in innovation and invention. We expect this country to invest more money and time training scientists and engineers. In short, the level and type of human capital accumulated depend on the level and type of technology being used in an economy. Technology is considered by many economists to be the main determinant of economic growth.[14]

Technology

For economists, the simplest definition of technology is that it is the interaction of labour and capital. Technology is embedded in machines and factories but it also exist in the ways workers use machines and processes of production. Better technology typically translates into more efficient methods of production and therefore more national output. For a country, the goal is to increase its own level of technology and potential for economic growth. There are essentially three ways to obtain higher level of technology and the ability to implement any of these three will have a large effect on the economic growth of a country.

The first is for the citizens of a country to invent new technology. This approach requires a substantial level of existing technology and human capital. There are prerequisite necessary for certain innovations. A country needs telephones in order to invent answering machines and computers to write software. Among the countries listed in Table 18.2 Denmark, France, Germany, Ireland, Italy, Japan, South Korea, the UK and the US are all countries doing a significant amount of technological innovation. The standard measurement of innovation is the number of patents filed in the United States.[15] Unsurprisingly these are the rich countries that have shown a large degree of growth already. They are poised, given their existing technology, to augment their technological lead through invention and innovation. It is a virtuous cycle where their past innovation has made them rich enough to afford the R&D that will make future innovations more likely.

For example, as measured by US patents granted in 1997, the top five countries represent 10.4% of the world's population, yet they filed 87.2% of the total patent throughout the world in that year. These same top five countries accounted for 41% of the world's GNP that year. Innovation and invention pay.[16]

The second approach for accumulating new technology is to adopt already existing technology that has been developed elsewhere. This however requires not only a certain degree of technical expertise, but also an ability to purchase the technology. Such countries would be considered technological adopters and include Poland and certain regions of China and India. These technology adopters have certain advantages namely, location and education. For example, as can be seen in Table 18.3, Poland has a well-educated population, and its location on the border of the European Union gives it access to high technology goods. Adopting new technology is easier. Some regions of China and India, most notably the coastal regions, also benefit from their proximity to Hong Kong, Singapore and other East Asian markets.

Finally, the third approach to increase a nation's level of technology is to encourage foreign investment in factories and businesses. Foreign firms bring their technology and their processes to a host nation. Domestic workers learn new techniques and other local firms benefit from the example set by the foreign multinational. If there is a large degree of 'spill over' of knowledge between foreign multinationals and domestic firms, the amount of new technology can be significant. This has been the approach of countries like Ireland and China as discussed earlier under globalisation and foreign direct investment.

If a country cannot use one of these three approaches to accumulate new technology, then it is excluded, for the most part, from using any new techniques and machines. These countries may not be rich enough to afford top scientific research to innovate themselves, and they may also be too poor to buy and adopt existing technology. Furthermore, if the country is not an attractive place for foreign investment, then the rate of technology acquisition may be quite slow or even non-existent. Among the countries listed in Table 18.2, Egypt, Ethiopia, Venezuela and the inland regions of India and China are excluded through poverty and isolation from accumulating technology. These areas are caught in a vicious cycle of being too poor to acquire new technology and hence remaining poor because of the lack of new technology.[17]

These four factors or characteristics illustrate that economic growth across countries may differ, not just because of savings rates, the capital stock and labour as predicted by the Solow growth model, but also because of institutional or structural aspects of an economy. The main implication is that even countries with similar technology or human capital may face quite different futures if other aspects of their economies such as their degree of openness or their political systems differ.

In real terms, the lessons that the 'winners' of the economic growth race can teach are quite varied. The lessons for growth are not that countries such as Egypt, Ethiopia and India should suddenly start innovating or importing technology. That is not feasible given their current national income and level of human capital. Rather, they should start by opening their economies to more foreign direct investment and work on establishing a healthy relationship between their governments and the economy. As for economies such as Germany, France, Denmark and the UK, they are not growing as rapidly as Ireland. What lessons can an economy like Ireland's teach these countries? That question is discussed next.

18.3 LESSONS FROM THE IRISH EXPERIENCE

Finally, we turn to the economic history of Ireland over the past number of decades. Having discussed the theory of economic growth and compared the growth experience of a number of different countries around the world, what are the lessons about economic growth that we can learn from the experience of Ireland?

If we were to tell the conventional story about how a country develops and grows it might sound like the following: A country starts out with an economy dependent largely on agriculture. The agricultural sector becomes more mechanised with tractors and other farm machinery and this leads to fewer people employed on farms. The large number of people displaced from farms provides a ready and cheap labour force for industries, which have started to appear. These new industries, in the early stages of a country's growth, are largely in light manufactured goods, like textiles and simple goods.

Eventually, as the country's economy grows, the goods that it manufactures become more complex and more highly valued, like steel, ships and cars. As the country develops further and acquires more technology and knowledge, it may begin to manufacture electronics, computers and software. At this stage the country has a small agricultural sector relative to the whole economy and its manufacturing sector is heavily weighted in favour of high tech and high value products. Then, in the advanced stages of economic growth, a process of de-industrialisation occurs.[18] With less actual manufacturing taking place, the economy of an advanced industrial state sees an increase in the size of its service sector, providing goods like design, research, tourism and entertainment.

This story of development is similar to that which occurred in the United Kingdom, Japan, France, Germany and the United States, just to name a few countries. The countries of China, Egypt, Ethiopia, India, South Korea and Venezuela are at different stages of this process. As for Ireland, the story is a little bit different, although it starts out the same.

Ireland has historically had a large agricultural sector, and that sector has been subject to the same stresses of mechanisation as elsewhere in the world. In practical terms, it means that fewer workers can do more work. Hence each farm supports fewer people. Now, in other countries the surplus labour that is displaced from farms would be welcome in growing industries, and those industries would be attracted by the abundant and therefore cheap labour.

However, because of Ireland's proximity to the UK and the ease with which people could emigrate there and to the US, Canada, Australia, New Zealand and elsewhere, Ireland did not have the large amount of cheap labour that would attract industry and help it develop. The wage in Ireland was kept high by large emigration. One could almost consider Ireland a regional economy within Europe.[19] Certainly with its mobile labour force and its proximity to the UK, when jobs were scarce in Ireland, workers left. This left fewer people behind and a smaller supply of workers. This relative scarcity of workers kept the wage higher than expected in a developing country. Hence manufacturing of simple goods with low technology never truly developed in Ireland to the same extent as in other countries.

The second way in which Ireland's economic growth differs from the conventional story is that Ireland moved almost directly from an agricultural based economy to a high tech manufacturing and services economy. There was a jump in development and Ireland did not develop much of the heavy manufacturing that characterises other newly industrialised countries.

A brief history of the twentieth century Irish economy would read as follows. Though the economy was largely agricultural, the industry that did exist tended to locate in the Northeast, close to Belfast. As industries started to locate there, it became an attractive place for other industries to locate as well. This is known as clustering. After independence and partition, the fledgling Irish republic was left with few indigenous industries. Its agriculture sector was then faced with an increasing mechanisation in which farming supported fewer people. Many farm workers were displaced and left without work.

Starting in the 1930s and continuing until the 1960s, the government introduced protectionist policies aimed at increasing economic activity domestically. These included tariffs on imported goods and subsidies to some industries. And while some industries were helped, the main result of this protectionism and inward focus of economic policy was that the industries that did develop tended to be inefficient because they were no subject to international competition. These industries also tended to focus on producing goods mainly for domestic consumption, and given the relatively small size of the Irish home market, their growth was limited.

The major change in economic policy in the 1960s was a shift toward encouraging a more outward oriented economy. This shift did not mean simply the abolishment of tariffs. Rather, the government actively sought to grow through exports and the attraction of foreign direct investment. It was, in short, an opening of the Irish economy to the global economy. As seen in Table 18.1, this largely worked. GDP per capita grew at a much higher rate after 1965, growing by over 15% in every five-year period except 1980–85.

All of this historical explanation and storytelling just tells us about the foundation of the 'Celtic Tiger' and current Irish economic growth. In short, Ireland industrialised very rapidly by increasing exports and attracting more foreign businesses. The growth has been so quick because Ireland has been catching up to the rest of Europe and the other industrialised countries. Growth from 1960–90 has been very good compared to richer, more developed countries, but this is what the Solow growth model would predict. As such, it is good news for the Irish economy, but not necessarily earth-shattering news to the rest of the world.

But what has astonished many economists and brought Irish economic growth to the attention of the world has been its performance in the 1990s. By some economic measures, Ireland is not just catching up to the level of Europe, but surpassing it. This fact has caused much debate among Irish economists and questioning by economists everywhere. All of them are looking for the lessons for economic growth that can be learned from Ireland.

First, let us look at the actual growth in the Irish economy in the 1990s.

Table 18.4: Recent Irish economic growth

	1990	1991	1992	1993	1994	1995	1996	1997	1998	1999*
Gross National Product at 1995 prices (million €)	37,473	38,328	39,222	40,549	43,108	46,631	50,067	54,732	59,023	63,643
Gross National Product at 1995 prices (million £)	29,512	30,186	30,890	31,935	33,950	36,725	39,431	43,105	46,484	50,123
Annual % change in GNP	..	2.3%	2.3%	3.4%	6.3%	8.2%	7.4%	9.3%	7.8%	7.8%
GNP per capita (€)	10,689	10,870	11,033	11,345	12,021	12,950	13,808	14,950	15,930	16,994
GNP per capita (£)	8,418	8,561	8,689	8,935	9,467	10,199	10,875	11,774	12,546	13,384

* Preliminary

Source: CSO, *National Income and Expenditure 1999*, August 2000.

The most notable aspect of recent economic growth in Ireland is the high growth in the period 1994–99. Up to this point economic growth had certainly been respectable, but growth rates of 6% and higher are exceptional. And while the process of economic growth started in the 1960s with the introduction of globally oriented economic policies, it was not until the late 1980s that Ireland's economic prospects really took off.

In the late 1980s, the government introduced cuts in its spending to reign in its deficits and debts. Government spending had grown so much that the level of the national debt was larger than the size of the economy. At that level, a substantial portion of government spending is on interest payments alone. Part of the pressure for reducing government debt and hence spending was international, coming from such bodies as the International Monetary Fund and the European Union. Around the same time, a national wage agreement was signed in 1987 that brought about wage restraint in exchange for reductions in income taxes. These two factors set the stage for the high growth in the 1990s.

So from the statistics in Table 18.4, we can see that the Irish economy is growing strongly, but the magnitude of the change in the Irish economy can be illustrated in other, more tangible ways. For example, unemployment has fallen from 11% as recently as 1997 to as low as 5% in the summer of 2000. Instead of one in ten people being out of work, only one in twenty people are still without jobs. A second visible sign that the economy is doing well is the recent change in migration. More people are moving to Ireland than are leaving: contrast this with the fact that half of the people who left school in the 1950s had also left the country by 1961. The number of automobiles bought in 1999 was 25% higher than the number bought in 1998.[20] Strong economic growth exhibits itself in a variety of ways.

As for explanations of this growth, there are a number of possibilities. The most common are the high level of foreign investment, the well-educated workforce, the level of European Union subsidies and social partnership. Of course, there is also the theory that current Irish economic growth, no matter how robust, is nothing more than the continuation of growth that has been occurring since the 1960s (see Case Study). Let us look at a number of these explanations for Ireland's growth and see what lessons and stories can be told.

Foreign investment

The clearest sign that Ireland has benefited greatly from foreign direct investment is the large difference between Gross National Product and Gross Domestic Product. Currently in Ireland, GDP is much larger than GNP. The discrepancy is largely due to foreign firms repatriating profits to their home countries. The ability to attract foreign investment has made it possible for Ireland to acquire technology and human capital. So, Ireland, instead of moving from light manufacturing to heavy manufacturing and then to high tech products, has actually skipped a few steps. The recent foreign investment has been in software, electronics and medical equipment, to name just a few sectors. For example, by the end of 1994, investment from the US alone has totalled almost $3,000 per person. This compares to $2,000 per person in Britain and $500 per person in France and Germany.[21]

Ireland's ability to attract foreign investment is due to a number of factors. These include, but are not limited to the following:

1. Ireland is an English speaking nation within the euro area.
2. Ireland's workforce is relatively young and a high percentage of the labour force have a third level degree.[22]
3. The cluster effect: a number of firms have already invested in Ireland and that makes it more likely that other, similar firms will invest in Ireland. For example, investments by Apple Computer, Inc. mean that Gateway Computer Inc. is more likely to invest because of the existence of trained workers and secondary markets geared for the computer industry.
4. Social partnership has brought stable wages and moderate wage increases over the years.
5. Tax on manufacturing industry is one of the lowest in the EU.

The educated workforce

This point is more debated than foreign investment, partly because of the problems involved in trying to tie educational spending and attainment to specific trends in growth. Suffice it is to say that currently Ireland is enjoying a demographic boom. Its workforce is among the youngest in Europe, and as can be seen in Table 18.3, it spends a larger percentage of its GDP on education than many other rich nations. When these characteristics are coupled with a national wage agreement promising wage restraint and when the labour costs are already among the lowest in western Europe, the labour market is a strong factor for growth. Perhaps a more important factor for economic growth is not the education of a workforce or its cost but rather its flexibility. Many economists argue that Ireland's recent reduction in unemployment is due, in part, to the flexibility of its labour market. On the one hand, this flexibility leads to large migration in and out of Ireland. On the other hand, it has allowed Ireland to reduce its unemployment rate to below 5% while many areas in the rest of Europe still wrestle with double-digit unemployment rates.

The European Union

Critics of Irish economic growth typically say that all of the growth is due to European Union subsidies. In fact, the level of subsidies has stayed at roughly the same level while the growth rate continues to climb. If the growth was due solely to EU aid, then continued growth would necessitate larger and larger subsidies from the EU. So while Ireland has benefited from transfers from the EU, it is not the only reason for growth. Rather, membership in and of itself has probably done more for Irish economic growth than direct monetary aid. When joining the EU in 1973, Ireland was committing itself to a process of opening itself to the European and global economies. This openness increased competition and hence forced Irish companies to be more efficient. Furthermore, the process of deregulating industries such as airlines and telecommunications lowered the costs for consumers and other businesses. This has produced a knock-on effect so that Irish businesses thrive due to lower costs of telephone calls and energy.

Social partnership

Irish economic growth is sometimes portrayed as a shining example of the benefits of partnership between firms, unions and the government. Certainly, the benefit of partnership agreements has been a very stable wage environment in which wage increases are restrained and industrial actions are curtailed. However, this is not a characteristic unique to the Irish economy. Other countries such as Germany and Austria have also exhibited a large degree of co-operation between unions, businesses and the government.[2] The major benefit of having a national wage agreement is its attraction to foreign businesses looking to invest. However, maintaining the social partnership may not be easy and could pose one of many problems for economic growth.

Irish economic growth over the last forty years and in particular the last ten years has been spectacular, but there are a number of dangers. As the economy grows it is placed under a variety of stresses. Firstly, it is hard to continue to grow at a rapid pace without experiencing large rises in prices. Until 1999 and 2000, this problem of inflation did not exist in the general economy, though house prices and some wages did increase sharply. As inflation picks up, it is more difficult for social partnership to last, as businesses and the government cannot make a convincing case for continued wage restraint. Secondly, as the Irish economy grows, it may run into shortages, particularly of some types of labour. The computer software and pharmaceutical sectors are examples where firms have openly expressed their concerns about a shortage of qualified and skilled workers. Thirdly, infrastructural bottlenecks (in the areas of transport, housing, the environment) are evident, as the recent economic growth stretches Ireland's productive capacity. Fourthly, Ireland is not the only destination for foreign direct investment, nor is Ireland the only country actively seeking such investment. Other countries may become more attractive places for firms to locate. Finally, Ireland may be too heavily dependent on certain industrial sectors. The current economic growth is due largely to growth in the computer, electronic and biotechnology fields. When those industries experience downturns, as they are likely to do, they may drag the Irish economy into a recession.[24]

CASE STUDY

Extract from *The Irish Times*
Economic miracle long time coming
State's growth has merely been in line with figures laid down in 1950
by Prof. Cormac Ó Gráda and Dr Kevin O'Rourke

As the 21st century dawns, official Ireland is feeling smug. Between 1994 and 1999, per capita income (GNP) grew at an astonishing 7.9 per cent. Between 1987 and 1998, per capita output (GDP) grew at 6.7 per cent in Ireland, but at only 1.7 per cent in the US and 1.8 per cent in the rest of western Europe. Some commentators seem to think this headlong growth will last, while some politicians seem to think it ought to. Meanwhile, the Economist magazine, which once referred to Ireland as 'The Poorest of the Rich' now muses about 'what Ireland can teach the rest'. However, an historical and comparative view of the Irish boom yields a more sobering perspective.

One of the most robust facts about European growth over the past 50 years has been that poorer countries tend to grow faster than richer countries: thus, the fastest growing economies have been Greece and Portugal, while the slowest growing economies have been Switzerland and Britain (which has, in turn, grown slightly faster than the US). This 'convergence' tendency reflects the ability of laggards to catch up on economic leaders by importing both capital and best practice technology. Between 1950 and 1987, the outstanding exception to this general rule was Ireland, which only managed to grow at 2.8 per cent per annum (the same rate as affluent Belgium), while its peripheral peers were clocking up growth rates in excess of 4 per cent.

. . .

Viewed in this light, the interesting question is not why Ireland has done so well in the last decade, but why it took so long to catch up. A useful comparison is provided by Italy, another traditionally agricultural economy whose per capita output was roughly the same as Ireland's in 1950. By 1998, its per capita output (if not its income) was 8.8 per cent lower, but it would be wrong to view this as a case of Irish success and Italian failure. By 1973, GDP per capita was almost 60 per cent higher in Italy than in Ireland, a gap which persisted as late as 1990. The net present value of Irish income, discounted back to 1950, would have been 28.9 per cent higher had it grown at the same pace as Italy throughout, rather than making up for lost ground in the 1990s. The moral is that if you are going to converge on richer countries, then the sooner you do so the better. If Ireland's long-run performance has not been exceptional, then neither ⸱e the mechanisms by which we

achieved our belated success. Indeed, Ireland's 'Golden Age' bears a striking resemblance to the Golden Age the rest of western Europe enjoyed four decades earlier, and which lasted from 1950 to 1973.

Then as now, growth was largely due to convergence; then as now, the economies concerned received substantial external funding, giving governments a little extra room for manoeuvre; then as now, this led to a more structured approach towards economic and infrastructural planning; then as now, the bestowers of this largesse (the US government in the earlier episode, Brussels in the later) insisted that market-friendly reforms be adopted by recipient governments.

. . .

The argument that recent Irish success is due to our educational system has been oversold. For one thing, the timing is wrong: trends in educational spending cannot account for the sharp improvement in our fortunes which occurred from 1987 on. Second, it is not enough to educate the young, . . . Job creation has played a crucial role during this boom . . . This suggests that social partnership was critically important, just as it was in Europe in the 1950s and 1960s.

An historical perspective makes it clear why current growth rates cannot last: rapid growth is only possible while economies converge on the frontier economy (in practice, the US). Once all possible convergence has been achieved, further growth will only be at the rate at which the frontier itself expands, or, historically, 2 per cent. Even boosters of the 'new economy' and the Nasdaq only claim that long-run frontier growth has increased from 2 per cent to 3 per cent. It would be folly to expect that Ireland could do much better than this in the long run. Indeed, US technology firms have played such a crucial role in Irish growth that it is tempting to conclude that

→

our boom has been largely a product of the Greenspan boom. On this view, the possible implications of an American crash are worrying.

History also emphasises the political nature of the Irish boom. Labour's share of national income has declined steadily during the 1990s, but workers have until now been bought off with tax cuts (rather than the improved welfare benefits which mollified an older generation of European workers). Europe's Golden Age ended when the oil crises heightened distributional tensions to the point where they became unmanageable. We look forward to speculating about why Ireland's social partnership experiment finally collapsed – was it the political scandals? the McCreevy budgets? or EMU entry and the consequent housing crisis? – when we have an adequate historical perspective on the question. Say 50 years from now.

Source: *The Irish Times*, 9 June 2000.

QUESTIONS

1. How unique has Ireland's economic growth been?
2. What is the problem of citing education as a reason for economic growth in Ireland?
3. What are the short-term and long-term prospects for the Irish economy?

Answers on website

SUMMARY

1. This chapter examines economic growth and the performance of an economy over a long period of time. Factors that influence economic growth in the long run include changes in population, capital and technology.
2. The Solow growth model details a relationship between labour L, capital stock K and national income, Y. Part of this relationship is savings. A country must save part of its output to use as capital stock in future years; the remainder of its output is consumption.
3. The Solow growth model predicts that countries with similar characteristics tend to grow together and converge in terms of income per capita. Dissimilar countries may actually grow apart with wealthy countries growing much faster than poorer ones.
4. Based on experiences from countries around the world, factors such as political systems, education, degree of openness to the world economy and levels of technology play significant roles in the economic growth of a country.
5. Ireland's economic growth has taken its own unique path. Recent strong economic growth can be considered a continuation of growth that started in the 1960s.
6. Factors that have contributed to Ireland's recent strong economic growth include the amount of foreign investment, membership in the European Union, an educated workforce and social partnership.

KEY TERMS

Solow growth model
Capital stock
Labour
Production function
Depreciation
Steady state level of capital
Golden Rule level of capital
Export-led growth
Foreign direct investment
Human capital
Celtic Tiger
Clustering
Social partnership

REVIEW QUESTIONS

1. What is the main equation for the Solow growth model and what does it tell us about economic growth in a country?
2. What is foreign direct investment and how can it help a country's economy grow?
3. List four factors that can influence a country's economic growth.
4. Explain why a poorer country is likely to grow faster than a wealthier one.
5. List four factors that have influenced Ireland's economic growth over the past decade.
6. In the context of the Irish economy, explain the economic problems that might arise from excessive growth.

MULTI-CHOICE QUESTIONS

1. The Golden Rule level of capital refers to the:
    (a) level of capital at which a country grows most quickly over time;
    (b) level of capital with the largest amount of savings over time;
    (c) level of capital with the largest amount of consumption over time;
    (d) level of capital with the largest amount of gold in an economy;
    (e) level of capital with the most technology.

2. In the simple Solow growth model, if savings is larger than the depreciation of the capital stock:
    (a) the country will lose capital;
    (b) the country will accumulate capital;
    (c) consumption will increase;
    (d) growth will slow down;
    (e) capital will depend on the level of technology.

3. All of the following are factors that influence the long-term economic growth of a country, except:
    (a) level of technology;
    (b) the political system;
    (c) the level of education;
    (d) interest rates;
    (e) the degree of openness to the world economy.

4. Invention and innovation are more likely to occur in wealthier, highly developed countries because:
    (a) wealthier countries exploit their workers more efficiently;
    (b) wealthier countries have the resources to spend on R&D;
    (c) wealthier countries already have existing technology and knowledge;
    (d) wealthier countries are able to exploit poorer countries;
    (e) both (b) and (c).

5. Which of the following is not a reason for Ireland's recent economic success?
    (a) the economic policies of the 1960s;
    (b) membership in the European Union;
    (c) the level of foreign direct investment;
    (d) tough government policies on immigration and asylum seekers;
    (e) a well educated workforce.

6. The very strong growth in Ireland in the 1990s implies that:
    (a) Ireland will have the largest economy in the world eventually;
    (b) Ireland's economy will keep growing at this pace forever;
    (c) Ireland's GDP per capita is quickly matching the GDP per capita of other EU nations;
    (d) Ireland's economy will never enter a recession again;
    (e) none of the above.

TRUE OR FALSE (SUPPORT YOUR ANSWER)

1. A country is poor because it chooses to be poor.

2. A country will grow quickly only if it is wealthy.

3. Poorer countries tend to catch up to wealthier countries in terms of economic growth.

4. The Golden Rule level of capital entails the highest consumption for people in a country over time.

5. A country can acquire technology through foreign direct investment.

6. The only reason Ireland's economy grew in the last 10 years is because of money from the European Union.

CASE STUDY

Extract from the *Irish News*
Irish lessons for UK economy
by Jonathan Turner

The Republic could teach Britain a lesson about economic growth, a report published today says. Financial consultancy Business Strategies said Britain's economic performance could be improved by adopting some of the policies that have helped the south's impressive growth over the last six years. Since 1994, the Republic – dubbed by some as the 'Celtic Tiger' – has seen output grow by an average nine per cent a year, compared to 2.7 per cent in the UK, while jobs have increased by 25 per cent, compared to the UK's six per cent.

Business Strategies said its successful strategies had included targeting and developing high-growth sectors like pharmaceuticals, electronics and services, mainly by attracting inward investment. Ireland has also put an emphasis on identifying sectors and niche areas that have high, long-term growth potential. Jane Croot, managing economist at Business Strategies said: 'In seeking foreign direct investment, the Irish have made a point of targeting only the most successful companies in a sector, primarily those producing for export markets, being careful not to displace existing domestic industries.' She said in contrast with the UK, growth in Ireland had been led by manufacturing, driven by tremendous growth in exports.

. . .

Ireland had also benefited by raising skill levels in the young workforce by its emphasis on completing upper secondary and tertiary education. Business Strategies added that, although education was largely a matter for national policy, the UK could focus its regional education policies on raising skill levels in the workforce. However, the report said that although learning from Irish strategies would benefit the UK, the impact on economic growth would not be on the same scale that Ireland has experienced. It added that the Republic's economic growth could be seen partly as a result of reversing policy mistakes of the past.

Source: *Irish News*, 3 July 2000.

QUESTIONS

1. What aspects of Ireland's strategy have been globally oriented?
2. What is special about the way that Ireland has attracted foreign direct investment?
3. If the UK were to imitate Irish economic policy, would the UK economy begin to grow at 9% per year?

ENDNOTES

CHAPTER 1

1   Barbara Wootton, *Lament for Economics*, Allen, 1938.
2   George Bernard Shaw, attributed.
3   Milton Friedman, *Capitalism and Freedom*, University of Chicago Press, 1982.
4   Ibid. He states, 'Every extension of the range of issues for which explicit agreement is sought further strains the delicate threads that hold society together . . . The wider the range of activities covered by the market, the fewer the issues on which explicit political decisions are required and hence on which it is necessary to achieve agreement.'
5   Ibid.
6   This discussion is based on the work of Ingrid Rima, *Development of Economic Analysis*, Irwin Press, 1986.
7   Thorstein Veblen, *The Theory of the Leisure Class*, New American Library, a division of Penguin Books, 1953 (originally published by Macmillan, 1899).
8   Ibid.
9   Ingrid Rima, *Development of Economic Analysis*, 4th edition, Irwin Press, 1986.
10 To find out more about Marx and Engels, read Robert C. Tucker, editor, *The Marx–Engels Reader*, 2nd edition, W. W. Norton & Company, 1978. For a contemporary treatment of Marxian economics, read E. K. Hunt and Howard J. Sherman, *Economics: An Introduction to Traditional and Radical Views*, 6th edition, HarperCollins Publishers, 1990.
11 Pope Leo XIII, May 15, 1891, *On the Conditions of Workers Rerum Novarum*, Office of Publishing and Promotion Services United States Catholic Conference. For a more current discussion of the Catholic Church's view of the labour market see Pope John Paul II, May 1, 1991, *On the Hundredth Anniversary of Rerum Novarum Centesimus Annus*, Office of Publishing and Promotion Services United States Catholic Conference.
12 R. D. Dickenson, *A Dictionary of Philosophy*, Ballantyne Press, 1887.
13 Paul W. Humphreys, 'Induction' in *The New Palgrave: A Dictionary of Economics*, edited by J. Eatwell, M. Milgate, P. Newman, 3, Macmillan, 1987.
14 Rima, 1986.

CHAPTER 2

1   George Bernard Shaw, 'Socialism and Superior Brains', *The Fortnightly Review*, April 1894.
2   Alfred Marshall, *Principles of Economics*, 8th edition, Macmillan, 1920.
3   It appears that Giffen did not make this observation. It was Alfred Marshall that attributed this observation to Giffen. See Marshall, *Principles of Economics*.
4   'We might as reasonably dispute whether it is the upper or the under blade of a pair of scissors that cuts a piece of paper, as whether value is governed by utility or cost of production.' Marshall, *Principles of Economics*.
5   J. FitzGerald and D. O'Connor, 'Economic Consequences of CAP Reform' in J. Bradley, J. FitzGerald and D. McCoy, *Medium-Term Review: 1991–96*, ESRI, 1991.

CHAPTER 3

1 *The Random House Dictionary of the English Language*, the unabridged edition, Random House, 1967.
2 W. Stanley Jevons, *The Theory of Political Economy*, 5th edition, A. M. Kelley, 1957.

CHAPTER 4

1 See Bonar's Preface to *Letters of Ricardo to Malthus*, Clarendon Press, 1887.
2 Jevons, *The Theory of Political Economy*.
3 He went on to say 'Nothing is more useful than water: but it will purchase scarce any thing; . . . A diamond, on the contrary, has scarce any value in use; but a very great quantity of other goods may frequently be had in exchange for it.' Adam Smith, *An Inquiry into the Nature and Causes of The Wealth of Nations*, edited by Edwin Cannon, reprinted, Methuen and Co. Ltd, 1961. (Originally printed in 1776.)
4 Researchers now believe that Giffen never made this claim. It appears that Paul Samuelson was responsible for accrediting Giffen with this observation. In addition, there is no evidence to suggest that the consumption of potatoes increased during the famine years. Indeed, with the potato blight damaging the crop, it is hard to imagine how the consumption of potatoes could have increased. This adds credence to the argument made in Chapter 2 that a Giffen good, although theoretically possible, is seldom observed in reality.
5 Marshall, *Principles of Economics*.

CHAPTER 5

1 Augustin Cournot, *Researches into the Mathematical Principles of the Theory of Wealth*, trans. Nathan T. Bacon, Macmillan, 1897. (Originally published in 1838.)
2 Joan Robinson, 'What is Perfect Competition?', *Quarterly Journal of Economics*, Nov. 1934.
3 John Stuart Mill, *Principles of Political Economy*, edited by Sir W. J. Ashley, A. M. Kelley, 1961. (Originally published in 1848.)
4 The economist who first developed the envelope curve was Jacob Viner in 1931. In the drafting of the envelope curve he and his draftsman, a brilliant mathematician at the University of Chicago, made what has become a famous error. He drew the LAC curve from the minimum points of the SATC curves. He acknowledged his mistake in a supplementary note written in 1950 where he wrote 'future teachers and students may share the pleasure of many of their predecessors of pointing out that if I had known what an "envelope" was, I would not have given my excellent draftsman the technically impossible and economically inappropriate assignment of drawing an AC curve which would pass through the lowest cost points of all the ac curves and yet not rise above any ac curve at any point.' However, this error does not, in any way, take from Viner's contribution to the theory of costs. The name of the article, regarded as a classic, is 'Cost Curves and Supply Curves', *Zeitschrift fur Nationalokonomie*, 3 1931. Finally, the explanation of the envelope curve which is to be found in the text is rather brief. A fuller explanation is left to authors of intermediate textbooks.
5 The average revenue received is simply the price of the product. This can be confirmed as follows:

$$TR = P \times Q$$

Divide both sides by Q:

$$\frac{TR}{Q} = \frac{P.Q}{Q}$$

The left-hand side is equal to AR. The right-hand side simplifies to P with the cancellation of Q above and below the line. Thus AR = P.

6 Commission of the European Communities, *Completing the Internal Market; Cockfield White Paper, Brussels/Luxembourg*, June 1985.

CHAPTER 6

1 Joan Robinson, 'What is Perfect Competition?'.
2 Smith, *An Enquiry into the Nature and Causes of the Wealth of Nations*.
3 We noted in Chapter 3 that the elasticity of demand for a good is determined by the number of available substitutes. The greater the number of readily available and close substitutes, the more elastic is demand. Under conditions of perfect competition, there are many close substitutes for the firm's product. The result is an elastic demand curve. It is important to recognise that this feature does not apply to the market demand curve. The market as an entity can only sell a greater amount of goods if it lowers its price. There exists a negatively sloped market demand curve.
4 Edward Chamberlin, *The Theory of Monopolistic Competition*, 1933, Joan Robinson, *The Economics of Imperfect Competition*, 1933, Piero Sraffa, *The Law of Return under Competitive Conditions*, 1926.
5 See P. M. Sweezy, 'Demand under Conditions of Oligopoly,' *Journal of Political Economy*, 47, August 1939 and R. L. Hall and C. J. Hitch, 'Price Theory and Business Behaviour', *Oxford Economic Papers*, No. 2, May 1939. Sweezy was interested in the downward stickiness of prices which was evident during the Great Depression.

CHAPTER 7

1 Karl Marx, 'First Manuscript' in *Early Writings, (of) Karl Marx*, trans. Rodney Livingstone and Gregor Bentan, introduced by Lucio Colletti, Penguin, 1975.
2 Frederick B. Hawley, *Enterprise and the Productive Process*, G. P. Putnam and Sons, 1907.
3 The American economist J. Bates Clark is accredited with writing the most comprehensive book on marginal productivity theory. The book entitled The *Distribution of Wealth: A Theory of Wages, Interest and Profits* (1899) became the basis for the theory of income distribution. The idea for the book came from issues raised by his fellow American Henry George (see endnote 10). The marginal productivity theory has a number of shortcomings. First, it is extremely difficult to calculate the marginal productivity of labour. Second, it assumes that all other factor inputs are constant. This is unlikely in reality. Third, it fails to account for wage differentials. Fourth, it ignores imperfections in the market. Fifth, it is difficult to separate out the marginal products of the various factor inputs. Notwithstanding these limitations, the marginal productivity theory makes a significant contribution to factor markets and the theory of income distribution.
4 For arguments by economists who favour the imposition of the minimum wage, see David Card and Alan B. Kruger, *Myth and Measurement: The New Economics of the Minimum Wage*, Princeton University Press, 1995.
5 Inter-Departmental Group on Implementation of a National Minimum Wage, *Interim Report of the Inter-Departmental Group on Implementation of a National Minimum Wage*, October 1998, The Stationery Office.
6 Barry O'Keefe, 'Minimum wage would hurt business, says SFA survey', *The Irish Times*, December 1997.
7 Rent was defined by Ricardo as '. . . that portion of the produce of the earth which is paid to the landlord for the use of the original and indestructible powers of the soil'. See Ricardo, *The Principles of Political Economy and Taxation*.

8   Economic rent is to factor markets what consumer surplus is to product markets. In Chapter 4 we defined consumer surplus as the difference between the price the consumer pays for the good and the maximum price he is willing to pay for the good. Economic rent can be defined in the same terms: it is the difference between the actual factor price that the owner receives and the minimum factor price at which the owner is willing to supply the factor input.

9   In reality, the supply of land is not necessarily fixed and there are alternative uses. Irrigation, other forms of reclamation and fertilisers allow for the existing parcels of land to be extended or improved. For the sake of simplicity, however, we assume a fixed supply of land with no alternative uses.

10   As land is in fixed supply and has zero supply cost, all its earnings are economic rent. Any change in demand, small or large, will have no effect on the supply. It is unearned income and it is for this reason that a tax on land is often proposed. Rent could be subject to tax in the knowledge that the supply of land will remain unchanged. Those who argue against a land tax maintain that with all the alternative uses, land is not fixed in reality. In addition, they argue that there are many other factors which earn economic rent and are viable sources of tax, e.g. income tax levied on the salaries of movie actors or professional sports stars. For a definitive analysis on the reasons for why landowners should be subject to tax, read Henry George's (of the single tax movement) classic *Progress and Poverty*, (1879).

11   Classical economic theory divided factor income into three rather than four categories – wages (the return on labour), rents (the return on land) and profits (the return on capital). For classical economists, profit and interest were indistinguishable. This reflected the structure of the corporate sector in the nineteenth century when the role of the capitalist and the entrepreneur were combined.

12   F. Knight, *Risk, Uncertainty and Profit*, Houghton Mifflin Co., 1921.

13   Henry Ergas, *Why Do Some Countries Innovate More Than Others?* CEPS Paper No. 5, Centre for European Policy Studies, 1984.

14   Ibid.

15   Ibid.

16   For example, in 1991, the special consideration applied if the wage increase of 4% had an effect of less than £5 per week in the worker's gross pay. For this to occur, the worker's pay was less than £125 per week, 54% of the average manufacturing wage.

17   For a balanced discussion on the benefits and problems associated with social partnership, read Brigid Reynolds, S. M. and Sean Healy, S. M. A., editors, *Social Partnership in a New Century*, Dublin: Justice Commission, Conference of Religious of Ireland, March 1999.

18   Ricardo, *The Principles of Political Economy and Taxation*.

CHAPTER 8

1   George Bernard Shaw, *John Bull's Other Island*, Penguin Books, 1984. (First published 1907.)

2   Thomas Fuller, *Gnomologia: adages and proverbs; wise sayings and witty sentences, ancient and modern*, 1932. (Originally published 1732.)

3   If producers produce goods that consumers do not want, then they will go out of business. In addition, if producers do not sell at the lowest conceivable price, then the forces of competition will drive them out of business.

4   B. Mandeville, *The Fable of the Bees*, edited by P. Harth, Penguin Books, 1970. (First published 1714.)

5   Pigou, *The Economics of Welfare*.

6   R. H. Coase, 'The Problem of Social Cost', *Journal of Law and Economics*, 3, 1960.

7   P. A. Samuelson, 'The Pure Theory of Public Expenditure', *Review of Economics and Statistics*, 36, 1954. Also, 'A Diagrammatic Exposition of a Theory of Public Expenditure', *Review of Economics and Statistics*, 37, 1955.

CHAPTER 9

1 These two basic allowances were standard-rated in 1999/00; Ireland has, in effect, adopted a tax-credits system. As such, the maximum values of the two basic allowances to an individual are £1,100/€1,396.71 (20% of £5,500/€6,983.56) and £400/€507.90 (20% of £2,000/€2,539.48). The purpose behind the standard rating of allowances is to equalise the (maximum) value of these allowances across taxpayers.

2 For example, a further distinction was introduced in the tax code between one income married couples with children and one income married couples without children. The interested reader should consult specialist publications in taxation and/or a tax accountant for further details.

3 First time buyers have a raised ceiling of £2,500/€3,174.35 (£5,000/€6,348.69).

4 Employees also pay a health levy. The contribution is 2% of gross income; employees earning less than £280/€355.53 per week are exempt from these levies.

5 A discussion on unemployment traps and poverty traps can be found in the unemployment section of Chapter 17.

6 The individual profit-maximising firm, whether in perfect competition or monopoly, produces a level of output at which marginal revenue is equal to marginal cost, i.e. MR = MC. From the individual firm's perspective in perfect competition, however, marginal revenue is equal to price, i.e. MR = P. Therefore, in perfect competition, the individual firm produces a level of output at which price is equal to marginal cost, i.e. P = MC.

7 However, a high own-price elasticity of demand (in absolute terms) does not necessarily imply the absence of substantial market power. Such a result would show that the firm is not able to profitably increase price beyond the present price – it does not, in itself, show that the firm has not, in the past, increased price substantially above the cost of production.

8 The reduction in demand caused by these increased prices comes from two sources – demand substitution by consumers and supply substitution by new competitors. Demand substitution represents the reduction in consumer demand caused by the increased prices and supply substitution by new competitors represents the response of new competitors in terms of producing new (relatively close substitute) products in response to the increased prices.

9 G. Stigler, *The Organisation of Industry*, Irwin, 1968.

10 J. Bain, *Barriers to New Competition*, Harvard University Press, 1956.

11 The breadth (or scope) of a natural monopoly may be determined by the existence, and degree of, so-called economies of scope. Technically, economies of scope arise if, $C(Q_A, Q_B) < C(Q_A,0) + C(0,Q_B)$, where A and B represent different products. Economies of scope arise where it is cheaper for one firm to produce two different products than it is for two firms to each produce one of the two products; wool and mutton offers an obvious example. The provision of a national electricity grid and the provision of a national natural gas grid represent a possible example in the context of natural monopolies.

12 The term 'X-inefficiency' is used to denote a situation in which the costs of a monopolist are higher than the costs of a perfectly competitive firm.

CHAPTER 10

1 Simon Kuznets, *Economic Growth and Structure: Selected Essays*, Heinemann, 1966.

2 Paul Ormerod, *The Death of Economics*, Faber and Faber, 1995.

3 Quesnay was one of the leading physiocrats (see Chapter 11 for an explanation on the physiocrats) of the eighteenth century. His main work *Tableau Économique (Economic Table)* was published in 1758. This table analysed the circulation of wealth in the economy and it is believed that it was one of the first models to describe the macroeconomy in a circular flow fashion.

4　Kuznets' contribution to macroeconomics was recognised by the profession in 1971 when he was awarded the Nobel prize in economics for his work on accounting and measurement techniques. At the same time, work was been carried out in the UK on the construction of the national accounts by Richard Stone and James Meade. In recognition of his work Stone received the 1984 Nobel prize in economics.

5　Many commentators argue that Irish GDP is artificially inflated because of 'transfer pricing'. Transfer pricing refers to a practice of transferring tax liabilities abroad. This is where multinational corporations use their foreign subsidiaries that operate in a low tax jurisdiction (e.g. Ireland) to reduce their overall tax burden. Partially manufactured inputs, manufactured by a subsidiary in another country, are imported into Ireland. Some processing occurs in this country and the intermediate or final good is exported. The 'value added' by the manufacturing process which takes place in Ireland is inflated to take advantage of the low Irish corporate tax rate. In doing so, the multinationals minimise their tax bill. The Irish measure of GDP is overvalued as a result of this practice.

6　E. Friedman, S. Johnson, D. Kaufman, P. Zoido-Lobarton,*Dodging the Grabbing Hand; The Determinants of Unofficial Activity in 69 Countries*, 1999.

7　In more recent times, national statistics offices have tried to incorporate an evasion adjustment into their calculation of GDP in order to capture activity in the hidden economy.

8　Economists and sociologists have attempted to develop satisfactory measures of economic and social wellbeing. A review of the international research is included in S. Scott, B. Nolan and T. Fahey, *Formulating Environmental and Social Indicators for Sustainable Development*, Economic and Social Research Institute, 1996.

9　T. Callan, R. Layte, B. Nolan, D. Watson, C. T. Whelan, J. Williams and B. Maitre, *Monitoring Poverty Trends*, June 1999. Research commissioned by the Department of Social, Community and Family Affairs and the Combat Poverty Agency and undertaken by the ESRI. Dublin: The Stationery Office and the Combat Poverty Agency.

10　A. B. Atkinson, L. Rainwater, and T. M. Smeeding, *Income Distribution in OECD Countries: Evidence from the Luxembourg Income Study*, OECD, 1995; V. J. Verma, *Robustness and Comparability in Income Distribution Statistics*, Stockholm, 1998.

11　Tim Callan and Brian Nolan, 'Income Inequality in Ireland in the 1980s and 1990s', in F. Barry, editor, *Understanding Ireland's Economic Growth*, Macmillan, 1999.

12　World Bank, *World Development Report, 1998/99*, 1999.

13　James Tobin was a member of President Kennedy's Council of Economic Advisers and a winner of the Nobel prize in economics in 1981. William Nordhaus served as a member of President Carter's Council of Economic Advisers from 1977 to 1979.

CHAPTER 11

1　J. R. Hicks, 'Mr. Keynes and the "Classics"; A Suggested Interpretation', *Econometrica*, 5, April 1937.

2　Quoted by Benjamin Higgins, *What do Economists Know?*, Melbourne University Press, 1951.

3　It is generally believed that Keynes got his inspiration for the title of *The General Theory* from Einstein's general theory of relativity. The classical doctrine was a special case in economics that held under specific conditions with Keynes' analysis being described as the general case just as Sir Isaac Newton's (also a Professor at Cambridge University) classical Newtonian mechanics was a special case of Einstein's General Theory. This general/special case relationship and his criticism of the special case are evident from the opening words of *The General Theory*: 'I shall argue that the postulates of the classical theory are applicable to a special case only and not to the general case, the situation which it assumes being a limited point of the possible positions of equilibrium. Moreover, the characteristics of the special case assumed by the classical theory happen not to be those of the economic society in which we actually live, with the result that its teaching is misleading and disastrous if we attempt to apply it to the facts of experience.' *The General Theory of Employment, Interest and Money*, Macmillan, 1936.

4   Quoted in R. F. Harrod, *The Life of John Maynard Keynes*, Macmillan, 1951.
5   J. M. Keynes, *The General Theory of Employment, Interest and Money*.
6   Letter to George Bernard Shaw, 1 January 1935.
7   The 1944 UK White Paper on *Employment Policy* was also heavily influenced by the Beveridge Report of 1942. The welfare state as we know it today has its origins in the writings of Lord Beveridge.
8   A similar crash occurred on Monday, 19 October 1987 when the Dow Jones Industrial average on Wall Street fell 508 points and in the process wiped over 22% off share values. This collapse on Black Monday was almost double the drop on the worst day of the 1929 crash. In London £50 billion, or 10%, was wiped off the value of publicly-quoted companies. The major difference between the 1929 crash and the 1987 crash was not the extent of the collapse on any one day but the economic decline that followed. The first crash was followed by the Great Depression whereas a similar downturn in economic activity was avoided after the second crash of 1987. This was due to the deliberate actions taken by the authorities after October 1987.
9   'The Past', *Business Week*, 3, September 1979.
10 The actual responses from the US and the UK administrations varied. In Washington President Hoover requested extra funds from Congress for a federal programme to create jobs. Yet in the depths of the depression, he also increased taxes, justifying it by the need to balance the federal budget. In fact, Hoover was criticised by his opponent, Franklin Roosevelt, in the election of 1932 for not cutting government expenditure and for failing to balance the budget (Roosevelt himself was to oversee some 'Keynesian-style' policies in the second period of the New Deal). In London the Labour government announced a public works programme. Opposition parties were critical of the government's response and called for urgent action on the jobs front. In particular the Liberals, led by Lloyd George, proposed an increase in the amount of public works programmes. He was advised by a young radical economist by the name of John Maynard Keynes. The advice given was based on the model of income determination (see Section 12.1).
11 Keynes, *The General Theory of Employment, Interest and Money*.
12 Ibid.
13 J. M. Keynes, *A Tract on Monetary Reform*, Macmillan, 1923.

CHAPTER 12

1   L. Tarshis, 'Keynesian Revolution' in *The New Palgrave: A Dictionary of Economics* edited by J. Eatwell, M. Milgate, P. Newman, 3, Macmillan, 1987.
2   Keynes, 'National Self-Sufficiency', *Studies*, 22, 1933.
3   Keynes, *The General Theory of Employment, Interest and Money*.
4   The terms 'aggregate demand' and 'total expenditure' are also used to describe the aggregate expenditure function. We use aggregate expenditure rather than aggregate demand in order to avoid confusion with the aggregate demand curve which is derived and explained in Chapter 16.
5   In order to keep our model simple we assume that taxes are zero (T = 0). A more complex analysis would incorporate taxes as autonomous (T = $\bar{T}$) or as a function of income (T = tY).
6   Keynes, *The General Theory of Employment, Interest and Money*.
7   The equation

$$€1,000 + €750 + €562.50 + €421.875 + €316.40625 + \ldots$$

can be written as

$$€1,000 + (€1,000 × .75) + (€1,000 × <.75^2>) + (€1,000 × <.75^3>) + (€1,000 × <.75^4>) + . . .$$
$$= €1,000 (1 + <.75> + <.75^2> + <.75^3> + <.75^4> + . . .)$$

8   Infinite geometric progressions can be summed if the absolute value of the multiplying coefficient is less than 1. In this case the sum of the infinite series $1 + b + b^2 + b^3 + b^4 . . .$ is equal to $\frac{1}{1 - b}$. From our description of the MPC we know it to be less than 1. Our series can be summed and in this particular case it adds to 4. Appendix 12.3 contains the formal derivation of the Keynesian multiplier.

9   The new equilibrium level of income can be calculated by using the formula as derived in the text. In this case:

$$\bar{A} = \bar{C} + \bar{I} + \bar{G} = 50 + 100 + 90 = €240$$
$$b = .75$$

Thus,

$$Y = \bar{A} × \frac{1}{1 - b} = 240 × \frac{1}{1 - .75} = 240 × 4 = £960.$$

10   This contrasts sharply with those economists who argue that inappropriate monetary policy by the Fed was the significant factor in explaining the Great Depression of the 1930s. A good account of this view is given by Milton and Rose Friedman in *Free to Choose*, Penguin, 1980.

11   If consumer expenditure is determined by disposable income (gross income minus taxation), the multiplier is equal to $\frac{1}{MPS + MPM + bMPT}$.

12   These values are taken from Walsh and Leddin's *The Macroeconomy of Ireland*. Norton's estimates are slightly different. For more, read B. Walsh and A. Leddin, *The Macroeconomy of Ireland*, 4th edition, Gill & Macmillan, 1998; and D. Norton, *Economics for an Open Economy: Ireland*, Oak Tree Press in association with Graduate School of Business UCD, 1994.

13   The relatively small size of the Keynesian multiplier for small open economies was noted as far back as 1956 by T. K. Whitaker when he wrote "In the real world, however, there are few, if any, completely isolated economies and the effects of the creation of new incomes are, therefore, not wholly retained within the system", 'Capital Formation, Saving and Economic Progress', reprinted in *Interests*, Institute of Public Administration, 1983. O. Katsiaouni came to the same conclusion in his paper 'Planning in a Small Economy: The Republic of Ireland' read to the Statistical and Social Inquiry Society of Ireland in May 1978. He explicitly referred to the Irish situation when he wrote "demand management, thus is rendered ineffectual . . ." Des Norton emphasises the point in his open economy textbook *Economics for an Open Economy: Ireland*. He writes "The tax leakage aside, Ireland's high marginal propensity to import explains why national income multipliers for the small open economy of Ireland are quite low." Finally, on account of a high MPM, a domestic fiscal boost may only succeed in aggravating the trade balance between Ireland and the rest of the world (see Chapter 15).

14   Budgets are to be distinguished from plans or programmes. In Ireland the relationship between the annual budget and government plans has been, at times, rather loose and ambiguous. Another component of fiscal policy is the Book of Estimates. The expenditure estimates are published in advance of the Budget. It shows predicted current government spending for the fiscal year. With so much information available prior to the publication of the Budget, Budget day itself has declined in importance.

15 The first capital budget was introduced by Patrick McGilligan, the Finance Minister, in 1950. Some economic commentators view this as the first evidence of Keynes' influence on the Irish budgetary process. In terms of personalities, Patrick Lynch (Professor of Political Economy at UCD) was one of the first Irish academics to espouse Keynesian economics. On a political level, it was Sean Lemass (former Taoiseach) who enthusiastically embraced the economics of Keynes. T. K. Whitaker, the person primarily responsible for the First Programme for Economic Expansion, devoted a section to the Keynesian multiplier in his seminal paper 'Capital Formation, Saving and Economic Progress' of 1956. Interestingly, two of the people who were involved in a debate on 'full-employment' back in April 1945 at the Statistical and Social Inquiry Society of Ireland were Patrick Lynch and T. K. Whitaker. It is also far from coincidental that the public speech given by the then Taoiseach, John A. Costello, in 1949 on the need for a sufficient level of demand in the economy was drafted by Patrick Lynch, his adviser.

16 The responsibility for managing the National Debt has changed hands from the Department of Finance to the National Treasury Management Agency (NTMA).

17 The 'business cycle' is the term used to explain fluctuations in the level of national income. Terms such as troughs, peaks, booms, slumps, recession, depression and recovery relate to different phases of the business cycle. The business cycle is a well-established economic phenomenon, observed since the industrial revolution. However, there is little consensus among economists and academics on the causes of such fluctuations. The one economic factor, however, which is constantly referred to in the literature on business cycles is investment expenditure and its inherent volatility. This suggests a role for government policy, which is aimed at stabilising the economy close to its potential output level. This is referred to as stabilisation policy. This is simply a collective term to describe various short-term demand-side policies such as fiscal, monetary, incomes and exchange rate policy which attempt to smooth out fluctuations in output and keep the actual level of output close to its potential level, i.e. the output level that results in the full employment of resources.

18 This does not suggest that Keynes, a former member of the Apostles and the Bloomsbury group which advocated personal freedom and liberty, approved of Hitler's authoritarian methods. Solving unemployment at the expense of freedom was not to be tolerated, according to Keynes.

19 The Phillips curve depicts the relationship between the unemployment rate and wage inflation. Supporters of Keynesian economics who were disenchanted with the simple fixed-price Keynesian model used this concept to develop a more sophisticated theory of inflation and explain how price changes were related to the changes in demand, output and unemployment. The Phillips curve is explained in Appendix 17.1.

20 Whereas the Labour party in Ireland was constrained in its use of fiscal policy by the Maastricht criteria, President Clinton disappointed many of his supporters by adopting more 'conservative-style' policies.

21 A good example of this was the advice given by Keynes at the first Finlay lecture in UCD in 1933. In his address 'National Self-Sufficiency' he congratulated the De Valera government in its commitment to maintaining protectionism in order to support indigenous industry. Almost seventy years later, the same advice would be rejected by the vast majority of the economics profession, even if given by Keynes. This article can be found in *Studies*, 22, 1933.

22 This is not to suggest that Keynesian ideas lacked support in Ireland before the 1970s. In fact, Keynes had many followers in Ireland, including Sean Lemass, Taoiseach from 1959 to 1966. Lemass had a keen interest in economics. Before he ever entered politics he had read many books on Keynes and his policies. However, Lemass was more interested in adopting Keynesian policies to enhance the long-term development of the country. It was not until the early 1970s that short-term Keynesian policies were adopted in Ireland. To find out more about Lemass and his interest in economics in general and Keynes in particular read M. O'Sullivan, *Sean Lemass: A Biography*, Blackwater Press, 1995.

23 *Budget 1972*, Government Publications Office, 1972.

24 *Budget 1976*, Government Publications Office, 1976.

25 The Tallaght Strategy, of supporting the government's austere fiscal measures, receives its name because it began with a speech given by the then leader of the main opposition party, Mr Alan Dukes, in Tallaght, Dublin.

26 The phrase 'Expansionary Fiscal Contraction' originated from work done by F. Giavazzi and M. Pagano at the University of Bologna in 1990.

CHAPTER 13

1 George Bernard Shaw, *John Bull's Other Island: and Major Barbara, Also How He Lied to Her Husband*, Constable, 1911.

2 J. R. Hicks, *Critical Essays in Monetary Theory*, Clarendon Press, 1967.

3 This system dates back to the Middle Ages when people deposited gold with goldsmiths. Over time, goldsmiths noticed that it was unlikely that all depositors would withdraw their gold all at once. On recognising this, they kept some gold in reserve to meet the immediate demands of their depositors. The remainder was lent out to new clients. This is the way in which the early banking system developed.

4 This assumption is rather restrictive. In reality, a portion of the loan may not find its way back into the banking system but instead end up in the form of cash. This implies that the subsequent increase in the money supply will not be as large as originally suggested. This curtailment in the money creation process may also happen if the bank decides to keep reserves over and above the minimum amount that is required by law. See Appendix 13.1 on the money multiplier.

5 Required reserve ratios are common features in any modern banking system. Pre-1999, credit institutions in Ireland were required to maintain a reserve ratio, called the 'liquidity' ratio. The primary liquidity ratio is the ratio of required holdings of primary liquid assets to relevant resources. Its purpose when introduced in 1972 was to avoid a 'run' on the banking system and also to control the amount of lending. Although they are an essential part of monetary policy, they should also be seen as prudential protection for depositors. Since the launch of the euro, credit institutions across the participating member states are subject to reserve requirements, imposed by the Eurosystem.

    Credit institutions are continually faced with the conflict between profitability and liquidity where liquidity is the ease with which an asset can be converted into cash without financial loss. In order for financial institutions to make a profit, they must engage in the act of lending. On the other hand, credit institutions must always be ready to meet the daily demands of their clients, both personal and corporate. Maintenance of a reserve ratio helps to resolve this conflict and in doing so, contributes to a relatively secure banking system.

6 Its derivation is similar to the derivation of the expenditure multiplier. The sum of the created deposits forms a geometric series. It can be proven that this sum is equal to the reciprocal of the reserve ratio. This is called the deposit multiplier. With 10% kept in reserves, reserves increase by €1,000. Hence, bank deposits increase by €10,000. In practice, the multiplier will be much smaller than the above example suggests. This is because the public is likely to hold some of their borrowings in the form of cash. Also, some banks may decide to hold a greater amount of their deposits on reserve than is generally required.

7 Firms can also finance capital goods from retained earnings. However, their decision will still be determined by the interest rate. We can think of the interest rate as the opportunity cost. The opportunity cost of purchasing capital goods is the best opportunity forgone. If the interest rate is high, the firm could earn the market rate of interest. If the firm earns more by lending than investing, we must assume that at higher rates of interest, their demand for capital goods is low.

8   This assertion depends on the relative strengths of substitution and income effects arising from changes in interest rates. See Chapter 7 for a similar discussion.

9   A bond or a fixed-interest security is a government IOU. It is an instrument in which one party (the debtor/borrower) promises to repay the other party (lender/investor) the amount borrowed plus interest. They can be bought or sold on the equity (capital) market. Bonds are known as gilts in the UK and Ireland.

10 Keynes, *The General Theory of Employment, Interest and Money*.

11 The negative relationship that exists between the price of a bond and the interest rate can be explained by defining the price of a bond as the present value of a set of future cash flows. The lower the interest rate that is earned on any sum invested today, the greater is the amount that needs to be invested (today) in order to realise a specified value (in the future). Hence, for a given future value at some specified time in the future, the lower the interest rate, the higher the present value. By now applying the definition as above, we observe the negative relationship that exists between interest rates and the price of a bond.

12 The Swedish Central Bank is the oldest, dating back to 1668. The Bank of England was established shortly afterwards in 1694. In contrast, the US Federal Reserve System ('Fed' for short) was set up in 1913. The Central Bank of Ireland was established as recently as 1943. In 1998, The European Central Bank was formally established.

13 The Irish pound has a chequered history. We begin in 1689 when an exchange rate of 13:12 was set for the Irish pound/British pound. In 1826 the two currencies were amalgamated. Over a century later, the Banking Commission of 1927 established the Saorstat pound, which was set at parity with sterling. Parity was maintained until 1979 when the Irish pound became a member, unlike the British pound, of the Exchange Rate Mechanism (ERM) in the European Monetary System. With this the 153-year, one-for-one, fixed link with sterling ended. In January 1999, the Irish pound became irrevocably fixed to the euro, effectively bringing about the demise of the Irish pound. By 2002, Irish notes and coins will be replaced by euro notes and coins.

14 We know from the discussion on money creation that the amount of money which the banking system can create is a multiple of the amount of reserves that they hold. Hence, if the monetary authorities can control the amount of reserves which the banks hold, they can then regulate the amount of money which they can create. For example, by simply creating more reserves, it provides the banks with the opportunity to make more loans and consequently more deposits. As a result, money supply increases. The three tools of monetary policy which are described in the chapter are, in effect, ways of controlling the supply of reserves rather than the supply of money, *per se*.

15 The Keynesian cross diagram which we used in the previous chapter was based on the assumption that investment is exogenous. In this analysis investment is dependent on the rate of interest. Panel (b) depicts this relationship between interest rates and investment. Consequently, there is an adjustment to the AE function. There is more material on this in the next chapter.

16 D. Romer, 'Comment on Bosworth', *The Brookings Papers on Economic Activity*, no. 1, 1989.

17 Some of the material used to describe the ineffectiveness of monetary policy for a SOE is unfamiliar. A more detailed explanation of this and other material is contained in Chapter 15.

18 One party to the contract agrees to the spot purchase (sale) of one currency for another. This is one part of the swap. The other part of the swap is the forward sale (purchase).

19 Paul Tansey, 'Money Matters', *Magill*, August 1989.

20 Maurice Doyle, 'Monetary Policy – The Hidden Stabiliser', *Central Bank Annual Report 1988*, Spring 1989.

21 The objective of monetary policy in Ireland was price stability. There was no commitment to other goals. In other countries, the US for example, central banks are committed to achieving a number of objectives, including low inflation, low unemployment and high growth rates.

22 'Monetary Policy Statement 1992', *Central Bank Report*, Spring 1992.

23 Officially, the currencies of the EU member states that do not participate in the single currency are linked to the euro by means of the new Exchange Rate Mechanism (ERM II), membership of which is voluntary.

24 In the future we will need to assess whether or not the governors of the national central banks are willing to put the interests of the EU above their national interests, particularly if the two interests conflict.

25 The reference value of 4.5% per annum was derived from the quantity theory of money relationship. MV = PY, which is explained in Chapter 17. Using the definition of price stability as defined by the ECB and the assumptions for trend GDP growth and M3 income velocity, a value for M3 growth of 4.5% results. See the ECB *Monthly Bulletin* November 2000 for a detailed explanation.

26 A useful reference for monetary policy in the context of European monetary union is Paul De Grauwe, *The Economics of Monetary Union*, Oxford University Press, 2000.

CHAPTER 14

1 Christopher Bliss, 'John R. Hicks' in *The New Palgrave: A Dictionary of Economics*.

2 Jordi Gali, 'How Well Does the IS-LM Model Fit Postwar U.S. Data?', *Quarterly Journal of Economics*, 67, May 1992.

3 Hicks has received most of the credit for the development of the IS/LM framework and, as a result, for spreading the Keynesian doctrine among his contemporaries and to the general public. Although Alvin Hansen did not receive the same acknowledgments his contribution was of no lesser importance. His book succeeded in spreading Keynes' ideas to countless academic institutions and universities throughout the US. See A. Hansen, *A Guide to Keynes*, McGraw-Hill, 1953.

4 Prices are incorporated into the macro model in Chapter 16, and again in Chapter 17.

5 We know from Chapter 12 that equilibrium in the goods market (without the government sector) can be expressed in terms of investment and savings. It is this view of equilibrium (investment, I = savings, S) which gives us the name the IS curve. This simple injections-leakages approach is useful in explaining the negative relationship that exists between interest rates and income levels in the goods market. The lower interest rate level induces lower savings and higher investment. This increase in investment causes a multiplier effect which will result in higher income levels. Hence, with an initial reduction in interest rates, equilibrium is maintained in the goods market (I = S) through a subsequent increase in national income.

6 With interest rates as an explanatory variable, the resulting AE function is different from that presented in Chapter 12. In Chapter 12, the AE function was of the form $AE = \bar{A} + bY$. In this chapter the AE function is of the form $AE = \bar{A} - di + bY$ (see Figure 14.2). The algebraic derivation of this function is contained in Appendix 14.1.

7 In the analysis of the money market, we are concerned with the supply of real balances $(\frac{\bar{M}}{P})$. Hence, our discussion is limited to the real money stock (and not nominal money supply, M_s) and the real money supply curve.

8 This can be explained by reference to the upper panel (the Keynesian cross diagram) of Figure 14.2. Point A would coincide with a point corresponding to income level Y^0 and interest rate level i^1. This point lies on a higher aggregate expenditure curve than AE^0. This means that the demand for goods exceeds the level of output, i.e. there is an excess demand for goods.

9 This can be explained by reference to the right-hand panel (the money market diagram) of Figure 14.3. Point A would coincide with a point corresponding to interest rate, i^1 and

an income level, Y^0. This point lies on a lower money demand curve than $L(Y^1)$. With the demand for money less than the supply of money, an excess supply of money will result.

10 An important aspect of expansionary fiscal policy is the method of financing. Two methods exist. First, the government can finance the additional spending through an expansion of the money supply. This method is called monetary financing. Second, additional spending can be financed by issuing government bonds or gilts to the non-bank public. This method is commonly known as bond financing. The effectiveness of expansionary fiscal policy may depend on whether the additional spending is monetary or bond financed. For example, additional spending financed from monetary sources tends to be accompanied by increases in the money supply. With no subsequent rise in interest rates, the risk of crowding out is reduced. Alternatively, additional spending financed by the sale of bonds to the non-bank public may push interest rates higher.

11 The presentation of expansionary fiscal policy in this format is helpful. For example, the effectiveness of fiscal policy depends largely on the strength of each link in the chain and, in particular, between [increases Y → increases L] and [increases i → reduces I]. As an exercise the student should change the slope of the LM curve to see the impact on interest rates and national income.

12 In Chapter 16 we will see that fiscal expansion can lead to higher inflation. This possibility is not considered here because the IS/LM is a fixed-price model.

CHAPTER 15

1 Margaret Thatcher, *The Downing Street Years*, HarperCollins Publishers, 1993.

2 Bernard Connolly, *The Rotten Heart Of Europe*, Faber and Faber, 1995.

3 The trade balance must be distinguished from the terms of trade which is simply the ratio of export prices to import prices, i.e. it reflects relative prices Px/Py. An improvement in the terms of trade implies that the prices of exports have risen relative to the prices of imports. In other words, we need to export less in order to secure a given quantity of imports.

4 With two currencies involved, there are two ways to express the exchange rate. We can express it as the number of euros per one dollar or as the number of dollars per one euro. On this side of the Atlantic it is customary to express the €/US$ exchange rate as the number of dollars per one euro. The euro is called the base currency and the US dollar is called the counter currency.

5 In particular, we make no explicit reference in the text to the role that the price elasticity of demand for imports plays in determining the supply of the base currency. The supply curve will only appear as a 'normal' upward sloping curve if the demand for imports is elastic, i.e. a lower exchange rate (higher import prices) leads to less imports and hence a lower quantity of euros supplied. This assumption is implicit in the text when we discuss the supply of euros. In the case of inelastic demand, the supply curve will have a negative slope. Norton in his book *Economics for an Open Economy: Ireland* points out that this possibility could arise if the 'Home' country were ' . . . a large country relative to the rest of the world'. A discussion on the price elasticity of demand for imports (and exports) usually leads to some debate on the related topics of the J-curve effect and the Marshall-Lerner condition. A good description of both is included in Sloman's *Economics*, 4th edition, Prentice Hall, 2000.

6 Market participants, in the belief that the value of the euro will be lower, sell the euro today (known as selling short) with the intention of buying it back some time in the future at a lower rate. If this happens, the traders are left with a tidy profit from this euro trade.

7 The deficits and surpluses recorded in the balance of payments are an indicator of whether a country is a net borrower from or a lender to the rest of the world. For example, under a flexible exchange rate system a current account deficit is matched by a surplus in the capital account. The deficit in the current account is financed by either running down its

8 assets or borrowing from abroad. The latter is done by the sale of bonds and other financial assets, recorded in the capital account as a surplus. This signals that the country is a net borrower from the rest of the world. A country is defined as a net debtor when it owes more to the rest of the world than it is owed; a net creditor is owed more from the rest of the world than it owes.

8 The two great fixed exchange rate systems were the Gold Standard (1815–1914) and the Bretton Woods system (1945–71). The Gold Standard fixed the value of each participating currency in terms of gold. The Bretton Woods system, set up at the end of World War II, fixed all currencies in terms of the dollar. Not surprisingly, it was also called the Dollar Exchange Standard. An interesting feature of the Bretton Woods system was the adjustable peg, i.e. although currencies were pegged to each other, adjustments were permitted in the event of persistent imbalances.

9 The US dollar is an example of a managed float. The value of the dollar was the main topic for consideration at both the Plaza Accord (1985) and the Louvre Agreement (1987). The former acknowledged that the dollar was overvalued and set as its aim a reduction in the value of the US dollar. The Louvre Agreement, although less concerned with the dollar's value, acknowledged the danger of volatile foreign exchange markets and called for greater co-ordination of monetary policy in order to provide a more stable economic environment.

10 'The Exchange-Rate Mechanism of the European Monetary System', *Central Bank Annual Report 1978*, Spring 1979. This article includes a detailed discussion on how the ERM operated.

11 From 1979 to 1987 the ERM operated as an adjustable peg system. Realignments were quite common in those early years. The convergence of many economic indicators such as interest rates, government borrowing and inflation rates among member states was partly responsible for the change in the system to a semi-fixed exchange rate system by the late 1980s. Until the autumn of 1992, member states were reluctant to realign their currencies. By August 1993, the bands of fluctuation were widened to 15% either way for all but two member states. In reality, the ERM had become more of a managed floating system rather than a semi-fixed exchange rate system.

12 The German mark is taken as an example because in practice it played the same central role within the ERM as the dollar played in the Bretton Woods system. Over the years the German mark assumed the role of an anchor currency.

13 'Hedging' is practised by importers and exporters in order to reduce possible losses arising from fluctuations in the exchange rate. For example, suppose the Galway dealership for Toyota contracts for 10 billion yen of automobiles and has to pay for them in 30 days. If the euro depreciates against the Japanese yen during these 30 days, the cost of the automobiles in euros will increase. To ensure against an exchange rate loss the automobile dealer contracts to buy 10 billion yen at the forward exchange rate. This protects the dealer against loss due to depreciation. As he is locked into an agreement at a specified rate, the automobile dealer will not benefit from an appreciation of the euro *vis-à-vis* the Japanese yen. The practice of hedging involves a transaction cost. It is generally not used by small firms.

14 Economic and social cohesion is an essential component of monetary union and the single currency. In practice, this involves the transfer of funds from the wealthy nations to the weaker nations. Ireland has benefited substantially from these EU funds. For years, Ireland was the largest net beneficiary per head of EU funding. These funds have been used in the areas of human resources, agriculture, industry and physical infrastructure. Many worthwhile projects, beyond the means of the Irish state and the private sector, have been co-financed from the EU exchequer.

15 On 1 January 2002 (e-day), Euro notes and coins will go into circulation. Under EU law, there can be a dual circulation period of up to six months at most. As this period can be shortened by national law, the Euro Changeover Board of Ireland has recommended that

this period should end on 9 February 2002. This will mean that the legal tender status for Irish notes and coins will be withdrawn.

16 The Council and Commission of the European Communities, *The Treaty on European Union*, Office for Official Publications of the European Communities, 1992.

17 Honohan, Patrick, 'Fiscal Adjustment and Disinflation in Ireland: Setting the Macro Basis of Economic Recovery and Expansion, in F. Barry, editor, *Understanding Ireland's Economic Growth*, Macmillan, 1999.

18 This division, incidentally, is similar to the split in the fortunes of the ERM itself. In the first few years realignments were quite common, exchange rates were volatile and little or no convergence between the member states took place. By the late 1980s things had changed. Realignments were fewer, exchange rates were stable and greater convergence was evident between member states. In fact, many commentators viewed the ERM by the turn of the decade as a *de facto* fixed exchange rate system. We take 1992 as an end point because of the currency crisis and its effect on the ERM.

19 A comprehensive analysis of the costs and benefits to Ireland of membership in the EMU was carried out by the Economic and Social Research Institute. For more, read *Economic Implications for Ireland of EMU*, edited by T. Baker, J. FitzGerald and P. Honohan, Economic and Social Research Institute, no. 28, July 1996. For alternate conclusions, see P. Neary and R. Thom, *Punts, Pounds and Euros*, Centre for Economic Research UCD; and F. Barry, 'The Dangers for Ireland of an EMU without the UK: some Calibration Results', *Economic and Social Review*, 1997.

20 The existence of a gap between the richest nations and the poorest member states of the EU has always been a lively issue. The structural funds and the EU commitment to 'economic and social cohesion' arose out of the debate on the 'wealth gap'. The progress of the peripheral countries, as a group, has been patchy. Ireland has achieved most of the four (the others being Spain, Portugal and Greece) in the past twenty-five years. In 1975 Ireland's GDP per capita was 64.1% of the EU average. In 1999 it was in excess of 100% according to the European Commission.

21 A weaker version of PPP is written as follows:

$$\Delta E = \Delta P_{US} - \Delta P_{UK}$$

where

$$\Delta E = \text{the change in the exchange rate}$$
$$\Delta P_{US} = \text{change in the US price level, i.e. US inflation rate}$$
$$\Delta P_{UK} = \text{change in the UK price level, i.e. UK inflation rate.}$$

This weaker version states that changes in the exchange rate arise out of inflation rate differentials.

22 'Big MacCurrencies', *The Economist*, 29 April 2000. $2.51 is actually the average price of a Big Mac in four American cities, of which one is New York. Ideally, an internationally traded good should be used in any discussion of PPP.

23 *The New Palgrave: A Dictionary of Economics.*

CHAPTER 16

1 Alan S. Blinder, 'Hard Heads, Soft Hearts', *Tough-Minded Economics for a Just Society*, Addison-Wesley, 1987.

2 Mark Brownrigg, *Understanding the Economy*, Addison-Wesley, 1990. A good description of supply-side economics is given in Chapter 10 of this textbook.

3 The real balance effect owes its prominence in the economics literature to A. C. Pigou and Donald Patinkin who independently worked on the existence of such an effect.

4　We generally discuss the negative aspects of government policy when we discuss the 'supply side'. For example, according to economists who focus on the supply side, demand-management policy is ineffective and inflationary. However, there are some government policies which are advocated by these economists. 'Positive' supply-side policies promote the research and adoption of new technologies and programmes to provide relevant training opportunities for labour. These measures actually push the AS curve out and to the right, increasing the potential output of the economy.

5　At full employment, the economy is at a point on its production possibility frontier (see Chapter 1). Supply-side policies attempt to push out the boundaries of the nation's production possibility frontier. In other words, a rightward shift of the long-run AS curve is equivalent to an outward shift of the production possibility frontier.

6　A. Protopapadakis, 'Supply-Side Economics: What Chance For Success?' in *The Supply-Side Solution* edited by B. Bartlett and T. P. Roth, Macmillan, 1983.

7　In response to the lacklustre performance of Irish industry during the 1980s, the then Minister of Industry and Commerce, Des O'Malley, established the Industrial Policy Review Group. Its role was to assess the performance of Irish industry and, in particular, Irish-owned companies and to recommend appropriate policy changes. The report entitled *A Time for Change: Industrial Policy for the 1990s* was published in January 1992 (Government Publications Office). It is commonly referred to as the *Culliton report*.

8　D. Ó Cearbhaill, 'The same, and more', *Fortnight*, February 1992.

9　Paul Tansey, *Ireland at Work; Economic Growth and the Labour Market 1987–1997*, Oak Tree Press, 1998.

CHAPTER 17

1　John F. Kennedy. Speech, 1962.

2　Benjamin Franklin, *Thoughts on Commercial Subjects*.

3　The Household Budget Survey is conducted by the CSO. Between 7,000 and 8,000 rural and urban households complete the survey which is designed to provide details concerning the allocation of their income.

4　M. Friedman, 'The Quantity Theory of Money – A Restatement', in *Studies in the Quantity Theory of Money*, Chicago University Press, 1956.

5　In this chapter, we draw the AS curve as a straight line. Our basic assumptions still hold.

6　Remember that the supply curve of labour is based on the assumption that work causes disutility. An increase in the real wage compensates for the disutility caused by work. For this reason, the relationship between the number of hours worked or the number of people working and the real wage is positive. Workers should be interested in their real wage, rather than their nominal wage because they are concerned about the quantity of goods and services which they can purchase.

7　Wincott Memorial lecture, London, 16 September 1970.

8　If the number of unemployed decreases by 5,000 between 2000 and 2001, the number of people counted at the end of 2001 is 5,000 less than the number of people counted at the end of 2000. However, 15,000 new people may have become unemployed because they lost their jobs, finished school or returned home from abroad and could not find employment. On the other hand, 20,000 people must have found jobs, retired from the labour force or emigrated. In other words, a small change in the stock of the unemployed may mask larger flows of people into and out of unemployment.

9　The natural rate of unemployment is a term used by monetarists and new classical economists. When the economy is at full employment, frictional unemployment is inevitable. The rate of unemployment associated with full employment is called the natural rate of unemployment. It is also the unemployment rate which is consistent with a stable rate of inflation, hence the name 'the non-accelerating inflation rate of unemployment' or simply NAIRU.

10 Marx and Keynes had very different views on the long-term prospects for the capitalist system. Whereas Keynes was largely optimistic about the future, Marx predicted a total collapse of the capitalist system. To date, Marx is wrong.

11 The insider-outsider theory is a relatively new way of looking at the behaviour of participants in the labour market. The insiders are those who already have jobs whereas the outsiders are those who are unemployed. Given the conservative nature of the labour market which confers advantages on the insiders at the expense of the outsiders, this model predicts no great change in the unemployment structure.

12 *The Jobs Crisis*, edited by Colm Keane, Mercier Press, 1993.

13 The increase in the price of oil was both price inflationary and demand deflationary for oil-importing countries, including Ireland. Expansionary fiscal policy only fuels inflation whereas contractionary fiscal policy slows down economic activity further. Policy-makers were faced with a dilemma. The Irish authorities opted for an expansion of fiscal policy. Yet, unemployment numbers increased, inflation rose, the budget deficit soared and the balance of payments deteriorated.

14 Although there are valid economic arguments in favour of borrowing to finance productive investment, there is less justification for borrowing to finance current spending. Current spending is usually financed out of tax revenue.

15 It is argued that for fiscal policy to be effective, it must be counter-cyclical. During the mid-1970s the Irish economy was experiencing strong growth. The domestic economy was benefiting from an increase in world trade. Hence, restrictive fiscal policy was required. The incumbent government, however, opted for an expansionary phase. In the early 1980s economic activity was sluggish. The international background was unfavourable. Yet, driven by the urgent need to restore order to the public finances, a highly contractionary fiscal policy was implemented. In both these periods Irish fiscal policy appeared to be pro-cyclical. Although the contractionary policy of the early 1980s was inappropriate on theoretical grounds, the Irish authorities were forced to practise fiscal rectitude because of the poor state of the public finances. In retrospect, the decision taken seems to have been the correct one. The same cannot be said for the experience of the mid-1970s. With the economy growing at a satisfactory rate, there was little or no need for a fiscal stimulus by the state. The long-term costs of such a policy outweighed the short-term gains.

16 The Coalition government of the early 1980s began to tackle the problem of the public finances. Both capital spending and taxation were targeted. Increases in capital spending were to be curtailed while at the same time tax rates were increased in order to boost revenue. Current spending was left largely intact. This policy mix, however, was flawed. Capital expenditure, assuming it is productive, is essential for the long-term prosperity of the economy. Moreover, capital expenditure was not the problem. The primary source of the high budget deficits was the growth in current expenditure. Yet the increases in current spending went largely unchecked. The increase in the tax rates was also considered as unhelpful. Tax rates were already penal. The revenue raised from the hike in the tax rates was not enough to compensate for the damage done to both the demand side and the supply side of the labour market.

17 There is considerable debate over each of these issues and their contribution to Irish unemployment. For example, the Irish authorities had little control over the level of interest rates. Hence, should blame be apportioned to our counterparts in Europe rather than to the monetary authorities in Ireland? The same argument applies to the value of the Irish pound. Membership of the ERM and the link with the German mark were helpful in achieving price stability. Was this achieved, however, at the cost of thousands of job losses? Finally, did the employed benefit, in terms of pay increases, at the expense of the

unemployed? Were the centralised pay agreements successful or was there a need for local wage bargaining given the high unemployment numbers?

18   The evidence of a link between replacement ratios and unemployment rates is not conclusive. For a synopsis of the international and Irish studies, read 'Implications of Incentives for Employment. A review of the Economic Evidence', in *Expert Working Group Report on the Integration of the Tax and Social Welfare Systems*, Government Publications Office, June 1996.

19   Paul Tansey, *Making the Irish Labour Market Work*, Gill & Macmillan, 1991.

20   Arthur Andersen & Co., 'Reform of the Irish Tax System from an Industrial Point of View', a report to the Industrial Policy Review Group. A table of the tax wedge for the different countries is reprinted in NESC No. 96, *A Strategy for Competitiveness, Growth and Employment*, National Economic and Social Council, November 1993.

21   *OECD Economic Surveys: Ireland, 1990/91*, Organisation for Economic Co-operation and Development, 1991.

22   Dermot McAleese, 'Solutions and Political Implications' in *The Dark Shadow of Unemployment in the Republic and Northern Ireland*, Studies, 82, no. 325, Spring 1993.

23   See M. Emerson, 'Regulation or Deregulation of the Labour Market', *European Economic Review*, 32, no. 4, 1988. In contrast, Goodhart claimed that Ireland, along with the UK and Denmark, were the 'three most *laissez-faire* countries when it comes to closures and sackings'. See D. Goodhart, 'Ground Rules for the Firing Squad', *Financial Times*, 15 February 1993. This view was endorsed by the OECD in their 1994 *Jobs Study* report.

24   Brendan Walsh has written extensively on this topic. Among his latest works include the following: *The Macroeconomics of Ireland* (1998), 4th edition with Anthony Leddin; 'What's in Store for the Celtic Tiger?' (1999) in the *Irish Banking Review*; and 'Cyclical and Structural Influences on Irish Unemployment' (2000) in *Oxford Economic Papers*.

25   Studies include G. Kenny, 'Economic growth in Ireland: Sources, Potential and Inflation', *CBI Bulletin*, Autumn 1996; J. Nugent, 'Corporate Profitability in Ireland: Overview and Determinants', *CBI Bulletin*, Winter 1998; OECD *Economic Surveys: Ireland, 1999*. An interesting account of Ireland's growth is given by F. Barry and N. Crafts in 'Some Comparative Aspects of Transformation', *Irish Banking Review*, 1999.

26   'Poorest of the Rich: A Survey of the Republic of Ireland', *The Economist*, 16 January 1988 and 'Europe's Shining Light', *The Economist*, 17 May 1997.

27   Adam Smith, *An Inquiry into the Nature and Causes of the Wealth of Nations*.

28   David Ricardo, *The Principles of Political Economy and Taxation*.

29   Eli Heckscher, *The Effect of Foreign Trade on the Distribution of Income*, Ekonomisk Tidskerift, 21, 1919. Bertil Ohlin, *Interregional and International Trade*, Harvard University Press, 1933.

30   W. M. Corden, *The Theory of Protection*, Clarendon Press, 1971.

31   W. M. Corden, *Trade Policy and Economic Welfare*, Clarendon Press, 1974.

32   Mancur Olson, *The Logic of Collective Action*, Harvard University Press, 1965.

33   Paul Krugman, 'Increasing Returns, Monopolistic Competition and International Trade', *Journal of International Economics*, 9, 1979. Also, 'Scale Economies, Product Differentiation and the Pattern of Trade', *American Economic Review*, 1980.

34   Of course it could be argued that these regions would have remained poor even if they were not engaged in free inter-regional trade. But if this were true, it merely serves to highlight that free trade will not necessarily bring great economic advancement to a region with poor resources.

35   A. W. Phillips, 'The Relation between Unemployment and the Rate of Change of Money Wages in the United Kingdom 1861–1957', *Economica*, 25, November 1958.

36   The theory of rational expectations dates from the early 1960s and to a seminal paper written by John Muth and entitled 'Rational Expectations and the Theory of Price Movements', *Econometrica*, 29, 1960.

37   J. M. Keynes, *A Tract on Monetary Reform*, Macmillan, 1923.

CHAPTER 18

1 J. K. Galbraith, *The Affluent Society*, Hamish Hamilton, 1958.

2 P. J. O'Rourke, *Eat the Rich*, Picador, 1998.

3 The concept of using stories to explain economic growth rather than relying solely on a formal model is advocated by David Colander in 'Telling Better Stories in Introductory Macro', *AEA Papers and Proceedings*, May 2000.

4 GDP per capita is used for most international comparisons rather than GNP per capita. For a full explanation of the difference between GNP and GDP see Chapter 10. For Ireland, GNP is the more accurate measurement because it measures the output of Irish firms and workers and it does not include some of the distorting effects of foreign companies using Ireland as an export base.

5 The table is derived from the Penn-World tables, version 5.6. Values for GDP per person and capital stock per worker are given in 1985 international prices. The capital stock per worker data only date back to 1965. The tables are available on-line at the following address: http://datacentre.chass.utoronto.ca/pwt/index.html.

6 Barry, Frank, 'Irish Growth in Historical and Theoretical Perspective', Chapter 2 in Frank Barry, editor, *Understanding Ireland's Economic Growth*, Macmillan, 1999. This idea will be discussed more in Section 18.3.

7 Robert Solow, 'A Contribution to the Theory of Economic Growth', *Quarterly Journal of Economics*, 70, February 1956.

8 For a brief synopsis of Robert M. Solow's life and contribution to economics, read P. Samuelson, 'Paul Robert Solow: An Affectionate Portrait', *Journal of Economic Perspectives*, Volume 3(3), Summer 1989.

9 *World Development Report 1999/2000*, The World Bank.

10 Edward Phelps, 'The Golden Rule of Accumulation: A Fable for Growthmen', *American Economic Review*, 51, September 1961.

11 The columns containing GNP/capita for 1998 and annual growth 1997–98 are from the *World Development Report 1999/2000* of the World Bank. The last column on the right was derived from the Penn-World tables version 5.6 and author's calculations. It lists the average annual growth in GDP. For most of the countries the difference between GDP and GNP is minor. Ireland is an exception and this will be discussed in Section 18.3. A few points should be made: a) Ethiopia growth only covers the years 1950–86. b) Germany's growth refers only to West Germany. c) Poland's growth covers only the years 1970–92. d) South Korea's growth is only for the years 1953–92.

12 The relationship between growth rates and doubling in GNP per capita illustrates the 'rule of 72'. Divide 72 by your annual growth rate and this yields the number of years it takes for GNP per capita to double. For example, an economy growing at 4% per year will double in size in 72 ÷ 4 = 18 years.

13 The Asian crisis of 1997 and the crisis in Mexico in 1994 were caused in part because international investors tried to pull their investments out of these countries very quickly. This mass exit of money caused the currencies to fall drastically in value.

14 In fact, technology is so important that one major variation of the Solow growth model includes technology and the rate of growth in national income per capita equals the rate of technological growth.

15 Jeffrey Sachs, 'A new map of the world', *The Economist*, 24 June 2000.

16 Ibid.

17 Ibid.

18 De-industrialisation does not mean economic decline. On the contrary, there is evidence to suggest that it is an important step in a rich economy's development. See 'It's wise to deindustrialise', *The Economist*, 26 April 1997.

19   This point is made by Frank Barry, 'Irish Growth in Historical and Theoretical Perspective', Chapter 2 in Frank Barry, editor, *Understanding Ireland's Economic Growth*, Macmillan Press, 1999 and by Paul Krugman, 'Good News from Ireland: A Geographical Perspective', in Alan Gray, editor, *International Perspectives on the Irish Economy*, Indecon, 1997.

20   'Europe's tiger economy', *The Economist*, 17 May 1997 and 'Hot and Sticky in Ireland', *The Economist*, 29 July 2000. A note about automobiles: the introduction of the National Car Test for older cars probably hastened many automobile purchases. Nevertheless, by July 2000, County Galway had registered over 10,000 autos for the first time ever.

21   'Europe's tiger economy', *The Economist*, 17 May 1997.

22   Ibid.

23   Cormac Ó Gráda and Kevin O'Rourke, 'Economic miracle long time coming', *Irish Times, Business This Week*, 9 June 2000.

24   Ibid.

GLOSSARY OF TERMS

Absolute advantage A country has an absolute advantage if it can produce more of a commodity than any other country with the same amount of resources.

Aggregate demand is the total output which is demanded at each price level holding all other variables constant.

Aggregate demand curve This shows the level of national output demanded at different price levels.

Aggregate expenditure is the amount that households and firms plan to spend on goods and services.

Aggregate supply describes the total quantity of national output supplied by all producers at each level of price.

Aggregate supply curve It shows the output of GDP produced at different price levels.

Arbitrage refers to the buying and selling of goods in different markets in order to exploit price differentials and to make a riskless profit.

Arc elasticity measures the elasticity of demand over a price range using the midpoint or average price as the base.

Average product is the total output divided by the number of units of the variable input employed.

Average revenue is a firm's total revenue divided by the quantity sold.

Average total cost is total cost divided by the number of units produced.

Balance of payments It is a set of accounts showing all economic transactions between residents of the home country and the rest of the world in any one year.

Balance of payments capital and financial account This is a record of a country's inflows and outflows of capital or assets.

Balance of payments current account This records all visible and invisible trade.

Broad money supply is defined as M1 plus deposit account balances.

Budget line It illustrates the maximum combination of two goods that the consumer can purchase, given her level of income and prices.

Capital goods are durable assets used during the production process.

Capital stock is all of the capital goods controlled by a firm.

Cartel A group of firms in a particular market who collude on price and output decisions in an effort to earn monopoly profits.

Ceteris paribus means that all other variables are held constant.

Comparative advantage A country has a comparative advantage in producing a commodity if it can produce that commodity at a lower opportunity cost than any other country.

Complements are goods that are bought and consumed together. This implies that if the price of one good falls, demand for the other good increases and vice versa.

Concentration ratio measures the total market share of a given number of the largest firms.

Constant returns to scale exist when a change in inputs results in an equal change in output.

Consumer price index This index is designed to measure the average change in the level of the prices paid for consumer goods and services by all private households in the country.

Consumer surplus is the excess of what a person is willing to pay for a good over what the person actually pays.

Consumption function It shows consumer expenditure at different levels of income.

Cost push inflation occurs when the source of upward pressure on prices is the rising costs of the factors of production in the absence of any corresponding increase in productivity.

Cross-price elasticity measures the sensitivity of quantity demanded of one good to a change in the price of another good.

Deflation is a fall in the general level of prices.

Demand is the quantity of a good or service that consumers purchase at each conceivable price during a particular time period.

Demand, law of refers to the inverse or negative relationship between price and quantity demanded, *ceteris paribus*.

Demand management is the collective term used to explain various government policies which influence the level of aggregate expenditure in the economy.

Demand pull inflation occurs when the total demand for goods and services is greater than the total supply of goods and services.

Demand schedule A table which indicates the quantity of a particular good which consumers are willing to purchase at various prices during a specified time period.

Deposit multiplier The multiple by which deposits will increase for every unit increase in reserves.

Depreciation is the value of capital which has been used up during the production process.

Derived demand for an input means that it is not demanded for its own sake but for its use in the production of goods and services.

Devaluation refers to a reduction in the value of a currency *vis-à-vis* other currencies in a fixed or semi-fixed exchange rate regime.

Diminishing marginal utility, principle of It states that the more of a commodity we consume, the less extra satisfaction we gain.

Diminishing returns, law of means that if at least one factor is fixed, a point is reached when an additional unit of a variable factor adds less to total product than the previous unit.

Discount rate The rate which the Central Bank charges financial institutions that borrow from it for purposes of maintaining the reserve requirement.

Discounting is the process of reducing the future value of a sum of money or a flow of revenues to the present value.

Discretionary fiscal policy refers to deliberate, as opposed to automatic, changes in government expenditure or tax rates in order to influence national income.

Diseconomies of scale exist where an increase in the scale of production leads to higher costs per unit produced.

Disinflation is a reduction in the rate of inflation.

Double counting occurs if the expenditure on intermediate goods is included in the calculation of national output.

Economic profit is the difference between revenue and economic costs.

Economic rent is a payment in excess of the opportunity cost.

Economies of scale exist where an increase in the scale of production leads to lower costs per unit produced.

Effective exchange rate index for a currency is the weighted average of the value of the currency against its largest trading partners.

Elasticity measures the change in one variable in response to a change in another variable.

Equi-marginal principle This states that utility is maximised when the utility for the last euro spent on each good is the same.

Equilibrium implies a state of balance, a position from which there is no tendency to change

Exchange rate The exchange rate between two currencies is the price of one currency in term of another.

Exchequer Borrowing Requirement This is the total amount of money that the central government borrows in any one fiscal year if current and capital expenditure exceeds current and capital revenue.

Excise duties are imposed to discourage consumption and production of goods and services which have detrimental effects on individuals other than direct consumers or producers.

Expenditure multiplier It is the ratio of the change in income to the change in autonomous spending.

External reserves refer to the stock of foreign currency held by the Central Bank for the purpose of intervention in the foreign exchange market.

Externalities are positive or negative by-products of production or consumption decisions.

Factors of Production are the resources of an economy. They include land, labour, capital and enterprise.

First degree price discrimination occurs when every buyer is charged the maximum price that he is willing to pay.

Fiscal policy refers to the use of government expenditure and taxation in order to influence aggregate expenditure and, in turn, national output.

Fixed exchange rate system A system where member states' currencies are pegged to each other at rates which are usually agreed by their respective Central Banks.

Fixed incomes People are on fixed incomes if their income is set at a particular nominal amount which is not adjusted for inflation.

Flexible exchange rate system This operates on the basis of market forces whereby the exchange rate between two currencies is determined by demand and supply.

GDP at constant prices measures economic activity in the prices of a fixed or base year.

GDP at current prices is a measure of economic activity based on the current prices of the goods and services produced.

GDP deflator This is the ratio of nominal GDP to real GDP expressed as an index.

General Government Deficit is calculated by adding the EBR to the borrowings of local authorities and non-commercial state-sponsored bodies.

Giffen good A very inferior good with an upward sloping demand curve.

Golden Rule level of capital is the steady state with the highest level of consumption.

Gross domestic product is the value of all goods and services produced domestically in the economy, regardless of the nationality of the owners of the factors of production.

Gross national product is the value of all goods and services produced by a country's productive factors regardless of their geographical location.

Herfindahl-Hirschman index is the sum of the squared percentage share of all firms of the relevant variable in the market.

High-powered money is equal to currency plus reserves held by the Central Bank.

Income effect It is the adjustment of demand to a change in real income.

Income elasticity of demand measures the responsiveness of the quantity demanded for a good to a change in income.

Increasing marginal returns means that an additional unit of a variable factor adds more to total product than the previous unit.

Indifference curve It shows all the bundles of two goods that give the same level of utility to the consumer.

Inferior good A good is classified as inferior if demand for that good falls when income increases and vice versa.

Inflation A rise in the general or aggregate price level.

Inflation rate The percentage change in the price level from one period to the next period.

Inflationary gap An inflationary gap exists when the equilibrium of the economy is greater than the full-employment level of output.

Interest is the amount that is paid on a loan or the amount that is received on a deposit.

Interest rate This is the interest amount expressed as a percentage of the sum borrowed or lent.

Investment expenditure is the corporate or business expenditure on machinery, fixtures and fittings, vehicles and buildings. It also includes inventory build-ups of raw materials, semi-finished and finished goods.

IS curve It depicts the combination of interest rates and income levels that is consistent with equilibrium in the goods market.

Isocost line It shows all the combinations of two inputs that can be employed for a certain amount of money.

Isoquant It is a locus of points, showing the various combinations of two inputs that can be used to produce a given level of output.

Labour force includes those who are employed and those who are unemployed.

Law of demand refers to the inverse or negative relationship between price and quantity demanded, *ceteris paribus*.

Liquidity preference is the desire by households to hold assets in liquid form.

LM curve It depicts the combination of interest rates and income levels that is consistent with equilibrium in the money market.

Long run This is a period of time when all the factors of production can be varied in quantity.

Macroeconomics is concerned with the operation of the economy as a whole.

Main refinancing operations are reverse transactions using tenders and are normally executed weekly, with a maturity of two weeks.

Managed floating exchange rate system A system characterised by an exchange rate which changes with the market forces of demand and supply. However, the Central Bank intervenes periodically, particularly when the currency is very weak or very strong.

Marginal cost is the extra cost incurred from producing an additional unit of output.

Marginal product is the change in total output obtained from an additional unit of a variable input, holding other inputs constant.

Marginal propensity to consume is the fraction of each additional unit of disposable income that is spent on consumer goods and services.

Marginal propensity to import is the fraction of an increase in income that is spent on imports.

Marginal propensity to save is the proportion of a change in disposable income that is saved.

Marginal propensity to tax is the proportion of any increment in income paid in taxes.

Marginal rate of substitution indicates the willingness of the consumer to give up a certain amount of one good in order to obtain one unit of the other good without changing utility.

Marginal rate of technical substitution is the amount of an input that can be replaced by one unit of another input without changing the level of output.

Marginal revenue is the change in total revenue resulting from a one unit change in output.

Marginal revenue product is the addition to revenue from the employment of an extra unit of an input.

Marginal social cost is the total cost to society from producing an additional unit of output.

Marginal utility is the extra or additional satisfaction that the consumer gains from consuming one extra unit of a good or service.

Market It is any arrangement that facilitates the buying and selling of a good, service, factor of production or future commitment.

Menu costs refer to costs which are associated with adjustments in prices. Examples include the printing of price lists and the reticketing of merchandise.

Merchandise trade balance This is a record of transactions of merchandise exports and imports during a year.

Microeconomics studies individual decision-making units.

Monetary policy refers to the use of money supply, credit and interest rates to achieve economic objectives.

Monetary transmission mechanism is the process where a change in monetary policy affects aggregate expenditure and national output.

Narrow money supply is defined as the notes and coins in circulation plus current account balances at credit institutions.

Natural monopoly exists if total output can be produced more cheaply by a single firm than by two or more firms.

Net factor income from the rest of the world is the outflows of income earned by foreigners operating in Ireland minus the inflows of income earned by foreign subsidiaries of Irish companies.

Nominal rate of interest The actual rate of interest which is charged when money is borrowed.

Normal good There is a positive relationship between income and demand. Demand for a normal good increases with income. If income falls, demand for the normal good falls.

Normal profit is the amount or percentage of profit which the entrepreneur requires to supply his or her expertise.

Okun's Law depicts the inverse relationship between output growth and unemployment.

Open market operations involves the buying and selling of government securities.

Opportunity cost The opportunity cost of an activity is measured in terms of the highest valued alternative foregone.

Pareto efficiency means that there is no available alternative that keeps all individuals at least as well off, but makes at least one person better off.

Potential output represents the maximum level of output that can be produced given a country's productive capacity.

Present value is the estimate of what the revenue stream of a capital asset is worth today.

Price can be defined as that which is given in exchange for a good or service.

Price ceiling is a form of price control. To help consumers, the government legislates that the selling price cannot exceed this maximum price.

Price controls are government regulations which limit the ability of the market to determine price.

Price discriminating monopolist is a monopolist who charges different prices to different customers for the same product for reasons other than differences in costs.

Price elastic The demand for a good is price elastic if the percentage change in quantity demanded is greater than the percentage change in price.

Price elasticity of demand measures the responsiveness of quantity demanded to changes in the price of the same good or service.

Price elasticity of supply measures the responsiveness of quantity supplied to changes in price.

Price floor is a form of price control designed to help producers. The selling price is not allowed to fall below a minimum price legislated by government.

Price index A price index measures the level of prices in one period as a percentage of the level in another period called the base period.

Price inelastic The demand for a good is price inelastic if the percentage change in quantity demanded is less than the percentage change in price.

Product differentiation means that the good produced by one firm is different from the good produced by the firm's competitor.

Production function This shows the relationship between the amounts of inputs used and the maximum amount of output generated.

Production possibility frontier shows all possible combinations of two goods that can be produced using available technology and all available resources.

Public goods must be consumed by everyone in the same amount and no one can be excluded from consumption.

Rate of return on capital is a measure of the productivity of a particular capital asset.

Real rate of interest is the nominal rate of interest adjusted for the inflation rate.

Reserve requirement This is the percentage of deposits which banks are legally obligated to lodge at the Central Bank.

Returns to scale refers to the long-run relationship between changes in inputs and subsequent changes in output.

Revaluation is an increase in the value of one currency *vis-à-vis* other currencies in a fixed or semi-fixed exchange rate regime.

Savings function It shows the relationship between savings and disposable income.

Semi-fixed exchange rate system is a system where member states set the value of their currencies in relation to other participating currencies. However, currencies are permitted to fluctuate above and below these rates.

Short run This is a period of time where there is at least one factor of production which does not change.

Shutdown price is less than the short-run average variable cost of producing a unit of output.

Small open economy refers to an economy that is so small relative to the world economy that domestic economic events have no effect on the rest of the world. The domestic economy is a price taker: it accepts world prices. Also, external trade (exports and imports) represents a high proportion of the country's GDP.

Steady state level of capital consists of a level of capital and a savings rate such that the level of savings and investment equal the capital that is lost due to depreciation.

Substitutes Two goods are substitutes if consumers consider one good as an alternative for the other good. If the price of one good falls, demand for the other good falls and vice versa.

Substitution effect It is the change in consumption that is caused by the change in the relative prices of the two goods.

Supply is the quantity of the good that sellers offer at each conceivable price during a particular period of time.

Supply schedule A table which indicates the quantity of a particular good which producers are willing to supply at various prices, over a particular period of time.

Supply-side policies are targeted at increasing the productive capacity of the economy.

Supply-side shock This refers to changes in the conditions of productivity or costs which in turn impacts on aggregate supply.

Tariffs A tariff is a tax on imports and is usually *ad valorem* which means that a percentage of the price is added to the price of the imported good.

Third degree price discrimination occurs when firms separate consumers into classes and establish a different price for each class.

Total utility is the total satisfaction that a consumer gains from the consumption of a given quantity of a good or service.

Total factor productivity growth is the change in output that arises from technological progress.

Transfer earnings is what a resource could earn in its best alternative use.

Transfer payments redistribute wealth. They include pensions, unemployment benefit, disability allowances and other payments.

Unemployed The unemployed include those who are not working and who are available for, and are actively seeking, work.

Unemployment rate The number of people unemployed divided by the labour force.

Unit elastic The demand for a good is unit elastic if the percentage change in quantity demanded is equal to the percentage change in price.

Utility is the satisfaction or pleasure that is derived from consuming a good or service.

Value Added Tax is an integrated sales tax levied at each stage of production and distribution.

Yield curve This shows the way in which the yield on a security varies according to its maturity or expiry date.

INDEX